1 & 2 Kings

Continental Commentaries

Old Testament

Genesis 1–11, Genesis 12–36, Genesis 37–50
Claus Westermann

Psalms 1–59
Hans-Joachim Kraus

Psalms 60–150
Hans-Joachim Kraus

Theology of the Psalms
Hans-Joachim Kraus

The Song of Songs
Othmar Keel

Isaiah 1–12, Isaiah 13–27, Isaiah 28–39
Hans Wildberger

Obadiah and Jonah
Hans Walter Wolff

Micah
Hans Walter Wolff

Haggai
Hans Walter Wolff

* * * *

New Testament

Matthew 1–7
Ulrich Luz

Galatians
Dieter Lührmann

Revelation
Jürgen Roloff

VOLKMAR FRITZ

1 & 2 KINGS

A Continental Commentary

Translated by
Anselm Hagedorn

FORTRESS PRESS
MINNEAPOLIS

1 & 2 KINGS
A Continental Commentary

First English language edition published by Fortress Press, 2003.

Translated by Anselm Hagedorn from Volkmar Fritz, *Das Erste Buch Könige* and *Das Zweite Buch Könige,* Zürcher Bibelkommentar 10, published by Theologischer Verlag, Zurich, Switzerland, copyright © 1996, 1998.

ISBN 0-8006-9530-5

The paper used in this publication meets the minimum requirements of American National Standard for Information Sciences — Permanence of Paper for Printed Library Materials, ANSI Z329.48-1984.

Manufactured in the U.S.A.
07   06   05   04   03   1   2   3   4   5   6   7   8   9   10

Contents

Abbreviations   ix
Translator's Note   xiii

Introduction   1
1 Kings 1–11   The Reign of Solomon   5
1:1—2:46   Solomon's Rise to the Throne   5
3:1-3   Opening   33
3:4-15   Theophany at Gibeon   36
3:16-28   Solomon's Wisdom in Judgment   41
4:1-6   Solomon's Administrative Officers   44
4:7-19   The Provinces   47
4:20—5:8   Additions [ET = 4:20-28]   53
5:9-14   Solomon's Wisdom [ET = 4:29-34]   56
5:15-26   The Treaty with Hiram of Tyre [ET = 5:1-12]   59
5:27-32   Conscripted Labor [ET = 5:13-18]   63
6:1-38   Building and Setup of the Temple   66
7:1-12   The Palace   76
7:13-51   The Bronze Works for the Temple   80
8:1-11   The Transfer of the Ark into the Temple   87
8:12-13   The Consecration Proverb for the Temple   90
8:14-66   The Dedication of the Temple   93
9:1-9   The Second Theophany   103
9:10-14   The Loss of the Land of Cabul   106
9:15-25   Conscripted Labor and Further Building Projects   108
9:26-28   The Journeys to Ophir   115
10:1-13   The Visit of the Queen of Sheba   117
10:14-29   Wealth and Splendor of the Solomonic Era   122

Contents

11:1-40	The Reasons for the Division of the Empire	128
11:41-43	Concluding Formula for Solomon	138

1 Kings 12—2 Kings 17   The Divided Monarchy of Israel and Judah   139

12:1-25	The Installation of Jeroboam as King	139
12:26-33	The Cultic Measures of Jeroboam	146
13:1-34	The Man of God from Judah	148
14:1-18	The Prophet Ahijah of Shiloh	153
14:19-20	Concluding Formula: Jeroboam	157
14:21-31	Rehoboam of Judah	159
15:1-8	Abijam of Judah	163
15:9-24	Asa of Judah	165
15:25-32	Nadab of Israel	169
15:33—16:7	Baasha of Israel	171
16:8-14	Elah of Israel	173
16:15-28	Zimri, Tibni, and Omri	175
16:29-34	Introductory Formula for Ahab	178
17:1-24	Elijah at Wadi Cherith and at the Widow of Zarephath	181
18:1-46	The Trial by Ordeal on Mount Carmel	186
19:1-18	Elijah at the Mountain of God	195
19:19-21	The Call of Elisha	200
20:1-43	The Wars against the Arameans	202
21:1-29	The Judicial Murder of Naboth	209
22:1-38	The Death of Ahab in the Campaign against the Arameans	216
22:39-40	Concluding Formula for Ahab	222
22:41-51	Jehoshaphat of Judah [ET = 22:41-50]	224
22:52-54	Ahaziah of Israel [ET = 22:51-53]	227
2 Kings 1:1-17a	The Death of Ahaziah of Israel	228
1:17b-18	Concluding Formula for Ahaziah	232
2:1-18	Elisha Succeeds Elijah	233
2:19-22	Elisha's Miracle at the Spring	237
2:23-25	The Cursing of the Boys	239
3:1-3	Introductory Formula for Jehoram of Israel	241
3:4-27	The Campaign against Mesha of Moab	242
4:1-7	The Miracle of the Oil	247
4:8-37	The Son of the Shunammite Woman	249

Contents

4:38-41	Death in the Pot	253
4:42-44	The Feeding Miracle	255
5:1-27	The Healing of Naaman	257
6:1-7	The Floating Ax	262
6:8-23	The Tricking of the Arameans	263
6:24—7:20	The Miraculous Deliverance of Samaria	266
8:1-6	The King as a Guarantor of Justice	272
8:7-15	The Death of Ben-hadad	274
8:16-24	Jehoram of Judah	276
8:25-27	Introductory Formula for Ahaziah of Judah	278
8:28—10:17	The Revolution of Jehu	279
10:18-27	The Eradication of the Worshipers of Baal	290
10:28-33	The Judgment of Jehu	292
10:34-36	Concluding Formula for Jehu	294
11:1-20	The Fall of Queen Athaliah	295
12:1-4	Introductory Formula for Jehoash of Judah	301
12:5-17	The Temple Repaired	302
12:18-19	Hazael Threatens Jerusalem	305
12:20-22	Concluding Formula for Joash of Judah	306
13:1-9	Jehoahaz of Israel	307
13:10-11	Introductory Formula for Jehoash of Israel	310
13:12-13	Concluding Formula for Joash of Israel	311
13:14-21	Elisha's Prophecies of Victory and His Death	312
13:22-25	The Victories over Aram	314
14:1-7	Introductory Formula for Amaziah of Judah	316
14:8-14	The Victory of Jehoash of Israel against Amaziah of Judah	318
14:15-17	Concluding Formula for Jehoash of Israel	321
14:18-22	Concluding Formula for Amaziah of Judah	322
14:23-29	Jeroboam of Israel	324
15:1-7	Azariah of Judah	327
15:8-12	Zechariah of Israel	330
15:13-16	Shallum of Israel	331
15:17-22	Menahem of Israel	332
15:23-26	Pekahiah of Israel	334
15:27-31	Pekah of Israel	335
15:32-38	Jotham of Judah	338

Contents

16:1-4	Introductory Formula for Ahaz of Judah	340
16:5-9	The Conquest of Damascus by Tiglath-pileser	342
16:10-18	The New Altar in the Temple at Jerusalem	344
16:19-20	Concluding Formula for Ahaz	346
17:1-2	Introductory Formula for Hoshea of Israel	347
17:3-23	The Downfall of Israel	348
17:24-41	The Foreign Nations in the Cities of Samaria	353
2 Kings 18–25	**The Kingdom of Judah after the Destruction of Israel**	**358**
18:1-8	Introductory Formula for Hezekiah	358
18:9-12	Shalmaneser's Advance on Samaria	361
18:13-16	Hezekiah Pays Tribute to Sennacherib	362
18:17—19:37	Sennacherib at Jerusalem	365
20:1-11	Hezekiah's Illness and Recovery	380
20:12-19	The Threat against Hezekiah	383
20:20-21	Concluding Formula for Hezekiah	386
21:1-18	Manasseh	388
21:19-26	Amon	393
22:1-2	Introductory Formula for Josiah	395
22:3-11	The Discovery of the Book of the Law	397
22:12-20	The Prediction of the Prophetess Huldah	399
23:1-3	The Covenant	402
23:4-27	The Cult Reform of Josiah	404
23:28-30	Concluding Formula for Josiah	410
23:31-35	Jehoahaz of Israel	412
23:36—24:7	Jehoiakim	414
24:8-17	Jehoiachin	416
24:18—25:7	Zedekiah	418
25:8-21	The Destruction of Jerusalem	420
25:22-26	Gedaliah	423
25:27-30	The Pardon of Jehoiachin	425
Select Bibliography		427
Index of Ancient Sources		437
Index of Divine Names		444
Index of Geographical Names		445

Abbreviations

AASOR	Annual of the American Schools of Oriental Research
AB	Anchor Bible
ABD	*Anchor Bible Dictionary,* edited by David Noel Freedman, 6 vols., 1992
ABLAK	Martin Noth, *Aufsätze und biblischen Landes- und Altertumskunde,* 2 vols., 1971
ABRL	Anchor Bible Reference Library
ADPV	Abhandlungen des deutschen Palästina-Vereins
AfO	*Archiv für Orientforschung*
AJSL	*American Journal of Semitic Languages and Literature*
AnBib	Analecta Biblica
ANEP	*Ancient Near East in Pictures Relating to the Old Testament,* 2d ed., edited by James B. Pritchard, 1969
ANET	*Ancient Near Eastern Texts Relating to the Old Testament,* 3d ed., edited by James B. Pritchard, 1969
Ant.	Josephus, *Antiquities of the Judeans*
AOAT	Alter Orient und Altes Testament
AOS	American Oriental Series
ASOR	American Schools of Oriental Research
ATD	Das Alte Testament Deutsch
BA	*Biblical Archaeologist*
BAR	*Biblical Archaeology Review*
BASOR	*Bulletin of the American Schools of Oriental Research*
BerO	Berit Olam
BHH	*Biblisch-historisches Handwörterbuch,* edited by Bo Reicke and Leonhard Rost, 4 vols., 1962–66
BHS	Biblia Hebraica Stuttgartensia
Bib	*Biblica*
BibSem	Biblical Seminar
BIOSCS	*Bulletin of the International Organization for Septuagint and Cognate Studies*
BJS	Brown Judaic Studies
BKAT	Biblischer Kommentar, Alte Testament
BN	*Biblische Notizen*

Abbreviations

BRL	*Biblisches Reallexikon,* 2d ed., edited by Kurt Galling, 1977
BZAW	Beihefte zur ZAW
CAD	*Assyrian Dictionary of the Oriental Institute of the University of Chicago,* edited by Ignace Gelb et al., 1956–
CBQ	*Catholic Biblical Quarterly*
CBOT	Coniectanea biblica. Old Testament Series
CHier	Collectanea Hierosolymitana
DamFor	Damaszener Forschungen
DDD²	*Dictionary of Deities and Demons,* 2d ed., edited by Karel van der Toorn et al., 1999
DMOA	Documenta et monumenta orientis antiqui
DSBOT	Daily Study Bible—Old Testament
EA	Amarna Tablets
ErIsr	*Eretz Israel*
FOTL	Forms of the Old Testament Literature
FRLANT	Forschungen zur Religion und Literatur des Alten und Neuen Testaments
HAT	Handbuch zum Alten Testament
HCOT	Historical Commentary on the Old Testament
HSM	Harvard Semitic Monographs
HTIBS	Historical Texts and Interpreters in Biblical Scholarship
HUCA	*Hebrew Union College Annual*
IBC	Interpretation: A Bible Commentary for Teaching and Preaching
ICC	International Critical Commentary
IEJ	*Israel Exploration Journal*
JANESCU	*Journal of the Ancient Near Eastern Society of Columbia University*
JAOS	*Journal of the American Oriental Society*
JBL	*Journal of Biblical Literature*
JNES	*Journal of Near Eastern Studies*
JNSL	*Journal of Northwest Semitic Languages*
JSOTSup	Journal for the Study of the Old Testament Supplement Series
JSS	*Journal of Semitic Studies*
KAI	*Kanaanäischen und aramäischen Inschriften,* 3 vols., edited by Herbert Donner and Wolfgang Röllig, 3d ed., 1971–76
KHC	Kurzer Hand-Commentar zum Alten Testament
KS	*Kirjath-Sepher*
LÄ	*Lexikon der Ägyptologie,* 7 vols., edited by Wolfgang Helck und Eberhard Otto, 1972–92
LAI	Library of Ancient Israel
LXX	Septuagint

MT	Masoretic text
NBL	*Neues Bibel-Lexikon,* 3 vols., edited by Manfred Görg and Bernhard Lang, 1988–2001
NCB	New Century Bible Commentary
NEAEHL	*New Encyclopedia of Archaeological Excavations in the Holy Land,* edited by Ephraim Stern, 4 vols., 1993
NIBC	New International Biblical Commentary
NRSV	New Revised Standard Version
NT	New Testament
OBO	Orbis biblicus et orientalis
OLZ	*Orientalistische Literaturzeitung*
OT	Old Testament
OTL	Old Testament Library
PEQ	*Palestine Exploration Quarterly*
PJ	*Palästina-Jahrbuch*
PW	*Paulys Realencyclopädie der classischen Altertumswissenschaft,* edited by August Friedrich Pauly, revised by Georg Wissowa, 49 vols., 1980
RLA	*Reallexikon der Assyriologie,* edited by Erich Ebeling et al., 1928–
SBT	Studies in Biblical Theology
SBTS	Sources for Biblical and Theological Study
SHAJ	Studies in the History and Archaeology of Jordan
SHANE	Studies in the History of the Ancient Near East
SHBC	Smith and Helwys Bible Commentary
SHCANE	Studies in the History and Culture of the Ancient Near East
SOTSMS	Society for Old Testament Study Monograph Series
ST	*Studia theologica*
STTB	Suomalaisen Tiedeakatemian Toimituksia, Series B
TA	*Tel Aviv*
TDOT	*Theological Dictionary of the Old Testament,* edited by G. Johannes Botterweck and Helmer Ringgren, 1974–
TGI	*Textbuch zur Geschichte Israels,* 2d ed., edited by Kurt Galling, 1968
ThBü	Theologische Bücherei
ThWAT	*Theologisches Wörterbuch zum Alten Testament,* edited by G. Johannes Botterweck and Helmer Ringgren, 1970–
TOTC	Tyndale Old Testament Commentary
TRE	*Theologische Realenzyclopädie,* edited by Gerhard Krause and Gerhard Müller, 1977–
TUAT	*Texte aus der Umwelt des Alten Testaments,* edited by Otto Kaiser, 1984–
UF	*Ugarit-Forschungen*

Abbreviations

VT	*Vetus Testamentum*
VTSup	VT Supplements
WBC	Word Biblical Commentary
WMANT	Wissenschaftliche Monographien zum Alten und Neuen Testament
WO	*Die Welt des Orients*
ZAW	*Zeitschrift für die alttestamentliche Wissenschaft*
ZDMG	*Zeitschrift der deutschen morgenländischen Gesellschaft*
ZDPV	*Zeitschrift des deutschen Palästina-Vereins*

Translator's Note

It has been an honor to be invited to make this book available to English readers and of course a major challenge. Translating an author's thoughts into another language always bears difficulties, and one runs the risk of destroying the original impetus of the language. I have tried to stay as close as possible to the original German (without germanizing the English, I hope), only correcting printing errors.

Volkmar Fritz has written a lucid and readable commentary to the book of Kings. His work addresses literary questions of the origin of the books and offers archaeological insights. All this is done in a very accessible way. Without a massive apparatus of footnotes, Fritz is able to explain the literary processes behind the individual texts. Right from the start it will become apparent to the reader that Fritz's long archaeological activity as the director of the German Evangelical Institute of the Holy Land has deeply influenced his approach to the text. He aims to place the two biblical books in their historical context of Syro-Palestine, offering many comparative insights. The reader will especially welcome the identification of the biblical place-names with modern locations.

As far as the English version of the biblical text is concerned, the NRSV is used and adaptations are made when the author's translation differs significantly from it. After the translation, a brief paragraph on the passage as a whole is followed by a detailed, verse-by-verse commentary. This prevents a fragmentation of the text as a whole and draws attention to the overall composition.

K. C. Hanson has composed the Select Bibliography for English readers; this is intended as a guide to the reader to further reading and progress in scholarship. Of course the literature on the book of Kings is legion, and providing a complete bibliography of everything published since the original appearance of the commentary in 1996 would be a research project in itself. Nevertheless, we have tried to list all commentaries published in the English language since that date, since we believe it will be useful to the reader to compare Fritz's approach to the text with that of other commentators. Much debate has focused in recent years on the question of the Deuteronomistic history. Here the volume edited by de Pury, Römer, and Macchi will provide a good description of the state of affairs,[1] and the volume edited by Knoppers and McConville contains many classic articles—some of them translated into English for the first time.[2] Finally, I want to draw attention to simply one passage in the commentary: As it becomes apparent from the commentary on 1 Kgs 1:1—2:46, Fritz firmly believes in the existence of a so-called succession narrative but is reluctant to ascribe any historical value to the passage: "Rather, we can assume that the single episodes have been put down in writing from the very beginning and that the author was able to draw on a detailed knowledge of the situation at the court. The vividness of the narrative in particular proclaims it as a literary fiction of great artistic value." Here he is moving in the direction of current trends in scholarship that doubt very much the existence of a succession narrative already in the tenth century.[3]

For brevity sake, references in the footnotes to the major commentaries (e.g., Cogan and Tadmor, Noth, and Würthwein) are cited in shortened form. The reader will find the full citations in the bibliography.

After the completion of a project it is a pleasure to give thanks to the people directly or indirectly involved. First of all I would like to thank Volkmar Fritz and K.C. Hanson from Fortress Press for entrusting me with the enterprise. K.C. Hanson has been the careful editor every author and translator wishes for.

Secondly I have to record my deepest gratitude and thanks to Constanze Güthenke. She not only read every sentence I translated but also helped to bring volume two into its current form. Without her valuable assistance this translation would not have been possible.

---

[1] Albert de Pury, Thomas Römer, and Jean-Daniel Macchi, eds., *Israel Constructs Its History: Deuteronomistic Historiography in Recent Research,* JSOTSup 306 (Sheffield: Sheffield Academic, 2000).

[2] Gary N. Knoppers and J. Gordon McConville, eds., *Reconsidering Israel and Judah: Recent Studies on the Deuteronomistic History*, SBTS 8 (Winona Lake, Ind.: Eisenbrauns, 2000).

[3] Compare, for example, Albert de Pury and Thomas Römer, eds., *Die sogenannte Thronfolgegeschichte Davids: Neue Einsichten und Anfragen,* OBO 176 (Göttingen: Vandenhoeck & Ruprecht, 2000).

Introduction

The two books of Kings originally formed a single document, but following the example of the Septuagint and the Vulgate it was divided into two separate books by the end of the Middle Ages. The current division gives the impression of some sort of randomness, since it separates the introductory and concluding formula to the reign of Ahaziah, which can now be found in two different books. This formula originally formed a unit, which was only interrupted by the note in 2 Kgs 1:1. In the original document, the history of kingship after David was divided into three major parts

1 Kings 1–11	The Reign of Solomon
1 Kings 12—2 Kings 17	The Divided Monarchy of Israel and Judah
2 Kings 18–25	The Kingdom of Judah after the Destruction of Israel

Thus the books of Kings provided a continuous account of the history from Solomon to the end of the kingdom of Judah in connection with the destruction of Jerusalem and the temple by the Babylonians. In two additional parts two later incidents are briefly mentioned: the murder of the Babylonian governor Gedaliah, and the release from prison of the former king Jehoiachin in the Babylonian exile. This account of the history of kingship serves a twofold purpose: on the one hand to maintain the memory of the previous glory of the monarchy under Solomon, and on the other hand to emphasize the guilt of the succeeding kings and their responsibility for the vanishing of the kingdoms of Israel and Judah. The guiding principle for the evaluation of the kings of Israel and Judah is their behavior toward the cult and thus their view of the temple in Jerusalem. As the temple is the only proper place of worship, so is the worship of Yahweh alone the only right attitude in the question of gods. With the recognition of Yahweh as the only God all polytheistic practices are excluded. The faith in the one and only God is the only measurement for the kings and people.

The decisive element of connection within the work is the chronological frame as it is found in the so-called synchronisms. In these notes the reign of each king is dated according to the regnal year of the king in the neighboring kingdom. In addition to that we find a note on the age of each king at the time of his accession and the indication of the length of his reign. For the centuries of the monarchies of Israel and Judah, these notes also refer to external sources such as annals and chronicles, none

1

of which has survived, however. The frequent references to a "Book of the Acts of Solomon" (1 Kgs 11:41), "The Book of the Annals of the Kings of Israel" (14:19), and "The Book of the Annals of the Kings of Judah" (14:29) indicate that the author has used a source for the chronological and biographical notices that is now long lost. Also in other parts of the books of Kings already existing traditions have been used, whose origins and collections can no longer be illuminated.

The two books of Kings are part of a larger literary composition generally called the Deuteronomistic History. This extensive account of history consists of the books Deuteronomy, Joshua, Judges, 1 and 2 Samuel, and 1 and 2 Kings, and has been handed down to us in its entirety. The Deuteronomistic History not only describes the history of the people of Israel from their journey through Transjordan, the conquest of Canaan, and the emergence of kingship to the end of the monarchy in 587, but also explains the course of history as a result of the disobedience against the book of the law (Deuteronomy) and its principal demand that Yahweh alone has to be worshiped at the place that he has chosen, the temple in Jerusalem. In retrospect the exile is understood as a result of the turning away from Yahweh. Here the kings are especially guilty, since they encouraged the people to worship other gods and thus violated divine law. Accordingly all kings of the northern monarchy are condemned because they followed the evil example of their ancestor Jeroboam manifested by the setting up of rival sanctuaries in Bethel and Dan. Of the southern kings next to Joash only the "reformers" Hezekiah and Josiah are viewed in a positive light because they tried to establish the worship of Yahweh alone in the temple of Jerusalem. The stipulation of the centralization of the cult as found in Deuteronomy 12 is thus the guiding principle for the verdict on each epoch, especially in the books of Kings. Next to that, there is a second feature of the presentation of the history: the motif of prophecy and fulfillment.

There is no scholarly consensus regarding the formation of the Deuteronomistic History. After Martin Noth's discovery of the unity of the extensive textual corpus, scholars have proceeded to develop two models to explain the complex composition of the work.

The "stages model" (*Stufenmodell*) argues for a first edition completed by the end of the kingship that has subsequently been expanded during the exile. The point of departure for such a hypothesis is the recognition that the framing remarks for the last four Judean kings differ significantly from the notes on their predecessors. The necessity of a new edition with corresponding continuation and change resulted from the new historical situation as provided by the end of the monarchy, the loss of the cultic center, and the leading from the land into the exile. According to this hypothesis the first edition served the purpose of creating a national identity during the time of the monarchy, whereas the supplemented edition was determined by the changed historical situation.

The "strata model" (*Schichtenmodell*) argues for a basic literary stratum that was systematically revised at least twice in a process during which extensive additions were made. According to this model the Deuteronomistic History was first composed during the time of the exile and only in postexilic times expanded by redactors into the work we have today. This hypothesis also assumes different "editions" of the work actualized by redactors in such a way that more narratives or individual scenes have been added.

Both models assume the incorporation of already existing written narrative complexes, but the extent of each of these complexes is debated. Also a subject of debate is the question of how far these literary complexes were already joined together at a pre-Deuteronomistic stage. Absolute certainty of the literary stage before the Deuteronomistic History cannot be reached. This commentary is not intended as a contribution to the solution of the problems mentioned, because its main aim is not the presentation of literary-critical results, but rather the attempt to elucidate the often alien world of the Bible by explaining its presuppositions. Nonetheless, it is also necessary to distinguish between different literary layers and to assess the value of the traditions in order to reach a historically sound result of the course of Israel's history. For the author of the Deuteronomistic History the course of Israel's history was determined by the will of Yahweh. Today's reader understands history almost exclusively as the act of persons. Given the close link of the history of God with his people, the differentiation between event and explanation remains a necessary criterion in the search for the truth of history that does not dissolve in the truth of faith.

1 Kings 1–11

The Reign of Solomon

1 Kings 1:1—2:46

Solomon's Rise to the Throne

Text

1:1 King David was old and advanced in years; and although they covered him with clothes, he could not get warm. 2 So his servants said to him, "Let a young virgin be sought for <our>a lord the king, and let her wait on the king, and be his attendant; let her lie in <his>b bosom, so that my lord the king may be warm." 3 So they searched for a beautiful girl throughout all the territory of Israel, and found Abishag the Shunammite, and brought her to the king. 4 The girl was very beautiful. She became the king's attendant and served him, but the king did not know her sexually.

5 Now Adonijah son of Haggith exalted himself, saying, "I will be king"; he prepared for himself chariots and horsemen, and fifty men to run before him. 6 His father had never at any time displeased him by asking, "Why have you done thus and so?" He was also a very handsome man, and he was born next after Absalom. 7 He conferred with Joab son of Zeruiah and with the priest Abiathar, and they supported Adonijah. 8 But the priest Zadok, and Benaiah son of Jehoiada, and the prophet Nathan, [. . .]c and David's own warriors did not side with Adonijah.

9 Adonijah sacrificed sheep, oxen, and fatted cattle by the stone Zoheleth, which is beside En-rogel, and he invited all his brothers, the king's sons, and all the royal officials of Judah, 10 but he did not invite the prophet Nathan or Benaiah or the warriors or his brother Solomon.

11 Then Nathan said to Bathsheba, Solomon's mother, "Have you not heard that Adonijah son of Haggith has become king and our lord David does not know it? 12 Now therefore come, let me give you advice, so that you may save your own life and the life of your son Solomon. 13 Go in at once to King David, and say to him, 'Did you not, my lord the king, swear to your

servant, saying: Your son Solomon shall succeed me as king, and he shall sit on my throne? Why then is Adonijah king?' 14 Then while you are still there speaking with the king, I will come in after you and confirm your words."

15 So Bathsheba went to the king in his room. The king was very old; Abishag the Shunammite was attending the king. 16 Bathsheba bowed and did obeisance to the king, and the king said, "What do you wish?" 17 She said to him, "My lord, you swore to your servant by the LORD your God, saying: Your son Solomon shall succeed me as king, and he shall sit on my throne. 18 But now suddenly Adonijah has become king, though you,[d] my lord the king, do not know it. 19 He has sacrificed oxen, fatted cattle, and sheep in abundance, and has invited all the children of the king, the priest Abiathar, and Joab the commander of the army; but your servant Solomon he has not invited. 20 <Now>,[e] my lord the king—the eyes of all Israel are on you to tell them who shall sit on the throne of my lord the king after him. 21 Otherwise it will come to pass, when my lord the king sleeps with his ancestors, that my son Solomon and I will be counted offenders."

22 While she was still speaking with the king, the prophet Nathan came in. 23 The king was told, "Here is the prophet Nathan." When he came in before the king, he did obeisance to the king, with his face to the ground. 24 Nathan said, "My lord the king, have you said, 'Adonijah shall succeed me as king, and he shall sit on my throne'? 25 For today he has gone down and has sacrificed oxen, fatted cattle, and sheep in abundance, and has invited all the king's children, Joab the commander[f] of the army, and the priest Abiathar, who are now eating and drinking before him, and saying, 'Long live King Adonijah!' 26 But he did not invite me, your servant, and the priest Zadok, and Benaiah son of Jehoiada, and your servant Solomon. 27 Has this thing been brought about by my lord the king and you have not let your servants know who should sit on the throne of my lord the king after him?"

28 King David answered, "Summon Bathsheba to me." So she came into the king's presence, and stood before the king. 29 The king swore, saying, "As the LORD lives, who has saved my life from every adversity, 30 as I swore to you by the LORD, the God of Israel, 'Your son Solomon shall succeed me as king, and he shall sit on my throne in my place,' so will I do this day." 31 Then Bathsheba bowed with her face to the ground, and did obeisance to the king, and said, "May my lord King David live forever!"

32 King David said, "Summon to me the priest Zadok, the prophet Nathan, and Benaiah son of Jehoiada." When they came before the king, 33 the king said to them, "Take with you the servants of your lord, and have my son Solomon ride on my own mule, and bring him down to Gihon. 34 There let the priest Zadok [. . .][g] anoint him king over Israel; then blow the trumpet, and say, 'Long live King Solomon!' 35 You shall go up following him. Let him enter and sit on my throne; he shall be king in my place; for I have

appointed him to be ruler over Israel and over Judah." 36 Benaiah son of Jehoiada answered the king, "Amen! May the LORD, the God of my lord the king, so ordain. 37 As the LORD has been with my lord the king, so may he be with Solomon, and make his throne greater than the throne of my lord King David."

38 So the priest Zadok, the prophet Nathan, and Benaiah son of Jehoiada, and the Cherethites and the Pelethites, went down and had Solomon ride on King David's mule, and led him to Gihon. 39 There the priest Zadok took the horn of oil from the tent and anointed Solomon. Then they blew the trumpet, and all the people said, "Long live King Solomon!" 40 And all the people went up following him, playing on pipes and rejoicing with great joy, so that the earth quaked at their noise.

41 Adonijah and all the guests who were with him heard it as they finished feasting. When Joab heard the sound of the trumpet, he said, "Why is the city in an uproar?" 42 While he was still speaking, Jonathan son of the priest Abiathar arrived. Adonijah said, "Come in, for you are a worthy man and surely you bring good news." 43 Jonathan answered Adonijah, "No, for our lord King David has made Solomon king; 44 the king has sent with him the priest Zadok, the prophet Nathan, and Benaiah son of Jehoiada, and the Cherethites and the Pelethites; and they had him ride on the king's mule; 45 the priest Zadok [. . .]ʰ has anointed him king at Gihon; and they have gone up from there rejoicing, so that the city is in an uproar. This is the noise that you heard. 46 Solomon now sits on the royal throne. 47 Moreover, the king's servants came to congratulate our lord King David, saying, 'May God make the name of Solomon more famous than yours, and make his throne greater than your throne.' The king bowed in worship on the bed 48 and went on to pray thus, 'Blessed be the LORD, the God of Israel, who today has granted one of my offspring to sit on my throne and permitted me to witness it.'"

49 Then all the guests of Adonijah got up trembling and went their own ways. 50 Adonijah, fearing Solomon, got up and went to grasp the horns of the altar. 51 Solomon was informed, "Adonijah is afraid of King Solomon; see, he has laid hold of the horns of the altar, saying, 'Let King Solomon swear to me first that he will not kill his servant with the sword.'" 52 So Solomon responded, "If he proves to be a worthy man, not one of his hairs shall fall to the ground; but if wickedness is found in him, he shall die." 53 Then King Solomon sent to have him brought down from the altar. He came to do obeisance to King Solomon; and Solomon said to him, "Go home."

2:1 When David's time to die drew near, he charged his son Solomon, saying: 2 "I am about to go the way of all the earth. Be strong, be courageous, 3 and keep the charge of the LORD your God, walking in his ways and keeping his statutes, his commandments, his ordinances, and his testimonies, as it is written in the law of Moses, so that you may prosper in all that you do and wherever you turn. 4 Then the LORD will establish his word that he spoke concerning me: 'If your heirs take heed to their way, to walk before me in faithfulness with all their heart and with all their soul, there shall not fail you a successor on the throne of Israel.'

5 "Moreover, you know also what Joab son of Zeruiah did to me, how he dealt with the two commanders of the armies of Israel, Abner son of Ner, and Amasa son of Jether, whom he murdered, <taking vengeance>[i] in time of peace for blood that had been shed in war, and putting <innocent>[j] blood on the belt around his waist, and on the sandals on his feet. 6 Act therefore according to your wisdom, but do not let his gray head go down to Sheol in peace. 7 Deal loyally, however, with the sons of Barzillai the Gileadite, and let them be among those who eat at your table; for with such loyalty they met me when I fled from your brother Absalom. 8 There is also with you Shimei son of Gera, the Benjaminite from Bahurim, who cursed me with a weak curse on the day when I went to Mahanaim; but when he came down to meet me at the Jordan, I swore to him by the LORD, 'I will not put you to death with the sword.' 9 Therefore do not hold him guiltless, for you are a wise man; you will know what you ought to do to him, and you must bring his gray head (stained) with blood down to Sheol."

10 Then David slept with his ancestors, and was buried in the city of David. 11 The time that David reigned over Israel was forty years; he reigned seven years in Hebron, and thirty-three years in Jerusalem. 12 So Solomon sat on the throne of his father David; and his kingdom was firmly established.

13 Then Adonijah son of Haggith came to Bathsheba, Solomon's mother. She asked, "Do you come peaceably?" He said, "Peaceably." 14 Then he said, "May I have a word with you?" She said, "Go on." 15 He said, "You know that the kingdom was mine, and that all Israel expected me to reign; however, the kingdom has turned about and become my brother's, for it was his from the LORD. 16 And now I have one request to make of you; do not refuse me." She said to him, "Go on." 17 He said, "Please ask King Solomon—he will not refuse you—to give me Abishag the Shunammite as my wife." 18 Bathsheba said, "Very well; I will speak to the king on your behalf."

19 So Bathsheba went to King Solomon, to speak to him on behalf of Adonijah. The king rose to meet her [. . .][k]; then he sat on his throne, and had a throne brought for the king's mother, and she sat on his right. 20 Then she said, "I have one small request to make of you; do not refuse me." And the king said to her, "Make your request, my mother; for I will not refuse you." 21 She said, "Let Abishag the Shunammite be given to your brother Adonijah as his wife." 22 King Solomon answered his mother, "And why do you ask Abishag the Shunammite for Adonijah? Ask for him the kingdom as well! For he is my elder brother; ask not only for him but also for the priest Abiathar and for the <commander>[l] Joab." 23 Then King Solomon swore

by the L<small>ORD</small>, "So may God do to me, and more also, for Adonijah has devised this scheme at the risk of his life! 24 Now therefore as the L<small>ORD</small> lives, who has established me [as king] and placed me on the throne of my father David, and who has made me a house as he promised, today Adonijah shall be put to death." 25 So King Solomon sent Benaiah son of Jehoiada; he struck him down, and he died.

26 The king said to the priest Abiathar, "Go to Anathoth, to your estate; for you deserve death. But I will not at this time put you to death, because you carried the ark of the Lord G<small>OD</small> before my father David, and because you shared in all the hardships my father endured." 27 So Solomon banished Abiathar from being priest to the L<small>ORD</small>, thus fulfilling the word of the L<small>ORD</small> that he had spoken concerning the house of Eli in Shiloh.

28 When the news [of this] came to Joab—for Joab had supported Adonijah though he had not supported Absalom—Joab fled to the tent of the L<small>ORD</small> and grasped the horns of the altar. 29 When it was told King Solomon, "Joab has fled to the tent of the L<small>ORD</small> and now is beside the altar," Solomon sent Benaiah son of Jehoiada, saying, "Go, strike him down." 30 So Benaiah came to the tent of the L<small>ORD</small> and said to him, "The king commands, 'Come out.'" But he said, "No, I will die here." Then Benaiah brought the king word again, saying, "Thus said Joab, and thus he answered me." 31 The king replied to him, "Do as he has said, strike him down and bury him; and thus take away from me and from my father's house the guilt for the blood that Joab shed without cause. 32 The L<small>ORD</small> will bring back his bloody deeds on his own head, because, without the knowledge of my father David, he attacked and killed with the sword two men more righteous and better than himself, Abner son of Ner, commander of the army of Israel, and Amasa son of Jether, commander of the army of Judah. 33 So shall their blood come back on the head of Joab and on the head of his descendants forever; but to David, and to his descendants, and to his house, and to his throne, there shall be peace from the L<small>ORD</small> forevermore." 34 Then Benaiah son of Jehoiada went up and struck him down and killed him; and he was buried in his <grave>^m near the wilderness. 35 The king put Benaiah son of Jehoiada over the army in his place, and the king put the priest Zadok in the place of Abiathar.

36 Then the king sent and summoned Shimei, and said to him, "Build yourself a house in Jerusalem, and live there, and do not go out from there to any place whatever. 37 For on the day you go out, and cross the Wadi Kidron, know for certain that you shall die; your blood shall be on your own head." 38 And Shimei said to the king, "The sentence is fair; as my lord the king has said, so will your servant do." So Shimei lived in Jerusalem many days.

39 But it happened at the end of three years that two of Shimei's slaves ran away to King Achish son of Maacah of Gath. When it was told Shimei, "Your slaves are in Gath," 40 Shimei arose and saddled a donkey, and went to

Achish in Gath, to search for his slaves; Shimei went and brought his slaves from Gath. 41 When Solomon was told that Shimei had gone from Jerusalem to Gath and returned, 42 the king sent and summoned Shimei, and said to him, "Did I not make you swear by the LORD, and solemnly adjure you, saying, 'Know for certain that on the day you go out and go to any place whatever, you shall die'? And you said to me, 'The sentence is fair; I accept.' 43 Why then have you not kept your oath to the LORD and the commandment with which I charged you?" [44 The king also said to Shimei, "You know [. . .]ⁿ all the evil that you did to my father David; so the LORD will bring back your evil on your own head. 45 But King Solomon shall be blessed, and the throne of David shall be established before the LORD forever."] 46 Then the king commanded Benaiah son of Jehoiada; and he went out and struck him down, and he died.

So the kingdom was established in the hand of Solomon.

^a Following *BHS;* cf. NRSV "my."

^b Following *BHS;* cf. NRSV "your."

^c NRSV "and Shimei, and Rei"; these people have nothing to do with the parties at the court, and must be a later addition, since they have nothing to do with the course of the narrative.

^d Here NRSV follows the versions; see *BHS.*

^e Following *BHS;* NRSV "But you."

^f Here NRSV follows a Greek version, as does *BHS.*

^g The words "and the prophet Nathan" are a late addition; see 1:39. The Hebrew verb form has to be changed to singular.

^h See note g.

ⁱ See *BHS.*

^j See *BHS;* cf. NRSV "blood of war."

^k The words "and bowed down to her" do not fit the context and have to be regarded as a gloss.

^l See *BHS;* cf. NRSV "son of Zeruiah."

^m See *BHS;* cf. NRSV "own house."

ⁿ The words "in your own heart" are a secondary addition; see *BHS.*

Analysis

The first two of the eleven chapters of the Solomon tradition differ fundamentally from the account that follows. Certainly, in the following chapters we find narratives next to lists and descriptions, but none of these can live up to the compositional style and standard of the succession narrative. The large number of acting persons, the artistic structure, the use of direct speech, and the graphic description of the events by using only a concise choice of words are impressive. Here, in the opening chapters, we encounter a vivid and clear narrative that enables the reader or hearer to participate actively, almost personally, in the events. In a brilliant fashion, the narrator has constructed the course of events in such a way that the listener or hearer is drawn into the events and becomes persuaded of the rightness of the decisions and results.

Given this artistic structure and careful composition, a long oral tradition of the material is unlikely. Rather, we can assume that the single episodes have been put down in writing from the very beginning and that the author was able to draw on a detailed knowledge of the situation at the court. The vividness of the narrative in particular proclaims it as a literary fiction of great artistic value. It is impossible to verify the narrative historically. It is only possible to assume that—already during the last days of David—Solomon was made king over Israel and Judah against the rightful claim of his older brother Adonijah with the help and skillful intervention of a certain party at the court.

On a literary level these two chapters form the conclusion of a larger work; its original cohesion was destroyed through the separation into single books at a later stage. The narratives in 1 Kings 1–2 are the conclusion and climax of the so-called Narrative of the Succession to the Throne of David. This work encompasses the whole complex of 2 Samuel 9–20 and contains all essential details from the circumstances that were connected with the birth of Solomon to the revolt and death of Absalom and finally the enthronement of Solomon. The intention of this extended narrative is to describe all the circumstances connected with the succession of David, and the final ascension of Solomon to the throne is portrayed as the conclusion of a potentially explosive development that lasted for several decades. Thus 1 Kings 1–2 continues 2 Samuel 9–20 and brings the long narrative strand, which covers at least twenty years, to a happy end. Not only is the question of who shall sit on the throne of David answered, but also the continuation of the Davidic dynasty and the existence of his empire have been secured.

Originally 1 Kings 1–2 and 2 Samuel 9–20 formed a literary unit. The interrupting chapters 2 Samuel 21–24 are later additions to the Davidic tradition that already presuppose the division of the text into different books dealing with David and Solomon, respectively. The assumed character of 2 Samuel 9–20 and 1 Kings 1–2 as a unit results from its composition, style, and intention. Just like 2 Samuel 9–20, 1 Kings 1–2 consists of single narratives that are sometimes linked through backward references but generally follow a straight sequence of events. However, the narrative sequence of 1 Kings 1–2 is not always uniform. Its core is the long narrative of the ascension of Solomon in 1:5-53, to which other episodes have been added before and after. Apart from the introduction and conclusion, the narrative is structured into three scenes—the middle one, concerning the investiture of Solomon, is the center and framed by the other two. Thus 1:5-53 has the following structure:

1:5-10	Introduction: the coup of Adonijah
1:11-37	First scene: Nathan's intrigue
1:38-40	Second scene: Solomon's investiture
1:41-50	Third scene: the fate of Adonijah
1:51-53	Conclusion: Solomon's mercy

The plot is firmly constructed, although the description of the actual investiture in the second scene in 1:38-40 is kept remarkably brief. This central event of the installation of Solomon is, however, repeated in the messenger's report in 1:43-45 and thus appropriately emphasized. In the third scene the exposition is taken up again to bring the narrative strand to a satisfactory end in which not only the kingship of Solomon is stressed but also the fate of Adonijah is clarified. Within the third scene, 1:46-48 seems to be a secondary addition, since the place of the action changes to David in the palace and certain theological judgments regarding the royal dignity of Solomon are repeated. Originally, the narrative might have consisted of 1:5-45, 49-53 only. The remark in 2:12 may once have served as the final statement of the narrative as a whole.

With 1:1-4 a short piece has been added to this narrative that aims to clarify the situation at the court: David is still alive, but due to his failing health he is unable to engage actively in political decisions. This little narrative is essentially an illustration of the statement in 1:15b and may have been composed because of the remark of the weak health of David. In 1 Kings 2 four individual narratives follow the opening speech by David (vv. 1-9) and the final formulaic statement (v. 10); they continue the succession narrative by describing Solomon's dealings with his opponents. The instructions of David to Solomon in 2:1-9 refer back to events within the succession narrative and probably have to be regarded as a later composition to justify the actions of Solomon and bind him to the fulfillment of duties that have arisen in the past. With the general statements in 2:10-11 the history of David concludes. The statement mentioning death, burial, and duration of reign belong to the formula that can be found for every king.

Four subsequent narratives describe the fates of Adonijah, Abiathar, Joab, and Shimei. These events happened much later than the actual enthronement of Solomon, but they are added here to stress the consolidation of his reign. With the killing of Adonijah (2:13-25) the dangerous rival is finally gone. With Abiathar (2:26-27) an old follower of David is sidelined. Joab suffers the same fate as Adonijah (2:28-35), thus a further supporter of David is killed. The portrayal of the killing of Joab as blood vengeance in 2:13b is probably a later addition to the section. With Shimei (2:36-46a), who only played a minor part in the succession narrative, Solomon demonstrates the indispensable validity of royal orders. The final sentence, 2:46b, takes up statements of 2:12 and constitutes a literary frame. The events narrated in 1 Kings 2 were hardly original parts of the succession narrative. Rather they were added to the original narrative in 1 Kings 1 during the process of expanding the Solomon tradition. The unity of style is surprising but does not allow any conclusions regarding the author.

The style of the entire narrative of the succession to the throne of David is extraordinarily lively and realistic. The events span a long period. In comparison to other single narratives—for example, those about the patriarchs Abraham, Isaac, and Jacob—the number of acting persons is relatively large. Direct speech is used frequently, creating a vivid impression. The characters are portrayed with all their weaknesses. Especially David is described as extraordinarily human so that despite all his grandness and achievements his limitations also become apparent. The course of events is seen as the result of human decisions and acts. The human person alone is responsible for his or her actions; if one does wrong, one is called to account by others. Nothing happens due to divine intervention. As the Lord of history God remains hidden. "There is no miracle, and no charismatic leader appears. Events unwind themselves according to the laws of their own nature."[1] The narrative drives itself since every human act bears consequences that have to be followed up in the course of the events. Overall, the literary composition of 2 Samuel 9–20 and 1 Kings 1–2 is high-level historiography that demonstrates the course of events over a long period. Moreover, the history of one family determines the history of the state.

The intention of this narrative opus is disputed, especially since the character of the work is difficult to determine. On the one hand, everything leads to the ascension of Solomon, the son of Bathsheba, to the throne, since all other contenders eliminate themselves. Thus the narrative legitimates Solomon as the rightful successor to David. On the other hand there are critical undertones. The circumstances of Solomon's birth stand in sharp contrast to law and morality. Nothing distinguishes Solomon from the other sons of David so that he would be predestined to become his successor. Only the intrigue by the court prophet Nathan brings him to power, a power that he then uses in sharp contrast to the order created by David. With regard to his actions in particular, Solomon is not at all a suitable candidate for the throne of David. Thus the legitimating and the critical tendencies are mixed in the narrative. The path to power has been paved by the interplay of several factors, but with regard to the prevailing order in Israel Solomon is far from being the ideal monarch for the people. Too many acts cast too long a shadow; therefore his ascension to the throne cannot be portrayed with the aura of universal agreement. However, the picture of Solomon in 1 Kings 1–2 is generally a positive one that corresponds to the portrayal we find in the remaining chapters, 3–11, even if there the positive view is above all linked to elements such as his wisdom, building activity, and the expansion of power.

Commentary

[1:1-4] This section serves as a prelude to stress the age of David and to highlight the problems connected with it. From the note in 2 Sam 5:4-5 we learn that David must have been about seventy years old toward the end of his life. His debility is not further explained but graphically described. David is pictured as a freezing old man whose energy, which once distinguished him, has burned out. The measures taken by his followers are unsuccessful. Behind their actions lies the belief that his lost energy can be recovered by the presence of a young maiden. For this, Abishag of Shunem is chosen. In addition to her origin, only her beauty is mentioned. Shunem (modern

---

[1] Gerhard von Rad, "The Beginning of Historical Writing in Ancient Israel," in idem, *The Problem of Hexateuch and Other Essays,* trans. E. W. T. Dicken (New York: McGraw-Hill, 1966), 201 [166-204].

Solem), her place of birth, is located on the eastern edge of the plain of Jezreel and belongs, according to Josh 19:18, to the tribal territory of Issachar. Abishag is thus described as an Israelite. Furthermore, the Shunammite Abishag has nothing to do with the Shulammite of the Song of Songs.

The procedure to provide a woman for the king is not perceived as offensive in a society that knows of and practices polygamy. That a young woman would be a virgin until her marriage was expected. As stated in 1:4b, a change of her condition did not happen. With this note attention is drawn to two facts: First, the king is unable to participate actively in life and is thus in principle also unable to exercise his power. Second, the legal status of Abishag as an unmarried woman has not changed, for the marriage has not been consummated. Thus it is confirmed with regard to 2:13-25 "that Abishag did not belong to the royal harem."[2]

The duties of Abishag are described as fourfold: "to wait on the king" means the continuous readiness to serve the king (see 10:8). Here it is assumed that Abishag is always present in the rooms inhabited by the king, an abnormal situation for one of David's women, who lived together in a different part of the palace. The Hebrew word for "to be the king's attendant" is used only in this context. It describes Abishag's daily care for the king and includes, due to David's condition, nursing care. Thus the word does not describe any legal standing or official office but only emphasizes the fulfillment of the daily duties in dealing with the king.

"To lie in his bosom" is a euphemistic description for sexual intercourse. Here it becomes clear why an exceptionally beautiful woman had been looked for within Israel. Beauty does not necessarily have to be understood as a "sign of youthfulness,"[3] since beauty not only describes bodily perfection but also reflects the inner personality. By stressing her beauty the author pictures Abishag in the light of complete femininity. Vitality is intrinsically connected with sexual potency. The warming of David's bosom is to restore his diminished vitality by rekindling the lost potency with the help of a young woman. The restoration of the virility of the king is not just a nursing act, but also—according to ancient Near Eastern tradition—the well-being of the country depends entirely on the physical capability of its monarch. Even if in the narrative context the debility of David has to be understood as mainly a weakness in reaching decisions, the phrase "to lie in his bosom" also stresses the connection of vitality and sexual act. Thus it is necessary to look out for a young woman who still possesses the unfailing plentitude of life.

The plan fails, however, and the duties of Abishag are limited to "serving" the king. The broad term *šrt* (שרת) stresses personal services of a wide variety. The last designation seems to be an explanation for the looking after.

The followers of the king are not specified. The Hebrew word *ʿebed* (עבד) refers to all men in the service of the king. This can be slaves who carry out the basic

---

[2] Martin Noth, *Könige,* 14.
[3] Ibid.

services or members of the upper class who, as officials, run the bureaucracy. Since a question of high importance is debated by them, the followers are most likely high officials from the royal government who appear in the following narrative as independently acting persons.

[1:5-53] The narrative of Solomon's accession to the throne is shaped in a highly artistic way as the events in several places and with numerous acting persons are intertwined. The introduction (1:5-10) is followed by three scenes (1:11-37, 38-40, and 41-45, 49-50) of which the middle one reports the enthronement as such while the conclusion (1:51-53) depicts Solomon already exercising royal authority. Despite all details Solomon remains in the background and comes across as strangely passive. He does not take part in the intrigue, and everything happens without his involvement. Even the claim of Adonijah takes care of itself. Solomon only appears to show mercy toward his rival. The whole narrative is shaped in such a way that the enthronement happens almost inevitably. Solomon's ascension to the throne is triggered by the rash actions of Adonijah, engineered by the prophet Nathan, and determined by the old but still ruling King David.

[1:5-10] The introduction places Adonijah and his misbehavior at the center. Adonijah—with the programmatic name "Yahweh is my Lord"—was the fourth son born to David in Hebron, as stated in the list of David's sons in 2 Sam 3:1-5. Of his three elder brothers Amnon, Chileab, and Absalom, Amnon was killed by Absalom (2 Sam 13:28-29), Absalom in turn was killed by Joab (2 Sam 18:14-15), and the fate of Chileab is not mentioned in the sources—maybe he died a natural death. By his position among the sons of David, Adonijah was the next contender for the throne. Even though we do not find any statements for a succession according to birth in Israel, this seems to have been the normal procedure. Adonijah appears to have been very conscious of his special position.

[1:5] As a visible sign of his claim to the throne he musters a group of bodyguards, as Absalom had done before him (see 2 Sam 15:1), an act only the crown prince could afford to do. His chariot was drawn by two horses driven by a charioteer so that Adonijah could stand next to him and fight. The number of the horsemen is not stated, but it is unlikely to have exceeded ten. The cavalry is a new development that was unknown during the time of David. The infantry of fifty men was also part of the escort of the king's son that probably ran before the chariot to clear space. This entourage secured a royal appearance for the contender to the throne that reflected his status as crown prince. Since this small army had to be accommodated and provided for at the court, its setting up could not have been done without David's consent.

[1:6] The claim of Adonijah is criticized in that it is described as arrogance resulting from a lack of reprimand. The self-confident behavior displayed by Adonijah is thus pictured as a character deficiency; his striving for power is portrayed as the sign of a weak character. The special mention of his handsome appearance is similar to the description of David (1 Sam 20:18) and Absalom (2 Sam 14:25); according to biblical mentality the external appearance mirrors the internal disposition of a human being. Beauty does not mean the idealization of the physical appearance but represents the view that a beautiful person manifests the grace of Yahweh. Additionally, the claim of Adonijah is stressed by the remark that he was born after Absalom. This alone can be the meaning of the sentence, because Absalom had a different mother by the name of Maacah, a daughter of King Talmai of Geshur (2 Sam 3:3).

[1:7-8] The parties at the court are introduced without any reason for their existence. As long as the new king has not been installed, siding with one party or another is a life-or-death decision. If the son whom one supported got access to the throne, this would result in a strengthening of one's own position. If not, one would be suspected of disloyalty and could lose not only one's position but also one's life. With Joab and Abiathar—who probably had good reasons—two loyal followers of David who had served him faithfully for decades sided with Adonijah. Both held high offices in the state: Joab was head of the army, and Abiathar, as priest, was the mediator at sacrifices. Due to his descent from the priestly family of Nob (Ras el-Mesharif, 3 km. north of Jerusalem), Abiathar was probably close to the ancient Israelite cultic tradition but cannot be labeled as "a representative of a conscious Yahweh tradition."[4] The sole survivor of the slaughter of the priests of Nob, Abiathar came down to David to serve as priest (1 Sam 22:20-23; 23:6-9; 30:7). Next to Zadok he then became priest at the royal sanctuary in Jerusalem (2 Sam 20:25) and later bequeathed this office to his son (8:17). During the revolt of Absalom he and Zadok remained loyal to David (15:24-29). Joab was the head of the army (8:16; 20:23) and as a son of a sister of David also the king's nephew (1 Chr 2:16). He was not only loyal to David and next to him "the leading political and military head,"[5] but also a representative of old Israelite ideas and patterns of behavior to which David also adhered.

The rival party that did not see Adonijah as the legitimate successor, because it sided with a different son of David, consisted of Zadok, Benaiah, and Nathan. Zadok, probably a former priest at the Canaanite sanctuary in Jerusalem, became royal priest next to Abiathar after David's conquest of the city (2 Sam 20:25; see 8:17) so that he was not connected to the king by origin, but only by his office and the duty to be completely loyal to the king.

Benaiah, who is always described as "son of Jehoiada," was the commander of the Cherethites and Pelethites (2 Sam 8:18; 20:23). The terms "Cherethites" and "Pelethites" can no longer be adequately explained, but they seem clearly to be used

---

[4] Ernst Würthwein, *Könige,* 1:11.
[5] Ibid.

to describe David's personal army that served as bodyguards in Jerusalem and were under his personal command. They consisted of men from outside Israelite society who probably belonged to the groups of Aegean origin that settled in the southern coastal plain and its borders.[6] The commander Benaiah once belonged to the group of David's heroes who distinguished themselves by their brave military acts so that the king promoted him to head of his bodyguard (23:20-23). His place of origin is Kabzeel, a place in the Negev that cannot be identified (see Josh 15:21). Thus he belongs to the southern tribes that merged with Judah. His career is almost typical for somebody who was not a member of the Davidic family: he owed his office solely to his bravery. Whether he—as commander of the bodyguard—stood in any tension to Joab as head of the army is not known but could have been possible. It is never mentioned, however, that he had set an eye on Joab's position.

The third person of the rival party is Nathan the prophet, who had great authority at the court. According to 2 Sam 12:25 he was especially close to Solomon, since David entrusted Nathan with Solomon's education or at least placed Solomon under Nathan's protection. Nathan's origin remains unknown; he is absent from the list of David's officers, since he does not receive any orders from the king but is—as the messenger of God—quite independent from David, as his appearance in 2 Sam 12:1-15 demonstrates.

The rival party is thus far from homogeneous since it consisted of officers who were close to the court and also of Nathan with his special position. What binds them together is the conviction that Adonijah could not win them for his coalition due to the special relationship of Nathan and Solomon. Especially the following events are then determined by the initiative taken by Nathan in favor of Solomon. After the description of the parties, the reader or hearer is now adequately prepared for the following conflict.

[1:9-10] The meal given by Adonijah for his party happens by the stone Zoheleth next to En-rogel. The Rogel spring is identical to Job's well (Bir Ayyub), which can be located 300 m. south of the southern corner of the city of David in Wadi en-Nar, a continuation of the Kidron Valley. The well, which still today has plenty of water, had possibly been a spring during Davidic times that disappeared after the valley raised up. The contemporary name can be traced back to a cave just east of Job's well where, according to Arabic tradition, Job lived in order to be healed by the water.[7] The surroundings of the Rogel spring provided a suitable area for a banquet that could be easily accessed from Jerusalem. The stone Zoheleth (stone of snakes) is hardly "a monument of ancient Semitic snake worship,"[8] but rather a special stone formation or a single rock in the vicinity of the Rogel spring that has vanished over the last three

---

[6] See Noth, *Könige,* 25–26.

[7] Gustaf Dalman, *Jerusalem und sein Gelände* (Gütersloh: Gütersloher, 1930), 163–67.

[8] Würthwein, *Könige,* 1:3 n. 2.

thousand years due to natural circumstances. Thus the stone did not have any cultic implications.

The invited sons of the king are probably members of the royal family who were educated together and whom Adonijah sought as allies. Adonijah is not proclaimed king during the banquet. Such a premature step by Adonijah is only alleged by Nathan in 1:11. Rather, the banquet was supposed to create a special bond between the participants and to forge a better alliance.[9] Of course, Adonijah aimed at the crown in the near future but did not plan to usurp his father. The banquet of Adonijah has to be seen on the same level as the festivals of the sons of the king described in 2 Sam 13:23-27. The invitation of his party-liners Joab and Abiathar is not explicitly mentioned; they are most likely included in the group of the king's followers. Both high officials and palace servants can be called followers. That the rival party has not been invited is explicitly stressed in v. 10, although Zadok is not mentioned again.

The heroes are distinguished fighters who form a separate group and have to be seen as some sort of elite. Their special status is further emphasized by the fact that their names are mentioned in 2 Sam 23:8-12, 18-39.[10] As worthy fighters they marched into battle with the rest of the army but were put into action for single combat or individual missions (see 2 Sam 2:2-16). Their heroic deeds were in part transmitted in short notices; compare 2 Sam 21:15-22 and 23:12-17.

[1:11-37] The first scene (vv. 11-37) consists of different speeches that find their fulfillment in the investiture of Solomon as new king in the second scene (vv. 38-40). The speeches by changing protagonists serve as preparation for the act as such; they provide the necessary explanation for the actions. The individual speeches follow one another immediately:

vv. 11-14	Nathan to Bathsheba
vv. 15-21	Bathsheba in front of David
vv. 22-27	Nathan to David
vv. 28-31	David's promise to Bathsheba
vv. 32-35	order of the king
vv. 36-37	confirmation by Benaiah

[1:11-14] In his speech to Bathsheba, Nathan first interprets the events reported in the introduction (vv. 5-10) before developing his plan for the enthronement of Solomon. The banquet of Adonijah is understood by Nathan as an investiture as king. This interpretation of the narrative is never questioned and is thus assumed to be correct; the interpretation becomes a fact, a fact that in turn will be responsible for the following actions by the party of Solomon. The moving force behind all actions is Nathan, who

---

[9] Ibid., 13.

[10] See Karl Elliger, "Die dreissig Helden Davids," in *Kleine Schriften zum Alten Testament* (Tübingen: Mohr/Siebeck, 1966), 72–118.

knows how to use Bathsheba for his purposes to persuade David eventually to issue an order in favor of Solomon (vv. 32-35). Right from the beginning it is made abundantly clear that no other contender for the throne will stand a chance against the confirmation of Solomon by the king. The actions of Nathan presuppose that it has been his plan for a long time to make Solomon, to whom he has since his birth had a special relationship, as the pet name Jedidiah ("Yahweh is [my] beloved"; see 2 Sam 12:25) shows, the successor to David. Thus Nathan has to be seen as the driving force behind the ascension of Solomon. Bathsheba, Solomon's mother, is only a "willing tool."[11]

[1:12] He reminds her that all is at stake now: the future of her son as king and her own future as queen mother, who occupied a special place at the court. However, there could not have been any immediate danger for either her or her son. As one of David's wives she belonged to the royal harem, which is never mentioned but whose existence is assumed in 2 Sam 16:21-22. In spite of the culpable circumstances in which David had won Uriah's wife, the narrative in 2 Sam 11:1—12:25 detects a certain love and care of David for this woman. Nathan uses her for his plans not only as the mother of Solomon but also as the lover of David.

[1:13-14] For the implementation of his plan, Nathan provides Bathsheba with detailed orders for her appearance before the king. Here it is assumed that Bathsheba always had free access to the king. She is to remind David of his oath that Solomon will be his successor. Such an oath, however, is never reported in the succession narrative. If David really made such a commitment by oath this would explain the tensions between the two parties. If such an oath never existed the whole setting can be understood as skillful staging by Nathan in favor of his protégé that takes the debility of David into account. This question cannot be answered. Since the narrator does not mention the oath in the course of his succession narrative, "he provides his judgment of the circumstances under which Solomon came to the throne: he views them as a result of dishonest manipulations by the unscrupulous Nathan."[12] The instruction to Bathsheba closes in v. 14 with Nathan's promise to take care of the whole affair after Bathsheba has prepared it and to bring it to a happy end.

[1:15-21] The entrance of Bathsheba provides insights into the protocol at the royal court: even the wife of the king has to bow down (a *proskynesis*) before the king and is allowed to speak only after being spoken to (v. 16). Bathsheba's change of place from the women's apartments of the palace, where Nathan had visited her, to the quarters of the king is silently presupposed. Even though we do not possess any detailed knowledge of the royal palace, one can assume that it consisted of different

---

[11] Noth, *Könige*, 20.
[12] Würthwein, *Könige*, 1:14.

parts with different functions. The palace was probably the ancient fortress that David took when he conquered the city (see 2 Sam 5:9), since we learn of new building work done by Solomon only at a later stage (see 7:1-12). The exact location of the fortress is unknown; in analogy with other cities one can assume that it was placed in the center of Jerusalem.

[1:17-21] Bathsheba's speech follows exactly the pattern proposed by Nathan: she takes on the interpretation of Adonijah's banquet as a royal proclamation and repeats the words of the oath formulated by Nathan. She confronts the king in a skillful manner with claim and reality and leaves the decision of who should solve such a conflict to him. The speech is extremely sophisticated, since it leaves the king no choice but to side with Solomon and to take actions toward his enthronement. At the end of her speech she puts additional pressure on the king by alluding to the immediate danger for Solomon's and her own life resulting from his oath, since Adonijah will be forced after David's death to kill everybody who has a rightful claim to the throne.

[1:24-27] In his speech Nathan compares in masterly fashion the alleged acts with the will of David. The king is now trapped between his oath and the actions of Adonijah as interpreted by Nathan; thus he is forced to make a decision. Skillfully, Nathan expands and intensifies the details: the banquet becomes a sacrifice and the elevation of Adonijah to being king is implied in the use of the proclamation formula: "Long live King Adonijah." Here Nathan supposes that David endorsed the actions of Adonijah. The king has to answer to this challenge: the intrigue is perfect. The manipulation of old David has worked. The reader or hearer is dragged into the speculative and fictive string of arguments, and after the third repetition by Nathan that Adonijah has been proclaimed king the report has become a truth that is no longer questioned and that justifies all following actions.

[1:28-31] As expected the trapped king accepts the implied solution and calls for Bathsheba to tell her his decision. At this point the actions on the personal level come to an end. As the first one who had reminded David of his earlier promise, Bathsheba is now the first to receive note of his decision. Thus the reader or hearer is acquainted with the solution before any order is issued to implement the decision. David confirms his oath to the once loved and desired woman to keep his promise. David formulates his promise by means of an oath. Using a formula already encountered in 2 Sam 4:9, he refers to the "life of Yahweh," which guarantees the oath unswervingly, and to the help received by Yahweh.[13] Bathsheba's reaction corresponds to the court protocol. After her dismissal she does not appear again as an actor in the story.

[1:32-37] The whole scene ends with the order of David to crown Solomon at the Gihon spring. As known from Nathan's speech in v. 26, the party of Solomon is

---

[13] Noth, *Könige*, 23.

responsible for the realization of the order. The enthronement is to consist of the following elements: riding the royal mule to Gihon, anointing by Zadok the priest, cheering on the specified signal, and occupying the throne. David's statement gives the impression that the king set the pattern for the investiture. However, the ritual consists of traditional elements, which were necessary for the proper execution of an enthronement. The anointing was the decisive cultic act, which had already made David king. The cheering in connection with the blowing of the horn has to be seen in the same context. It is a constitutive element of the investiture, since it had already played an important role in the crowning of Absalom at Hebron (2 Sam 15:10). The enthronement of a new king while the old king is still alive makes him fellow ruler. The riding of the royal mule is determined by the choice of place for the investiture, because Gihon is located outside the city in the Kidron Valley.

The spring can be clearly identified with today's Spring of Mary (En Sittī Miryam = En Umm ed-Deraǧ). It owes its Hebrew name to the fact that the water does not flow on a regular basis but only bubbles out at certain intervals from a subterranean basin. Its present name is due to the legend that Mary washed the diapers of Jesus there.[14] The choice of Gihon as the place of the anointing of Solomon is not further justified but was probably determined by the common view of the purifying character of water, although the crowning ritual did not contain an element of purification. In any case, the choice of Gihon was due not to the sacred character of the place, but rather to the public character of the enthronement: a place had to be chosen that could accommodate all the people, something that was difficult to do within the densely built city walls.

Riding the royal mule is not really part of the investiture but still "an honor that points to royal standing."[15] Before the introduction of the horse, the donkey or mule served as the riding animal par excellence, emphasizing the high social status of the rider (see Judg 5:10; 10:4; 2 Sam 13:29). The entourage is only vaguely described as "followers," but one can assume that the whole court participated in an event such as a coronation.

Anointing and proclamation are the crucial acts of the investiture. The anointing with oil was a sacred act and was therefore executed by a priest; David ordered it himself as a sign that he was still in power. In any case, the anointing is always independent of the person ordering it. The anointing of the king can be prompted by the people (2 Sam 2:4; 5:3; 2 Kgs 11:12; 23:30) or by Yahweh (1 Sam 9:16; 10:1; 15:17; 16:12-13; 2 Sam 12:7; 2 Kgs 9:36). The anointing is the appointment to office; with it the new king gains power, strength, and honor, and at the same time a special relationship with Yahweh (see 1 Sam 24:7, 11; 26:9, 11, 16, 23; 2 Sam 1:14, 16; 19:22). With the anointing a divine act is performed on the king that makes him capable of his office and places him under the special protection of Yahweh. The cheering

---

[14] Dalman, *Jerusalem,* 168–73.
[15] Würthwein, *Könige,* 1:15.

signifies the recognition of the new king by the people. The blowing of the trumpet only gives the signal and has no further meaning. With the cry "Long live the king" the enthronement comes to an end and is publicly ratified. Thus Solomon is made coregent of the still living King David. In a further step, Solomon is to sit on the throne of David. Thus the new honor is clearly displayed. We do not know whether the enthronement of Solomon coincides with the abdication of David and his renunciation of power. The narrator focuses only on the installment of Solomon, and he emphasizes that this act is always in accordance with David's will.

The Hebrew word for "ruler," *nagid* (נגיד), is a fixed term for the king designate, although it is not possible to decipher its precise meaning (see 1 Sam 9:16; 10:1; 13:14; 25:30; 2 Sam 5:2; 6:21; 7:8; 1 Kgs 14:7; 16:2; 2 Kgs 20:5). At least it can be said with certainty that it was not simply a term for the crown prince but always includes the election by Yahweh.

[1:36-37] The order of David is brought to an end by Benaiah's wish for the confirmation through Yahweh. The words of Benaiah correspond to the ideology expressed in 2 Samuel 7 that the Davidic dynasty will endure forever. The words of Benaiah are neither tactless nor offensive but describe the kingship as an institution that is endorsed and supported by Yahweh and whose continuation depends not only on the character of the ruler but also on divine will. Benaiah's use of the ceremonial formula "Amen" confirms the special status of the ordered event.

[1:38-40] The execution in the second scene remains within the frame of the issued order. The correspondence between direct speech and reported action is a characteristic feature of Hebrew narrative style. Only at a few points are small details added, but this does not amount to an embellishment of the narrative. Of the participating people only the Cherethites and the Pelethites are mentioned, of whom Benaiah was commander. The bodyguards do not have any special duty but their presence is a further display of royal authority. Another detail that is mentioned is the horn of oil from the tent. David erected the tent as a sanctuary for the ark; before its abandonment by Solomon it also served as the place of sacrifice (2 Sam 6:17) since it contained an altar. The special mention of the place of origin of the oil confirms the view that the anointing is a sacral act that represents a consecration. Also the role of the people is stressed further. The cheering for the new king is pictured as boundless joy. The role of the people is not limited to proclaiming the new king; rather, they celebrate his enthronement like a festival where the joy of having a new king is so boundless that— metaphorically—the earth quakes at their noise.

[1:41-45, 49-50] The narrator moves back to Adonijah in the third scene. It is implied that Adonijah's festival continued during the enthronement of Solomon. Only the cheering of the people draws the attention of the guests to the events that happened some hundred meters further north; it is Joab who voices the amazement of the guests. The investiture of Solomon as the new king is next reported by a messenger—the important message is repeated to the reader or hearer for the third time. The messenger, Jonathan, son of the priest Abiathar, is already known as a loyal follower of David from 2 Sam 15:36; 17:17ff.

[1:46-48] The addition to the messenger's report repeats the tribute paid by Benaiah in v. 37 and stresses once more the dynastic character of the succession. In addition, the praise of God with which he is worshiped is put in David's mouth (see Pss 41:14; 89:53; 106:48; 119:12; 135:21). The mention of David's bed does not demonstrate his debility but simply marks the place of the action—David's chamber.

The guests' reaction to the report is depicted as a hasty departure and panic. The narrator shows that the guests have realized for whom the bell tolls. There is no sign of resistance or taking up the challenge; the party of Adonijah simply falls apart in a blind panic. Adonijah's situation is so serious that he seeks asylum in the tent of worship directly by the altar, whose horns he grasps. Adonijah seeks the protection of the altar even though there is no sign of bloodguilt. The asylum is a specially protected quarter where an unjustly pursued victim is safe from his persecutors. The horns of the altar are raised blocks of stone on each of the four corners; these "horns" were regarded as the seat of holiness (see Lev 16:18; Exod 30:10). The character of the asylum was especially effective in places of special holiness within the sacred quarter, since here the divine presence removed the victim from human persecution.[16] As a rival to Solomon, Adonijah is in danger, since he obviously does not show the expected loyalty by forming a party to support his claim to the throne of David. By seeking asylum in the sanctuary Adonijah tries to prevent Solomon from having him killed and hopes to obtain an act of grace.

[1:51-53] At the end of the whole narrative the scene of action changes again, and for the first time puts Solomon conscientiously in the spotlight. The intention is twofold: first, the fate of Adonijah has to be resolved; second, the magnanimity of Solomon is stressed because his first decision as king is to show mercy toward Adonijah. Thus at the end of the narrative the two rivals meet. The paragraph is composed as a messenger speech and climaxes in the promise of freedom for Adonijah. Previous to that Adonijah has to subordinate himself to the king, here expressed in the address of Solomon as king and the self-predication of Adonijah as follower. The life and death of Adonijah will depend on his future behavior; Solomon stresses that he will not tolerate any deviation from the expected loyalty. The formula of mercy, "Go home," does not imply any restriction of Adonijah's freedom or even his banishment from the court, but makes him dependent on Solomon's mercy, since he can now decide if

---

[16] Noth, *Könige*, 29.

Adonijah will ever again occupy a public office. The further fate of Adonijah depends entirely on his loyalty toward the king.

Thus the conflict between the two sons ends in favor of Solomon, because Nathan was able to force David to reach a decision regarding his succession. Whether the narrative ever ended with 2:12 or a similar remark can no longer be established. In the current context, the final remark of the narrator can only be found in 2:46b at the end of the added narratives. The additional episodes in 2:1-9 and 10-11 interrupt the flow of the narrative in 1:5-53 with several individual measures of Solomon regarding his opponents.

[2:1-9] The last words of David are a secondary composition. The first part (vv. 1-4) contains several Deuteronomistic formulas, while the second half (vv. 5-9) prepares for the following events. Apart from the introduction to the direct speech (v. 1) there is no framing narrative, which is hardly necessary anyway due to the numerous references to David in the previous parts of the narrative. David's speech begins in v. 2 with the announcement of his imminent death, which is euphemistically described as "to go the way of all the earth," just as in Josh 23:14. The first part of David's speech (vv. 3-4) is shaped by fairly traditional language. The formula of exhortation is similar to Deut 31:67; Josh 1:6, 7, 9; 10:25; 2 Sam 10:12. The words "keep the charge" appear in Deut 11:1; Josh 22:3. The phrase "walking in his ways" is a standard formula of the Deuteronomistic History as a whole (see Deut 8:6; 10:12; etc.). Often we find formulas such as "so that you may prosper" (see Deut 29:8; Josh 1:7) or "with all your heart and all your soul" (see Deut 4:29). Finally, the call to keep and to obey "his statutes, his commandments, his ordinances, and his testimonies" is repeated over and over again in the Deuteronomistic History.[17] Here David appears as the keeper of the Torah of Moses as no king did after him.

Toward the end this speech refers to the situation of the establishment of the dynasty. Nathan's promise of 2 Sam 7:12-15 is interpreted in such a way that only the observance of the law results in the fulfillment of the divine promise.[18] With these words an obligation is placed on Solomon to keep the Deuteronomic law. In these words to his successor, David is pictured as an outstanding king; no other king exhorts his son in a similar way. The only comparison is Yahweh's programmatic exhortation of Joshua as successor to Moses at the beginning of the book of Joshua (Josh 1:2-9).

[2:5-9] The second part of David's speech has to be understood as the preparation for the four following narratives (vv. 13-46). The fate reported in vv. 13-25 is not mentioned, however, since this had already been prepared for in 1:51-53. Also the expul-

---

[17] See Norbert Lohfink, *Das Hauptgebot: Eine Untersuchung literarischer Einleitungsfragen zu Dtn 5–11*, AnBib 20 (Rome: Pontifical Biblical Institute Press, 1963), 64ff., 299ff.

[18] Noth, *Könige*, 30.

sion of Abiathar is not mentioned. His deposition as priest in Jerusalem has been added in vv. 27-28, because his fate was closely linked to that of Adonijah. In contrast, the reward of Barzillai (v. 7) for his loyal attitude to David during his flight from Absalom has only been added to show that not all commandments of David were of a negative kind.[19] The punishment or reward decreed by David is in all cases justified by the previous behavior of the persons concerned. At the same time these justifications are references back to other parts of the Deuteronomistic History.

The basic principle behind the orders concerning the treatment of the different persons is the idea of poetic justice. The individual is in all circumstances responsible for his actions; good behavior is rewarded, whereas bad conduct is punished. Behavior that contradicts law and morality is perceived as bad or evil. Loyalty was the constitutive element in the behavior toward the king. This unconditional loyalty had been taken over from tribal society, just like the institution of blood vengeance that demanded the murderer's death for the blood shed. Thus the demands of David have to be placed within the context of clan ethos and cannot be seen as innovations of the recently established kingship. David's orders had the sole purpose of releasing Solomon from the responsibility for the questionable and probably controversial treatment of Joab and Shimei.[20] The decision is ascribed to David; its execution is only a consequence of Joab's and Shimei's former acts.

[2:5-6] Joab falls victim to blood vengeance because he had murdered Abner and Amasa. The justification refers back to 2 Sam 3:26-30 and 20:9-10; both acts characterize Joab as a person who does not shrink back from murder to decide situations in favor of David. (The killing of Absalom has to be understood along the same lines. It is not mentioned here since the truth about his end has been kept secret from David; see 2 Sam 18:9-15.) Normally blood vengeance serves to protect life. It rests on the notion that the shedding of innocent blood can be expiated only by the killer's blood. The vengeance is normally carried out by a relative but can also be the duty of the king. Generally speaking atonement can also be granted without a human act if God accounts for the expiation of the bloodguilt.[21]

[2:7] The order to provide for the descendants of Barzillai as guests at the court is justified by an episode during David's flight before Absalom. Next to two other landowners by the name of Shobi son of Nahash and Machir son of Ammiel, Barzillai the Gileadite provided food and household goods for David and his army at Mahanaim, a place yet unidentified on the banks of the Jabbok (2 Sam 17:24-29). Due to his old age Barzillai had declined the offer of David to follow him to the court

---

[19] Würthwein, *Könige,* 1:20.

[20] Noth, *Könige,* 30.

[21] See Klaus Koch, "Der Spruch, 'Sein Blut bleibe auf seinem Haupt' und die israelitische Auffassung vom vergossenen Blut," *VT* 12 (1962) 396–416.

at Jerusalem (2 Sam 19:32-41). Such a provision was most likely not really an alternative for a big landowner.

[2:8-9] The treatment of Shimmei too is justified by an episode from the flight of David to Mahanaim. Near Bahurim, a place east of Jerusalem, Shimei had thrown stones at David and his followers and had cursed him (2 Sam 16:5-14). A curse is a powerful word; its impact emerges from itself. This curse did not have any effect; thus David can call it "weak." The oath "I will put you to death with the sword" stands in strict contrast to the behavior of David during the event and after his return to Jerusalem, when David assured him, against the advice of Abishai, the brother of Joab, that he would be spared and not punished (2 Sam 19:24). The behavior of Shimei is explained by his allegiance to the clan of Saul; out of his solidarity with the dead King Saul he had to show dislike for David. The contrast of the order in v. 9 with the original behavior of David that aimed at mercy and fear of God in 2 Sam 16:11-12 demonstrates particularly clearly that this order here has been composed to justify Solomon's treatment of Shimei. It is not royal despotism but rather Shimei's own wrong behavior that is responsible for his treatment and forces Solomon to seek vengeance. David was bound by his oath; Solomon on the other hand can act free from any old obligation or responsibilities.

The use of the phrase "to go down to Sheol" as a description for dying implies the old Israelite image of life after death. According to this view, the dead person moves to the underworld, called Sheol in Hebrew. The origin and meaning of the term are not clear; it is a place underneath the earth where the dead persons assemble as shadows with no hope of a return to the realm of the living. The image of Sheol corresponds to the Greek concept of Hades—life continues in a restricted form but without the fundamental experiences of life such as love and pain.[22] "The darkness of Hades covers all the dead with the veil of equality. Tensions and differences that make life happy and miserable no longer exist: the small are like the great, the servant is no longer subject to his master (Job 3:19), and thus all storms of lust and passion have died down."[23] Quietness and silence are the characteristic features of the underworld, "for there is no work or thought or knowledge or wisdom in Sheol" (Eccl 9:10).

[2:10-11] The concluding formula for David interrupts the flow of the narrative. It deviates from the normal pattern of these formulas as they are found with later kings in that the duration of his reign is repeated from 2 Sam 5:4-5 and the expression "and X succeeded him" is missing. The figure of speech "to sleep with his ancestors" presupposes a burial in a family tomb that was in use for many generations. The image

---

[22] See Victor Maag, "Tod und Jenseits nach dem Alten Testament," in *Kultur, Kulturkontakt und Religion: Gesamelte Studien zur allgemeinen und alttestamentlichen Religionsgeschichte,* ed. Victor Maag (Göttingen: Vandenhoeck & Ruprecht, 1980), 181–202.

[23] Ibid., 186–87.

of the burial with the ancestors need not be viewed in contrast to the going down to Sheol, since Hebrew thought is able to combine both aspects without giving any explanation or harmonization.

Irrespective of numerous variants, the tomb hewn from stone and accessible by steps consisted of a square chamber leading on to several neighboring chambers with recesses at a certain height above the ground. The dead bodies were placed on these benches; after decaying the bones were collected and placed in a pit underneath the floor. This type of tomb is called a "bench tomb" after the mode of burial. There are several burial grounds of this kind in the necropolises around Jerusalem. For a concrete example compare the burial ground from the period of the kings near the École Biblique.[24] The burial place of the kings of Judah is unknown; however, a place within the city walls is unlikely, for the term "city of David" has to be understood to include the surrounding areas where the necropolis is situated. The two tunnels, labeled T1 and T2, excavated by R. Weill on the southeastern hill, are so different from the tombs typical of the epoch that it is impossible to regard them as royal tombs.[25] This scholarly view still found in the literature has to be abandoned because no traces typical of tombs have been found there.

The assessment of David's years of government is divided according to the two capitals. David reigned first in Hebron, the urban center of Judah, as king of Judah. Only after his promotion to king of the northern tribes and the conquest of Jerusalem (2 Sam 5:1-10) did David choose the city, now called "city of David," as his seat of government. One reason was its geographical position on the border between Judah and the northern tribes. Another is that David, as conqueror of the city, was also the king of Jerusalem and could thus determine the development and organization according to his will—a privilege inherited by his successors.[26] Even though the personal union of the city kingship is not explicitly mentioned in the sources, the renaming of the city as "city of David" demonstrates a certain sovereignty of the king with regard to his city.

[2:12] The mention of the successor in the final remark could be omitted, since v. 12 serves as the conclusion of the succession narrative of 1:5-53. Adding further narratives made it necessary to repeat the statement in 2:46b. Given the difficulties of the enthronement, the security of the Solomonic rule is now stressed. It is only now that the attention of the reader or hearer is drawn to the fact that the elimination of Adonijah and his party has not been the automatic consequence as suggested by the narrative so far. At the same time the remark leads on to the following narratives, which stress the aspect of the security of the kingship of Solomon with regard to his

---

[24] Gideon Barkay, A. Kloner, and Amihai Mazar, "The Northern Necropolis of Jerusalem during the First Temple Period," in *Ancient Jerusalem Revealed,* ed. Hillel Geva (Jerusalem: Israel Exploration Society, 1994), 119–27.

[25] Raymond Weill, *La cité de David* (Paris: Geuthner, 1920), 157–75.

[26] See Albrecht Alt, "Jerusalems Aufstieg," in *Kleine Schriften* (Munich: Beck, 1959), 3:243–57.

adversaries from within; however, one cannot help but think that his behavior as a whole was quite unscrupulous.

[2:13-25] Adonijah's final fate is narrated as of his own making, even though the order to kill him is issued by the king. Apart from the narrative frame, which is extraordinarily brief and presupposes knowledge of 1 Kings 1, the events are related in direct speech. Again, Bathsheba serves as a willing tool; her position as the king's mother seems to enable her in a special way to ask a favor for Adonijah in front of Solomon. No doubts are left that she is convinced of the guilelessness of Adonijah's request, especially since Adonijah in his speech accepts the kingship of Solomon as a divinely given fact. The king's mother occupied a special position of honor that is expressed in her sitting on a throne next to the king during public appearances. Thus rivalries between the women who lived together in special quarters of the palace were limited. Women were part of the court but did not play any important political role. The high standing of the king's mother is graphically expressed by the honor paid to her by Solomon.

The politeness of the king ends, however, when he hears Adonijah's request presented by Bathsheba. Instead of keeping his promise, Solomon responds with an oath to kill Adonijah. In Solomon's eyes, the "small favor" becomes a claim to kingship. In this overreaction the narrator aims at showing the insecurity of the new king. In the dialogue Solomon reveals the sore point of his enthronement that is also the reason for his weak self-confidence. The narrator emphasizes that Adonijah's claim to succeed David is justified and that Solomon's enthronement as the new king is not beyond doubt. The prevailing of Solomon during the struggle for succession does not imply legitimacy. The conflict over the kingship is merely alluded to and only its results are reported. The followers of David are almost all set aside and their offices filled with new men.

Many have speculated why asking for Abishag of Shunem sealed Adonijah's fate. As far as her legal status is concerned, she does not belong to the king's harem, since David does not have sexual intercourse with her. But as a servant of David Abishag belongs to the court, and thus Adonijah has to ask Solomon to leave her to him. Solomon regards the request as a claim to affiliation that has to be seen as on the same level as Adonijah's claim to the throne; this claim remains as long as the contender lives. The request of Adonijah therefore provides Solomon with a suitable opportunity to rid himself of his rival forever.

Here Solomon's behavior stands in sharp contrast to his mercy at the end of the succession narrative (1:51-53). Since the freedom granted to Adonijah does not remove the potential danger implied by his presence, Solomon has to dispose of him altogether; the request for Abishag is then a welcome occasion. The narrative justifies why Solomon did away with his rival; it makes the act understandable. Still the narrator did not manage to justify the act completely, because the killing of Adonijah at the hands of Benaiah after a royal order remains an act of despotism. The narrator presents the event in such a way that Solomon uses the request of Adonijah to suspect him of still harboring some aspirations for the throne and to draw consequences from it.[27] The offense of Adonijah is too insignificant to justify the consequences; only in Solomon's view does it represent a mortal crime.

Despite the fact that the narrator is prepared to let the picture of Solomon as a merciful king be tainted, he cannot persuade the reader or hearer that Solomon's actions are entirely justified. The murder of Adonijah is understandable within the framework of the struggle for the succession of David but does not fit the picture of the wise and just king to which the narrative is committed since 1:51-53 and which shapes the character of the later tradition. The blood of Adonijah sticks to the hands of Solomon; his unscrupulous behavior cannot be covered up or even justified by the narrative.

[2:26-27] After removing his rival Adonijah, Solomon systematically eliminates Adonijah's party. Since the narrative element is absent from the banishment of Abiathar to Anathoth (vv. 26-27), the episode could be a later addition to provide details for the measure taken in 2:35b. Abiathar is removed from office and exiled to his estate in Anathoth (Khirbet Der es-Sidd near Anata). It is doubtless the right of a new king to appoint new personnel, but the removal of the acting priest is explicitly mentioned without further explanation, since Abiathar is already known from 1:5-53 as a member of Adonijah's party. The reference to the curse over the Elides, the priestly family at the sanctuary of Shiloh (1 Sam 2:27-36), is not very convincing, since Abiathar is a descendant of the priests of Nob. In reality his removal seems to have been a political decision. As a follower of David, Abiathar was replaced by Zadok to make way for a new generation of officials who represent and advance the idea of merging Canaanite and ancient Israelite elements of the state. Solomon represented a new idea of kingship as an institutionalized form of power and needed new officials to put his concept into practice.

The reference to the loyalty of Abiathar toward David in difficult times (1 Sam 22:20-22; 23:6, 9; 30:7) is used as an explanation for having spared his life. Abiathar is no longer allowed to sacrifice for the king at the royal sanctuary, but he cannot lose the inherited qualification as priest. The exile to Anathoth means the restriction to private life and provision by his land only. The pointed use of the term "today" in Solomon's speech must refer to the day of his enthronement and not to the previously reported removal of Adonijah.

[2:28-35] On a literary level the narrative of the end of Joab continues the narrative of the enthronement of Solomon in 1:5-53. Joab belonged to the guests of Adonijah (1:41) and like them fled after Jonathan had delivered the message of Solomon's enthronement (1:49). The news of mercy toward Adonijah had obviously prompted

---

[27] Noth, *Könige,* 34.

Joab too to seek protection by the altar of the sanctuary in the tent. The dialogue between Solomon and Benaiah has the function to clarify who is responsible for the murder of Joab, during which the asylum of the sanctuary is disregarded and the place of sacrifice profaned. Even the usually quite violent Benaiah has tried to maintain the asylum of the sanctuary, but Solomon orders the removal and disregards the laws of the sacred realm. The narrator makes quite clear that the death of Joab is an act of royal despotism in which Solomon transgresses his boundaries. Thus the narrative serves to correct the picture of Solomon. The order to kill Joab stands also in sharp contrast to the act of mercy to which Adonijah owes his life. Solomon is pictured as a king who unscrupulously uses his newly acquired power and disregards the law of asylum; Benaiah as his obedient servant is a helping hand.

The murdered Joab is buried in a family tomb located in the Judean desert near Bethlehem, the place of Joab's origin (see 2 Sam 2:31). Verses 31b-33 add to the justification in 2:5 of why Joab had to be killed. The office of head of the army, now vacant, goes to Benaiah, who has so far been the commander of the bodyguard. With the killing of Joab another of David's followers has been removed and replaced by a new official who is completely loyal to Solomon. The note on Zadok is not quite correct, since he had already been priest next to Abiathar under David (see 2 Sam 2:25); however, he has now risen to be the sole occupant of the priestly office.

[2:36-46a] The narrative of the death of Shimei is a literary appendix but presupposes that Solomon has had Shimei killed. The plot is structured in such a way that Solomon appears cleared of any charges; however, the reader is given the impression that Solomon has had Shimei killed for a trivial reason. The narrative demonstrates the king's determination to rid himself of actual or alleged adversaries. The real reason why Shimei is counted among the enemies of the state can no longer be determined. (The events in connection with the flight of David to Mahanaim are only alluded to in the short addition 2:44-45 to verify the fulfillment of David's order in 2:8-9.)

In any case Shimei is placed under house arrest in Jerusalem; failure to comply to that will result in his death. The reason for this measure might have been that Shimei was not allowed to return to his Benjaminite home in Bahurim because Solomon suspected or feared opposition there. Bahurim has not yet been identified. Wolfgang Zwickel has proposed Barruka in the Wadi el-Lehham as a possible location, since, according to the pottery found there, the site was occupied during the Iron Age.[28] Over the course of the narrative Shimei's oath is given a prominent position to underline that he is himself responsible for his fate. Particularly with the formula "your blood shall be upon your own head" blame is apportioned unambiguously; because of his earlier consent Shimei has forfeited his life.

---

[28] Wolfgang Zwickel, "Baḥurim und Nob," *BN* 61 (1991) 84–93.

The whole narrative can easily be recognized as literary fiction. The reason for the death sentence is constructed from fairly simple motives. The escape of two slaves is a common event. Achish of Gath is known as the feudal lord of David from the history of David's rise (see 1 Sam 21:1-16; 27:1—28:2), his figure has probably been taken from there. The Philistine town was probably located at the fringe of the Shephelah at Tell eṣ-Ṣafi outside the state territory. Even though Shimei just wanted to reclaim his property, the king had to execute the death sentence relentlessly; again he uses Benaiah to carry out the order to kill Shimei.

[2:46b] The concluding remark brings the previous events to a close and arrives at a preliminary summary of the reign of Solomon. The measures taken so far appear to be logical decisions in support of his kingship. Solomon secures his reign by ridding himself of potential rivals.

The narratives relating to the enthronement of Solomon and to the subsequent events are not historical despite the fact that they pretend to give insights into the secret dealings at the court. Rather, they represent a fictive form of the events in connection with the enthronement of Solomon; at the same time the narrator wants to convey a certain judgment. This judgment is quite differentiated and not easy to reduce to a common denominator. On the one hand the legitimacy of Solomon's succession to the throne is pointed out: it happens in accordance with the will of David and it follows the proper rites. On the other hand there is a certain criticism of Solomon in that his first measures to secure his reign, which result in the killing of several possible rivals, are portrayed as pure despotism. The picture of Solomon in 1:5-53 as the well-meaning son of David with good intentions is corrected by the literary additions in 2:13-25, 28-35, and 36-46a; here Solomon is portrayed as a ruthless ruler who uses every possible means to remove Adonijah and his party. The justification for his brutal acts at the beginning of his reign is quite meager, and this creates a certain distance between the reader and the new ruler. The reality behind the narratives can only be guessed at. The characters are undoubtedly historical figures, and the fate of Adonijah and his party is not pure invention; the circumstances, however, are purely fictitious. Thus the narratives cannot simply be regarded as reports of factual events; rather, they represent the attempt to portray the beginning of Solomon's reign in such a way that the dark side of the new ruler comes clearly to the fore.

The whole narrative of the succession to David reaches its climax in the enthronement of Solomon in 1:5-53. In the light of the failure of the princes Amnon and Absalom, it is understandable that the succession cannot be solved according to rank of birth. It cannot be concealed, however, that a certain group at the court with Nathan as its leader was responsible for the investiture of Solomon as king. He must have known his protégé as well as the circumstances at the court, since he was able to take the necessary steps.

A suspicion remains that the proceedings were not as clear as suggested by the narrator. The enthronement of Solomon is skillfully portrayed as a reaction to the rash behavior of Adonijah, and the rival parties at the court are equally skillfully set against each other. With Solomon a son of David ascends to the throne who was not born to him in Hebron and who was educated by Nathan. He was no longer dependent on the tribal tradition but focused more on the Canaanite element of the population. The expansion of his empire was only possible if he managed to unite the different groups and tendencies into one state. It is emphasized by the tradition; the transition from a tribal kingship to a state secured by military and bureaucracy happened during Solomon's reign. Several measures point to this claim to realize control over all aspects of private, public, and religious life, a claim that is characteristic for ancient Near Eastern monarchs. In view of the subsequent narrative the court party headed by the prophet Nathan supported the right person. Solomon's lifework, the integration of the different groups of the population into one state, failed in the end due to the resistance of the radical supporters of the tribes; yet this cannot refute the correctness of the development introduced and maintained by Solomon.

Opening

Text

3:1 Solomon made a marriage alliance with Pharaoh king of Egypt; he took Pharaoh's daughter and brought her into the city of David, until he had finished building his own house and the house of the LORD and the wall around Jerusalem. 2 The people were sacrificing at the high places, however, because no house had yet been built for the name of the LORD. 3 Solomon loved the LORD, walking in the statutes of his father David; only, he sacrificed and offered incense at the high places.

Analysis

These verses represent an intermediate piece that consists of several different separate notes. It neither belongs to the previous narrative nor to the following paragraph, vv. 4-15, which has its own introduction. Its content (v. 1) consists of a note on the marriage and accommodation of the daughter of Pharaoh and a summary statement regarding sacrificial practice (vv. 2-3). The paragraph is therefore different from both the sporadic notes added to the Solomon narrative (4:20—5:5; 9:15-28; 10:14-29) and the usual introductory statements found elsewhere. Still, these verses have to be understood as a programmatic introduction to the further account of Solomon.

Commentary

[3:1] Here it is surprising that the note regarding the marriage to an Egyptian princess is put in a prominent place at the very beginning of v. 1. The emphasis shows the importance of the event. Unfortunately the princess does not have a name, so it is impossible to verify the circumstances of the wedding. That we also find a daughter of Pharaoh among Solomon's wives cannot be doubted; at least there must have been an Egyptian woman who was labeled as such. The marriage to one of Pharaoh's daughters is also presupposed in 7:8 and 9:16-17, 24; here it could have been a daughter of Pharaoh Siamum (978–960), even though he is not mentioned in the biblical account.[1] Despite the fact that details cannot be determined, the union fits the marriage pattern of the pharaohs as reflected in the Eighteenth Dynasty (1540–1295 BCE).[2] The exchange of princesses was a common custom to secure diplomatic relations as well as to safeguard the Egyptian foreign political and economic interests. The reign of Solomon coincides with a new rise of Egyptian power that commenced with Siamun, the last king of the Twenty-first Dynasty, and reached a preliminary climax with the military campaign to Palestine by Sheshonk (Shishak) I (945–924 BCE), the first king of the Twenty-second Dynasty. The note stresses that the marriage to the Egyptian princess happened before the erection or completion of the temple and palace so that it was necessary to accommodate her in the royal palace of the city of David. After the completion of the new palace complex the woman was given her own house (7:8), as is fitting for her status.

The verse uses traditional material and does not contain any new information. Given the normal bias of the Deuteronomistic Historian toward cultic matters, it is somewhat unusual that the introductory formula should start with a note of political content. Maybe the glory of Egypt should reflect upon Solomon in the shape of the daughter of Pharaoh, while the rest of the tradition is constructed around the theme of wisdom.

[3:2] The subject of v. 2 is the people, whose sacrificial practice on the cultic heights is condemned but at the same time also excused, since the temple has not yet been built. The remark is an addition to v. 3 by the Deuteronomistic redactor, since it does not contain any new information. According to the Deuteronomistic view, offering sacrifices at the high places was the main abomination of the kings that was responsible for the downfall of kingship in the end; the people are included in this practice of disregarding the command to sacrifice only at the temple.

[3:3] In v. 3 Solomon is essentially judged in a positive manner by the Deuteronomistic Historian. "To love God" is the main principle of Deuteronomistic theology; this love has to be understood as sole and complete loyalty to Yahweh to the exclusion of worship of any foreign gods (see Deut 6:5; 11:1; 13:14). After all, the love of God embraces the whole sphere of life in the sense of a devotion to God that includes absolute loyalty. It is also stressed that the political and ethical dimensions of Solomon's actions are within the norms of the Deuteronomistic Historian's tradition. It is not general moral principles that are envisaged here; rather, the formulation has to be understood against the background of the Deuteronomic law (Deuteronomy 12–26), because this legal corpus contained, next to several religious stipulations, also commandments regulating life in the political and personal realms.

---

[1] See Abraham Malamat, "Aspects of the Foreign Policies of David and Solomon," *JNES* 22 (1963) 1–17, esp. 11–12.

[2] See *LÄ*, 2:1104–7.

The sacrifices at the high places are regarded negatively. "High place" is a term established by the Deuteronomistic Historian for all cultic places outside Jerusalem. Whether we are dealing just with cultic places or with sanctuaries has to remain open. It cannot be determined either whether these high places were situated within or outside the settlements—the terminology suggests that we are dealing with places situated on hilltops close to settlements (see 1 Sam 9:13-19). Due to the general use of the word, the layout and significance of the high places cannot be determined. The term only implies a very negative stance toward all cultic places outside Jerusalem. Since the temple in Jerusalem is the only legitimate place for sacrifice and the worship of Yahweh in the theology of Deuteronomy (see Deuteronomy 12), all other cultic places outside Jerusalem had to be viewed as illegitimate and are thus labeled "high places."

The negative judgment on Solomon is limited, since the temple as the only legitimate place of worship is built during his reign. Overall Solomon is judged altogether positively in the first statement of v. 3. The opening serves as a transitional passage from the rather dramatic beginnings of Solomon's reign to the subsequent historical narrative. The theophany at Gibeon (3:4-15) adds to this evaluation.

Theophany at Gibeon

Text

3:4 The king went to Gibeon to sacrifice there, for that was the principal high place; Solomon used to offer a thousand burnt offerings on that altar. 5 At Gibeon the LORD appeared to Solomon in a dream by night; and God said, "Ask what I should give you." 6 And Solomon said, "You have shown great and steadfast love to your servant my father David, because he walked before you in faithfulness, in righteousness, and in uprightness of heart toward you; and you have kept for him this great and steadfast love, and have given him a son to sit on his throne today. 7 And now, O LORD my God, you have made your servant king in place of my father David, although I am only a little child; I do not know how to go out or come in. 8 And your servant is in the midst of the people whom you have chosen, a great people, so numerous they cannot be numbered or counted. 9 Give your servant therefore an understanding mind to govern your people, able to discern between good and evil; for who can govern this your great people?"

10 It pleased the LORD that Solomon had asked this. 11 God said to him, "Because you have asked this, and have not asked for yourself long life or riches, or for the life of your enemies, but have asked for yourself understanding to discern what is right, 12 I now do according to your word. Indeed, I give you a wise and discerning mind; no one like you has been before you and no one like you shall arise after you. 13 I give you also what you have not asked, both riches and honor all your life; no other king shall compare with you. 14 If you will walk in my ways, keeping my statutes and my commandments, as your father David walked, then I will lengthen your life."

15 Then Solomon awoke; it had been a dream. He came to Jerusalem where he stood before the ark of the covenant of the LORD. He offered up burnt offerings and offerings of well-being, and provided a feast for all his servants.

36

Analysis

The theophany to Solomon serves as a programmatic prelude to the following historical narrative. Apart from the introduction in v. 4 and the end in v. 15, the passage does not report any action but consists only of direct speeches in the following order: Yahweh—Solomon—Yahweh. The speeches are so strongly shaped by Deuteronomistic language that the Deuteronomistic Historian is the most likely author. It is impossible to extract an older version that served as a literary *Vorlage* from this text. The narrative as a whole is legendary. The revelation of the dream is an event that solely concerns Solomon, and the fictional content of the narrative serves to clarify certain traits of Solomon's character as exemplary. The essential message is the ability to reign, captured in the phrase "listening heart" (NRSV "understanding mind") and setting the example for future kings. This legendary narrative first marks Solomon as the ideal king who places his whole reign under the faith in Yahweh.

Commentary

[3:4] The theophany is situated at Gibeon and stands in the context of numerous sacrifices. According to the Deuteronomistic view, sacrifices at high places are illegitimate, but it is unproblematic to report Solomon's offering at the altar of Gibeon, since it happened before the building of the temple. Gibeon was a former Canaanite city that was protected by a special treaty with Israel (Joshua 9) and situated at el-Jib, about 8 km. northwest of Jerusalem in the middle of the tribal territory of Benjamin. Despite this protective agreement, Saul had carried out a massacre in the city for which blood vengeance was claimed in the time of David (2 Sam 21:1-9).[1] The cultic place at which Solomon sacrificed probably has to be understood as a Canaanite sanctuary, because the sacrifice on a non-Israelite altar would not cause any problems, since no conflict arose with the Deuteronomistic ideology of Jerusalem as the only legitimate cultic place. Thus far it is impossible to locate such a sanctuary archaeologically.[2] The choice of Gibeon as the place of the theophany to Solomon was determined by the author's aim to locate the revelation of the dream at a place close to Jerusalem that was known to possess a sanctuary. Detailed historical knowledge or an ancient tradition cannot be read off the location.

[3:5] The dream is a normal vehicle for a revelation (see Gen 26:3; 28:16; 31:10-11, 24; 40:5; 46:2ff.; 1 Sam 3:4ff.). It is remarkable that the introduction or self-presentation by Yahweh is absent here. The address is a call that Solomon answers. The fairly common motif of granting a request at a crucial point in life is used here to equip the person for duties and deeds in the future.

---

[1] See Henri Cazelles, "David's Monarchy and the Gibeonite Claim," *PEQ* 87 (1955) 165–75.

[2] See James B. Pritchard, "Gibeon's History in the Light of Excavations," in *Congress Volume: Rome 1968,* VTSup 17 (Leiden: Brill, 1969), 1–12.

[3:6-9] Solomon shows himself deserving of his request. Before he utters his wish for a "listening heart," he refers to the circumstances to which he is obligated. First he mentions David, the founder of the dynasty who walked before God "in faithfulness, in righteousness, and in uprightness of heart." Essentially these three terms form a biblical teaching on virtue: "faithfulness" is cleaving to the one God, "righteousness" represents the realization of a communal relationship with the people, and "uprightness of heart" describes the unity of thought and deed. Kingship is understood to be divinely given; here the one chosen by God is elevated while humbling himself as being too young for the office of king.

The people are described as "numerous," representing the fulfillment of the promise to the patriarchs that reaches its goal during the time of David and Solomon (see Gen 12:2; 13:16; 15:5; 22:17; 26:4; 28:14). The reference to the number of the people is a recognition not only of the divine blessing but also of the fulfillment of the promise to the fathers. Thus the plan of God with his people, as given and foretold to the fathers, is confirmed in the institution of kingship.

The term "election" characterizes the special relationship between God and his people. The election is based on a divine decision that a human person can neither influence nor change; it not only establishes Israel's special place among the other nations but also its exceptional obligation toward the one God: Yahweh as the one God has chosen Israel so that this people can worship this one God as the only one (see Deut 7:6-8; 10:14-15; 14:2). Election is based on God's love and asks from the chosen one little more than to love God alone. Election looks to the people, among which Israel is particularly elevated.

[3:9] Solomon's request is directed only toward the "listening heart." According to the biblical understanding the heart is not the place of feelings but the center of understanding and will. The heart determines the spiritual direction of a person, which is also the place through which God influences and determines the human person.[3] To be in line with divine advice and will the human being has to listen to God in his or her heart. This is the reason why Solomon asks that God guide his deliberations. Thus "listening heart" is a metaphor for the unity of the human being with God in one's thoughts, a unity that determines every act.

Here two qualities that are necessary for a successful reign are united: judgment and the ability to distinguish between good and bad. To sit in judgment and to speak righteous verdicts are the two most important duties of the king. Normally the judicial authority belonged to the local communities, whose representatives met in the city gates to speak justice and to attend court. It is not possible to determine the

---

[3] See Hans Walter Wolff, *Anthropology of the Old Testament*, trans. Margaret Kohl (Philadelphia: Fortress Press, 1974), 40–58.

relationship between the royal court and the local ones.[4] The advent of kingship in Israel did not result in the creation of a new judicial system. The local courts remained intact, but special cases could have been referred to the king to be decided by him. Possibly the king served as a court of appeal. He certainly had to serve as judge in cases that concerned persons who were dependent on him, since court officials did not belong to the sphere of local courts due to their special position. In any case the king was a new authority in Israel's judicial constitution.

The ability to distinguish between good and bad is not only a necessary prerequisite to reach a verdict but also a basic qualification to lead a proper life. Good is what is in accordance with law and morality because only then is a peaceful existence possible. Bad is the opposite of good, the disturbance of the unity of the ethos of the clan and thus of society as a whole. "Good and bad" are therefore not abstract values that the individual has to obey but take shape in the communal life as they realize the demands made of a person. Therefore all actions can be regarded and evaluated by their results.

[3:10] The intermediate statement in v. 10 leads on to the decisive divine speech.

[3:11-14] In his response Yahweh moves beyond the request of Solomon: he promises him riches, honor, and a long life. "Riches" describes material wealth and indicates success. Of all the kings of Israel only the riches of Solomon are singled out especially. Reveling in abundance is a characteristic trait of his reign. It is manifest in his building works and the journeys to Ophir. The vast riches distinguish Solomon from all other kings; the material wealth is manifest in the abundance of gold, which was larger in Solomonic times than in any other epoch. "Honor" is the prestige that Solomon acquired in his office; it is given by God and distinguishes the king in a special way. In the same way, "a long life" is a sign of divine affection. All these qualities are not natural but expressions of divine favor. The promise of Yahweh points to the incomparability of Solomon.

[3:15] The final verse describes Solomon's awakening and his return to Jerusalem. By marking the event as a dream it is once more characterized as a revelation. In this dream the whole reign of Solomon is placed under the promise of the blessing of God. The mention of the ark in this context emphasizes that in traveling to Gibeon Solomon did not deviate from the proper cult of Yahweh.

The ark is a wooden case that represented the presence of Yahweh in a special way. The origin of this crucial symbolic item for the worship of Yahweh cannot be determined. Historically, the ark first appears at the sanctuary of Shiloh. It was lost in

---

[4] See G. Christian Machholz, "Die Stellung des Königs in der israelitischen Gerichtsverfassung," *ZAW* 84 (1972) 157–81.

the wars against the Philistines; after the conquest of Jerusalem by David he recaptured it from Kiriath-jearim (Tell el-Azhar) and placed it in the tent sanctuary (1 Samuel 4–6). Until the building of the temple by Solomon this was the only place of worship for Yahweh in the capital of the kingdom.

Sacrifices were offered on the altar of the tent of worship (1 Kgs 1:28-29).[5] For a burnt offering the slaughtered animal was burned completely. This most important type of sacrifice was made on all public occasions. The origin of the burnt offering is unknown; most likely the practice was adopted from surrounding cultures. The meaning of the sacrifice is expiation. By offering a slaughtered animal the human person returns to God what belonged to the Godhead and thus expiates the guilt of killing.[6] Offerings of well-being are always mentioned in connection with burnt offerings (see Exod 20:24; 32:6; Deut 27:6; Josh 8:30; Judg 20:26; 21:4; 1 Sam 13:9; 18:8; 2 Sam 6:17-18; 1 Kgs 8:64; 9:25; 2 Kgs 16:13). During this sacrifice the burning of the fat and the sprinkling of blood are crucial elements. We can assume that the remaining parts of the animal were consumed by those offering the sacrifice in a communal meal with God just like during the normal sacrifice, which is not explicitly mentioned here; the blood rite symbolized expiation. After the cultic event the king hosts a feast for the members of his court, as would be expected of a generous king.

---

[5] For the different types of sacrifice see Rolf Rendtorff, *Studien zur Geschichte des Opfers im alten Israel,* WMANT 24 (Neukirchen-Vluyn: Neukirchener, 1967).

[6] See Bernd Janowski, *Sühne als Heilsgeschehen: Studien zur Sühnetheologie der Priesterschrift und zur Wurzel KPR im Alten Orient und im Alten Testament,* 2d ed., WMANT 55 (Neukirchen-Vluyn: Neukirchener, 2000).

Solomon's Wisdom in Judgment

Text

3:16 Later, two women who were prostitutes came to the king and stood before him. 17 The one woman said, "Please, my lord, this woman and I live in the same house; and I gave birth while she was in the house. 18 Then on the third day after I gave birth, this woman also gave birth. We were together; there was no one else with us in the house, only the two of us were in the house. 19 Then this woman's son died in the night, because she lay on him. 20 She got up in the middle of the night and took my son from beside me while your servant slept. She laid him at her breast, and laid her dead son at my breast. 21 When I rose in the morning to nurse my son, I saw that he was dead; but when I looked at him closely in the morning, clearly it was not the son I had borne." 22 But the other woman said, "No, the living son is mine, and the dead son is yours." The first said, "No, the dead son is yours, and the living son is mine." So they argued before the king.

23 Then the king said, "The one says, 'This is my son that is alive, and your son is dead'; while the other says, 'Not so! Your son is dead, and my son is the living one.'" 24 So the king said, "Bring me a sword," and they brought a sword before the king. 25 The king said, "Divide the living boy in two; then give half to the one, and half to the other." 26 But the woman whose son was alive said to the king—because compassion for her son burned within her—"Please, my lord, give her the living boy; certainly do not kill him!" The other said, "It shall be neither mine nor yours; divide it." 27 Then the king responded: "Give the first woman the living boy; do not kill him. She is his mother." 28 All Israel heard of the judgment that the king had rendered; and they stood in awe of the king, because they perceived that the wisdom of God was in him, to execute justice.

Analysis

Like the previous narrative of the theophany at Gibeon, the story of the judgment of Solomon at the beginning of the Solomon tradition is placed in a programmatic fashion. While the theophany demonstrated the divine confirmation of Solomon's acces-

41

sion to the throne, the narrative of the judgment exemplifies—as the final sentence (v. 28) stresses—the wisdom of the new king. The sequence of events is narrated fairly scantily; the reader or hearer gains all necessary information from the speeches that report the court scene. The contradictory reports of the two anonymous women move the narrative toward its climax; the tension is resolved only when the king names the true mother toward the end of the judicial procedure. Despite its simplicity the narrative is skillfully constructed, because the solution of the case remains open until the very end of the story.

The king is confronted with a legal case that is apparently impossible to decide because of its lack of witnesses to call upon. Why both women are labeled prostitutes is unclear; maybe the case could only be exemplified by using two single women who stand outside the complex kinship network of Israel. A degradation of the acting persons is certainly not intended; the narrative does not judge the social status of the women, but only exposes them as good or bad in the sense of a common humanity through their own behavior. The selfless mother is the good woman because she wants to keep her child alive at all costs. The preservation of the innocent life is thus the criterion of law and morality.

Commentary

[3:16-23] Just like the king, the reader or hearer is immediately confronted with the case. The report of one woman (vv. 17-21) is contradicted by the other (v. 22). Pondering the case the king stresses once more the impossibility of reaching a solution by pointing out its essential crux: one word stands against the other (v. 23).[1] At the same time the significance of the solution found by Solomon is highlighted: even in what seems an impossible case he is able to reach a just verdict with great persuasive power.

[3:24-27] In v. 24 the king takes the initiative; the command "bring me a sword" adds to the drama of the events. The proposal to divide the child is certainly ambivalent. On the one hand the claims of both sides will be satisfied; on the other hand the child will be killed. In her rejection of the solution (v. 26) the true mother is found: she waives her claim in order to save her child. It is she who is therefore granted the child by the king (v. 27).

The narrative of the two women who quarrel over a child has a fairy-tale character, and it has numerous parallels in Indian and Far Eastern cultures; Gressmann has collected these parallels.[2] Even though all variants of the circulating narratives are later than the biblical material, we find here a narrative topic that was in currency and that has been taken up, reshaped, and applied to Solomon by the narrator. The craftsmanship in the exposition of the biblical narrative becomes apparent when it is com-

---

[1] Würthwein, *Könige,* 1:37.

[2] Hugo Gressmann, "Das salomonische Urteil," *Deutsche Rundschau* 33 (1907) 212–28.

pared with another version of the material. The Indian version from the collection of fairy tales called "Vikramodaya" may serve as an example.[3]

Apart from the differences in detail the result is the same: the false mother is discovered and the true mother receives her child. Yet in the biblical version the course of events is entirely determined by the superiority of the king. It is stated clearly at the end that by his knowledge he is the one who is able to shed light on the hidden truth. The self-reflections of v. 23 are not an expression of his helplessness but have the sole purpose of stressing the difficulty of reaching a verdict. The king publicly displays the truth, since his proposal to divide the child forces both women to take a stand that will reveal their true character. Only after the reader or hearer has realized the true circumstances is a judgment made.

This conspicuous feature of the verdict is also maintained in those versions where a decision is reached by the fact that the judge orders the two quarrelling women to seize the child and the true mother lets go so that the frail body of the child is not damaged.[4] Later, Klabund and Bertolt Brecht have utilized the conspicuous display of the judgment in their dramatic works. Even if the biblical circumstances are not that of the present, the material professes such a closeness to life concerns that the conflict can be used time and again to exemplify a fundamental decision for humanity.

[3:28] In v. 28 the Deuteronomistic Historian comments on the traditional narrative and integrates it into his framework of the Solomon narrative: all acts of Solomon are determined by divine wisdom that proves itself especially in the royal duty of speaking justice. The verdict in favor of the true mother serves as an example: the king is not influenced by wrong statements but is able to find truth and thus justice because of his exceptional wisdom.

---

[3] See ibid., 219.

[4] Hermann Gunkel, *The Folktale in the Old Testament,* trans. Michael D. Rutter, HTIBS 6 (Sheffield: Almond, 1987) 155–56.

Solomon's Administrative Officers

Text

4:1 King Solomon was king over all Israel, 2 and these were his high officials: Azariah son of Zadok, priest; 3 Elihoreph and Ahijah sons of Shisha, scribes; Jehoshaphat son of Ahilud, recorder; 4 Benaiah son of Jehoiada was in command of the army; [. . .]ᵃ 5 Azariah son of Nathan was over the officials; Zabud son of Nathan [. . .]ᵇ and king's friend; 6 Ahishar was in charge of the palace; Adoniram son of Abda was in charge of the forced labor.

ᵃ "Zadok and Abiathar were priests" is an incorrect addition from 2 Sam 20:25.
ᵇ The word "priest" is missing from the LXX; I consider it an addition.

Commentary

[4:1] After the interruption by the two narratives in chap. 3, 4:1 continues 2:46b and again underlines the new reign. The verse provides the necessary literary link to the following lists that have been taken over from official documents.

[4:2-6] We do not know in which form these documents were recorded or kept; in any case we can assume that scribes recorded these lists of persons to document current affairs. The author of the Deuteronomistic History or the composer of the Solomon narrative has used such documents in his work without any further editing. In this way several original documents are handed down to us that allow insights into the administration of the kingdom. The list of the officials in vv. 2-6 is such a document; it names the bearers of high offices without any further narrative ornamentation. Since a date is not mentioned, it is not possible to place the list more accurately within Solomon's reign. Since appointments to these offices were normally made for life, however, a change of official is always exceptional.

Two such lists of officials are known already from the time of David. An older version is found in 2 Sam 8:15-18 and a later one in 2 Sam 20:23-26. Since the office of the overseer of forced labor points to a reorganization of the state, the list has to be dated in the second half of David's reign. During Solomon's reign the number of officials increased; new offices are: head of the officials, head of the palace, and the "king's friend." The office "head of the bodyguard" no longer exists, probably because this group had been either dissolved or integrated into the army (we do not possess a more detailed knowledge of the organization of the army). Two of the offices are exclusively concerned with running the palace to handle the increased demands. This might be a hint that these offices were introduced only after the completion of the building of the palace. Such a view is, of course, not compelling, since new offices were normally introduced at the beginning of a new reign. The listed officials can be compared with the secretaries of state in modern governments. Due to their special abilities they were appointed for life by the king. A dismissal was not envisaged but could happen under special circumstances (see 2 Kgs 2:26-27). Priest and scribe were the only hereditary offices.

Three of the officials had already served under David: Jehoshaphat and Adoniram remained in office under Solomon, and Benaiah was promoted after the murder of Joab from head of the bodyguard to head of the army (see 2:35). Thus new men were appointed only to the new offices: Azariah and Zabud were sons of Nathan, while the origin of Ahishar remains uncertain. Overall, the duties of the officials allow a glimpse at the administration of the country, but due to the scarcity of sources it is impossible to track this further development.

[4:2] The list commences with the mention of the priests. After the banishment of Abiathar solely the Zadokites became priests at the sanctuary in Jerusalem, which consisted of the tent keeping the ark. After the building of the temple by Solomon (see 1 Kings 6) the Zadokites became high priests at the state sanctuary and served there until the dismissal of Onias IV by the Seleucids in 162 BCE. For legitimating purposes the family tree of Zadok was traced back to Aaron in postexilic times (1 Chr 5:29-34). This became necessary because Zadok was probably the priest of the pre-Israelite city god called Zedek in Jerusalem and became priest for David only after the conquest of the city. In place of the king, Zadok and his descendants served as high priests at the state sanctuary. (After the end of Israelite kingship the office received a certain promotion, expressed in the title "high priest," since the bearer of the office was the highest representative of the Jewish people.)

[4:3] "Scribe" and "recorder" were two offices created by David after Egyptian examples. Not only did the scribe have to write the documents and annals for the royal archives, but he was also responsible for conducting diplomatic correspondence with the neighboring states. He was probably also head of the scribal school that served, like its Near Eastern counterparts, to educate new scribes. Through the expansion of the administration and international relations the duties of the scribes increased; an appointment of two officials is therefore justified. An extended bureaucracy was necessary to organize the different duties of the people, such as taxes and forced labor; in addition, letters, statutes, and orders of the king had to be sent by messengers to all parts of the kingdom. The office of the recorder is difficult to grasp. By analogy to the Egyptian herald he could have been partly responsible for the court ceremony. Maybe he served as the secretary of state, who oversaw the execution of royal orders.

Saul had already created the office of "commander of the army," to which he had appointed Abner, a man from his own family (see 2 Sam 2:8). During David's reign, Joab, the head of the army, was the most powerful person in the state after the king. His importance is emphasized by his mention in first place in both lists of David's officials (2 Sam 8:16; 20:23). Under Solomon the importance of this office decreases in connection with the establishment of a standing army in place of the tribal league. The commander of the army replaces the king in battle and is responsible for victory or defeat.

[4:5] The office of overseer of the officials is an innovation connected to the division of the country into different provinces (4:7-19). While David was still able to meet the demand of the royal court by the supplies from the crown's estate, Solomon created twelve provinces of which one was responsible every month to meet the increased demands of the court. A governor, who in turn was controlled by the overseer of the officials, administrated these provinces. This new division into provinces was not only an administrative measure but also created a new structure of the state and new offices. The other new office, "friend of the king," corresponds to the Egyptian office of the "acquaintance of the king." He is the adviser of the king in public and private affairs.

[4:6] The person in charge of the palace administered the personal property of the king, including the land owned by the crown; he was the manager of the crown's estate and thus responsible for the running of the estates and the tithes. The crown's estate supplied the royal family and the court but could no longer cover the increased demands; thus new forms of tithes had to be added. "Forced labor" consisted of work for the royal projects such as buildings. This institution had already existed under David, but Solomon expanded it in order to realize his ambitious projects in Jerusalem and elsewhere. The narrative of the events after Solomon's death demonstrates how much the population suffered from this forced labor: Since his son and successor Rehoboam did not want to make any concessions regarding forced labor, the northern tribes split from the Davidic dynasty and elected Jeroboam their own king (12:1-19).

The Provinces

Text

4:7 Solomon had twelve officials over all Israel, who provided food for the king and his household; each one had to make provision for one month in the year. 8 These were their names: Ben-hur, in the hill country of Ephraim; 9 Ben-deker, in Makaz, Shaalbim, [Beth-shemesh, and Elon-beth-hanan]; 10 Ben-hesed, in Arubboth (to him belonged Socoh and all the land of Hepher); 11 Ben-abinadab, in all Naphath-dor (he had Taphath, Solomon's daughter, as his wife); 12 Baana son of Ahilud, in Taanach, Megiddo, (and all Beth-shean, which is beside Zarethan below Jezreel, and from Beth-shean to Abel-meholah, as far as the other side of Jokmeam); 13 Ben-geber, in Ramoth-gilead (he had the villages of Jair son of Manasseh, which are in Gilead, and he had the region of Argob, which is in Bashan, sixty great cities with walls and bronze bars); 14 Ahinadab son of Iddo, in Mahanaim; 15 Ahimaaz, in Naphtali (he had taken Basemath, Solomon's daughter, as his wife); 16 Baana son of Hushai, in Asher and Bealoth; 17 Jehoshaphat son of Paruah, in Issachar; 18 Shimei son of Ela, in Benjamin; 19 Geber son of Uri, in the land of Gilead, (the country of King Sihon of the Amorites and of King Og of Bashan). (And there was one official in the land of Judah.)

Commentary

[4:7-19] The list of the twelve governors of Solomon and their provinces is one of the few original documents incorporated into the Deuteronomistic History. Since this text was most likely written in the royal scribal school, it is of extraordinary historical value. The Deuteronomistic Historian simply added an introduction to the original document in vv. 7, 8a. Later redactions added vv. 9b, 10b, 12b, 13b, 19b to describe the territories in more detail. These supplements serve as a more precise description of the provinces. The list seems to be fragmented at the beginning, since we do not know the names of the first four and of the sixth. Bealoth or Aloth, the name after Asher, is unclear. Since Asher designates tribal territory, the unclear term seems to have been the name of a certain territory. To change it into Zebulun is hardly possible since—according to Josh 19:10-16—the tribal territory belonging to this tribe is part of the fifth province. Thus it is recommended to follow Noth and to keep the name.[1] The reference to the "Ladder of Tyre" (see 1 Macc 11:59; Josephus, *Ant.* 13.146, etc.) is not very helpful; it is more likely to think of Aloth as being the plateau Sahl Battof, which was not included in the tribal territory of Asher but did belong to Israelite settlements. Certainty cannot be gained without emending the text of the rather difficult passage.

Two groundbreaking observations by A. Alt can serve as points of departure for a definition of the single provinces: (1) The separation into provinces concerns only the northern tribes, including the Transjordan territory. Judah is not part of the system. (2) The naming of the provinces is done according to two different systems: some provinces are described according to tribes or territories, while others are labeled according to cities.[2] It has to be added to his observation that all these provinces had to have the same economic power. Due to the difference in the size of farmable land it cannot be assumed that all provinces covered the same amount of territory. However, each province must have had an acceptable number of settlements to be able to pay the taxes. Thus densely populated areas could have been smaller than less populated ones.

The specifications of the document can be used to determine the geographical location and extent of the provinces. Even though the borders of the single provinces cannot be determined with absolute confidence, the provinces can be separated from one another.

I. The use of the term "hill country of Ephraim" shows that a territory is envisaged that extends beyond the territory conquered by the tribe of Ephraim. According to the description in Josh 16:4-9, Ephraim borders Benjamin in the south and extends north up to the height of Tappuach (Tell Seh Abu Zarad). Since Benjamin is the eleventh province, the term "hill country of Ephraim" can only designate the mountain range in the south near Bethel, while its northern extent cannot be determined exactly. In any case the mountain range north of Tappuach on the same latitude as Shechem (Tell Balatah) has certainly to be included; here Wadi Nablus to the west and Wadi el-Fârʿa to the southeast form natural boundaries. Under no circumstances is "hill country of Ephraim" used to describe the middle Palestinian mountains up to the plain of Jezreel and the bay of Beth-shean as a whole, because the mountainous regions north of Shechem are called "mount of Samaria" (Amos 4:1; 6:1) and "mount of Gilboa" (1 Sam 31:1, 8; 2 Sam 1:5; 1 Chr 10:1, 8), and Mount Carmel is located outside the territory in question. As the designation of a landscape the label "hill country of Ephraim" included only the central part of the western Jordanian moun-

---

[1] Noth, *Könige,* 56.
[2] Albrecht Alt, "Israels Gaue unter Salomo," in *Kleine Schriften* (Munich: Beck, 1953), 2:83–85 [76–89].

tains. The borders in the east and west are determined by the slopes toward the Jordan and the coast.

II. The second province is marked by the names Makaz, Shaalbim, and Beth-shemesh; for clarification purposes a redactor has also added the names Elon (Aialon) and Beth-hanan. As far as they can be identified they describe places bordering on the mountains. Shaalbim has to be identified with Selbit, Beth-shemesh with Khirbet er-Rumele, and Elon/Aialon with Yalo. Thus the province encloses the mountainous territory north of Wadi es-Sarar; the places south of this line probably belonged to Judah. The northern extent of the province is unknown; toward the east it borders on the eleventh province, Benjamin. It was possibly limited to the lower hill country west of the mountains and did not include the coastal plains, since they were Philistine territory.

III. The description of the third province is difficult, since the geographical place of Arubboth is unknown. Of the two added names only Socoh can be localized with certainty. Following A. Alt, I do not think this Socoh is identical with the two places of the same name in Judah (see Josh 15:35, 48, etc.) but has to be identified with Suweke, 3 km. north of Tulkarm.[3] Thus Socoh is located at a convenient place on the eastern fringe of the coastal plain called Sharon toward the end of Wadi Zemir, which continues east as Wadi Nablus and served as an important western gateway to the middle Palestinian mountains. Socoh probably marks off the farthest western expansion of this province. Arubboth probably served as the seat of the governor and could have been in the mountains north of Shechem. Hepher occurs in Josh 12:17 together with Tappuach and also in the genealogy of Manasseh (Num 26:32-33). It belonged to the mountain range and could be located on Tell el-Muhaffar on the northern fringe of the plain called Sahl 'Arraba.[4] If one presumes that Hepher was situated in the mountains, the third province occupied the northern part of the middle Palestinian mountains between Shechem in the south and the plain of Jezreel in the north. Thus it was situated between provinces I and V and shared a border with the fourth province in the west.

IV. The term Naphath-dor, "wooded plain of Dor," is an archaic designation for the northern part of the coastal plain that is later called Sharon and that was tree-covered during the Iron Age.[5] How far it stretched south is difficult to say; the border could have been Jarcon (Nahr el-'Auga). The port of Dor (et-Tantura) was situated at the northern end where the coastal strip is just a few kilometers wide. During the early time of the kings the population density of the coastal strip was sparse, and most settlements were on the eastern fringe.

---

[3] Ibid., 78–79.

[4] See G. Ernest Wright, " The Provinces of Solomon," *ErIsr* 8 (1967), 63* [58–68*]. See also Volkmar Fritz, "Die Sogennante Liste der Besiegten Könige in Josua 12," *ZDPV* 85 (1969) 136–61.

[5] M. Ben-Dov, "Rapha—A Geographical Term of Possible 'Sea People' Origin," *TA* 3 (1976) 71–72.

V. The original designation of the fifth province has been expanded several times for clarification purposes. Taanach (Ta'anek) and Megiddo (Tell el-Mutesellim) describe the two main settlements of the province. That included the plain of Jezreel, which originally did not belong to the settlement of the Israelite tribes. The cities were only annexed to Israel by Solomon. The "bay of Beth-shean" has been added by a redactor to the province despite being geographically an extension of the Jordan Valley.

VI. The seat of the governor of the sixth province is Ramoth-gilead. The addition of v. 13b does not add anything to the determination of the territory. According to Gustaf Dalman the administrative headquarters of Ramoth-gilead have to be located on the mighty Tell el-Husn, 15 km. southwest of er-Remta.[6] Thus the sixth province comprised the hill country south of the Yarmuk excluding the Jordan Valley, since that was the seventh province. The southern border is determined by the twelfth province, the country Gilead. The exact border cannot be determined, since the name Gilead is also used for the mountains north of the Jabbok. One can assume, however, that the Jabbok formed the southern border. The geographical borders of the sixth province are determined by the phasing out of the Iron Age settlements at Wadi es-Sellale. The rather large size of the province is due to the lack of density in population.

VII. Only the administrative headquarters (Mahanaim) of the governor of the seventh province is mentioned. Despite the as yet unclear geographical site of Mahanaim, it can be located at the lower course of the Jabbok from its mention in Gen 32:3 and in the list of Sheshonk. The role played by Mahanaim in the early monarchy (see 2 Sam 2:8-10; 17:24, 27; 19:33; 2 Kgs 2:8) suggests that it was an important place in the middle Jordan Valley that has not yet been discovered.[7] The territory of the province equals the Jordan Valley; during the Iron Age the eastern side was densely populated. Marked off by mountains in the east and west, the province extended south to the Dead Sea and north at least to the bay of Beth-shean, which belonged—following the redactor in v. 12b—to the fifth province.

VIII. Naphtali is the first in the list of provinces described by tribal names. According to Josh 19:32-39 the territory of this tribe consisted of east Galilee up to the same latitude as Kedesh (Qedesh) in the north and up to Tabor in the south. The Jordan Valley above Lake Huleh was sparsely settled, since it consisted of marshland with several watercourses. Otherwise the territory extended up to the Sea of Galilee with the mighty fortress Kinnereth, which was responsible for giving the lake its name during the time of the kings (Num 34:11; Deut 3:17; Josh 12:3; 13:27) and which had been fortified by David. The border to the west is Ramah

---

[6] Gustaf Dalman, "Jahresberichte des Instituts für das Arbeitsjahr 1912/13; 8. Zeitreise: Auf den Suche nach Mahanaim," *PJ* 9 (1913) 64.

[7] See Robert A. Coughenour, "A Search for Mahanaim," *BASOR* 273 (1989) 57–66.

(Khirbet Zertun er-Rame, about 3 km. southeast of er-Rame) and thus on the same latitude as Tabor.

IX. The tribal territory of Asher was located in western Galilee next to that of Naphtali. The most northern place was probably Abdon (Khirbet 'Abde) on the same latitude as Achzib (ez-Zīb). To the south the territory extended at least up to the plateau Sahl Battof but also encompassed southwestern Galilee. The plain of Acre probably did not belong to the ninth province, since Solomon had handed it over to the potentate of Tyre (see 9:10-14). The coastal strip north of Acre also belonged to the territory under the influence of Tyre.

X. According to Josh 19:24-31, the territory claimed for Issachar connects south with the one of Naphtali and has to be located south and east of Tabor in Lower Galilee. Southward it borders the bay of Beth-shean, westward the plain of Jezreel, probably including the town of Jezreel (Zerʿīn). The territory of the tenth province was quite small, but Lower Galilee was well suited for intensive agricultural use, so that it possessed the necessary economic power.

XI. The tribal territory of Benjamin in Josh 18:11-20 is characterized by a description of its border as a combination of the southern border of Ephraim (16:2-3a) and the northern one of Judah (15:5b-9). Thus the territory consisted of the small strip of hill country between Bethel (Betin) and Jerusalem; the hollow of Jordan probably did not belong to it. The territory of Benjaminite settlements had been firmly defined since premonarchic times, because Benjamin is mentioned as an individual tribe in the Song of Deborah (Judg 5:14). The dense population ensured the necessary economic power of the province.

XII. The designation "land of Gilead" probably already reflects an expansion of an original term for a landscape to a broader territory. The name in still in use today as the place names Jebel Gelʿad, 'En Gelʿad, and Khirbet Gelʿad in its vicinity show. Originally Gilead described the hill country that is called Ard el-'Arde today; the province "land of Gilead" probably consisted of the territory south of the Jabbok. The twelfth province thus enclosed the middle East Jordan between Jabbok and the northern end of the Dead Sea; in the east it bordered the country of the Ammonites.

The twelve provinces form the Solomonic state with the exception of Judah, which remained outside the administrative division. The reason for the special status of Judah is unknown, but it probably reflects the special treatment of this tribal territory by the introduction of taxes by the king. How much these taxes and forced labor influenced the independent tribal life becomes clear in the disputes after Solomon's death when demands to ease the forced labor culminated in the separation of the empire (12:1-19).

Apart from the territory that had been extended with the help of fortresses deep into the Negev, the Solomonic empire formed a closed territory that consisted of parts of the coastal plain, the middle Palestinian mountains, Galilee, the plain of Jezreel, Jordan, and East Jordan. The coastal plain south of Jarkon that was under Philistine influence, the almost uninhabited Mount Carmel and the plain of Acre that had been ceded to the king of Tyre, the marshland of the Upper Jordan Valley, and the plateau east of the Dead Sea up to Arnon did not belong to the royal territory.

The territory of the northern tribes within the Solomonic empire was made up of the settlement area of the Israelite tribes and of the settlements of former Canaanite city-states. Of the ten tribes of the Song of Deborah (Judg 5:13-18), Naphtali, Asher, Issachar, and Benjamin are directly listed (provinces VIII–XI) and Ephraim and Gilead indirectly together with landscapes (provinces I and XII); due to territorial changes for the remaining tribes—Machir, Zebulun, Reuben, and Dan—the provinces could not be set up according to tribal territory.

Provinces II–VII included those parts of the country that did not belong to the original settlement area of premonarchic Israel and that were not placed under royal authority. Thus the territory is rounded off, and an ethnically diverse population is made into a political unity. While a premonarchic Israel had to prevail against an autochthonous population in the Solomonic empire, all inhabitants of the land were part of one state regardless of their ethnic origin. As a result the former Canaanite population was assimilated into the one Israel. The division into provinces was not only an administrative measure, but—despite the division after the death of Solomon—also served the purpose of political consolidation of the tribes with the rest of the people in the land into a unified state and a unified people.

Additions [ET = 4:20-28]

Text

4:20 Judah and Israel were as numerous as the sand by the sea; they ate and drank and were happy. 5:1 Solomon was sovereign over all the kingdoms from the Euphrates [. . .]ᵃ even to the border of Egypt; they brought tribute and served Solomon all the days of his life.

2 Solomon's provision for one day was thirty cors of choice flour, and sixty cors of meal, 3 ten fat oxen, and twenty pasture-fed cattle, one hundred sheep, besides deer, gazelles, roebucks, and fatted fowl. 4 For he had dominion over all the region west of the Euphrates from Tiphsah to Gaza, over all the kings west of the Euphrates; and he had peace on all sides. 5 During Solomon's lifetime Judah and Israel lived in safety, from Dan even to Beer-sheba, all of them under their vines and fig trees. 6 Solomon also had <fourteen hundred>ᵇ stalls of horses for his chariots, and twelve thousand horsemen. 7 Those officials supplied provisions for King Solomon and for all who came to King Solomon's table, each one in his month; they let nothing be lacking. 8 They also brought to the required place barley and straw for the horses and swift steeds, each according to his charge.

ᵃ The phrase "to the land of the Philistines" is an addition that was mistakenly placed here.
ᵇ The figure 40,000 in MT is far too high and has already been corrected to 4,000 in 2 Chr 9:25. Since the note is taken over from 1 Kgs 10:26, the figure provided there is used here.

Analysis

This section consists of a collection of several notes whose origin and historical value have to be determined individually. Since 5:7 repeats the closure of the list of the provinces in 4:7 (4:8-19), the phrase probably comes from the hand of the Deuteronomistic Historian. All further notes (4:20; 5:1—6:8) are secondary redactional additions to the text. Since the content of each statement varies greatly, each of these statements has to be examined individually.

Commentary

[5:7] Compared with 4:7, 5:7 does not contain any new information. The number of the officials is determined by the twelve months of a calendar year. The system assumes that each province was of equal economic power. "King Solomon's table" is a description for the circle of persons who are looked after at the court. A requirement for such a provision was to have an official function at the court, but the king could also grant it (see 2 Sam 9:1-13).

[5:2-3] The concluding remark in 5:7 is the reason for the note on the needs of the royal court (vv. 2-3), divided into corn, cattle, and game. The figures seem to be grossly exaggerated and cannot be accurate. A cor is a dry measurement and equals approximately 400 liters; thus we have the huge amount of 12,000 liters of choice flour and twice as much meal for a single day. In view of the average provision it is highly unlikely that herds of cattle were slaughtered on a daily basis. The game is not specified, but was probably part of the provisions for the royal table. The grossly exaggerated amount of wheat and the high numbers of slaughtered animals do not represent actual facts but serve to emphasize the size of the court and thus the mightiness of the Solomonic rule.

[5:1, 4] Verses 1 and 4 describe the expansion of the Solomonic empire. The phrase "west of the Euphrates" is the language of the Persian period and describes the territories southeast of the river that are called Syria today (see Ezra 8:36; Neh 2:7, 9; 3:7). Verse 1 assumes that the empire of Solomon has stretched beyond the vassal states up to the Euphrates. The same view can be found in Gen 15:18, but it probably does not reflect reality; rather the Davidic rule over some Aramaic kings (see 2 Sam 8:1-14) is extended to the whole territory of Aramaic states up to the Euphrates to push the northern border of the state as far as possible. In correspondence to that the southern border moves far into the coastal plain; here the "wadi of Egypt" (Wadi el-'Arish) is designated as the border of the land in postexilic times (see Num 34:5; Josh 15:4, 47; 1 Kgs 8:65; 2 Kgs 24:7; Isa 27:12).[1]

This image of the expansion of the Solomonic territory is further emphasized in v. 4 by mention of the two towns Tiphsah and Gaza. Tiphsah can be identified as ancient Thapsakos, which, according to Greek sources, was located on the bend of the Euphrates.[2] An exact location cannot yet be given. The place is not mentioned again in the Bible, and knowledge of it is hardly possible before the deportations of 588/587 by the Babylonians. Gaza (Gazze) is the most southern of the five Philistine cities and was located about 30 km. northeast of the estuary of Wadi el-'Arish into the Mediterranean Sea. It is also used elsewhere in descriptions of the expansion of the land to describe the point furthest south (see Josh 10:41; 15:47; 2 Kgs 18:8).

---

[1] Gustaf Dalman, *PJ* 20 (1924) 54–57.
[2] *PW,* VA/1, 1272–80.

[5:5] The peace already stressed in v. 4 is again mentioned in v. 5. The phrase "under their vines and fig trees" uses metaphorical imagery that can be found in later prophetic texts to describe the peace of the period of salvation (see Mic 4:4; Zech 3:10). In such a way during postexilic times one looked to the time of Solomon: here the reality expected for the eschatological future had already been realized.[3] In contrast to 5:1, 4, the expansion of the empire is described with the traditional formula "from Dan even to Beer-sheba." By mentioning the most northern place, Dan (Tell el-Qadi), and the southern bordertown of Beer-sheba (Bīʾr es-Sebaᶜ), this formula describes the territory settled by Israelite tribes and therefore the real territory of Solomonic rule (see Judg 20:1; 1 Sam 3:20; 17:11; 24:2, 15). In terms of its content v. 5 is a redactional addition from postexilic times.

[4:20] "As numerous as the sand of the sea" is a traditional formula used to show the fulfillment of the promise to the fathers during the time of Solomon (see Gen 22:17; 32:13). A postexilic redactor added the phrase, despite the fact that it does not fit the context.

[5:6-8] Verse 8 stresses the provision for the horses and the cavalry. The verse assumes that the tithes are also used for the army. This additional comment resulted in the addition of the horses that had to be cared for in v. 6. The figures are taken from 10:26, but here the text distinguishes between "horses" and "swift steeds." Despite its redactional character the statements of v. 6 are reliable, since they use a reliable source. For details see the commentary on 16:26.

---

[3] Würthwein, *Könige,* 1:471.

Solomon's Wisdom [ET = 4:29-34]

Text

5:9 God gave Solomon very great wisdom, discernment, and breadth of understanding as vast as the sand on the seashore, 10 so that Solomon's wisdom surpassed the wisdom of all the people of the east, and all the wisdom
of Egypt. 11 He was wiser than anyone else, wiser than Ethan the
Ezrahite, and Heman, Calcol, and Darda, children of Mahol; his fame
spread throughout all the surrounding nations. 12 He composed three
thousand proverbs, and his songs numbered a thousand and five. 13 He
would speak of trees, from the cedar that is in the Lebanon to the hyssop
that grows in the wall; he would speak of animals, and birds, and reptiles,
and fish. 14 People came from all the nations to hear the wisdom of
Solomon; they came from all the kings of the earth who had heard of his
wisdom.

Analysis

The passage exemplifies Solomon's wisdom, a topic already mentioned during the
theophany in 3:12 and in the addition to the judgment of Solomon in 3:28. The theme
will be mentioned again in 5:26, but only with the episode of the visit of the Queen
of Sheba in 10:1-10, 13 is Solomon's wisdom truly put to the test.[1] The passage is
loosely placed in the context without any literary relations to other elements of the
Solomonic tradition.[2] Here the Deuteronomistic Historian has probably used a piece
from a pre-Deuteronomistic author of the history of Solomon. One can ponder
whether vv. 12-13 might represent a later addition; such a view is supported by the
fact that "nature" wisdom (flora and fauna) has no relation to the judicial wisdom of
Solomon or to the daily wisdom represented in the wisdom literature. But also the
other statements in vv. 9-11, 14 cannot be used for a description of the personality of
Solomon, since they merely stylize the picture of Solomon as the wise monarch.

---

[1] Hans Peter Müller, *TDOT*, 4:375.
[2] Noth, *Könige*, 80.

Commentary

[5:9-11, 14] These verses characterize the wisdom of Solomon by a general comparison with wisdom regarding the environment. According to the ancient Near Eastern royal ideology, Solomon is portrayed as the wise king par excellence, whose wisdom surpasses that of others. "Wisdom" and "discernment" are mentioned elsewhere together. Here "wisdom" describes the exhaustive knowledge of natural phenomena and experience of life. "Nature wisdom" attempts to understand the phenomena by creating lists; "wisdom of life" on the other hand tries to discover a suitable behavior of the human person toward himself/herself as well as toward others in the light of the experience of danger and need. Both forms of knowledge were highly developed in the surrounding cultures. "Discernment" accompanies wisdom in that it is only possible to arrive at wisdom via the recognition and spiritual penetration of the world and life (compare Prov 4:1, 5, 7; 16:16; 23:23). "The breadth of understanding" (lit. "the wide heart") has been added, since it is the actual seat of wisdom and so has the ill-fitting comparison with the sand on the seashore, which is normally used in relation to offspring (compare 4:20).

Ethan, Heman, Calcol, and Darda cannot be identified; in 1 Chr 2:6 they have metamorphosed into grandchildren of Judah and are thus placed within an old Israelite genealogy. They must belong to the context of wisdom; they are probably men who represent the wise person as such. Similarly the "people of the east" cannot be identified. The phrase is as general as our statement *ex oriente lux* ("light from the east"). The origin of wisdom is placed in the east; how far or near is impossible to determine. The attempt to connect the three sons of Mahol with the bedouin of the eastern steppe and desert is not persuasive, since wisdom is a cultural phenomenon that is closely connected with literacy and thus with the use of writing in different cultures.

As far as ancient Israel is concerned, the advent of wisdom literature is closely connected with the development of the institution of kingship. Despite its possible roots within oral family traditions, wisdom is foremost a courtly phenomenon that represents the education and social status of the individuals.[3] In comparison to other kings, Solomon occupies first place; the sending of presents represents here a Near Eastern custom within diplomatic relations. The presents also articulate the superiority of Solomon. At the same time, the stress on the wide heart confirms Yahweh's promise to him in 3:12.

[5:12-13] These verses list in detail the extent and contents of the tradition. The figures of three thousand proverbs and one thousand and five songs are probably the result of gematria, the calculation according to the numerical value of a Hebrew

---

[3] See Hans Jürgen Hermisson, *Studien zur israelitischen Spruchweisheit,* WMANT 28 (Neukirchen-Vluyn: Neukirchener, 1968).

letter.[4] In any case they are round figures that do not represent actual numbers. The note cannot be separated from the fact that the biblical books of Proverbs and Song of Songs are attributed to Solomon. The portrait of the wise king is repeated in later tradition; at the same time, the nature wisdom stressed in this passage took second place to the knowledge/wisdom of life. The sapiential knowledge of natural phenomena is summarized by certain examples. The mighty cedar is contrasted with the insignificant hyssop. This plant, which grows on walls, has not been identified but was used during purification offerings (compare Exod 12:12; Lev 14:4, 6, 49, 51-52; Num 19:6, 18).[5] The statement about the trees emphasizes that wisdom covers everything from the cedar to the shrub. The animals are divided into four groups with no further classification. With both verses the common knowledge of Solomon is increased.

---

[4] See Carl Steuernagel, *ZAW* 30 (1910) 70–71.

[5] Gustaf Dalman, *Arbeit und Sitte in Palästina* (Gütersloh: Bertelsmann, 1928), 1.2:543–45.

The Treaty with Hiram of Tyre
[ET = 5:1-12]

Text

5:15 Now King Hiram of Tyre sent his servants to Solomon, when he heard that they had anointed him king in place of his father; for Hiram had always been a friend to David. 16 Solomon sent word to Hiram, saying, 17 "You know that my father David could not build a house for the name of the LORD his God because of the warfare with which his enemies surrounded him, until the LORD put them under the soles of his feet. 18 But now the LORD my God has given me rest on every side; there is neither adversary nor misfortune. 19 So I intend to build a house for the name of the LORD my God, as the LORD said to my father David, 'Your son, whom I will set on your throne in your place, shall build the house for my name.' 20 Therefore command that cedars from the Lebanon be cut for me. My servants will join your servants, and I will give you whatever wages you set for your servants; for you know that there is no one among us who knows how to cut timber like the Sidonians."

21 When Hiram heard the words of Solomon, he rejoiced greatly, and said, "Blessed be the LORD today, who has given to David a wise son to be over this great people." 22 Hiram sent word to Solomon, "I have heard the message that you have sent to me; I will fulfill all your needs in the matter of cedar and cypress timber. 23 My servants shall bring it down to the sea from the Lebanon; I will make it into rafts to go by sea to the place you indicate. I will have them broken up there for you to take away. And you shall meet my needs by providing food for my household." 24 So Hiram supplied Solomon's every need for timber of cedar and cypress. 25 Solomon in turn gave Hiram twenty thousand cors of wheat as food for his household, and twenty cors of fine oil. Solomon gave this to Hiram year by year. 26 So the LORD gave Solomon wisdom, as he promised him. There was peace between Hiram and Solomon; and the two of them made a treaty.

Analysis

The treaty between Solomon and Hiram of Tyre is described in narrative form; the course of the narrative as such is fictitious, but it correctly assumes trade relations. Stylistically the Deuteronomistic Historian has shaped it as the preparation for the building of the temple. The structure is simple: the introduction in v. 15 is followed by the exchange of diplomatic notes; here Hiram grants Solomon in vv. 21 and 23 what he had requested in vv. 16-20. Finally, the content of the treaty is reported in vv. 24-25, followed by a general statement about Solomon in v. 26. Despite its fictitious character the narrative contains some information about the preparation of the building of the temple as well as some details on the proceedings of economic relations. From a formal point of view the story is structured quite simply, and the course of the narrative appears monotonous.

Commentary

[5:15] The introductory verse refers back to Solomon's accession to the throne and mentions the friendly relations between Hiram and David. The exchange of messengers after the enthronement of a new king was quite common.[1] Outside the Bible, Hiram of Tyre, who is also called "king," is mentioned only in an excerpt from Menander of Ephesus quoted by Josephus.[2] According to this literary source, Hiram was the second ruler of a dynasty founded by his father that came to an end with his grandson Abdastratos, son of Beleazar. Despite the fact that most of Josephus's information is taken from the Bible, the excerpt from the lost history of Menander of Ephesus demonstrates the historicity of this ruler as a contemporary of Solomon. His rule from about 969 to about 936 BCE is roughly parallel with that of Solomon (965–926 BCE).

Tyre (Ṣur) was the southernmost of the Phoenician coastal cities and is mentioned frequently in Egyptian, Akkadian, and Ugaritic sources. The city was originally located on an island just off the coast; it was connected with the mainland only when Alexander the Great built a dam during his siege. Founded during the third millennium BCE, Tyre managed to remain an independent city-state until its conquest by Alexander. After the general collapse of the Mycenean and Canaanite culture around 1200 BCE, which resulted in the termination of trade in the eastern Mediterranean, Tyre managed to achieve a prominent position among the cities of Phoenicia, a position that it lost to Sidon during the first millennium BCE (this is why later texts speak of the Phoenicians as Sidonians; see 1 Kgs 5:20). By the eleventh century BCE trade had been reestablished, and the delivery of wood to Solomon during the tenth century

---

[1] See EA 33:9; 2 Kgs 20:12-15.

[2] See Josephus, *Apion* 17-18, 106-27, 1.18; *Ant.* 8.3; see also H. Jacob Katzenstein, *The History of Tyre, from the Beginning of the Second Millenium B.C.E. until the Fall of the Neo-Babylonian Empire in 539 B.C.E.* (Jerusalem: Schocken, 1973), 116–28.

was simply routine. Ever since the third millennium the timber from the forests of Lebanon was the most important commodity of the Phoenicians and the source of their wealth.

[5:16-20] The message of Solomon to Hiram first explains the delay in the building of the temple; the statement serves as preparation for the actual building in 1 Kgs 6:1-38. It does not refer to the divine command in the prophecy of Nathan (2 Sam 7:12-13) but only mentions the wars of David as a reason for the delay. In contrast to David, who was constantly forced to wage war, Yahweh has granted Solomon peace and quiet: no enemy from outside, no plague from within presses him.[3] The idea of the presence of the name of Yahweh in the temple is part of the typical Deuteronomic theology (see Deut 12:11; 14:23; 16:2, 6, 11; 26:2). Thus the presence of the transcendent God in the temple is emphasized. The author is eager to anchor the temple theology already firmly in the preparation and planning of the building; organizational and economic problems are therefore pushed to the background and are emphasized only toward the end of the narrative. Due to their extreme firmness, the cedars (*Cedrus libani barrel*) with a height of up to thirty meters were indispensable in the construction; felling and transport of the mighty trunks required special skills.

[5:21-23] Next to the cedars, Hiram's answer also mentions cypresses (*Cypressus semper virens L.*); their wood was probably used for paneling as well as for the floors, since it was much easier to cut. The wood was transported over the sea; this assumes the existence of a port in the Mediterranean, but such a place is not mentioned. Only the Chronicler mentions Jaffa in 2 Chr 2:15 for clarifying purposes. The difficulties of transport via land to Jerusalem are not mentioned; however, such an operation required a proper road, since the timber could not be transported by donkeys and had to be put on wagons. The timber was made into rafts that were probably towed by ships. As a quid pro quo, Hiram requests food. Since the coastal strip near the Phoenician towns has always been fairly narrow, it was difficult to meet the agricultural needs of the population.

[5:24-25] These additions list only the Israelite part of the exported goods. The price paid by Solomon is huge: 20,000 cors of wheat equal 800 tons; 20 cors of fine oil equal about 8,000 liters. The Deuteronomistic Historian probably grossly exaggerates these huge amounts, since Israel was hardly able to produce such a large surplus. Despite the fact that the timber for the temple and palace was imported from Lebanon (as the name "House of the Forest of Lebanon" in 7:2 stresses), the details of the exchange of goods do not stem from an actual historical source, but are rather vague and imprecise. The extent of the deliveries mainly stresses that Solomon is a king with a huge surplus that can be used for prestigious building projects.

---

[3] Würthwein, *Könige,* 1:53.

[5:26] The final comment states the agreement between the two partners and describes the economic exchange as a covenant, that is, a treaty between equal partners. The choice of words fits the general nomenclature of the Deuteronomistic Historian: the economic relationship is styled as a peace treaty. Finally, the verse repeats the picture of the wise king and adds to it the notion of the peaceful, treaty-making king.

Conscripted Labor [ET = 5:13-18]

Text

5:27 King Solomon conscripted forced labor out of all Israel; the levy numbered thirty thousand men. 28 He sent them to the Lebanon, ten thousand a month in shifts; they would be a month in the Lebanon and two months at home; Adoniram was in charge of the forced labor. 29 Solomon also had seventy thousand laborers and eighty thousand stonecutters in the hill country, 30 besides Solomon's three thousand three hundred supervisors who were over the work, having charge of the people who did the work. 31 At the king's command, they quarried out great, costly stones in order to lay the foundation of the house with dressed stones. 32 So Solomon's builders and Hiram's builders and the Giblites did the stonecutting and prepared the timber and the stone to build the house.

Analysis

The notes about the conscripted labor are added to the narrative of the treaty between Solomon and Hiram, since they belong to the same context, that is, the preparation for the building of the temple. Verses 27-28 deal with conscripted labor in connection with the delivery of the timber, and vv. 29-31 are concerned with the stonecutting but do not mention the catchword "forced labor" again. The addition of the paragraph prompted a new concluding remark on the collaboration in v. 32.

Commentary

[5:27-28] The note in vv. 27-28 stands in opposition to v. 23, where Hiram promises that native workers will take care of the felling and shipping of the trees; the previous narrative does not state that workers were sent to Lebanon. It is not clear why it is stated that the workers spent one month in Lebanon and two months at home. Forced labor for the accomplishment of certain royal projects is well attested in the ancient Near East.[1] The even figure of thirty thousand men has probably not been taken from

---

[1] See Anson F. Rainey, "Compulsory Labour Gangs in Ancient Israel," *IEJ* 20 (1970) 191–202.

a reliable source; the mention of Adoniram with reference to his father is taken from 4:6. Thus the addition is probably not based on an authentic remark, but it is equally impossible to find a reason for a later addition. Maybe the participation of Solomon in the organization of the timber is intended to limit the role of Hiram during the building of the temple. At the same time the burden of the forced labor is eased by the system of spending a month in Lebanon and two months at home. In any case, the note is hardly reliable and probably an invention of the later narrator.

[5:29-31] It is only the literary context that allows us to understand the other preparations also as forced labor. It is assumed that the stones were cut in quarries close to Jerusalem and were then transported to the construction site.[2] It is not possible to locate the quarries in greater detail; it is possible, however, that they operated under royal supervision, since only the royal building projects required hewn stones. Local limestone was used for construction, since it is very easy to work. In deviation from the common technique of broken stones, the text mentions "dressed stones," that is, square hewn stones. This technique appears first in the early monarchy during the Iron II period and probably shows Phoenician influence.[3] The note on the foundation developed from 7:10-11. The use of dressed stones for the foundation emphasizes the precious character of the building, since the foundations were normally made from undressed stones.

The numbers of the forced laborers are vastly exaggerated and are not taken from a historical source; rather, the high figure demonstrates the size and extent of the Solomonic building project. The number of supervisors is not reliable either. How grossly these numbers are exaggerated is demonstrated by a comparison with the estimated population of the early monarchy. Based on the density and extent of Iron Age settlements during the time of the monarchy, estimates are that the population around 1000 BCE was approximately 150,000 adults in the land west of the Jordan. Only later, during the period of the monarchy up until the Assyrian invasion, did the population rise to 400,000 people.[4] Only the imagination of later redactors, who picture Solomon as a Near Eastern potentate, was able to create such exaggerated figures that do not comply with reality.

[5:32] The final remark stresses again the cooperation between Solomon and Hiram. We can no longer determine to what extent this cooperation influenced planning and building of temple and palace as such. We can assume that the Phoenicians, due to

---

[2] See Yigal Shiloh and Avigdor Horowitz, "Ashlar Quarries of the Iron Age in the Hill Country of Israel," *BASOR* 217 (1975) 37–48.

[3] See Yigal Shiloh, "The Proto-Aeolid Capital and Israelite Ashlar Masonry," *Qedem* 11 (1979).

[4] See Yigal Shiloh, "The Population of Iron Age Palestine in the Light of a Sample Analysis of Urban Plans, Areas and Population Density," *BASOR* 239 (1980) 25–35; Magen Broshi and Israel Finkelstein, "The Population of Palestine in Iron Age II," *BASOR* 287 (1992) 47–60.

their skill, took an active part in the building rather than only delivering building materials. In contrast to 5:20, the Phoenicians are called Giblites after the Phoenician city of Gebal (Jebeil), which the Greeks called Byblos. In the third millennium this city exercised great influence on the city-states along the Levantine coast. Despite the late character of the passage, this information is probably correct, because archaeology has shown the spread of Phoenician building techniques.[5] This note indicates knowledge of Phoenician participation during the building of the temple. Because of the character of the temple as the sole place for sacrifice, this knowledge was most likely not invented. In the following report of the building of the temple this cooperation is not mentioned again.

---

[5] See Ephraim Stern, "The Phoenician Architectural Elements in Palestine during the Late Iron Age and the Persian Period," in Aharon Kempinski and Ronny Reich, eds., *The Architecture of Ancient Israel: From the Prehistoric to the Persian Periods: In Memory of Immanuel (Munya) Dunayevsky* (Jerusalem: Israel Exploration Society, 1992), 302–9.

Building and Setup of the Temple

Text

6:1 In the four hundred eightieth year after the Israelites came out of the land of Egypt, in the fourth year of Solomon's reign over Israel, in the month of Ziv, which is the second month, he began to build the house of the Lord. 2 The house that King Solomon built for the Lord was sixty cubits long, twenty cubits wide, and thirty cubits high. 3 The vestibule in front of the nave of the house was twenty cubits wide, across the width of the house. Its depth was ten cubits in front of the house. 4 For the house he made windows with recessed frames. 5 He also built a structure against the wall of the house, running around the walls of the house, both the nave and the inner sanctuary; and he made side chambers all around. 6 The lowest story was five cubits wide, the middle one was six cubits wide, and the third was seven cubits wide; for around the outside of the house he made offsets on the wall in order that the supporting beams should not be inserted into the walls of the house.

7 The house was built with stone finished at the quarry, so that neither hammer nor ax nor any tool of iron was heard in the temple while it was being built.

8 The entrance for the middle story was on the south side of the house: one went up by winding stairs to the middle story, and from the middle story to the third. 9 So he built the house, and finished it; he roofed the house with beams and planks of cedar. 10 He built the structure against the whole house, each story five cubits high, and it was joined to the house with timbers of cedar.

11 Now the word of the Lord came to Solomon, 12 "Concerning this house that you are building, if you will walk in my statutes, obey my ordinances, and keep all my commandments by walking in them, then I will establish my promise with you, which I made to your father David. 13 I will dwell among the children of Israel, and will not forsake my people Israel."

14 So Solomon built the house, and finished it. 15 He lined the walls of the house on the inside with boards of cedar; from the floor of the house to the rafters of the ceiling, he covered them on the inside with wood; and he covered the floor of the house with boards of cypress. 16 He built twenty cubits of the rear of the house with boards of cedar from the floor to the rafters, and he built this within as an inner sanctuary, as the most holy place. 17 The house, that is, the nave in front of the inner sanctuary, was forty cubits long. 18 The cedar within the house had carvings of gourds and open flowers; all was cedar, no stone was seen. 19 The inner sanctuary he prepared in the innermost part of the house, to set there the ark of the covenant of the LORD. 20 The interior of the inner sanctuary was twenty cubits long, twenty cubits wide, and twenty cubits high; he overlaid it with pure gold. He also overlaid the altar with cedar. 21 Solomon overlaid the inside of the house with pure gold, then he drew chains of gold across, in front of the inner sanctuary, and overlaid it with gold. 22 Next he overlaid the whole house with gold, in order that the whole house might be perfect; even the whole altar that belonged to the inner sanctuary he overlaid with gold.

23 In the inner sanctuary he made two cherubim of olivewood, each ten cubits high. 24 Five cubits was the length of one wing of the cherub, and five cubits the length of the other wing of the cherub; it was ten cubits from the tip of one wing to the tip of the other. 25 The other cherub also measured ten cubits; both cherubim had the same measure and the same form. 26 The height of one cherub was ten cubits, and so was that of the other cherub. 27 He put the cherubim in the innermost part of the house; the wings of the cherubim were spread out so that a wing of one was touching the one wall, and a wing of the other cherub was touching the other wall; their other wings toward the center of the house were touching wing to wing. 28 He also overlaid the cherubim with gold.

29 He carved the walls of the house all around about with carved engravings of cherubim, palm trees, and open flowers, in the inner and outer rooms. 30 The floor of the house he overlaid with gold, in the inner and outer rooms.

31 For the entrance to the inner sanctuary he made doors of olivewood; the lintel and the doorposts were five-sided. 32 He covered the two doors of olivewood with carvings of cherubim, palm trees, and open flowers; he overlaid them with gold, and spread gold on the cherubim and on the palm trees.

33 So also he made for the entrance to the nave doorposts of olivewood, four-sided each, 34 and two doors of cypress wood; the two leaves of the one door were folding, and the two leaves of the other door were folding. 35 He carved cherubim, palm trees, and open flowers, overlaying them with gold evenly applied upon the carved work. 36 He built the inner court with three courses of dressed stone to one course of cedar beams.

37 In the fourth year the foundation of the house of the LORD was laid, in the month of Ziv. 38 In the eleventh year, in the month of Bul, which is the eighth month, the house was finished in all its parts, and according to all its specifications. He was seven years in building it.

Analysis

The detailed report of the setup and dedication of the temple in 1 Kings 6–8 has to be seen as the center of the story of Solomon. The other narratives and short notes about Solomon's wisdom, his building projects, and his trade in 1 Kings 3–5 and 9–10 serve as a frame to this central piece, which can be divided into the following sections of different lengths:

6:1-38	Building of the temple
7:1-12	The palace
7:13-51	Bronze work for the temple
8:1-11	Transportation of the ark
8:12, 13	Dedication
8:14-61	Temple prayer
8:62-66	Sacrifices

The introduction and final remark show that chap. 6 has to be regarded as a closed unit to which other sections were added. To this end, the Deuteronomistic Historian used an earlier report in 6:1—7:51 and independently formulated and added the temple prayer. The understanding of the whole complex is rather difficult, and its riddles have not yet been solved by scholarly discussion.

1. The text uses several technical terms that are not clear and cannot be deciphered. In addition, several colloquial words are used with a technical meaning that is unknown to us. Several details therefore remain obscure.

2. The text is not a single unit but has been supplemented by additions, and it is not clear if these additions are mere ornamentation or correct additions. In any case, the text grew slowly into its current shape, and it is not always easy to keep track of the developments.

3. The intention of the single parts is not always clear, especially in chap. 6. Since I. Benzinger scholars tend to speak of a building report written by an eyewitness, who was not necessarily a contemporary of Solomon.[1] M. Noth moved beyond this view and called the basic layer in 6:2-36 a written account of the planning of the temple.[2] In the light of unevenness and several other difficulties, it is hardly likely that we have a blueprint here according to which the actual temple had been built and

---

[1] Immanuel Benzinger, *Die Bücher der Könige: Mit neun Abbildungen im Text, einem Plan des alten Jerusalem und einer Geschichtstabelle*, KHC 9 (Freiburg: Mohr/Siebeck, 1899), 25.

[2] Noth, *Könige*, 104.

decorated. Rather it is a description written after the erection of the building that is—despite the obvious splendor of the building—full of gaps and missing details. The report is more likely a description of the building by an author whose time of origin cannot be determined. In any case, this report was written by an eyewitness, who was not only familiar with several technical terms, but also acquainted with the design as a whole as well as with several details concerning the building. Whether the author was a priest is difficult to determine but probably unlikely.

4. Apart from the framing verses 1 and 37-38, the building report can be divided into two larger parts: the masonry work (vv. 2-14) and the timber work (vv. 15-25); a remark on the enclosure walls in v. 36 concludes both parts. Of the timber work, the inner sanctuary (vv. 16-20), the cherubim (vv. 23-27), and the doors (vv. 31-34) are described in detail. All parts were reworked at a later stage and additions were made; the notes on the gold ornamentation in particular are later additions.[3]

Commentary

[6:1] This verse gives the date of the beginning of the building, following the standard formula giving the month and year of the king's rule. The month is determined by the lunar calendar; since a lunar phase consists of 29 days, 12 hours, and 44 minutes, the length of the month is either 29 or 30 days. The day of the new moon, a holiday, was always the beginning of the month. The months of a year were originally numbered successively, but toward the end of the monarchy the Babylonian names were adopted. The gloss of Ziv as the second month presupposes the beginning of the new year in spring. The use of the name shows that the dating is that of the Deuteronomistic Historian, who in mentioning the fourth year places the building of the temple at the beginning of Solomon's reign.

The identification "in the four hundred eightieth year after the Israelites came out of the land of Egypt" makes a connection between the building of the temple and this profound event of salvation. Historically, the even number is not very reliable; it consists of twelve generations of forty years each. Nevertheless, it can be reconciled with the general chronological time frame of the Deuteronomistic History. According to the chronology of the book of Judges, the whole period of the judges lasted 349 years. For the period between Samson as the last judge and the fourth year of Solomon one can add 86 years. Including the forty years in the desert but without the conquest and the distribution of the land by Joshua, one arrives at 349 + 86 + 40 = 475 years. To make these 475 years and the 480 years of 6:1 fit, one has to assume that the conquest of the land lasted five years. Within the Deuteronomistic History we thus find a consistent chronology that is nevertheless useless for any historical reconstruction since it is based on the assumption that one generation lasted forty years. Despite the absence of any comparable chronology, one can date the period of the

---

[3] See ibid., 105.

reign of Solomon between 965 and 926; thus—according to the Deuteronomistic Historian—the construction of the temple began in 962.

On a literary level the paragraph on the masonry work is not a unity, as is shown by the repetition of the concluding formula in vv. 9a and 14. This doublet is determined by the addition of vv. 9b, 10, and 11-13. The real conclusion of the masonry work is found in v. 7; thus also v. 8 has to be regarded as another addition to the annex. Moreover, the rather detailed descriptions of the annex do not fit the frame of the description and are most likely additions. The description of the masonry work is rather concise and consists only of the following elements: measurements (vv. 2-3), windows (v. 4), annex (v. 5), building technique (v. 7), and concluding formula (v. 9a).

[6:2-3] The measurements in vv. 2-3 are the outside measurements, but in vv. 16-29 we find similar figures for the inside. According to this, the house, including the vestibule, was 70 cubits long, 20 cubits wide, and 30 cubits high. The standard measurement of a cubit changed during the time of the kings from the old 44.5 cm. to the royal measurement of 51.8 cm. Thus the building as such had either a size of 31.15 m. x 8.90 m. x 13.35 m. or 36.26 m. x 10.36 m. x 15.54 m. The graphic reconstruction leads to a longhouse with vestibule with the distorted proportions of 7:2:3. The length of the building is not in proportion to its width, and its height in particular is far too great. The missing balance of height, length, and width and the even figures lead to the assumption that the measurements are not the real ones but simply an estimate by the author.

From the information we can deduct that the Solomonic temple was a longhouse with a vestibule in which the shrine was placed (vv. 16-20). This long-room temple had been quite common in Syria from the end of the third millennium, and slowly the wide-room temple in the southern Levant was replaced from the second millennium onward. In the light of several parallels for this type of temple up to the last example from Tell Ta'yinat from the eighth century, one has to conclude that the form of the Solomonic temple was taken over from the Canaanite environment and belonged to the Syrian form of the longhouse temple.[4]

[6:4] The windows mentioned in v. 4 cannot be verified. They were possibly openings high up in the walls that served as a source of light for the inner room; these openings were then framed with grids of stone.

[6:5] The annex sets against the outer walls of the temple. According to the addition in v. 5, the building had three floors, while the addition in v. 10—with its note on a height of five cubits—assumes only one floor (it is possible that v. 6 refers to a later extension of the building). The form and function of the annex cannot be determined from the text, because the meaning of the word usually translated "rib" or "side"

---

[4] See *BRL*, figs. 85:15, 17-21, 28-30.

(NRSV "side chambers") remains unclear. According to the example of the Iron Age temple at 'En Dara we can assume a gallery on three sides of the temple.[5] The function of this gallery cannot be determined; given its structure it could have been an element that facilitated unseen access to certain parts of the inner room of the temple. Such a view presupposes connecting doors between gallery and temple that were not found at 'En Dara. The state of preservation of this temple is so bad, however, that one cannot exclude that there were such access doors. This annex distinguishes the temple in Jerusalem (and the temple at 'En Dara) from other longhouse temples in Syria-Palestine during the Late Bronze Age and the Iron Age.

[6:7] The remark in v. 7 presupposes that the stones for the building were finished at the quarry and only put into place on the construction site. By sticking to certain norms further work on them was rendered superfluous. This process, here described as being almost a miracle, was the normal practice with hewn stones, which were always manufactured and delivered according to a standardized measure so that they could be joined together without any further work. In contrast to the normal form of construction using unhewn stones, the use of such stones is extraordinary; the intensive labor connected with such hewn stones reserved their use for royal building projects. The best example of this technique is the palace built by Omri in Samaria during the ninth century; here the standardized hewn stones were placed according to an architectural plan. The description of the masonry work concludes with the note in v. 7. Only the general concluding note in v. 9 follows, which—in view of v. 38— seems to come too early.

[6:6] The description of the annex continues with the additional v. 6. It is only here that the gallery becomes an annex with three stories, whose function and aim are not described. Here the intact character of the temple is stressed, since the stories and the roof rest on specially built offsets so that the supporting beams would not be inserted into the walls of the house. At the same time the annex becomes an integral part that encompasses the temple building in a harmonious way.

[6:8] The theme of the addition in v. 8 is the mode of access to the annex. According to this description it was possible to enter only via a door on the ground floor on the northern side. The two other stories were accessible only through inside stairs. This description stresses that there were no other stairs on the outside, so the facade was even.

[6:9b] The added remark in v. 9b is impossible to understand, since the meaning of the two relevant terms is unknown. It seems to have been a remark on the construction of

---

[5] See Ali Abou-'Assaf, *Der Tempel von Ain Dara,* DamFor 3 (Mainz: von Zabern, 1990), 17–19, fig. 18.

the roof that remains unclear. Nevertheless, we can assume a flat roof that rested on beams, but we have to presuppose that the gaps between the beams were covered with planks.

[6:10] This verse adds the height of the annex; the five cubits mentioned can only refer to a story. The further statement assumes that the temple also had outside paneling made of cedar. This statement comes a bit too early, since the woodwork is only described from v. 15 onward. In addition, such outside paneling is quite superfluous—stonewalls did not need any additional cover. With the covering of the walls from outside the redactor wanted to increase the splendor of the appearance.

[6:11-13] This interpolation has the form of a Yahweh speech and is shaped in its entirety by Deuteronomistic language. The verses interrupt the context and have nothing to do with the building of the temple. As in the temple speech of Jeremiah (Jeremiah 7), it is stressed that not merely the existence of the temple but only the obedience toward the stipulations of Yahweh can guarantee salvation. The building of the temple and the sacrifices do not replace a conduct of life according to the law. The proximity of Yahweh, vouched for by the existence of the temple, is only guaranteed as long as the king follows the law. This connection between obedience and the course of life is a characteristic feature of Deuteronomistic theology, a feature that is stressed again and again in longer speeches, such as 1 Kings 8. Here a redactor has added this feature.

The description of the timber work can be divided into the following parts:

v. 15	interior lining
vv. 16-20	shrine
vv. 23-27	cherubim
v. 29	wall carvings
vv. 31-34	doors

[6:14] This verse repeats the concluding formula of v. 9a. This repetition is necessary due to the interpolation of vv. 11-13.

[6:15] The description of the woodwork commences with a note on the lining of the walls and the floor covering. We do not know how well stone walls could be covered by wooden paneling. This lining of the wall is understandable only if one takes the ornamentation of v. 29 into account. The paneling corresponds to the orthostats on the lower parts of the wall in Assyrian palaces that were decorated with reliefs. It has to remain open whether the author is describing the actual state. Also, the covering of the floor with wood is highly unusual, given both the value of the material and its durability. Next to floors made from fortified clay, stone is fairly common; wooden floors have not yet been excavated. It can no longer be determined why boards of cypress were used for the floor; maybe they was easier to cut than the fairly hard wood of the cedar.

[6:16-17, 20] The shrine was a built-in wooden cube, whose sides were 20 cubits long—here the outer measures of vv. 2-3 are used as inner ones. The shrine thus stretched across the whole width of the building and used a third of its length. As far as its height is concerned, it did not reach up to the ceiling. This fact has given rise to much speculation, but the problem can be solved by regarding the shrine as part of the inner decoration of the temple. The free space on top of the shrine just remained empty.[6] The shrine was a special room where the cherubim were placed. Further details of its appearance cannot be deduced from the textual evidence; it did not occupy a special symbolic function. Thus the built-in shrine created a special room for the presence of Yahweh so that the shrine corresponded to the separation of the adytum from the cella in the temple buildings of the first millennium.

[6:20] The remark on the gold overlay is an addition that in turn resulted in the further comments in vv. 21-22. According to this, the whole interior was overlaid with gold. The chains as a further decorative element cannot be explained. The lining of the interior with gold moves beyond any decoration known and wants to stress the special status of the Solomonic temple, which exceeds any other cultic building in the milieu. The decoration does not reflect reality but expresses the wish to glorify the temple of Jerusalem.

[6:22] According to v. 22 the altar mentioned in the same context stood in front of the shrine. This fixture could only have been a small altar for burnt offerings on which incense was burned; generally the burnt offering was placed in a bowl on the altar.[7] This altar has a parallel in the two small altars on the steps leading to the niche in the temple of Arad.[8]

[6:18-19] The description of the shrine interrupts the flow of the text and is a redactional addition. Furthermore, the description of the woodwork is interrupted several times by remarks that its inside was overlaid by pure gold. These notes on the gold works (vv. 20, 21, 22, 28, 30, 35b) are secondary additions. The overlaying of the doors of the shrine with gold seems, in contrast, to have been an original part of the description.

---

[6] See Noth, *Könige,* 121.

[7] On this mode of offering see Wolfgang Zwickel, *Räucherkult und Räuchergeräte: Exegetische und archäologische Studien zum Räucheropfer im Alten Testament,* OBO 97 (Göttingen: Vandenhoeck & Ruprecht, 1990).

[8] See Volkmar Fritz, *Tempel und Zelt: Studien zum Tempelbau in Israel und zu den Zeltheiligtum der Priesterschrift,* WMANT 47 (Neukirchen-Vluyn: Neukirchener Verlag, 1977).

The addition of v. 18 refers to v. 15 and specifies the paneling of the wall so that "no stone was seen." The carvings are only mentioned in v. 29. The additional v. 19 repeats v. 16, giving a new purpose to the shrine. In contrast to v. 23, which states that the wooden cherubim were placed in the inner sanctuary, v. 19 mentions the shrine as the place for the ark of the covenant. According to 8:1-11 the ark was indeed brought into the temple after the completion of the building works (see 8:4). Despite the fact that undoubtedly the ark was placed in the inner sanctuary, the temple was not built especially to house the ark. Its building is connected with the imagination of Yahweh's dwelling in the temple (see 8:12-13).

[6:23-28] Two cherubim made of olivewood were carved to be placed in the shrine. The measures given do not provide any exact detail, but the statues were probably larger than lifesize. Their exact appearance is not described; the text emphasizes only that they were standing statues with outstretched wings. By analogy to figures known from pictorial evidence among Israel's neighbors where such creatures accompanied the gods, we have to imagine them as winged figures with possibly a human body. As carriers of the theophany (see Ps 18:11 par. 2 Sam 22:11) the cherubim accompanied the divinity but did not themselves possess divine character. Also, the cherubim do not serve as cultic mediators between the human person and the godhead, although they represent the god in that they stress the presence of the god. Thus the cherubim can serve as the symbol for the presence of Yahweh. Since Yahweh sits enthroned upon the cherubim (see 1 Sam 4:4; 2 Sam 6:2; 2 Kgs 19:15; 1 Chr 13:6; Pss 80:2; 99:1; Isa 37:16), they serve as the visible sign of the invisible God. In them, Yahweh manifests his presence at the place. Since they were carved from wood, each cherub probably consisted of several individual pieces; v. 28 adds that they also were overlaid with gold. Most likely these cherubim were burned during the siege and destruction of Jerusalem by the Babylonians in 587 BCE; the shrine of the Second Temple was empty.

[6:29-30] According to v. 29 the paneled inside walls were decorated with carvings of cherubim, palm trees, and garlands. The cherubim were mixed creatures whose appearance is not described. Palm tress occur quite frequently in ancient Near Eastern art, since they represent the tree of life. Garlands are bands of ornaments or floral patterns that could be extended at will. All motifs are well known from ivory carvings of the royal period.[9] Further details are not mentioned; the additional remark on the golden overlay is missing, since this fact had already been stressed for the temple as a whole in vv. 21-22. Verse 30 mentions that the floor too was overlaid with gold, a rather senseless addition.

---

[9] See J. W. Crowfoot and Grace M. Crowfoot, *Early Ivories from Samaria,* Samaria-Sebaste (London: Palestine Exploration Fund, 1938).

[6:31-35] The details of the doors for shrine and temple conclude the description of the woodwork. Each door had two wings that were divided into coffers. These consisted of projected coffers as decoration (the mention of the cherubim, palm trees, and garlands for which there was no space on the doors is determined by v. 29 and is probably a secondary addition). It is not clear why the doors to the inner sanctuary were made from olivewood while the outer doors were made from cypress wood. The note on the overlaying of the doors with gold seems to be authentic, but whether this decoration really existed cannot be said for sure. Since we find bronze paneling on doors in Assyria such a method cannot be excluded. The wooden doorposts display a special design too; here one could think of staggered doors that are sometimes found in public buildings in Syria and Mesopotamia.

[6:36] The temple precinct is separated from the palace by a wall. This boundary creates a separate court for the temple and shows the separation of the cultic realm, determined by the holiness of God, from the profane one. The technique mentioned, with three courses of dressed stones and one course of cedar beams, is quite common in the southern Levant during the Bronze Age and Iron II. It is a measure against earthquakes and serves as additional protection for the temple.

The exact location of the temple is not mentioned. The visible rock under the Dome of the Rock was by no means included in the temple. Since this rock probably was freestanding during the period of the kings, it cannot serve as an indication for the site of the temple. According to the geographical condition of the area one can assume that the temple stood just south of the visible rock, but there are no traces that allow for a detailed determination of the exact spot. The temple stood, in any case, within the palace precinct and originally served as the chapel for the palace. It cannot be said if it was open to common people from the beginning or just to members of the palace. The temple was planned and built as a royal sanctuary; only during the period of the kings did it become the national sanctuary and cultic center of all the people.

[6:37-38] The concluding formula mentions the dates for the foundation and completion of the building. Despite the fairly detailed dates it is not a note from the royal annals. The duration of seven years is a standard figure that stresses the length of the building project. As in v. 1, the Deuteronomistic Historian wants to integrate the building of the temple into his view of history, and this is done by giving an exact date. Although the building of the temple is only part of the general construction of the palace, the Deuteronomistic Historian not only describes the temple fairly extensively but also places it at the beginning of his report of the building projects, thereby stressing its importance. Within the Deuteronomistic History, the temple occupies a special role as the cultic center. The building of the palace comes only second and is described in much shorter fashion.

The Palace

Text

7:1 Solomon was building his own house thirteen years, and he finished his entire house.

2 He built the House of the Forest of the Lebanon one hundred cubits long, fifty cubits wide, and thirty cubits high, built on four rows of cedar pillars, with cedar beams on the pillars. 3 It was roofed with cedar on the forty-five rafters, fifteen in each row, which were on the pillars. 4 There were window frames in the three rows, facing each other in the three rows. 5 All the doorways and doorposts had four-sided frames, opposite, facing each other in the three rows.

6 He made the Hall of Pillars fifty cubits long and thirty cubits wide. There was a porch in front with pillars, and a canopy in front of them.

7 He made the Hall of the Throne where he was to pronounce judgment, the Hall of Justice, covered with cedar from floor to floor.

8 His own house where he would reside, in the other court back of the hall, was of the same construction. Solomon also made a house like this hall for Pharaoh's daughter, whom he had taken in marriage.

9 All these were made of costly stones, cut according to measure, sawed with saws, back and front, from the foundation to the coping, and from outside to the great court. 10 The foundation was of costly stones, huge stones, stones of eight and ten cubits. 11 There were costly stones above, cut to measure, and cedarwood. 12 The great court had three courses of dressed stone to one layer of cedar beams all around; so had the inner court of the house of the LORD, and the vestibule of the house.

Analysis

In comparison to the exposition of the temple, the description of the palace is rather brief. The palace consists of five buildings in total, which are surrounded by a wall and thus form a separate entity:

1. House of the Forest of the Lebanon
2. Colonnade
3. Hall of the Throne
4. Living quarters
5. House for Pharaoh's daughter

Only the House of the Forest of the Lebanon is described in detail; the author either knew the building himself or he had a detailed oral or written report of it. It is not possible to get a detailed picture of the other buildings. It is remarkable that the public buildings seem to outnumber the private ones, but it is impossible to check the completeness of the list of buildings. The palace was situated on a hill north of the city, which is today occupied by the Temple Mount. So far, no archaeological remains of it have been found, and probably never will be found, since later buildings replaced the older ones, whose remains have probably been cleared away in the process.

Commentary

[7:1] The statement on the duration of the building cannot be verified, but we learn from the dating that the construction of the temple was completed before the completion of the palace. The palace is called "the house of Solomon" and is thus distinguished linguistically from the temple as "the house of Yahweh."

[7:2-5] According to this description, the House of the Forest of the Lebanon was a rectangular shaped building 100 cubits long, 50 cubits wide, and 30 cubits high. Converted into meters the ground of this building covered either 44.5 x 22.25 m. or 51.8 x 25.9 m., making it much larger than the temple. Its height of either 13.35 or 15.54 m. is the same height as the temple. All measurements seem to be round figures, which are probably exaggerated, to stress the size of the building.

Despite the details given it is not possible to sketch out a picture of the building. The name of the building comes from the wood of the cedars of Lebanon used for the pillars (see 1 Kgs 5:15-26). The place of the entrances is not mentioned, but the note about doors and windows suggests that it was a closed building. To support the roof, the pillars were probably lined up lengthwise in four even rows so that the whole building was separated in five parallel rooms of even size. The position of the beams above the pillars is explicitly mentioned, as is the wooden ceiling, which has to be imagined as a coffered ceiling. The terminology does not explicitly state that there was not an additional floor above the ceiling, but such a thing would have been against the design of the building. Light for this representative room came from three rows of windows. The shape of windows and doors is explicitly mentioned.

The purpose of the building is not stated. It is possible that this building served as the "lounge" for the members of the court if they did not have their own rooms or offices. Comparable buildings have not been unearthed in Palestine or Syria during the second or first millennium. Similar halls have been found only in the thirteenth-century Hittite palace at Hatussa and in the eighth/seventh century citadel of Godin Tepe in ancient Iran.[1] An architectural placement of the building is therefore not yet possible. In any case, the House of the Forest of the Lebanon was a representative hall, which is found only in palace quarters. That the Phoenicians were able to erect such buildings is proven by the tenth/ninth-century Phoenician temple of Kition on Cyprus, which covers an area of 33.5 x 22 m. and has four rows of seven pillars each.[2]

[7:6] According to the measurements given in v. 6, the so-called Hall of Pillars was much smaller than the House of the Forest of the Lebanon. The specially mentioned porch allows us to think also of a freestanding building, but it is not possible to decide if this building was a long or a wide room. It is out of the question to think of the Syrian architectural style of Hilani, because this style of building did not migrate to the southern Levant.[3] The use of the term "hall" possibly shows that the building was not enclosed by walls on all four sides but was probably open on one side. Such a view of the hall as an early form of a stoa is contradicted by the mentioning of the porch, which—in analogy to the temple—seems to hint at a rectangular building. If the Hall of Pillars was indeed a longhouse it was probably named after the rows of pillars that divided the interior space. The measurements are comparable to the one of the temple but they probably just reflect the approximate size. The purpose of the building is not stated.

[7:7] The Hall of the Throne is not described in great detail, but it also had a wooden ceiling. Maybe it was a long rectangular building of fair size. Thus, next to the living quarters, the palace consisted of three buildings for public or general purposes: the House of the Forest of the Lebanon, the Hall of Pillars, and the Hall of the Throne, which was also used to pronounce judgment there. On the judicial duties of the king see 1 Kgs 3:6-9.

[7:8] The royal residence containing the living and sleeping quarters is only mentioned, not described in detail. The building probably also had a kitchen. We do not get any information about the plan of the building and as a comparison can only use Megiddo palace 1723, which can be dated to the tenth century.[4] In analogy to this building we can assume that the Solomonic residential palace had several rooms, which were placed around one or more courtyards. The details, however, remain

---

[1] See Winfried Orthmann, *Der alte Orient,* Propyläen-Kunstgeschichte 14 (Berlin: Propyläen, 1975), 396, fig. 116; 410, fig. 123a.

[2] See Vassos Karageorghis, *Cyprus: From the Stone Age to the Romans,* Ancient People and Places 101 (London: Thames and Hudson, 1982), 124, fig. 95.

[3] See Volkmar Fritz, "Die syrische Bauform des Hilani und die Frage seiner Verbreitung," *Damaszener Mitteilungen* 1 (1983) 43–58.

[4] Ibid., 54–56.

obscure. It is also not certain whether the royal harem was situated in this part of the palace. Due to her special status at the court, a special house is built and furnished only for the daughter of the pharaoh. We do not know whether this house resembled the Egyptian houses with their strict architectural plans. The adoption of the Egyptian mode of building is possible, however, since we do know that the model of so-called Amarna houses was fairly widespread in premonarchic times.[5] It is not quite certain, however, whether v. 8b is not simply a literary addition to stress the elevated status of the daughter of Pharaoh, since this happens elsewhere in the narrative.

[7:9-11] Just like 6:7, vv. 9-11 mention again the building materials. Like the temple, the buildings of the palace were made of hewn stones. The use of hewn or cut stones stands in sharp contrast to the usual mode of building using uncut stones; all this stresses the special character of the building. The use of these hewn stones had to follow a certain norm since they were cut elsewhere and then delivered (see 6:7). However, the measurements of 10 and 8 cubits (= 4.35/5.18 m. and 3.56/4.14 m.) for the stones are exaggerated—stones of this length were used only in Hellenistic times. The stones used for the palace in Samaria differ in size from period to period. For the foundational phase the stretchers measure 0.94–1.13 m. in length and the headers 0.21–0.47 m. in width by a height of 0.45–0.47 m. In the additional phase the blocks are 1–1.10 m. long, 0.30–0.35 m. wide, and 0.5 m. high. These are obviously the measurements common in the period of the kings, although the foundation phase uses the shorter cubit and the addition phase the longer one as a standard. According to this, the dressed stones could not have been longer than between 2 and 2.5 cubits. Moreover, the walls of Samaria show that dressed stones were already used for the foundations to provide a secure basis for the building.[6] The mention of the cedarwood shows that the walls of the building were regularly interrupted by wooden beams to increase their stability.

[7:12] According to v. 12 the great outside wall enclosed all parts of the palace, with the wall of the temple distinguished from it and called the inner wall. Thus the single buildings of the palace stood around a great court and did not form a closed complex. The note on the outside wall shows that the temple formed a special part of the palace. How far it could be immediately accessed, that is, without entering the palace, cannot be said. Due to the elevated location in the north of Davidic Jerusalem, palace and temple formed the new acropolis of the city.

---

[5] See Volkmar Fritz, "Die Verbreitung des sogennanten Amarna-Wohnhauses in Kanaan," *Damaszener Mitteilungen* 3 (1988) 27–34.

[6] See J. W. Crowfoot, Kathleen M. Kenyon, and E. L. Sukenik, *The Buildings at Samaria,* Samaria-Sebaste (London: Palestine Exploration Fund, 1942), 93–100. Reprinted London: Dawson, 1966.

The Bronze Works for the Temple

Text

7:13 Now King Solomon invited and received Hiram from Tyre. 14 He was the son of a widow of the tribe of Naphtali, whose father, a man of Tyre, had been an artisan in bronze; he was full of skill, intelligence, and knowledge in working bronze. He came to King Solomon, and did all his work.

15 He cast two pillars of bronze. Eighteen cubits was the height of the one, and a cord of twelve cubits would encircle it; the second pillar was the same. 16 He also made two capitals of molten bronze, to set on the tops of the pillars; the height of the one capital was five cubits, and the height of the other capital was five cubits. 17 There were nets of checker work with wreaths of chain work for the capitals on the tops of the pillars; seven for the one capital, and seven for the other capital. 18 He made the columns with two rows around each latticework to cover the capitals that were above the pomegranates; he did the same with the other capital. 19 Now the capitals that were on the tops of the pillars in the vestibule were of lily-work, four cubits high. 20 The capitals were on the two pillars and also above the rounded projection that was beside the latticework; there were two hundred pomegranates in rows all around; and so with the other capital. 21 He set up the pillars at the vestibule of the temple; he set up the pillar on the south and called it Jachin; and he set up the pillar on the north and called it Boaz. 22 On the tops of the pillars was lily-work. Thus the work of the pillars was finished.

23 Then he made the molten sea; it was round, ten cubits from brim to brim, and five cubits high. A line of thirty cubits would encircle it completely. 24 Under its brim were panels all around it, each of ten cubits, surrounding the sea; there were two rows of panels, cast when it was cast. 25 It stood on twelve oxen, three facing north, three facing west, three facing south, and three facing east; the sea was set on them. The hindquarters of each were toward the inside. 26 Its thickness was a handbreadth; its brim was made like the brim of a cup, like the flower of a lily; it held two thousand baths.

27 He also made the ten stands of bronze; each stand was four cubits long, four cubits wide, and three cubits high. 28 This was the construction of the stands: they had borders; the borders were within the frames; 29 on the borders that were set in the frames were lions, oxen, and cherubim. On the frames, both above and below the lions and oxen, there were wreaths of beveled work. 30 Each stand had four bronze wheels and axles of bronze; at the four corners were supports for a basin. The supports were cast with wreaths at the side of each. 31 Its opening was within the crown whose height was one cubit; its opening was round, as a pedestal is made; it was a cubit and a half wide. At its opening there were carvings; its borders were four-sided, not round. 32 The four wheels were underneath the borders; the axles of the wheels were in the stands; and the height of a wheel was a cubit and a half. 33 The wheels were made like a chariot wheel; their axles, their rims, their spokes, and their hubs were all cast. 34 There were four supports at the four corners of each stand; the supports were of one piece with the stands. 35 On the top of the stand there was a round band half a cubit high; on the top of the stand, its stays and its borders were of one piece with it. 36 On the surfaces of its stays and on its borders he carved cherubim, lions, and palm trees, where each had space, with wreaths all around. 37 In this way he made the ten stands; all of them were cast alike, with the same size and the same form.

38 He made ten basins of bronze; each basin held forty baths, each basin measured four cubits; there was a basin for each of the ten stands. 39 He set five of the stands on the south side of the house, and five on the north side of the house; he set the sea on the southeast corner of the house.

40 Hiram also made the pots, the shovels, and the basins. So Hiram finished all the work that he did for King Solomon on the house of the LORD: 41 the two pillars, the two bowls of the capitals that were on the tops of the pillars, the two latticeworks to cover the two bowls of the capitals that were on the tops of the pillars; 42 the four hundred pomegranates for the two latticeworks, two rows of pomegranates for each latticework, to cover the two bowls of the capitals that were on the pillars; 43 the ten stands, the ten basins on the stands; 44 the one sea, and the twelve oxen underneath the sea.

45 The pots, the shovels, and the basins, all these vessels that Hiram made for King Solomon for the house of the LORD were of burnished bronze. 46 In the plain of the Jordan the king cast them, in the clay ground between Succoth and Zarethan. 47 Solomon left all the vessels unweighed, because there were so many of them; the weight of the bronze was not determined.

48 So Solomon made all the vessels that were in the house of the LORD: the golden altar, the golden table for the bread of the Presence, 49 the lampstands of pure gold, five on the south side and five on the north, in front of the inner sanctuary; the flowers, the lamps, and the tongs, of gold; 50 the cups, snuffers, basins, dishes for incense, and firepans, of pure gold; the

sockets for the doors of the innermost part of the house, the most holy place, and for the doors of the nave of the temple, of gold.

51 Thus all the work that King Solomon did on the house of the LORD was finished. Solomon brought in the things that his father David had dedicated, the silver, the gold, and the vessels, and stored them in the treasuries of the house of the LORD.

Analysis

The paragraph on the bronze works continues the description of the temple that had been interrupted in vv. 1-12 by the description of the palace. The report has its own introduction in vv. 13-14 and then continues to describe the pillars in vv. 15-22, the molten sea in vv. 23-26, as well as the stands and basins in vv. 27-30. Verses 40-47 serve as a summary that mentions further items made from bronze, followed in vv. 48-50 by the list of the vessels of gold. A concluding formula in v. 51 ends the section as a whole.

Commentary

[7:13-14] The introduction attributes the bronze works to a certain Hiram of Tyre. The correspondence in name with the king of Tyre, known from 5:15-26, is striking and can be explained only by assuming that this craftsman is a fictitious person; in the following section he appears again in vv. 40 and 45. The introduction tries to give to the description the character of a narrative. With the introduction of this person we suddenly get a certain tension between Solomon as the commissioner of the works and Hiram as the person who is responsible for carrying out the project. Whether the introduction really reflects this tension cannot be determined. In any case, the author was convinced that the extensive bronze works were only possible under the supervision of and with the help of specialists from Tyre.

The origin of the metal is unknown mainly because the author did not know it or simply could not imagine it. According to v. 46 the casting of bronze was done in a workshop in the Jordan Valley between Succoth and Zarethan. Succoth has not yet been located, but Zarethan has to be located on Tell Umm Hammad.[1] The location of the smelting works in the Jordan Valley is surprising, since the casting of bronze requires fairly high temperatures and correspondingly large amounts of charcoal; however, the slopes of the hills of the East Jordan had still enough trees during the period of the monarchy. The amount of metal that was necessary probably came from the mines of Fenan on the eastern fringe of the Arabah where, after a long interruption of about one thousand years, the production of copper had been taken up in the eleventh century. In any case, the production of copper was widespread in Israel during premonarchic times and thus also known in the early period of the monarchy.

---

[1] Volkmar Fritz, "Die syrische Bauform des Hilani um die Frage nach seiner Verbreitung," *Damaszener Mitteilungen* 1 (1983) 48 [43–58].

[7:15-22] The description of the single items begins with the two pillars in vv. 15-22. The height of the shaft of the pillar is said to be 18 cubits (= 8.01 or 9.32 m.) and the circumference 12 cubits (radius = 1.70 or 1.98 m.); but these figures are probably not very accurate. The measurements assume that both pillars were huge, but that their height and circumference are in proper relation to the stated measurements of the temple. In view of their height it was unlikely that both pillars were made of one piece, but we do not get to know any details. The surface must have been smooth, without any further ornaments. Due to the preciousness of the metal and the technical difficulties of casting bronze, the mentioned thickness of the walls given as four fingers (= 7.2 cm., according to Jer 52:21b) is highly unlikely. Rather, we should assume that the pillars were made of wood and covered with bronze plates. The bronze works were thus a necessary protection against the weather for the two pillars that stood outside. The bases of the pillars are not described. Maybe they are not mentioned because they were made from stone and not from bronze. We cannot, in any case, exclude the existence of bases, since the widespread occurrence of bases in Syria during Iron Age I seems to support their existence. The massive pillars were topped by two equally massive capitals, whose height is said to have been 5 cubits (2.25 or 2.59 m.).

The original description consisted just of vv. 17-18—the remaining verses (vv. 19-22) are explanatory additions that do not always help to clarify matters. Despite several uncertainties with regard to terminology it is possible to reconstruct the form of the capitals by using Iron Age findings from Syria.[2] To top pillars with capitals required a certain form of fashioning that was done by using bronze applications (it was also possible to attach such applications to capitals made from stone, as examples from Assyria show). According to the addition in v. 20 the capitals were placed on top of a rounded projection that had the shape of a round plate and was placed between pillar and capital. According to the addition in v. 19 the capital as such had the shape of an opening flower; this calyx was shaped like the opening of a lotus flower, which is used quite frequently in Phoenician art. According to v. 17, a round addition of unknown height was placed on such a capital in the form of a barrel, which was decorated with nets of checker work. On top of that we have the last element of the north Syrian capital, the typical wreath of leaves. There was no additional cover, and it would appear that the beams of the ceiling were placed directly on top of the double wreath of leaves, which formed the completion of the capital. Most likely, the single parts were fastened on a circular wooden core.

According to the addition in v. 21 the pillars were placed "at the vestibule of the temple"; their position is therefore not exactly determined. A lot has been speculated about their exact place. Since the pillars have to be regarded as an integral part of the vestibule, they cannot be placed—as often found in reconstruction—in front of

---

[2] See Volkmar Fritz, "Die Kapitelle der Säulen des salomonischen Tempels," *ErIsr* 23 (1992) 36*–42*.

the temple building as such. Comparing it with Iron Age architecture we can assume two possible places inside the vestibule. Depending on whether one assumes an open or a closed vestibule, the pillars were either placed inside the vestibule between the protruding long walls of the building (so-called position *in antes*), or they flanked the entry standing in a niche of the portal. Since the description of the woodwork in 6:31-35 mentions only the two doors for the shrine and for the main room (cella), we can assume that the vestibule was open quite like the Syrian long-room temple. Thus the position of the pillars in between the antes seems to be most likely. Such a position for pillars is clearly supported by evidence from temples from the Late Bronze and Early Iron Age in Syria, the best example here being the eighth-century temple at Tell Ta'yinat on the Orontes River.[3]

There has been much speculation about the two names, Jachin and Boaz, and the explanation of the names is disputed. Both names can be found elsewhere in the OT as personal names. Jachin means "he [Yahweh] will ascertain," and Boaz can be translated as "strength is in him [Yahweh]." There is no special symbolism in these two names, and one cannot assume that they were inscribed on the pillars. Both designations identify the pillars as persons and seem to have originated in folklore tradition that personifies the elements of the temple visible on the outside. Due to the names it is now possible to address the pillars directly; thus they receive a meaning beyond their architectural function. Last but not least, both names reflect trust in Yahweh. Similarly, both pillars manifest the special status of Yahweh that precedes each sacrifice and cultic action; visitors to the temple would have gained comfort for themselves and for their people.[4]

[7:23-26] The molten sea described in vv. 23-26 was a round basin with an outwardly bent and decorated rim whose exact form cannot be determined. The extraordinary proportion does not reflect reality. The weight of thirty-six tons especially shows how exaggerated the statement is, because the technological possibilities of the time did not allow manufacture or transport of a basin of such size.[5] The basin was filled with water, which was used for cleansing purposes. According to the late interpretation in 2 Chr 4:6, the water in the molten sea was employed by the priests for their ritual washings. One should not regard it as a symbol for the primeval ocean, even though Israel shares the common idea that the earth floated on the primeval ocean.

The basin was placed on twelve oxen, whose manufacture is not described. Since these statues carried the weight of the basin and its contents as a whole, it is possible that they were carved from stone. As carriers of cultic objects, oxen can serve as symbols for prowess and fertility. In the ancient Near East stones were fre-

---

[3] See Richard C. Haines, *Excavations in the Plain of Antioch* (Chicago: Univ. of Chicago Press, 1971), 2:53–55, pl. 103.

[4] Würthwein, *Könige,* 1:77.

[5] Weight calculated by T. A. Busink, *Der Tempel von Jerusalem von Salomon bis Herodes,* Vol. 1: *Der Tempel Salomos,* Studia Francisci Scholten Memoriae Dicata 3 (Leiden: Brill, 1970), 331.

quently used as pedestals (cf. 1 Kgs 12:25-32). The oxen were probably portrayed as standing and made as round sculptures, but it is entirely possible that only the heads were manufactured three-dimensionally (as is the case with the gateposts) while their sides were carved in a large stone relief. We cannot be sure about the details. When Ahaz proceeded to build a stone altar in front of the temple, he removed the molten sea from the oxen and placed it simply on the ground somewhere else in the courtyard (2 Kgs 16:17).

[7:27-39] The description of the stands is not clear in all its details, but the artifacts found at Megiddo and at Larnaca (Cyprus) provide a good impression of the appearance of such cultic items.[6] According to this evidence the stands were of a square shape, with four wheels fixed on each corner girder. Between these corner girders figures of lions, oxen, and cherubim were attached. On top of the square stand there was a round supplement on which the specially made basin was placed. The description is influenced by the sheer amazement about the artistic work. The fixing of the cast wheels onto axles is mentioned especially. Next to the animal figurines the decoration with geometric patterns is stressed; maybe they were spiral shaped bands, which are known from elsewhere for the decoration of metal objects.

As with all items, the dimensions are grossly exaggerated. This becomes apparent not only in comparison with a movable stand from Larnaca, which is only 39 cm. high and 23 cm. wide, but also in Busink's calculation of the weight: a total weight of 2.5 tons is far beyond any reality or practicability.[7] These comparative items show that such stands were well known in the environment and were probably taken over from neighboring cultures; the animals depicted do not hint at any specific Israelite symbolism. Cherubim belonged to the standard furnishings of a temple (cf. 6:23-27). Oxen symbolize fertility and abundance, the lion unrestrained power/force (cf. 2 Sam 1:23; Judg 14:18; Prov 30:30).

Nothing is said about the function of these stands in the cult. According to 2 Chr 4:6 the water from these tanks was used to wash the pieces for the burnt offering. This would explain the mobility of the stands: they could be wheeled to the place of slaughter of the sacrificial animal and there provide the water necessary for cleaning the pieces. This practice would also explain the relatively high number of these tank wagons: it was then possible to prepare several burnt offerings at the same time in the temple court. After the construction of a stone altar by Ahaz, these wagons, just like the molten sea, were no longer required—showing a change in sacrificial practice.

[7:40-47] The summary lists again the pieces already described without providing any further details. Only the description of the capitals as "bowls" shows that these

---

[6] See Silvia Schroer, *In Israel gab es Bilder: Nachrichten von darstellender Kunst im Alten Testament,* OBO 74 (Göttingen: Vandenhoeck & Ruprecht, 1987), figs. 5 and 21.

[7] Busink, *Tempel,* 1:349.

capitals were not solid but rather have to be understood as appliqués. In addition, pots, shovels, and basins are mentioned in vv. 40 and 45 without giving any details regarding their manufacture. These pieces cannot be identified. The pots of unknown shape served for the preparation of the sacrificial meal. The shovels were probably used for the ashes of the altar, and they were clearly not smoke pans, which are known from Roman times. For parallels one can probably look to iron shovels with a long handle found in Iron Age Dan.[8] The basins were probably richly decorated metal bowls, which are quite common in the ancient Near East and were possibly manufactured by Phoenician artisans.[9] The author did not possess any figures for the quantity of the used metal, and instead of giving an estimate he provides his readers with a note on an increase beyond measure.

[7:48-50] The enumeration of the golden vessels is an addition, which serves the glorification of Solomon.[10] For some items, the use of gold makes no sense. We thus have here a later compilation, which lists items used for the temple service but for which it is not possible to determine their exact use. The golden altar has probably been taken over from the addition to the Priestly description of the sanctuary in the tent in Exod 30:1-10. The golden table probably stems from the same source (Exod 25:23-30).[11] A lampstand is mentioned in Exod 25:31-39 in connection with the desert sanctuary, but it is neither listed among the abducted vessels from the temple in 2 Kgs 25:13ff. nor does it occur in the fictitious account in Ezekiel 40–48. These findings show that the lampstands were taken over from the priestly conception of the sanctuary; the number ten is governed by the number of tanks. The items called "flowers" remain obscure; lamps and tongues belonged to the objects used to light the temple. Bowls and basins are ordered according to size, the knives made of gold were useless. All in all we find cultic items that have been added from the description of the priestly sanctuary in Exodus 25–32, as well as items that were necessary for the temple service. Their description as made from gold not only stresses the wealth and splendor of Solomon but also elevates the temple way beyond the human imagination.

[7:51] The new concluding formula assumes that some of the instruments were not used but stored in some sort of treasury. This remark mirrors the vast wealth of Solomon with which he furnished the temple. The note on the things that were already dedicated by David marks a certain later tendency to give David a part in building and furnishing the temple.

---

[8] Avraham Biran, *Biblical Dan,* trans. Joseph Shadur (Jerusalem: Israel Exploration Society, 1994), fig. 33.

[9] H. von Bissing, "Untersuchungen über die phoinikischen Metallschalen," *JAI* 38/39 (1923–24) 180–241; R. D. Barnett, "Layard's Nimrod Bronzes and Their Inscriptions," *ErIsr* 8 (1967) 1*–7*.

[10] Würthwein, *Könige,* 1:84.

[11] See Volkmar Fritz, *Tempel und Zelt: Studien zum Tempelbau in Israel und zu dem Zeltheiligtum der Priesterschrift,* WMANT 47 (Neukirchen-Vluyn: Neukirchener, 1977).

The Transfer of the Ark
into the Temple

Text

8:1 Then Solomon assembled the elders of Israel and all the heads of the tribes, the leaders of the ancestral houses of the Israelites, before King Solomon in Jerusalem, to bring up the ark of the covenant of the LORD out of the city of David, which is Zion. 2 All the people of Israel assembled to King Solomon at the festival in the month Ethanim, which is the seventh month. 3 And all the elders of Israel came, and the priests carried the ark. 4 So they brought up the ark of the LORD, the tent of meeting, and all the holy vessels that were in the tent; the priests and the Levites brought them up. 5 King Solomon and all the congregation of Israel, who had assembled before him, were with him before the ark, sacrificing so many sheep and oxen that they could not be counted or numbered. 6 Then the priests brought the ark of the covenant of the LORD to its place, in the inner sanctuary of the house, in the most holy place, underneath the wings of the cherubim. 7 For the cherubim spread out their wings over the place of the ark, so that the cherubim made a covering above the ark and its poles. 8 The poles were so long that the ends of the poles were seen from the holy place in front of the inner sanctuary; but they could not be seen from outside; they are there to this day. 9 There was nothing in the ark except the two tablets of stone that Moses had placed there at Horeb, where the LORD made a covenant with the Israelites, when they came out of the land of Egypt. 10 And when the priests came out of the holy place, a cloud filled the house of the LORD, 11 so that the priests could not stand to minister because of the cloud; for the glory of the LORD filled the house of the LORD.

Commentary

[8:1-6] The paragraph about the transfer of the ark into the temple appears fairly crowded. On the one hand several remarks about the ark and the transfer in general are added in vv. 7 and 10-11; on the other hand there are short notices suggesting that only the priests came in contact with the ark. The kernel of the narrative seems to be vv. 1-6, but this is already a late literary piece, attached to the report of the building of the temple.

Despite the fact that the ark is not mentioned again at a later stage, we can assume that it has been placed in the inner sanctuary of the temple. Support for such a view is found in those OT passages that mention the ark as the footstool of Yahweh sitting enthroned in the temple (see Isa 6:19). The temple has not been built for the ark. The cherubim were standing in the inner sanctuary as a visible sign for the invisible God. The transfer of the ark to the shrine resulted in an unreflected duplication, because the ark was also connected with the concept of the presence of Yahweh. The ark was a wooden box that during premonarchic times stood in the sanctuary at Shiloh and then was lost to the Philistines (1 Samuel 4–6). It was only David who transferred the ark to Jerusalem and placed it in a tent sanctuary (2 Samuel 6).[1] With the introduction of the ark, the temple has now two symbols of divine presence that normally exclude each other and that are only connected in the Priestly conception of the sanctuary in the desert.[2] The author of the passage does not perceive this as a problem, since he is only interested in the whereabouts of the tent sanctuary erected by David after the completion of the temple. His narrative solution is entirely guided by the Solomonic temple: the sanctuary in the tent is superseded by the temple when the ark is transferred to the temple. There the ark did not have any further function, since the concept of the tie of divine presence to the ark has been replaced by the concept of God's dwelling in the temple.[3] The text emphasizes that Solomon and the elders—as representatives of the tribes—were involved in the transfer. In addition, it stresses that sacrifices were made in connection with this act. Naturally, priests function in the temple.

[8:7-8] The additions mention further aspects in connection with the ark. Verses 7-8 describe the exact position of the ark under the cherubim. The poles used to carry the ark are mentioned only in the Priestly conception in Exod 25:13-15; thus they demonstrate that the verses are a later addition. According to this, the ark was placed in a longitudinal direction in the shrine, and the ends of the poles were visible only from a point close to the door to the shrine.

[8:9] This verse aims at preventing any speculation about the content of the ark. The ark was originally empty; only according to Deuteronomic/Deuteronomistic theology

---

[1] On the history of the ark see Johann Maier, *Das altisraelitische Ladeheiligtum,* BZAW 93 (Berlin: Töpelmann, 1965).

[2] See Exod 25:10-22 and Volkmar Fritz, *Tempel und Zelt: Studien zum Tempelbau in Israel und zu dem Zeltheiligtum der Priesterschrift,* WMANT 47 (Neukirchen-Vluyn: Neukirchener, 1977), 112–57.

[3] See Jörg Jeremias, "Lade und Zion," in *Probleme biblischer Theologie: Gerhard von Rad zum 70. Geburtstag,* ed. Hans Walter Wolff (Munich: Kaiser, 1971), 183–98.

were the two tablets with the Ten Commandments connected with the ark in such a way that it became the container for this covenantal document (see Deut 10:1-5). The venerable cultic item was thus connected with the covenant on Mount Sinai. At the same time, the reference back to Moses connects the temple as the new cultic institution intrinsically with the fundamental event of the past; thus the divine endowment of the covenant is present in the temple. Following Deuteronomistic theology the author of this addition connected the constitutional granting of the covenant indissoluble with the central sanctuary.

[8:10-11] These verses are also found in Exod 40:34-35. After the completion of the tabernacle Yahweh appears in glory to legitimize the newly erected sanctuary with his presence. In accordance with the Priestly view the text states that after the transfer of the ark, the Solomonic temple is no less sanctified with the presence of Yahweh than was the case with the desert sanctuary in Mosaic times.[4] The cloud accompanies God and provides protection from the divine power, which a human person cannot endure. Like Moses, who could not enter the tent of meeting during a theophany, the priests are unable to serve in the temple when it was filled with God's presence and glory.[5]

---

[4] Noth, *Könige,* 180–81.

[5] For the concept of theophany and presence see R. E. Clements, *God and Temple: The Idea of the Divine Presence in Ancient Israel* (Oxford: Blackwell, 1965); Jörg Jeremias, *Theophanie: Die Geschichte einer alttestamentliche Gattung,* 2d ed., WMANT 10 (Neukirchen-Vluyn: Neukirchener, 1977). [Ed.] See also J. Kenneth Kuntz, *The Self-Revelation of God* (Philadelphia: Westminster, 1967).

The Consecration Proverb
for the Temple

Text

8:12 Then Solomon said:
    "‹The LORD has placed the sun in the heavens›,[a]
       he has decided that he would dwell in thick darkness.
  13 I have built you an exalted house,
       a place for you to dwell in forever."[b]

[a] Translation according to the Greek and Old Latin textual tradition; see J. Wellhausen, *Die Composition des Hexateuchs und der historischen Bücher des Alten Testaments,* 3d ed. (Berlin: Reimer, 1899), 269.

[b] The addition of the LXX, "is that not written in the Book of the Song," does not necessarily have to be part of the original text, since the LXX could have formed the remark by analogy to Josh 10:13 and 2 Sam 1:18 to stress the authenticity of the proverb.

Analysis

The Hebrew text of the consecration proverb for the temple has come down to us only in fragmentary form, but with the help of the Septuagint it is possible to restore it. The proverb as it stands is totally isolated and does not have any connection to the following context, but since it can be understood independently it does not seem to need a literary context.

Formally it consists of two verses constructed in parallel. Despite the fact that it is impossible to prove its old age, it is possible that the proverb originated during the early monarchy and referred right from the beginning to the temple. The change from the third person in the first verse to the first person in the second verse is noticeable. There is no parallel for such a form of a proverb and for an attribution to the so-called house blessings;[1] biblical or other comparative material is missing. The songs

---

[1] Noth, *Könige,* 181.

mentioned by G. Dalman in connection with the building of a house generally mock or praise the master builder.[2] Here more is at stake because the dwelling of Yahweh is picked out as the central theme. Only the proverb determines the meaning and purpose of the building of the temple: the creation of a dwelling place for Yahweh. Thus the idea of God's dwelling in the temple has been transferred to the sanctuary in Jerusalem.

Commentary

[8:12] The first verse contains a statement about the sun as a divine creation before contrasting the heavenly body of the day with the darkness and thus with the hidden God. The thick darkness alludes to the natural phenomena of rain and thunder clouds, which are especially impressive in the Near East since they stand in sharp contrast to the blazing sky. These dark clouds are the cosmic signs of the weather-god. In the catchword "thick darkness" Yahweh is described in analogy to the weather-god and thereby portrayed in close allusion to the Ugaritic god Baal. Just like Baal, who can be described as riding on clouds in Ugaritic texts, Ps 18:10-11 speaks of Yahweh:

> "He rode on a cherub, and flew;
>> he came swiftly upon the wings of the wind.
> He made darkness his covering around him,
>> his canopy thick clouds dark with water."

Even during his theophany God remains hidden in the darkness of clouds; the darkness is his place. Despite his seclusion, Yahweh created the sun and thus the light for the world. Human reality and the hidden reality of Yahweh are contrasted with each other.

[8:13] In the second verse Solomon himself speaks and qualifies the temple built by him as the earthly palace of God. The image of Yahweh's dwelling in the first verse is thus supplemented, stressing that with the temple he has received a dwelling place on earth. This image moves beyond the concept of the presence of God encompassed by the ark. Now the heavens as the dwelling place for Yahweh correspond to the earthly dwelling. Jerusalem receives a special presence of Yahweh that is mentioned elsewhere. For example, Ps 132:13-14 calls Zion the habitation of Yahweh:

> "For the LORD has chosen Zion;
>> he has desired it for his habitation:
> 'This is my resting place forever;
>> here I will reside, for I have desired it.'"

---

[2] Gustaf Dalman, *Palästinischer Diwan: Als Beitrag zur Volkskunde Palästinas* (Leipzig: Hinrichs, 1901), 58–64.

The point of departure for all further statements about the dwelling of Yahweh on earth is the idea connected with the temple, that here Yahweh has his palace on earth.[3] The theology of the temple corresponds to the ancient Near Eastern view: temples are erected to connect the godhead to a certain place. This view is well attested in Ugaritic texts.[4] The consecration proverb transfers a standard view of the surrounding nations to the sanctuary in Jerusalem that thereby receives a new dimension: with his dwelling in the temple, Yahweh is eternally connected to this place, as emphasized by the songs of Zion (Psalms 46, 48, 76). The temple thus determines a strong theology of presence that reaches its climax in the statement that Yahweh is in our midst (see Jeremiah 7). It is only with Deuteronomistic theology that the conception of the dwelling is spiritualized; it argues that the habitation is only concerned with the name of Yahweh and no longer with Yahweh as a person. In the following prayer of Solomon in 1 Kgs 8:14-53 the concept of the dwelling put forth by the consecration proverb is corrected by the Deuteronomistic Historian.

---

[3] See Martin Metzger, "Himmlische und irdische Wohnstatt Jahwes," *UF* 2 (1970) 139–58.

[4] See Otto Eissfeldt, "Die Wohnsitze der Götter von Ras Schamra," in *Kleine Schriften,* 6 vols., ed. Rudolf Sellheim und Fritz Maass (Tübingen: Mohr/Siebeck, 1963), 2:502–6.

The Dedication of the Temple

Text

8:14 Then the king turned around and blessed all the assembly of Israel, while all the assembly of Israel stood. 15 He said, "Blessed be the LORD, the God of Israel, who with his hand has fulfilled what he promised with his mouth to my father David, saying, 16 'Since the day that I brought my people Israel out of Egypt, I have not chosen a city from any of the tribes of Israel in which to build a house, that my name might be there; but I chose David to be over my people Israel.' 17 My father David had it in mind to build a house for the name of the LORD, the God of Israel. 18 But the LORD said to my father David, 'You did well to consider building a house for my name; 19 nevertheless you shall not build the house, but your son who shall be born to you shall build the house for my name.' 20 Now the LORD has upheld the promise that he made; for I have risen in the place of my father David; I sit on the throne of Israel, as the LORD promised, and have built the house for the name of the LORD, the God of Israel. 21 There I have provided a place for the ark, in which is the covenant of the LORD that he made with our ancestors when he brought them out of the land of Egypt."

22 Then Solomon stood before the altar of the LORD in the presence of all the assembly of Israel, and spread out his hands to heaven. 23 He said, "O LORD, God of Israel, there is no God like you in heaven above or on earth beneath, keeping covenant and steadfast love for your servants who walk before you with all their heart, 24 the covenant that you kept for your servant my father David as you declared to him; you promised with your mouth and have this day fulfilled with your hand. 25 Therefore, O LORD, God of Israel, keep for your servant my father David that which you promised him, saying, 'There shall never fail you a successor before me to sit on the throne of Israel, if only your children look to their way, to walk before me as you have walked before me.' 26 Therefore, O God of Israel, let your word be confirmed, which you promised to your servant my father David.

27 "But will God indeed dwell on the earth? Even heaven and the highest heaven cannot contain you, much less this house that I have built! 28 Regard your servant's prayer and his plea, O LORD my God, heeding the cry and the prayer that your servant prays to you today; 29 that your eyes may be open night and day toward this house, the place of which you said, 'My name shall be there,' that you may heed the prayer that your servant prays toward this place. 30 Hear the plea of your servant and of your people Israel when they pray toward this place; O hear in heaven your dwelling place; heed and forgive.

31 "If someone sins against a neighbor and is given an oath to swear, and comes and swears before your altar in this house, 32 then hear in heaven, and act, and judge your servants, condemning the guilty by bringing their conduct on their own head, and vindicating the righteous by rewarding them according to their righteousness.

33 "When your people Israel, having sinned against you, are defeated before an enemy but turn again to you, confess your name, pray and plead with you in this house, 34 then hear in heaven, forgive the sin of your people Israel, and bring them again to the land that you gave to their ancestors.

35 "When heaven is shut up and there is no rain because they have sinned against you, and then they pray toward this place, confess your name, and turn from their sin, because you punish them, 36 then hear in heaven, and forgive the sin of your servants, your people Israel, when you teach them the good way in which they should walk; and grant rain on your land, which you have given to your people as an inheritance.

37 "If there is famine in the land, if there is plague, blight, mildew, locust, or caterpillar; if their enemy besieges them in any of their cities; whatever plague, whatever sickness there is; 38 whatever prayer, whatever plea there is from any individual or from all your people Israel, all knowing the afflictions of their own hearts so that they stretch out their hands toward this house; 39 then hear in heaven your dwelling place, forgive, act, and render to all whose hearts you know—according to all their ways, for only you know what is in every human heart—40 so that they may fear you all the days that they live in the land that you gave to our ancestors.

41 "Likewise when a foreigner, who is not of your people Israel, comes from a distant land because of your name 42—for they shall hear of your great name, your mighty hand, and your outstretched arm—when a foreigner comes and prays toward this house, 43 then hear in heaven your dwelling place, and do according to all that the foreigner calls to you, so that all the peoples of the earth may know your name and fear you, as do your people Israel, and so that they may know that your name has been invoked on this house that I have built.

44 "If your people go out to battle against their enemy, by whatever way you shall send them, and they pray to the LORD toward the city that you have

chosen and the house that I have built for your name, 45 then hear in heaven their prayer and their plea, and maintain their cause.

46 "If they sin against you—for there is no one who does not sin—and you are angry with them and give them to an enemy, so that they are carried away captive to the land of the enemy, far off or near; 47 yet if they come to their senses in the land to which they have been taken captive, and repent, and plead with you in the land of their captors, saying, 'We have sinned, and have done wrong; we have acted wickedly'; 48 if they repent with all their heart and soul in the land of their enemies, who took them captive, and pray to you toward their land, which you gave to their ancestors, the city that you have chosen, and the house that I have built for your name; 49 then hear in heaven your dwelling place their prayer and their plea, maintain their cause 50 and forgive your people who have sinned against you, and all their transgressions that they have committed against you; and grant them compassion in the sight of their captors, so that they may have compassion on them 51 (for they are your people and heritage, which you brought out of Egypt, from the midst of the iron-smelter). 52 Let your eyes be open to the plea of your servant, and to the plea of your people Israel, listening to them whenever they call to you. 53 For you have separated them from among all the peoples of the earth, to be your heritage, just as you promised through Moses, your servant, when you brought our ancestors out of Egypt, O Lord GOD."

54 Now when Solomon finished offering all this prayer and this plea to the LORD, he arose from facing the altar of the LORD, where he had knelt with hands outstretched toward heaven; 55 he stood and blessed all the assembly of Israel with a loud voice:

56 "Blessed be the LORD, who has given rest to his people Israel according to all that he promised; not one word has failed of all his good promise, which he spoke through his servant Moses. 57 The LORD our God be with us, as he was with our ancestors; may he not leave us or abandon us, 58 but incline our hearts to him, to walk in all his ways, and to keep his commandments, his statutes, and his ordinances, which he commanded our ancestors. 59 Let these words of mine, with which I pleaded before the LORD, be near to the LORD our God day and night, and may he maintain the cause of his servant and the cause of his people Israel, as each day requires; 60 so that all the peoples of the earth may know that the LORD is God; there is no other. 61 Therefore devote yourselves completely to the LORD our God, walking in his statutes and keeping his commandments, as at this day."

62 Then the king, and all Israel with him, offered sacrifice before the LORD. 63 Solomon offered as sacrifices of well-being to the LORD twenty-two thousand oxen and one hundred twenty thousand sheep. So the king and all the people of Israel dedicated the house of the LORD. 64 The same day the king consecrated the middle of the court that was in front of the house of the

LORD; for there he offered the burnt offerings and the grain offerings and the fat pieces of the sacrifices of well-being, because the bronze altar that was before the LORD was too small to receive the burnt offerings and the grain offerings and the fat pieces of the sacrifices of well-being.

65 So Solomon held the festival at that time, and all Israel with him—a great assembly, people from Lebo-hamath to the Wadi of Egypt—before the LORD our God, seven days. 66 On the eighth day he sent the people away; and they blessed the king, and went to their tents, joyful and in good spirits because of all the goodness that the LORD had shown to his servant David and to his people Israel.

Analysis

Solomon's prayer of dedication of the temple is characterized in its entirety by Deuteronomistic language and viewpoint and was probably composed by the Deuteronomistic Historian as the conclusion of his report on the building of the temple. He obviously regarded the erection of the temple as a decisive point in the history of Israel, for only at such turning points does the Deuteronomistic Historian introduce extensive speeches that serve the sole purpose of expressing his theological view of history and pointing out the standpoint reached in regard to the future (cf. the speech of Joshua with the loyalty oath of the tribes to Yahweh in Joshua 24 and the farewell speech of Samuel in 1 Samuel 12).[1] The prayer of dedication is not a unified whole; despite several later additions, it can be structured into four large parts:

vv. 14-21	speech of Solomon
vv. 22-29	prayer for the preservation of the dynasty
vv. 30-53	grand intercession
vv. 54-61	blessing and exhortation

Within the grand intercession the two last paragraphs, vv. 44-53, are most likely an addition. The speech concludes in vv. 62-66 with a report of sacrifice and a feast for the dedication of the temple.

Commentary

[8:14-16] Verse 14 connects the speech of Solomon with the report of the transfer of the ark in vv. 1-11 and the consecration proverb for the temple in vv. 12-13. The following actions of Solomon are understood as a blessing through which the people present participate in the given salvation. The speech commences in vv. 15-16 with

---

[1] See also Hans Walter Wolff, "The Kerygma of the Deuteronomic Historical Work," in Walter Brueggemann and H. W. Wolff, *The Vitality of Old Testament Traditions*, 2d ed. (Atlanta: John Knox, 1982), 83–100.

the praise of Yahweh that aims to thank God in view of the completion of the temple. Here the building of temple is connected with two fundamental salvific events: the exodus from Egypt and the election of David. Thus the temple itself is elevated to a salvation event. Just as the exodus from Egypt triggered the constitution of Israel as a free people and just as David had created the kingship as a governmental form for this people, so does the temple create for the people the necessary place for the worship of Yahweh.

[8:17-20] For the Deuteronomistic Historian these three salvation events belong together. According to the Deuteronomistic worldview, the reality of the salvation provided by Yahweh is reached only with the temple as the cultic center.[2] Just like 1 Kgs 5:17, vv. 17-20 pick out the delay of the building of the temple as their central theme. The reason given here is not the same as in chap. 5; rather, Solomon presents himself as the executor of the will of David. Behind such reasoning stands the view that the building of the temple normally belongs at the beginning of a dynasty. All promises were made with regard to the founder—Solomon just executes the paternal will. The impression is carefully avoided that Solomon is elevated above his father due to the building of the temple—that is one of the central points of the Deuteronomistic History, and it is already prepared for by Deuteronomy 12. In accordance with 2 Sam 7:13 it is stressed again that the delay in the building of the temple was not a result of David's indecisiveness or incapability, but rather happened due to an order of Yahweh.

The statement about the dwelling of the name corresponds with Deuteronomistic theology (see Deut 12:5, 11, 21; 14:23-24; 16:2, 6, 11; 26:2). This name theology marks a spiritualization of the concept of the presence of Yahweh. Yahweh himself is not present in the cultic place, but only his name as a guarantee for his promise of salvation; Israel has to cling to it alone as the sufficient form of revelation.[3] The meaning of such name theology is therefore to keep the significance of the temple as the place of the effective presence of God in the light of natural transcendence.[4]

[8:21] Following Deuteronomistic theology, v. 21 connects the ark with the temple. Since according to Deut 10:1-5 the ark contained the two tablets of the Decalogue, the ark was in the Deuteronomistic view the guarantor of the covenant between God and his people on Mount Horeb, after the Decalogue had been repeated in Deuteronomy 5. The Deuteronomistic Historian as the author of the prayer has given a new significance to the temple: the temple is not only the place of the dwelling of the

---

[2] See F. Dumermuth, "Zur Deuteronomistischen Kulttheologie und ihren Voraussetzungwn," *ZAW* 70 (1958) 59–98.

[3] Gerhard von Rad, *Studies in Deuteronomy*, trans. David Stalker, SBT 1/9 (Chicago: Regnery, 1953), 38–39.

[4] Würthwein, *Könige*, 1:103.

divine name and thus the place of the presence of God, but also because of the ark the guarantor of the covenant that Yahweh made with his people.[5]

[8:22-29] Solomon speaks the prayer as such by spreading out his hands to heaven. The raising of the hands was a common gesture of prayer that is now also attested by the depictions on a pithos from Kuntillet 'Ajrūd.[6] The act of kneeling is only added later in the addition of v. 54. The praise in the opening of the prayer stresses the incomparability of Yahweh in comparison with other gods. The praise is concerned with the continued existence of the dynasty that has already been promised by the oracle of Nathan in 2 Sam 7:16. The firm establishment of the dynastic principle in the will of God results in the eternally unassailable and indissoluble character of Davidic kingship. On the other hand the preservation of kingship is linked to obeying God. This demand of obedience is the reason for the future development of the history. The end of the monarchy as a result of the Babylonian conquest in 587 is explained in view of this demand, namely the disobedience of the king and the people toward the will of God embodied in the Deuteronomistic law. With its reflection on the incomprehensibility of God, v. 27 is a later addition that interrupts the current context. Here the image of God's dwelling expressed in the consecration proverb is confronted with the notion of Yahweh's incomprehensible greatness.

[8:30] This verse leads up to the prayer in which God is beseeched for support during time of need. Each of the seven plights is introduced by a conditional "if." In the grand intercession the king ceased to play an active role; the plea to hear concerns only the prayers of the individual or the people. The seven plights refer to a situation that assumes the further spiritualization of the temple. True, the temple occupies a special place, but the dwelling of Yahweh in it is not mentioned; rather his presence in heaven is assumed. All requests are shaped by postexilic Deuteronomic-Deuteronomistic theology; most likely they do not belong to the original literary layer of the Deuteronomistic History but are additions of a later redactor, just as vv. 44-53 represent further additions.

[8:31-32] The first case deals with unjust curses. The cursed person can subject himself to a trial by ordeal that will either acquit or convict him. This procedure takes place at the altar in the temple, but further details are not mentioned. The curse is understood as a powerful word that hits the cursed person without human interference. A removal of the curse is thus absolutely necessary if it was unlawfully uttered.

[8:33-34] The second case concerns military defeat, which—according to the Deuteronomistic view—is always because of a turning away from Yahweh. The

---

[5] See Lothar Perlitt, *Bundestheologie im Alten Testament,* WMANT 36 (Neukirchen-Vluyn: Neukirchener, 1969).

[6] See Pirhiya Beck, "The Drawings from Ḥorvat Teiman (Kuntillet ʿAjrud)," *TA* 9 (1982) 6, pl. 3 [3–68].

phrase "to bring again to the land" already presupposes the Babylonian exile; thus the plea refers to the return of the exiles to the land that Yahweh promised to the fathers (see Gen 12:7; Exod 32:13; Ps 105:8, 11; Ezek 47:14; 1 Chronicles 15–18).

[8:35-36] The third case concerns drought caused by lack of rainfall. Being the lord of nature, Yahweh rules over all natural phenomena; here rain is the necessary prerequisite for growth. If the people transgress, Yahweh can keep away the rain as a form of punishment and thus endanger the basis of life. Along with prayer, the return to Yahweh is expected and with it to give up the worship of all other gods. To emphasize this a special penitential rite including fasting and self-humiliation develops during postexilic times (see Neh 9:1).

[8:37-40] The fourth case concerns general afflictions that affect the people as a whole as well as the individual person. The following collective afflictions are mentioned: famine, plague, mildew, locusts, and vermin. Famine is caused by crop failure, which is the result of lack of rain. The plague is an uncontrollable disease that from time to time endangers the existence of the people (see Exod 9:3, 15; Num 14:12; Pss 78:50; 91:3, 6; Ezek 14:19; Hab 3:5). Mildew can be caused by fungi or the hot east wind that causes crops to ripen prematurely, resulting in the death of the ears of grain. Since barley and wheat were the basic foodstuffs of Israel, crop failure inevitably led to famine. Locusts are feared since they completely destroy the entire vegetation of the land.[7] "Vermin" is a collective term for all other pests that endanger the harvest. From among the individual afflictions, the illness (plague) mentioned is especially dangerous since there was no cure for it. All afflictions are considered as caused by the humans themselves, because they are understood as having transgressed God's commandment. Absolution as the conclusion to a rite is limited, since it is connected to behavior. This reflects the ethics developed by the Deuteronomistic theology: not the cultural act as such but the conduct of life is reason for forgiveness.

[8:41-43] The plea to hear is expanded to the foreigner. The foreigner has to be distinguished from the resident alien; his place of origin is therefore specified as "from a distant land." It is presupposed that this foreigner recognizes Yahweh as God and is thus able to worship him in the Jerusalem temple. Here we have the beginning of the view that Yahweh will be worshiped by all people, a view already present in Deut 4:35 and then especially prevalent in Deutero-Isaiah.[8]

---

[7] See Gustaf Dalman, *Arbeit und Sitte in Palästina* (Gütersloh: Bertelsmann, 1932), 2:346–48.

[8] See Isa 44:6 and Hans Wildberger, "Der Monotheismus Deuterojesajas," in *Beiträge zur alttestamentlichen Theologie: Festschrift für Walther Zimmerli zum 70. Geburtstag*, ed. Herbert Donner, Robert Hanhart, and Rudolf Smend (Göttingen: Vandenhoeck & Ruprecht, 1977), 506–30.

[8:44-45] The two additions deal with matters of warfare. Here it is presupposed that the way leading into battle has been determined by an oracle and thus by Yahweh. The plea to hear does not refer to Yahweh's participation in battle, as it does in the case of holy war, where God fights on the side of his people. Rather, Yahweh is called upon for support, which is prerequisite for any success in battle. The general formulation does not suggest any closer link to a special form of war. The conflicts with the great powers Assyria and Babylon, which reached their climax during the end of the seventh and the beginning of the sixth century, could be after the battles with other surrounding neighbors the background for the plea.

[8:46-53] The last case presupposes the exile. The plea is not concerned with the liberation and return of the exiles, but asks for well-being in foreign lands. The direction of the prayer is determined by mentioning the land, city (Jerusalem), and temple three times. The plea is underlined by the remembrance of the exodus from Egypt. The drastic description of Egypt as an iron-smelter occurs elsewhere only in Deut 4:20 and Jer 11:4 and is thus a late metaphor. That the late author of the paragraph asks only for merciful treatment and not for the return points to a time in which the exiles accepted their fate and started to settle in foreign lands.[9] This all indicates postexilic times. Living in the land is not important; only clinging to election matters. The term "heritage" or "inheritance," normally used for the land (see Deut 1:38; 3:28; 31:7; Isa 1:6; 11:23; 13:6-7), is used here for the people in order to stress the special relationship between the people and God, who grants its possession. The integration into the divine promise allows Israel to live under the protection of God, even in the exile.

[8:54-61] The paragraph vv. 54-61 follows the prayer in vv. 22-30; within the blessing, vv. 59-60 are a later addition. During the blessing, Solomon acts as priest just as he did at the dedication of the temple. The blessing shall ensure the presence of Yahweh for the people. Verse 56 is not exactly a blessing but a praise that is not specifically composed for the building of the temple; rather it is stressed that all salvific actions of Yahweh toward Israel have come to an end.[10] The promise made to Moses has now been fulfilled. In the building of the temple the order of life communicated by the Torah in the speech of Deuteronomy 12–26 is made manifest. Further acts of salvation are not to be expected; the temple cannot be superseded and remains, in contrast to the monarchy, eternally. With the reference back to Moses the temple is linked with the eternal validity of the Torah.

In a similar way the pleas of vv. 57-58 do not contain a blessing, but display a desire that reflects the situation of the author in exilic or postexilic times. The image of a God who walks with someone becomes the example for the closeness of God in the present time. Keeping the situation of the fathers in view, the people are ensured of the presence of God. The commandments, stipulations, and ordinances mediated

---

[9] Würthwein, *Könige,* 1:100.
[10] Ibid., 101.

by Moses provide the path to salvation; as long as Israel keeps the Torah of Moses everything will turn out well. Obedience to the law is the path to salvation.[11]

[8:62-66] The note on the sacrifices concludes the dedication of the temple. The short paragraph can be understood as an explanation of v. 5 and has probably been written by the Deuteronomistic Historian, the author of the report of the building of the temple as a whole. According to his view, the temple was foremost a place for sacrifice, that is, a place where the reconciliation between Yahweh and his people is carried out.[12] The figure given for the sacrificial animals is grossly exaggerated, stretching beyond human imagination, but stressing once more the uniqueness of the temple. At the same time it is made clear that the altar made from bronze does not suffice for such extensive offerings so that sacrifices had to be made in the middle of the court. We can assume then that the Solomonic temple did not possess an altar for burnt offerings; only Ahaz erects such an altar in the temple, for which he needed to move the bronze altar and the molten sea (2 Kgs 16:10-17).[13]

The main types of sacrifice are summarized: burnt offerings, grain offerings, and sacrifices of well-being, although the sacrifical praxis was even more extensive.[14] Despite the sparse remarks and the obvious postexilic character of the procedure for different sacrifices described in Leviticus 1–7, which reflects the practice of the Second Temple, different forms of sacrifice have existed since the time of the monarchy. During the normal sacrifice, the animal is eaten by the participants in a communal meal and only the fat is burned on the altar. For the communal sacrifice one can assume a similar ritual during which the blood of the animal is sprinkled on the altar as an act of expiation. The communal sacrifice was originally linked with the burnt offering but was later separated from it to merge with the common sacrifice.[15] In any case, common sacrifice and communal sacrifice are already used synonymously in our passage.

At the burnt offering the animal as a whole is consumed by fire on the altar. The origin of this form of sacrifice is not clear; it was possibly taken over from the neighboring cultures since Canaan, Phoenicia, and Greece knew the burnt offering as the most distinguished form of sacrifice. As the most important form of sacrifice it is used on public occasions, shown by the fact that the building of an altar is always

[11] Ibid.

[12] See Bernd Janowski, *Sühne als Heilsgeschehen: Studien zur Sühnetheologie der Priesterschrift und zur Wurzel KPR im Alten Orient und im Alten Testaments,* WMANT 55 (Neukirchen-Vluyn: Neukirchener, 1982).

[13] See Volkmar Fritz, "Bis an die Hörner des Altars," in *Gottes Recht als Lebensraum: Festschrift für Hans Jochen Boecker,* ed. Peter Mommer, Werner, H. Schmidt, and Hans Strauss (Neukirchen-Vluyn: Neukirchener, 1993), 61–70.

[14] See Rolf Rendtorff, *Studien zur Geschichte des Opfers im alten Israel,* WMANT 24 (Neukirchen-Vluyn: Neukirchener, 1967).

[15] See Bernd Janowski, "Erwägungen zur Vorgeschichte des israelitischen šelāmîm-Opfer," *UF* 12 (1980) 231–59.

connected with a burnt offering (see Gen 8:20; Num 23:1-2, 14, 29-30; Judg 6:26; 2 Sam 24:25). The burnt offering is a sacral act of killing livestock during which the whole animal is offered to God without giving part of it to anyone else. The expiatory character of the sacrifice is therefore stressed. In contrast to this, the common sacrifice is characterized by the aspect of feeding the deity; here vegetarian offerings were placed in bowls on special benches. Such benches can be found in several temples in Israel's environment as well as in the Israelite temple at Arad.[16] The dedication of the temple concludes on the eighth day with the dismissal of the people from the sacred sphere of the sanctuary.

[8:65] The later addition of v. 65 connects the dedication with the Feast of Tabernacles/Sukkoth. This pilgrimage feast to celebrate the successful harvest (Deut 16:13) was held at the temple only after the centralization of the cult in the later period of the monarchy. Moreover, the addition stresses the participation of all Israel.

The geographical view of the national territory places the verse in close proximity to 1 Kgs 5:4. The border of the Solomonic empire to the south is the Wadi of Egypt (Wadi el Gazze; see 5:1), while its northernmost point is said to be Lebo-hamath; this corresponds to the Priestly view (see Num 43:8), and the place is also mentioned elsewhere as a border (see Num 13:21; Josh 13:5; Judg 3:3; 2 Kgs 14:25; Amos 6:14). Lebo-hamath can be located on the northern end of Lebanon and be identified with el-Lebwe on route from the Biqaᶜ to the bay of Ribla.[17] The size of the territory again stresses the greatness of Solomon.

The feast is dated in an addition: in the MT the duration is "seven days and seven days, fourteen days," which can only be understood in the sense that the dedication of the temple was celebrated after the Feast of Tabernacles, making it a period of fourteen days. The dedication of the temple is thus placed in the context of the ancient Israelite festival calendar, without losing its special status. The return home is described using traditional language, where "tent" designates the dwelling place as such (see Deut 16:7; Josh 22:4, 6-8).

---

[16] See Volkmar Fritz, *Tempel und Zelt: Studien zum Tempelbau in Israel und zu dem Zeltheiligtum der Priesterschrift,* WMANT 47 (Neukirchen-Vluyn: Neukirchener, 1977).

[17] See Benjamin Mazar, "Lebo-hammath and the Northern Border of Canaan," in idem, *The Early Biblical Period: Historical Studies,* ed. Shmuel Ahituv and Baruch A. Levine, trans. Ruth Rigbi and Elisheva Rigbi (Jerusalem: Israel Exploration Society, 1986), 189–202.

The Second Theophany

Text

9:1 When Solomon had finished building the house of the LORD and the king's house and all that Solomon desired to build, 2 the LORD appeared to Solomon a second time, as he had appeared to him at Gibeon. 3 The LORD said to him, "I have heard your prayer and your plea, which you made before me; I have consecrated this house that you have built, and put my name there forever; my eyes and my heart will be there for all time. 4 As for you, if you will walk before me, as David your father walked, with integrity of heart and uprightness, doing according to all that I have commanded you, and keeping my statutes and my ordinances, 5 then I will establish your royal throne over Israel forever, as I promised your father David, saying, 'There shall not fail you a successor on the throne of Israel.'

6 "If you turn aside from following me, you or your children, and do not keep my commandments and my statutes that I have set before you, but go and serve other gods and worship them, 7 then I will cut Israel off from the land that I have given them; and the house that I have consecrated for my name I will cast out of my sight; and Israel will become a proverb and a taunt among all peoples. 8 This house will become a heap of ruins; everyone passing by it will be astonished, and will hiss; and they will say, 'Why has the LORD done such a thing to this land and to this house?' 9 Then they will say, 'Because they have forsaken the LORD their God, who brought their ancestors out of the land of Egypt, and embraced other gods, worshiping them and serving them; therefore the LORD has brought this disaster upon them.'"

Analysis

The second theophany immediately follows the report on the building of the temple and refers back to 1 Kgs 3:3-15. Its scene is the royal sanctuary. Judging by its language and style, one would have to conclude that the Deuteronomistic Historian wrote the report.

Two statements follow each other: vv. 3-5 promise once again the continued existence of the dynasty, followed by the threat of punishment in the case of disobedience in vv. 6-9. This discrepancy shows that vv. 6-9 are a later addition that already knows of the fate of the people after the destruction of the Solomonic temple at the hand of the Babylonians in 587. The first part can be understood as God's answer to Solomon's prayer in 8:22-29. The promise is given to Solomon immediately in a theophany without any cultic personnel acting as mediator. In the long history of Yahweh's revelations since the time of the fathers, Solomon is the last person who receives such a direct announcement of the divine will. The event is thus of special importance.[1]

Commentary

[9:1-5] The introduction, v. 1, does not report any further details because the Deuteronomistic Historian is generally not a very good narrator. The theophany as such consists of a speech of Yahweh, vv. 3-5, without describing the reaction of Solomon. Since the piece responds to the prayer of 8:22-29, there is nevertheless an element of dialogue. The promise of Yahweh means that he has heard the prayer; the temple is the place where God placed his name forever, to let it dwell there. The presence of eyes and heart refers to the permanent solidarity and attention of Yahweh with regard to his place. At the same time, the notion of habitation is spiritually superseded because Yahweh participates in the temple in a special form. The prominence of the temple depends on God—this unusual quality cannot be reversed.[2] The promise of the continuation of the dynasty in vv. 4-5 corresponds to the plea in 8:25, but is closely linked with the observance of Deuteronomic law (see the explanation of 8:25). The Deuteronomistic Historian stresses the responsibility of the king for the promise to be fulfilled.

[9:6-9] The addition in vv. 6-9 extends this requirement of correct and lawful behavior to the people as a whole, and stresses that the worship of other gods, as the abomination per se, will necessarily lead to the destruction of the temple. Behind such a viewpoint is the Deuteronomistic demand to worship Yahweh alone, a demand that is mentioned time and again in programmatic speeches (see Joshua 24; 1 Samuel 12). The demand of the Deuteronomistic school to worship Yahweh alone is connected to a theological view of history. Since Yahweh is the only God of his people, every worship of other gods is a break of this unique relationship with all its consequences. If the exclusive recognition of Yahweh is not obeyed, the people have to suffer the results of his turning away.

Given the inevitability of the historical fate, the demand of the exclusive worship of Yahweh receives a last tightening: the temple will become a "heap of ruins,"

---

[1] Würthwein, *Könige,* 1:105.
[2] Ibid.

signifying that Yahweh has forsaken his chosen dwelling place. Foreign gods mean the loss of Yahweh's care and at the same time bring inevitable disaster. The later redactor therefore envisages the course of Israel's history with its fatal end as an end that was unavoidable, since Yahweh had to answer to the violation of the divine sphere with the withdrawal of the divine promise of salvation. When other gods are worshiped, God can break the promise manifested in the exodus and the building of the temple.

The vision of the destruction of the temple and its ruins is answered with hissing by the people, a measure to cast away the demons. The antagonism between the salvation embodied by the temple and the punishment announced could hardly be expressed in more graphic terms: the worship of other gods leads to the downfall and destruction of the only legitimate place for the worship of Yahweh.

The Loss of the Land of Cabul

Text

9:10 At the end of twenty years, in which Solomon had built the two houses, the house of the LORD and the king's house, 11 King Hiram of Tyre having supplied Solomon with cedar and cypress timber and gold, as much as he desired, King Solomon gave to Hiram twenty cities in the land of Galilee. 12 But when Hiram came from Tyre to see the cities that Solomon had given him, they did not please him. 13 Therefore he said, "What kind of cities are these that you have given me, my brother?" So they are called the land of Cabul to this day. 14 But Hiram had sent to the king one hundred twenty talents of gold.

Analysis

This section is not a literary unity. The quantity of gold in v. 14 seems to be a later addition, specifying the amount of gold as 120 talents, either 4,112 or 4,935 kg. Verses 10-11 are a simple statement, while vv. 12-13 seem to be a narrative comment of anecdotal character. It looks as if the statement of vv. 10-11 has been expanded by Hiram's remark at a later stage. The statement of vv. 10-11b is interrupted by the parenthesis in v. 11a, which repeats the delivery of wood for the buildings, already known from 5:15-26, adding to it Hiram's financial support. The piece is therefore not a narrative, but rather belongs to the short notes attached to the report of the building of the temple dealing with the Solomonic construction works.

Commentary

[9:10-11] These verses are apparently older than 5:25, since there the deliveries made by Hiram are paid for in kind. The building of the temple and palace results in the transfer of twenty cities in Galilee to Hiram. On the one hand, the costly imports for wood and precious metals had to be settled in appropriate form. On the other hand, the report shows the desire of the Phoenician city-state to expand its territory through an adequate hinterland. Unfortunately we know next to nothing about the territorial relations between Israel and Tyre at the time of Solomon. From ceramic evidence found at Achzib (ez-Zīb) and the graves surrounding the settlement, Achzib appears to have been a Phoenician settlement during the tenth century. We do not know whether the coastal strip next to Achzib belonged to the territory of influence of the Phoenicians. Generally speaking, each Phoenician port required a certain hinterland to supply its inhabitants with food. The transfer of twenty cities in Galilee to Hiram has to be seen in the context of the expansion of the hinterland of Tyre. The exact location of these places is not mentioned; they were probably a kind of enclave excluded from the territory and placed under the jurisdiction of Tyre.

[9:12-14] This transfer of territory to Hiram must have caused some offense not long after, because the consequences of the transfer described in vv. 12-13 provide an indirect excuse for Solomon's actions. This anecdotal narrative places the twenty towns in the region of Cabul and qualifies them as inferior. The name Cabul continued to exist in the Arabic village of Kabūl situated on the northern fringe of the plain of Acre; the Israelite settlement was probably located close to the village but has not yet been identified. A place called Cabul is also attested among the towns of Asher in Josh 19:27. In any case, Kabūl provides a clue for the situation of the twenty places that Solomon transferred; they were probably located on the western fringe of the Galilean hill country. In contrast to the cities of the fertile plain, they were small places or villages in the hills, whose economic value did not satisfy Hiram. The note about Hiram's disapproval serves as an excuse for Solomon. He may have transferred Israelite settlements to a foreign ruler, yet they were just inferior places Israel could afford to give up. The popular etymology hinted at in the text cannot be deciphered, but it seems to be a derogatory comment on the land encapsulated in the name Cabul.

The historical events behind this section are difficult to grasp, since we lack geographical details. The transfer stands in contrast to the statement mentioning the trade in 1 Kgs 5:15-26. The present passage assumes that the expenses were paid by a transfer of territory. The background could be the loss of certain Galilean towns to the Phoenicians, and an eastward Phoenician expansion along the coastal strip did certainly happen during the tenth century. Excavations on Khirbet Rās ez-Zētūn 2 km. northeast of Kabūl have shown that the excavated fortress was a Phoenician military post during the tenth and ninth centuries; it was only during the eighth century that an Israelite settlement emerged next to the deserted fortress.[1] The border between the Solomonic empire and Phoenicia on the western fringe of Galilee cannot be determined; but it is entirely possible that the boundary line changed, that the conflict with Phoenicia over its claim to the hinterland of the coastal plain resulted in a change of affiliation for certain areas. The section does not prove the practice of exchange of land for building materials; rather, it is a later explanation for a change of the borderline during the early period of the monarchy.

---

[1] See Zvi Gal, *Excavations and Surveys* 9 (1990) 195–96; and 10 (1991) 84.

Conscripted Labor and
Further Building Projects

Text

9:15 This is the account of the forced labor that King Solomon conscripted to build the house of the LORD and his own house, the Millo, and the wall of Jerusalem, Hazor, Megiddo, Gezer 16 (Pharaoh king of Egypt had gone up and captured Gezer and burned it down, had killed the Canaanites who lived in the city, and had given it as dowry to his daughter, Solomon's wife; 17 so Solomon rebuilt Gezer), Lower Beth-horon, 18 Baalath, Tamar in the wilderness, within the land, 19 as well as all of Solomon's storage cities, the cities for his chariots, the cities for his cavalry, and whatever Solomon desired to build, in Jerusalem, in Lebanon, and in all the land of his dominion. 20 All the people who were left of the Amorites, the Hittites, the Perizzites, the Hivites, and the Jebusites, who were not of the people of Israel— 21 their descendants who were still left in the land, whom the Israelites were unable to destroy completely—these Solomon conscripted for slave labor, and so they are to this day. 22 But of the Israelites Solomon made no slaves; they were the soldiers, they were his officials, his commanders, his captains, and the commanders of his chariotry and cavalry.

23 These were the chief officers who were over Solomon's work: five hundred fifty, who had charge of the people who carried on the work.

[24 But Pharaoh's daughter went up from the city of David to her own house that Solomon had built for her; then he built the Millo.

25 Three times a year Solomon used to offer up burnt offerings and sacrifices of well-being on the altar that he built for the LORD, offering incense before the LORD. So he completed the house.]

Analysis

This section contains a summary in the form of several individual notices of Solomon's building projects. The concise character of the statements does not necessarily vouch for their historicity. They are more likely traditions that have not been transformed into narratives; they can certainly not be regarded as excerpts from the royal annals. Instead, statements of a diverse kind were put together that demonstrate a vague knowledge of the royal activities. It is only in those cases where critical analysis cannot discount their credibility that we can assume historical facts. The section is structured as follows:

vv. 15, 17-19	Solomon's building projects outside Jerusalem
vv. 20-23	the organization of conscripted labor
vv. 16, 24	postscript concerning the daughter of Pharaoh
v. 25	postscript to the sacrifices of Solomon

Just as in 5:27-32, all of Solomon's building projects are put down to conscripted labor in vv. 15, 17-19, but this time no figures are mentioned (see 5:27-28). The explanation of vv. 20-23, that only the descendants of foreign nations were conscripted for labor, looks like an addition. The statements about the daughter of Pharaoh in vv. 16 and 24 are also additions. The postscript concerning the sacrifices takes up 8:62-66 and is probably a later redactional addition that refers to the repetition of the sacrifices during each of the three pilgrim festivals.

Commentary

[9:15] Apart from the temple and palace the building projects of Solomon include the Millo and the city wall in Jerusalem. Millo is a name for a certain area in Jerusalem that remained undeveloped until the time of Solomon. The area is already called by this name in the report of David's conquest of the city (2 Sam 5:9), and it is again mentioned here in 9:24, in 11:28, and in 2 Kgs 12:21. The geographical location is not given; it was most likely an artificially filled-in plateau in the north of the city, where Solomon started to build private houses.[1] Additional building of undeveloped areas became necessary due probably to a rise in population. The need for space led probably also to the abandonment of the Davidic palace within the city precinct and the building of a new palace and temple north of the city. The exact location of the temple and palace cannot be determined, since at the later stage of building all previous traces were removed. In any case it is certain that the Solomonic temple was situated within the area of the temple court encircled by the Herodian wall. Tenth-century city walls have not yet been found.[2]

---

[1] Only further excavations can verify whether the stepped structure excavated by Y. Shiloh on the eastern fringe of the southeastern hill (which can be dated to the thirteenth/twelfth century) was a terraced wall for the plateau; see Jane M. Cahill and David Tarler, "Excavations Directed by Yigal Shiloh at the City of David 1978-1985," in *Ancient Jerusalem Revealed*, ed. Hillel Geva (Jerusalem: Israel Exploration Society, 1994), 34–35 [31–45].

[2] For a possible reconstruction see Dan Bahat, *The Illustrated Atlas of Jerusalem,* trans. Shelomo Ketko (New York : Simon & Schuster, 1990), 24–33.

Of the building projects outside Jerusalem, the rebuilding of Hazor, Megiddo, and Gezer are specifically mentioned. The reference to these cities is probably not taken from any official documents; rather, the author has grouped together three important cities as well as composing an addition in vv. 17-18. The form that the rebuilding took is not mentioned, but the statement has correctly been linked to the construction of fortifications. The refoundation of Hazor and its fortification by a six-chambered gate and a freestanding casemate wall (stratum X) has been proven by archaeological evidence.[3] For Megiddo the dating of the six-chambered gate is disputed.[4] The Solomonic city lies at stratum VA.[5] At Gezer also the dating of the six-chambered gate to Solomonic times is not entirely certain, even though we can prove a certain density of population in the tenth century.[6] Even though not all six-chambered gates of Hazor, Megiddo, and Gezer can be attributed to Solomon,[7] it is nevertheless possible to verify the statement from the point of settlement history.

[9:16] Verse 16 is an additional interjection, stimulated by the mention of Gezer in v. 15. The destruction of Gezer is attributed to an anonymous pharaoh; it cannot be verified from Egyptian sources. Prerequisite for the statement is the archaeological fact that Gezer continued to exist as a Canaanite town during the twelfth and eleventh centuries (it is disputed if the city was walled). Since a repopulation by Israelites is not mentioned, one can assume that Gezer and its population were integrated into the Solomonic empire; the takeover of the city is justified by saying that the city was the dowry of the daughter of Pharaoh. Despite the fact that a conquest of Gezer in the mid-tenth century by a pharaoh cannot be proven, it becomes clear that Gezer and its non-Israelite inhabitants have belonged to Israel only since Solomonic times. In the tradition the annexation of Gezer is made to look like a present of Pharaoh to Solomon. The note is of no historical value, because a military expedition of a pharaoh during the time of the reign of Solomon cannot be verified. Even the identification of the anonymous pharaoh is disputed, but he is generally equated with Siamun, the penultimate ruler of the Twenty-first Dynasty.[8] The note is not historical.

[9:17-18] The name Gezer is repeated in vv. 17-18, where the three places Bethhoron, Baalath, and Tamar are added. A plausible order of the names cannot be deter-

---

[3] See Yigael Yadin, *Hazor: The Rediscovery of a Great Citadel of the Bible* (London: Weidenfeld and Nicolson, 1975), 187–99.

[4] See David Usshishkin, "Was the 'Solomonic' City Gate at Megiddo Built by Solomon?" *BASOR* 239 (1980) 1–18.

[5] See Aharon Kempinski, *Megiddo: A City-State and Royal Centre in North Israel*, Materialien zur allgemeinen und vergleichenden Archäologie 40 (Munich: Beck, 1989), 90–98, and plan 11.

[6] See William G. Dever, "Late Bronze Age and Solomonic Defenses at Gezer: New Evidence," *BASOR* 262 (1986) 9–34; David Ussishkin, "Notes on Megiddo, Gezer, Ashdod and Tel Batash in the Tenth to Ninth Centuries B.C.," *BASOR* 277/278 (1990) 72–91.

[7] As assumed by Yigael Yadin, "Solomon's City Wall and Gate at Gezer," *IEJ* 8 (1958) 80–86.

[8] See the considerations of A. R. Green, "Solomon and Siamun: A Synchronism Between Dynastic Israel and the Twenty-First Dynasty of Egypt," *JBL* 97 (1978) 353–67.

mined. Beth-horon (Bēt ʿŪr) is situated along the old ascent to Jerusalem and is thus an important post to secure the road leading from the plain to the hills. Baalath is identical with the place of the same name in the middle part of the coastal plain that is mentioned in Isa 19:44. The exact geographical location cannot be determined, but one can assume it is either Qatre or el-Muǧar;[9] the place was probably a fortified outpost against the Philistine cities of the southern coastal plain. Tamar is probably ʿĒn Ḥusb, about 32 km. southwest of the Dead Sea.[10]

The purpose of erecting a fortress in this place was to secure the road leading through the Arabah to Ezion-geber on the Gulf of Aqabah, and hence being part of the grid of outposts in the steppe and desert south of the Solomonic territory.[11] Excavations have uncovered two fortresses, which can be dated to the tenth and ninth/eighth centuries. The three names are to verify Solomon's attempt to secure his territory and its entries by building cities and erecting fortresses. In contrast to the lists of the book of Joshua, the enumeration looks purely accidental, and one cannot assume that the list was taken over from official documents; its composition was more likely modeled on a general view of events. Since the statement cannot be dated it does not necessarily reflect the period of Solomon; rather, we have to allow for the fact that the author reported the circumstances of his own time.

[9:19] Verse 19 reports in summary form the building of further cities. The terms "storage cities," "cities for his chariots," and "cities for his cavalry" do not denote a certain type of city but rather describe the functions connected with some of them. Archaeology has shown that following the collapse of the Canaanite city-states, urbanization started anew only after the origin of a state under David and Solomon. The tenth-century cities were usually encircled by a wall and accessible only through a single gate; their buildings consisted mainly of private houses. Public buildings were rather exceptional, but their number increased during the period of the monarchy. Next to the palaces at Megiddo, Samaria, and Lachish and the sanctuary at Arad, we find the so-called houses of poles, whose use is disputed.[12]

The term "storage cities" is also mentioned in connection with the narrative of Israel's time in Egypt (Exod 1:11). A storage economy for ancient Israel during the period of the monarchy has yet to be verified. The label refers to general provisions more than to concrete building projects by the king.

The "cities of his chariots" cannot be verified either. The term is probably created by analogy to the notes on the chariots that presuppose the formation of an army

---

[9] Y. Aharoni, "The Northern Boundary of Judah" *PEQ* 90 (1958) 30 [27–31].

[10] See Y. Aharoni, "Tamar and the Roads to Elath," *IEJ* 13 (1963) 30–42.

[11] See Y. Aharoni, "Forerunners of the Limes: Iron Age Fortresses in the Negev," *IEJ* 17 (1967) 1–17; R. Cohen, "The Iron Age Fortresses in the Central Negev," *BASOR* 236 (1979) 61–79.

[12] See Volkmar Fritz, *The City in Ancient Israel,* BibSem 29 (Sheffield: Sheffield Academic, 1995).

of chariots (see 1 Kgs 10:26). The term "cities of his chariots" links the building projects with the formation of an army. We do not have any knowledge about the storage of the chariots and the stables for the horses. Since this part of the army operated only on the open battlefield, it is highly unlikely that it was housed within city walls. Also there are no notices to verify the development of a cavalry; it is only since the time of Ashurbanipal (668–631 BCE) that we know of the existence of a cavalry as a special part of the army.[13] In connection with the Solomonic building projects, the term "cities of his chariots" sounds like an anachronism since the conditions of the later monarchy are projected back onto the time of Solomon (the notice about the horses in 10:28-29 definitely refers to chariots). Since it is not possible to argue for the existence of a cavalry in the tenth century, the statement must be written by a later redactor. The different kinds of cities do not correspond to any verifiable reality; thus the notice simply aims at stressing the glory of Solomon as builder.

[9:20-23] This insertion stresses that only non-Israelites were forced to do conscripted labor. This idea does not reflect historical reality so much as the views of the Deuteronomistic Historian. According to the Deuteronomic law of warfare, Deut 20:16-18, all previous inhabitants of the land shall be extinguished by waging a war of extermination against them. The ban consisted of the transference of the spoil to God; this transfer is done by killing humans and animals with the sword and by burning their possessions with fire or by bringing them into a sanctuary. Following this pattern, the book of Joshua describes the conquest of the land as a war of extermination against its inhabitants (see Deut 2:34-35; 3:6-7; 7:2, 26). We have already realized that several Canaanite cities continued to exist during the period of the monarchy, which makes a program of total extermination seem unlikely. Judges 1 adds a negative list of Israel's possessions, mentioning those cities that remained in the hands of Canaanites after the conquest of the land.[14]

In a similar way, the insertion of vv. 20-23 presumes that a remnant of the previous population survived the conquest of the land by the Israelites; according to the usual terminology these people are called Amorites, Hittites, Perizzites, Hivites, and Jebusites. The names have no connection with foreign peoples mentioned elsewhere, but are part of a stereotypical enumeration found elsewhere in the Bible (see Exod 3:8, 17; 13:5; 23:23; 43:11; Deut 7:1; 20:17; Josh 3:10; 9:1; 11:3; 12:8; 24:11; Judg 3:5). The origin of the arrangement is unclear, and it does not reflect any historical accuracy or knowledge of ethnicity.

In the biblical writings "Amorites" is used synonymously with "Canaanites," but the term refers generally to the inhabitants of the land east of the Jordan (see Num 21:13; Josh 2:10; 9:10; 24:8; Judg 10:8; 11:20). The word is of Assyrian and Baby-

---

[13] See Yigael Yadin, *The Art of Warfare in Biblical Lands in the Light of Archaeological Discovery* (New York: McGraw-Hill, 1963), 2:383–89.

[14] See A. Graeme Auld, "Judges I and History: A Reconsideration," *VT* 25 (1975) 261–85.

Ionian origin, with Amurru denoting at first a certain territory and later the whole of the north Syrian realm. In the Bible it is used as a general description for the pre-Israelite population of the land without any ethnic specification.[15]

The Hittites, a people of Indo-Germanic origin, originally migrated into Asia Minor at the beginning of the second millennium BCE; their empire vanished during the invasion of the Sea Peoples around 1200 BCE. 1 Kings 10:29 and 2 Kgs 7:6 claim that Hittite kingdoms existed in Syria, but the texts probably refer to successor states of former vassal states of the Hittite Empire with Luwian population. The Bible in any case distinguishes an ethnic group called Hittites from the Aramean and Phoenician inhabitants of Syria; this group does not necessarily have to be composed of descendants of those inhabiting the Hittite heartland in Anatolia.

The Perizzites cannot be separated from the similar sounding Hebrew word for a certain part of the population. The term for a certain social group was changed into an ethnic designation that has nothing to do with the original meaning of the term.

There are no extrabiblical sources for the Hivites; the term is already used in the non-Priestly patriarchal narrative (Gen 36:2; 43:2) to designate the autochthonous population of the land. They are probably a small local group that—according to Josh 11:3 and Judg 3:3—lived in the northern part of the land. The Hivites are thus a small non-Israelite ethnic minority living in Canaan that is added to the foreign nations.

The name Jebusites derives from the name of the place and the city of Jebus (see Josh 15:8; 18:16). In the equation of Jebus with Jerusalem (Josh 15:63; 18:28; Judg 1:21; 1 Chr 11:4) it becomes the "city of the Jebusites" (Judg 19:11). It is likely that the city of Jebus was situated close to Jerusalem.[16]

The names of the non-Israelite population are taken over from the tradition of Deuteronomistic theology and do not reflect any specific historical circumstances. What is stressed is the general demand to exterminate the nations. The descendants of these nations are now forced to do conscripted labor, introduced under Solomon, while the Israelites will become warriors, officials, charioteers, and officers.

The different responsibilities are directly linked to the development of the monarchy. The monarchy creates a standing army that replaces the tribal league and introduces the professional soldier paid by the king. The officials are personal employees of the king; the commanders serve within the bureaucracy. The list of the officials is preserved in 1 Kgs 4:2-6, but one can assume that there were more officials on a local level, corresponding to today's civil servants. The charioteers form a special group. A chariot would usually be manned with a driver and an archer whose skill in this special form of combat could be acquired or maintained only by intensive training. Just like the army, the charioteers had their own commander.

---

[15] See John Van Seters, "The Term 'Amorites' and 'Hittite' in the Old Testament," *VT* 22 (1972) 64–81.

[16] See J. Maxwell Miller, "Jebus and Jerusalem: A Case of Mistaken Identity," *ZDPV* 90 (1974) 115–27.

All these details are not copied from an official document but probably deduced from the narrative about Solomon. The author did not possess any official documents. The figure 550 given for the number of officials cannot be verified. The interpolation divides the population into two classes: the Israelites form the class of free men of the state while all the other inhabitants are viewed as second-class citizens with limited rights. The population of the early kingdom consisted of different ethnic groups; among them the descendants of the Canaanite city-states formed the majority. The division into two classes whose social differentiation corresponds to their ethnic one reflects the wishful thinking of a late redactor. The additions aim at the exoneration of Solomon, trying to clear him of the fact that he turned the people into slaves by subjecting them to forced labor. To do so, the mixed population is split into two groups so that only the non-Israelites were subjected to labor while the Israelites were free from it.

[9:24] Verse 24 mentions again the move of Pharaoh's daughter, after the palace for this particular wife had already been described in 1 Kgs 7:8 (see 3:1). The notice forms an addition to v. 16. The building of Millo repeats the information given in v. 15, making the verse a redactional addition.

[9:25] Verse 25 is another addition that ensures the sacrifices of Solomon during each of the pilgrim festivals. The information is taken from the explanations at the end of the report of the building of the temple (see 8:62-64). The formula "So he completed the house" takes up formulations from 6:14, 38, but uses a different verb. The sections in chap. 9 are thereby connected to the report of the building of the temple.

The Journeys to Ophir

Text

9:26 King Solomon built a fleet of ships at Ezion-geber, which is near Eloth on the shore of the Red Sea, in the land of Edom. 27 Hiram sent his servants with the fleet, sailors who were familiar with the sea, together with the servants of Solomon. 28 They went to Ophir, and imported from there four hundred twenty talents of gold, which they delivered to King Solomon.

Commentary

[9:26-28] The journeys to Ophir have a close parallel in the two notices regarding the trading enterprises undertaken with Hiram in 10:11-12 and 10:22. The catchword Ophir is also mentioned in 10:11-12, while 10:22 just mentions ships of Tarshish crossing the Mediterranean Sea. As far as 10:11-12 is concerned, the text here seems to be a secondary addition to the context and has thus to be regarded as a later literary construct. The relationship between 9:26-28 and 10:22 is more difficult to define. The text here is definitely not an excerpt from the royal annals; instead the verses are formulations constructed on the basis of the trade with Hiram of Tyre and created in view of the sheer wealth of Solomon. Despite the use of concrete place names, 9:26-28 is only concerned with the increase of the gold; 10:22 thus seems to be the older notice, since it mentions several different trading goods. The notice about the trading journeys on the Red Sea seems to have been formulated on the basis of 10:22; it therefore does not reflect a historical background.

The mention of Ezion-geber provides us with a geographical point of departure for the journeys to Ophir. The place can in all likelihood be equated with Tell el-Hulēfi on the southern point of the Arabah. The excavations under the direction of Nelson Glueck unearthed two fortresses that—because of their square shape—correspond to similar constructions of the period of the monarchy. To the extent that the data can be verified, the site was founded during the eighth century and then occupied until the fourth century. The building of the fortresses could not have been done under

Solomon.[1] The construction and dispatch of ships from the northern point of the Gulf of Aqabah cannot be verified at Ezion-geber, a place that did not exist during Solomonic times, even though its existence can be presumed for the time in which the author of the text is writing.

The text also transmits only vague ideas. The absence of a harbor in this region is not surprising since it was common practice to pull the ships up on the beach. The question of the origin of the wood needed for the construction of the ships is the more pressing one. The whole area is an arid zone that even in Solomonic times did not have any significant tree growth. The building of ships could only have happened if the timber had been transported overland from far away. This cannot, of course, be ruled out, but it certainly affects the reliability of the remark.

The biggest problem, however, is the mention of Ophir as the land from where the gold was imported. The only extrabiblical occurrence on an ostracon from Tell Qasīle is rather obscure and does not contribute anything to its identification.[2] Genesis 10:29 and 1 Chr 1:23 mention Ophir as lying between Sheba and Hawila, both designations for countries or regions of southern Arabia (see also 1 Kgs 10:1). Even though the author did not seem to have any exact knowledge of the geographical location of Ophir, it seems reasonable to look for this land of gold in the southwest of the Arabian peninsula.[3] The region around Asīr in particular with its rivers carrying gold would be a possible location for Ophir, but without any further evidence it is impossible to equate Ophir with that region. Its mention in Job 22:24 shows that Ophir was understood to be the land of gold as such. Most likely the author used this famous name in connection with Solomon to stress his wealth even further.

The amount of 420 talents equals a weight of either 14,394 or 17,272 kg., depending if one calculates with 50 or 60 shekels per talent. These figures, too, are grossly exaggerated, especially if one takes into account the amount of gold available; the whole report of the journeys to Ophir thus seems pure fantasy. The notice on the trade in the area of the Red Sea undertaken by Solomon and Hiram is revealed to be a fiction based on the idea that Ophir was a land of gold and that this land was located in Arabia. Within the framework of the Solomonic narrative, the journeys to Ophir only covered part of Solomon's demand for gold; thereby his wealth is elevated to fantastic proportions.

---

[1] See Gary D. Pratico, *Nelson Glueck's 1938–1940 Excavations at Tell el-Kheleifeh: A Reappraisal,* ASOR Archaeology Reports 3 (Atlanta: Scholars, 1993).

[2] Benjamin Maisler [Mazar], "Two Hebrew Ostraca from Tell Qasile," *JNES* 10 (1951) 265–67.

[3] See B. Moritz, *Arabien: Studien zur physikalischen und historischen Geographie des Landes* (Hannover: Lafaire, 1923), 84ff.

The Visit of the Queen of Sheba

Text

10:1 When the queen of Sheba heard of the fame of Solomon, (fame due to the name of the LORD), she came to test him with hard questions. 2 She came to Jerusalem with a very great retinue, with camels bearing spices, and very much gold, and precious stones; and when she came to Solomon, she told him all that was on her mind. 3 Solomon answered all her questions; there was nothing hidden from the king that he could not explain to her. 4 When the queen of Sheba had observed all the wisdom of Solomon, the house that he had built, 5 the food of his table, the seating of his officials, and the attendance of his servants, their clothing, his valets, and his burnt offerings that he offered at the house of the LORD, there was no more spirit in her.

6 So she said to the king, "The report was true that I heard in my own land of your accomplishments and of your wisdom, 7 but I did not believe the reports until I came and my own eyes had seen it. Not even half had been told me; your wisdom and prosperity far surpass the report that I had heard. 8 Happy are your wives! Happy are these your servants, who continually attend you and hear your wisdom! 9 Blessed be the LORD your God, who has delighted in you and set you on the throne of Israel! Because the LORD loved Israel forever, he has made you king to execute justice and righteousness." 10 Then she gave the king one hundred twenty talents of gold, a great quantity of spices, and precious stones; never again did spices come in such quantity as that which the queen of Sheba gave to King Solomon.

11 Moreover, the fleet of Hiram, which carried gold from Ophir, brought from Ophir a great quantity of almug wood and precious stones. 12 From the almug wood the king made supports for the house of the LORD, and for the king's house, lyres also and harps for the singers; no such almug wood has come or been seen to this day. 13 Meanwhile King Solomon gave to the queen of Sheba every desire that she expressed, as well as what he gave her out of Solomon's royal bounty. Then she returned to her own land, with her servants.

Analysis

The compilation of several single notices of diverse content in 9:15-28 and 10:14-19 is interrupted by the narrative of the visit of the queen of Sheba. This episode has clearly been formulated in retrospect during the course of the monarchy, as the comparative note in v. 10 shows. Even if we assume a long tradition process, it is not possible to trace the narrative back to the time of the early monarchy. Its purpose is to glorify the unique wisdom of Solomon; thus the narrative picks up an aspect of Solomon's image that only originated with the expansion of the report on the king. A historical kernel of the narrative cannot be determined. The queen herself is anonymous, and the exact circumstances of her visit remain somewhat colorless in the narrative. The few details that are mentioned were also valid in later monarchic times. It is not possible to show that a certain vague knowledge of the queens of pre-Islamic Arabia influenced the composition of the narrative.[1]

The narrative is shaped consistently: it reaches its climax with the speech of the queen in vv. 6-8, in which she praises the incomparable wisdom of Solomon. Despite this stringent composition, the narrative is interrupted by several additions. In vv. 4b-5a the theme of wisdom is abandoned to narrate other achievements of Solomon. The statement "there was no more spirit in her" should therefore immediately follow the sentence "when the queen of Sheba had observed all the wisdom of Solomon." The praise of Yahweh in v. 9 is also ill-fitting in its current context and thus an addition. This glorification, supplemented with several formulas, is not a confession of Yahweh, but only the common acknowledgment of the national deity by the foreign visitor, who realizes the mighty and good acts of the god in his domain.[2] Finally, the statement on the almug wood is an addition that belongs to the paragraph on the journeys to Ophir in 1 Kgs 9:26-28. Verses 11-12 are also an addition that does not belong to the original narrative.

Apart from that the narrative is clearly structured and forms a unity. Other people are not mentioned; the exchange of gifts is part of the court ceremony and is used in the present context to demonstrate that both actors are on a par in regard to wealth. The centerpiece is the contest of wisdom, which Solomon wins. In her speech the queen of Sheba stresses the glory of Solomon in the world and thus elevates him far above any other wise king.

Commentary

[10:1] Verse 1 gives Sheba as the place of origin of the anonymous queen. This points to the Sabean empire of southern Arabia, known from inscriptions since the ninth century, and not to the tribe of the same name, mentioned in Assyrian inscriptions,

---

[1] See N. Abbot, "Pre-Islamic Arab Queens," *AJSL* 58 (1941) 1–22.
[2] Noth, *Könige,* 226.

that resided in north Arabia.[3] In any case, the narrator was not concerned with the exact geographical situation of the empire, but rather wanted to stress that Sheba was a faraway land, thus emphasizing that the fame of Solomon was exceptionally wide-spread.[4]

The purpose of the visit is to test Solomon's wisdom by riddles. It is in the nature of a riddle to contain a question that has to be answered.[5] This question distinguishes the riddle from all other sapiential forms of speech, and it ensures that a riddle is put by one person to another person or group with the intention to receive an answer. A certain contest or test is implied, where the guessing person demonstrates her/his equality, knowledge, and wit and thus emphasizes and manifests her/his own claim to wisdom. To answer a riddle can be seen as a test that reveals the distinctions between two people. Every riddle therefore includes a struggle for power that each person tries to win. On the one hand, this is achieved by making the question exceptionally difficult; on the other hand fame and equality are gained when the opponent solves the riddle. Josephus employed this form of debate to the relationship between Solomon and Hiram (see *Ant.* 8.141-43). As far as the biblical literature is concerned, riddles are only preserved in the narrative of Samson's wedding in Judg 14:1-19.

[10:2] Solomon defends his fame in the sapiential contest with a woman of equal status. The speechlessness of the queen of Sheba signifies her amazement after Solomon has answered all her questions. Without mentioning any precise questions or details, Solomon's wisdom exceeds the wisdom of the world. The gifts in v. 2 stress again the motif of wealth. The camels presuppose a long way through the desert; the gifts of spices, gold, and precious stones aim to emphasize the wealth of the queen and her equality with Solomon. The gifts befit her Arabian homeland. The "spices" are probably balsam oil, which is extracted from the stem of the balsam bush that grows in the mountains of southern Arabia; the oil has a strong fragrance and is used for cosmetic purposes (see Cant 4:10, 14, 16; 5:1, 13; 6:2; 8:14). Gold is the most precious metal and thus fitting for royal gifts. According to Isa 60:6 and Ezek 27:22, Sheba is a land that could supply gold. The precious stones are not specified. Since precious stones are not found in Israel, all pieces found during excavations were imported. The lists in Exod 28:17-20 and Ezek 28:13 show that several kinds of precious stones were known and used to make jewelry and seals. Like gold, precious stones were gifts of high value. The three gifts are repeated in v. 10; here the amount of gold is the same as in 1 Kgs 9:14: 120 talents (i.e., either 4,112 kg. or 4,945 kg.).

---

[3] See Hermann von Wissmann, *Das Grossreich der Sabäer bis zu seinem Ende im frühen 4. Jh. v. Chr.,* ed. Walter W. Müller (Vienna: Verlag der Österreichischen Akademie der Wissenschaften, 1982).

[4] Noth, *Könige,* 224.

[5] See André Jolles, *Einfache Formen: Legende, Sage, Mythe, Rätsel, Spruch, Kasus, Memorabile, Märchen, Witz,* 2d ed. (Darmstadt: Wissenschaftliche Buchgesellschaft, 1958), 129.

[10:3-4a, 5b] These verses state explicitly that Solomon has won the wisdom contest. Solomon is able to answer all the questions, proving that his wisdom is greater than the wisdom of the rest of the world. The queen of Sheba is left to admire the knowledge of Solomon, which exceeds all other knowledge. The contest remains rather vague overall, since no examples of the questions are given. The text assumes that riddles existed in Israel along with sapiental knowledge to test this knowledge. Apart from the different collections of daily wisdom as they are found in the book of Proverbs, we do not possess any collections of natural wisdom or riddles. The Sumerian collections of riddles of the third millennium show that riddles could have been concerned with the knowledge of the course of nature; however, these riddles already have the characteristic feature of pictorial coding.[6]

[10:6-8] The narrative reaches its climax with the speech of the queen in vv. 6-8, during which she acts as a representative of the whole world. Solomon's wisdom receives from her mouth the universal acknowledgment it deserves. All expectations are exceeded, and those around the king are praised as lucky since they can participate daily in his wisdom. The mention of women by a woman should not surprise here despite the fact that the social reality is completely dominated by men.

[10:13] The final remark shows that gifts are expected in return without giving any details. These gifts to his guest depict Solomon as a generous ruler, fulfilling all expectations. The return of the queen to her homeland concludes the events.

[10:11-12] The addition in vv. 11-12 stresses the augmentation of Solomon's wealth and does not seem to fit the current context to which it has been added. Apart from gold and precious stones the almug wood is mentioned, whose import is connected with the journeys to Ophir (see 9:26-28). This kind of wood, described with a foreign word, cannot be determined. The use of the word in Ugaritic and Akkadian texts lets one guess that it is a certain kind of wood without allowing a more detailed explanation.[7] It is possible that the wood came from nearby and was used to manufacture musical instruments. The addition also demonstrates the great distance between the author and the time of Solomon.

Only a few biblical narratives have had such a widespread reception history as the episode of the visit of the queen of Sheba. Already the Qur'an used the story and expanded it in view of the conversion of a pagan woman to the right faith (Sura 27:14-44). Here we find the first allusion to the motif of the exposed legs of the queen because Solomon in his palace tricked her into thinking she had to cross deep water by using glass floors. In Arabic literature the queen is later called Bilqis, the riddles

---

[6] See H. Ph. Römer, *TUAT*, 3:44–46.

[7] See Jonas C. Greenfield and H. Mayerhofer, *Hebräische Wortforschung: Festschrift zum 80. Geburtstag Walter Baumgartner,* VTSup 16 (Leiden: Brill, 1967), 83–89.

are expanded, and a romantic attachment between her and Solomon is added. The Jewish tradition expands the riddles by connecting them to biblical narratives; also her marriage to Solomon is described and ornamented in great detail. Additional expansions are found in Yemen and Ethiopia up to the present.[8]

---

[8] See Werner Daum, ed., *Die Königen von Saba: Kunst, Legende und Archäologie zwischen Morgenland und Abendland* (Stuttgart: Belser, 1988). [Ed.] See also idem, ed., *Yemen: 3000 Years of Art and Civilisation in Arabia Felix* (Frankfurt: Umschau, 1987).

Wealth and Splendor
of the Solomonic Era

Text

10:14 The weight of gold that came to Solomon in one year was six hundred sixty-six talents of gold, 15 besides that which came from the traders and from the business of the merchants, and from all the kings of Arabia and the governors of the land. 16 King Solomon made two hundred large shields of beaten gold; six hundred shekels of gold went into each large shield. 17 He made three hundred shields of beaten gold; three minas of gold went into each shield; and the king put them in the House of the Forest of the Lebanon. 18 The king also made a great ivory throne, and overlaid it with the finest gold. 19 The throne had six steps. The top of the throne was rounded in the back, and on each side of the seat were arm rests and two lions standing beside the arm rests, 20 while twelve lions were standing, one on each end of a step on the six steps. Nothing like it was ever made in any kingdom. 21 All King Solomon's drinking vessels were of gold, and all the vessels of the House of the Forest of the Lebanon were of pure gold; none were of silver—it was not considered as anything in the days of Solomon. 22 For the king had a fleet of ships of Tarshish at sea with the fleet of Hiram. Once every three years the fleet of ships of Tarshish used to come bringing gold, silver, ivory, apes, and peacocks.

23 Thus King Solomon excelled all the kings of the earth in riches and in wisdom. 24 The whole earth sought the presence of Solomon to hear his wisdom, which God had put into his mind. 25 Every one of them brought a present, objects of silver and gold, garments, weaponry, spices, horses, and mules, so much year by year.

26 Solomon gathered together chariots and horses; he had fourteen hundred chariots and twelve thousand horses, which he stationed in the chariot cities and with the king in Jerusalem. 27 The king made silver as common in Jerusalem as stones, and he made cedars as numerous as the

sycamores of the Shephelah. 28 Solomon's import of horses was from Egypt and Kue, and the king's traders received them from Kue at a price. 29 A chariot could be imported from Egypt for six hundred shekels of silver, and a horse for one hundred fifty; so through the king's traders they were exported to all the kings of the Hittites and the kings of Aram.

Analysis

The collection contains notices of diverse contents; together they serve the sole purpose to glorify the era of Solomon further. Most statements are of a general kind and cannot be regarded as historically reliable. Even those statements that seem to reflect reality are back projections from the later period of the monarchy. All in all these notices do not contain any traditions taken from official documents.

Commentary

[10:14-15] A redactor summarizes again Solomon's income of gold in vv. 14-15, stressing that we have an annual income here. The weight of 666 talents (22,825 kg. or 29,390 kg.) is roughly the sum of the 120 talents of Hiram (9:14) plus 420 talents from Ophir (9:28) plus the 120 talents of the queen of Sheba (10:10). The statement thus presupposes these redactional additions. Apart from the amount gained by trade and gifts, other income is specified; but the text of v. 15 is hardly understandable without additions and emendations. The only thing we learn from the verse is that Solomon raked off the profits of the merchants/traders and that different groups made unspecified contributions. The levying of taxes, duty, and tributes presupposes a working bureaucracy, about whose origin we learn nothing. Normally silver, chopped in small pieces and weighed against the standard of the shekel, was the common form of payment; but it is entirely possible that gold was also used for payments, despite the fact that such a process is neither textually not archaeologically verified. The verses seem to be a late—textually corrupt—summary of the theme of gold that aims at the glorification of the sheer wealth of the reign of Solomon.

[10:16-17] The golden shields served a representative purpose and were kept in the House of the Forest of the Lebanon. Their manufacture from alloyed gold is part of the usual exaggeration, since the amount of precious metal cannot correspond to reality. According to the statement 600 shekels (6.85 kg.) of gold were used for one large shield, while three minas or 1.71 (2.05 kg.) were used for a round shield. The different measurements for both forms of shields are remarkable. The large shield had a rectangular form, was slightly bent, and could be placed on the ground to protect the whole man. The round shield was significantly smaller, was carried on the left arm, and protected only the upper body. Both shields served as protection against attacks by sword, arrow, or spear.

Since the golden shields are mentioned again in 14:26 it is difficult to doubt their existence. However, they were hardly made from pure gold. It is more likely that wooden shields were covered by a golden overlay. The author knew of the golden shields but had no idea regarding their manufacture. The coating with gold foil was as common during the first millennium as covering with bronze plates. The royal bodyguard carried the shields during official ceremonies. Both types of shields have not been verified by archaeological finds but seem to correspond to types used in neighboring cultures.[1]

[10:18-20] Even if the description of the throne could be traced back to an eyewitness report, it nevertheless gives a rather general impression. Only special parts of the decoration are stressed, while other details remain open. The coating of the ivory throne with gold seems to point to a contradiction. It cannot be excluded that the throne had several decorative elements made of gold, but the complete covering of it with gold seems to indicate that for the author all important items of temple and palace have to be either made of pure gold or are at least covered by it. All we need to say here is that the ivory mentioned in the context must have been part of the decorative elements, since ivory is not suitable for the manufacture of larger objects.

According to the description the throne had two armrests and a bull's head, whose size is not mentioned, on the reverse of the backrest. The throne stood elevated on a pedestal that was reached by six steps that were flanked by lions on both sides. Two more lions were placed on each side of the armrest. As the most dangerous of the local animals, the lion symbolizes force and invincibility, both traits that are also attributed to the king. The statues of the lion point to the unique position of the king: in his reign over the people he equals a lion in strength and claim to power. Further decorative details of the throne are not mentioned.[2]

Despite possible differences in the details, two throne depictions from the immediate context can be used to illustrate the possible shape of the throne. One can be found on an ivory sketch from Megiddo and stems from the Canaanite realm of the end of the Late Bronze Age; the other one is found on the long side of the Ahiram sarcophagus from tenth-century Byblos.[3] Sphinxes carry both thrones; a similar function and position can be assumed for the lions next to the armrests of the Solomonic throne. In addition, both thrones have a footrest, which is not mentioned for the throne of Solomon but can probably be assumed. Even if the description is based on a throne of one of the later kings of Judah, it is entirely possible that such a throne can be traced back to the furnishing of the palace by Solomon. With the throne Solomon

---

[1] See Yigael Yadin, *The Art of Warfare in Biblical Lands in the Light of Archaeological Discovery,* 2 vols. (New York: McGraw-Hill, 1963).

[2] For the design of such furniture see Helmut Kyrieleis, *Throne und Klinen: Studien zur Formgeschichte altorientalischer und griechischer Sitz- und Liegemöbel vorhellenistischer Zeit,* Jahrbuch des Deutschen archäologischen Instituts, 24 (Berlin: de Gruyter, 1969).

[3] *ANEP*, nos. 332 and 458.

creates the indispensable status symbol of every Near Eastern monarch. The throne was placed in the reception hall of the palace called the throne room, whose shape is not described in 1 Kgs 7:7.

[10:21] The drinking vessels and vessels of the House of the Forest of the Lebanon are mentioned in v. 21 only in summary form to state their manufacture from pure gold. With the remark on the silver, after gold the most precious metal, the wealth of Solomon is increased beyond measure. The meaning of the addition corresponds to v. 27, where the silver is compared with the countless stars of heaven and the precious wood of the cedar with the uncountable sycamores of the Shephelah to stress the wealth of the king who succeeded David and to attribute a fabulous glory to Solomon.[4]

This expansion of the Solomon narrative clashes with the archaeological evidence, judging by which one cannot argue for any wealth during the era of Solomon. Despite several new foundations of cities, the material culture remained comparatively poor, and finds of objects made from precious metal seem to be the exception. In contrast to the premonarchic period, we do have a certain economic and cultural improvement during the tenth century; but in comparison to the epochs of the Middle and Late Bronze Ages the time of the reign of Solomon was not very spectacular.

[10:22] The theme of sea trade is taken up again. Like the journeys to Ophir in 9:26-28, the journeys in question here are seen as a joint venture with Hiram of Tyre. The word "sea" does not necessarily refer to the Mediterranean Sea, since the notice can be seen in analogy to the journeys on the Red Sea mentioned in 9:26-28. The destination of the journeys is not mentioned. (Only the Chronicler concluded that Tarshish must have been the destination since the ships are called Tarshish ships, and he adds the name in 2 Chr 9:21; the problem of the location of Tarshish can then be disregarded in our context.) Tarshish ships are seaworthy sailing vessels that have a large loading capacity so that long-distance journeys could be undertaken in a profitable way (see Isa 2:16). The term originates only during the monarchic period; hence the notice is an addition and historically useless.

Apart from precious metal, ivory, apes, and baboons are mentioned as freight. The ivory trade, well established since the second millennium—as shown by several finds of carvings—is attributed to Solomon. The apes and baboons are described with loanwords from Egyptian and can come only from Africa; such exotic animals probably arrived sometimes as curiosities at the court in Jerusalem. The author uses those exotic animals that are similar to humans to underscore the special character of the Solomonic era.

[10:23-25] After the sheer wealth of Solomon his wisdom is addressed directly. With the conviction that all wisdom is given by God, the sentences refer back to the first

---

[4] Würthwein, *Könige,* 1:126.

theophany in 3:4-15. The sapiential theme had already been taken up in 5:9-14. Wisdom is a gift from God, wealth the result of personal success. The wealth is further increased by gifts. The gifts listed are taken over from literary conventions and do not reflect historical reality. The mention of vessels refers to v. 21, the weapons to vv. 16-17, the oil to 10:2, 10, and the horses and mules to 5:6. Only the garments have not yet been mentioned, but since clothes were preferred personal gifts their listing here is hardly surprising. To heap presents upon Solomon is part of the expansion of the portrait of Solomon and is a motif of his immense wealth. The ruler is thus glorified in a way beyond human imagination.

[10:26] This verse presumes the establishment of a standing army, but only the special units of chariots and cavalry are listed. The chariot was developed in the ancient Near East during the second millennium, in conjunction with the breeding of horses.[5] It was an open vehicle with two wheels that was usually pulled by two horses and equipped with one charioteer and one archer.[6] During David's time the chariot was unknown, but his sons Absalom and Adonijah already made use of it (1 Sam 15:1; 1 Kgs 1:5). With the help of chariots, archers could be employed quickly and over great distances. The origin of the cavalry at the beginning of the first millennium cannot yet be dated exactly. It is possible that the mention of the cavalry is anachronistic, since events of a later time are projected back to the Solomonic era. In any case, the cavalry as part of an army can be verified by inscriptions since the ninth century. The list of the army of the enemy of the anti-Assyrian coalition in the battle at Qarqar in the so-called monolith inscription of Shalmaneser III serves as a good comparison. According to this inscription the alliance fielded the following contingents for the battle against the Assyrians:

Aram	1,200 chariots	1,200 cavalry	20,000 soldiers
Hamath	700 chariots	700 cavalry	10,000 soldiers
Israel	2,000 chariots		10,000 soldiers
Koe			500 soldiers
Musri			1,000 soldiers
Irqanata	10 chariots		10,000 soldiers
Arvad			200 soldiers
Usanata			200 soldiers
Sian	30 chariots		10,000 soldiers
Arabia		1,000 camels	
Ammon			[. . .]000 soldiers

---

[5] See Yadin, *Art of Warfare*.
[6] See the illustrations in *ANEP*, nos. 165, 172, 184, 356–60.

The list of the booty distinguishes between chariots, cavalry, and horses "that were put under the yoke." As is common for Assyrian inscriptions, the numbers for some of the opponents are grossly exaggerated. Nadav Na'aman has proposed that especially for Israel one should only assume a contingent of 200 chariots.[7] The 1,400 chariots attributed to Solomon are therefore hardly realistic, and the cavalry of 12,000 is likewise a rather fantastic figure. The notice is not a reliable witness for the creation of a new army by Solomon. In addition, the existence of chariot cities has not yet been verified. Also the stables mentioned were used only to accommodate troops and not horses.[8] Chariots and cavalry add to the picture of Solomon: the new troops not only display his wealth but also portray him as a judicious commander.

[10:28-29] The passage on the horse trade with its details of the import countries and the prices seems to be reliable at first glance. But this note too seems to come from the later period of the monarchy. The note on the import of horses is too sparse to come from any official document of the royal administration. The countries of origin are called Musri (NRSV: Egypt) and Kue. Kue is a name for the plains of Cilicia,[9] and Musri is probably the area of the Taurus Mountains; both names occur next to each other in the monolith inscription of Shalmaneser III, according to which horses were imported from the southeastern part of Asia Minor that was famous for its horse breeding.[10] The chariots on the other hand are from Egypt, where they had been built and used since the New Kingdom.

The prices show the high value of the commodities and the incredibly large amount of silver that was spent on this special force; here a chariot is four times as valuable as a horse. The price is calculated in shekels, which can be, following several found weights, determined as 11.42 g. A chariot would then cost 6.852 kg. of silver and a horse 1.713 kg. of silver. The high price is only revealed by comparison with similar items: the value of a slave is said to be 30 shekels (342.6 g.) of silver (Exod 21:32). A horse thus costs five times as much as a slave. However, the figures cannot be verified, and it is entirely possible that they are exaggerated to stress the wealth of Solomon.

The reference to the Hittite kings has in mind the chiefdoms of the late Hittite rulers in northern Syria; the kings of Aram are the rulers of the Aramean states in Syria. The notice is not a historical report on the horse trade during the time of Solomon, since all information regarding prices and places can equally stem from later periods.

---

[7] Nadav Na'aman, "Two Notes on the Monolith Inscription of Shalmaneser III from Kurkh," *TA* 3 (1976) 89–106.

[8] See Volkmar Fritz, "Bestimmung und Herkunft des Pfeilerhauses in Israel," *ZDPV* 93 (1977) 30–45.

[9] Noth, *Könige*, 235.

[10] *ANET*, 279.

The Reasons for the Division
of the Empire

Text

11:1 King Solomon loved many foreign women along with the daughter of Pharaoh: Moabite, Ammonite, Edomite, Sidonian, and Hittite women, 2 from the nations concerning which the LORD had said to the Israelites, "You shall not enter into marriage with them, neither shall they with you; for they will surely incline your heart to follow their gods"; Solomon clung to these in love. 3 Among his wives were seven hundred princesses and three hundred concubines; and his wives turned away his heart. 4 For when Solomon was old, his wives turned away his heart after other gods; and his heart was not true to the LORD his God, as was the heart of his father David. 5 For Solomon followed Astarte the goddess of the Sidonians, and Milcom the abomination of the Ammonites. 6 So Solomon did what was evil in the sight of the LORD, and did not completely follow the LORD, as his father David had done. 7 Then Solomon built a high place for Chemosh the abomination of Moab, and for Molech the abomination of the Ammonites, on the mountain east of Jerusalem. 8 He did the same for all his foreign wives, who offered incense and sacrificed to their gods.

9 Then the LORD was angry with Solomon, because his heart had turned away from the LORD, the God of Israel, who had appeared to him twice, 10 and had commanded him concerning this matter, that he should not follow other gods; but he did not observe what the LORD commanded. 11 Therefore the LORD said to Solomon, "Since this has been your mind and you have not kept my covenant and my statutes that I have commanded you, I will surely tear the kingdom from you and give it to your servant. 12 Yet for the sake of your father David I will not do it in your lifetime; I will tear it out of the hand of your son. 13 I will not, however, tear away the entire kingdom; I will give one tribe to your son, for the sake of my servant David and for the sake of Jerusalem, which I have chosen."

14 Then the Lᴏʀᴅ raised up an adversary against Solomon, Hadad the Edomite; he was of the royal house in Edom. 15 For when David was in Edom, and Joab the commander of the army went up to bury the dead, he killed every male in Edom 16 (for Joab and all Israel remained there six months, until he had eliminated every male in Edom); 17 but Hadad fled to Egypt with some Edomites who were servants of his father. He was a young boy at that time. 18 They set out from Midian and came to Paran; they took people with them from Paran and came to Egypt, to Pharaoh king of Egypt, who gave him a house, assigned him an allowance of food, and gave him land. 19 Hadad found great favor in the sight of Pharaoh, so that he gave him his sister-in-law for a wife, the sister of Queen Tahpenes. 20 The sister of Tahpenes gave birth by him to his son Genubath, whom Tahpenes weaned in Pharaoh's house; Genubath was in Pharaoh's house among the children of Pharaoh. 21 When Hadad heard in Egypt that David slept with his ancestors and that Joab the commander of the army was dead, Hadad said to Pharaoh, "Let me depart, that I may go to my own country." 22 But Pharaoh said to him, "What do you lack with me that you now seek to go to your own country?" And he said, "No, do let me go."

23 God raised up another adversary against Solomon, Rezon son of Eliada, who had fled from his master, King Hadadezer of Zobah. 24 He gathered followers around him and became leader of a marauding band, after the slaughter by David; they went to Damascus, settled there, and made him king in Damascus. 25 He was an adversary of Israel all the days of Solomon, making trouble as Hadad did; he despised Israel and reigned over Aram.

26 Jeroboam son of Nebat, an Ephraimite of Zeredah, a servant of Solomon, whose mother's name was Zeruah, a widow, rebelled against the king. 27 The following was the reason he rebelled against the king. Solomon built the Millo, and closed up the gap in the wall of the city of his father David. 28 The man Jeroboam was very able, and when Solomon saw that the young man was industrious he gave him charge over all the forced labor of the house of Joseph. 29 About that time, when Jeroboam was leaving Jerusalem, the prophet Ahijah the Shilonite found him on the road. Ahijah had clothed himself with a new garment. The two of them were alone in the open country 30 when Ahijah laid hold of the new garment he was wearing and tore it into twelve pieces. 31 He then said to Jeroboam: Take for yourself ten pieces; for thus says the Lᴏʀᴅ, the God of Israel, "See, I am about to tear the kingdom from the hand of Solomon, and will give you ten tribes. 32 One tribe will remain his, for the sake of my servant David and for the sake of Jerusalem, the city that I have chosen out of all the tribes of Israel. 33 This is because he has forsaken me, worshiped Astarte the goddess of the Sidonians, Chemosh the god of Moab, and Milcom the god of the Ammonites, and has not walked in my ways, doing what is right in my sight

and keeping my statutes and my ordinances, as his father David did.
34 Nevertheless I will not take the whole kingdom away from him but will
make him ruler all the days of his life, for the sake of my servant David
whom I chose and who did keep my commandments and my statutes;
35 but I will take the kingdom away from his son and give it to you—that is,
the ten tribes. 36 Yet to his son I will give one tribe, so that my servant
David may always have a lamp before me in Jerusalem, the city where I
have chosen to put my name. 37 I will take you, and you shall reign over all
that your soul desires; you shall be king over Israel. 38 If you will listen to
all that I command you, walk in my ways, and do what is right in my sight by
keeping my statutes and my commandments, as David my servant did, I will
be with you, and will build you an enduring house, as I built for David, and I
will give Israel to you. 39 For this reason I will punish the descendants of
David, but not forever." 40 Solomon sought therefore to kill Jeroboam; but
Jeroboam promptly fled to Egypt, to King Shishak of Egypt, and remained
in Egypt until the death of Solomon.

Analysis

The long narrative preparing the division of the empire is not a unified whole but was
assembled from several single pieces to arrive at the current form. After giving the
basic reasons for the events in Solomon's wrong behavior in vv. 1-13, the narrative
moves on to depict Jeroboam as a renegade and unlawful usurper in vv. 26-28, 40.
The conflict of Jeroboam with his master Solomon is only hinted at, however, not
reported, because the course of the narrative is interrupted by a lengthy prophetic
story. This story legitimizes the kingship of Jeroboam by tracing it back to the will of
God. This attempted justification is added to the older narrative instead of reporting
the rift between the office bearer and Jeroboam and King Solomon. The narratives
about Hadad the Edomite (vv. 14-22) and Rezon the Aramean (vv. 23-25) are placed
between the introductory paragraph in vv. 1-13 and the narrative in vv. 26-28, 40;
both narratives expand the theme of the general danger for the Solomonic empire due
to foreign rabble-rousers.

Four reasons are given altogether for the separation of the northern tribes
from the house of David: First, Solomon's behavior is responsible for the split (vv. 1-
13); second, there are adversaries from outside (vv. 14-22, 23-25); third, Jeroboam
always sought to achieve power and glory (vv. 26-28); finally, God snatches away the
main part of the people from the Davidic dynasty because of the worship of foreign
gods by Solomon (vv. 29-39). All four pieces have to be seen as separate attempts to
explain the division of the empire.

Commentary

[11:1-13] The Deuteronomistic Historian speaks in this section; he hardly uses older
traditions, but levels general accusations against the king and combines several argu-

ments: the foreign women encourage Solomon to worship foreign gods, and this idolatry causes the division of the monarchy. To avoid any contradiction with the glory of the Solomonic rule, the turning away from Yahweh under the influence of foreign women is placed in the period "when Solomon was old" (v. 4). Specifically, a negative attitude against non-Israelite women is assumed that originated during exilic-postexilic times. Marriage to a foreign woman was probably the exception during the monarchical period but not necessarily a reason for concern, as the Aramean women in the harem of David show (cf. 2 Sam 3:3). It is only the Deuteronomic law written toward the end of the monarchy that generally forbids the marital union with the non-Israelite population (Deut 7:1-4), but also allows for certain exceptions (Deut 21:10-14). This ban on certain forms of marriage is intensified in postexilic times; Ezra judges mixed marriages in a negative way and enforces their dissolution.

The number of Solomon's wives is said to be one thousand; as usual, this is probably an exaggeration, and the number has no significance for the course of the narrative. It only matters that his love for the women causes Solomon's heart to turn away from Yahweh as the only God. The Deuteronomistic Historian firmly roots Solomon's idolatry in his biography.

Next to Milcom and Chemosh, the gods of the Ammonites and Moabites (v. 7), an addition also mentions Astarte (v. 5). Astarte was a fertility goddess who was worshiped in the whole Syro-Palestinian area; here she is said to be a deity of the Sidonians. Whether the numerous figurines found during excavations can be regarded as depictions of Astarte has to remain open.[1] Outside the Bible, Milcom, the main deity of the Ammonites, is only known from personal names.[2] In contrast, the Moabite deity Chemosh is well attested in texts. In the Mesha inscription he is mentioned several times as the god who enables Mesha's success.[3] All three gods are mentioned again in connection with the cultic reforms of Josiah (2 Kgs 23:13); for the Deuteronomistic Historian they serve as standard examples for the adoption of foreign cults.

The sanctuaries built for Chemosh and Milcom are explicitly described as high places and could have been situated near Jerusalem on the hill Bāṭen el-Hawa above Silwān east of the city. The type of the sanctuary is not mentioned, but one should not assume an open cultic place without a temple, since the term "high place" (*bamah*) usually serves as a general description for illegitimate cultic places without providing any information regarding place or appearance. Verse 8 assumes further cultic places where the foreign wives of Solomon sacrificed to their gods.

---

[1] See James B. Pritchard, *Palestinian Figurines in Relation to Certain Goddesses Known through Literature*, AOS 24 (New Haven: American Oriental Society, 1943). Reprinted New York: Kraus, 1967.

[2] See Ulrich Hübner, *Die Ammoniter: Untersuchungen zur Geschichte, Kultur und Religion eines transjordanischen Volkes im 1. Jahrtausend v. Chr.*, ADPV 16 (Wiesbaden: Harrassowitz, 1992), 252–56. [Ed.] See also Emile Puech, "Milcom," in *DDD*[2], 575–76.

[3] *TGI*, 5–53. Cf. Udo Worschech, "Der Gott Kemosch," *UF* 24 (1992) 393–401. [Ed.] See also Hans-Peter Müller, "Chemosh," in *DDD*[2], 186–89.

[11:9-13] As usual for Deuteronomistic theology, Solomon is made responsible for his actions (vv. 9-10). The worship of foreign gods breaks with the demand to worship Yahweh alone, a demand that can only be fulfilled by turning away from foreign gods.[4] Solomon's breaking away from Yahweh provokes Yahweh's anger and punishment; this is mentioned in a divine speech in vv. 11-13. This divine speech is constructed as a counterpart to the theophanies in 3:4-14 and 9:1-9. Already 9:6-8 mentions punishment for breaking away from Yahweh; the worship of foreign gods is—according to the Deuteronomistic Historian—the main misdemeanor for which king and people can be held responsible (cf. 1 Sam 12:20; 2 Kgs 18:6). The punishment envisaged is the division of the kingdom resulting from the separation of the northern tribes.

[11:11-13] Solomon himself is thus made responsible for the events after his death. Verse 11 pronounces a verdict. Since Solomon did not keep the covenant made with God, God in turn will not keep his promise regarding the united monarchy; rather he will give the kingship to a servant of Solomon. Taking the historical situation into account, this unconditional judgment is corrected in vv. 12-13. The disaster will not happen during Solomon's lifetime, and the tribe of Judah will remain in the hand of the Davidic dynasty. Thus the Deuteronomistic Historian interprets the course of history according to his worldview and disregards the facts and actual events. This is done according to two basic assumptions: first, human beings are responsible for their actions; second, the turning away from Yahweh is understood as the breaking of the covenant—which results in the loss of the basic means of salvation.

[11:14-22] The two episodes on Hadad and Rezon were added in vv. 14-27, to demonstrate the endangering of the Solomonic empire by enemies from outside. The narrative of the flight and return of Hadad the Edomite in vv. 14-22 gives an impression of incompleteness since it ends in the middle of a dialogue between Hadad and Pharaoh. At least from the narratological point of view one would expect a concluding sentence reporting the return and seizure of power by Hadad; such a sentence was probably dropped after the addition of the following episode in vv. 23-25. The Edomite Hadad, a member of the royal lineage, is hardly identical with the king bearing the same name mentioned in an Edomite king list in Gen 36:31-39, since this enumeration of Edomite names is probably of postexilic origin.[5]

The Edomites take their name from the land they inhabited. Originally, Edom ("the red one") was the name for the small strip of cultivated land on the eastern fringe of the Transjordanian high plateau, but the name is also used to describe the

---

[4] See Timo Veijola, "Höre Israel! Der Sinn und Hintergrund von Deuteronomium VI 4-9," *VT* 42 (1992) 528–41.

[5] See Ernst Axel Knauf, "Alter und Herkunft der edomitischen Königsliste Gen. 36,31-39," *ZAW* 97 (1985) 245–53.

whole territory east of the Arabah. In the Bible Edom is used synonymously with Seir ("the hairy one"), originally the name for the middle layer of the mountains consisting of Nubian limestone and used together with Teman ("the southern one"). The territory extends to the north up to Wādi el-Ḥesā, which forms the border with Moab; in the south it reaches as far as the Gulf of Aqabah. Toward the west the steep slope from the high plateau down to the Arabah forms an obstacle difficult to overcome, while in the east the transition from steppe to desert land is rather fluid. In the second millennium, Edom did not belong to the realm of the Canaanite city-states. From the Early Iron Age onward, remains of settlements suggest the transformation from a nomadic to a settled existence. Taking up agriculture changed the nomadic lifestyle. The founding of fortified cities can only be verified from the eighth century onward. The transition to a state with a king took part probably during this urbanization.

[11:15-17] It is not clear to which military campaign the events in v. 15 refer; the subjugation of the Edomites by David (2 Sam 8:13-14) presupposes the preservation of the people. The flight of the royal family during a conquest is a normal scenario, and Egypt seems to be an exiles' destination par excellence (cf. v. 40). The escape route was via Midian and Paran. Midian lies south of Edom in the northwestern part of the Arabian peninsula. The name Midian is preserved in the city Madiama/Madyan that is mentioned by ancient Arabic geographers and probably situated near the oasis el-Bada; east of the Gulf of Aqabah. The land of Midian was probably not only the surrounding territory of this oasis but extended to the coastal mountains and the plateau of el-Ḥisiā.[6] Paran is probably a term for the southern part of the Sinai peninsula, where the name is preserved in the oasis Fēran in the Wādi Fēran. To use this escape route one had to cross the Gulf of Aqabah.

[11:18-20] In Egypt the fugitives were assigned food and land according to their social position (v. 18). In addition, it was possible for Hadad to marry a woman from the royal family (v. 19). The name of the sister of the woman called Tahpenes could be the transliteration of Egyptian *t³ ḥm.t nsw,* "the wife of the king," so that the name is not really a personal name. The name of the son is also attested in Old North Arabic, and he is educated together with the princes at the royal court (v. 20). These details detract from the original aim of the narrative, but they seem to serve the purpose of describing the special status of Hadad as an adversary of Solomon.

[11:21-22] Along similar lines, the dialogue between Hadad and Pharaoh describes this opponent as determined and purposeful. The continuation and the end of the narrative are not preserved. It becomes clear from the narrative, however, that a member from the royal lineage returns to Edom to reestablish the kingship by crowning him-

---

[6] See Alois Musil, *The Northern Hegâz: A Topographical Itinerary* (New York: American Geographical Society, 1926), 278–82.

self king and making Edom an independent state. This procedure reverses the measures introduced by David to make Edom a dependent state. The reestablishment of the kingship in Edom results in the loss of a territory conquered by David; the power of Solomon is thus weakened. Despite the fact that Hadad is mentioned as king of the Edomites in Gen 36:35, the prelude to his accession to the throne is based on the use of conventional literary and geographical topoi that belong to the realm of common knowledge. The narrator probably used a well-known story to provide a reason for the reestablishment of the kingship in Edom under Hadad.

[11:23-25] The narrative of Rezon, who became king over the Aramean state of Damascus, is even shorter and more general. The exposition in v. 23 is an obvious imitation of the narrative of the fate of Jeroboam in vv. 26-28, 40, whose middle part is not preserved. Hadadezer, king of Zobah, here mentioned as the master of Rezon, is known from 2 Sam 8:3-8; all the other details remain rather vague and simply end in the enthronement. In contrast to Hadad, Rezon, as captain of a marauding band, is portrayed negatively. Further details are not given, but the accession to the throne could only have happened by usurpation. Rezon's kingship is not based on any legal principle but on brute force and on a group of faithful followers. The negative impression is nurtured further in v. 25 by referring to his personal character. Rezon is not attested extrabiblically as king of Damascus, but he could be identical with King Hezion, mentioned in 1 Kgs 15:18.

Damascus remained the capital of the Aramean state until the conquest by Tiglath-pileser III in 732. The Aramean city was probably located in the place of the current old city of Damascus.[7] Since according to 2 Sam 8:5-6 David subdued the Aramean kingdom of Damascus and instituted governors there, the reestablishment of the kingship there meant a diminution of the power of Solomon. The piece assumes prior knowledge of the situation created under David and can probably be traced back to the changes in Solomonic times; in its current form, however, it is a literary product that does not describe but only reflects historical reality.

[11:26-28, 40] The story of Jeroboam here is not complete, since its whole middle part is missing. Nevertheless, the course of the story can be reconstructed from the introduction that anticipates the result. The only missing part is therefore the reason why the client of Solomon became a political fugitive who had to seek asylum in Egypt. One can assume that the flight was made necessary after a severe crime so that the existing loyalty between the king and his official was broken.

Jeroboam is introduced as the son of Nebat from Zeredah (v. 26). His hometown Zeredah was situated at the place of the village Dēr Ğassāne in the southwest of the Samaritan hill country because the name survives in the spring ʿĒn Ṣerēda that

---

[7] See Dorothée Sack, *Damaskus: Entwicklung und Struktur einer orientalisch-islamischen Stadt,* DamFor 1 (Mainz: von Zabern, 1989), 9.

can be found close by.[8] The mention of his mother Zeruah is unusual and probably a sign of her independence after the death of her husband. The phrase "to raise the hand" is unique and seems at first to imply physical action. It can, however, also be used in a metaphorical sense to describe a rebellion against the king, such as not fulfilling a duty or acting independently.

The note on the building projects of Solomon in Jerusalem (v. 27) could derive from tradition since the building of the Millo and the closure of a gap in the wall is mentioned explicitly in 9:15. Thus the narrator uses known details from the period of Solomon's reign. The reference to the forced labor also takes up details from tradition (cf. 5:27-30; 9:20-22). The organization of the forced labor is not mentioned; the narrator only presupposes a division according to tribes. According to this, Jeroboam does not belong to the highest officials (he is not mentioned in the list), but his ability gave him a high rank in the royal bureaucracy. The details of his rise are not mentioned, but the extraordinary career of the young man is alluded to: the son of a widow became a man of high standing in the state. The missing continuation of the narrative probably mentioned a crime or infraction of Jeroboam that forced him to flee to Egypt to avoid punishment by the king. Jeroboam is thus put in the wrong.

The reference to Pharaoh Shishak places the narrative in a historical context but is probably taken over from 14:25-26, where he is mentioned in connection with the reign of Rehoboam. Shishak is the first ruler of the Twenty-second Dynasty; he ruled from 945 to 924. The details of the narrative of the revolt of Jeroboam are taken over from literary tradition and are not based on actual events. The whole piece is therefore a fictitious report with the aim to stigmatize the first king of the northern kingdom as an unfaithful servant even before his accession to the throne. The narrative has to be seen as a piece of Judean propaganda.

[11:29-39] The description of the conflict between Solomon and Jeroboam was broken off when the prophetic narrative (vv. 29-39) was included. Instead of a personal dispute we thus find a new justification of the historical events expressed by a divine word. The prophetic narrative contains a symbolic action that is explained by a long divine speech. The purpose of the whole action is the designation of Jeroboam as a king who is legitimized by a prophet—a normal process (cf. 1 Sam 9:27—10:1; 2 Kgs 9:5-6). The prophet Ahijah of Shiloh appears again in 1 Kgs 14:1-18 as a messenger of divine judgment. The meeting of Jeroboam and Ahijah happens without any witnesses, and the symbolic action remains secret. Witnesses are unnecessary since the actions only serve the legitimization of Jeroboam. Here it is stressed explicitly that Jeroboam was clothed with a new cloak, since for a symbolic action to become valid immediately requires an unblemished object.[9] The act as such is based on the

---

[8] See William F. Albright, "Archaeological and Topographical Exploration in Palestine and Syria," *BASOR* 48 (1933) 26–28.

[9] Noth, *Könige,* 259.

model of 1 Sam 15:27-28, a story that is adapted here for current historical purposes. The twelve pieces of the cloak represent the twelve tribes of Israel. Thus the narrative presupposes the later view that the Solomonic empire consisted of twelve tribes. (The tribe as a closed unit is already mentioned in the list of the provinces in 1 Kgs 4:8-19, but the definition of twelve tribes only stems from the later period of the monarchy.)

The speech of the prophet is not a unified entity. On the one hand it assumes that, after the split of Benjamin, the northern kingdom consisted only of ten tribes, a condition only reached in the course of the period of the monarchy. On the other hand, the reference to the one tribe refers to the situation shortly after the death of Solomon, that is, that only Judah is ruled by the Davidic dynasty. Most likely a basic layer (vv. 31, 33a, 34abα, 35abα, 37) later was expanded by a redactor (vv. 32, 33b, 34bβ, 36, 38abα).[10] The basic layer announces that the ten tribes will be taken from Solomon because of his apostasy and be given to Jeroboam; here it is taken into account that it is not Solomon but his son who loses the kingship over the ten tribes.[11] This announcement is amended in the redactional layer in such a way that the Davidic dynasty will keep one tribe because of the promise Yahweh made to David and because of the election of Jerusalem.

The same historical event is thus commented upon from two different viewpoints: the one layer is concerned with the legitimation of Jeroboam's rule over the ten tribes, the other one with the conservation of Davidic rule over Judah.[12] The point of departure for both interpretations is the apostasy of Solomon manifested in his worship of foreign gods; as in vv. 5 and 7, Astarte, Chemosh, and Milcom are mentioned. The reproach for worshiping foreign gods, already stated in vv. 1-3, is taken up again. Both layers are influenced by Deuteronomistic theology and have to be seen as later additions to the narrative of the conflict between Jeroboam and Solomon.

Instead of explaining the division of the monarchy on the basis of personal differences, the text states that God himself commissioned Ahijah of Shiloh to designate Jeroboam as king. For the Deuteronomistic redactors who are responsible for both layers of the narrative, the historical events are not the result of social or economic conflicts (as alluded to in 12:1-19); rather, history is determined by the will of God. The human person is the cause only in that God reacts to his behavior: the turning away from Yahweh inevitably results in punishment; here even promises made can be partly revoked. The prophetic narrative explains with regard to the division of the monarchy why God not only allowed such a crucial event but also wanted it to happen.[13] The connection between human and divine actions are made apparent; the human person determines the course of history only indirectly, since the orientation

---

[10] See Walter Dietrich, *Prophetie und Geschichte: Eine redaktionsgeschichtliche Untersuchung zum deuteronomistischen Geschichtswerk,* FRLANT 108 (Göttingen, Vandenhoeck & Ruprecht, 1972), 15ff.

[11] Würthwein, *Könige,* 1:141.

[12] Ibid., 144.

[13] Ibid., 145.

to the divine command determines his fate: by being faithful to Yahweh the human person keeps the divine covenant; the breaking of this covenant inevitably results in punishment that manifests itself in history.

The piece vv. 29-39 sets out what was already alluded to in vv. 11-13: judged against the demand of the sole worship of Yahweh, Solomon failed, because he made allowances for other gods. In his responsibility as king, Solomon has failed, despite all qualifications; he thus gambled away the destiny of the kingdom. At the same time such a judgment on the division of the monarchy glorifies the unification of all Israel under one king as a salvific time given by God; this time comes to an end because of the behavior of Solomon. Deuteronomistic theology leaves no doubt that the united monarchy was the divinely granted form of government that was rendered invalid due to human failure.

The Concluding Formula for Solomon

Text

11:41 Now the rest of the acts of Solomon, all that he did as well as his wisdom, are they not written in the Book of the Acts of Solomon? 42 The time that Solomon reigned in Jerusalem over all Israel was forty years. 43 Solomon slept with his ancestors and was buried in the city of his father David; and his son Rehoboam succeeded him.

Commentary

[11:41-43] The concluding formula for Solomon differs in two points from the general standard. On the one hand, there is no reference to the "Book of the History of the Kings of Judah (or Israel)" but to the "Book of the Acts of Solomon." This reference is, however, fictitious; it is used in order to make the description appear authentic and based on sources. Since Solomon ruled over both parts of the kingdom, the Deuteronomistic Historian assumes a special source for his history. Such a "Book of the Acts of Solomon" never existed. The author of a pre-Deuteronomistic description of the history of Solomon has probably used authentic source material, but this material is so sparse that one cannot argue for a special collection of events of the Solomonic era.

On the other hand the years of his reign are mentioned because they are missing in the introductory formula in 1 Kgs 3:3. The figure 40 corresponds—as has been the case with David (2:11) to the length of a generation and marks the duration of his reign. In addition, the wisdom of Solomon is mentioned. Furthermore, his death and burial as well as the name of his successor are stated in a formulaic way. The enthronement of his son as his successor is not described, since a dynastic succession is assumed. Since in ancient Israel burial happened very shortly after death, a quick succession within several days after a period of mourning can be assumed. The formulaic expression stresses the naturalness of the event.

1 Kings 12—2 Kings 17
The Divided Monarchy
of Israel and Judah

1 Kings 12:1-25

The Installation
of Jeroboam as King

Text

12:1 Rehoboam went to Shechem, for all Israel had come to Shechem to make him king. 2 When Jeroboam son of Nebat heard of it (for he was still in Egypt, where he had fled from King Solomon), then Jeroboam returned from Egypt. 3 And they sent and called him; and Jeroboam and all the assembly of Israel came and said to Rehoboam, 4 "Your father made our yoke heavy. Now therefore lighten the hard service of your father and his heavy yoke that he placed on us, and we will serve you." 5 He said to them, "Go away for three days, then come again to me." So the people went away.
6 Then King Rehoboam took counsel with the older men who had attended his father Solomon while he was still alive, saying, "How do you advise me to answer this people?" 7 They answered him, "If you will be a servant to this people today and serve them, and speak good words to them when you answer them, then they will be your servants forever." 8 But he disregarded the advice that the older men gave him, and consulted with the young men who had grown up with him and now attended him. 9 He said to them, "What do you advise that we answer this people who have said to me, 'Lighten the yoke that your father put on us'?" 10 The young men who had grown up with him said to him, "Thus you should say to this people who spoke to you, 'Your father made our yoke heavy, but you must lighten it for us'; thus you should say to them, 'My little finger is thicker than my father's loins. 11 Now, whereas my father laid on you a heavy yoke, I will add to your yoke. My father disciplined you with whips, but I will discipline you with scorpions.'"

12 So Jeroboam and all the people came to Rehoboam the third day, as the king had said, "Come to me again the third day." 13 The king answered the people harshly. He disregarded the advice that the older men had given him 14 and spoke to them according to the advice of the young men, "My father made your yoke heavy, but I will add to your yoke; my father disciplined you with whips, but I will discipline you with scorpions." 15 So the king did not listen to the people, because it was a turn of affairs brought about by the LORD that he might fulfill his word, which the LORD had spoken by Ahijah the Shilonite to Jeroboam son of Nebat.

16 When all Israel saw that the king would not listen to them, the people answered the king,
"What share do we have in David?
We have no inheritance in the son of Jesse.
To your tents, O Israel!
Look now to your own house, O David."
So Israel went away to their tents. 17 But Rehoboam reigned over the Israelites who were living in the towns of Judah. 18 When King Rehoboam sent Adoram, who was taskmaster over the forced labor, all Israel stoned him to death. King Rehoboam then hurriedly mounted his chariot to flee to Jerusalem. 19 So Israel has been in rebellion against the house of David to this day.

20 When all Israel heard that Jeroboam had returned, they sent and called him to the assembly and made him king over all Israel. There was no one who followed the house of David, except the tribe of Judah alone.

21 When Rehoboam came to Jerusalem, he assembled all the house of Judah and the tribe of Benjamin, one hundred eighty thousand chosen troops to fight against the house of Israel, to restore the kingdom to Rehoboam son of Solomon. 22 But the word of God came to Shemaiah the man of God: 23 "Say to King Rehoboam of Judah, son of Solomon, and to all the house of Judah and Benjamin, and to the rest of the people, 24 'Thus says the LORD, You shall not go up or fight against your kindred the people of Israel. Let everyone go home, for this thing is from me.'" So they heeded the word of the LORD and went home again, according to the word of the LORD.

25 Then Jeroboam built Shechem in the hill country of Ephraim, and resided there; he went out from there and built Penuel.

Analysis

The centerpiece of the narrative is the vain attempt by Rehoboam to become king over the northern tribes. The return of Jeroboam and his installation as king is mentioned only in the marginal comments in vv. 2, 3a, and 20a. The two different contents are not joined. This allows the conclusion that the remarks on Jeroboam's success were added at a later stage to the narrative of the failure of Rehoboam in vv. 1, 3b, 4-19. The narrative now climaxes in the installation of Jeroboam as king over the northern tribes. To this narrative a notice on the erection and transferal of the capital is added (v. 25). This verse stands quite isolated, since a redactor added a narrative on the prevention of Rehoboam's war against the northern tribes (vv. 21-24).

The narrative in vv. 1, 3b, 4-19 is an artistically shaped unity; only the back reference in v. 15 and the comments in vv. 17 and 20b can be regarded as later additions; the original narrative consisted of vv. 1, 3b, 4-14, 16, 18, 19. Maybe the Deuteronomistic Historian used an already existing narrative, added v. 19, and incorporated it into his history. The narrative is hardly a documentary report.[1] Rather, the division of the monarchy because of the forced labor—the main reproach against the kingship (see 1 Sam 8:10-17)—has to be explained; here the lack of experience and clumsiness of the young Rehoboam is added as a further motif. The mention of Adoram in v. 18 shows the lack of historical reliability: according to 2 Sam 20:24 he already belonged to the officials of David and was then the overseer of the forced labor under Solomon (1 Kgs 4:6). In view of the long reign of Solomon it is hardly likely that Adoram continued to occupy this office under Rehoboam; rather one can assume that the pre-Deuteronomistic author used names known from tradition.

Even if the narrative does not contain a historical report, the motif reflects that the forced labor during the period of the monarchy was regarded as a burden, and already in the addition 1 Kgs 9:20-22 the true circumstances of the forced labor are covered up. The narrative is shaped by the view that the forced labor represents an unbearable aspect of the reign of Solomon and thus cannot be justified as a price for the recognition of the Davidic dynasty.

Commentary

[12:1] The exposition in v. 1 states clearly the aim of the northern tribes: Rehoboam alone bears responsibility for the failure of his installation as king over all Israel. Here it is assumed that the northern tribes form an independent group, and, furthermore, that the assumption of the kingship is tied to the consent of the people. The northern tribes made David king in a special procedure (2 Sam 5:3) during which the relationship between king and people was regulated by a treaty. In contrast, Solomon's kingship was the result of a palace intrigue, and the participation of the people was limited to acclamation by the inhabitants of Jerusalem who were present (1 Kgs 1:11-40). The narrative assumes that the northern tribes do not doubt the dynastic principle but that they desire an agreement with the new king. The need of acceptance by the northern tribes shows that they occupy special status and special rights and that they are aware of them.[2]

The failure of the negotiations results in the failure of the unity of the northern tribes with Judah under one king. Deliberately, the negotiations take place at Shechem. Shechem is not only the first capital of Jeroboam; it also occupies a special

---

[1] Würthwein, *Könige,* 1:159.

[2] Ibid., 1:153.

place in the tradition. Already in Genesis 34, Joshua 24, and Judges 9, Shechem is the site where important events in the history of premonarchic Israel take place. This locale reflects that Shechem was the most important town in the north before the foundation of Samaria (for the location see the comment on 1 Kgs 12:25).

[12:2-3a] The note on the return of Jeroboam from Egypt interrupts the course of the narrative. As far as its content is concerned, it presupposes the narrative of 11:26-40. The overcrowding of the statement is caused by the later addition of v. 3a. The note on Jeroboam's return in v. 2 forms a necessary literary bridge that prepares the further events mentioned in v. 20. In any case we certainly do not have a short excerpt from some annals here.[3] An independent narrative of Jeroboam's accession to the throne never existed; rather the basic facts are added in the form of short comments (vv. 2, 20a, 25).

[12:3b-4] These verses mention the forced labor as the main reason for the breaking away of the northern tribes from the Davidic dynasty. The duty to do work for the king was probably introduced at the same time as the kingship itself, but only during the massive building projects of Solomon did the forced labor amount to an unbearable load (see 9:15-25). The socage is the reason for the split of the northern tribes from the Davidic dynasty, since Rehoboam refuses to ease the load. However, the remark in v. 16 shows that the cause for the dissolution of the united monarchy was rooted in the fundamental discrepancy between north and south. The heaviness of the forced labor is illustrated by the use of the metaphor of the yoke. The yoke was used to hitch up draught animals for a wagon or a plough (both are equally difficult to pull); the yoke thus illustrates the inevitability as well as the burden.[4]

[12:5-11] The decision about the demand is first postponed so that Rehoboam can seek advice on the matter in v. 5. The council (vv. 6-11) forms the main part of the whole narrative in which the future of kingship and of the state are decided. This part consists mostly of direct speech in which the advice of the older men is opposed to the opinion of the younger ones. The inexperienced hotheads are the decisive force. Rehoboam is exonerated but he is not freed from responsibility. Since he follows the advice of the young he is placed in the group of those who lack experience in life and therefore wisdom. The elders are explicitly introduced as counselors of Solomon. It is their advice to ease the forced labor for the sake of maintaining the unity of the kingdom. The young ones, on the other hand, plead to impose the royal will and claim to power. Their position is stressed by a proverb that uses vulgar imagery and is intended to stress their self-confidence: my little (finger) is thicker than my father's loins. The loins are a euphemistic circumscription for the penis, which manifests the

---

[3] Ibid., 1:150.
[4] See Gustaf Dalman, *Arbeit und Sitte in Palästina* (Gütersloh: Bertelsmann, 1932), 2:93–105.

might of the loins. The comparison opposes the little finger of the hand with the penis of the father and thus taunts him. Moreover, the comparison emphasizes the superiority of the speaker while putting down the self-esteem of the addressee. The proverb thus serves as an expression of superciliousness. In comparing virility, one's own potency is praised while that of the opponent is ridiculed. This blind confidence in one's own power is opposed to the balanced advice of the elders. Thus it is demonstrated that lack of reason, lack of experience, and ruthless use of power will inevitably lead to disaster.

[12:12-15] The answer of the king after three days does not ease the forced labor but instead promises its aggravation. The comparison that is used could have originated from colloquial speech. The whip consisted of several narrow strips of leather attached to a grip and was used to drive cattle or working slaves. The contrast implied in the metaphor "to discipline you with scorpions" means an intensification, since the sting of a scorpion is very painful. A lash from a whip may leave a painful wound, but the sting of a scorpion is even more painful. To answer the request of the people to ease the forced labor by promising its increase is contrary to all human forms of behavior and can only be described as folly. The arrogant answer of Rehoboam destroys every prospect to continue the reign over the northern tribes. According to the narrative Rehoboam is responsible for the failure of the united monarchy.

[12:16] The reaction of the people is unambiguous and is expressed by a proverb of two double lines. A similar form of this proverb is found as the unifying motto during Sheba's rebellion, where it serves as the succinct formula for the northern tribes in opposition to the Davidic dynasty. The circumstances of the northern tribes differ: there is no kinship tie to David and his house, thus the northern tribes are not obliged to be loyal and faithful to the Davidic monarchy. The cry "To your tents, O Israel" probably takes up an old formula that was used to release the army from their camp to return back home.[5] The last statement, "Look now to your own house, O David," is even more explicit: from now on, the Davidic dynasty is limited to Judah; a later gloss emphasizes this again in v. 20b. The whole proverb assumes that a tendency to move away from the Davidic dynasty existed among the northern tribes from very early on during the monarchic period. The narrator uses an older proverb to shape his material. The foolish behavior of Rehoboam is made to trigger a development already in progress. The northern tribes were not rooted in the united monarchy, despite the long reign of David and Solomon; thus they used the change from one king to another to realize their long desired independence. By using the proverb in v. 16 the narrator incorporates the element of a general existing tension between north and south into his description of the events.

---

[5] See Albrecht Alt, "Zelte und Hütten," in idem, *Kleine Schriften zur Geschichte des Volkes Israel* (Munich: Beck, 1959), 3:240 [233–42].

[12:18-19] The events take their expected course. As if he wanted to exceed his folly, Rehoboam sends the taskmaster over the forced labor to deal with the conflict. His attempt to push through his claim to power had to fail in light of the heated atmosphere. The people exercise their power and stone Adoram to death. This is a pitiful end for a faithful servant to the kingship. Rehoboam on the other hand managed to save his life and his kingship over Judah. The chariot helps the endangered king to make a quick escape. The final clause of v. 19 summarizes the event from a Judaic perspective. The separation of the northern tribes from the Davidic dynasty results in a final rift and in the parallel existence of two nations.

[12:20] Verse 20a continues the events already mentioned in v. 2: as a countermove Jeroboam is proclaimed king over the northern tribes. Further details about the process are not mentioned. The narrative stresses only that all the decisions and actions are done by the people who elect a new king to rule over them after Solomon's successor refused to give in to their rightful demand to ease the forced labor. The narrator portrayed these events as a logical result and uses the unbearable conditions of the forced labor and the inexperience of Rehoboam as an explanation.

However, another reason for the division seems to lurk behind the term used by the narrator in v. 16. The Davidic monarchy never had the strong support needed among the northern tribes to ensure the continuation of its kingship. Since a personal union held the empire together, the unbridgeable differences between the two parts must have resulted sooner or later in a division of both parts.[6] The narrator attempted to evaluate the reasons for the failure. It is not the institution of kingship that is at fault; rather the motive for the failure has to be seen in the old rivalry between the northern tribes and Judah—a rivalry that was felt strongly, even after the reign of two kings, so that it made the development toward a separate kingship for the northern tribes inevitable.

[12:21-24] The short narrative on the prevention of the war between the brothers Israel and Judah is a late piece. This impression is confirmed by the fact that the decision about the historical reality is made by a word of God that is announced by a prophet. Shemaiah, the man of God, is not mentioned again in the Deuteronomistic History; only the Chronicler attributes further words to him and presents him as a court prophet of Rehoboam (see 2 Chr 12:5-8). It is hardly possible to secure the historicity of this person. Just as in the addition in 1 Kgs 11:29-30, the course of history is seen as the will of God, who nevertheless remains hidden. King and people just carry out the divine counsel.

There is likely an older tradition behind the narrative, containing a report of a war of Rehoboam to win back the kingship. The details mentioned are sparse, the

---

[6] See Albrecht Alt, "The Monarchy in Israel and Judah," in idem, *Essays on Old Testament History and Religion,* trans. R. A. Wilson (Oxford: Blackwell, 1966), 239–59.

number of the mustered men is exaggerated. We know of wars between the two kingdoms during the period of the monarchy especially over the possession of the tribal area of Benjamin and therefore over the course of the border, but an attempt to restore the united monarchy is not attested. The passage considers the division of the monarchy finished. Since the decision corresponds to God's will, humankind is not allowed to try and nullify the division. The narrative in vv. 21-24 legitimizes the division as an act of God. The later author moves beyond all previous explanations by rooting the events in the will of God.

[12:25] The notice on the building of the two capitals does not stem from royal annals but simply uses a common tradition that could have been handed down orally. The verse mentions only the two cities of Shechem and Penuel but does not provide any details about the building projects or decoration of the cities chosen as seats of government. Shechem was situated at Tell Balāṭa east of today's Nablus, ancient Neapolis, in the valley between Mounts Ebal and Gerizim. According to archaeological evidence the city was founded in the Middle Bronze Age IIa (1950–1750 BCE) but destroyed in the twelfth century and not rebuilt, which means that it was deserted for two centuries. Only during the tenth century do we find new traces of settlements (stratum X), and during the last quarter of the tenth century the city is repopulated and fortified.[7] Stratum IX can probably be connected with the building of the city by Jeroboam; further details on the buildings and the fortifications have not yet been published. Penuel was situated in the East Jordan on the lower reaches of the Jabbok (see Gen 32:32; Judg 8:8, 9, 17). Its exact place has not yet been determined, but the identification with Tell dēr ʿAllā proposed by André Lemaire is quite likely, since it was populated from Late Bronze II until the end of the Iron Age.[8]

The note is incomplete in that the residence is moved to Tirzah, where it remained until the foundation of Samaria by Omri (see 1 Kgs 14:17). The reasons for the double move of the capital are not known. It seems that none of the newly founded cities in the realm of the northern tribes in the tenth century was able to house a royal court for a long period. It becomes apparent that Jeroboam wanted to place his capital either in the region of the middle Palestinian hill country or in the neighboring Jordan Valley and not to move it to the fringes. This absence of a tie to one city only is contrasted by his attempt to create lasting cultic traditions through the foundation of royal sanctuaries.

---

[7] See G. Ernest Wright, *Shechem: The Biography of a Biblical City* (New York: McGraw-Hill, 1965).

[8] André Lemaire, "Galaad et Makir: Remarques sur le tribu de Manasse à l'est du Jourdain," *VT* 31 (1981) 50–52 [39–61].

The Cultic Measures of Jeroboam

Text

12:26 Then Jeroboam said to himself, "Now the kingdom may well revert to the house of David. 27 If this people continues to go up to offer sacrifices in the house of the LORD at Jerusalem, the heart of this people will turn again to their master, King Rehoboam of Judah; they will kill me and return to King Rehoboam of Judah." 28 So the king took counsel, and made two calves of gold. He said to the people, "You have gone up to Jerusalem long enough. Here are your gods, O Israel, who brought you up out of the land of Egypt." 29 He set one in Bethel, and the other he put in Dan. 30 And this thing became a sin, for the people went to worship before the one at Bethel and before the other as far as Dan. 31 He also made houses on high places, and appointed priests from among all the people, who were not Levites. 32 Jeroboam appointed a festival on the fifteenth day of the eighth month like the festival that was in Judah, and he offered sacrifices on the altar; so he did in Bethel, sacrificing to the calves that he had made. And he placed in Bethel the priests of the high places that he had made. 33 He went up to the altar that he had made in Bethel on the fifteenth day in the eighth month, in the month that he alone had devised; he appointed a festival for the people of Israel, and he went up to the altar to offer incense.

Analysis

The Deuteronomistic Historian probably wrote the section on cultic measures, but it is not a unity. Verse 30b looks like an addition to the first narrative, vv. 26-30, so that this piece came to an end with v. 30a. To the basic layer describing the erection of bulls in Bethel and Dan (vv. 26-30a) further comments on the illegitimate cultic practice were added in vv. 31-32; furthermore, v. 33 serves as a redactional bridge to the narrative following in 13:1-34 about the man of God from Judah in Bethel.

Commentary

[12:26-30] The erection of the two bulls is seen as the fundamental transgression of Israel that will lead eventually to the destruction of the state. For Deuteronomistic

146

theology, the exclusive worship at the cultic center chosen by God (Deuteronomy 12) is the standard by which the new sanctuaries at Bethel and Dan are condemned. According to this theology, one can worship Yahweh only at the temple in Jerusalem because this place alone represents his presence on earth (see 1 Kgs 8:12-13). From the standpoint that one is allowed to sacrifice exclusively in Jerusalem, all other sanctuaries have to be seen as illegitimate and must be condemned. The Deuteronomistic Historian emphasizes this condemnation when he mentions the foundation of the sanctuaries by Jeroboam.

According to Amos 7:13 the cultic places in Bethel and Dan were royal sanctuaries. Existing cultic places were most likely transformed into temples of the kingdom so that one need not assume any rebuilding by Jeroboam. Their furnishing with bulls cannot be verified, but these bulls were most probably pedestals that, like the cherubim in the temple of Jerusalem, manifested the presence of the invisible Godhead. Also, these two bulls cannot be separated from the bull in the narrative of Exodus 32, which describes the manufacture of such bulls (or calves) by Aaron during the stay at Mount Sinai. This narrative is probably based on a tradition that traces the bulls in Bethel back to Aaron and thereby legitimizes them. In any case, bull and narrative seem to belong together in a way that cannot be determined any longer; the negative judgment of this cultic object relies on Deuteronomistic theology and its orientation to the temple of Jerusalem. Although the cultic centers of the northern kingdom are most likely older than the temple of Solomon, they are condemned from the outset since the existence of another temple next to the place chosen by God himself in Jerusalem is thought impossible. Despite extensive archaeological excavations, the sanctuaries in Bethel and Dan have not yet been found. The temple in Bethel (Bētīn) stood probably at a place that has not been excavated.[1] The area labeled "holy district" in Dan (Tell el-Qāḍi) did not possess any cultic function in pre-Hellenistic times and was probably an extensive palace.[2]

[12:31-32] The additions continue to pile up and intensify the reproaches. Judged by the absolute claim of the Jerusalem temple, every cultic place in the north and every form of cultic practice has to be denounced as unlawful or illegitimate. The use of the term "high place" already disqualifies the cultic institution. In addition, even the attempt to fix the cultic calendar in accordance with the pilgrimage festivals in Jerusalem is regarded as an unlawful intervention in the only valid cultic order as manifested in Jerusalem. Judged by the standard applied to Jerusalem, every form of cultic practice in Israel has to be seen as a royal presumption.

---

[1] See James L. Kelso, *The Excavation of Bethel (1934–1960)*, ASOR Annual 39 (Cambridge: American Schools of Oriental Research, 1968).

[2] Differently, Avraham Biran, *Biblical Dan* (Jerusalem: Israel Exploration Society, 1994), 147–233.

The Man of God from Judah

Text

13:1 While Jeroboam was standing by the altar to offer incense, a man of God came out of Judah by the word of the LORD to Bethel 2 and proclaimed against the altar by the word of the LORD, and said, "O altar, altar, thus says the LORD: 'A son shall be born to the house of David, Josiah by name; and he shall sacrifice on you the priests of the high places who offer incense on you, and human bones shall be burned on you.'" 3 He gave a sign the same day, saying, "This is the sign that the LORD has spoken: 'The altar shall be torn down, and the ashes that are on it shall be poured out.'" 4 When the king heard what the man of God cried out against the altar at Bethel, Jeroboam stretched out his hand from the altar, saying, "Seize him!" But the hand that he stretched out against him withered so that he could not draw it back to himself. 5 The altar also was torn down, and the ashes poured out from the altar, according to the sign that the man of God had given by the word of the LORD. 6 The king said to the man of God, "Entreat now the favor of the LORD your God, and pray for me, so that my hand may be restored to me." So the man of God entreated the LORD; and the king's hand was restored to him, and became as it was before. 7 Then the king said to the man of God, "Come home with me and dine, and I will give you a gift." 8 But the man of God said to the king, "If you give me half your kingdom, I will not go in with you; nor will I eat food or drink water in this place. 9 For thus I was commanded by the word of the LORD: You shall not eat food, or drink water, or return by the way that you came." 10 So he went another way, and did not return by the way that he had come to Bethel.

11 Now there lived an old prophet in Bethel. One of his sons came and told him all that the man of God had done that day in Bethel; the words also that he had spoken to the king, they told to their father. 12 Their father said to them, "Which way did he go?" And his sons showed him the way that the man of God who came from Judah had gone. 13 Then he said to his sons, "Saddle a donkey for me." So they saddled a donkey for him, and he

148

mounted it. 14 He went after the man of God, and found him sitting under an oak tree. He said to him, "Are you the man of God who came from Judah?" He answered, "I am." 15 Then he said to him, "Come home with me and eat some food." 16 But he said, "I cannot return with you, or go in with you; nor will I eat food or drink water with you in this place; 17 for it was said to me by the word of the LORD: You shall not eat food or drink water there, or return by the way that you came." 18 Then the other said to him, "I also am a prophet as you are, and an angel spoke to me by the word of the LORD: Bring him back with you into your house so that he may eat food and drink water." But he was deceiving him. 19 Then the man of God went back with him, and ate food and drank water in his house.

20 As they were sitting at the table, the word of the LORD came to the prophet who had brought him back; 21 and he proclaimed to the man of God who came from Judah, "Thus says the LORD: Because you have disobeyed the word of the LORD, and have not kept the commandment that the LORD your God commanded you, 22 but have come back and have eaten food and drunk water in the place of which he said to you, 'Eat no food, and drink no water,' your body shall not come to your ancestral tomb." 23 After the man of God had eaten food and had drunk, they saddled for him a donkey belonging to the prophet who had brought him back. 24 Then as he went away, a lion met him on the road and killed him. His body was thrown in the road, and the donkey stood beside it; the lion also stood beside the body. 25 People passed by and saw the body thrown in the road, with the lion standing by the body. And they came and told it in the town where the old prophet lived.

26 When the prophet who had brought him back from the way heard of it, he said, "It is the man of God who disobeyed the word of the LORD; therefore the LORD has given him to the lion, which has torn him and killed him according to the word that the LORD spoke to him." 27 Then he said to his sons, "Saddle a donkey for me." So they saddled one, 28 and he went and found the body thrown in the road, with the donkey and the lion standing beside the body. The lion had not eaten the body or attacked the donkey. 29 The prophet took up the body of the man of God, laid it on the donkey, and brought it back to the city, to mourn and to bury him. 30 He laid the body in his own grave; and they mourned over him, saying, "Alas, my brother!" 31 After he had buried him, he said to his sons, "When I die, bury me in the grave in which the man of God is buried; lay my bones beside his bones. 32 For the saying that he proclaimed by the word of the LORD against the altar in Bethel, and against all the houses of the high places that are in the cities of Samaria, shall surely come to pass."

33 Even after this event Jeroboam did not turn from his evil way, but made priests for the high places again from among all the people; any who wanted to be priests he consecrated for the high places. 34 This matter became

sin to the house of Jeroboam, so as to cut it off and to destroy it from the face of the earth.

Analysis

The narrative of the man of God from Judah comes in two parts. The first one deals with a word against Jeroboam and with two miracles concerning the king (vv. 1-10). The second one reports the strange circumstances of the death of the man of God on his way from Bethel to Judah (vv. 11-31). Verse 32 is an addition, and vv. 33-34 are later supplements that deal again with the theme of the transgressions of Jeroboam. Both narratives are connected by the motif of the immediate return of the man of God to Judah; originally, however, they were independent narratives. Despite the independent meaning of the stories, the miracle is more important than the proclamation of the word.[1]

Commentary

[13:1-10] The first narrative, with its double miracle of the withered and subsequently healed hand, demonstrates the power of God over the king through his prophet. The introduction in v. 1 is quite short and mentions along with the two acting characters only the place where the events take place; the events are not placed in time. The starting point is the word of the man of God against the altar at Bethel in vv. 2-3 to which 2 Kgs 23:16 explicitly refers. Würthwein assumes correctly that the threat of the man of God was originally directed against the king himself; it was only the Deuteronomistic Historian who changed this older word of Yahweh in favor of a threat that will be fulfilled under Josiah.[2] The late v. 5 refers explicitly to this. The double miracle with which the man of God demonstrated that the power of God exceeds the power of the king was originally the center of the narrative in vv. 4, 6. The hand with which Jeroboam underscored his order to seize the man of God withers but is healed again after the king begs for it. No matter what the actual threat may have been, the man of God demonstrates with his miracle not only that Jeroboam is unable to do anything against him but also that the king is dependent on the will of God mediated by him.

The man of God appears as a miracle worker equipped with special powers; his sending and proclamation are supported by signs that exceed the humanly possible and thus they have to come from God. The man of God has to decline the offer of a reward in v. 7, since the execution of the divine will is tied to certain conditions in vv. 8-9.

Verse 10 concludes the narrative of the miracle on Jeroboam. In its current context the narrative shows the king's lack of understanding despite the fact that he had

---

[1] Würthwein, *Könige,* 1:169.
[2] Ibid.

experienced the power of God himself. At the same time Bethel is discredited as a cultic place, since the fate of its altar has already been announced in connection with the cultic actions of the king.

[13:11-31] The second narrative reports the death of the man of God and his burial at Bethel. Its center is not a miracle by the man of God, but a special event that is thought to originate in God. The narrative is uniform, but due to its incorporation into the Deuteronomistic History it was expanded by additions in vv. 16-18, 20-22, and 32.[3] Originally, it dealt only with the death and burial of a man of God from Judah at Bethel. The narrative has a tight plot. In v. 11 the introduction mentions all circumstances necessary for the further course of the narrative. The first scene, vv. 12-15, 19, deals with the hospitality shown to the man of God. The second scene, vv. 23-25, describes the death of the man of God under miraculous circumstances. The third scene, vv. 26aα, 27-30, portrays the burial of the dead man by the prophet at Bethel. A decree by the prophet about his own burial in the same grave concludes the story (v. 31).

The narrative presupposes the existence of the grave of an anonymous man of God in the vicinity of the city that can be traced back to the fulfillment of a human duty by a prophet from Bethel. That he himself is buried in the same grave assumes the tradition of a burial of two prophetic figures in one grave at Bethel. This strange circumstance of the burial of two prophets in one grave is explained by the story of the strange death of the man of God by a lion on his way home to Judah. The center of the narrative is the surprising fact that the lion killed the man but did not eat him. This exceptional behavior of the animal is used to explain the special holiness of the man of God that leads to his burial in a foreign land and the special honor attached to his grave. The corpse possesses a special dignity, because the lion has not touched it; the lion reveals the special status of the man of God and so he is buried by the prophet in his own grave and lamented by him. Since the prophet decreed that his own burial be in the same grave, this grave shown near Bethel that contained two holy men from the north and south became a symbol for the community of the prophets of Israel and Judah.[4]

[13:16-18, 20-22] The Deuteronomistic Historian used this narrative connected with a grave in the vicinity of Bethel and reshaped it by making several additions. The center is now the ban by God on the return and the taking of food or drink. In his actions the man of God ignored the ban of God, and he is punished for his lack of obedience when he is killed by a lion. The additions fundamentally change the intention of the narrative; now, the story confirms the unconditional validity of the divine order. Its violation by the man of God is punished by death. The special behavior of the lion no

---

[3] Ibid., 171.
[4] Ibid., 170.

longer proves the special status of the man of God, but simply demonstrates that it is according to the will of God.

[13:32] The addition in v. 32 takes up again the threat of vv. 2-3. All in all the Deuteronomistic Historian reshaped the narrative according to his understanding of the word of God; here he uses the stipulation for the behavior given in vv. 8-9. The narrative thus serves as an explanation for the unconditional validity of a command given by God; the result of disobedience is reported in a drastic way. The lion executes God's punishment of the man of God because of his disobedience; this view of the events is added in v. 26aβb. The original aim of a double burial of the two prophets is pushed back in favor of the connection between the strange death of the man of God from Judah and his disobedience. The additions of the Deuteronomistic Historian do not change the course of the narrative, but they transform its intention.

[13:33-34] The redactional additions refer again to the sin of Jeroboam that consists in the erection of new sanctuaries in the northern kingdom. These measures show the turning away from the only legitimate cultic place: the temple in Jerusalem.

The Prophet Ahijah of Shiloh

Text

14:1 At that time Abijah son of Jeroboam fell sick. 2 Jeroboam said to his wife, "Go, disguise yourself, so that it will not be known that you are the wife of Jeroboam, and go to Shiloh; for the prophet Ahijah is there, who said of me that I should be king over this people. 3 Take with you ten loaves, some cakes, and a jar of honey, and go to him; he will tell you what shall happen to the child."

4 Jeroboam's wife did so; she set out and went to Shiloh, and came to the house of Ahijah. Now Ahijah could not see, for his eyes were dim because of his age. 5 But the LORD said to Ahijah, "The wife of Jeroboam is coming to inquire of you concerning her son; for he is sick. Thus and thus you shall say to her."

When she came, she pretended to be another woman. 6 But when Ahijah heard the sound of her feet, as she came in at the door, he said, "Come in, wife of Jeroboam; why do you pretend to be another? For I am charged with heavy tidings for you. 7 Go, tell Jeroboam, 'Thus says the LORD, the God of Israel: Because I exalted you from among the people, made you leader over my people Israel, 8 and tore the kingdom away from the house of David to give it to you; yet you have not been like my servant David, who kept my commandments and followed me with all his heart, doing only that which was right in my sight, 9 but you have done evil above all those who were before you and have gone and made for yourself other gods, and cast images, provoking me to anger, and have thrust me behind your back; 10 therefore, I will bring evil upon the house of Jeroboam. I will cut off from Jeroboam every male, both bond and free in Israel, and will consume the house of Jeroboam, just as one burns up dung until it is all gone. 11 Anyone belonging to Jeroboam who dies in the city, the dogs shall eat; and anyone who dies in the open country, the birds of the air shall eat; for the LORD has spoken.' 12 Therefore set out, go to your house. When your feet enter the city, the child shall die. 13 All Israel shall mourn for him and bury him; for he alone of Jeroboam's family shall come to the grave, because in him there is found something pleasing to the LORD, the God of Israel, in the house of Jeroboam. 14 Moreover the LORD will raise up for himself a king over Israel, who shall cut off the house of Jeroboam today, even right now!

15 "The LORD will strike Israel, as a reed is shaken in the water; he will root up Israel out of this good land that he gave to their ancestors, and scatter them beyond the Euphrates, because they have made their sacred poles, provoking the LORD to anger. 16 He will give Israel up because of the sins of Jeroboam, which he sinned and which he caused Israel to commit."

17 Then Jeroboam's wife got up and went away, and she came to Tirzah. As she came to the threshold of the house, the child died. 18 All Israel buried him and mourned for him, according to the word of the LORD, which he spoke by his servant the prophet Ahijah.

Analysis

An old prophetic narrative that has been heavily expanded by Deuteronomistic additions in vv. 7-11 and vv. 13aβb, 14-16 forms the basis of the section. The narrative was originally concerned with the announcement of the death of Jeroboam's son by Ahijah of Shiloh (vv. 1-6, 12-13aα, 17, 18); only with the expansions is a judgment on the house of Jeroboam added. These additions are not all from the same Deuteronomistic author.[1] The speech of reproof in vv. 7-8a, 9, and the word of threat in vv. 10-11, which announces the downfall of the house of Jeroboam, seem to form a unity. In contrast, v. 14 refers ahead to Baasha, Jeroboam's successor, while v. 15 points to the destruction of Israel and its deportation.

The original narrative is closely connected with the person of Ahijah and probably originated in Shiloh. Ahijah belonged to that group of early prophets who were visited to receive mediation of the divine will and who were also able to perform miracles. First Kings 11:29-39 attributes the designation of Jeroboam as king to Ahijah of Shiloh, who mediated the divine will. Just like other men of God, Ahijah is not only asked about the future; rather, the vision of a powerful word implies hope that a word of God will make the matter of the inquiry as a whole turn out well, manifesting that God himself intervenes in the events. In premonarchic times Shiloh was an important place, because the local sanctuary contained the ark, the old tribal symbol, before this cultic item was transferred to Jerusalem (cf. 1 Samuel 1–4 and 2 Samuel 6). So far, archaeological excavations have established proof of an Early Iron Age settlement but could not yield information about the old cultic place.[2]

---

[1] See Walter Dietrich, *Prophetie und Geschichte: Eine redaktionsgeschichtliche Untersuchung zum deuteronomistichen Geschichtswerk*, FRLANT 108 (Göttingen: Vandenhoeck &Ruprecht, 1972), 51ff.

[2] See Israel Finkelstein, ed., *Shiloh: The Archaeology of a Biblical Site* (Tel Aviv: Institute of

The narrative clearly shows the high standing of the prophet as the person who proclaims the will of God. The blindness of Ahijah, due to old age and the disguise of the wife of Jeroboam, underscores that his words are the result of divine intuition. Since both motifs seem to cancel each other out, one can assume that a later redactor added one of them. Despite that, the narrative moves straight toward its climax of the oracle concerning the death of the ill royal son, Abijah. A reason for his death is not given: God determines life and death and the human person cannot question that. The death of the child remains mysterious and is connected with the sin of the house of Jeroboam only at a later stage (v. 13aβb). The Deuteronomistic authors have used this narrative, which did not contain any negative judgment on Jeroboam, to express their rejection of Israelite kingship and to demonstrate its consequences.

Commentary

[14:1] This verse is rather concise: place and time, as well as the age and social position of the child, are not mentioned. Despite the fact that the fate of a royal son always concerned the succession, this narrative shows above all the exemplary behavior of Jeroboam and his wife, both of whom are concerned about the welfare and health of their child.

[14:2-3, 5-6] The narrative commences with the order Jeroboam gives to the mother of the child. Her mission is to clarify the fate of the son; this seems to imply a long-term illness. That she takes food for Ahijah shows that such a gift was common. The disguise of the otherwise anonymous queen would make her look like any common woman so that the inquiry will be free from any bias. The additional v. 5 stresses that Ahijah receives his knowledge from God. Despite his blindness, Ahijah recognizes the wife of Jeroboam because of his visionary ability, and he stresses the futility of her disguise, which cannot fool a prophet (v. 6). Although the motifs of disguise and blindness are mutually exclusive, they are used here to enforce the reliability of the divine message.[3]

[14:12] The word of doom is uttered; all further hope will be in vain—the son will die and the mother herself will become the messenger of death. She is condemned to carry death into the house, since the son will die the moment she returns.[4] The narrative contains a tragic element: with its announcement the tragic message is fulfilled.

[14:13] The further prophecy in v. 13aα is difficult to understand. The burial with its rites of mourning will be a public rather than a private affair. The rites of mourning

---

Archaeology of Tel Aviv University, 1993). See also Donald G. Schley, *Shiloh: A Biblical City in Tradition and History,* JSOTSup 63 (Sheffield: JSOT Press, 1989).

[3] Würthwein, *Könige,* 1:175.

[4] Ibid., 176.

express the pain of the loss of a person and consist of lamentation, tearing garments, putting ash on the head, and wearing special clothes. The extent of the dirge can only show the extraordinary loss. A royal son is always a person on whom hopes have been pinned, and the participation of all of Israel in the mourning demonstrates the dimension of this untimely death that concerns the state as a whole. The narrative assumes an untroubled relationship between the royal household and the people.

[14:17-18] The end of the narrative reports the fulfillment of the announced events; here the fulfillment of the word, spoken by the prophet, is stressed explicitly. The return to Tirzah presumes that the royal residence had been moved there in the meantime (see 1 Kgs 12:25).

[14:7-8a, 9] The reproof speech mentions again the reproach of the carving of images of foreign gods. This accusation of forsaking Yahweh refers back to 12:26-30a, where the author regards the erection of the bulls at Bethel and Dan as a sin.

[14:8b] The further addition of v. 8b intensifies this reproach by contrasting the transgression of the king chosen by God with the exemplary behavior of David. Judged by the Deuteronomistic standards of centralization of the cult in Jerusalem, Jeroboam did not fulfill the expectations as a king chosen by God.

[14:10-11] The word of threat thus announces the destruction of the royal family in no uncertain terms. The common practice of killing all male members of a family to wipe out any claim to the throne is in this case traced back to the will of God. The turning away from Yahweh is punished by the destruction of the royal family as a whole.

[14:14] This verse announces a new king who will replace the dynasty of Jeroboam. Baasha seizes the kingship in a revolt against Nadab, the son of and successor to Jeroboam, only two years after Jeroboam's death (see 15:27-28).

[14:15-16] The addition of vv. 15-16 foresees the downfall of the state following the Assyrian conquest and the deportation of the upper classes after the fall of Samaria. The fate of the northern kingdom is linked to the sin of Jeroboam, manifested in idolatry. The sacred poles or asherahs mentioned were wooden poles representing the goddess Asherah, who appears in Canaanite mythology not only as the consort of the fertility-god Baal but also as a guarantor and maintainer of fertility herself. The asherahs were thus a visible sign of the widespread fertility cult that stood in opposition to the universal claim of Yahweh as the lord of life.[5]

---

[5] On Asherah and asherahs see Johannes C. de Moor, "Asherah," in *TDOT*, 1:438–44; Hartmut Gese, in idem, Maria Höpfer, and Kurt Rudolph, *Die Religionen Altsyriens, Altarabiens und der Mandäer*, Die Religionen der Menschheit 10/2 (Stuttgart: Kohlhammer, 1970), 149–55. See also John Day, "Asherah," in *ABD*, 1:483–87; Susan Ackerman, "The Queen Mother and the Cult in Ancient Israel," *JBL* 112 (1993) 385–401; Nicholas Wyatt, "Asherah," in *DDD²*, 99–105; Judith M. Hadley, "Yahweh and 'His Asherah': Archaeological and Textual Evidence for the Cult of the Goddess," in *Ein Gott Allein?* ed. Walter Dietrich and Martin Klopfenstein, OBO 139 (Göttingen: Vandenhoeck & Ruprecht, 1994), 235–68.

Concluding Formula: Jeroboam

Text

14:19 Now the rest of the acts of Jeroboam, how he warred and how he reigned, are written in the Book of the Annals of the Kings of Israel. 20 The time that Jeroboam reigned was twenty-two years; then he slept with his ancestors, and his son Nadab succeeded him.

Analysis

The concluding formula for Jeroboam deviates from the standard pattern in that it mentions the duration of his reign. The reason for this deviation is that we lack his introductory formula and that it was difficult to fit the information in the narrative of his accession to the throne in 1 Kgs 12:1-25. The added narratives in chaps. 13 and 14, however, demanded a particular statement of the end of the reign of Jeroboam, according to the standard formula.

Commentary

[14:19-20] The "Book of the Annals of the Kings of Israel" is hardly a record in the form of annals kept at the court, of which the books of Kings did not have any knowledge. Rather, the reference has to be regarded as fictitious; it was used to fake extensive source material for the depiction of the period of the monarchy. Such a *Vorlage* for the work of the Deuteronomistic Historian never existed, but he was nevertheless able to use narratives and notices that were already fixed in written form. The extent and content of this pre-Deuteronomistic tradition can no longer be determined. All in all we can assume that the Deuteronomistic Historian was confronted with scarce source material rather than a plethora of it. In view of the scarcity of his depiction one cannot assume that the author of the Deuteronomistic History had access to concrete historical reports that he did not use or incorporate.

The place of burial is not mentioned, but one can assume that the family grave was located in the vicinity of Tirzah. Royal graves were not marked specifically and probably corresponded to the rock tombs common during the monarchic period. Nadab is introduced as son and successor only in 15:25-32, since the reign of the parallel kings Rehoboam, Abijam, and Asa of Judah had to be dealt with first (14:21-31; 15:1-8; 15:9-24).

Rehoboam of Judah

Text

14:21 Now Rehoboam son of Solomon reigned in Judah. Rehoboam was forty-one years old when he began to reign, and he reigned seventeen years in Jerusalem, the city that the LORD had chosen out of all the tribes of Israel, to put his name there. His mother's name was Naamah the Ammonite. 22 Judah did what was evil in the sight of the LORD; they provoked him to jealousy with their sins that they committed, more than all that their ancestors had done. 23 For they also built for themselves high places, pillars, and sacred poles on every high hill and under every green tree; 24 there were also male temple prostitutes in the land. They committed all the abominations of the nations that the LORD drove out before the people of Israel.

25 In the fifth year of King Rehoboam, King Shishak of Egypt came up against Jerusalem; 26 he took away the treasures of the house of the LORD and the treasures of the king's house; he took everything. He also took away all the shields of gold that Solomon had made; 27 so King Rehoboam made shields of bronze instead, and committed them to the hands of the officers of the guard, who kept the door of the king's house. 28 As often as the king went into the house of the LORD, the guard carried them and brought them back to the guardroom.

29 Now the rest of the acts of Rehoboam, and all that he did, are they not written in the Book of the Annals of the Kings of Judah? 30 There was war between Rehoboam and Jeroboam continually. 31 Rehoboam slept with his ancestors and was buried with his ancestors in the city of David. His mother's name was Naamah the Ammonite. His son Abijam succeeded him.

Analysis

The paragraph on Rehoboam is very concise and, along with the introductory formula (vv. 21-24) and the concluding formula (vv. 29-31), features only a report on the consequences of the campaign of Shishak (vv. 25-28).

Commentary

[14:21-24] The introductory formula, which occurs here for the first time, has the following elements:

- synchronic date of the beginning of his reign
- age of the king
- duration of his reign
- place of residence
- name of the king's mother
- evaluation of his piety

For the kings of the northern kingdom, their age and the name of the mother are generally missing. It is most likely that notices on the age of the Israelite kings did not exist and that there was no such office as the mother of the king. There is no synchronic date for Rehoboam, since the northern kingdom was established only after his accession to the throne. Age and duration of reign were probably recorded in lists. The mention of Jerusalem as the place of residence has been expanded by a reference to the election by Yahweh. This comment is used by the Deuteronomistic Historian to demonstrate the special preference of Jerusalem over every other Israelite residence.[1]

The queen mother, impartially called an Ammonite here, occupied an important place in the Davidic dynasty; in contrast to the wives of the king, she occupied a special position, which is also emphasized by the title "mistress" (see 15:13; 2 Kgs 10:13; Jer 13:18; 29:2). The office was probably connected with special rights and duties that are not known. In any case, she had to be present during official royal functions, and her person guaranteed the dynastic succession. The office is also known from neighboring cultures and was probably taken over from them, together with the main elements of the royal protocol for the court in Jerusalem.

The judgment on Rehoboam is—as usual for most of the kings of Judah and all of the kings of Israel—a negative one. The standard for the assessment of piety is the attitude of the king toward the central sanctuary in Jerusalem. Every single actual or hypothetical deviation from the Deuteronomic demand to regard Jerusalem as the only legitimate place for the worship of Yahweh leads to a negative judgment of the king in question. The accusations leveled against Rehoboam are of a general kind and are not specified any further: all places outside Jerusalem are "high places," since they are illegitimate according to Deuteronomic-Deuteronomistic theology. The "pillars" were erect stones that were worshiped, since they were understood as symbols of the deity, possessing numinous force. "Sacred poles" or asherahs are wooden poles representing the goddess Asherah in connection with special practices of the fertility cult. All three cultic items or institutions are often mentioned together and con-

---

[1] Würthwein, *Könige,* 1:181.

demned as not befitting the cult of Yahweh (see Lev 21:1; Deut 16:22; 2 Kgs 3:2; 10:27; 18:4; 23:14; Hos 10:2; Mic 5:12). The phrase "on every high hill and under every green tree" is fairly stereotypical (see Deut 12:2; Jer 2:20; Hos 4:14). Behind it stands the practice that worship often happened on hilltops and under trees since the deity was thought to be especially close there.

The "sanctified ones" (NRSV "temple prostitutes") are often connected with cultic prostitution, but there are no signs of sexual acts committed at cultic places in Israel. Rather one should think of the segregation of certain people for a deity; this would contradict the common thought of a life fulfilled by producing offspring. It is currently impossible to determine the character of the group any further; in any case, the custom of cult prostitution at a sanctuary is not attested—in contrast to normal prostitution, which was practiced in Israel.

[14:25-28] The emphasis of the report on the campaign of Pharaoh Shishak is on its consequences for the royal protocol. The shields made by Solomon are lost and brought to Egypt either as tribute or as booty. In consequence, the officers of the guard who accompany the king during official engagements are equipped with less valuable bronze shields. Both shields were ceremonial items that emphasize military strength during public appearances of the king. The feature mentioned here gives an impression how the appearance of the king was—in analogy to other royal courts—exalted by splendor.

The pharaoh mentioned was the founder of the Twenty-second Dynasty. His military campaign against the territories on both sides of the Jordan seems to have been an attempt to reestablish Egyptian rule over this land as it had existed during the time of the New Kingdom. The enterprise is attested by a long list of place names inscribed on the so-called Bubastide portal of the temple of Karnak. According to this list, Shishak crossed the Negev and the northern kingdom but did not enter the Judean mainland. This seems to indicate that Rehoboam paid tribute to avoid a conquest. The campaign of Shishak can be verified by an extrabiblical source, but as far as further details are concerned we learn from this list only of the places that were destroyed. Although it is not possible to identify all the names, we are able to reconstruct the course of the campaign.[2] The list of cities fortified by Rehoboam mentioned in 2 Chr 11:5-12 does not belong to the same context and is probably of a later date.[3]

---

[2] See Martin Noth, *ABLAK*, 2:73–93; Benjamin Mazar, "The Campaign of Pharaoh Shishak to Palestine," in *Volume du Congres: Strasbourg, 1956,* VTSup 4 (Leiden: Brill, 1957), 57–66; Kenneth A. Kitchen, *The Third Intermediate Period in Egypt* (Warminster: Aris and Phillips, 1973), 293–300.

[3] See Volkmar Fritz, "The 'List of Rehoboam's Fortresses' in 2 Chr 11:5-12—A Document from the Time of Josiah," *ErIsr* 15 (1981) 46*–57*; Nadav Na'aman, "Hezekiah's Fortified Cities and the LMLK Stamps," *BASOR* 261 (1986) 5–21.

[14:29-31] Along with the standard reference to the Annals of the Kings of Judah, the common note on the death and burial, and the mention of the successor, the concluding formula contains a notice on the continuing war between both states. A similar remark is found in 15:7, 16, 32; the notice was probably written by the Deuteronomistic Historian to emphasize the tension between the two states. However, there was no attempt in the course of history to reestablish the unity of the monarchy by a war; the conflict was most likely limited to incidents at the border.

Abijam of Judah

Text

15:1 Now in the eighteenth year of King Jeroboam son of Nebat, Abijam began to reign over Judah. 2 He reigned for three years in Jerusalem. His mother's name was Maacah daughter of Abishalom. 3 He committed all the sins that his father did before him; his heart was not true to the LORD his God, like the heart of his father David. 4 Nevertheless for David's sake the LORD his God gave him a lamp in Jerusalem, setting up his son after him, and establishing Jerusalem; 5 because David did what was right in the sight of the LORD, and did not turn aside from anything that he commanded him all the days of his life, except in the matter of Uriah the Hittite. 6 The war begun between Rehoboam and Jeroboam continued all the days of his life. 7 The rest of the acts of Abijam, and all that he did, are they not written in the Book of the Annals of the Kings of Judah? There was war between Abijam and Jeroboam. 8 Abijam slept with his ancestors, and they buried him in the city of David. Then his son Asa succeeded him.

Commentary

[15:1-8] Next to the information contained in the standard scheme, no further details on the short reign of Abijam are given. Only the praise for David, who, as the founder of the dynasty, sets the standard for all his successors, is interpolated between introductory and concluding formulas. The synchronic list of kings commences with Abijam, that is, the beginning of the reign of a king is dated according to the reign of the king of the neighboring state. Here the years of reign are counted from the New Year in the fall, but in such a way that the months from the death of the predecessor until the New Year were counted as the first year (so called predating) and from the New Year onward as the second year of the new reign.[1]

In view of this chronology the date for Abijam contains a discrepancy that cannot be removed: the seventeen years of the reign of Rehoboam (14:21) cannot be rec-

---

[1] Würthwein, *Könige,* 1:185.

onciled with the eighteenth year of Jeroboam, since both kings came to the throne at roughly the same time (see 12:1-25). The judgment on Abijam is clearly negative.

The concluding formula contains again the notice on the continuing war, which according to the Deuteronomistic Historian came to an end only during the reign of Asa of Judah, when the tribal territory of Benjamin was conquered by Judah (see 15:22). The meaning of the name is disputed; to take it as a nominal sentence, "(the god) Yamm is my father," is possible but cannot be verified. In the later tradition Abijam is changed to Abijah, "Yah (is) my father" (see 2 Chr 12:16; 13:1, 2, 4, 22, 23). The short reign of only three years is not explained.

Asa of Judah

Text

15:9 In the twentieth year of King Jeroboam of Israel, Asa began to reign over Judah; 10 he reigned forty-one years in Jerusalem. His mother's name was Maacah daughter of Abishalom. 11 Asa did what was right in the sight of the LORD, as his father David had done. 12 He put away the male temple prostitutes out of the land, and removed all the idols that his ancestors had made. 13 He also removed his mother Maacah from being queen mother, because she had made an abominable image for Asherah; Asa cut down her image and burned it at the Wadi Kidron. 14 But the high places were not taken away. Nevertheless the heart of Asa was true to the LORD all his days. 15 He brought into the house of the LORD the votive gifts of his father and his own votive gifts—silver, gold, and utensils.

16 There was war between Asa and King Baasha of Israel all their days. 17 King Baasha of Israel went up against Judah, and built Ramah, to prevent anyone from going out or coming in to King Asa of Judah. 18 Then Asa took all the silver and the gold that were left in the treasures of the house of the LORD and the treasures of the king's house, and gave them into the hands of his servants. King Asa sent them to King Ben-hadad son of Tabrimmon son of Hezion of Aram, who resided in Damascus, saying, 19 "Let there be an alliance between me and you, like that between my father and your father: I am sending you a present of silver and gold; go, break your alliance with King Baasha of Israel, so that he may withdraw from me." 20 Ben-hadad listened to King Asa, and sent the commanders of his armies against the cities of Israel. He conquered Ijon, Dan, Abel-beth-maacah, and all Chinneroth, with all the land of Naphtali. 21 When Baasha heard of it, he stopped building Ramah and lived in Tirzah. 22 Then King Asa made a proclamation to all Judah, none was exempt: they carried away the stones of Ramah and its timber, with which Baasha had been building; with them King Asa built Geba of Benjamin and Mizpah. 23 Now the rest of all the acts of Asa, all his power, all that he did, and the cities that he built,

are they not written in the Book of the Annals of the Kings of Judah? But in his old age he was diseased in his feet. 24 Then Asa slept with his ancestors, and was buried with his ancestors in the city of his father David; his son Jehoshaphat succeeded him.

Analysis

A report on the conflict between Asa and Baasha of Israel is interpolated between the introductory formula in vv. 9-16 and the concluding formula in vv. 23-24.

Commentary

[15:9-10] According to v. 9 Asa reigned for 41 years; only Manasseh was king longer (see 2 Kgs 21:1). The queen mother is again Maacah, the daughter of Abishalom as she was under Abijam in v. 10. Since her identity cannot be doubted, two explanations are possible. Either Abijam and Asa had the same mother and are therefore brothers, or Maacah remained in office after the death of Abijam, so that "queen mother" is a title rather than a description of the family relationship. The matter cannot be decided.

[15:11-12] Asa is the first king since Solomon who is judged positively; this judgment is justified by his actions concerning the purity of the cult. On the one hand he stopped the custom of sanctifying people, and on the other hand he put away the idols (v. 12; see the comment on 14:21-24). Both remarks are not very concrete and can probably be regarded as Deuteronomistic commendation.

[15:13] In contrast to that, the removal of the queen mother seems to have been an actual event. This was such a special procedure that it has been handed down separately. The exact circumstances and the name of her possible successor are not mentioned. The procedure has a parallel in the dismissal of Tawananna by the Hittite King Muršilis.[1] The reason that is given for this remarkable procedure is the erection of an abominable image for Asherah by the queen mother either in Jerusalem or its vicinity. Asa removed this cultic symbol and thus purified the cult of Jerusalem.

[15:14-15] The positive judgment on Asa is qualified by stating that he did not remove all high places (v. 14). With his remarks on Asa, the Deuteronomistic Historian moves his concern about the purity of the cult far back. Furthermore, the adding of cultic items to the temple is mentioned positively (v. 15). The attitude of the king to the temple in Jerusalem is the sole standard for his evaluation by the Deuteronomistic Historian.

---

[1] See Albrecht Goetze, *Kleinasien,* 2d ed. (Munich: Beck, 1957), 93.

[15:16] The general statement on the war between Judah and Israel serves as a literary bridge for the concrete example during the time of Baasha. The episode is added here despite the fact that his accession to the throne is mentioned only in vv. 27-28. The historicity of the conflict must not be doubted, since all its details can be verified. From the standpoint of Judah the episode reflects the desire to secure the territory north of Jerusalem by annexing the tribal territory of Benjamin.

[15:17-22] The piece in vv. 17-22 formulates the historical events quite clearly: When Baasha started to fortify Rama (er-Ram, about 8 km. north of Jerusalem) as a border post against Judah, Asa sent a "present" together with a petition for help to Ben-hadad of Damascus, asking him to attack Israel from the north. Due to the invasion of the Arameans Baasha had to give up the fortification of Ramah, and Asa himself used the building material provided to fortify Geba (Jebaʿ) and Mizpah (Tell en-Naṣbe). The border of Judah was thus moved about 12 km. to the north and the road to Jerusalem was secured accordingly.

King Ben-hadad cannot be found in extrabiblical sources, but he has to be distinguished from the king of the same name mentioned in 20:1-34; he reigned in the first third of the ninth century until 870.[2] A nonaggression pact apparently existed between Ben-hadad and Baasha. When Asa felt threatened by Israel, he sent a petition for help to the powerful Aramean state in Damascus. The petition for an alliance is supported by the payment of an unspecified tribute. As a result, Damascus changed sides and attacked Israel from the north. Whether the fragmentary inscription mentioning the "house of David," found at Dan has to be interpreted in connection with this military campaign against the northern kingdom must remain open.[3] The three conquered cities, Ijon (Tell Dibbīn), Dan (Tell el-Qāḍī), and Abel-beth-maacah (Tell Ābel el-Qamḥ), were situated in the far north of the country, but the campaign reached as far as the territory of Chinneroth, the plain el-Ǧuwēr south of Tell el-ʿOrēme and the tribal territory of Naphtali west of the Sea of Galilee. Ben-hadad had in this way reached Galilee.

In the face of this threat Baasha returns to his capital Tirzah. The removal of the danger is not mentioned. Asa, however, uses this chance to fortify Geba and Mizpah as border posts to provide Judah with a buffer zone and to secure the road to Jerusalem.[4] In a cunning maneuver Asa achieves a correction of the borderline and thus maintains an advantage for Judah. The marginal existence of Jerusalem in the

---

[2] See Gotthard G. G. Reinhold, *Die Beziehungen Altisraels zu den aramäischen Staaten in der israelitisch-judäischen Königszeit,* Europäische Hochschulschriften 23/368 (Frankfurt: Lang, 1989), 106–16.

[3] See Avraham Biran and Joseph Naveh, "An Aramaic Stele Fragment from Tel Dan," *IEJ* 43 (1993) 81–98.

[4] On the topographical questions see Herbert Donner, "Der Feind aus dem Norden: Topographische und archäologische Erwägungen zu Jes 10, 276-34," *ZDPV* 84 (1968) 46–54.

north of the Judean territory is changed by the annexation of the tribal territory of Benjamin.

[15:23-24] Next to the standard notices, the concluding formula mentions an unspecified disease of the feet. This comment shows that there existed short notices with personal information about the individual kings. The Deuteronomistic Historian used these oral or written traditions to expand his formula and to provide further details.

Nadab of Israel

Text

15:25 Nadab son of Jeroboam began to reign over Israel in the second year of King Asa of Judah; he reigned over Israel two years. 26 He did what was evil in the sight of the LORD, walking in the way of his ancestor and in the sin that he caused Israel to commit.

27 Baasha son of Ahijah, of the house of Issachar, conspired against him; and Baasha struck him down at Gibbethon, which belonged to the Philistines; for Nadab and all Israel were laying siege to Gibbethon. 28 So Baasha killed Nadab in the third year of King Asa of Judah, and succeeded him. 29 As soon as he was king, he killed all the house of Jeroboam; he left to the house of Jeroboam not one that breathed, until he had destroyed it, according to the word of the LORD that he spoke by his servant Ahijah the Shilonite— 30 because of the sins of Jeroboam that he committed and that he caused Israel to commit, and because of the anger to which he provoked the LORD, the God of Israel.

31 Now the rest of the acts of Nadab, and all that he did, are they not written in the Book of the Annals of the Kings of Israel? 32 There was war between Asa and King Baasha of Israel all their days.

Commentary

[15:25-30] After the introductory formula (vv. 25-26), only the premature end of his reign due to the revolt of Baasha (vv. 27-30) is reported of Nadab, the son of Jeroboam. Nadab had reigned over Israel less than two years and is judged negatively, like every king of Israel. He is killed by an unspecified opposition during a military campaign against the Philistines to secure the territory. The resistance to the successor of Jeroboam was either against the new ruler directly or against the dynastic principle. This procedure of getting rid of a dynasty by killing the son and successor is repeated a number of times in the history of Israel (see 16:2; 2 Kgs 15:10, 14, 25, 30). It was probably the rivalry among the tribes and a certain independence toward the king that prevented the establishment of a dynasty, so that the kingship in the northern kingdom is marked by a frequent change of the royal family.

The uprising of Baasha happens in the military camp during the siege of Gibbethon and was probably supported by the majority of the army. Gibbethon can be located on Tell el-Melāt about 9 km. north of Ekron (Khirbet el-Muqannaᶜ) and was probably the most northern city on Philistine territory.[1] An uprising with the help of the army outside the residential city meant success, since there was no need to overcome the administrative structures in the capital that were established to secure royal power.

[15:29-32] In order to stifle all other claims to the throne, the royal family had to be extinguished (v. 29aα). The note on the fulfillment in v. 29aβb, 30 is a later interpretation by the Deuteronomistic redactor. The word spoken by Ahijah is not stated. The reference is to the conviction that a change in royal authority and dynasty must be traced back to the will of Yahweh, uttered by a prophet. The notice on death and burial is absent from the concluding formula; since Nadab was removed by murder, he was probably buried where he was killed, that is, far from the family grave. Verse 32 repeats v. 16 and is probably an addition.

---

[1] See Gerhard von Rad, "Das Reich Israel und die Philister," *PJ* 29 (1933) 30–42.

Baasha of Israel

Text

15:33 In the third year of King Asa of Judah, Baasha son of Ahijah began to reign over all Israel at Tirzah; he reigned twenty-four years. 34 He did what was evil in the sight of the LORD, walking in the way of Jeroboam and in the sin that he caused Israel to commit.

16:1 The word of the LORD came to Jehu son of Hanani against Baasha, saying, 2 "Since I exalted you out of the dust and made you leader over my people Israel, and you have walked in the way of Jeroboam, and have caused my people Israel to sin, provoking me to anger with their sins, 3 therefore, I will consume Baasha and his house, and I will make your house like the house of Jeroboam son of Nebat. 4 Anyone belonging to Baasha who dies in the city the dogs shall eat; and anyone of his who dies in the field the birds of the air shall eat."

5 Now the rest of the acts of Baasha, what he did, and his power, are they not written in the Book of the Annals of the Kings of Israel? 6 Baasha slept with his ancestors, and was buried at Tirzah; and his son Elah succeeded him. [7 Moreover the word of the LORD came by the prophet Jehu son of Hanani against Baasha and his house, both because of all the evil that he did in the sight of the LORD, provoking him to anger with the work of his hands, in being like the house of Jeroboam, and also because he destroyed it.]

Commentary

[15:33-34] The introductory formula for Baasha follows the convention and does not contain any additional details. Like his predecessors he reigned in Tirzah. The duration of his reign (24 years) shows that he was able to maintain his power after he had seized it. Of course, the judgment on him is a negative one. The concluding formula (16:5) explicitly stresses his burial at Tirzah and the succession of his son.

[16:1-4] The word sent to the prophet Jehu, son of Hanani, announcing the destruction of the family of Baasha, is interpolated between the two formulas. This threat is closely related to similar words against the royal households of Israel (see 14:7-11; 21:20bβ-24; 2 Kgs 9:7-10a) and expresses the Deuteronomistic Historian's understanding of history. History is the execution of the word of God, spoken by the prophet. Nothing important happened because of some political, sociological, personal, or similar constellation of events, but only because Yahweh has decreed so through one of his prophets.[1] The metaphorical speech corresponds essentially to 1 Kgs 14:10-11; 21:23-24; 2 Kgs 9:10. Here the same fate repeats itself: the warrior chosen by God for the worship of Yahweh follows the sin of Jeroboam and has to be punished. Thus the words of the prophets express the Deuteronomistic view of history and are later additions.

[16:7] This understanding is expressed again in a shortened form in a further addition (v. 7a). The other addition (v. 7b) is made possible because Baasha acted without prophetic instruction; otherwise the Deuteronomistic redactor keeps to his interpretive pattern that forsaking Yahweh also results in destruction for the person who was originally chosen to be the tool of God.

---

[1] Walter Dietrich, *Prophetie und Geschichte: Eine redaktionsgeschichtliche Untersuchung zum deuteronomistichen Geschichtswerk,* FRLANT 108 (Göttingen: Vandenhoeck & Ruprecht, 1972), 107–8.

Elah of Israel

Text

16:8 In the twenty-sixth year of King Asa of Judah, Elah son of Baasha began to reign over Israel in Tirzah; he reigned two years. 9 But his servant Zimri, commander of half his chariots, conspired against him. When he was at Tirzah, drinking himself drunk in the house of Arza, who was in charge of the palace at Tirzah, 10 Zimri came in and struck him down and killed him, in the twenty-seventh year of King Asa of Judah, and succeeded him.

11 When he began to reign, as soon as he had seated himself on his throne, he killed all the house of Baasha; he did not leave him a single male of his kindred or his friends. 12 Thus Zimri destroyed all the house of Baasha, according to the word of the LORD, which he spoke against Baasha by the prophet Jehu— 13 because of all the sins of Baasha and the sins of his son Elah that they committed, and that they caused Israel to commit, provoking the LORD God of Israel to anger with their idols. 14 Now the rest of the acts of Elah, and all that he did, are they not written in the Book of the Annals of the Kings of Israel?

Commentary

[16:8-10] The introductory formula for Elah (v. 8) has been shortened drastically, since vv. 9-10 immediately report his murder at the hand of Zimri. The reasons for the murder of the king are not given. Again, the uprising prevents the establishment of a dynasty. The description of the circumstances does not shed a favorable light on Elah. The leader of the revolt, who then makes himself king, belongs to the charioteers and was, as one of their two commanders, a person of special standing. The overthrow of the king happens in an attack during a banquet; here the drunkenness of Elah is reported as a discriminatory fact.

[16:11-13] The addition portrays the extermination of the whole family of Baasha as the fulfillment of the prophecy spoken by Jehu in 16:1-4. The Deuteronomistic redactor understands history as the execution of the will of God spoken by his prophet. The concluding formula for Elah is shortened, because it is not possible to report a proper burial for a murdered person.

Zimri, Tibni, and Omri

Text

16:15 In the twenty-seventh year of King Asa of Judah, Zimri reigned seven days in Tirzah. Now the troops were encamped against Gibbethon, which belonged to the Philistines, 16 and the troops who were encamped heard it said, "Zimri has conspired, and he has killed the king"; therefore all Israel made Omri, the commander of the army, king over Israel that day in the camp. 17 So Omri went up from Gibbethon, and all Israel with him, and they besieged Tirzah. 18 When Zimri saw that the city was taken, he went into the citadel of the king's house; he burned down the king's house over himself with fire, and died— 19 because of the sins that he committed, doing evil in the sight of the Lord, walking in the way of Jeroboam, and for the sin that he committed, causing Israel to sin. 20 Now the rest of the acts of Zimri, and the conspiracy that he made, are they not written in the Book of the Annals of the Kings of Israel?

21 Then the people of Israel were divided into two parts; half of the people followed Tibni son of Ginath, to make him king, and half followed Omri. 22 But the people who followed Omri overcame the people who followed Tibni son of Ginath; so Tibni died, and Omri became king. 23 In the thirty-first year of King Asa of Judah, Omri began to reign over Israel; he reigned for twelve years, six of them in Tirzah.

24 He bought the hill of Samaria from Shemer for two talents of silver; he fortified the hill, and called the city that he built, Samaria, after the name of Shemer, the owner of the hill.

25 Omri did what was evil in the sight of the Lord; he did more evil than all who were before him. 26 For he walked in all the way of Jeroboam son of Nebat, and in the sins that he caused Israel to commit, provoking the Lord, the God of Israel, to anger by their idols. 27 Now the rest of the acts of Omri that he did, and the power that he showed, are they not written in the Book of the Annals of the Kings of Israel? 28 Omri slept with his ancestors, and was buried in Samaria; his son Ahab succeeded him.

Commentary

[16:15-20] After the introductory formula for Zimri (v. 15), his ignominious end is reported in vv. 16-18. The reasons for his failure are given in v. 19, followed by the concluding formula in v. 20.

Zimri reigned for only seven days, because his enthronement led to the proclamation of the counterking Omri. As leader of the army, Omri could probably rely on the military, but it is not clear whether we are dealing here with a conscripted or a professional army. The proclamation of Omri as king is said to have happened at Gibbethon, but this place is already mentioned during the conspiracy of Baasha in 15:27. Most likely the Deuteronomistic Historian used this place because of a lack of any concrete localization and placed the events relating to Omri there later. Nevertheless, the quick action of Omri and his siege of Tirzah seem to be historically probable. As a result, Zimri surrenders and is killed in the burning palace. Whether he himself set fire to it, as alleged by the text, cannot be verified; the evil act is probably attributed to the evil enemy. The ignominious end underscores the unlawfulness—manifested in its failure—of the attempt to seize the kingship. The reasons given for the failure correspond to typical Deuteronomistic phraseology, v. 19 ignoring the fact that due to his very short reign he could not possibly have done all the sins he is charged with.

The concluding formula (v. 20) contains the stereotypical phrases minus the reference to the burial. Since Zimri was burned in his own palace, a proper burial was made impossible. One has to ask why Zimri and his extremely short reign were included at all in the chronicle of the kings of Israel. The Deuteronomistic Historian probably wanted to present his source for the succession of the Israelite kings as fully as possible. On the other hand he was also keen to contrast the continuing attempts of a coup d'état with the much more stable situation in Judah. The Deuteronomistic Historian managed to fit Zimri as far as possible into his formulas, and he added a report on the end of his reign. This report can be traced back to the Deuteronomistic Historian, since the quick end of Zimri is portrayed one-sidedly as his own action in view of the siege of Tirzah.

[16:21-22] The double monarchy in the time between Zimri and Omri is omitted from the chronology of the kings here. Despite Omri's triumph over Zimri, another election of a king has happened. The exact circumstances of the investiture of Tibni are not reported. The people were split between two kings, but it is not clear if this split happened on a regional or social basis, that is, if the tribes or certain groups of people were loyal to one or the other king. A civil war is not mentioned, but we can assume that the conflict between the two rivals over the kingship was not exactly a peaceful process. The natural death assumed for Tibni seems to cover the fact that the struggle for power was a fight for life and death that only ended when one rival had been exterminated. According to the dates given in vv. 15 and 23, the double kingship lasted for three to four years. It was probably an advantage for Omri that he was able to reside in the capital after the conquest of Tirzah and the victory over Zimri. The duration of the reign of Omri is counted from the elimination of Tibni and the start of his supreme reign.

[16:23-26] The introductory formula for Omri is expanded by a notice on the move of the capital from Tirzah to Samaria. No reasons for the change of the capital are given. The new foundation not only had the advantage that one was not forced during the planning to take existing structures into account, but also made Omri the local king over the city so that he could exercise absolute power without consideration for the structures of the local community.

Samaria, the city founded by Omri, receives its name from the owner of the hill, Shemer; during the Roman period Herod renamed the city Colonia Lucia Septima Sebaste; the present village Sebastye east of the great hill of settlement maintained the Latin name. Excavations on the top of the hill unearthed the acropolis that was surrounded by a wall. Next to some administrative buildings the palace of Omri was situated in this specially fenced off territory of 178 x 89 m. The preserved parts show that the rooms were situated around a quadrangle but further courtyards seem to point toward a more wide-ranging area.[1] Samaria remained the capital until the conquest by the Assyrians in 722; thus it replaced the geographically unknown Tirzah.[2]

[16:27-28] Like all the other kings of Israel, Omri is judged negatively by the Deuteronomistic Historian. Further deeds and achievements by him are not mentioned. The concluding formula mentions the creation of a burial site outside the city walls; it was probably a rock chamber tomb on the slope of the hill. The enthronement of his son Ahab as successor creates a dynasty for the first time in the history of the northern kingdom.

---

[1] See *BRL*, 267.

[2] On the further history of the city see Albrecht Alt, "Der Stadtstaat Samaria," in idem, *Kleine Schriften* (Munich: Beck), 3:258–301.

Introductory Formula for Ahab

Text

16:29 In the thirty-eighth year of King Asa of Judah, Ahab son of Omri began to reign over Israel; Ahab son of Omri reigned over Israel in Samaria twenty-two years. 30 Ahab son of Omri did evil in the sight of the LORD more than all who were before him.

31 And as if it had been a light thing for him to walk in the sins of Jeroboam son of Nebat, he took as his wife Jezebel daughter of King Ethbaal of the Sidonians, and went and served Baal, and worshiped him. 32 He erected an altar for Baal in the house of Baal, which he built in Samaria. 33 Ahab also made a sacred pole. Ahab did more to provoke the anger of the LORD, the God of Israel, than had all the kings of Israel who were before him. 34 In his days Hiel of Bethel built Jericho; he laid its foundation at the cost of Abiram his firstborn, and set up its gates at the cost of his youngest son Segub, according to the word of the LORD, which he spoke by Joshua son of Nun.

Analysis

The introductory formula for Ahab corresponds to the concluding formula in 1 Kgs 22:39-40. An extensive block of prophetic narratives has been interpolated in between (17:1—22:38). The following description of the history of Ahab is closely connected with this prophetic tradition. According to the introductory formula, Ahab reigned 22 years in Samaria; the formula is expanded by several additional details:

- marriage to a Sidonian princess, v. 31b
- building of a temple for Baal in Samaria, v. 32
- manufacture of an asherah, v. 33
- rebuilding of Jericho by Hiel, v. 34

Marriage, building of a temple in Samaria, and the manufacture of an asherah are used to intensify the negative judgment on Ahab. The rebuilding of Jericho is mentioned, because the events connected with it are regarded as the fulfillment of the curse in Josh 6:26. Since this curse belongs to a later redactional layer of the book of Joshua, this notice too has to be regarded as a redactional addition.

Commentary

[16:31] The marriage of Ahab with Jezebel cannot be doubted, since such family unions generally served to enforce and secure already existing political relations. We do not yet have any epigraphical attestations for Ethbaal, the king of Sidon and father of the princess; nevertheless, the name Itobaal is typical for Phoenicia. Sidon is a coastal city 35 km. north of Tyre (Ṣūr) that is called Ṣēda today. The name *Yzbl* on a seal of unknown origin from the monarchic period can hardly be related to the queen.[1] Given Ahab's concern for the purity of the cult of Yahweh, expressed by the ban on mixed marriages, the marriage with a Phoenician princess is seen as a break away from Yahweh because this princess is made responsible for the introduction of the cult of Baal. The worship of Baal is regarded as worse than the transgression of Jeroboam.

[16:32] The excavations in Samaria have not yet produced a temple of Baal. One can assume that this temple stood inside the palace district, but the buildings in this area are badly preserved due to later destruction. After El, the father of the gods, Baal was the most powerful god of the Canaanite pantheon. The Ugaritic myth describes his takeover and exercise of power in a special cycle.[2] During the second millennium, Baal was equated with the weather-god Hadad and at the same time regarded as the lord of vegetation and fertility; thus he was seen as the lord of life as such. Both aspects demonstrate his universal claim to rule over the earth.[3] He was therefore an immediate rival for Yahweh; this explains the harsh polemics against this god during the period of the monarchy.

[16:33] To manufacture a sacred pole or asherah belongs to the stereotypical reproaches leveled against the kings who are judged negatively (see 14:15, 23; 2 Kgs 17:10, 16; 21:2); nevertheless, it is mentioned explicitly here. An asherah is a wooden symbol of the deity that was worshiped; thus it stood in contrast to the claim of Yahweh to be worshiped alone.

[16:34] The mention of the rebuilding of Jericho is foremost concerned with the fulfillment of the curse uttered by Joshua in Josh 6:26. Jericho was populated through-

---

[1] Nachman Avigad, "The Seal of Jezebel," *IEJ* 14 (1964) 274–76.

[2] See Karl-Heinz Bernhardt, in *Near Eastern Religious Texts relating to the Old Testament,* ed. Walter Beyerlin, trans. John Bowden, OTL (Philadelphia: Westminster, 1978), 192–221.

[3] See Hartmut Gese, in idem, Maria Höfer, and Kurt Rudolph, *Die Religionen Altsyriens, Altarabiens und der Mandäer,* Religionen der Menschheit 10.2 (Stuttgart: Koklhammer, 1970), 119–34.

out the whole monarchic period; a special rebuilding program during the time of Ahab cannot be verified but it cannot be excluded either.[4] Since a rebuilding by a single private person seems unlikely, the notice on the building projects by Hiel refers probably only to single buildings. Two sons of Hiel died apparently during the building project, a fact referring to the fulfillment of the curse. Verse 34 cannot be used as proof for child sacrifice connected to building projects.[5]

The introductory formula for Ahab (1 Kgs 16:29-34) is followed by several different narratives interpolated before the concluding formula in 22:39-40. First, chaps. 17–19 contain a string of prophetic narratives with Elijah as the central figure. Second, the narratives of the wars against the Aramean coalition in 20:1-43 and 22:1-38 form further additions. Here traditions are taken over that originated and were handed down in the circles of the prophet's followers. It is their purpose to glorify the figure of the prophet Elijah by using reports of his prophecy against King Ahab and his miracles, so that he is portrayed as a prophet of God.

Chapters 17–18 seem to be a larger composition, centering on the theme of draught. The following narratives belong to the basic layer of this composition:

1. Elijah's miraculous feeding at Wadi Cherith (17:2-7)
2. the feeding miracle in Zarephath (17:8-16)
3. the arrival of rain (18:1, 2a, 41-46)

This textual basis has been expanded by narratives that are determined by the view that Elijah has been commissioned by Yahweh and that he acts in his name:

1. the revival of the dead child (17:17-24)
2. the encounter with Obadiah (18:2b-16)
3. the fight with the priests of Baal (18:17-40)

The composition as a whole is introduced by a redactional bridge in 17:1. Originally, the conflict between prophet and king had to be seen as a struggle for the power of Yahweh. In view of the unlawful cult of Baal, Yahweh manifests himself as the sole ruler of the world, so that he alone deserves honor and worship.

---

[4] See Helga Weippert and Manfred Weippert, "Jericho in der Eisenzeit," *ZDPV* 92 (1976) 105–48.

[5] See Otto Kaiser, "Des Erstgeborenen deiner Söhne sollst du mir geben," in idem, *Von der Gegenwartsbedeutung des Alten Testaments: Gesammelte Studien zur Hermeneutik und zur Redaktionsgeschichte,* ed. Volkmar Fritz et al. (Göttingen: Vandenhoeck & Ruprecht, 1984), 142–66.

Elijah at Wadi Cherith and at the Widow of Zarephath

Text

17:1 Now Elijah the Tishbite, of Tishbe in Gilead, said to Ahab, "As the LORD the God of Israel lives, before whom I stand, there shall be neither dew nor rain these years, except by my word." 2 The word of the LORD came to him, saying, 3 "Go from here and turn eastward, and hide yourself by the Wadi Cherith, which is east of the Jordan. 4 You shall drink from the wadi, and I have commanded the ravens to feed you there." 5 So he went and did according to the word of the LORD; he went and lived by the Wadi Cherith, which is east of the Jordan. 6 The ravens brought him bread and meat in the morning, and bread and meat in the evening; and he drank from the wadi. 7 But after a while the wadi dried up, because there was no rain in the land.

8 Then the word of the LORD came to him, saying, 9 "Go now to Zarephath, which belongs to Sidon, and live there; for I have commanded a widow there to feed you." 10 So he set out and went to Zarephath. When he came to the gate of the town, a widow was there gathering sticks; he called to her and said, "Bring me a little water in a vessel, so that I may drink." 11 As she was going to bring it, he called to her and said, "Bring me a morsel of bread in your hand." 12 But she said, "As the LORD your God lives, I have nothing baked, only a handful of meal in a jar, and a little oil in a jug; I am now gathering a couple of sticks, so that I may go home and prepare it for myself and my son, that we may eat it, and die." 13 Elijah said to her, "Do not be afraid; go and do as you have said; but first make me a little cake of it and bring it to me, and afterward make something for yourself and your son. 14 For thus says the LORD the God of Israel: The jar of meal will not be emptied and the jug of oil will not fail until the day that the LORD sends rain on the earth." 15 She went and did as Elijah said, so that she as well as he and her household ate for many days. 16 The jar of meal was not emptied, neither

181

did the jug of oil fail, according to the word of the LORD that he spoke by Elijah.

17 After this the son of the woman, the mistress of the house, became ill; his illness was so severe that there was no breath left in him. 18 She then said to Elijah, "What have you against me, O man of God? You have come to me to bring my sin to remembrance, and to cause the death of my son!" 19 But he said to her, "Give me your son." He took him from her bosom, carried him up into the upper chamber where he was lodging, and laid him on his own bed. 20 He cried out to the LORD, "O LORD my God, have you brought calamity even upon the widow with whom I am staying, by killing her son?" 21 Then he stretched himself upon the child three times, and cried out to the LORD, "O LORD my God, let this child's life come into him again." 22 The LORD listened to the voice of Elijah; the life of the child came into him again, and he revived. 23 Elijah took the child, brought him down from the upper chamber into the house, and gave him to his mother; then Elijah said, "See, your son is alive." 24 So the woman said to Elijah, "Now I know that you are a man of God, and that the word of the LORD in your mouth is truth."

Commentary

[17:1] Elijah is introduced as the person who proclaims the powerful word of God; a further description of his office is not given. According to his place of origin he is called "the Tishbite" (see 21:17; 2 Kgs 1:3, 8, etc.). The exact geographical location of Tishbe in Gilead is unknown and is not mentioned again in the Bible. Just like Elisha, Elijah regards himself as standing in the service of Yahweh (see 1 Kgs 18:15; 2 Kgs 3:14; 5:16). Thus the announcement of the drought is not a sign of his hostility toward Ahab, but rather a powerful expression of the will of Yahweh. God as the lord of nature will retain rain and dew to demonstrate who is responsible for the course of nature. Yahweh will force Israel to accept him as the only God by withdrawal of vital water.

The background for this announcement of punishment is the worship of Baal, which interferes with Yahweh's claim to exclusivity. In the following narratives the anticipated drought is understood not as being a natural disaster but as a punishment caused by Yahweh because of the inappropriate behavior of the king. The whole cycle of narratives is thus placed under the will of God. Just as he can withhold rain and dew, he is also able to grant both things again. The drought belongs to the natural phenomena that cause severe harm for the people, since the absence of harvest and water threaten the basis of life. Human beings are helpless against drought. The text does not consider that the consequences of the drought not only concern the king but also affect the rest of the people.

The superscription provides a new dimension for all the other narratives, since they are now part of the struggle between prophet and king over the acceptance of

Yahweh. The announcement that the vital rain and dew will fail to appear places the whole narrative under the aspect of asserting the divine will. The tension is eased only by the narrative of the appearance of the rain in 1 Kgs 18:1, 2a, 41-46.

[17:2-7] At the beginning we find a narrative about the miraculous feeding of Elijah that was not originally connected with the drought; in its current context the passage stresses that Yahweh takes care of his prophet. On Yahweh's command Elijah retires to Wadi Cherith. The wadi is probably one of the tributaries from the east Jordan hills to the river Jordan, but this cannot be specified any further. There Elijah lives the life of a hermit. Despite being far away from any humans, he does not need to starve: he could drink from the wadi, and ravens supplied him with bread and meat.[1]

While the provision with water happens in a natural way, the provision of food by ravens points to a miracle. Ravens, which are normally regarded as scavengers and as aggressive birds, serve as carriers of food. The daily meat included in the provision moves beyond the average diet since meat was normally eaten only on feast days. Because of the miraculous supply, Elijah is free from concerns; as a man of God he does not need any help and the drought does not concern him. Elijah is already portrayed as an obedient prophet, led by the word of Yahweh because he does not act on his own initiative but follows the orders of Yahweh. It is not his own power but the help of Yahweh that secures his survival in a time of need triggered by a drought.

[17:8-16] These verses are a miracle story in which the laws of nature are rendered void because of divine intervention. This narrative also commences with a divine command. The portrayal of the poor widow describes the consequences of a drought in a drastic way: shortage of food leads to famine and generally results in the death of the people. The widow does not complain about her poverty but only describes her desperate situation. As a widow, who could probably be recognized by her special clothes (cf. Gen 38:14), the woman belonged to the lower social stratum, which suffered most from economic want, since she lacked the means of social sustenance. Originally, the story narrated how a prophet helped the widow in her desperate situation through miraculous intervention. This version of the story still shimmers through, even though the miracle does not only help the widow but also serves to provide food for Elijah. The motif of a certain supply in a jar or a bottle that never ceases is found elsewhere in literature, for example, in the fairy tale, "Sweet Porridge," by the brothers Grimm.

Now, the narrative results in the provision of food by Yahweh even far from home. Zarephath belongs to the territory of the Phoenician city Sidon (Ṣēdā) and can be identified with Rās Ṣarafandi. The place did not belong to Israelite territory but to the foreign country of Phoenicia (cf. Luke 4:26). Even in non-Israelite surroundings

---

[1] Würthwein, *Könige,* 2:212.

Yahweh is therefore able to guarantee the survival of the prophet. As the prophet of Yahweh he is guided and fed by his God far from home.[2] Here the miracle does not serve the purpose of producing a surplus but the feeding of the persons concerned. The famine is not removed, but the need of the widow and her son is eased in connection with the feeding of the prophet. Thus the narrative is completely concerned with the personal fate of the individual. In this respect it is quite different from the narrative of the "bread from heaven" (Exodus 16) in the desert, where the plight of the whole people is lifted by divine intervention. The miracle of Elijah is outdone only by the narratives of the feeding of the five thousand by Jesus in Mark 6:30-44 (par. Matt 14:13-21 and Luke 9:10-17) and Mark 8:1-9.

[17:17-24] These verses contain a further miracle story that had nothing to do with the previous one and was only placed in its current context by the transitional phrase "After this." Also, the mother of the child, here introduced as "mistress of the house," is not identical with the poor widow of the previous narrative in 17:8-16. It is presupposed that Elijah has visited this woman; to welcome a stranger as a guest was not only a natural process but also an honorable act; furthermore, according to the narrative, the woman recognized right from the start that Elijah had a special status as a "man of God." Only in this narrative and in 2 Kgs 1:9-16 is Elijah called a "man of God." Apart from Elijah only Samuel (1 Sam 9:6), Elisha (2 Kgs 4:7), an anonymous man from Judah (1 Kgs 13:1), and Moses (Deut 33:1) are referred to by this title. Elijah manifests himself as a "man of God" by the miracle on the dead child, because the address spoken by the women refers to his special ability. The title emphasizes the special connection of the miracle worker with God, because it is only God who provides him with special powers needed for the miracle.[3] It is remarkable that the miracles of the man of God happen in the personal and private sphere and that they belong to the natural rather than the historical realm.[4]

In addition to the miraculous act, the announcement of the powerful word of God and the ability to grasp concealed things also belong to the features of the man of God. The address by the woman in 17:18 reflects the fear that Elijah will be able to uncover unknown things and that he will evoke punishment by Yahweh. Elijah counters this fear by healing the child. We are given no details about the event in the upper room, and it is stressed that the event happens without the presence of any witnesses. Elijah evokes God as the lord over death and life twice, and v. 22 stresses explicitly that it is God who revives the child—Elijah serves only as his mediator. It is not Elijah but Yahweh himself who works the miracle. The narrative does not there-

---

[2] Ibid., 213.

[3] See Gottfried Quell, "Das Phänomen des Wunders im Alten Testament," in *Verbannung und Heimkehr: Beiträge zur Geschichte und Theologie Israels im 6. und 5. Jahrhundert vor Chr. Wilhelm Rudolph zum 70. Geburtstage,* ed. Arnulf Kuschke (Tübingen: Mohr/Siebeck, 1961), 253–300.

[4] Claus Westermann, in *BHH* 3:1499.

fore stress the miraculous powers of the prophet but the hearing by Yahweh; this pre-supposes Elijah's special connection to Yahweh, expressed in the double invocation.

In its current context the story clearly describes the raising of a dead person, the only one described in the Hebrew Bible. Normally, in the understanding of ancient Israel, the fate of death is irreversible. After the intercession of a prophet, Yahweh alone, as the creator of humanity and the world, is able to overcome the finality of death; this intercession displays the special ability of the man of God. Only in the Jesus narratives concerning the waking of the dead in Mark 5:21-43 (par. Matt 9:18-26 and Luke 8:40-56) and John 11:1-45 are dead persons restored to life, since the coming of Jesus marks the beginning of the reign of God during which the validity of death is rendered null and void by eternal life.

The Trial by Ordeal
on Mount Carmel

Text

18:1 After many days the word of the LORD came to Elijah, in the third year, saying, "Go, present yourself to Ahab; I will send rain on the earth." 2 So Elijah went to present himself to Ahab. The famine was severe in Samaria. 3 Ahab summoned Obadiah, who was in charge of the palace. (Now Obadiah revered the LORD greatly; 4 when Jezebel was killing off the prophets of the LORD, Obadiah took a hundred prophets, hid them [. . .]ᵃ in a cave, and provided them with bread and water.) 5 Then Ahab said to Obadiah, "Go through the land to all the springs of water and to all the wadis; perhaps we may find grass to keep the horses and mules alive, and not lose some of the animals." 6 So they divided the land between them to pass through it; Ahab went in one direction by himself, and Obadiah went in another direction by himself.

7 As Obadiah was on the way, Elijah met him; Obadiah recognized him, fell on his face, and said, "Is it you, my lord Elijah?" 8 He answered him, "It is I. Go, tell your lord that Elijah is here." 9 And he said, "How have I sinned, that you would hand your servant over to Ahab, to kill me? 10 As the LORD your God lives, there is no nation or kingdom to which my lord has not sent to seek you; and when they would say, 'He is not here,' he would require an oath of the kingdom or nation, that they had not found you. 11 But now you say, 'Go, tell your lord that Elijah is here.' 12 As soon as I have gone from you, the spirit of the LORD will carry you I know not where; so, when I come and tell Ahab and he cannot find you, he will kill me, although I your servant have revered the LORD from my youth. 13 Has it not been told my lord what I did when Jezebel killed the prophets of the LORD, how I hid a hundred of the LORD's prophets fifty to a cave, and provided them with bread and water? 14 Yet now you say, 'Go, tell your lord that Elijah is here'; he will surely kill me." 15 Elijah said, "As the LORD of hosts lives, before whom I

stand, I will surely show myself to him today." 16 So Obadiah went to meet Ahab, and told him; and Ahab went to meet Elijah.

17 When Ahab saw Elijah, Ahab said to him, "Is it you, you troubler of Israel?" 18 He answered, "I have not troubled Israel; but you have, and your father's house, because you have forsaken the commandments of the LORD and followed the Baals. 19 Now therefore have all Israel assemble for me at Mount Carmel, with the four hundred fifty prophets of Baal and the four hundred prophets of Asherah, who eat at Jezebel's table."

20 So Ahab sent to all the Israelites, and assembled the prophets at Mount Carmel. 21 Elijah then came near to all the people, and said, "How long will you go limping with two different opinions? If the LORD is God, follow him; but if Baal, then follow him." The people did not answer him a word. 22 Then Elijah said to the people, "I, even I only, am left a prophet of the LORD; but Baal's prophets number four hundred fifty. 23 Let two bulls be given to us; let them choose one bull for themselves, cut it in pieces, and lay it on the wood, but put no fire to it; I will prepare the other bull and lay it on the wood, but put no fire to it. 24 Then you call on the name of your god and I will call on the name of the LORD; the god who answers by fire is indeed God." All the people answered, "Well spoken!" 25 Then Elijah said to the prophets of Baal, "Choose for yourselves one bull and prepare it first, for you are many; then call on the name of your god, but put no fire to it." 26 So they took the bull that was given them, prepared it, and called on the name of Baal from morning until noon, crying, "O Baal, answer us!" But there was no voice, and no answer. They limped about the altar that they had made. 27 At noon Elijah mocked them, saying, "Cry aloud! Surely he is a god; either he is meditating, or he has wandered away, or he is on a journey, or perhaps he is asleep and must be awakened." 28 Then they cried aloud and, as was their custom, they cut themselves with swords and lances until the blood gushed out over them. 29 As midday passed, they raved on until the time of the offering of the oblation, but there was no voice, no answer, and no response.

30 Then Elijah said to all the people, "Come closer to me"; and all the people came closer to him. First he repaired the altar of the LORD that had been thrown down; 31 Elijah took twelve stones, according to the number of the tribes of the sons of Jacob, to whom the word of the LORD came, saying, "Israel shall be your name"; 32 with the stones he built an altar in the name of the LORD. Then he made a trench around the altar, large enough to contain two measures of seed. 33 Next he put the wood in order, cut the bull in pieces, and laid it on the wood. 34 He said, "Fill four jars with water and pour it on the burnt offering and on the wood." Then he said, "Do it a second time"; and they did it a second time. Again he said, "Do it a third time"; and they did it a third time, 35 so that the water ran all around the altar, and filled the trench also with water.

36 At the time of the offering of the oblation, the prophet Elijah came near and said, "O LORD, God of Abraham, Isaac, and Israel, let it be known this day that you are God in Israel, that I am your servant, and that I have done all these things at your bidding. 37 Answer me, O LORD, answer me, so that this people may know that you, O LORD, are God, and that you have turned their hearts back." 38 Then the fire of the LORD fell and consumed the burnt offering, the wood, the stones, and the dust, and even licked up the water that was in the trench. 39 When all the people saw it, they fell on their faces and said, "The LORD indeed is God; the LORD indeed is God." 40 Elijah said to them, "Seize the prophets of Baal; do not let one of them escape." Then they seized them; and Elijah brought them down to the Wadi Kishon, and killed them there.

41 Elijah said to Ahab, "Go up, eat and drink; for there is a sound of rushing rain." 42 So Ahab went up to eat and to drink. Elijah went up to the top of Carmel; there he bowed himself down upon the earth and put his face between his knees. 43 He said to his servant, "Go up now, look toward the sea." He went up and looked, and said, "There is nothing." Then he said, "Go again seven times." 44 At the seventh time he said, "Look, a little cloud no bigger than a person's hand is rising out of the sea." Then he said, "Go say to Ahab, 'Harness your chariot and go down before the rain stops you.'" 45 In a little while the heavens grew black with clouds and wind; there was a heavy rain. Ahab rode off and went to Jezreel. 46 But the hand of the LORD was on Elijah; he girded up his loins and ran in front of Ahab to the entrance of Jezreel.

^a NRSV: fifty to a cave.

Commentary

[18:1-2a] The theme of the drought comes to an end in 18:1, 2a, 41-46; thus the composition is finished. The introduction, vv. 1-2a, was added at a later stage to precede the narrative in vv. 41-45, which in turn has been expanded by v. 46. Verses 1-2a again place all the events under the order of Yahweh, to stress once more that Elijah does not act on his own account but only carries out the orders given by Yahweh. Just as God is able to withhold the rain for the land, so he will now send it to ease the deprivation caused by the drought. The power of Yahweh will be demonstrated to Ahab. The place where Ahab dwells is not mentioned; only toward the end of the narrative does he travel in a chariot to his place of residence in Israel. Most likely, the palace of the Omrides in Samaria is envisaged as the meeting place. This is, however, uncertain, although one can see the Mediterranean Sea from there too.

Elijah prays on Mount Carmel, a northwestern extension of the Samaritan hill country. The prayer looks almost like a magic incantation. The crouched position with the head between the knees has to be understood as an expression of special concentration. Sending his companion away seven times underscores the miraculous character of the event: after nothing has happened for a long time, the cloud finally announces the arrival of rain. Elijah works the miracle alone in the solitude of the mountains but announces it to Ahab, who becomes a witness of the events when the rain surprises him during his journey from Samaria to Jezreel. The addition in v. 46 makes Elijah accompany the event, since he ran in front of Ahab to Jezreel; this shows superhuman powers possible only for an ecstatic, since he is able to cover a distance of 35 km. on foot faster than a chariot. This trait of Elijah is only found in this verse, which adds to the tradition the picture of the miracle-working man of God.

[18:2b-4] The narrative of Elijah's encounter with Obadiah (vv. 2b-16b) is not a literary unit, but the literary-critical questions can be set aside here.[1] The encounter with Obadiah, who shall announce to the king his upcoming encounter with a prophet, is the focal point. The introduction (vv. 2b-4) presents Obadiah as the person who is in charge of the palace and responsible for the personal possessions of the king and the administration of the court (see 4:6). As an official of the inner circle of the king, he was regarded as a devout follower of Yahweh, who hid and took care of a large number of prophets persecuted by Ahab. Being the overseer of the provisions for the court probably facilitated his actions but also put him in opposition to the king to whom he had sworn loyalty.

[18:5-6] The description of the attempt to find watering places sets the scene for a meeting between Elijah and Obadiah when he is alone. The participation of the king in the search for springs in wadis is hardly likely. This trait of the narrative wants to emphasize the deprivation in the land: even the king is concerned about his horses and mules—the crisis has reached the royal court. The king is described as someone who realizes the consequences of the drought, that is, he is not protected from grim reality either.

[18:7-16] During the scene describing the encounter in vv. 7-15, Obadiah explicitly mentions the danger he is put in through Elijah's request to announce his appearance. In his answer, Obadiah provides some insights into the persecution of the prophets faithful to Yahweh in order to describe the situation under Ahab. According to Obadiah, Elijah was regarded as an enemy of the state who was searched for even abroad. The situation in Israel under Ahab is described as follows: the extermination of the prophets faithful to Yahweh by the king suppresses all prophecy in the name of Yahweh and thus the word of God in Israel. The request by Elijah to announce his appearance to the king puts Obadiah in danger, since the loyalty to the king demands the immediate arrest of the prophet wanted by Obadiah. Therefore the conversation results in Elijah's decision to appear immediately (i.e., on the same day) in front of

---

[1] See Würthwein, *Könige,* 2:221.

Ahab. The concluding notice (v. 16) states the execution of Elijah's commission and decision.

[18:17-40] The narrative of the ordeal forms an independent tradition closely connected with Elijah. It has been placed in its current context to illustrate the fundamental conflict of Elijah, as a representative of prophecy faithful to Yahweh, with the prophecy of Baal, preferred by the court. Glosses and tensions in the course of the narrative point to several reworkings of the original version.[2] The additions did not change the actual intention. The purpose of the narrative is not only to establish the proof that Yahweh is the true God of Israel, but also to show that Yahweh is the one and only God. In its current form, the narrative can be separated into several scenes; nevertheless, it moves resolutely toward its climax—the execution of the sacrifice by Yahweh in v. 38. Including all additions, we find the following structure:

vv. 17-20	introduction
vv. 21-25	preparation of the ordeal
vv. 26-29	mocking of the foreign god
vv. 30-35	preparation for sacrifice
vv. 36-38	prayer and sacrifice
vv. 39-40	profession to Yahweh

The introduction places the piece into the larger context of the cycle of narratives relating to the drought. The short encounter between Elijah and Ahab triggers the subsequent events. Elijah takes the initiative while Ahab only issues the necessary order to assemble the prophets on Mount Carmel. Mount Carmel is part of a mountain range 20 km. long northwest of the Samaritan mountains between the plain of Jezreel and the northern coastal plain. Due to its exposed location, it favored the foundation of cultic centers in all times. In addition to that, the lower mountains of Carmel belonged to mountains with their own mythical quality. They were not only considered a seat of a deity but were also idolized themselves. The connection of the Elijah tradition with the rock terrace el-Muḥraqa today cannot be traced back to Byzantine times; it only originated during the Middle Ages in connection with the Crusades.[3] Originally, the ordeal was not localized any further.

Ahab's role comes to an end with the summoning of the prophets; the king is absent from the remaining narrative. The whole prelude has probably been added to the narrative at a later stage. Elijah is the sole actor in the course of the remaining narrative; he alone faces the prophets of Baal and the people.

---

[2] See ibid., 215–17.

[3] See Clemens Kopp, *Elias und Christentum auf dem Karmel,* CHier 3 (Paderborn: Schöningh, 1929).

[18:21-25] The preparatory scene sets the conditions for the ordeal. The opening states clearly that it will be a choice between Yahweh and Baal; just like Joshua in his speech in Joshua 24, Elijah confronts the people with the option to follow Yahweh or to follow the foreign god. The whole narrative is marked by a monotheistic standpoint, that is, the worship of Yahweh as the sole God (see 1 Kgs 18:39). There can only be one God. Only the god who will, after an invocation, send fire on the sacrifice is the true God, because he alone is a living god. The metaphorical expression "to go limping with two different opinions" demonstrates the necessity for a decision, because in the view of the narrator the people are only safe in the worship of the true God. The silence of the people demonstrates their helplessness and at the same time their lack of profession and thus their distance from Yahweh; hence it has to be seen in sharp contrast to the vivid profession of v. 38.

The list of figures dramatizes the situation: one prophet of Yahweh stands against 450 prophets of Baal. When setting the conditions, equality is stressed. At the same time it is determined how the ordeal will be decided: it has to happen by divine intervention without any human mediation. Any doubt of the correctness of the sign is thus excluded from the start. By choosing a bull and placing the sacrificial animal on wood it becomes clear that the ordeal is envisaged as a burnt offering during which the whole animal, as a gift to the godhead, is consumed by fire.[4] The igniting of the burnt offering by the deity shall serve as an answer to the invocation. Thus the god invoked reveals himself as the living god.

[18:26-29] The fruitlessness of the efforts of the prophets of Baal is described right from the start of this paragraph. The reader realizes that a nonexistent god cannot answer. The prophets of Baal accompany their efforts by a cultic dance around the altar with the prepared sacrifice; in Israel too a dance can accompany the cultic festival (see 2 Sam 6:14; Pss 149:3; 150:4; Jer 31:13). As in Greece, dancing was foremost an expression of joy; here, however, it seems to have an incantational function and serves as a medium to reach an ecstatic condition, explicitly alluded to in vv. 28 and 29. Elijah uses the absence of an answer to mock the prophets of Baal. The general conviction of ancient Near Eastern religions that the deity follows the same daily activities as humans is the basis for the mockery. A god could be traveling or be asleep and thus unable to hear the voice of the praying person. The general conviction that divine life is analogous to human life is mocked with sharp irony.

[18:28-29] Verses 28-29 deal explicitly with the ecstasy of Baal's prophets. Ecstasy is a state of enrapture that is deliberately reached and regarded as divine inspiration.

---

[4] On this mode of offering see Rolf Rendtorff, *Studien zur Geschichte des Opfers im Alten Israel*, WMANT 24 (Neukirchen-Vluyn: Neukirchener, 1967).

According to 1 Sam 10:5-12; 19:18-24; 2 Kgs 3:15, the phenomenon was also known in ancient Israel. It is an altered state of consciousness during which the divinity takes complete possession of the human person so that one no longer feels any pain. Ecstasy served as a medium to receive revelations, because, according to the Israelite view, God speaks directly through persons other than himself. Stressing the absence of every form of divine answer, it becomes clear that in the case of a god who does not exist, ecstasy as a medium of receiving a divine word has to fail. The narrator thus utters a devastating judgment on Baal: the day passes but there is no answer, because a god like Baal, who does not exist, cannot answer. The scene expresses the defeat of Baal's prophets.

[18:30-35] Only after the failure of the prophets of Baal does Elijah himself start to prepare the sacrifice. Here the remarks about the altar contradict each other. On the one side Elijah rebuilds a destroyed altar of Yahweh (v. 30b); on the other side he builds it using twelve stones and encircles it with a special ditch that separates the altar and its special holiness from its surroundings (vv. 31-32). Both remarks are probably later additions, which stress the correct execution of the sacrifice according to the cultic prescriptions.[5] The original narrative was able to report the preparation of a sacrifice without mentioning the erection of an altar as the place for the sacrifice; nevertheless, the wood necessary for the burnt offering was mentioned. Even though digging a ditch around the altar and pouring water over the sacrifice could have corresponded to common sacrificial practice, these details serve here merely to increase the miraculous character of the process.

[18:36-38] The next scene contains the climax of the narrative: the igniting of the sacrifice. The fire from heaven shows not only that Yahweh is the more powerful god, but also that he himself is the only living God. The event is preceded by Elijah's prayer, which once more depicts the prophet in the role of an advocate. Yahweh is addressed as the God of Abraham, Isaac, and Israel (Jacob). This formula, which is, in addition to Exod 3:6, 13, 15-16; 4:5, found quite often in the Deuteronomistic History and the Chronicler's History, emphasizes the continuity of the worship of God in Israel since the time of the patriarchs (Genesis 12–37).[6] The formula of the "God of the fathers" does not point to an older stage of Yahwistic religion but represents a special form of address to stress the personal relationship with God. In this context the formula expresses that Yahweh has always been the God of the people; they invoked him and were bound to him. Elijah invokes Yahweh as the God of the fathers and thus places

---

5 On the burnt offering see Volkmar Fritz, "'Bis an die Hörner des Altars,' Erwägungen zur Praxis des Brandopfers," in *Gottes Recht als Lebensraum: Festschrift für Hans Jochen Boecker,* ed. Peter Mommer et al. (Neukirchen-Vluyn: Neukirchener, 1993), 61–70.

6 See Matthias Köckert, *Vätergott und Väterverheissungen: Eine Auseinandersetzung mit Albrecht Alt und seinen Erben,* FRLANT 142 (Göttingen: Vandenhoeck & Ruprecht, 1988).

himself in the long history of the worship of Yahweh. By answering Elijah's intercession Yahweh himself decides the ordeal and manifests himself as the only God.

The narrative of the trial by ordeal on Mount Carmel does not contain a historical kernel transformed into a saga;[7] rather it is a didactic narrative that expresses in an ideal scene the faith in Yahweh as the only God; next to him Baal (and all other gods) are rendered void.[8] Since fire is generally a sign of theophany (see Exod 3:2; 19:18), the climax has to be seen as a self-revelation of Yahweh. Since the narrative was localized on Mount Carmel only at a later stage, it cannot be regarded as an etiology for a sanctuary on Mount Carmel and as an old local tradition; rather, the narrative was created from within the horizon of Deuteronomistic theology to demonstrate the singularity of Yahweh.

[18:39-40] The conclusion then naturally results in the confession by the people of Yahweh as the only God. Yahweh is addressed from a monotheistic point of view as the only God in the formula, "Yahweh indeed is God." Here monotheism means the worship of Yahweh as the only God, excluding the existence of any other gods. The formula is also found in Deut 4:35 (see 4:39), here with the explanatory addition, "there is no other besides him." This claim to exclusiveness is then repeated in the self-introduction in Isa 45:5-6, 18. "I am Yahweh and there is no other" can only be understood as "besides me there is no god" (see Isa 44:6 and 46:9). According to these monotheistic statements Yahweh as the only God is also the God of the whole world; he is its creator and maintainer; other gods do not exist.[9] This decision for the one God was taken up in the formula of Deut 6:4, which can be seen as the profession to the uniqueness of Yahweh: "Listen Israel, Yahweh is our God, Yahweh alone!"[10] With the final profession to the one God Yahweh, the people commit themselves to his truth in faith. Yahweh is solely and exclusively recognized as the God of Israel and of the whole world, because the narrative teaches that Baal does not exist and thus he cannot be god. Thus the narrative demonstrates that no other gods exist next to Yahweh.

In the spirit of this monotheism, Elijah leads the people back to the path of truth. The prophets of Baal are not only defeated, they are also eventually killed because they have denied Yahweh's exclusiveness by worshiping another god. The butchering of Baal's prophets at Wadi Kishon is paralleled with the massacre of the

---

[7] See Albrecht Alt, "Das Gottesurteil auf dem Karmel," in idem, *Kleine Schriften zur Geschichte des Volkes Israel* (Munich: Beck, 1953) 2:147 [135–49].

[8] Würthwein, *Könige,* 2:218.

[9] See Georg Braulik, "Deuteronomy and the Birth of Monotheism," in *The Theology of Deuteronomy,* trans. Ulrika Lindblad (N. Richland, Tex.: Bibal, 1994), 99–130; Hans Wildberger, "Der Monotheismus Deuterojesajas," in *Beiträge zur alttestamentlichen Theologie: Festschrift für Walther Zimmerli zum 70. Geburtstag,* ed. Herbert Donner et al. (Göttingen: Vandenhoeck & Ruprecht, 1977), 506–30.

[10] See Timo Veijola, "Höre Israel! Der Sinn und Hintergrund von Deuteronomium VI 4-9," *VT* 42 (1992) 528–41.

Baal worshipers by King Jehu in 2 Kgs 10:18-27. Wadi Kishon is a brook running through the plain of Jezreel and along the northern foot of Carmel, before flowing into the Mediterranean Sea south of the bay of Acre. A more detailed location of the place at Wadi Kishon is not given. The consequences of such a triumph of the legitimate prophet of Yahweh over the false prophets of Baal may seem puzzling to us, but they were in accordance to the way of thinking in ancient Israel: a coexistence of different forms of worship of different gods could not be tolerated. The proof that Baal was a "non-god" is therefore followed by the physical destruction of his erring prophets. In accordance with the exclusiveness of Yahweh, the worship of Baal is abolished by killing his prophets. A tolerant behavior toward other forms of cultic practice is not envisaged here; such an attitude developed only after the encounter of Judaism with other religions.

Elijah at the Mountain of God

Text

19:1 Ahab told Jezebel all that Elijah had done, and how he had killed all the prophets with the sword. 2 Then Jezebel sent a messenger to Elijah, saying, "So may the gods do to me, and more also, if I do not make your life like the life of one of them by this time tomorrow." 3 Then he was afraid; he got up and fled for his life, and came to Beer-sheba, which belongs to Judah; he left his servant there.

4 But he himself went a day's journey into the wilderness, and came and sat down under a solitary broom tree. He asked that he might die: "It is enough; now, O LORD, take away my life, for I am no better than my ancestors." 5 Then he lay down under the broom tree and fell asleep. Suddenly an angel touched him and said to him, "Get up and eat." 6 He looked, and there at his head was a cake baked on hot stones, and a jar of water. He ate and drank, and lay down again. 7 The angel of the LORD came a second time, touched him, and said, "Get up and eat, otherwise the journey will be too much for you." 8 He got up, and ate and drank; then he went in the strength of that food forty days and forty nights to Horeb the mount of God. 9 At that place he came to a cave, and spent the night there.

Then the word of the LORD came to him, saying, "What are you doing here, Elijah?" 10 He answered, "I have been very zealous for the LORD, the God of hosts; for the Israelites have forsaken your covenant, thrown down your altars, and killed your prophets with the sword. I alone am left, and they are seeking my life, to take it away."

11 He said, "Go out and stand on the mountain before the LORD, for the LORD is about to pass by." Now there was a great wind, so strong that it was splitting mountains and breaking rocks in pieces before the LORD, but the LORD was not in the wind; and after the wind an earthquake, but the LORD was not in the earthquake; 12 and after the earthquake a fire, but the LORD was not in the fire; and after the fire a sound of sheer silence. 13 When Elijah heard it, he wrapped his face in his mantle and went out and stood at the entrance

of the cave. Then there came a voice to him that said, "What are you doing here, Elijah?" 14 He answered, "I have been very zealous for the LORD, the God of hosts; for the Israelites have forsaken your covenant, thrown down your altars, and killed your prophets with the sword. I alone am left, and they are seeking my life, to take it away." 15 Then the LORD said to him, "Go, return on your way to the wilderness of Damascus; when you arrive, you shall anoint Hazael as king over Aram. 16 Also you shall anoint Jehu son of Nimshi as king over Israel; and you shall anoint Elisha son of Shaphat of Abel-meholah as prophet in your place. 17 Whoever escapes from the sword of Hazael, Jehu shall kill; and whoever escapes from the sword of Jehu, Elisha shall kill. 18 Yet I will leave seven thousand in Israel, all the knees that have not bowed to Baal, and every mouth that has not kissed him."

Analysis

The narrative of Elijah's stay at the mountain of God is incomplete in that the return of the prophet is not mentioned. Rather, the piece finishes with a long speech of Yahweh (vv. 15-18) that is not a fitting closure of the narrative. In addition, the placement of the climax is disjointed; Yahweh speaks to Elijah in v. 13, but without any description of the theophany especially introduced in v. 11. Thus the action is coherent, yet lacking a refined structure. Most likely, an older tradition of an appearance of Yahweh to Elijah at Mount Horeb has later been reworked to make it fit with Elijah's conflict with the king. Elijah's journey to Horeb is then seen as a flight from Jezebel (vv. 1-3) to make the narrative fit into the context. In its current form the narrative consists of the following scenes:

vv. 1-3	introduction
vv. 4-8	Elijah's journey to Horeb
vv. 9-12	Elijah's stay in a cave
vv. 13-18	Elijah's conversation with Yahweh

Commentary

[19:1-3] The introduction explicitly blames Jezebel for the persecution of the Yahweh-fearing prophet. The wife of Ahab was a daughter of Ethbaal of Tyre (Ṣūr); see 16:31. As a Phoenician princess, she did not belong to the worshipers of Yahweh and was regarded as the representative par excellence for the worship of foreign gods. Therefore, she is portrayed as the driving force behind the destruction of the prophets of Yahweh. As the woman behind Ahab, she is seen in a very negative light, since she is made responsible for the evil acts of Ahab; she is killed under Jehu, who, in a violent uprising, overthrows the Omride dynasty (2 Kgs 9:30-37).

Elijah's first stop during his flight from Jezebel was Beer-sheba, a place in the Negev near Bīʾr es-Sebaʿ. Already part of the steppe, Beer-sheba was the starting point for all long-distance journeys to the southern deserts and probably also for the journey to the mountain of God. Why he left his servant there is unclear; maybe Elijah wanted to spare him the dangerous journey through the desert.

[19:4-8] On his way through the desert, Elijah again experiences the miraculous help of God. The scene presupposes that Elijah started his journey without any provisions of water or food. His wish to die uttered after just one day's journey does not fit the picture painted of the prophet in other texts. Elijah is provided for, in a miraculous way, on his way to the mountain of God with water and bread by a messenger of God just as in Wadi Cherith by the raven (17:2-7) and in Zarephath by the widow (17:8-16). Yahweh's special care for his prophet is stressed again. Elijah does not need to make any provisions for his needs, because God himself takes care of him. Thus the prophet is elevated far beyond any normal human being. The forty days emphasize the length of the journey and correspond to Moses' stay on Mount Sinai in Exod 34:28.

The geographical location of the mountain of God is not given nor is it known from other sources. In the historical works preceding the Priestly writer the mountain is connected with the exodus and therefore located on the Sinai peninsula (see Exodus 18–19). It is possible, however, that the mountain could be in northwestern Arabia on Midianite territory, but there are no pointers supporting such a location.[1] Horeb is the term for the mountain of God in the Deuteronomistic History (see Deut 1:2, 6, 19; 4:10, 15; 5:2; 9:8; 18:16; 28:69; 1 Kgs 8:9).

[19:9-12] Elijah stays overnight in a cave on the mountain of God and receives the announcement of a theophany. The cave offers some protection during a longer stay; the mountain itself, as a place of divine presence, is holy and thus possesses a special numinous quality. According to the narrative Elijah's stay at the mountain of God is an exceptional event; but indicators for a pilgrimage to that holy mountain in ancient Israel are missing, and the list of places given in Numbers 33 cannot be regarded as a pilgrimage map to the mountain of God. Describing the situation in v. 10, Elijah enumerates all the transgressions of Israel; this is repeated, using similar expressions, in the addition in v. 14.

In Deuteronomistic theology the term "covenant" describes the relationship between God and Israel. This covenant is a binding treaty that Yahweh imposes on Israel; at the same time it is an obligation to recognize Yahweh as the one and only God, and the covenant includes the fulfillment of the will of God mediated in the stipulations.[2] By worshiping foreign gods Israel has broken this covenant, because the

---

[1] See Alois Musil, *The Northern Hegaz: A Topographical Itinerary* (New York: American Geographical Society, 1926), 296–98.

[2] See Lothar Perlitt, *Bundestheologie im Alten Testament,* WMANT 36 (Neukirchen-Vluyn: Neukirchener, 1969), 54–128.

people no longer follow the stipulations. The altar is the only legitimate place for sacrifice; since the meaning of sacrifice is expiation, cultic practice and thus a reconciliation with Yahweh are no longer possible after the destruction of the altars. The killing of the prophets emphasizes again the general persecution of the worshipers of Yahweh; the notice that Elijah is the only remaining prophet of Yahweh stresses his significance and elevates his personal status.

[19:11-12] The report of the coming of God is missing from the original narrative, but in vv. 11-12 we find a description of a theophany. The accompanying features like storm, shaking of the earth, and fire are enumerated, but each time it is added that Yahweh is not in them. The traditional attributes of a theophany are rejected, since the coming of Yahweh is always connected with a description of natural events; his coming assumes a cosmic dimension (see Exod 19:16-18; Judg 5:4-5; Ps 18:8-16). Most likely, the connection of natural events and theophany has been taken over from the surrounding nations.[3] In contrast to this, the text stresses the silence. Elijah recognizes the presence of Yahweh only in the hardly audible murmur. This statement is influenced by a reflection on the event of the presence of Yahweh and thus mediates a new image of God that moves beyond traditional views.[4] One can experience God only in the silence that focuses the individual on himself or herself and on the act of listening; this silence is appropriate to the nature of God and to the experience of God through his word. God reveals himself mysteriously.

[19:13-18] After Elijah has realized the presence of God, he answers by stepping out from the cave and covering his face; then he receives a new mission through a speech of Yahweh. The mission consists of three parts or three acts of anointing: the appointment of Hazael as king over the Arameans, the designation of Jehu as king over Israel, and the investiture of a successor for Elijah. The instructions point ahead to the further history of Israel, and they are determined by the view that Yahweh as the lord of history influences the course of history.

The execution of the instructions is reported in several different ways in the further narrative. Hazael will not be anointed by Elijah, but in an encounter with Elisha in 2 Kgs 9:1-15 he is addressed as the future king of the Arameans, who will wage war against Israel. The anointing of Jehu happens in 2 Kgs 9:1-14a by a prophet sent by Elisha; the Omride dynasty ends with Jehu. The call of Elisha is reported in 19:19-21 and establishes a prophetic succession without any anointing. Thus the announcement presupposes the further course of history and has to be regarded as a "prophecy after the event" (*vaticinum ex eventu*). At the same time the further history is placed under the notion of judgment. There is no escape from the fate of a violent death; surprisingly, Elisha is placed with those who have to accept this fate. The

---

[3] See Jörg Jeremias, *Theophanie*, WMANT 10 (Neukirchen-Vluyn: Neukirchener, 1965), 73–90.
[4] Würthwein, *Könige*, 2:230.

further history of Israel, with the wars against the Aramean coalition in the ninth century and the violent coup d'état by Jehu, is seen as a punishment in that the death in battle is not considered a heroic feat but rather an untimely end of life. Death has to be accepted as an unchangeable fact, but only if life reaches its natural end in old age; untimely death in younger years is seen as preventing the normal course of life. The context stresses that the terror of war is caused by Yahweh as a punishment for the worship of foreign gods.

Judging by the population as a whole, which can be calculated as a quarter of a million, the number of seven thousand true worshipers of Yahweh is quite small. A redactor explains in vv. 15-18 the further course of history as Yahweh's judgment on his people because of the worship of foreign gods. This judgment is not final, since some people remain. In the face of a terrible future there is hope of survival for all those who cling to Yahweh.

The Call of Elisha

Text

19:19 So he set out from there, and found Elisha son of Shaphat, who was plowing. There were twelve yoke of oxen ahead of him, and he was with the twelfth. Elijah passed by him and threw his mantle over him. 20 He left the oxen, ran after Elijah, and said, "Let me kiss my father and my mother, and then I will follow you." Then Elijah said to him, "Go back again; for what have I done to you?" 21 He returned from following him, took the yoke of oxen, and slaughtered them; using the equipment from the oxen, he boiled their flesh, and gave it to the people, and they ate. Then he set out and followed Elijah, and became his servant.

Analysis

The call of Elisha by Elijah belongs to the tradition of the prophet Elisha. Its genre can be described as a short narrative whose events are reduced to the absolutely necessary; nevertheless, due to the direct speech, it appears quite lively. As in 1 Kgs 2:1-15, the story links the two men who are otherwise described as being totally different.

Commentary

[**19:19**] The call to service happened in a symbolic action. In v. 19 Elijah throws his mantle over Elisha. The mantle is filled with the power of its owner; in the gesture Elisha becomes Elijah's property and is forced to serve him.[1] The mantle symbolizes the new bond and marks the change of affiliation. Elisha immediately understands Elijah's claim to power and acts accordingly. Elisha is pictured as a farmer, who plows his field. The twelve yoke of oxen do not necessarily point to wealth and could also be understood as a hint that certain tasks in farming were carried out collectively.

[**19:20**] The call means a break in the life of Elisha that results in his giving up his normal routine and bidding farewell to his parents. Both are briefly described. The

---

[1] Würthwein, *Könige*, 2:233.

hearty farewell from his parents in v. 20 shows that Elisha departs on good terms to be free for the new task. Only the parents are mentioned here. This means that Elisha still lives in his parents' home and did not have a family of his own. With the farewell kiss Elisha fulfills the commandment to honor father and mother (see Exod 20:12).

[19:21] The break with the traditional profession appears far more radical. Elisha exchanges the life of a farmer tied to a plot of land that provides for himself and his family with the insecure existence of a prophet, who does not have a regular income and has to depend on alms. The parting from both profession and land is described in radical terms: Elisha destroys his tools and thus gives up every thought of a possible return. In addition, he slaughters his oxen to prepare a farewell feast for his fellow villagers. The place of the actions is not mentioned. According to 19:16 Elisha comes from Abel-meholah. This place is probably also the place of the events mentioned here and can be located at Tell Abū Sus southeast of Beth-shean.[2]

The relationship to Elijah is thought of as a personal discipleship that results in succession, just as the "servant" Joshua had become the successor to Moses (see Exod 24:13; 33:1; Num 11:28; Josh 1:1). Elisha secures the continuation of the Yahwistic prophecy represented by Elijah even though his mission deviates in details from that of Elijah (see the commentary on 17:17-24). Second Kings 2:1-8 describes Elisha's succession to Elijah. The narrative is exceptionally short and displays the unconditional nature of the office of the prophet. Elijah's answer to Elisha's request must not be understood in the sense of the call to discipleship in Matt 8:28-29 and Luke 9:61-62. A separation of Elisha from his family is expected, but this separation does not mean a detachment from society. Elisha will live with his group of prophets on the margins of society, but he remains connected with society as a prophet (see 2 Kgs 6:1-7).

---

[2] See Hans-Jürgen Zobel, "Abel Mehola," *ZDPV* 82 (1966) 83–108.

The Wars against the Arameans

Text

20:1 King Ben-hadad of Aram gathered all his army together; thirty-two kings were with him, along with horses and chariots. He marched against Samaria, laid siege to it, and attacked it. 2 Then he sent messengers into the city to King Ahab of Israel, 3 and said to him: "Thus says Ben-hadad: Your silver and gold are mine; your fairest wives and children also are mine." 4 The king of Israel answered, "As you say, my lord, O king, I am yours, and all that I have." 5 The messengers came again and said: "Thus says Ben-hadad: I sent to you, saying, 'Deliver to me your silver and gold, your wives and children'; 6 nevertheless I will send my servants to you tomorrow about this time, and they shall search your house and the houses of your servants, and lay hands on whatever pleases them, and take it away."

7 Then the king of Israel called all the elders of the land, and said, "Look now! See how this man is seeking trouble; for he sent to me for my wives, my children, my silver, and my gold; and I did not refuse him." 8 Then all the elders and all the people said to him, "Do not listen or consent." 9 So he said to the messengers of Ben-hadad, "Tell my lord the king: All that you first demanded of your servant I will do; but this thing I cannot do." The messengers left and brought him word again. 10 Ben-hadad sent to him and said, "The gods do so to me, and more also, if the dust of Samaria will provide a handful for each of the people who follow me." 11 The king of Israel answered, "Tell him: One who puts on armor should not brag like one who takes it off." 12 When Ben-hadad heard this message—now he had been drinking with the kings in the booths—he said to his men, "Take your positions!" And they took their positions against the city.

13 Then a certain prophet came up to King Ahab of Israel and said, "Thus says the LORD, Have you seen all this great multitude? Look, I will give it into your hand today; and you shall know that I am the LORD." 14 Ahab said, "By whom?" He said, "Thus says the LORD, By the young men who serve the district governors." Then he said, "Who shall begin the battle?" He answered, "You."

15 Then he mustered the young men who serve the district governors, two hundred thirty-two; after them he mustered all the people of Israel, seven thousand.

16 They went out at noon, while Ben-hadad was drinking himself drunk in the booths, he and the thirty-two kings allied with him. 17 The young men who serve the district governors went out first. Ben-hadad had sent out scouts, and they reported to him, "Men have come out from Samaria." 18 He said, "If they have come out for peace, take them alive; if they have come out for war, take them alive."

19 But these had already come out of the city: the young men who serve the district governors, and the army that followed them. 20 Each killed his man; the Arameans fled and Israel pursued them, but King Ben-hadad of Aram escaped on a horse with the cavalry. 21 The king of Israel went out, attacked the horses and chariots, and defeated the Arameans with a great slaughter.

22 Then the prophet approached the king of Israel and said to him, "Come, strengthen yourself, and consider well what you have to do; for in the spring the king of Aram will come up against you."

23 The servants of the king of Aram said to him, "Their gods are gods of the hills, and so they were stronger than we; but let us fight against them in the plain, and surely we shall be stronger than they. 24 Also do this: remove the kings, each from his post, and put commanders in place of them; 25 and muster an army like the army that you have lost, horse for horse, and chariot for chariot; then we will fight against them in the plain, and surely we shall be stronger than they." He heeded their voice, and did so.

26 In the spring Ben-hadad mustered the Arameans and went up to Aphek to fight against Israel. 27 After the Israelites had been mustered and provisioned, they went out to engage them; the people of Israel encamped opposite them like two little flocks of goats, while the Arameans filled the country. 28 A man of God approached and said to the king of Israel, "Thus says the LORD: Because the Arameans have said, 'The LORD is a god of the hills but he is not a god of the valleys,' therefore I will give all this great multitude into your hand, and you shall know that I am the LORD." 29 They encamped opposite one another seven days. Then on the seventh day the battle began; the Israelites killed one hundred thousand Aramean foot soldiers in one day. 30 The rest fled into the city of Aphek; and the wall fell on twenty-seven thousand men that were left.

Ben-hadad also fled, and entered the city to hide. 31 His servants said to him, "Look, we have heard that the kings of the house of Israel are merciful kings; let us put sackcloth around our waists and ropes on our heads, and go out to the king of Israel; perhaps he will spare your life." 32 So they tied sackcloth around their waists, put ropes on their heads, went to the king of Israel, and said, "Your servant Ben-hadad says, 'Please let me live.'" And he said, "Is he still alive? He is my brother." 33 Now the men were watching for an omen; they quickly took it up from him and said, "Yes, Ben-hadad is your brother." Then he said, "Go and bring him." So Ben-hadad came out to him; and he had him come up into the chariot. 34 Ben-hadad said to him, "I will restore the towns that my father took from your father; and you may establish bazaars for yourself in Damascus, as my father did in Samaria." The king of Israel responded, "I will let you go on those terms." So he made a treaty with him and let him go.

35 At the command of the LORD a certain member of a company of prophets said to another, "Strike me!" But the man refused to strike him. 36 Then he said to him, "Because you have not obeyed the voice of the LORD, as soon as you have left me, a lion will kill you." And when he had left him, a lion met him and killed him. 37 Then he found another man and said, "Strike me!" So the man hit him, striking and wounding him. 38 Then the prophet departed, and waited for the king along the road, disguising himself with a bandage over his eyes. 39 As the king passed by, he cried to the king and said, "Your servant went out into the thick of the battle; then a soldier turned and brought a man to me, and said, 'Guard this man; if he is missing, your life shall be given for his life, or else you shall pay a talent of silver.' 40 While your servant was busy here and there, he was gone." The king of Israel said to him, "So shall your judgment be; you yourself have decided it." 41 Then he quickly took the bandage away from his eyes. The king of Israel recognized him as one of the prophets. 42 Then he said to him, "Thus says the LORD, 'Because you have let the man go whom I had devoted to destruction, therefore your life shall be for his life, and your people for his people.'" 43 The king of Israel set out toward home, resentful and sullen, and came to Samaria.

Analysis

Two narratives are connected under the theme of the conflict with the Arameans: the battle for Samaria (vv. 1-21) and the battle for Aphek (vv. 26-43). Both pieces are joined by an interlude (vv. 22-25). A prophet appears in both narratives who announces the victory of Yahweh by using formulaic expressions (vv. 13-14, 28); these verses can be regarded as additions. Finally, vv. 35-42 are additions in which the sparing of the enemy is disapproved of; this supplement represents a later interpretation by a redactor. Otherwise both narratives in vv. 1-12, 15-21, and vv. 26-27, 29-34, 43 are full of drama, and the joy of the victory over the enemy shines through.

The quick change between scenes is characteristic for this type of narrative—the flow of action is moved forward by the decisions of the kings, who are the main actors. Since Ahab is mentioned by name only in v. 2 and in the addition of vv. 13-14 (otherwise the narrative speaks of the "king of Israel"), some have suggested that the narrated events should be dated to the time of Jehoaz or Joash.[1] Since it was only Joash who managed, with significant military success, to ban the threat posed by the Arameans, the dating of the narrated events to his time is entirely probable. The Ben-hadad mentioned in the text would then be Ben-hadad II, the successor to Hazael. It is impossible to extract further historical details from the narratives. Rather, the chapter is a fictive composition of events in connection with the victories over the Arameans during the sieges of Samaria and Aphek.

Commentary

[20:1-12, 15-21] The first narrative takes place in Samaria. Samaria was the capital of the state of Israel (see 16:24) since the transfer of the residence of the kings of Israel to this newly built city under Omri. Ben-hadad, the king of the Aramean state of Damascus, musters not only his own troops for the war against Israel but also contingents of his vassals (v. 1). The king in the besieged city is in a desperate situation. In view of his hopeless situation he promises payment of a tribute and the provision of hostages (vv. 2-4). It is only the further demand of looting and the unconditional surrender of the city that strengthens the resistance of the Israelite king (vv. 5-9).

The measures mentioned in the negotiations were part of ancient Near Eastern warfare. The tribute allowed the defeated party to buy themselves out and thus stop further battle and looting. In a way, this payment was regarded as a replacement for the lost booty. The hostages provided would secure the negotiated peace. The purpose of the looting of a city was to take as much booty as possible. This booty included the inhabitants, who were either sold as slaves or became part of the now increased property of the victor. Thus tribute was to spare the inhabitants. The demand of Ben-hadad is unacceptable in that it does not guarantee the legal status of the inhabitants that was negotiated by the tribute. According to Ben-hadad the handing over of the city equals its capture. In view of this demand, the representatives of Samaria decide against surrender without a fight and opt for a further defense of the city.

[20:10-12, 15-18] The following scenes portray Ben-hadad as an arrogant general, whose wrong judgments are responsible for his defeat. First, he praises the size of his army to demonstrate his military strength (v. 10). The king of Israel answers this display of power with the proverb that one cannot be sure of victory before the end of battle (v. 11). The meaning of the proverb is roughly: "Don't count your chickens before they hatch." A celebration is only justified after the end of an event, because even during a favorable course of events a sudden turn is possible.

The king of Israel answers the danger he is in with a sally. During a siege this was the only way for the besieged to defeat the enemy. Such an attack was a risky

---

[1] See J. Maxwell Miller, "The Rest of the Acts of Jehoahaz, 1 Kings 20, 22:1-38," *ZAW* 80 (1968) 337; Hans-Christoph Schmitt, *Elisa: Traditionsgeschichtliche Untersuchungen zur vorklassischen nord-israelitischen Prophetie* (Gütersloh: Gütersloher, 1972), 60–61.

enterprise, since its success could not be foretold. The order to take hostages rather than to encounter the enemy on a military basis results in disaster (vv. 17-18). Furthermore, Ben-hadad is portrayed as a drunkard who tries to counter the boredom of this military campaign with drinking parties (vv. 12, 16). Also the Israelites make use of a ruse of war: they attack at midday. During this hour the readiness to fight diminishes due to the sweltering heat and the poor visibility in bright sunlight.

[20:19-21] The end of the battle is quickly narrated, using general formulas. The Israelites put the Arameans to flight and follow with a general pursuit. Ben-hadad avoids captivity through flight, and the king of Israel takes rich booty from the weapons, horses, and chariots. The victory of Israel is thus complete, the siege is ended, the enemy put to flight, and the danger averted.

[20:26-27, 29-34, 43] The second narrative is set in Aphek. Although the geographical location of the city is not given, the context seems to point to a place east of the Jordan, situated on a plateau (v. 23); Aphek is also mentioned in 2 Kgs 13:17. Eusebius already located Aphek near Hippo (Khirbet Susita/Qalʿat el-Ḥuṣu) east of the Sea of Genezareth (*Onomasticon* 22.20-21), but the equation with the hill of ruins called Fiq in the Golan has to be abandoned, since this city of the Middle Bronze Age was resettled only in Hellenistic-Roman times—despite the fact that its ancient name survived. Biblical Aphek can possibly be identified with the neighboring Tell Soreg, where a fortified settlement of Iron Age II has been excavated.[2]

The successful campaign against Aphek is narrated in conventional form. Apart from the reprieve of Ben-hadad and the agreements reached, no details are given. The time of the campaign is spring, since a war could start only after the rainy season (v. 26). Again, the Arameans are the aggressors. In the comparison of the two armies, the weakness of Israel is especially stressed. The battle is not described, but one can assume that it was fought in open territory (v. 29). The flight into the city of Aphek presupposes that this city was in Aramean hands (v. 30). Since we do not know the exact course of the border between Aram and Israel, we cannot comment on the original property situation; however, it would appear that the whole of the Golan territory was part of the Aramean state during the monarchic period. The battle of Aphek would then presuppose that the king of Israel was campaigning on foreign territory.

The subsequent narrative presumes that Aphek was surrounded, as an Aramean enclave, by the Israelite army after the victorious battle. The scene of reprieve (vv. 31-33) is in accordance with the rules of war at that time.[3] By submission to the victor the defeated party was able to save their lives and sometimes even the throne (see Isa 21:9; 38:17). Ben-hadad and his followers acknowledge the victorious opponent with rites of self-humiliation manifested by special garments. To put on clothing of

---

[2] See Mosheh Kochavi, *IEJ* 39 (1989) 6–9; *IEJ* 41 (1991) 181.
[3] Würthwein, *Könige,* 2:241.

poor quality is also part of the funeral rites, which are especially characterized by self-humiliation (see Gen 37:34; 2 Sam 3:31; 1 Kgs 21:27; 2 Kgs 6:30).

The king of Israel grants a pardon with words and a gesture emphasizing equality when he asks Ben-hadad to step on his chariot. The public act of pardon renders it legally binding. According to the rules of society, which are valid as unwritten laws, the reprieved person is bound to loyalty. After he has acknowledged the victor as the more powerful person, he remains obliged to him. This commitment, which results from submission, leads in the case of Ben-hadad to a treaty that presupposes the end of combat and a lasting peace (v. 34).

Ben-hadad not only gives back the conquered territories but also sets up "lanes" or "bazaars" for Israel in Damascus. A list of towns is missing; therefore neither the territory nor the new course of the border can be determined in more detail. Since the Golan Heights still belonged to the Aramean states of Geshur and Maachah during the tenth century, we can assume that the deep separating valley of the Yarmuk formed the natural border between the east Jordan territories of Israel and the Aramean states.[4] The exact function of the established "lanes" or "bazaars" is not clear; they may have been open spaces established for the victor in the defeated capital. They were probably not used as trading places, but could be used to demonstrate Israelite presence and to control the loyalty of the subjugated people. These places were most likely extraterritorial areas within the city that only the victor was allowed to use. The establishment of these "lanes" and the right to use them symbolizes the establishment of Israelite rule over the Aramean state of Damascus and the end of Israel's war with the Arameans. The narrative probably reflects the conditions during the reign of Joash at the beginning of the eighth century.[5] The pardon is therefore not a sign of selflessness but part of the rules of war; it serves to manifest the power of the victorious party. After the peace agreement, the king of Israel can return to his residence in Samaria (v. 43).

[20:22-25] The connecting piece between the two narratives places the events under a theological premise: the victory is really due to Yahweh, whom the Arameans had underestimated. The events narrated without any divine connection receive a special twist: Yahweh alone helped Israel to conquer the enemy; the success in battle—despite being a human enterprise—has to be traced back to the power of God. A later redactor thus adds his view of history. Such kerygmatic additions aim at keeping alive the hope in Yahweh in a critical situation.[6] The added word of the prophet stresses the contribution of Yahweh to the events, since in the narrative human action was the main focus, with no reflection upon the help of Yahweh.

---

[4] See Benjamin Mazar, "Geshur and Maachah," in idem, *The Early Biblical Period: Historical Studies,* ed. Shmuel Ahituv and Baruch A. Levine (Jerusalem: Israel Exploration Society, 1986), 113–15.

[5] See Alfred Jepsen, "Israel und Damaskus," *AfO* 14 (1941–44) 153–72.

[6] Würthwein, *Könige,* 2:243.

[20:13-14, 28] A similar intention is found in the two additions, vv. 13-14 and v. 28. The central statement of both anonymous prophetic words is that Yahweh gives the enemies into the hand of the king, so that he will know "that I am Yahweh." The phraseology is part of Deuteronomistic theology. The expression "to give into your hand" contains the promise of victory over the enemies and is a so-called hand-over formula, which is often found in connection with the wars of Israel (see Josh 2:24; 6:2; 8:1, 18; 10:8, 19). The demand to recognize Yahweh belongs to the common language pool of the Deuteronomistic History too (see Deut 4:35, 39; 7:9; Josh 2:11). The formula does not imply an act of spiritual recognition, but asks one to acknowledge Yahweh as the one and only God (see 1 Kgs 18:39). The external sign for this recognition is the worship of Yahweh alone and the exclusion of all other foreign cults. Success in war and turning to Yahweh as the only God are thus dependent on each other.

[20:35-42] The later interpretation in vv. 35-42 tries to bring the events into line with the stipulations of the Deuteronomic laws of warfare. According to them, all inhabitants are to be placed under the ban and therefore have to be killed. Not only did the ban remove the booty from the reach of the conquerors, but the killing of both people and animals placed the booty in Yahweh's hands. This cultic measure, given only in Deut 20:10-18, stands in stark opposition to the assumed rules of war in the narrative. It is almost expected that a prophet would threaten the king with death for not heeding the divine rules.

The short narrative is intensified by the prophet being incognito. Members of a certain group of prophets apparently wore a recognizable sign on their forehead that distinguished them from other people. This sign is hidden by a bandage that supposedly covers a wound and is only removed at the time of the oracle of judgment. The sign legitimizes the prophetic message. In the judgment of the prophet the military success of the king appears as a violation of divine law, which has to be punished.

The Judicial Murder of Naboth

Text

21:1 Later the following events took place: Naboth the Jezreelite had a vineyard in Jezreel, beside the palace of King Ahab of Samaria. 2 And Ahab said to Naboth, "Give me your vineyard, so that I may have it for a vegetable garden, because it is near my house; I will give you a better vineyard for it; or, if it seems good to you, I will give you its value in money." 3 But Naboth said to Ahab, "The LORD forbid that I should give you my ancestral inheritance." 4 Ahab went home resentful and sullen because of what Naboth the Jezreelite had said to him; for he had said, "I will not give you my ancestral inheritance." He lay down on his bed, turned away his face, and would not eat.

5 His wife Jezebel came to him and said, "Why are you so depressed that you will not eat?" 6 He said to her, "Because I spoke to Naboth the Jezreelite and said to him, 'Give me your vineyard for money; or else, if you prefer, I will give you another vineyard for it'; but he answered, 'I will not give you my vineyard.'" 7 His wife Jezebel said to him, "Do you now govern Israel? Get up, eat some food, and be cheerful; I will give you the vineyard of Naboth the Jezreelite."

8 So she wrote letters in Ahab's name and sealed them with his seal; she sent the letters to the elders and the nobles who lived with Naboth in his city. 9 She wrote in the letters, "Proclaim a fast, and seat Naboth at the head of the assembly; 10 seat two scoundrels opposite him, and have them bring a charge against him, saying, 'You have cursed God and the king.' Then take him out, and stone him to death." 11 The men of his city, the elders and the nobles who lived in his city, did as Jezebel had sent word to them. Just as it was written in the letters that she had sent to them, 12 they proclaimed a fast and seated Naboth at the head of the assembly. 13 The two scoundrels came in and sat opposite him; and the scoundrels brought a charge against Naboth, in the presence of the people, saying, "Naboth cursed God and the king." So they took him outside the city, and stoned him

to death. 14 Then they sent to Jezebel, saying, "Naboth has been stoned; he is dead."

15 As soon as Jezebel heard that Naboth had been stoned and was dead, Jezebel said to Ahab, "Go, take possession of the vineyard of Naboth the Jezreelite, which he refused to give you for money; for Naboth is not alive, but dead." 16 As soon as Ahab heard that Naboth was dead, Ahab set out to go down to the vineyard of Naboth the Jezreelite, to take possession of it.

17 Then the word of the LORD came to Elijah the Tishbite, saying: 18 Go down to meet King Ahab of Israel, who rules in Samaria; he is now in the vineyard of Naboth, where he has gone to take possession. 19 You shall say to him, "Thus says the LORD: Have you killed, and also taken possession?" You shall say to him, "Thus says the LORD: In the place where dogs licked up the blood of Naboth, dogs will also lick up your blood."

20 Ahab said to Elijah, "Have you found me, O my enemy?" He answered, "I have found you. Because you have sold yourself to do what is evil in the sight of the LORD, 21 I will bring disaster on you; I will consume you, and will cut off from Ahab every male, bond or free, in Israel; 22 and I will make your house like the house of Jeroboam son of Nebat, and like the house of Baasha son of Ahijah, because you have provoked me to anger and have caused Israel to sin. 23 Also concerning Jezebel the LORD said, 'The dogs shall eat Jezebel within the bounds of Jezreel.' 24 Anyone belonging to Ahab who dies in the city the dogs shall eat; and anyone of his who dies in the open country the birds of the air shall eat."

25 (Indeed, there was no one like Ahab, who sold himself to do what was evil in the sight of the LORD, urged on by his wife Jezebel. 26 He acted most abominably in going after idols, as the Amorites had done, whom the LORD drove out before the Israelites.)

27 When Ahab heard those words, he tore his clothes and put sackcloth over his bare flesh; he fasted, lay in the sackcloth, and went about dejectedly. 28 Then the word of the LORD came to Elijah the Tishbite: 29 "Have you seen how Ahab has humbled himself before me? Because he has humbled himself before me, I will not bring the disaster in his days; but in his son's days I will bring the disaster on his house."

Analysis

The story of the judicial murder of Naboth falls into two parts. Verses 1-16 narrate the case and its background, followed by the words of the prophet in vv. 17-29, which add a separate theological interpretation to the story. The narrative, which was originally independent and self-explanatory, is thereby moved into the interpretive framework of offense and punishment, characteristic of the Deuteronomistic History. The object of contention is the vineyard of Naboth, a free citizen, declared an "inheritance" by its owner. The inherited land is especially significant in that the term used for it is associated with Yahweh; "inheritance" does not mean inherited land only, but is also used to describe the land given by Yahweh as inheritance.[1] If the land essentially belongs to Yahweh, then its owner cannot offer it for sale; see Lev 25:23. The conflict between Ahab and Naboth, however, is not mainly "about the legal status of the plot of land."[2] "The plan of the king does not founder on the stipulations of land law but rather on the Israelite notion of kingship, which sees the will of the king curtailed by the will of a free citizen when his possession of land is concerned."[3] The dispute about the vineyard is a model case for showing up the limits of royal power and paradigmatic for the decline of the rule of law and for royal despotism.

The events take place at Jezreel (Zer'in), where the Israelite kings kept a palace (although no mention is made of its construction). Excavations have been able to confirm the location, but the residence proper has not yet been discovered.[4] With Jezreel lying on a plain, the cultivation of vines nearby is rather unlikely: vineyards would usually be planted on hill terraces, and we ought to conclude that the story does not rest on historical precedents but instead is a fictional example of royal despotism. The intention of the story is not to show that Ahab has taken possession of a vineyard for his own use by unlawful means, but rather that the kingship of Israel has removed itself from law and order to the extent where even a judicial murder and the shedding of innocent blood are not ruled out. In the hands of Ahab and his wife Jezebel royal power becomes an instrument of murder to which the free citizen is cruelly exposed. It is therefore not only land law that is at stake, but the rule of law as such. The kingship, instead of guaranteeing legal security, adds to the perversion of justice by using unlawful means in order to achieve a piece of land: those who object are executed on trumped up charges, so that the appearance of proper procedure is maintained. The narrative is dramatic and full of tension, making artful use of dialogue in particular.

Commentary

[21:1-4] The exposition establishes the parameters of the conflict. Naboth refuses to sell Ahab his vineyard, which borders on the royal palace. The king's intention to enlarge his estate meets with the firm decision of the owner not to sell or exchange his land. Ahab is so enraged by his failure that he takes himself to bed and refuses to eat, a behavior that forces those near him to act.

---

[1] See Friedrich Horst, "Zwei Begriffe für Eigentum," in *Verbannung und Heimkehr: Beiträge zur Geschichte und Theologie Israels im 6. und 5. Jahrhundert vor Chr. Wilhelm Rudolph zum 70. Geburtstage,* ed. Arnulf Kuschke (Tübing: Mohr/Siebeck, 1961), 135–50.

[2] Albrecht Alt, *Kleine Schriften zur Geschichte des Volkes Israels* (Munich: Beck), 3:357 n. 1.

[3] Würthwein, *Könige,* 2:248.

[4] See H. G. M. Williamson, "Jezreel in Biblical Texts," *TA* 18 (1991) 72–92; David Ussishkin and John Woodhead, "Excavations at Tel Jezreel, 1990–1991," *TA* 19 (1992) 3–56; idem, "Excavations at Tel Jezreel 1992-1993: Second Preliminary Report," *Levant* 26 (1994) 1–48.

[21:5-7] Thus, in the following scene, his wife Jezebel takes up the baton; it is she who is charged with the preparation and execution of the plot against Naboth. After she has asked Ahab about the reason for his anger, she promises to find a solution and assuage his fury. As a Tyrian princess, Jezebel was a foreigner in Israel and was considered capable of any form of debasement (see on 16:31-32). Here she almost comes to embody the evil spirit of Ahab, perverting the entire system of justice in Israel. The tender care shown for her husband covers only thinly her reckless determination to make royal power prevail at all costs, even if it means murder.

[21:8-13] The main section sees Jezebel plot her murderous intrigue against Naboth that involves practically the entire community in a manipulated law case against him. She has a written order issued against him and makes unauthorized use of the royal seal. She thereby not only exceeds her powers (she has, in fact, no governmental authority at all), but also orders the execution of what now appears as a royal decree, unknown to those acting on its behalf. The form in which the decree is issued implies that the king, who was probably illiterate, would dictate and then stamp his letters with a seal as a form of signature. We have evidence for this practice through a large number of seals and prints, with the seal usually attached to the folded document by a string. The seal would be inscribed with the name of its owner and thus be recognizable to the addressee.[5]

Jezebel's contemptuous plan is carried out by the city elders who share in her guilt by their placid consent. The role of the king in cultic and legal affairs of the community was obviously limited, yet Jezebel insists unscrupulously on the privilege of royal power. Jurisdiction in particular was in the hands of the people, or rather their representatives, that is, the elders of a family or clan, and not the king.[6]

Her first order is to announce a fast, together with a public assembly, the sign of a cultic act to expiate a wrongdoing and to turn away its effects from the community (see 1 Sam 7:6; Joel 1:14; 2:15). In postexilic times this rite of fasting was institutionalized in the great Day of Atonement (see Num 29:7). The fast is accompanied by prayer and acts of self-humiliation to gain God's forgiveness for trespasses.[7]

In the assembly in question Naboth is to be placed in such a way that every accusation leveled against him will de facto be made public. Once the stage is prepared the two false witnesses are to appear. According to Israelite legal custom, those witnesses were also the accusers. Since there was no office comparable to a public prosecutor, any witness was obliged to make charges himself. "Failing that, he himself became guilty . . . of letting an offense go past without punishment, an offense

---

[5] See Kurt Galling, "Tafel, Buch und Blatt," in *Near Eastern Studies in Honor of William Foxwell Albright*, ed. Hans Goedicke (Baltimore, Johns Hopkins Press, 1971), 207–23.

[6] See Christian Macholz, "Die Stellung des Königs in der israelitischen Gerichtsverfassung," *ZAW* 84 (1972) 157–81.

[7] See H. D. Preuss, "צום, fasting," in *TDOT* 12:297–301.

that, according to contemporary belief, would lie heavily on a community and have damaging effects on it."[8] The false accusation against Naboth is therefore voiced at a particularly opportune time. While the people are gathered in assembly to expiate for a sin, Naboth is accused of cursing against God and the king. The charge is not further specified, but in its context must appear as a conviction already. Naboth's (alleged) offense can be expiated only through death by stoning, according to Lev 24:16.

In order to guard oneself against false accusations, two witnesses had to be brought forward (see Num 35:30; Deut 17:6; 19:15). Jezebel has therefore arranged for two witnesses in advance, who accuse Naboth of cursing against God and the king. The curse is thought to be a mighty and damaging word whose power unfolds independently of its immediate context.[9] The curse against God violates the sanctity of Yahweh and infringes upon the sphere of God alone to which no human being must have access. The curse against the king diminishes his actions and status and subsequently is harmful to the people, whose well-being is closely connected to that of the king. The accusation against Naboth therefore blames him alone for all the misfortunes that have occurred to the people and have necessitated the assembly in the first place. God had to answer the infringement of his proper sphere with an act of punishment, while the king could no longer guarantee the prosperity of his people.

Someone who has done such injury to the community has to be excluded from it by a collective death sentence.[10] The collective act of stoning makes sure that no one attracts new bloodguilt that would lead to new vengeance in turn. What is crucial is not the death of the perpetrator but the purification from his guilt. The stoning is therefore not to be seen as a particularly gruesome way of killing, but rather as a necessary act of expiation. Verses 12-13 summarily report the execution of Jezebel's plan by the elders of Samaria.

[21:14-16] Finally, these verses bring the conflict outlined in vv. 1-4 to a conclusion. The execution of the judicial murder is reported back to the queen (v. 14), and she now asks Ahab to take possession of Naboth's vineyard. Now that the culprit has been put to death, the king can apparently dispose freely of his estate. Legal practice probably decreed that the possessions of those who were found guilty of a capital offense against the king were handed over not to the family but to the king instead. Ahab marks the actual taking of possession by entering the vineyard he has so passionately craved.

All the participants of the episode appear in a bad light, with the exception of

---

8 Würthwein, *Könige*, 2:250.

9 See Willy Schottroff, *Der altisraelitische Fluchspruch*, WMANT 30 (Neukirchen-Vluyn: Neukirchener, 1969).

10 See Hermann Schulz, *Das Todesrecht im Alten Testament: Studien zur Rechtsform der Mot-Jumat-Sätze*, BZAW 114 (Berlin: Töpelmann, 1969).

Naboth, who, after all, falls victim to false charges. Ahab is incapable of controlling his desires; Jezebel recklessly hatches a plot to eliminate the "adversary"; the representatives of the people, finally, disregard their duty toward freedom and law and become willing executioners of the power claimed by the kingship. The theme of the story is "the demise of the old Israelite legal order: the kingship oversteps its boundaries and hands a citizen over to judgment on trumped-up charges simply in order to annex his estate."[11] The story thus turns out to be heavily critical of the kingship: the king not only seizes what is not his to seize, but he also simply does away with a citizen's rights and possessions. The blame that is apportioned to Jezebel does not diminish Ahab's guilt in any way; the decision to marry a non-Israelite woman who is capable of such perversions of justice is, after all, his choice. The present story articulates a fundamentally negative attitude toward the kingship, compatible with the critical undercurrent of the entire Deuteronomistic History: because the kingship does not respect the inviolability of people and their possessions, it disregards the inalienable rights at the basis of the Israelite legal order.

[**21:17-29**] The prophetic words, which are added as an interpretation in vv. 17-29, underline once more the theme of divine punishment. Yahweh, the true guarantor of law, will not treat the king with impunity after he has resorted to murder to get his will. The original core is most likely vv. 17-19a, 20, 24. While Ahab is still in the vineyard, which he has now unlawfully acquired, Elijah is sent to confront him. The short dialogue between the king and the prophet shows clearly the imperviousness of the king. A shameful end is predicted for him and his family as punishment: after their death they will be eaten by animals (dogs and birds), which means that Ahab and his family will be left unburied. This is a threat amounting to eternal punishment: proper burial was a constitutive part of the Israelite notion of life and death. In death, one changes into a different state, being summoned to one's ancestors. This transition to the realm of the dead was tied to the burial in a proper tomb, usually a chamber hewn into the rock where stone benches served as biers for several generations of a family (see on 2:10-11). To leave a corpse to scavenging animals was therefore not only shameful, but it also barred any further existence, even if it was that of a shadow in the realm of the dead.

[**21:21-26**] Verses 21-22 change the stress slightly when they foretell the end of the dynasty. The future history with the usurpation of the throne by Jehu and the extinction of the royal family (2 Kings 10) is interpreted as a judgment over Ahab. Verse 23 extends the punishment to Jezebel. Verses 25-26 once more put the blame on the worship of foreign gods (see on 16:32-33).

---

[11] Würthwein, *Könige*, 2:251.

[21:27-29] A second reinterpretation mentions Ahab's repentance to justify the transfer of punishment to a later generation. All the additions use the formulaic language characteristic of the Deuteronomistic redactors. Those enlargements are of little historiographic value, as their main aim is to interpret history within the framework of Deuteronomistic theology and its all-encompassing concept of the justice of God. Even the undetected murderer will therefore meet his just punishment; and even if the king is not tried in a human court, he is part of the divine world order of retribution guaranteed by God himself.

The Death of Ahab
in the Campaign against the Arameans

Text

22:1 For three years Aram and Israel continued without war. 2 But in the third year King Jehoshaphat of Judah came down to the king of Israel. 3 The king of Israel said to his servants, "Do you know that Ramoth-gilead belongs to us, yet we are doing nothing to take it out of the hand of the king of Aram?" 4 He said to Jehoshaphat, "Will you go with me to battle at Ramoth-gilead?" Jehoshaphat replied to the king of Israel, "I am as you are; my people are your people, my horses are your horses."

5 But Jehoshaphat also said to the king of Israel, "Inquire first for the word of the LORD." 6 Then the king of Israel gathered the prophets together, about four hundred of them, and said to them, "Shall I go to battle against Ramoth-gilead, or shall I refrain?" They said, "Go up; for the LORD will give it into the hand of the king." 7 But Jehoshaphat said, "Is there no other prophet of the LORD here of whom we may inquire?" 8 The king of Israel said to Jehoshaphat, "There is still one other by whom we may inquire of the LORD, Micaiah son of Imlah; but I hate him, for he never prophesies anything favorable about me, but only disaster." Jehoshaphat said, "Let the king not say such a thing." 9 Then the king of Israel summoned an officer and said, "Bring quickly Micaiah son of Imlah." 10 Now the king of Israel and King Jehoshaphat of Judah were sitting on their thrones, arrayed in their robes, at the threshing floor at the entrance of the gate of Samaria; and all the prophets were prophesying before them. 11 Zedekiah son of Chenaanah made for himself horns of iron, and he said, "Thus says the LORD: With these you shall gore the Arameans until they are destroyed." 12 All the prophets were prophesying the same and saying, "Go up to Ramoth-gilead and triumph; the LORD will give it into the hand of the king."

13 The messenger who had gone to summon Micaiah said to him, "Look, the words of the prophets with one accord are favorable to the king; let your

216

word be like the word of one of them, and speak favorably." 14 But Micaiah said, "As the LORD lives, whatever the LORD says to me, that I will speak."

15 When he had come to the king, the king said to him, "Micaiah, shall we go to Ramoth-gilead to battle, or shall we refrain?" He answered him, "Go up and triumph; the LORD will give it into the hand of the king." 16 But the king said to him, "How many times must I make you swear to tell me nothing but the truth in the name of the LORD?" 17 Then Micaiah said, "I saw all Israel scattered on the mountains, like sheep that have no shepherd; and the LORD said, 'These have no master; let each one go home in peace.'" 18 The king of Israel said to Jehoshaphat, "Did I not tell you that he would not prophesy anything favorable about me, but only disaster?"

19 Then Micaiah said, "Therefore hear the word of the LORD: I saw the LORD sitting on his throne, with all the host of heaven standing beside him to the right and to the left of him. 20 And the LORD said, 'Who will entice Ahab, so that he may go up and fall at Ramoth-gilead?' Then one said one thing, and another said another, 21 until a spirit came forward and stood before the LORD, saying, 'I will entice him.' 'How?' the LORD asked him. 22 He replied, 'I will go out and be a lying spirit in the mouth of all his prophets.' Then the LORD said, 'You are to entice him, and you shall succeed; go out and do it.' 23 So you see, the LORD has put a lying spirit in the mouth of all these your prophets; the LORD has decreed disaster for you."

24 Then Zedekiah son of Chenaanah came up to Micaiah, slapped him on the cheek, and said, "Which way did the spirit of the LORD pass from me to speak to you?" 25 Micaiah replied, "You will find out on that day when you go in to hide in an inner chamber." 26 The king of Israel then ordered, "Take Micaiah, and return him to Amon the governor of the city and to Joash the king's son, 27 and say, 'Thus says the king: Put this fellow in prison, and feed him on reduced rations of bread and water until I come in peace.'" 28 Micaiah said, "If you return in peace, the LORD has not spoken by me." And he said, "Hear, you peoples, all of you!"

29 So the king of Israel and King Jehoshaphat of Judah went up to Ramoth-gilead. 30 The king of Israel said to Jehoshaphat, "I will disguise myself and go into battle, but you wear your robes." So the king of Israel disguised himself and went into battle. 31 Now the king of Aram had commanded the thirty-two captains of his chariots, "Fight with no one small or great, but only with the king of Israel." 32 When the captains of the chariots saw Jehoshaphat, they said, "It is surely the king of Israel." So they turned to fight against him; and Jehoshaphat cried out. 33 When the captains of the chariots saw that it was not the king of Israel, they turned back from pursuing him. 34 But a certain man drew his bow and unknowingly struck the king of Israel between the scale armor and the breastplate; so he said to the driver of his chariot, "Turn around, and carry me out of the battle, for I am wounded." 35 The battle grew hot that day, and the king was propped up in

his chariot facing the Arameans, until at evening he died; the blood from the wound had flowed into the bottom of the chariot. 36 Then about sunset a shout went through the army, "Every man to his city, and every man to his country!"

37 So the king died, and was brought to Samaria; they buried the king in Samaria. 38 They washed the chariot by the pool of Samaria; the dogs licked up his blood, and the prostitutes washed themselves in it, according to the word of the LORD that he had spoken.

Analysis

The account of the death of Ahab at Ramoth-gilead (vv. 1-4, 29-38) is interrupted by the prophetic narrative of Micaiah son of Imlah (vv. 5-28), a prophet who is not mentioned anywhere else. Its theme is the difficult relationship between true and false prophecy: here the prophecy in the name of Yahweh is true because it is fulfilled and thus verified. Verse 38 adds to the battle account the fulfillment of the prophecy to Ahab in 21:19b; the fate of the king is interpreted retrospectively as the sentence spoken over him by God. The account of the king's death in battle at Ramoth-gilead was originally there to elucidate that the king cannot avoid his fate, as it is ordained by Yahweh. A historical evaluation of the story is inappropriate, because we are dealing with a freely composed piece. The king of Israel is not once mentioned by name, and the reference to Ahab becomes obvious only in its larger context. The story is therefore not referring to a specific event, but rather shows in an exemplary fashion that no cunning can help to eschew death once the hour has approached. Even the king of Israel cannot escape the will of God. The battle account takes on the character of an exemplary didactic tale. Its application to Ahab illuminates the figure of the king from a critical angle.

Commentary

[22:1-4] The two kings of Israel and Judah are at the center of the battle account in vv. 1-4, 29-38, with the king of Israel being the dominating figure. The introduction (vv. 1-4) first establishes a link back to 20:1-43 in its mention of the three-year truce between Israel and Aram, which also dates the events. No reason is given for Jehoshaphat's visit to Samaria, but it may well have been a gesture of goodwill, following his accession to the throne, to confirm the improved relations between Judah and Israel. When Ahab outlines his plan to reclaim Ramoth-gilead, Jehoshaphat agrees to participate in the campaign.

Ramoth-gilead was the most important city in northern East Jordan and, according to 4:13, the seat of the governor of one of three East Jordanian provinces; its probable location is Tell el-Ḥusn. Jehoshaphat's pledge is tantamount to an alliance and the provision of Judean troops to be put under Ahab's order. The same formula is used in a different context in 2 Kgs 3:7, where it expresses the same unconditional support. Jehoshaphat shows no intention to evaluate the military situation first, nor are conditions imposed.

[22:29-33] The scene of Ahab in disguise follows immediately from v. 4. No details are provided regarding the type and strength of the armies; the focus is firmly on the two kings. Ahab himself suggests that he go into battle in disguise, whereas Jehoshaphat still wears his royal dress, a statement that implies that the king must have been recognizable by his splendid clothes even from afar. The intention is clear: Ahab wants to avoid being identified as the king leading an army into battle in order to avoid danger. While Jehoshaphat draws special attention to himself, Ahab fights under the guise of normal armor and remains undetected. This trick exposes Jehoshaphat to greater danger, while reducing Ahab's own. At first the plan appears to work. Jehoshaphat can escape and save his life only when his cry proves him not to be the king of Israel. Ahab had deliberately taken Jehoshaphat's death into account when he suggested his plan to the king of Judah; the plan is now foiled.

[22:34-35] The terse report of the wounding and death of Ahab is the high point of the narrative. He is hit by an arrow, as if accidentally, and not even the scales of his armor can protect him. Ahab is fatally injured and bleeds to death. As the leader known to his own people, he cannot leave the battle, despite his own wish, as this would have meant surrender. Thus he is propped up in his chariot to maintain an image of steadfastness for the enemy. It was a rule of war that the king would lead his troops into battle, standing in his chariot and visible to all. With the death of a king the battle was decided: without royal leadership no concerted attack was possible, but a counterattack was all the more likely, which could easily cause an army under no firm command to flee. The explicit notice that Ahab died in the evening is to insist that he saw his troops through battle while still conscious, a proviso to avoid charges of improper treatment of a corpse.

[22:36-37] These verses report the end of the battle without specifying the outcome. The shout, "Every man to his city and every man to his country!" releases the troops from their allegiance (see on 12:16). Ahab's corpse is brought back to Samaria to be buried with his ancestors. Regardless of his wrongdoings, the king is given a proper and appropriate burial. The tomb of the Omrides is unknown but is likely to have been very near Samaria.

[22:38] It is only the addition of v. 38 that refers explicitly to the fulfilled prophecy of 21:19b; however, the entire narrative already presents Ahab's end as a shameful death. To save himself Ahab puts Jehoshaphat at high risk to be killed in battle. "The mean plan has been foiled, the king of Judah could save his own life, but the king of

Israel is killed by a stray arrow."[1] Against our divinely ordained fate, we humans and our schemes are powerless, even if they seem as well devised as those of Ahab.

[22:5-28] The stock of characters links the battle account with the prophetic narrative; the narrative is not of a piece but is a compound of vv. 10-12, 19-23, and 24-25. Its proper theme is formulated clearly in v. 28: the truth of prophecy is manifest in its fulfillment. The predictions of victory do not come true, hence proving their prophets false, while the prophet of Yahweh foretelling misfortune is proven truthful. Israel's disastrous history is the yardstick of prophecy and Yahweh as the Lord of history reveals history through his prophets. The present prophetic narrative verifies Micaiah's prophecy of doom and paves the way for the prophetic judgments in the books of the prophets of the eighth and seventh centuries, Isaiah, Jeremiah, Hosea, Amos, and Micah. Its central figure is the prophet Micaiah, son of Imlah, who has to be distinguished from Micah of Moresheth-gath in Mic 1:1.

As in 1 Kgs 18:2b-15, Ahab is seen to persecute a Yahweh prophet. He holds Micaiah in custody, probably as a preventive measure (no proper sentence is mentioned) to keep the prophet from making inopportune public statements and to suppress prophetic truth. The narrative focuses on the direct conflict between the prophets of salvation and the one prophet of Yahweh, and Ahab orders Micaiah, son of Imlah, to appear for this purpose especially.

[22:17] The central word of Micaiah has all the hallmarks of a prophecy of doom: it is brief, it uses metaphorical language, and it is sufficiently vague for the listener or reader to draw the appropriate conclusions dictated by the historical outcome. The simile compares Israel to a scattered herd of sheep that have no shepherd. The meaning is obvious: like sheep without a shepherd, Israel without a leader cannot survive. The fact that Israel followed the ancient Near Eastern example and considered its king the shepherd of the people means that the vehicle and tenor of the image are all the more closely intertwined (see 2 Sam 5:2; Ps 78:72).[2] Yahweh himself relates the metaphor, in the second half, to the historical situation: without its king the Israelite army has no choice but to return home (v. 36). Only this second part points ahead to the battle account, while the first part remains vague about the future events. Given Ahab's plans, however, there was no doubt about the negative character of Micaiah's simile: Israel will emerge from battle like a herd without its shepherd. Ahab's death at Ramoth-gilead is indirectly but clearly foretold. The truthfulness of his prophecy

---

[1] Würthwein, *Könige,* 2:257.

[2] See G. Johannes Botterweck, "Hirt und Herde im Alten Testament und im Alten Orient," in *Die Kirche und ihre Ämter und Stände: Festgabe seiner Eminenz dem hochwürdigsten Herrn Joseph Kardinal Frings, Erzbischof von Köln zum goldenen Priesterjubiläum am 10. August 1969 dargeboten,* ed. Wilhelm Corsten et al. (Köln: Bachem, 1960), 339–52.

would have raised the esteem of Micaiah, confirmed as the true prophet of Yahweh, although no mention is made of his later fate.

[22:10-12, 24-25] The addition in vv. 10-12 underlines the predictions by the prophets of salvation with a symbolic action. The interpretation of a "telling" object, as we see here, is another trademark of early prophecy. Zedekiah, son of Chenaanah, the prophet wearing horns of iron, is put as the opponent of Micaiah, reappearing in vv. 24-25. In this later scene Micaiah answers his insult of a slap on the cheek with another simile: the impending disaster will make the prophet seek to hide in a shelter.

[22:19-23] The vision of the heavenly scene is particularly interesting, as it explains the words of the false prophets as part of Yahweh's will. In this scene, similar to those of Isa 6:13 and Job 2:1-6, Yahweh is seen on his heavenly throne, surrounded by his court. He decrees the future events, and a "lying spirit" is explicitly dispatched to cause confusion through the false prophets. The false prophets receive inspirations indeed, yet they are the words of the lying spirit sent by Yahweh. The inconsistency between prophecies is therefore ordained by Yahweh, which answers the problematic question why contradictory prophecies exist, and humans cannot resolve them. The false prophecies confirm the path to destruction and precipitate the divinely ordained fate; in the last resort, they themselves are part of the divine counsel.

Concluding Formula for Ahab

Text

22:39 Now the rest of the acts of Ahab, and all that he did, and the ivory house that he built, and all the cities that he built, are they not written in the Book of the Annals of the Kings of Israel? 40 So Ahab slept with his ancestors; and his son Ahaziah succeeded him.

Commentary

[22:39-40] The concluding formula for Ahab follows the standard pattern, apart from the brief mention of the ivory house and the building of some unspecified cities. There is archaeological evidence for building activity in the sense of the enlargement of the centers at Hazor and Megiddo in the ninth century, which can be attributed to the king.[1] There is also evidence for the ivory house: excavations in the palace area on the acropolis of Samaria have uncovered a building next to the palace, which contained numerous ivories, published as a separate volume of the excavation report.[2] The "ivory house" would therefore have been decorated with ivories, mainly in the form of wall decorations (e.g., more than seventy ivory palmettes) or as ivory plaques on furniture or wooden boxes. The same is true of the sculpted ivory lion.[3] The motifs are taken from the repertoire of Syrian and Phoenician ivory art, and they include fighting animals, sphinxes, grazing deer, the birth of Horus, and the "woman at the window."[4] The Samaria ivories are similar to the large finds from Arslan Tash and Nimrod, but are likely to have been manufactured in the north Syrian area and/or the Phoenician coastal towns, rich proof of the cultural connections between Israel and its surrounding areas during the reign of Ahab.

---

[1] See Volkmar Fritz, *The City in Ancient Israel,* BibSem 29 (Sheffield: Sheffield Academic, 1995).

[2] See J. W. Crowfoot and Grace M. Crowfoot, *Early Ivories from Samaria, 1938,* Samaria-Sebaste (London: Palestine Exploration Fund, 1938; reprinted 1972).

[3] *ANEP,* no. 129.

[4] See Richard D. Barnett, *Ancient Ivories in the Middle East and Adjacent Countries,* Qedem 14 (Jerusalem: Institute of Archaeology, 1982).

All the narratives that fill the space between the introductory and concluding formulas (16:29-34 and 22:39-40) are concerned with the battles between Israel and the Arameans of Damascus; no interest, however, is shown in the danger coming from Ashur. The monolith inscription of Shalmaneser III tells us that Israel and the Arameans, together with other allies, were trying to stop the Assyrian flow into the areas west of the Euphrates.[5] Ahab and Ben-hadad were at least temporarily allied, and in the battle of Qarqar in 853 Ashur had to face a coalition of the Phoenician coastal towns and the small states of Syria; to these last Ahab had contributed a large contingent of chariots and foot soldiers.[6] Shalmaneser claims a grand victory, but it would appear that the combined resistance against Assyrian hegemony was success-ful for awhile: Israel becomes a tributary only under Jehu in 841.[7]

We can only speculate why the Deuteronomistic History keeps silent on the conflict. The negative judgment of Ahab made any reference to his successes unlikely. It is Hezekiah who is credited by the Deuteronomistic Historian with averting the Assyrian danger, a king who is given an altogether positive judgment because of the cultic reforms he instigated (see 2 Kings 18–20). Ahab's death is apparently a peace-ful one, disregarding the prediction of his dreadful end in 21:34-35. No mention is made of his burial, reported already in 22:37.

---

[5] *TGI*, 50.

[6] See *ANET*, 278–79.

[7] See *TGI*, 51.

Jehoshaphat of Judah
[ET = 22:41-50]

Text

22:41 Jehoshaphat son of Asa began to reign over Judah in the fourth year of King Ahab of Israel. 42 Jehoshaphat was thirty-five years old when he began to reign, and he reigned twenty-five years in Jerusalem. His mother's name was Azubah daughter of Shilhi. 43 He walked in all the way of his father Asa; he did not turn aside from it, doing what was right in the sight of the Lord; 44 yet the high places were not taken away, and the people still sacrificed and offered incense on the high places. 45 Jehoshaphat also made peace with the king of Israel.

46 Now the rest of the acts of Jehoshaphat, and his power that he showed, and how he waged war, are they not written in the Book of the Annals of the Kings of Judah? 47 The remnant of the male temple prostitutes who were still in the land in the days of his father Asa, he exterminated.

48 There was no king in Edom; a deputy was king. 49 Jehoshaphat made ships of the Tarshish type to go to Ophir for gold; but they did not go, for the ships were wrecked at Ezion-geber. 50 Then Ahaziah son of Ahab said to Jehoshaphat, "Let my servants go with your servants in the ships," but Jehoshaphat was not willing. 51 Jehoshaphat slept with his ancestors and was buried with his ancestors in the city of his father David; his son Jehoram succeeded him.

Analysis

King Asa, the father and predecessor of Jehoshaphat, had reigned in Jerusalem for forty-one years (15:10), a long time during which he saw six different kings of the throne of Israel, namely Jeroboam, Nadab, Baasha, Elah, Zimri, and Omri, and proof that the political stability in the southern kingdom of Judah surpassed that of the northern kingdom, shaken by a number of violent changes of royal power.

Commentary

[22:41-44] According to the introductory formula, Jehoshaphat was only thirty-five years when he came to the throne, which makes him likely to be not the oldest son of Asa. His reign of twenty-five years covers that of Ahab, Ahaziah, and Jehoram of Israel. Like Asa, Jehoshaphat is judged positively, the only limitation being his failure to abolish the worship of foreign deities. Beyond the standard information some interesting details of his reign are mentioned; the section vv. 47-50 is an interpolation before the concluding formula.

[22:45] This verse characterizes his reign by the peaceful relations with Israel. Asa had turned Aramean pressure on Israel to his advantage and had gained the territory of the tribe of Benjamin for Judah, moving the border of his own territory northward. Nearly sixty years after the division of the realm, the tense relations between the two states had given way to a more peaceful coexistence. The politics of the two kingdoms were still different, though, since Israel was much more immediately threatened by foreign powers and its neighbors, Aram in particular. The new appeasement policy was strengthened by the marriage of Athaliah, daughter of Ahab and Jezebel, to Jehoram, the son of Jehoshaphat (2 Kgs 8:18).

[22:47] It is not clear who the *qedesh* are, whom Asa had already removed from the country. It is certainly a particular group of men or women dedicated to the cult, although it is hardly a case of cultic prostitution, which cannot be verified for Israel and Judah.[1] It is more likely that the *qedesh* were followers of a foreign cult and hence not tolerated.

[22:48] The remark on Edom should be taken to mean that there was no monarchy yet established there at the time, but that Edom was ruled by the king of Judah. The so-called Edomite king list in Gen 36:31-39 is not an argument against it, as its composition date is much later (see on 1 Kgs 11:14-22). Urbanization reached Edom only in the eighth century, as did probably the formation of a state. The administration of the Edomite desert areas by the king of Judah in the ninth century as it was done in Davidic times is therefore well within the realm of historical possibility, even if we lack definite proof.

[22:49] The revival of trade routes across the Red Sea came to nothing, probably because the ships sank in a storm before being launched. On the Tarshish ships see on 10:22; on Ophir, the legendary land of gold, and on Ezion-geber, see on 9:26-28. The

---

[1] See Mayer I. Gruber, "Hebrew *qedeshah* and Her Canaanite and Akkadian Cognates," *UF* 18 (1986) 133–48; Hans M. Barstad, *The Religious Polemics of Amos: Studies in the Preaching of Am 2,7B-8; 4,1-13; 5,1-27; 6,4-7; 8,14,* VTSup 34 (Leiden: Brill, 1984), 17–33.

administration of Edom and the plans for reviving trade from Ezion-geber are proof that the kings of Judah considered the steppe and desert of the south and southeast as part of their own territory.

[22:50, 46, 51] Ahaziah's offer to Jehoshaphat of a joint trade venture is declined (v. 50), a further sign of the independence of the king of Judah from the northern kingdom. The concluding formula, vv. 46, 51, interrupted by vv. 47-50, follows the standard model.

Ahaziah of Israel [ET = 22:51-53]

Text

22:52 Ahaziah son of Ahab began to reign over Israel in Samaria in the seventeenth year of King Jehoshaphat of Judah; he reigned two years over Israel. 53 He did what was evil in the sight of the LORD, and walked in the way of his father and mother, and in the way of Jeroboam son of Nebat, who caused Israel to sin. 54 He served Baal and worshiped him; he provoked the LORD, the God of Israel, to anger, just as his father had done.

Commentary

[22:52-54] The judgment on Ahaziah, like all the kings of Israel, is negative, with a particular stress on the continued worship of Baal, who had been introduced by Ahab, according to 16:32. Apart from his brief reign of only two years, we are told only about an insurrection in Moab, 2 Kgs 1:1. Second Kings 1:2-17 adds another prophetic narrative from the Elijah circle before the concluding formula in 2 Kgs 1:18.

The Death of Ahaziah of Israel

Text

1:1 After the death of Ahab, Moab rebelled against Israel.

2 Ahaziah had fallen through the lattice in his upper chamber in Samaria, and lay injured; so he sent messengers, telling them, "Go, inquire of Baal-zebub, the god of Ekron, whether I shall recover from this injury." 3 But the angel of the LORD said to Elijah the Tishbite, "Get up, go to meet the messengers of the king of Samaria, and say to them, 'Is it because there is no God in Israel that you are going to inquire of Baal-zebub, the god of Ekron?' 4 Now therefore thus says the LORD, 'You shall not leave the bed to which you have gone, but you shall surely die.'" So Elijah went.

5 The messengers returned to the king, who said to them, "Why have you returned?" 6 They answered him, "There came a man to meet us, who said to us, 'Go back to the king who sent you, and say to him: Thus says the LORD: Is it because there is no God in Israel that you are sending to inquire of Baal-zebub, the god of Ekron? Therefore you shall not leave the bed to which you have gone, but shall surely die.'" 7 He said to them, "What sort of man was he who came to meet you and told you these things?" 8 They answered him, "A hairy man, with a leather belt around his waist." He said, "It is Elijah the Tishbite."

9 Then the king sent to him a captain of fifty with his fifty men. He went up to Elijah, who was sitting on the top of a hill, and said to him, "O man of God, the king says, 'Come down.'" 10 But Elijah answered the captain of fifty, "If I am a man of God, let fire come down from heaven and consume you and your fifty." Then fire came down from heaven, and consumed him and his fifty.

11 Again the king sent to him another captain of fifty with his fifty. He went up and said to him, "O man of God, this is the king's order: Come down quickly!" 12 But Elijah answered them, "If I am a man of God, let fire come down from heaven and consume you and your fifty." Then the fire of God came down from heaven and consumed him and his fifty.

13 Again the king sent the captain of a third fifty with his fifty. So the third captain of fifty went up, and came and fell on his knees before Elijah, and entreated him, "O man of God, please let my life, and the life of these fifty servants of yours, be precious in your sight. 14 Look, fire came down from heaven and consumed the two former captains of fifty men with their fifties; but now let my life be precious in your sight." 15 Then the angel of the LORD said to Elijah, "Go down with him; do not be afraid of him." So he set out and went down with him to the king, 16 and said to him, "Thus says the LORD: Because you have sent messengers to inquire of Baal-zebub, the god of Ekron,—is it because there is no God in Israel to inquire of his word?—therefore you shall not leave the bed to which you have gone, but you shall surely die."

17a So he died according to the word of the LORD that Elijah had spoken.

Analysis

The two books of Kings form a single unit in the Hebrew tradition. The division into two parts occurred at first in the Greek manuscripts and was continued in the Vulgate; with the edition of the so-called Bombergiana in 1516, it became finally accepted in the printed Hebrew versions too. Only by this separation were the introductory and concluding formulas for Ahaziah split apart. Set between the introductory formula (1 Kgs 22:52-54) and concluding formula (2 Kgs 1:17b-18), the narrative of 1:2-17a explains the early death of the king after only two years. (These two years of government amount in fact to only just over twelve months; 1 Kgs 22:52 knows of Ahaziah's accession to the throne in the seventeenth year of Jehoshaphat, while, according to 2 Kgs 3:1, he died in the eighteenth year of Jehoshaphat.) The theological orientation of the narrative leads us to assume that it was shaped and consequently interpolated by the author of the Deuteronomistic History. It is certainly not based on an older anecdote that was later transposed to Ahaziah, as Würthwein thought.[1] The version before us is not of a piece, and the insertion of vv. 3-4 and 9-16 cause the plot to lose much of its original tension.

The Septuagint omits v. 17a, probably because the details are repeated in 3:1. On the discrepancy of its dating see the comments on 3:1.

Commentary

[1:1] The note preceding the narrative as such is echoed almost verbatim in 3:5. Factually this statement belongs within the context of the war against Mesha and Moab under the joint leadership of the kings of Judah and Israel reported in 3:4-27; to find the sentence in this position must therefore imply a redactional addition. The later insertion shows the interest of the redactor to offer more information on the reign of

---

[1] Würthwein, *Könige*, 2:267.

Ahaziah, although there was apparently no tradition readily available for this king. 2 Kgs 2:5—8:17a is little more than an elaboration of the judgment pronounced in 1 Kgs 22:54.

[1:2-17a] The story moves in a straight line toward its climax, the death of Ahaziah. Apart from the king only Elijah is named individually, although he does not appear on the scene as such. Only the unnamed messengers appear as characters beside the king. The stress is on the fulfillment of the word of God more than on the rather thin plot. The will of God is announced only indirectly though the speech of the messengers. It is assumed that only Yahweh can rule over human life and therefore only Yahweh can speak of it. By sending a delegation to a foreign god Ahaziah has broken trust, and he is duly punished with death. The story thus points up the fundamental tenet of Deuteronomistic theology: "Yahweh is God, there is no other besides him" (Deut 4:35). The claim of the one God to be acknowledged as such imposes strict limitations on the individual's free choice of which god to turn to. Yahweh alone is God and therefore the only one to be approached for counsel or help; to acknowledge Yahweh as the only God precludes the possibility of appealing to any other god. The story relies on the assumption that God alone rules over life and death.

[1:2] Threfore it is only logical when Ahaziah asks to learn the divine will regarding his illness. His illness is said to be the result of a fall within the palace. The exact circumstances remain in the dark, mainly because the meaning of the word translated "lattice" is unclear. Much has been speculated, but it is impossible to define the word more precisely than as a technical term for a structural part of the building. It would appear that the king has fallen from the first floor and has been seriously injured.

No mention is made of the reason why the mission is sent to Ekron. Ekron is one of the five cities of the Philistines (see 1 Sam 6:18; 18:30; 29:3, 4, 9, etc.) and can be located at Khirbet el-Muquanna' in the southern coastal plain. No other evidence is found for Baal-zebub as the name of the local deity, although he reappears in the Synoptic Gospels as the "Beelzebul" of early Jewish tradition, probably adopting postbiblical elements (Matt 10:25; Mark 3:22; Luke 11:15). The meaning of the name Baal-zebub as "lord of the flies" points strongly to a corruption of the original name Baal-zebal; Zebal appears as an epithet of Baal in Ugaritic texts (*zbl b'l*, "Prince Baal"). It is likely that the epithet was transmitted in its distorted form in order to underline disgust and contempt.

[1:5-8, 17a] The answer to the king's question is revealed only indirectly through the messenger's report, which predicts death for Ahaziah as a punishment for his offense, the disrespect shown to Yahweh by sending a mission to the god of Ekron. God's will is proclaimed by his man Elijah, well known from 1 Kings 17–21 as a radical defender of the exclusiveness of Yahweh. This information is imparted through the further questions asked by the king; Elijah could apparently be identified by his way of dressing and his unkempt hair, and we have to presume that this distinguished him from other men of God. He obviously did not wear a coat and, like the nazirites, he did not cut his hair. From his description as a man of God, Ahaziah has to deduce that the death sentence proclaimed on him is the will of Yahweh and hence irrevocable. The passage closes with the notice that Ahaziah died according to Elijah's prediction.

[1:3-4, 9-16] The original narrative mentions Elijah as the proclaimer of God's will only at the end. At "the center," however, of the two interpolations, vv. 3-4 and 9-16, "are the miraculous man of God, Elijah, and the right attitude toward him."[2] The first insertion (vv. 3-4) interprets the entire sequence of events as prompted by Yahweh. The second insertion (vv. 9-16) not only confirms Yahweh's superior power but also shows Elijah at the sickbed of Ahaziah. Here it is only through the figure of the third captain that the respect owed to the man of God is acknowledged. The captain personifies the insight that acceptance is the only appropriate response to the man of God as the representative of God's will. The example of the other two captains, in contrast, serves to demonstrate the infinite superiority of divine power over that of humans.

---

[2] Ibid., 268.

Concluding Formula for Ahaziah

Text

1:17b His brother, Jehoram succeeded him as king in the second year of King Jehoram son of Jehoshaphat of Judah, because Ahaziah had no son. 18 Now the rest of the acts of Ahaziah that he did, are they not written in the Book of the Annals of the Kings of Israel?

Commentary

[1:17b-18] The concluding formula points out in v. 17b that Ahaziah did not yet have a son to succeed him. Jehoram was the son of Ahab, as mentioned in his introductory formula in 3:1-3, and thus a brother of the deceased Ahaziah, a fact that the old translations (the so-called Lucianic recension of the LXX, the Peshitta, and the Vulgate) added to the text. Although the formula introducing Ahaziah in 1 Kgs 22:52-54 makes no mention of his age, we can conclude from his death without issue that he must have been still young when he acceded to the throne. If the line of succession proceeded according to age, Jehoram must have been about the same youthful age as Ahaziah; yet further speculation on this matter is futile. With Jehoram the dynasty founded by Omri comes to an end, as he is killed in the twelfth year of his reign by Jehu (see on 8:28—10:17). Ahaziah's reign was too short to have an impact on the history of Israel.

Elisha Succeeds Elijah

Text

2:1 Now when the LORD was about to take Elijah up to heaven by a whirlwind, Elijah and Elisha were on their way from Gilgal. 2 Elijah said to Elisha, "Stay here; for the LORD has sent me as far as Bethel." But Elisha said, "As the LORD lives, and as you yourself live, I will not leave you." So they went down to Bethel. 3 The company of prophets who were in Bethel came out to Elisha, and said to him, "Do you know that today the LORD will take your master away from you?" And he said, "Yes, I know; keep silent."

4 Elijah said to him, "Elisha, stay here; for the LORD has sent me to Jericho." But he said, "As the LORD lives, and as you yourself live, I will not leave you." So they came to Jericho. 5 The company of prophets who were at Jericho drew near to Elisha, and said to him, "Do you know that today the LORD will take your master away from you?" And he answered, "Yes, I know; be silent."

6 Then Elijah said to him, "Stay here; for the LORD has sent me to the Jordan." But he said, "As the LORD lives, and as you yourself live, I will not leave you." So the two of them went on. 7 Fifty men of the company of prophets also went, and stood at some distance from them, as they both were standing by the Jordan. 8 Then Elijah took his mantle and rolled it up, and struck the water; the water was parted to the one side and to the other, until the two of them crossed on dry ground.

9 When they had crossed, Elijah said to Elisha, "Tell me what I may do for you, before I am taken from you." Elisha said, "Please let me inherit a double share of your spirit." 10 He responded, "You have asked a hard thing; yet, if you see me as I am being taken from you, it will be granted you; if not, it will not." 11 As they continued walking and talking, a chariot of fire and horses of fire separated the two of them, and Elijah ascended in a whirlwind into heaven. 12 Elisha kept watching and crying out, "Father, father! The chariots of Israel and its horsemen!" But when he could no longer see him, he grasped his own clothes and tore them in two pieces.

13 He picked up the mantle of Elijah that had fallen from him, and went back

and stood on the bank of the Jordan. 14 He took the mantle of Elijah that had fallen from him, and struck the water, saying, "Where is the LORD, the God of Elijah?" When he had struck the water, the water was parted to the one side and to the other, and Elisha went over.

15 When the company of prophets who were at Jericho saw him at a distance, they declared, "The spirit of Elijah rests on Elisha." They came to meet him and bowed to the ground before him. 16 They said to him, "See now, we have fifty strong men among your servants; please let them go and seek your master; it may be that the spirit of the LORD has caught him up and thrown him down on some mountain or into some valley." He responded, "No, do not send them." 17 But when they urged him until he was ashamed, he said, "Send them." So they sent fifty men who searched for three days but did not find him. 18 When they came back to him (he had remained at Jericho), he said to them, "Did I not say to you, Do not go?"

Analysis

The story tells of the last event in the life of Elijah—his translation—and of the pronouncement of Elisha as his successor. It thus links the two eminent prophetic figures and their tradition within the framework of the Deuteronomistic History. The only other relation between predecessor and successor that is comparable in prominence is the transition of leadership from Moses to Joshua (see Num 27:18-23). By pronouncing Elisha, his specifically appointed disciple (1 Kgs 19:19-21), as his successor, Elijah passes on his own spirit and authority to the new prophet.

Because of its significance the narrative kept expanding even after it was fixed in written form. This expansion took two forms: the addition of narrative passages and the insertion of explanatory notes. The first addendum is vv. 2-6, where the groups of prophets of Bethel and Jericho alert Elisha to the imminent end of Elijah's activity. The second addition, in vv. 16-18, basically reaffirms, even if only indirectly, the exceptional nature of the event that is the translation of Elijah. In vv. 1a and 11b the redactor supplies further information; here the miraculous translation of Elijah is reinterpreted as an "ascent to heaven in a whirlwind." The original narrative, then, contained only vv. 1b, 7-11a, 12-15. It is set by the river Jordan and reports a legitimation miracle in addition to the miraculous translation of Elijah. The focus is on the two prophets, while the disciples of the prophets, who are also mentioned, fulfill merely the role of witnesses.

Commentary

[2:1, 7-11a, 12-15] Gilgal, the starting place of the narrative, has not yet been located. Following Josh 4:19; 5:9, 10; 2 Sam 19:16, 41, Gilgal is placed in the Jordan Valley, but we have to leave open the precise location of this Iron Age settlement. (The Gilgal of the Byzantine age, known from the Madeba Map, can be located at Tell Ǧalǧûl =

Tell es-Sultān, 5 km. southeast of Jerusalem.) From Gilgal Elijah and Elisha move to an unspecified place by the river Jordan where the remainder of the introduction is set.

[2:8] They both cross the river on dry ground after Elijah separates the waters with his mantle or cloak (v. 8). In this way he repeats the miracle of the crossing of the Jordan entering the land (Josh 3:4), which in turn mirrors the crossing of the sea during the exodus from Egypt (Exodus 14). The cloak by which the miracle is effected has already been introduced in the call narrative of 1 Kgs 19:19, where it signifies the power of its owner, Elijah. When Elisha takes up this very cloak in v. 13, its special quality is passed on to him, for all to see. Accordingly, Elisha works the same miracle in the same manner when crossing back in v. 14, a feat that marks him as the new prophet continuing the tradition of Elijah. Cloak and miracle may be said to legitimize Elisha. "The cloak can work miracles not on its own but only when it is handled by the bearer of the spirit."[1]

[2:9] Elisha asks for a share of this spirit, implying that its transfer is possible. "Spirit" is here understood as a special gift, bestowed by God alone. The spirit granted by Yahweh not only enables the prophet to proclaim God's will, but also lets him perform acts that surpass the limits of human strength and nature. Only the spirit gives authority and superiority to the prophet, as it is described in many of the stories, and it is only the spirit that Elisha claims as an inheritance. (The cloak, therefore, is only a ancillary.) Nothing is said about the kind or way of transfer; again, only God can enable it.

[2:11-12] The translation of Elijah is reported twice in v. 11, although the sentence "and Elijah ascended in a whirlwind to heaven" (v.11b) is redactional. Originally, the ascent to heaven was only alluded to by the "chariot of fire and horses of fire" (v.11a), to which Elisha's cry in v. 12 makes reference.[2] Elijah's end is not death and burial but translation to heaven. The chariot of fire has to be interpreted as a divine vehicle, since fire usually signifies the manifestation of divine presence (see Exod 3:2; 13:21; 19:18).

Of what follows next, nothing is said other than that the two prophets are separated. It is assumed that Elijah climbs onto the chariot sent from heaven and is translated there. Elijah is the only figure in the Hebrew Bible who enjoys this particular privilege. Even Moses, the greatest of the prophets so far, had to die in the land of Moab, although he was buried by God himself and his grave remained unknown (Deut 34:5-6). Otherwise, only Enoch was translated by God (Gen 5:24) and gained immortality. Elijah, too, ascends to immortality and thus lives on in the tradition,

---

[1] Würthwein, *Könige,* 2:275.
[2] See Jack R. Lundbom, "Elijah's Chariot Ride," *JSS* 24 (1973) 39–50.

especially in the context of waiting for the endtime.[3] That the fate of death is suspended nowhere else in the Hebrew Bible (apart from Enoch) is what makes Elijah's translation exceptional.

[2:12] Elisha responds to Elijah's ascent with a lament and the tearing of his clothes as a sign of grief. In the face of the unusual events Elisha still performs the usual rites of lamentation. The lament does not mention Elijah's name, yet the title "father" (lit. "my father") is one of honor. Elisha's close relationship with the prophet as a "disciple" justifies this familial address. In what follows he takes up what he has seen and transposes the image of the chariot and horses to the figure of Elijah ascended. The phrase is repeated in 13:14, this time referring to Elisha. To transpose the image onto the prophet is to underline and justify his leadership. As the king in his chariot visibly leads Israel into battle (e.g., 1 Kgs 22:29-37), so does the prophet lead Israel against false claims and foreign gods. With this trope, "The chariots of Israel and its horsemen," the Deuteronomistic author expresses his own judgment on early (pre-classical) prophecy.

[2:14-15] When, on the way back, Elisha works the same miracle by the river Jordan (v. 14) as Elijah had done (v. 8) before, he is expressly acknowledged as the legitimate successor of the prophet by his disciples. The acknowledgment takes the form of a proskynesis, an unusual gesture shown to a human being.

[2:16-18] This short epilogue is not entirely consistent with v. 15. While the disciples of the prophet had acknowledged Elijah's translation and had greeted Elisha as the new "father," the epilogue is built on a moment of doubt. The aim of the episode is to give proof that Elijah is no longer on this earth and has indeed been translated. Evidence comes through the unsuccessful search for him.

[2:2-6] This addition is to introduce the account of the translation. Bethel and Jericho here signify places where other groups of prophets had settled who acknowledged the tradition of Elijah. Through the speeches by the two prophets those communities are included in the events, alongside Gilgal.

---

[3] See N. Oswald, *TRE* 9:502–4.

Elisha's Miracle at the Spring

Text

2:19 Now the people of the city said to Elisha, "The location of this city is good, as my lord sees; but the water is bad, and the land is unfruitful." 20 He said, "Bring me a new bowl, and put salt in it." So they brought it to him. 21 Then he went to the spring of water and threw the salt into it, and said, "Thus says the LORD, I have made this water wholesome; from now on neither death nor miscarriage shall come from it." 22 So the water has been wholesome to this day, according to the word that Elisha spoke.

Commentary

[2:19] The first of the miracles performed by Elisha is set in Jericho. The narrator presumes the existence of the city in the ninth century, and there is indeed archaeological proof for a settlement at that time.[1] The spring in question is ʿĒn es-Sulṭān on the eastern edge of the settled hill. The narrative implies that the salt content of the water is spoiling the ground, rendering the land unfruitful. The use of salt as a remedy refers back to this phenomenon.

[2:20] The complaints by the population lead Elisha to immediate action. By applying salt he pronounces the spring cured. Elisha performs the miracle through a powerful word and a sign, not by an act of magic. A similar miracle is reported in Exod 15:23-25a, where Moses cured the spring of Marah with a piece of wood.[2] The choice of salt to accompany the procedure is not commented upon; its application was not a cultic act as such, although salt was an indispensable component in sacrifice (e.g.,

---

[1] See Helga Weippert and Manfred Weippert, "Jericho in der Eisenzeit," *ZDPV* 92 (1976) 105–48.

[2] For Marah's likely location on the western fringe of the Sinai desert see Volkmar Fritz, *Israel in der Wüste: Traditionsgeschichtliche Untersuchung der Wüstenüberlieferung des Jahwisten*, Marburger theologische Studien 7 (Marburg: Elwert, 1970), 37–41.

Exod 30:35; Lev 2:13; Ezek 43:24; Mark 9:49). The sprinkling of salt is also known as part of a curse in the context of the destruction of a city.[3]

[2:21] By sprinkling salt into the water Elisha realizes the miracle. The function of the salt was probably a purely symbolic one, although the choice of substance might owe to the general "purifying, apotropaic power" attributed to salt.[4]

[2:22] The section closes with a report of the success of Elisha's deed. Although the story is closely linked to its topographical marker, we are not dealing with an aetiology, since there is no name change of the spring involved. Neither is it related to Joshua's curse on the city in Josh 6:26, as we are only told of the spring and its water. The focus is rather on Elisha as performing miracles, "curing" the harmful water. Yet, as the next episode shows, the prophet's word brings not only health and life but can also lead to death.

---

[3] See Judg 9:45 and *KAI*, no. 222A.36; also F. C. Fensham, "Salt as a Curse in the Old Testament and in the Ancient Near East," *BA* 25 (1962) 48–50.

[4] Würthwein, *Könige,* 2:277.

The Cursing of the Boys

Text

2:23 He went up from there to Bethel; and while he was going up on the way, some small boys came out of the city and jeered at him, saying, "Go away, baldhead! Go away, baldhead!" 24 When he turned around and saw them, he cursed them in the name of the LORD. Then two she-bears came out of the woods and mauled forty-two of the boys. 25 From there he went on to Mount Carmel, and then returned to Samaria.

Analysis

The story is not given a specific location; its only presumption is that there were bears in the central Palestinian mountains during the monarchy. Excavations of bones have proven the existence of *ursus arctos syriacus.*[1] The episode cannot really be called an "anecdote";[2] instead, is a typical miracle story that is best characterized as a short narrative. This form dominates in the further tradition of Elisha in 2 Kings 4–6 and 8. Their point in common is that Elisha's powers enable him to perform acts that reach beyond human limitations.

Commentary

[2:23-24] In the present story, Elisha's curse brings death upon the boys jeering at him. The object of their mockery is his baldness, probably the result of a natural loss of hair rather than a "tonsure,"[3] although one could argue that Elisha had cut off his hair lamenting Elijah's departure. In any case, the irritating flock of shouting boys, a feature of the Near Eastern landscape still today, picks on the unusual appearance of the prophet. Elisha answers their jibes with a curse that is effectively out of proportion. The moral of the story is obvious: the prophet as a bearer of divine powers is

---

[1] See F. S. Bodenheimer, *Animal and Man in Bible Lands,* 2 vols. (Leiden: Brill, 1960), 1:45.
[2] Würthwein, *Könige,* 2:278.
[3] Ibid.

owed respect. The number of the boys mauled by the she-bears is, at 42, a figure associated with death elsewhere too.[4] The story is tightly woven around the figure of the prophet and demonstrates the power of the prophetic word, here uttered as a curse. Further reactions or consequences are not mentioned.

[2:25] According to v. 25 Elisha crosses Mount Carmel and goes on to the capital Samaria. The detour over Mount Carmel is probably explained by the fact that this forested and mainly uninhabited mountain area was considered an attractive habitat by the early prophets, whose way of living on their own or in a community of followers put them outside the social order of Israel.

---

[4] See J. Herrmann, "Die Zahl zweiundvierzig im AT," *OLZ* 13 (1910) 150–52.

Introductory Formula
for Jehoram of Israel

Text

3:1 In the eighteenth year of King Jehoshaphat of Judah, Jehoram son of Ahab became king over Israel in Samaria; he reigned twelve years. 2 He did what was evil in the sight of the LORD, though not like his father and mother, for he removed the pillar of Baal that his father had made. 3 Nevertheless he clung to the sin of Jeroboam son of Nebat, which he caused Israel to commit; he did not depart from it.

Commentary

[3:1-3] The formula introducing Jehoram follows the usual pattern. The pillar of Baal is, however, not mentioned among the cult objects of Ahab (1 Kgs 16:32-33). It is probably a standing stone, dedicated to Baal, of the type often used for cultic purposes.[1] The temple of Baal at Samaria was later destroyed by Jehu (2 Kgs 10:27). According to the chronology, Jehoram of Israel reigned until the year 845 and came to a violent end during the revolution of Jehu, together with Ahaziah, the king of Judah (see also on 9:11-29). Jehoram, the next in line of the sons of Ahab, succeeded to the throne, following the early death of his brother Ahaziah.

---

[1] See Carl Frank Graesser, "Standing Stones in Ancient Palestine," *BA* 35 (1972) 34–63.

The Campaign against
Mesha of Moab

Text

3:4 Now King Mesha of Moab was a sheep breeder, who used to deliver to the king of Israel one hundred thousand lambs, and the wool of one hundred thousand rams. 5 But when Ahab died, the king of Moab rebelled against the king of Israel. 6 So King Jehoram marched out of Samaria at that time and mustered all Israel. 7 As he went he sent word to King Jehoshaphat of Judah, "The king of Moab has rebelled against me; will you go with me to battle against Moab?" He answered, "I will; I am with you, my people are your people, my horses are your horses." 8 Then he asked, "By which way shall we march?" Jehoram answered, "By the way of the wilderness of Edom."

9 So the king of Israel, the king of Judah, and the king of Edom set out; and when they had made a roundabout march of seven days, there was no water for the army or for the animals that were with them. 10 Then the king of Israel said, "Alas! The LORD has summoned us, three kings, only to be handed over to Moab." 11 But Jehoshaphat said, "Is there no prophet of the LORD here, through whom we may inquire of the LORD?" Then one of the servants of the king of Israel answered, "Elisha son of Shaphat, who used to pour water on the hands of Elijah, is here." 12 Jehoshaphat said, "The word of the LORD is with him." So the king of Israel and Jehoshaphat and the king of Edom went down to him.

13 Elisha said to the king of Israel, "What have I to do with you? Go to your father's prophets or to your mother's." But the king of Israel said to him, "No; it is the LORD who has summoned us, three kings, only to be handed over to Moab." 14 Elisha said, "As the LORD of hosts lives, whom I serve, were it not that I have regard for King Jehoshaphat of Judah, I would give you neither a look nor a glance. 15 But get me a musician." And then, while the musician was playing, the power of the LORD came on him. 16 And he said,

"Thus says the LORD, 'I will make this wadi full of pools.' 17 For thus says the LORD, 'You shall see neither wind nor rain, but the wadi shall be filled with water, so that you shall drink, you, your cattle, and your animals.' 18 This is only a trifle in the sight of the LORD, for he will also hand Moab over to you. 19 You shall conquer every fortified city and every choice city; every good tree you shall fell, all springs of water you shall stop up, and every good piece of land you shall ruin with stones." 20 The next day, about the time of the morning offering, suddenly water began to flow from the direction of Edom, until the country was filled with water.

21 When all the Moabites heard that the kings had come up to fight against them, all who were able to put on armor, from the youngest to the oldest, were called out and were drawn up at the frontier. 22 When they rose early in the morning, and the sun shone upon the water, the Moabites saw the water opposite them as red as blood. 23 They said, "This is blood; the kings must have fought together, and killed one another. Now then, Moab, to the spoil!" 24 But when they came to the camp of Israel, the Israelites rose up and attacked the Moabites, who fled before them; as they entered Moab they continued the attack. 25 The cities they overturned, and on every good piece of land everyone threw a stone, until it was covered; every spring of water they stopped up, and every good tree they felled. Only at Kir-hareseth did the stone walls remain, until the slingers surrounded and attacked it. 26 When the king of Moab saw that the battle was going against him, he took with him seven hundred swordsmen to break through, opposite the king of Edom; but they could not. 27 Then he took his firstborn son who was to succeed him, and offered him as a burnt offering on the wall. And great wrath came upon Israel, so they withdrew from him and returned to their own land.

Analysis

The account of the campaign against Mesha of Moab is not of a piece. The central section on the prophet, vv. 9b-17, is easily identified as a later addition that links the events back to God's will. The same section is then enlarged once more to include vv. 18-19, although the proclamation in those verses is not fully consistent with the course of events. Thus the report proper of the campaign includes only vv. 4-9a and 20-27 with the following subsections:

vv. 4-5	exposition
vv. 6-9a	the coalition of the kings of Israel and Judah
vv. 20-24	the miraculous victory against the Moabites
v. 25	the conquest of Moab and the siege of Kir-hareseth
vv. 26-27	end of the campaign

By one of the rare fortunes in the study of biblical history, we have epigraphic evidence for the name of Israel's opponent, Mesha of Moab, from a nonbiblical source. The so-called Mesha inscription, named after the Moabite king, is from a black basalt stele found at Diban in 1868. The inscription begins with a personal introduction: "I am Mesha, son of Chemoshyat, king of Moab, the Dibonite," and records the conquest of the entire plateau north of the river Arnon.[1] Mesha further mentions Omri of Israel as a contemporary of Ahab. Although the king's defection mentioned in v. 5 cannot be dated, we can assume that the events recorded in the Mesha inscription took place before the campaign of the kings Jehoram and Jehoshaphat.[2]

It is likely that the Mesha inscription summarizes conquests that took place over a period of several years. This extension of Moabite power is probably the background against which the refusal to pay tribute to the Israelites has to be seen. At two hundred thousand animals the tribute is extraordinarily high. The number likely does not refer to the exact quantity, but rather signifies total subordination. Assyrian inscriptions too give unusually high figures when listing tributes.[3] To cease payment means to break the vassal treaty. This drastic change is then the starting point for the narration of military events.

Commentary

[3:4-9a] First, Jehoram urges the king of neighboring Judah to join forces. Jehoshaphat's words, "I am with you, my people are your people, my horses are your horses," echo 1 Kgs 22:4; rather than a voluntary declaration of support, they are the formula in which the weaker partner in an alliance confirms the obligation into which he has entered. The implied power relation lets us assume that Judah was politically dependent on Israel during the Omride period, although this dependency is not thematized here. That the king of Edom is unnamed equally points to an inferior position of Edom. The campaign remains essentially the task of the king of Israel, even if Judah and Edom participate (in the case of Judah probably without much choice).

[3:20-24] The marching route indicates the plan of attack. It leads from a ford at the south end of the Dead Sea through Edomite land, in order to conquer the heartland of Moab between the rivers Zered (Wadi el-Hesā) and Arnon (Sēl el Mōǧib) from the south. Israel can win a decisive battle on Edomite soil by way of an ambush (vv. 20-

---

[1] Translations in *ANET,* 320–21; *TGI,* 51–53; and *KAI,* 2:168–69. On the geography and history, see Yohanan Aharoni, *The Land of the Bible: A Historical Geography,* trans. Anson F. Rainey (Philadelphia: Westminster, 1979), 336–40.

[2] Karl-Heinz Bernhardt's dating of the campaign to the time of Joash ca. 800 is entirely mistaken; see his "Der Feldzug der drei Könige," in *Schalom: Studien zu Glaube und Geschichte Israels: Alfred Jepsen zum 70. Geburtstag,* ed. Karl-Heinz Bernhardt (Stuttgart: Calwer, 1971), 11–22.

[3] See Cogan and Tadmor, *II Kings,* 43, for examples.

24). The exact location is not given, and the miraculous character of the story is likely to derive from the phenomenon that stagnant pools are tinged blood-red by the rising sun. The mistaken perception of the Moabites is, however, exaggerated to a degree that renders the whole sequence of events unlikely. The narrator has obviously only a vague idea of the natural conditions on the Edomite steppe, recalled from a geographical and historical distance.

[3:25] The rest of the campaign is summarized in v. 25 without mentioning any further places or routes. The practice of destroying trees during conquest is explicitly banned in Deut 20:19. The stopping up of springs has been a staple of warfare everywhere and at all times. The passage consists mainly of commonplaces, which render the campaign only slightly credible. It finishes with the siege of Kir-hareseth, the capital of Moab. The site can be located at el-Kerak at the center of the Moabite plateau.

[3:26-27] The attempted sortie, which is to bring relief from the siege, ends in failure (v. 26). Events take a turn only after the king of Moab sacrifices his firstborn son (v. 27). The passage thus alleges that the practice of child sacrifice took place in Moab, a custom that was strictly banned in Israel.[4] There is no evidence for child sacrifice from any of the surrounding areas either.[5] It is unlikely that child sacrifice was practiced anywhere in the larger environment of Israel, which makes the allegation reflect rather more on the narrator and his circle. The description of events is governed by theological considerations. The siege is abandoned not for military reasons but out of disgust at the sacrifice by the king of Moab. The campaign yields no result, Moab retained its independence, even if it had to bear the "stigma" of human sacrifice.

This tendentiousness reveals the story to be a piece of anti-Moabite propaganda and unlikely to correspond to reality. The only historical element is the establishment of Moab as an independent political power on which the story is based. Apart from that, nothing can be historically verified. Rather than being a factual account of a campaign against Moab, the narrative reflects the desire at least to discredit the Moabites, even if they could not be beaten. A tendentious compilation without any historical value, it was possibly composed only by the Deuteronomistic redactor. It contains no significant historical detail apart from commonplaces familiar from military accounts, and cannot therefore be considered as a source for the history of Israel. An Israelite invasion of Moab never took place, and the battles fought over the cities on the plateau north of the Arnon, which are mentioned in the Mesha inscription, do not appear in biblical historiography.

---

[4] See Otto Kaiser, "Den Erstgeborenen deiner Söhne sollst du mir geben: Erwägungen zum Kinderopfer im AT," in idem, *Von der Gegenwartsbedeutung des Alten Testaments: Gesammelte Studien zur Hermeneutik und zur Redaktionsgeschichte,* ed. Volkmar Fritz et al. (Göttingen: Vandenhoeck & Ruprecht, 1984), 142–66.

[5] See Michel Gras, P. Ronillard, and Javier Teixidor, "The Phoenicians and Death," *Berytus* 39 (1991) 127–76, esp. 155–59.

[3:9b-17] This interpolation describes how Elisha saves the army from a water shortage. It repeats the motif of water from the main narrative, although here the flooding of the valley is prompted by Yahweh alone. Water is not merely the instrument of victory over the enemies (v. 22) but also the means of supply for the army. In this way Yahweh not only keeps the Israelites alive, he also effects the miracle by which Israel is victorious.

Elisha is fashioned as a seer who foretells the future in a state of trance induced by the playing of a lyre. The passage stresses Yahweh's miraculous actions in the face of contradictory appearances. Elisha is given a status above that of the kings, who have to come and seek him out. His different treatment of Jehoram and Jehoshaphat clearly expresses his attitude toward the king of Israel. The interpolated section offers a literary subplot where Yahweh himself, through the figure of Elisha, saves the army from their dire straits. To the word of Elisha in v. 17 was then added another proclamation.

[3:18-19] This addition uses the usual formula "hand over (the enemy)" (see Deut 2:24, 30; 3:2-3; 7:24; 20:13; 21:10). The granting of victory contradicts the eventual outcome. Verse 19 repeats the statements made in v. 25. There is no evidence elsewhere for the custom of throwing stones to prevent the cultivation of the fields. The formulaic character of the addition makes it likely to be the work of a Deuteronomistic redactor, while its main function is to underline again the authoritative position of Elisha as the proclaimer of God's will.

The Miracle of the Oil

Text

4:1 Now the wife of a member of the company of prophets cried to Elisha, "Your servant my husband is dead; and you know that your servant feared the LORD, but a creditor has come to take my two children as slaves." 2 Elisha said to her, "What shall I do for you? Tell me, what do you have in the house?" She answered, "Your servant has nothing in the house, except a jar of oil." 3 He said, "Go outside, borrow vessels from all your neighbors, empty vessels and not just a few. 4 Then go in, and shut the door behind you and your children, and start pouring into all these vessels; when each is full, set it aside." 5 So she left him and shut the door behind her and her children; they kept bringing vessels to her, and she kept pouring. 6 When the vessels were full, she said to her son, "Bring me another vessel." But he said to her, "There are no more." Then the oil stopped flowing. 7 She came and told the man of God, and he said, "Go sell the oil and pay your debts, and you and your children can live on the rest."

Analysis

With 4:1-7 begins a sequence of miracle stories that depict the prophet as a powerful man of God whose deeds surpass the human sphere. The focus is on the special care he bestows on the community of prophets as their leader. In this way the stories not only praise his miraculous power, but also point out the plight of the disciples and how to ameliorate it.

Commentary

[4:1-7] The plot is very straightforward. The widow of one of the prophet's disciples is threatened by a creditor to have her children taken from her, and so she turns to Elisha. If the sons are sold into slavery, they will no longer be able to support their mother, which adds to the seriousness of her distress. Elisha solves the financial problem of a family through the miraculous multiplication of oil. The description is

247

extraordinarily graphic: in order to gain the most from the sudden increase, the woman has to borrow vessels from her neighbors. Oil as a valuable natural produce has a high market value, although we do not have any more specific information. The story closes with Elisha's order to pay off the debt with the money gained from the sale of this oil. To the reader the problem is solved. The survival of the family has been guaranteed through Elisha's miraculous deed.

Like all miracle stories, the tale is short. The plot is reduced to its bare essentials. Elisha, as the main actor, is at center stage; his miraculous powers as a prophet are taken as a given. The emergence of such stories among his followers may have begun during his lifetime already. In this case, the miracles legitimate Elisha as a prophet.

The Son of the Shunammite Woman

Text

4:8 One day Elisha was passing through Shunem, where a wealthy woman lived, who urged him to have a meal. So whenever he passed that way, he would stop there for a meal. **9** She said to her husband, "Look, I am sure that this man who regularly passes our way is a holy man of God. **10** Let us make a small roof chamber with walls, and put there for him a bed, a table, a chair, and a lamp, so that he can stay there whenever he comes to us."

11 One day when he came there, he went up to the chamber and lay down there. **12** He said to his servant Gehazi, "Call the Shunammite woman." When he had called her, she stood before him. **13** He said to him, "Say to her, Since you have taken all this trouble for us, what may be done for you? Would you have a word spoken on your behalf to the king or to the commander of the army?" She answered, "I live among my own people." **14** He said, "What then may be done for her?" Gehazi answered, "Well, she has no son, and her husband is old." **15** He said, "Call her." When he had called her, she stood at the door. **16** He said, "At this season, in due time, you shall embrace a son." She replied, "No, my lord, O man of God; do not deceive your servant."

17 The woman conceived and bore a son at that season, in due time, as Elisha had declared to her.

18 When the child was older, he went out one day to his father among the reapers. **19** He complained to his father, "Oh, my head, my head!" The father said to his servant, "Carry him to his mother." **20** He carried him and brought him to his mother; the child sat on her lap until noon, and he died. **21** She went up and laid him on the bed of the man of God, closed the door on him, and left. **22** Then she called to her husband, and said, "Send me one of the servants and one of the donkeys, so that I may quickly go to the man of God and come back again." **23** He said, "Why go to him today? It is neither new moon nor sabbath." She said, "It will be all right." **24** Then she saddled the donkey and said to her servant, "Urge the animal on; do not hold back for me unless I tell you." 25 So she set out, and came to the man of God at Mount Carmel.

When the man of God saw her coming, he said to Gehazi his servant, "Look, there is the Shunammite woman; 26 run at once to meet her, and say to her, Are you all right? Is your husband all right? Is the child all right?" She answered, "It is all right." 27 When she came to the man of God at the mountain, she caught hold of his feet. Gehazi approached to push her away. But the man of God said, "Let her alone, for she is in bitter distress; the LORD has hidden it from me and has not told me." 28 Then she said, "Did I ask my lord for a son? Did I not say, Do not mislead me?" 29 He said to Gehazi, "Gird up your loins, and take my staff in your hand, and go. If you meet anyone, give no greeting, and if anyone greets you, do not answer; and lay my staff on the face of the child." 30 Then the mother of the child said, "As the LORD lives, and as you yourself live, I will not leave without you." So he rose up and followed her. 31 Gehazi went on ahead and laid the staff on the face of the child, but there was no sound or sign of life. He came back to meet him and told him, "The child has not awakened."

32 When Elisha came into the house, he saw the child lying dead on his bed. 33 So he went in and closed the door on the two of them, and prayed to the LORD. 34 Then he got up on the bed and lay upon the child, putting his mouth upon his mouth, his eyes upon his eyes, and his hands upon his hands; and while he lay bent over him, the flesh of the child became warm. 35 He got down, walked once to and fro in the room, then got up again and bent over him; the child sneezed seven times, and the child opened his eyes. 36 Elisha summoned Gehazi and said, "Call the Shunammite woman." So he called her. When she came to him, he said, "Take your son." 37 She came and fell at his feet, bowing to the ground; then she took her son and left.

Analysis

The episode of the son of the Shunammite woman has two parts. Verses 8-17, the promise of the birth of a son, is a self-contained narrative. However, because the story of the raising of the dead son, vv. 18-37, refers back to it explicitly (v. 28), both tales form a single unit. Apart from Elisha and his servant Gehazi none of the characters is named, which might indicate that the narrator was not relying on any specific models. The events are set far from the usual centers of prophetic activity: Shunem, which is also mentioned in Josh 19:18 and 1 Sam 28:4, is to be found at Sōlem on the eastern border of the Jezreel plain. (Shunem is also the place of origin of Abishag, who cared for David toward the end of his life; see 1 Kgs 1:1-4.) The geographical position requires that Elisha would occasionally leave his sphere of influence in the south of Israel, although the destination of his wanderings is not mentioned.

Commentary

[4:8-17] The first part of the narrative is coherent and proves the miraculous power of the prophet. The prophet shows the unnamed woman his gratefulness for the guest room she provides and announces to her the birth of a son. The birth of a son was not only essential for the survival of the family in ancient Israelite society but also meant the greatest fulfillment in the life of a woman. The Hebrew Bible therefore knows a number of stories about the promise of the desired birth of a child (Gen 17:15-22; Judges 13; 1 Sam 1:1-20). The fulfillment of the promise "at that season, in due time," proves the special ability of the prophet to influence the course of nature. The announcement in this form is not to be read as direct interference, however, but as an act of intercession with God, the Lord of nature. The realization of the prophet's promise is explicitly mentioned in v. 17.

[4:18-19] The episode gives a particular slant to the subsequent narrative, since the reader (or listener) now knows of the special circumstances surrounding the birth. This is not any child, but an only son whose existence is owed to the prophet. Verse 18 links the narrative explicitly to what went before. In v. 19 the death of the child is summarily told without mentioning its precise cause. It is assumed that the boy is still of childhood age. In what follows, the mother appears as an unfailing supporter of the prophet; it is from him that she expects help, even in the face of the death of her child. Although the nature of her expectations is not specified, it is obvious to all concerned what they are.

[4:20-24] The remarks on the new moon and the Sabbath in the preparatory section indicate that both days were specially celebrated in the time of the narrator. The new moon is the first day of the lunar month, and the Sabbath is the seventh day of the week; the Sabbath was taken out of a strict monthly context to which it had probably once belonged, in order to become a holiday independent of the monthly cycle.[1]

[4:25-31] The following scene is set on Mount Carmel. Elisha's companion Gehazi is probably included in order to underline the superiority of Elisha's behavior. Elisha grasps the seriousness of the situation immediately from the brief allusions made by the woman in v. 28. She is adamant that Elisha attend in person; her trust in the power of the prophet is unshakable. He alone can work the wonder of raising the dead. The measure carried out by Gehazi at Elisha's behest is, accordingly, to no avail whatsoever (v. 31).

[4:32-35] Elisha achieves the raising of the boy, described in vv. 32-35, through prayer and body contact. The aspect of prayer indicates that it is Yahweh alone, as the

---

[1] See M. Tsevat, "The Basic Meaning of the Biblical Sabbath," *ZAW* 84 (1972) 447–59.

Lord of creation, who can give back life. The body contact confirms the share that the prophet has in this singular event: the life force of Elisha is passed on to the dead boy through his touch. The return to life is confirmed by the boy's seven sneezes, with no further commentary added.

[4:36-37] These verses conclude the events with the boy's return to his mother. She is rewarded because she has trusted in the healing power of the prophet. Her trust has had the desired effect and she expresses her gratitude through reverence. Although her trust is not problematized as a question of belief, one could still say that, as in the miracle stories of the NT, her belief plays an important role in the events.

The narrative parallels that of the miracle of Elijah in 1 Kgs 17:17-24. Both miracle stories follow the same structural pattern, although in Elijah's case there is a stronger focus on prayer. It is likely that the story of Elisha raising the dead child is the older one, which was then transposed to Elijah.

Death in the Pot

Text

4:38 When Elisha returned to Gilgal, there was a famine in the land. As the company of prophets was sitting before him, he said to his servant, "Put the large pot on, and make some stew for the company of prophets." 39 One of them went out into the field to gather herbs; he found a wild vine and gathered from it a lapful of wild gourds, and came and cut them up into the pot of stew, not knowing what they were. 40 They served some for the men to eat. But while they were eating the stew, they cried out, "O man of God, there is death in the pot!" They could not eat it. 41 He said, "Then bring some flour." He threw it into the pot, and said, "Serve the people and let them eat." And there was nothing harmful in the pot.

Commentary

[4:38] The episode is one of a number of short miracle stories whose aim is to glorify Elisha's deeds. Its setting is Gilgal in the Jordan Valley near Jericho, where a large number of unmarried followers apparently lived together. "A simple lifestyle characterizes the members of these groups; in many instances they appear on the verge of starvation, and these stories recall Elisha's miraculous aid in their time of need."[1] It is implied that in times of famine people would live on wild plants growing on the open fields around the settlement.

[4:39] This is obviously the background for the mistake occurring in the story. Collecting mallows, a kind of shrub whose leaves could be cooked, one of the prophet's followers has chanced upon wild gourds, which he then made into a stew, not realizing that they are inedible. The colocynth or bitter apple is a creeper that, because of its appearance, is also called "wild gourd" (*Citrullus colocynthis*). "Its fruit is round, yellow in its ripened stage, and the size of an apple."[2] Its flesh is used as a remedy,

---

[1] Cogan and Tadmor, *II Kings,* 60.
[2] Michael Zohary, *Plants of the Bible* (London: Cambridge Univ. Press, 1982).

especially for stomach pains, but the plant is inedible otherwise. Only its seeds are eaten, which the bedouin grind and bake into a kind of bread in times of dearth. The confusion is probably due to its similarity with a regular gourd.

[4:40-41] The mistake is only discovered during the meal through its bitter taste, leading to the cry of horror: "There is death in the pot." As with the spring in Jericho (2:19-22), Elisha knows how to help. Using flour as a miraculous substance he turns the noxious dish into a wholesome one. Yet it is not the flour but the prophet's power over natural phenomena that has effected the miracle. "The flour is only the means by which he confirms his supernatural power."[3] Once more Elisha has proven himself as a miracle worker among his followers. The setting of the story among the followers of the prophet points to its composition within those circles, since they had a keen interest to promote their master as a great miracle worker.

---

[3] Würthwein, *Könige,* 2:295.

The Feeding Miracle

Text

4:42 A man came from Baal-shalishah, bringing food from the first fruits to the man of God: twenty loaves of barley and fresh ears of grain in his sack. Elisha said, "Give it to the people and let them eat." 43 But his servant said, "How can I set this before a hundred people?" So he repeated, "Give it to the people and let them eat, for thus says the LORD, 'They shall eat and have some left.'" 44 He set it before them, they ate, and had some left, according to the word of the LORD.

Commentary

[4:42-44] The story of the feeding miracle is set in Baal-shalishah, a place, like Gilgal, probably found in the area of the tribe of Benjamin (cf. 1 Sam 9:4). From an archaeological point of view it would make sense to locate it at Khirbet el-Marjameh next to the spring ʿĒn Sāmiya, although there is no definite proof.[1]

According to the cultic laws (Lev 2:14; 23:17-20) the loaves brought to Elisha would really belong to the priests, and it is not clear why the gift of firstfruits should reach the prophet. The unnamed man is obviously keen to safeguard the provision of the prophet too. Elisha immediately orders the distribution of the gift to a crowd of people surrounding his house. The miracle lies in the difference between the number of loaves available and the number of people present. Yet all those present receive a share of the loaves and witness the miracle of eating sufficiently. Once more Elisha has shown his miraculous power, signified in his supplying a hungry crowd.

The narrative is curt; the miracle is introduced through the question in v. 43 and expressly confirmed in v. 44. Although the story is likely an independent tradition, it associates the famine mentioned in v. 38, thus adding weight to the miracle of feeding the hundred. It might also be a redactional construct underlining the social com-

---

[1] Amihai Mazar, "Khirbet Marjane (ʿAin Samiya)," *IEJ* 26 (1976) 138–39.

mitment of the prophet.[2] The feeding miracle of Elisha is far surpassed by those of Jesus; see Mark 6:30-44 par. Matt 14:13-21; Mark 9:10b-17 and Mark 8:1-9 par. Matt 15:32-39.

---

[2] See Hans-Christoph Schmitt, *Elisa: Traditionsgeschichtliche Untersuchungen zur vorklassischen nordisraelitischen Prophetie* (Gütersloh: Gütersloher, 1972), 100.

The Healing of Naaman

Text

5:1 Naaman, commander of the army of the king of Aram, was a great man and in high favor with his master, because by him the LORD had given victory to Aram. The man, though a mighty warrior, suffered from leprosy. 2 Now the Arameans on one of their raids had taken a young girl captive from the land of Israel, and she served Naaman's wife. 3 She said to her mistress, "If only my lord were with the prophet who is in Samaria! He would cure him of his leprosy." 4 So Naaman went in and told his lord just what the girl from the land of Israel had said. 5 And the king of Aram said, "Go then, and I will send along a letter to the king of Israel."

He went, taking with him ten talents of silver, six thousand shekels of gold, and ten sets of garments. 6 He brought the letter to the king of Israel, which read, "When this letter reaches you, know that I have sent to you my servant Naaman, that you may cure him of his leprosy." 7 When the king of Israel read the letter, he tore his clothes and said, "Am I God, to give death or life, that this man sends word to me to cure a man of his leprosy? Just look and see how he is trying to pick a quarrel with me."

8 But when Elisha the man of God heard that the king of Israel had torn his clothes, he sent a message to the king, "Why have you torn your clothes? Let him come to me, that he may learn that there is a prophet in Israel." 9 So Naaman came with his horses and chariots, and halted at the entrance of Elisha's house. 10 Elisha sent a messenger to him, saying, "Go, wash in the Jordan seven times, and your flesh shall be restored and you shall be clean." 11 But Naaman became angry and went away, saying, "I thought that for me he would surely come out, and stand and call on the name of the LORD his God, and would wave his hand over the spot, and cure the leprosy! 12 Are not Abana and Pharpar, the rivers of Damascus, better than all the waters of Israel? Could I not wash in them, and be clean?" He turned and went away in a rage. 13 But his servants approached and said to him, "Father, if the prophet had commanded you to do something difficult,

would you not have done it? How much more, when all he said to you was, 'Wash, and be clean'?" 14 So he went down and immersed himself seven times in the Jordan, according to the word of the man of God; his flesh was restored like the flesh of a young boy, and he was clean.

15 Then he returned to the man of God, he and all his company; he came and stood before him and said, "Now I know that there is no God in all the earth except in Israel; please accept a present from your servant." 16 But he said, "As the LORD lives, whom I serve, I will accept nothing!" He urged him to accept, but he refused. 17 Then Naaman said, "If not, please let two mule-loads of earth be given to your servant; for your servant will no longer offer burnt offering or sacrifice to any god except the LORD. 18 But may the LORD pardon your servant on one count: when my master goes into the house of Rimmon to worship there, leaning on my arm, and I bow down in the house of Rimmon, when I do bow down in the house of Rimmon, may the LORD pardon your servant on this one count." 19 He said to him, "Go in peace."

But when Naaman had gone from him a short distance, 20 Gehazi, the servant of Elisha the man of God, thought, "My master has let that Aramean Naaman off too lightly by not accepting from him what he offered. As the LORD lives, I will run after him and get something out of him." 21 So Gehazi went after Naaman. When Naaman saw someone running after him, he jumped down from the chariot to meet him and said, "Is everything all right?" 22 He replied, "Yes, but my master has sent me to say, 'Two members of a company of prophets have just come to me from the hill country of Ephraim; please give them a talent of silver and two changes of clothing.'" 23 Naaman said, "Please accept two talents." He urged him, and tied up two talents of silver in two bags, with two changes of clothing, and gave them to two of his servants, who carried them in front of Gehazi. 24 When he came to the citadel, he took the bags from them, and stored them inside; he dismissed the men, and they left.

25 He went in and stood before his master; and Elisha said to him, "Where have you been, Gehazi?" He answered, "Your servant has not gone anywhere at all." 26 But he said to him, "Did I not go with you in spirit when someone left his chariot to meet you? Is this a time to accept money and to accept clothing, olive orchards and vineyards, sheep and oxen, and male and female slaves? 27 Therefore the leprosy of Naaman shall cling to you, and to your descendants forever." So he left his presence leprous, as white as snow.

Analysis

The story of the healing of Naaman the Aramean is carefully crafted, reaching its end point with his actual recovery (v. 14). The subsequent passage, vv. 15-27, is an addition that takes as its theme Naaman's conflict of loyalty and Gehazi's sin and subsequent punishment. Even without this addition the narrative falls into several scenes with changing characters, showing the great creativity and skill with which it is structured and formulated. The intention of the narrator is to offer further proof of Elisha's miracle powers.

Commentary

[5:1] The exposition in v. 1 refers to the wars with the Arameans described by 1 Kings 20 and 22 as well as 2 Kgs 6:24—7:20. The names of the kings are not mentioned; only the "hero" of the story proper is named and specified as the commander of the army of the Aramean king. The reference to his leprosy introduces the plot line. The disease is more likely to be a form of eczema than leprosy, which would agree with its description in v. 27 as "white as snow."

[5:2-3] The decisive advice is given in the interlude in vv. 2-3 by a slave girl captured in the war who happens to work in the house of Naaman. Through her Naaman is told to seek help in the right quarter, for leprosy was considered a disease that could only be healed through divine help, not human skill (cf. Numbers 12). This requires the mediation of a miracle-working prophet such as Elisha, who is introduced as being active in Samaria at the time.

[5:4-7] Naaman, as a powerful state official, can rely on the full support of his king, who turns to the king of Israel as his peer. The delivery of the royal message by Naaman only reaffirms what is already implied: the insight that no human can offer a remedy for the disease, not even the king of Israel himself. It is only God who can help. The acknowledged insufficiency of humans prepares for the true extent of Elisha's miracle.

[5:8-14] Elisha is introduced in the miracle story proper. No immediate encounter takes place between the commander and the prophet, who effects the healing from a distance. In Naaman's reaction the mutual demands of respect and veneration are skillfully played off against each other. Naaman can be persuaded to follow Elisha's order only by the insistence of his men. To mark Elisha, who speaks and acts in the name of Yahweh, as the more powerful one, who is not obliged to follow the rules of submission, renders Naaman's claim of power implicitly absurd.

[5:11-14] Naaman's words by the river Jordan (vv. 11-12) equally bear out the arrogance of this Aramean who considers himself superior. Abana and Pharpar are the rivers near Damascus that water its oasis, which antiquity compared to paradise. Abana can be identified as Bavadā, while Pharpar is el-Anwağ. The waters of the river Jordan are used as the medium for ritual purification. After seven immersions Naaman is completely and permanently healed. However, it is not the water that effects the healing, but the miraculous power of the prophet, who has the necessary strength for the deed. It is Yahweh alone who works miracles, with the prophet as his agent, although this is not said in such explicit terms.

[5:15-27] The following section supplies the theological message that had been missing so far. Moreover, it emphasizes the prophet's stance as being both consequent and binding, taking his rejection of gifts as the example. Verses 15-16 speak first of Naaman's reaction: he returns to the man of God to confirm the miracle he has worked on him and to show his gratitude. On this occasion he professes Yahweh as the only God on earth, which amounts to a statement of consequent monotheism such as developed only in the exilic and postexilic period. Monotheism is here understood as the worship of Yahweh as the only God to the extent of denying the existence of other gods. The claim that Yahweh is the one God not only of Israel but of the entire earth, which precludes the existence of other gods, is found first in Deut 4:35, 39 and Deutero-Isaiah (Isa 44:6; 45:5-6, 18). Given its theological assumptions, the passage relating Naaman's response has then to be dated to the postexilic period.

[5:17-18] These verses subsequently thematize the problem that results for Naaman: how can he stay true to his confession and still fulfill his duty as a state official? How can he be loyal both to his newly found God and to his king who worships other gods? The god Rimmon, who is mentioned by Naaman, appears in Aramaic and Neo-Assyrian sources as a separate deity, although his name is elsewhere an epithet of the weather-god Hadad.[1] The conflict lies in the exclusion of the worship of any other deity that the acknowledgment of Yahweh makes necessary, even if that worship occurs through loyalty to the king as master. Naaman asks forgiveness for his conduct, which is neither granted nor precluded by Elisha's response.

[5:19a] J. J. Stamm already saw that Elisha's formula "go in peace" leaves the question ultimately undecided: "He certainly does not grant his foreign guest definite forgiveness, rather he lets him hope for a certain lenience on the part of Yahweh."[2] The taking of two mule-loads of earth from the land of the God of Israel also relates to Naaman's future worship of Yahweh. "Foreign soil is considered unclean soil,"[3] as testified by Amos 7:17 and Hos 9:3. Soil from the land that belongs to Yahweh and to which he is connected in a particular way is therefore part of the proper worship of Yahweh. The problem arising from sacrifice in a different country is solved if a certain quantity of earth from the land of Israel is present when the cult is practiced in

---

[1] See Jonas C. Greenfield, "The Aramean God Ramman/Rimmon," *IEJ* 26 (1976) 195–98; and idem, "Hadad," in *DDD*[2] 377–82.

[2] Johann Jakob Stamm, *Erlösen und Vergeben im Alten Testament: Eine begriffsgeschichtliche Untersuchung* (Bern: Francke, 1940), 48–49.

[3] Würthwein, *Könige*, 2:301.

some other place, in order to represent Israel. As a result the worship of Yahweh is possible anywhere, while the special significance of the land of Israel is not compromised. The land itself thus assumes a theological quality; as the gift of Yahweh to his people it is at the same time the essential foundation for the lawful practice of the cult.

[5:19b-27] The later addition that follows speaks of the greed of Gehazi and of his punishment. The starting point is Naaman's wish to reward Elisha generously with silver and gold. When Elisha refuses the offer as improper, his servant Gehazi coaxes part of the silver from Naaman by using a lie. In the last scene (vv. 25-27) Elisha takes his companion to task and punishes him with the very same disease from which he has just healed Naaman. The reason for punishment is that Gehazi wanted to acquire the money unlawfully and, in addition, had lied to Elisha. More than that, this part of the addition turns out also to teach a lesson about the behavior becoming a follower: a prophet must not derive material benefits from his special gift, since the use of his power, granted by God, must only reflect on its creator.

The Floating Ax

Text

6:1 Now the company of prophets said to Elisha, "As you see, the place where we live under your charge is too small for us. 2 Let us go to the Jordan, and let us collect logs there, one for each of us, and build a place there for us to live." He answered, "Do so." 3 Then one of them said, "Please come with your servants." And he answered, "I will." 4 So he went with them. When they came to the Jordan, they cut down trees. 5 But as one was felling a log, his ax head fell into the water; he cried out, "Alas, master! It was borrowed." 6 Then the man of God said, "Where did it fall?" When he showed him the place, he cut off a stick, and threw it in there, and made the iron float. 7 He said, "Pick it up." So he reached out his hand and took it.

Commentary

[6:1-7] This miracle story is a typical short narrative. The events, again, take place by the river Jordan and within the circle of followers, offering yet another insight into their community life. The plot is told straightforwardly and without further decorations: during the felling of trees near the river an ax falls into the water. The iron tool is not only of high value as such, but is also borrowed, which increases the anxiety caused by its loss. Using a piece of wood as the miracle-working item Elisha fetches back the ax, making its iron body float on the water. Apart from giving evidence of his miracle-working power, Elisha also shows his superiority over his followers.

Nothing is said about the shape of the ax. It is probably an ax whose handle was put through a forged hole to connect the handle firmly to the blade. The point of the story lies in Elisha making the iron float on water. More than simply recovering the tool, Elisha here demonstrates his miracle-working powers that let him contradict the laws of nature.

The Tricking of the Arameans

Text

6:8 Once when the king of Aram was at war with Israel, he took counsel with his officers. He said, "At such and such a place shall be my camp." 9 But the man of God sent word to the king of Israel, "Take care not to pass this place, because the Arameans are going down there." 10 The king of Israel sent word to the place of which the man of God spoke. More than once or twice he warned such a place so that it was on the alert.

11 The mind of the king of Aram was greatly perturbed because of this; he called his officers and said to them, "Now tell me who among us sides with the king of Israel?" 12 Then one of his officers said, "No one, my lord king. It is Elisha, the prophet in Israel, who tells the king of Israel the words that you speak in your bedchamber." 13 He said, "Go and find where he is; I will send and seize him." He was told, "He is in Dothan." 14 So he sent horses and chariots there and a great army; they came by night, and surrounded the city.

15 When an attendant of the man of God rose early in the morning and went out, an army with horses and chariots was all around the city. His servant said, "Alas, master! What shall we do?" 16 He replied, "Do not be afraid, for there are more with us than there are with them." 17 Then Elisha prayed: "O LORD, please open his eyes that he may see." So the LORD opened the eyes of the servant, and he saw; the mountain was full of horses and chariots of fire all around Elisha. 18 When the Arameans came down against him, Elisha prayed to the LORD, and said, "Strike this people, please, with blindness." So he struck them with blindness as Elisha had asked. 19 Elisha said to them, "This is not the way, and this is not the city; follow me, and I will bring you to the man whom you seek." And he led them to Samaria.

20 As soon as they entered Samaria, Elisha said, "O LORD, open the eyes of these men so that they may see." The LORD opened their eyes, and they saw that they were inside Samaria. 21 When the king of Israel saw them he

said to Elisha, "Father, shall I kill them? Shall I kill them?" 22 He answered, "No! Did you capture with your sword and your bow those whom you want to kill? Set food and water before them so that they may eat and drink; and let them go to their master." 23 So he prepared for them a great feast; after they ate and drank, he sent them on their way, and they went to their master. And the Arameans no longer came raiding into the land of Israel.

Analysis

The narrative is set against the background of the Aramean wars, although no details are provided. The two rival kings are not named, for the intention is not to situate the miraculous events within their historical context, but rather to emphasize Elisha's supernatural powers and glorify them. The original narrative was extended by vv. 15b-17, which aims to illustrate the superior strength of the God fighting for Israel. Verses 18aβγ-b and 20 are likely to be another addition; here Elisha, who usually acts on his own, addresses Yahweh. The story presupposes a particular method of warfare: a ruler dispatches relatively small raiding troops into enemy territory to ransack villages or towns and to take away prisoners and goods. Such forays may not entirely beat the enemy, but they will certainly diminish the enemy's strength.

Commentary

[6:8-20] The central theme of the story is Elisha's supernatural power of perception. His foresight allows him to warn the king of Israel against the Aramean raids (vv. 8-10). Seeing his attacks fail, the king of Aram suspects treason, yet learns from his men about the powers of the prophet Elisha, which let him perceive things even when he is not present (vv. 11-12). The king of Aram subsequently gives order to have Elisha caught and in this way to stop this form of advance warning, but he has to witness the attempt end with the capture of his raiding troop instead (vv. 13-15a, 18aα, 19). In this context, the delusion of the troop stands in particularly sharp contrast to Elisha's clairvoyance.

The events take place at Dothan (Tell Dōtān), an important town about 20 km. north of Samaria on the edge of a fertile plain. The choice of place seems nonetheless rather arbitrary and allows no inferences to be made about an earlier version.[1] It was only the locality near Samaria as the setting of the last scene that was important to the narrator: for Elisha, by his supernatural powers, contrives to lead the troop that was sent against him in captivity to Samaria.

[6:21-23] The final scene tells of the sparing and the release of the prisoners. Elisha outspokenly objects to the death sentence envisaged by the king of Israel; in this way

---

[1] *Pace* Hans-Christoph Schmitt, *Elisa: Traditionsgeschichtliche Untersuchungen zur vorklassischen nordisraelitischen Prophetie* (Gütersloh: Gütersloher, 1972), 155–56.

he is revealed as a defender of life and justice even and especially concerning the enemy. In the background lingers the fact that the enemies, released after a feast, can now bear witness to Elisha's singular power. They can give proof from experience that all further action is futile and that even the king of Aram stands powerless against this omniscient man of God.

The Miraculous Deliverance of Samaria

Text

6:24 Some time later King Ben-hadad of Aram mustered his entire army; he marched against Samaria and laid siege to it. 25 As the siege continued, famine in Samaria became so great that a donkey's head was sold for eighty shekels of silver, and one-fourth of a kab of dove's dung for five shekels of silver. 26 Now as the king of Israel was walking on the city wall, a woman cried out to him, "Help, my lord king!" 27 He said, "No! Let the LORD help you. How can I help you? From the threshing floor or from the wine press?" 28 But then the king asked her, "What is your complaint?" She answered, "This woman said to me, 'Give up your son; we will eat him today, and we will eat my son tomorrow.' 29 So we cooked my son and ate him. The next day I said to her, 'Give up your son and we will eat him.' But she has hidden her son." 30 When the king heard the words of the woman he tore his clothes—now since he was walking on the city wall, the people could see that he had sackcloth on his body underneath— 31 and he said, "So may God do to me, and more, if the head of Elisha son of Shaphat stays on his shoulders today." 32 So he dispatched a man from his presence. Now Elisha was sitting in his house, and the elders were sitting with him. Before the messenger arrived, Elisha said to the elders, "Are you aware that this murderer has sent someone to take off my head? When the messenger comes, see that you shut the door and hold it closed against him. Is not the sound of his master's feet behind him?" 33 While he was still speaking with them, the king came down to him and said, "This trouble is from the LORD! Why should I hope in the LORD any longer?" 7:1 But Elisha said, "Hear the word of the LORD: thus says the LORD, Tomorrow about this time a measure of choice meal shall be sold for a shekel, and two measures of barley for a shekel, at the gate of Samaria." 2 Then the captain on whose hand the king leaned said to the man of God, "Even if the LORD were to make windows in the sky, could such a thing happen?" But he said, "You shall see it with your own eyes, but you shall not eat from it."

3 Now there were four leprous men outside the city gate, who said to one another, "Why should we sit here until we die? 4 If we say, 'Let us enter the city,' the famine is in the city, and we shall die there; but if we sit here, we shall also die. Therefore, let us desert to the Aramean camp; if they spare our lives, we shall live; and if they kill us, we shall but die." 5 So they arose at twilight to go to the Aramean camp; but when they came to the edge of the Aramean camp, there was no one there at all. 6 For the Lord had caused the Aramean army to hear the sound of chariots, and of horses, the sound of a great army, so that they said to one another, "The king of Israel has hired the kings of the Hittites and the kings of Egypt to fight against us." 7 So they fled away in the twilight and abandoned their tents, their horses, and their donkeys leaving the camp just as it was, and fled for their lives. 8 When these leprous men had come to the edge of the camp, they went into a tent, ate and drank, carried off silver, gold, and clothing, and went and hid them. Then they came back, entered another tent, carried off things from it, and went and hid them.

9 Then they said to one another, "What we are doing is wrong. This is a day of good news; if we are silent and wait until the morning light, we will be found guilty; therefore let us go and tell the king's household." 10 So they came and called to the gatekeepers of the city, and told them, "We went to the Aramean camp, but there was no one to be seen or heard there, nothing but the horses tied, the donkeys tied, and the tents as they were." 11 Then the gatekeepers called out and proclaimed it to the king's household. 12 The king got up in the night, and said to his servants, "I will tell you what the Arameans have prepared against us. They know that we are starving; so they have left the camp to hide themselves in the open country, thinking, 'When they come out of the city, we shall take them alive and get into the city.'" 13 One of his servants said, "Let some men take five of the remaining horses, since those left here will suffer the fate of the whole multitude of Israel that have perished already; let us send and find out." 14 So they took two mounted men, and the king sent them after the Aramean army, saying, "Go and find out." 15 So they went after them as far as the Jordan; the whole way was littered with garments and equipment that the Arameans had thrown away in their haste. So the messengers returned, and told the king.

16 Then the people went out, and plundered the camp of the Arameans. So a measure of choice meal was sold for a shekel, and two measures of barley for a shekel, according to the word of the LORD. 17 Now the king had appointed the captain on whose hand he leaned to have charge of the gate; the people trampled him to death in the gate, just as the man of God had said when the king came down to him. 18 For when the man of God had said to the king, "Two measures of barley shall be sold for a shekel, and a measure of choice meal for a shekel, about this time tomorrow in the gate

of Samaria," 19 the captain had answered the man of God, "Even if the LORD were to make windows in the sky, could such a thing happen?" And he had answered, "You shall see it with your own eyes, but you shall not eat from it." 20 It did indeed happen to him; the people trampled him to death in the gate.

Analysis

The story of the miraculous deliverance of Samaria is not of a piece but has been extended through a number of additions. Thus 6:27 and 31 add short explanations. A larger interpolation is the passage about the prophet in 6:32—7:2, between the first and second scenes. A later hand again added the explanation of the silence reigning over the camp of the Arameans in 7:6-7. This necessitated the repetition in 7:8a, which takes up 7:5. After the end of the narrative as such, in 7:16a, the fulfillment of the prophet's word is recounted in 7:16b-20. Quite apart from those additions, the narrative is skillfully constructed and falls into the following subsections:

6:24-25	Exposition
6:26, 28-30	The famine at Samaria
7:3-5, 8b-11	The discovery of the deserted Aramean camp
7:12-16a	The relief of the siege

Commentary

[6:24-25] The exposition lays out the situation and provides the necessary information. The siege of Samaria by the Aramean king Ben-hadad has led to a disastrous famine. Regarding the name of Ben-hadad we have to distinguish three Aramean kings in the biblical context: Ben-hadad I, the son of Tabrimmon, son of Hezion, was a contemporary of King Asa of Judah and King Baasha of Israel (1 Kgs 15:18-20). Ben-hadad II, according to 1 Kings 20, fought against Ahab, the details in this case being provided by the Deueronomistic redactor. Ben-hadad III is mentioned in 2 Kgs 13:24-25 as the son and successor of Hazael.[1] The king mentioned here is probably Ben-hadad II, who was a contemporary of the Omrides and who can be dated to the mid-ninth century.[2]

The aim of the siege was to starve Samaria into submission. Although the citizens were well protected by a city wall, this also meant they were cut off from necessary supplies of water and food. Nothing is said on the length of the siege, but the

---

[1] On the extrabiblical sources for the kings of this name see Stefan Timm, *Die Dynastie Omri: Quellen und Untersuchungen zur Geschichte Israels im 9. Jahrhundert vor Christus,* FRLANT 124 (Göttingen: Vandenhoeck & Ruprecht, 1982), 241–45.

[2] See also Benjamin Mazar, "The Aramean Empire and Its Relations with Israel," in *The Early Biblical Period: Historical Studies,* ed. Shmuel Ahituv and Baruch A. Levine, trans. Ruth Rigbi and Elisheva Rigbi (Jerusalelm: Israel Exploration Society, 1986), 151–72.

graphic description of the situation, as it is recalled in the first scene (vv. 6:26, 28-30), makes a duration of several months seem likely.

The effects of the siege are illustrated by the scarcity of food. The donkey was an unclean animal (see Lev 11:18 and Deut 14:3-8) whose meat was not usually eaten. All animals for slaughter having been consumed, however, it was inevitable to eat what was despised. H. Gunkel has pointed out a parallel in Plutarch, where during the war against the Caduzians the Persian army was forced to slaughter their beasts of burden when the famine was so great "that one could not buy a donkey's head for less than 60 drachmas."[3] The horror of the famine is symbolized by the price at which the donkey's head was traded; one "shekel" equals 11.42 g. of silver. In normal times the worth of a slave was 30 shekels (Exod 21:32). Thus 80 shekels for a donkey's head expresses the seriousness of the plight, because the named price would have been out of the reach of most inhabitants of the besieged city anyway.

The dove's dung, which is further mentioned, is probably not a replacement for salt (Josephus, *Ant.* 9.62) but instead a paraphrase for the fruits of the carob tree, as suggested by Akkadian lexicography.[4] Those pods were edible, but their bad taste let them be used mainly as animal feed. The term "kab" refers to the dry measure and equals a sixth of a seah. If one seah is 7.2 liters, the kab amounts to about 1.2 liters.

[6:26, 28-30] The story is made up of three scenes with changing characters. The first scene, 6:26, 28-30, offers a stark description of the effects of the famine wrought by the siege. The king is present during the siege, as he would be when leading his troops into battle, and so he is seen walking the ramparts (6:26). This explains why he can be addressed in public and without the usual court etiquette. The cry "Help, my lord king!" is an appeal for justice and support. The king answers the appeal inquiring about the particulars of the case (6:28). In this way the king learns about the cruel realities in the city resulting from the siege. The lack of food has already driven people to cannibalism. The slaughter of one's own children as a sign of extreme want is also mentioned in other biblical and Akkadian sources.[5] The portrayal of plight could not be more drastic: in order to survive, people destroy their own future. The king's response to the account of the dreadful legal case is to rend his clothes, a rite of lamentation, thereby expressing his shock as much as his helplessness.

[7:3-5, 8b-11] The second scene deals with the discovery of the deserted camp of the Arameans and prepares for the deliverance from the famine. The scene opens with the

---

[3] Hermann Gunkel, *Geschichten von Elisa,* Meisterwerke hebräischer Erzählungskunst 1 (Berlin: Curtius, 1925), 48.

[4] See Cogan and Tadmor, *II Kings,* 79.

[5] See Deut 28:52-58; Ezek 5:10; Lam 2:20; 4:10; Treaties of Esarhaddon, lines 448-50 and 547-50 (*TUAT,* I/2, 171–73).

four leprous men giving a realistic evaluation of the situation (7:3-4). Their disease is the reason why they are still outside the city. Considered unclean, they were excluded from the community of the city and were cared for outside its walls. "It is difficult to imagine what exactly their present situation would have been."[6] They come between two fronts, so to speak, and the narrator leaves no doubt that death looms on either side and no help is to be expected. Their decision to throw in their lot with the Arameans leads them to find the Aramean camp empty (7:5). At first, the four men take advantage of the situation, eat to the full of the deserted provisions, and make off with some of the valuables left behind (7:8b). It is only when their own needs have been satisfied that they remember the general plight (7:9). After they tell the guardians at the city gate, the changed circumstances are made known to the king (7:10-11).

[7:12-16a] In the third and final scene the story reaches its climax. Before that, however, the king's counsel introduces a retarding element: the course of events is suspended over deliberations whether the desertion could be a ploy of the Arameans (7:12). The enemy is to be lured out of the city under false pretenses, only to be destroyed in a surprise attack. Apparent desertion is a military tactic mentioned elsewhere (see Josh 8:10-22; Judg 9:34-41, 42-45; 20:29-48) that allowed one to conquer a city without having to take it by storm. The possibility of an ambush is excluded by dispatching two horsemen, who return to confirm the withdrawal of the Arameans and therefore the relief of the siege (7:13-15). No reason is given for the retreat of the enemy. The siege is finished unexpectedly, and the end of the famine is borne out with the looting of the camp (7:16a).

The historical truth of the story cannot be verified; "the memory of a siege of Samaria by the Arameans" is unlikely to be its background.[7] Rather, it is the miraculous deliverance of the city from great need and danger that is the central concern of the author. Information establishing the general background is kept vague, and the three scenes contain no specific details about the progress of the siege. Cogan and Tadmor, too, after considering all historical evidence, reach the conclusion that a siege of Samaria by the Arameans during the reign of the Omrides is highly unlikely.[8] The plot line supports the theory of a fictitious account, as it is driven along by common literary topoi. These include the description of the famine, as well as the surprising discovery of the withdrawal of the enemy. The entire narrative moves toward the miraculous deliverance from the hands of the enemy and the ending of the famine that ensues. The story is therefore better interpreted as a miracle story within the general framework of the Aramean wars, rather than as an account of historical events.

[6:32—7:2] The additions contribute to the miraculous character of the events. The interpolation in 6:32—7:2 reports an encounter between the king and Elisha, who

---

[6] Würthwein, *Könige,* 2:312.

[7] Contra ibid., 314.

[8] Cogan and Tadmor, *II Kings,* 84.

foretells that normality will be restored in the name of Yahweh, which implies the relief of the siege and the end of the famine. The prices for grain sold at the gate of Samaria will still be above the normal level, but they indicate the return to a regular provision of food. The measure of the seah equals about 7.2 liters, with semolina, made from wheat, being sold at twice the price of the less common barley.

The doubts about the fulfillment of the word of God, expressed by the captain, lead Elisha to utter a prophecy of doom against this same official, whose position is most likely to be that of a liaising officer. His rank cannot be determined more precisely but it may have been adopted from the division of charioteers ("third man").[9]

[7:6-7] This addition serves to explain the desertion of their camp by the Arameans. The hasty retreat is caused by the appearance of a large army including chariots. The delusion is the work of Yahweh, who thereby effects the pivotal turn of events in favor of Israel. The mention of the "kings of the Hittites" and the "kings of Egypt" cannot be related to a historical pretext; rather, those two empires are referred to as military powers against whom a small state could not survive. To mention those states is in fact an anachronism: the Hittite Empire had already fallen in the thirteenth century, and the hegemony of Egypt had declined since the Ramesside period in the twelfth century, to be supplanted eventually by the ascendancy of Assyria in the ninth century. Thus we are not dealing with allusions to an immediate historical context.[10]

[7:16b-20] Finally, the addition in vv. 16b-20 tells of the fulfillment of the word of Yahweh in 6:32—7:2. The section is tagged on to the end of the narrative in 7:16a to tie up the subplot: to doubt the word of God means to be punished with death. The captain, overseeing the gate after the end of the siege, is trampled to death by the masses—not an honorable death for an active army officer. The addition is, like the section 6:32—7:2, part of a redaction whose aim is to make the prophet the focus of the story and, moreover, to relate the events back to the will of Yahweh alone.

---

[9] For possibilities of interpretation see B. A. Mastin, "Was the *šališ* the Third Man in the Chariot?" in *Studies in the Historical Books of the Old Testament,* ed. J. A. Emerton, VTSup 30 (Leiden: Brill, 1979), 125–54.

[10] See already Gunkel, *Geschichten von Elisa,* 59.

The King as a Guarantor of Justice

Text

8:1 Now Elisha had said to the woman whose son he had restored to life, "Get up and go with your household, and settle wherever you can; for the LORD has called for a famine, and it will come on the land for seven years." 2 So the woman got up and did according to the word of the man of God; she went with her household and settled in the land of the Philistines seven years. 3 At the end of the seven years, when the woman returned from the land of the Philistines, she set out to appeal to the king for her house and her land. 4 Now the king was talking with Gehazi the servant of the man of God, saying, "Tell me all the great things that Elisha has done." 5 While he was telling the king how Elisha had restored a dead person to life, the woman whose son he had restored to life appealed to the king for her house and her land. Gehazi said, "My lord king, here is the woman, and here is her son whom Elisha restored to life." 6 When the king questioned the woman, she told him. So the king appointed an official for her, saying, "Restore all that was hers, together with all the revenue of the fields from the day that she left the land until now."

Analysis

This is the story of a legal case aiming to portray the king as a guarantor of justice. Only the scene in vv. 4-5 involving Gehazi is a later addition that identifies the unnamed woman with the woman of Shunem (4:8-17), whose son Elisha had raised from the dead. This identification was later also added to the story's beginning in v. 1. Other than that, the addition does not interfere with the course of the narrated events. The main point is that the king, as sovereign, restores to the woman her estate after she has returned from the Philistines, an act which establishes him as a just ruler.

Commentary

[8:1-3] The starting point is a famine, predicted by the prophet from his knowledge of the future. Seven years of famine, a general timespan mentioned elsewhere too, are a long time, given the short life expectancy.[1] Although there is evidence from other sources that people would try to flee from food shortages caused by crop failures, this appears to be the exception rather than the rule.[2] In effect, to leave one's ground meant to give up one's property. In cases of abandonment, as also in cases of the death penalty, land would be confiscated as the king's property. The ownership of land was dependent on the actual use of property, the legal claim therefore tied to its possession rather than mere ownership.

[8:4-6] The narrative shows that the king acknowledges the woman's property as her possession and releases it back to her out of the royal estate. The king's order implies that he is in fact the sovereign ruler of the land once owned by her, but that he willingly restores it to her. This restitution of an old legal claim constitutes an "act of grace,"[3] showing the king, as the guarantor of old Israelite land law, in a special light. His legal act is all the more significant precisely because he is under no obligation to restore her possession. Thus the main point of the narrative is clearly established: the king uses his regal privilege to reestablish a status quo to which there existed not even a rightful claim, thus proving himself to be a guardian of the downtrodden and a guarantor of justice.

---

[1] See, e.g., Gen 41:25-32 or the so-called Famine Stele, *ANET*, 31–32.

[2] See Ruth 1; Papyrus Anastasi VI, 51-61 (*TGI*, 40).

[3] Albrecht Alt, "Der Anteil des Königtums an der sozialen Entwicklung in den Reichen Israel und Juda," in idem, *Kleine Schriften zur Geschichte des Volkes Israels* (Munich: Beck), 3:364.

The Death of Ben-hadad

Text

8:7 Elisha went to Damascus while King Ben-hadad of Aram was ill. When it was told him, "The man of God has come here," 8 the king said to Hazael, "Take a present with you and go to meet the man of God. Inquire of the LORD through him, whether I shall recover from this illness." 9 So Hazael went to meet him, taking a present with him, all kinds of goods of Damascus, forty camel loads. When he entered and stood before him, he said, "Your son King Ben-hadad of Aram has sent me to you, saying, 'Shall I recover from this illness?'" 10 Elisha said to him, "Go, say to him, 'You shall certainly recover'; but the LORD has shown me that he shall certainly die." 11 He fixed his gaze and stared at him, until he was ashamed. Then the man of God wept. 12 Hazael asked, "Why does my lord weep?" He answered, "Because I know the evil that you will do to the people of Israel; you will set their fortresses on fire, you will kill their young men with the sword, dash in pieces their little ones, and rip up their pregnant women." 13 Hazael said, "What is your servant, who is a mere dog, that he should do this great thing?" Elisha answered, "The LORD has shown me that you are to be king over Aram." 14 Then he left Elisha, and went to his master Ben-hadad, who said to him, "What did Elisha say to you?" And he answered, "He told me that you would certainly recover." 15 But the next day he took the bed-cover and dipped it in water and spread it over the king's face, until he died. And Hazael succeeded him.

Analysis

This section is not a story of the prophet but explains the succession of Hazael to the throne. The same Hazael is mentioned in 13:24 as the father of Ben-hadad III, and he also appears in the inscriptions of Shalmaneser III, where he is, however, explicitly labeled the "son of a nobody," that is, a usurper.[1] The story states clearly that this suc-

---

[1] *TUAT*, I/4, 365; [Ed.] also in Daniel David Luckenbill, *Ancient Records of Assyria and Babylonia*, vol. 1 (Chicago: Univ. of Chicago Press, 1927).

cession to the throne at Damascus was not a peaceful or natural one, since Hazael had killed his lord and predecessor. The section with the dialogue between Elisha and Hazael is full of contradictions and inconsistencies. Following Würthwein, who reads vv. 10b-13 as part of a later redaction, the difficulties can be resolved.[2]

Commentary

[8:7-10a, 14-15] In this case vv. 7-10a, 14-15 form a consistent narrative with a clear plot. When Elisha is in Damascus Ben-hadad sends his confidant Hazael to him to ask about God's will regarding his illness. No further details are revealed about the nature of this illness, but it appears to be serious and long-lasting. The prophet's answer is clear and positive: God grants Ben-hadad's survival. This proclamation in no way agrees with Hazael's plans: he therefore suffocates the king with a wet blanket and kills him.

The plot is clearly fictitious, as it pretends to know about events at the court at Damascus that took place with no witnesses. We can, for this reason, not assume that we are reading a historical tradition. The point of the story is rather to contest that Ben-hadad had died a natural death. The narrator knows better: Hazael killed his predecessor in cold blood when he was ill, in order to usurp power. It is most likely that the narrative originated in prophetic circles; this would explain the link between the events and the prophecy of Elisha.

[8:10b-13] This addition not only preempts the final outcome but also offers a glimpse of the future, thus presenting the prophet as an omniscient seer. The prophecy of the future deeds of Hazael against the people of Israel makes use of certain literary topoi that paint a picture of the horrors of war.[3] To refer to oneself as a "dog" was contemporary linguistic usage too.[4] The interpolated section closes with the announcement of Hazael's future rule as king of the Arameans. Apart from the introduction of those literary topoi, however, the passage does not add anything to the narrative sequence vv. 7-10a, 14-15.

---

[2] Würthwein, *Könige,* 2:319.

[3] See 15:16; Amos 1:3, 13; Hos 14:1; and the Akkadian parallels in Mordechai Cogan, "'Ripping Open Pregnant Women' in Light of an Assyrian Analogue," *JAOS* 103 (1983) 755–57.

[4] See 1 Sam 24:14; 2 Sam 9:8; Lachish letters 2:4; 5:4; 6:3 (*ANET* 320–22; *TUAT,* I/6, 620–23); and Assyrian evidence in *CAD* 8:72.

Jehoram of Judah

Text

8:16 In the fifth year of King Joram son of Ahab of Israel, Jehoram son of King Jehoshaphat of Judah began to reign. 17 He was thirty-two years old when he became king, and he reigned eight years in Jerusalem. 18 He walked in the way of the kings of Israel, as the house of Ahab had done, for the daughter of Ahab was his wife. He did what was evil in the sight of the LORD. 19 Yet the LORD would not destroy Judah, for the sake of his servant David, since he had promised to give a lamp to him and to his descendants forever. 20 In his days Edom revolted against the rule of Judah, and set up a king of their own. 21 Then Joram crossed over to Zair with all his chariots. He set out by night and attacked the Edomites and their chariot commanders who had surrounded him; but his army fled home. 22 So Edom has been in revolt against the rule of Judah to this day. Libnah also revolted at the same time. 23 Now the rest of the acts of Joram, and all that he did, are they not written in the Book of the Annals of the Kings of Judah? 24 So Joram slept with his ancestors, and was buried with them in the city of David; his son Ahaziah succeeded him.

Analysis

A short notice on the political developments in Edom, vv. 20-22, is stuck between the introductory formula, vv. 16-19, and the closing formula of Jehoram, vv. 23-24.

Commentary

[8:16-19] The introductory formula justifies the negative evaluation of Jehoram through his connection to the Omride dynasty (v. 18). He married Athaliah, a daughter of Omri and sister of Ahab (NRSV: daughter of Ahab), a marriage that shows the good relations between the houses of Israel and Judah at the time. After the early death of her son Ahaziah, Athaliah herself took power in Jerusalem and reigned on the throne of David for six years. Her royal pedigree certainly helped her to become the only woman ever to hold this position and to take this unusual and daring step (see 11:1-20). Jehoram follows the direction of the kings of Israel, that is, he does not follow the way prescribed by Yahweh; the path he chooses is clearly commented on by his marriage to a princess from the northern kingdom.

[8:20-22] The notices on Edom can be considered historical; they could hardly be pure invention. Their origin is lost, but they possibly derive from the royal annals. Edom is originally the name attached to the small strip of arable land south of the Wadi el-Hesā (and not the mountains made from Nubian sandstone). The name was then transferred to the inhabitants of this area, which probably descend from the nomad tribes mentioned in the Egyptian sources of the New Kingdom.[1] There is evidence for settlements in this area as early as the eleventh century.[2] According to archaeological evaluation, however, "Edom remained a tribal fiefdom without urban institutions throughout the ninth and eighth centuries."[3] Even despite Judean sovereignty over Edom in Davidic times, we cannot assume a transition to a form of state organization much before the ninth century.

The notice on the defection of Edom reports two events: the installation of a king and a victory over the Judeans. Of the military defeat of Judah we are given only the location. According to Genesis 19, Zoar (Zair?) lies at the southern end of the Dead Sea, but following Deut 34:3; Isa 15:5; and Jer 48:4, it is a Moabite city. Lack of additional information does not allow us to define the location more precisely, but it is possible that Zoar was situated south of the estuary of the Wadi el-Hesā into the Dead Sea, near Tawahin es-Sukkar, the Byzantine-Arabic village of that name.[4] The Edomite contingent apparently took advantage of its knowledge of the area and launched a surprise attack on the Judeans, whose king and officers must have escaped by a hair's breadth.

We do not know whether the proclamation of a king led to the establishment of a permanent kingdom, but for the following two reasons this is rather unlikely: (1) Qausmalaka (or: Qaush-malaku) is named as the first Edomite king only under Tiglath-pileser III in the second half of the eighth century.[5] (2) The capital of Bozra (Busera) was founded only toward the end of the eighth century, judging by ceramic evidence. The notice on the installation of a king of Edom does prove, in any case, that the Edomite tribes would form a front under a single ruler when they felt threatened from outside, even if this did not mean the establishment of a formal state.

---

[1] See Raphael Giveon, *Les bédouins Shosou des documents égyptiens,* DMOA 18 (Leiden: Brill, 1971).

[2] Manfred Weippert, "Remarks on the History of Settlement in Southern Jordan during the Early Iron Age," *SHAJ* 1 (1982) 153–62.

[3] Ernst Axel Knauf, *NBL* 1:469.

[4] See Nelson Glueck, *Explorations in Eastern Palestine,* AASOR 15 (New Haven: American Schools of Oriental Research, 1935), 2:7–8.

[5] *TUAT* I/4, 375.

Introductory Formula
for Ahaziah of Judah

Text

8:25 In the twelfth year of King Joram son of Ahab of Israel, Ahaziah son of King Jehoram of Judah began to reign. 26 Ahaziah was twenty-two years old when he began to reign; he reigned one year in Jerusalem. His mother's name was Athaliah, a granddaughter of King Omri of Israel. 27 He also walked in the way of the house of Ahab, doing what was evil in the sight of the LORD, as the house of Ahab had done, for he was son-in-law to the house of Ahab.

Commentary

[8:25-27] In the case of Ahaziah of Judah there is no concluding formula to match the introductory formula. His being wounded and his death at Megiddo are, however, mentioned in 9:27, in the context of the revolution of Jehu. After the transport of his corpse to Jerusalem he was buried there in the family tomb (9:28). Such detailed information about the death and burial of Ahaziah render a separate concluding formula superfluous. His pedigree—with Athaliah as his mother he was a descendant of Omri—puts him on a par with the kings of Israel and subjects him to the same negative evaluation as that of his father, Jehoram. Apart from a visit to his cousin Jehoram, king of Israel, nothing is said about his short reign over Judah.

The Revolution of Jehu

Text

8:28 He went with Joram son of Ahab to wage war against King Hazael of Aram at Ramoth-gilead, where the Arameans wounded Joram. 29 King Joram returned to be healed in Jezreel of the wounds that the Arameans had inflicted on him at Ramah, when he fought against King Hazael of Aram. King Ahaziah son of Jehoram of Judah went down to see Joram son of Ahab in Jezreel, because he was wounded.

9:1 Then the prophet Elisha called a member of the company of prophets and said to him, "Gird up your loins; take this flask of oil in your hand, and go to Ramoth-gilead. 2 When you arrive, look there for Jehu son of Jehoshaphat, son of Nimshi; go in and get him to leave his companions, and take him into an inner chamber. 3 Then take the flask of oil, pour it on his head, and say, 'Thus says the LORD: I anoint you king over Israel.' Then open the door and flee; do not linger."

4 So the young man, the young prophet, went to Ramoth-gilead. 5 He arrived while the commanders of the army were in council, and he announced, "I have a message for you, commander." "For which one of us?" asked Jehu. "For you, commander." 6 So Jehu got up and went inside; the young man poured the oil on his head, saying to him, "Thus says the LORD the God of Israel: I anoint you king over the people of the LORD, over Israel. 7 You shall strike down the house of your master Ahab, so that I may avenge on Jezebel the blood of my servants the prophets, and the blood of all the servants of the LORD. 8 For the whole house of Ahab shall perish; I will cut off from Ahab every male, bond or free, in Israel. 9 I will make the house of Ahab like the house of Jeroboam son of Nebat, and like the house of Baasha son of Ahijah. 10 The dogs shall eat Jezebel in the territory of Jezreel, and no one shall bury her." Then he opened the door and fled.

11 When Jehu came back to his master's officers, they said to him, "Is everything all right? Why did that madman come to you?" He answered them, "You know the sort and how they babble." 12 They said, "Liar! Come on, tell

us!" So he said, "This is just what he said to me: 'Thus says the LORD, I anoint you king over Israel.'" 13 Then hurriedly they all took their cloaks and spread them for him on the bare steps; and they blew the trumpet, and proclaimed, "Jehu is king."

14 Thus Jehu son of Jehoshaphat son of Nimshi conspired against Joram. Joram with all Israel had been on guard at Ramoth-gilead against King Hazael of Aram; 15 but King Joram had returned to be healed in Jezreel of the wounds that the Arameans had inflicted on him, when he fought against King Hazael of Aram. So Jehu said, "If this is your wish, then let no one slip out of the city to go and tell the news in Jezreel." 16 Then Jehu mounted his chariot and went to Jezreel, where Joram was lying ill. King Ahaziah of Judah had come down to visit Joram.

17 In Jezreel, the sentinel standing on the tower spied the company of Jehu arriving, and said, "I see a company." Joram said, "Take a horseman; send him to meet them, and let him say, 'Is it peace?'" 18 So the horseman went to meet him; he said, "Thus says the king, 'Is it peace?'" Jehu responded, "What have you to do with peace? Fall in behind me." The sentinel reported, saying, "The messenger reached them, but he is not coming back." 19 Then he sent out a second horseman, who came to them and said, "Thus says the king, 'Is it peace?'" Jehu answered, "What have you to do with peace? Fall in behind me." 20 Again the sentinel reported, "He reached them, but he is not coming back. It looks like the driving of Jehu son of Nimshi; for he drives like a maniac."

21 Joram said, "Get ready." And they got his chariot ready. Then King Joram of Israel and King Ahaziah of Judah set out, each in his chariot, and went to meet Jehu; they met him at the property of Naboth the Jezreelite. 22 When Joram saw Jehu, he said, "Is it peace, Jehu?" He answered, "What peace can there be, so long as the many whoredoms and sorceries of your mother Jezebel continue?" 23 Then Joram reined about and fled, saying to Ahaziah, "Treason, Ahaziah!" 24 Jehu drew his bow with all his strength, and shot Joram between the shoulders, so that the arrow pierced his heart; and he sank in his chariot. 25 Jehu said to his aide Bidkar, "Lift him out, and throw him on the plot of ground belonging to Naboth the Jezreelite; for remember, when you and I rode side by side behind his father Ahab how the LORD uttered this oracle against him: 26 'For the blood of Naboth and for the blood of his children that I saw yesterday, says the LORD, I swear I will repay you on this very plot of ground.' Now therefore lift him out and throw him on the plot of ground, in accordance with the word of the LORD."

27 When King Ahaziah of Judah saw this, he fled in the direction of Beth-haggan. Jehu pursued him, saying, "Shoot him also!" And they shot him in the chariot at the ascent to Gur, which is by Ibleam. Then he fled to Megiddo, and died there. 28 His officers carried him in a chariot to Jerusalem, and buried him in his tomb with his ancestors in the city of David.

29 In the eleventh year of Joram son of Ahab, Ahaziah began to reign over Judah.

30 When Jehu came to Jezreel, Jezebel heard of it; she painted her eyes, and adorned her head, and looked out of the window. 31 As Jehu entered the gate, she said, "Is it peace, Zimri, murderer of your master?" 32 He looked up to the window and said, "Who is on my side? Who?" Two or three eunuchs looked out at him. 33 He said, "Throw her down." So they threw her down; some of her blood spattered on the wall and on the horses, which trampled on her. 34 Then he went in and ate and drank; he said, "See to that cursed woman and bury her; for she is a king's daughter." 35 But when they went to bury her, they found no more of her than the skull and the feet and the palms of her hands. 36 When they came back and told him, he said, "This is the word of the LORD, which he spoke by his servant Elijah the Tishbite, 'In the territory of Jezreel the dogs shall eat the flesh of Jezebel; 37 the corpse of Jezebel shall be like dung on the field in the territory of Jezreel, so that no one can say, This is Jezebel.'"

10:1 Now Ahab had seventy sons in Samaria. So Jehu wrote letters and sent them to Samaria, to the rulers of Jezreel, to the elders, and to the guardians of the sons of Ahab, saying, 2 "Since your master's sons are with you and you have at your disposal chariots and horses, a fortified city, and weapons, 3 select the son of your master who is the best qualified, set him on his father's throne, and fight for your master's house." 4 But they were utterly terrified and said, "Look, two kings could not withstand him; how then can we stand?" 5 So the steward of the palace, and the governor of the city, along with the elders and the guardians, sent word to Jehu: "We are your servants; we will do anything you say. We will not make anyone king; do whatever you think right." 6 Then he wrote them a second letter, saying, "If you are on my side, and if you are ready to obey me, take the heads of your master's sons and come to me at Jezreel tomorrow at this time." Now the king's sons, seventy persons, were with the leaders of the city, who were charged with their upbringing. 7 When the letter reached them, they took the king's sons and killed them, seventy persons; they put their heads in baskets and sent them to him at Jezreel. 8 When the messenger came and told him, "They have brought the heads of the king's sons," he said, "Lay them in two heaps at the entrance of the gate until the morning." 9 Then in the morning when he went out, he stood and said to all the people, "You are innocent. It was I who conspired against my master and killed him; but who struck down all these? 10 Know then that there shall fall to the earth nothing of the word of the LORD, which the LORD spoke concerning the house of Ahab; for the LORD has done what he said through his servant Elijah." 11 So Jehu killed all who were left of the house of Ahab in Jezreel, all his leaders, close friends, and priests, until he left him no survivor.

12 Then he set out and went to Samaria. On the way, when he was at

Beth-eked of the Shepherds, 13 Jehu met relatives of King Ahaziah of Judah and said, "Who are you?" They answered, "We are kin of Ahaziah; we have come down to visit the royal princes and the sons of the queen mother." 14 He said, "Take them alive." They took them alive, and slaughtered them at the pit of Beth-eked, forty-two in all; he spared none of them.

15 When he left there, he met Jehonadab son of Rechab coming to meet him; he greeted him, and said to him, "Is your heart as true to mine as mine is to yours?" Jehonadab answered, "It is." Jehu said, "If it is, give me your hand." So he gave him his hand. Jehu took him up with him into the chariot. 16 He said, "Come with me, and see my zeal for the LORD." So he had him ride in his chariot. 17 When he came to Samaria, he killed all who were left to Ahab in Samaria, until he had wiped them out, according to the word of the LORD that he spoke to Elijah.

Analysis

This detailed account of Jehu's revolution consists of several scenes, with Jehu at the center of events. Apart from some short comments that were added later, the text has been expanded at the end of each scene by several redactions.[1] The last scene with Jehonadab, son of Rechab, is likely to be an interpolation altogether, which wants to confirm Jehu's positive attitude toward the Rechabites. Otherwise, all scenes are preoccupied with murder and violence: apart from the house of Omri a great number of the royal family of Judah are killed too, a fact that, in turn, led to the succession of Athaliah as queen of Jerusalem (see on 11:1-3). This gives us the following overall sequence of events:

8:28-29	Exposition
9:1-6, [7-10a,] 10b	Anointing by a disciple of the prophet
9:11-14a, [14b-15a]	Proclamation of the king
9:15b-24, [25-26]	Murder of Jehoram
9:27-28, [29]	Murder of Ahaziah
9:30-35, [36-37]	Killing of Jezebel
10:1-9, [10-11]	Extinction of the Royal House
10:12-14	Extinction of the brothers of Ahaziah
[10:15-16	Co-optation of Jehonadab]
10:17	Closing remarks

The high point of the narrative is the murder of Jehoram and its dramatic preparation. The death of Jehoram seals the fate of the dynasty of the Omrides.

---

[1] On the textual criticism see Yoshikazu Minokami, *Die Revolution des Jehu,* Göttinger theologische Arbeiten 38 (Göttingen: Vandenhoeck & Ruprecht, 1989).

Commentary

[8:28-29] The war against the Arameans is made the starting point of the entire narrative in the exposition. Jehoram of Israel has been wounded in battle against Hazael, king of the Arameans. The succession of the usurper to the Aramean throne is reported in 8:7-15. The introductory formula for Jehoram of Israel is found as early as 3:1-3, but the narrative proper, beginning in 8:28, is separated from this introduction through several interpolated stories of the prophet and (fictitious) war accounts.

As already in 1 Kgs 22:1-38, the scene of battle is Ramoth-gilead, with no further details given. This settlement is to be found at Tell el-Ḥusn in northern Gilead (see on 1 Kgs 4:13), where it constituted an important defense point against Aramean assaults due to its geographical position. Ahab of Israel had already found his death here in battle against the Arameans (1 Kgs 22:1-38). Jehoram, too, is wounded and leaves his army to recover at his winter residence at Jezreel (Zerʿīn). Excavations at Jezreel have uncovered strategically planned fortifications but no traces of a royal palace.[2] Ahaziah's visit illustrates the good relations between Israel and Judah under the Omride dynasty, mirrored by the close family relations; Jehoram of Israel and Ahaziah of Judah were cousins, since Jehoram's father Ahab and Ahaziah's mother Athaliah were both children of Omri and hence siblings (NRSV differs). The visit of the king of Judah to Jezreel is most likely for family reasons, yet it is an official act all the same, and the meeting of the two kings is an important prerequisite for the events to follow.

[9:1-6, 10b] The first scene tells of the anointing of Jehu by a disciple of Elisha. The scene is still at Ramoth-gilead, apparently the headquarters of the Israelite army. Jehu belongs to a group of commanding officers who form a separate unit, although we have no exact information about his status. The anointing takes place with no witnesses present. As we do not know what building is involved, we also cannot speculate about the nature of the room where the act takes place. The anointing was an indispensable part of the crowning ritual (see 2 Sam 2:4; 5:3; 1 Kgs 1:34, 39; 2 Kgs 11:12; 23:30). As in the case of Saul and David, the anointing takes place secretly in order to designate a new successor to the kingship (see 1 Sam 10:1; 16:13). The anointing was the external sign to have been chosen by God.[3] The disciple takes to his heels once the deed is done and remains unrecognized and anonymous, a fact that stresses that the executing figure is little more than a tool to transmit God's will.

[9:7-10a] The coda adds to the anointing the legitimacy to extinguish the royal family. The subsequent acts of Jehu are given explicit justification by the words of

---

[2] See David Ussishkin and J. Woodhead, "Excavations at Tel Jezreel 1994–1996: Third Preliminary Report," *TA* 24 (1997) 6–72.

[3] See Ernst Kutsch, *Salbung als Rechtsakt im Alten Testament und im Alten Orient,* BZAW 87 (Berlin: Töpelmann, 1963).

Yahweh. One of the reasons invoked is the persecution the prophets suffered under the Omrides. Together with the prophets, the Yahweh cult was persecuted, and it is now to be reinstated as the only form of worship under Jehu.

The inappropriate and sinful worship contradicting Yahweh is here once more associated with the figure of Jezebel, daughter of the king of Sidon and wife of Ahab, who had introduced her foreign cult to Samaria (1 Kgs 16:32). The stories of Elijah in 1 Kings 17–19 and 21 in particular had thematized that conflict between the cult of Baal and that of Yahweh. The figure of Jezebel, as a representative of the worship of Baal, foreign and to be rejected, amounts more or less to the incarnation of evil in the books of Kings, even if the cult of Baal was much longer established in Israel than the alleged introduction under Ahab makes us assume. Still, Jezebel, as the wife of King Ahab, was associated with the cult in a way that retraced the origins of the worship of Baal to this non-Israelite princess.[4] This historical link serves as a justification to extinguish the entire male line, characterized literally as "the one who pisses against a wall." The same expression occurs in 1 Sam 25:22, 34; 1 Kgs 14:10; 16:11; 21:21; this need not be a vulgar expression. With sanitary systems lacking in old Israelite cities, this is no more than an accurate description of customary practice.

[9:10a] The curse uttered in v. 10a harks back to 1 Kgs 21:23 and it is realized in 2 Kgs 9:35. The curse not only foresees that Jezebel will be eaten by wild dogs like a carcass, but also implies that she cannot be buried appropriately and hence will not be able to enter into the realm of the dead. This means that her restless spirit will have to roam the world forever. This notion of remaining unburied and hence forever restless was one of terror across the ancient Near East.[5] The same is expressed in the Mesopotamian curse: "May dogs and pigs eat your flesh; may your [spirit] have no one who cares for the libations" (see also Jer 22:19).[6] The redactional addition of the curse shows the translation of rejection from the cult of Baal to the queen in a particularly spiteful light.

[9:11-14a] In the second scene Jehu is proclaimed king by his fellow commanders, who thereby desert King Jehoram. The proclamation of the king is a separate act in the ceremony of enthronement, and the same proclamation was made at Solomon's surprising succession to the throne in 1 Kgs 1:11, 13, 18. It marks the act of enthronement as such, because only public acknowledgment completes the succession to the office.[7] The proclamation is accompanied by signals from a ram's horn, another indi-

---

[4] See Stefan Timm, *Die Dynastie Omri: Quellen und Untersuchungen zur Geschichte Israels im 9. Jahrhundert vor Christus,* FRLANT 124 (Göttingen: Vandenhoeck & Ruprecht, 1982), 288–303.

[5] See Homer, *Iliad* 5.57–60.

[6] *ANET,* 538.

[7] See Baruch Halpern, *The Constitution of the Monarchy in Israel,* HSM 25 (Chico, Calif.: Scholars, 1981), 134–36.

cation of its public character. The spreading of cloaks is a sign of devotion, comparable to the modern phenomenon of the red carpet.

To conclude, the entire episode is interpreted as an act of transgression and conspiracy. The same Hebrew word was used in the context of revolutions in 1 Kgs 15:27; 16:9, 16, 20, and will be used again in 15:10, 15, 25, 30. It indicates "in principle a connection of people within a conspiratorial circle, that is, a conspiracy with the aim to topple and kill the governing ruler and to usurp the throne."[8]

[9:14b-15a] This addition explains that the special circumstances at Jezreel were caused by the absence of the king.

[9:15b-24] The third scene relates the high point of the entire narrative: the successful conspiracy and the assassination of Jehoram. Its dramatic structure increases the tension: only after two emissaries have not returned do Jehoram of Israel and Ahaziah of Judah order their chariots to be made ready to meet Jehu, whom the sentinel has already identified by his style of driving. The reader, familiar with the events, knows that they are moving inexorably toward their destiny. When Jehoram realizes they have been betrayed, it is already too late. Jehu hits the unguarded king with an arrow and kills him with his own hand. Thus the second requirement for his kingship is fulfilled; his proclamation as king is followed by the removal of the ruler, and the revolution now takes its destined course. From now on, the path to Jehu's reign is soaked in the blood of his victims.

[9:25-26] This little afterthought adds another justification for the death of Jehoram of Israel by referring to the figure of Naboth, whose innocent blood was shed by Ahab (see on 1 Kings 21). The extinction of the house of Omri is interpreted in terms of expiation for innocently shed blood. Since blood is the carrier of life, innocent bloodshed forfeits the life of the perpetrator, his own and that of his descendants. Bloodguilt can be expiated even without human intervention.[9] The murder of Jehoram is legitimated in retrospect by the injustice that Ahab did to Naboth. The deed then appears to fulfill Elijah's words to Ahab in 1 Kgs 21:19.

[9:22b] The addition characterizes the cult of Baal associated with Jezebel in no uncertain terms as "whoredom," in accordance with the judgment of Hosea (see Hos 1:2; 2:4; 4:11; 6:10).[10]

---

[8] J. Conrad, *TWAT,* 7:214.

[9] See Klaus Koch, "Der Spruch 'Sein Blut bleibe auf seinem Haupt' und die israelitische Auffassung vom vergossenen Blut, Spuren des hebräischen Denkens," in idem, *Gesammelte Aufsätze* (Neukirchen-Vluyn: Neukirchener, 1991), 1:128–45.

[10] See Hans Walter Wolff, *Hosea,* trans. Gary Stansell, Hermeneia (Philadelphia: Fortress Press, 1974), 13–16.

[9:27-28] The fourth scene offers a separate account of Ahaziah's fate. The king of Judah, taking to his heels at first, is eventually overtaken and fatally wounded. The place given as his destination, Beth-haggan, is mentioned only here; it lies east of Jezreel and can, given the similar names, probably be located in the vicinity of the modern town of Jenin, where excavations have discovered the remains of an Iron Age settlement. Further geographical data too points to the area surrounding Jenin. Ibleam, it is agreed, lies at Khirbet Bel'ame, about two km. south of Jenin. The ascent from Gur can then be identified with the upper area of the Wadi Semme, which is crossed even today by the road from Jenin to the south. The flight toward the northwest, on to Megiddo, is explained by the town's status as a garrison, expanded under the Omrides, where Ahaziah could take refuge. The plot is not entirely consistent at this point; if the royal guard is unable to save their master from Jehu, it is not clear why Megiddo should have been a safer heaven.

At any rate, we are not told about Ahaziah's death in any detail. The parallel version of the story in 2 Chr 22:9, which is drastically different, shows a lack of an authentic tradition: here Ahaziah hides at Samaria, where he is found and killed by Jehu. The transport of a corpse from Megiddo to Jerusalem is also mentioned in 2 Kgs 23:30a, here with regard to Josiah. This last verse surely goes back to the Deuteronomistic Historian, who claims that even the kings of Judah who die outside Jerusalem were buried in the family tomb in Jerusalem and who provides this information instead of the usual concluding formula.

[9:29] This comment is a redactional addition that repeats the synchronism of the introductory formula, 8:25.

[9:30-35] The fifth scene is devoted to the fate of Queen Jezebel. Her death finally establishes the rule of Jehu: as a worshiper of Baal she was also opposed to the monarchy loyal to Yahweh, represented and introduced by Jehu. Jehu enters Jezreel triumphantly to manifest his kingship. Jezebel, misjudging the new power relations, expects Jehu and greets him from her palace window. Her appearance at the window does not indicate an obscure cultic aspect; rather, the window was the only point of contact for a woman in the male-dominated public space (see Judg 5:28; 2 Sam 6:16; Cant 2:9). The woman at the window is one of the motifs of biblical literature, with no further cultic background.

In her ignorance, Jezebel awaits Jehu already upon his entry into the city, and the scene subsequently appears rather artificial. Her words of greeting are words of haughtiness, spoken as a judgment. The episode about the kingship of Zimri is found in 1 Kgs 16:15-20. Zimri not only killed his predecessor, Elah son of Baasha, but also lasted as king for only seven days, since the people made Omri king, and Zimri, now in the unfortunate position of an unsupported usurper, put an end to his life in the palace at Tirzah. When Jezebel addresses Jehu as Zimri she puts him in a line with other murderers of kings and, in addition, reminds him of their untimely deaths.

In what follows, Jehu uses the central issue of loyalty against the former queen to his advantage. The courtiers attending the women of the royal harem are eunuchs, as evidenced by Akkadian texts.[11] The courtiers, pressed for loyalty, side with whoever has power: they follow the order of Jehu and throw Jezebel, now the representative of dethroned authority, from the window. She dies from her fall and Jehu treads on her corpse as a manifestation of power. Her burial is ordered only after a feast, which is apparently part of the ritual of enthronement; yet the burial is thwarted when only parts of her corpse are found. There is no mention of what happened to the rest. It is assumed, rather, that the reader will still remember Elisha's pronouncement in 1 Kgs 21:24, which was already repeated in the redactional verse 2 Kgs 9:10a. Elisha prophesied that Jezebel would have no burial so that her spirit would wonder restlessly forever. Thus she has received the most severe punishment that was imaginable in ancient Israel.

[9:36-37] This redactional addendum clearly states the fulfillment of the prophecy: without burial Jezebel is "like the dung on the field." This fate amounts to the destruction of a human life that can no longer exist in the shadowy realm of the dead.[12]

[10:1-9] Jehu's bloody trail continues in the sixth scene. Part of safeguarding his power was to remove any rightful heir to the throne. The story at this point quotes in detail from the correspondence between Jehu and the princes' tutors. We can conclude that the princes, from a certain age, were educated together in preparation for their future military and administrative roles. Although no details are given, we can assume that the main focus of such an educational program was on the use of various arms and the chariot, in accordance with the royal leadership of the military. The number 70 is certainly a significant number; Judg 9:5 and the Aramaic inscriptions from Sam'āl mention the same number in the context of the murder of rightful heirs to the throne.[13]

The story underlines Jehu's cunning. The members of Samaria's ruling class decide to submit to Jehu when faced with the choice of either installing a rightful heir to the throne or acknowledging a usurper. Their decision is followed by Jehu's demand to have all of the former king's sons removed, a demand that amounts to the complete extinction of the royal family. The fate of the daughters and mothers is left unmentioned, since it was of little interest in male-dominated Israelite society. "The assiduousness and compliance by which the order is executed is clearly indicated: whoever is in power will find willing executioners who try to save their own lives."[14]

---

[11] See Hayim Tadmor, "Rab-saris and Rab-shakeh in 2 Kings 18," in *The Word of the Lord Shall Go Forth: Essays in Honor of David Noel Freedman,* ed. Carol L. Meyers and Michael O'Connor (Winona Lake, Ind.: Eisenbrauns, 1983), 279–85.

[12] See Ludwig Wächter, *Der Tod im Alten Testament,* Arbeiten zur Theologie 2/8 (Stuttgart: Calwer, 1967).

[13] *KAI,* 215:3.

[14] Würthwein, *Könige,* 2:336.

Jehu's will and claim to power is also borne out by the warning example of the stacked heads at the gate of Jezreel. Jehu's question is a rather cynical comment on the execution of the order and the display of severed heads, since he apportions the blame for the beheadings to the dutiful servants. This question originally closed the scene; it was up to the reader, knowing Jehu's order, to give an answer and find the murderous usurper guilty. A result of the events is that Jehu now holds firm power over Samaria too.

[10:10-11] This redactional addition reports the fulfillment of the threat uttered in 1 Kgs 21:24. In addition to the removal of the royal family, however, we are told of the extinction of the entire class of officials of the Omride dynasty. The change in kingship brings death and destruction to the governing elite bound to the dethroned king by loyalty. With this necessary exchange of officials Jehu has cunningly established the complete and irreversible changeover and, in consequence, his own kingship.

[10:12-14] In the seventh and final scene, Jehu's violent and bloody trail comes to an end with the murder of the royal family of Judah. The events take place in Beth-eked, which can be located neither at Beit Qad, about 5 km. east of Jenin, nor at Kefar Raʿi, about 17 km. southwest of Jenin,[15] since both those places lie away from the roads to Jezreel. Judah, too, practiced the communal upbringing and educating of the young princes, who are taken captive while on a visit and also killed. Although the narrative mentions explicitly Jehu's order for their apprehension only, the order to kill them has to have come from the highest authority. Jehu has now eradicated a large part of the Davidic dynasty and thus prepared the way for the actions of Athaliah, mentioned in 11:1-3.

[10:15-16] This scene of the granting of a favor is another later addition. It concerns the person of Jehonadab, son of Rechab, but it is only the description of the Rechabites in Jeremiah 35 that illuminates the scene more fully. The Rechabites, regarding themselves as descendants of their ancestor Rechab, lived a nomadic life characterized by the rejection of any form of agriculture or settlement. The personal encounter of Jehonadab, son of Rechab, with Jehu binds him in loyalty to the latter as the new king. It cannot be established whether the connection between Jehonadab and Jehu is historically verifiable. It is possibly the rejection of the cult of Baal by Jehu and the rejection of civilization by the Rechabites that serves as a common denominator here.[16]

---

[15] Albrecht Alt, "Das Institut in den Jahren 1929 und 1930," *PJ* 27 (1931) 32 [5–50].

[16] See Frank S. Frick, "The Rechabites Reconsidered," *JBL* 90 (1971) 279–87.

[10:17] The closing remark in 10:17a confirms once more how the eradication of all the members of Ahab's family has consolidated Jehu's power. The later addition, 10:17b, stresses, as all the redactions do, that the words of Yahweh spoken through the prophet Elijah have been fulfilled, thus declaring the revolution to be justified as the will of God.

The Eradication of the Worshipers of Baal

Text

10:18 Then Jehu assembled all the people and said to them, "Ahab offered Baal small service; but Jehu will offer much more. 19 Now therefore summon to me all the prophets of Baal, all his worshipers, and all his priests; let none be missing, for I have a great sacrifice to offer to Baal; whoever is missing shall not live." But Jehu was acting with cunning in order to destroy the worshipers of Baal. 20 Jehu decreed, "Sanctify a solemn assembly for Baal." So they proclaimed it. 21 Jehu sent word throughout all Israel; all the worshipers of Baal came, so that there was no one left who did not come. They entered the temple of Baal, until the temple of Baal was filled from wall to wall. 22 He said to the keeper of the wardrobe, "Bring out the vestments for all the worshipers of Baal." So he brought out the vestments for them. 23 Then Jehu entered the temple of Baal with Jehonadab son of Rechab; he said to the worshipers of Baal, "Search and see that there is no worshiper of the LORD here among you, but only worshipers of Baal." 24 Then they proceeded to offer sacrifices and burnt offerings.

Now Jehu had stationed eighty men outside, saying, "Whoever allows any of those to escape whom I deliver into your hands shall forfeit his life." 25 As soon as he had finished presenting the burnt offering, Jehu said to the guards and to the officers, "Come in and kill them; let no one escape." So they put them to the sword. The guards and the officers threw them out, and then went into the citadel of the temple of Baal. 26 They brought out the pillar that was in the temple of Baal, and burned it. 27 Then they demolished the pillar of Baal, and destroyed the temple of Baal, and made it a latrine to this day.

Analysis

The events reported in this section take place at the temple of Baal in Samaria, which Ahab had erected there. The Deuteronomistic Historian considers the worship of Baal

290

the utmost offense of Israel, finally leading to its destruction (see on 17:7-20). The narrative indicates that its original version knew only of the slaughter of the priests and prophets; in its present, enlarged form the story tells of the extinction of all worshipers of Baal, without further attention as to how this could have been achieved in detail. The course of events shows up the cunning of Jehu. Those called to the sacrifice are killed by decree of the king; the temple and its inventory are destroyed. The location of the temple is turned into a dumping ground for dung and a latrine.

Commentary

[10:18-27] Some details mentioned by the narrator reflect on the mentality of the time. The king, as the highest ruler of the cult, presents the sacrificial offering himself. The two types of sacrifice, for which separate terms are used, are distinguished by their kind. The burnt offering consists of the sacrificial animal that is burned in its entirety after being slaughtered on the altar, whereas in the act of the sacrifice the animal is eaten by the worshipers in communion with God. Both types of sacrifice are executed on the altar and serve for expiation.[1] The distribution of clothes before the sacrifice makes clear that the sacrifice had to be carried out in special attire. The guards and officers are the king's official entourage. Following 1 Kgs 14:27-28 and 2 Kgs 11:4, 6, the former are a kind of personal guard, while the latter are difficult to define more closely.[2] From the context it appears likely that the eighty men arrayed outside the temple are identical with the guard and officers.

There has, so far, been no archaeological evidence for a temple of Baal at Samaria. However, since the entire narrative, governed as it is by its cultural interests, can be regarded as fictitious, we cannot necessarily presuppose the existence of such a temple. The narrative follows the motto "the end justifies the means." Once Jehu has usurped the throne through violence and murder, he might as well have deceived and destroyed the worshipers of Baal.

In terms of its history, nothing can be said about the conflict between the cults of Yahweh and Baal. Jehu is considered here an ardent supporter of the exclusive cult of Yahweh. It is in this role that he is charged with the destruction of the cult of Baal and of his worshipers. Jehu's actions thus put an end to the worship of Baal in Samaria, associated originally with Ahab.

---

[1] See Bernd Janowski, *Sühne als Heilsgeschehen: Studien zur Sühnetheologie der Priesterschrift und zur Wurzel KPR im Alten Orient und im Alten Testament,* WMANT 55 (Neukirchen-Vluyn: Neukirchener, 1982).

[2] The word appears in this plural form only here and is usually used in the singular; see 1 Kgs 9:22; 2 Kgs 7:2, 7, 19; 15:25.

The Judgment of Jehu

Text

10:28 Thus Jehu wiped out Baal from Israel. 29 But Jehu did not turn aside from the sins of Jeroboam son of Nebat, which he caused Israel to commit—the golden calves that were in Bethel and in Dan. 30 The Lord said to Jehu, "Because you have done well in carrying out what I consider right, and in accordance with all that was in my heart have dealt with the house of Ahab, your sons of the fourth generation shall sit on the throne of Israel." 31 But Jehu was not careful to follow the law of the Lord the God of Israel with all his heart; he did not turn from the sins of Jeroboam, which he caused Israel to commit.

32 In those days the Lord began to trim off parts of Israel. Hazael defeated them throughout the territory of Israel: 33 from the Jordan eastward, all the land of Gilead, the Gadites, the Reubenites, and the Manassites, from Aroer, which is by the Wadi Arnon, that is, Gilead and Bashan.

Analysis

Jehu's concluding formula as such in 10:34-36 is prefaced by several notices. "Praise and criticism stand next to each other in a confusing and unbalanced way."[1] The overall judgment, however, is negative.

Commentary

[10:28-31] Although vv. 28-29 mention the destruction of the cult of Baal approvingly, what follows criticizes the continuing sins of Jeroboam, which consisted in turning from the temple in Jerusalem as the only rightful place of worship of Yahweh, together with the building of public sanctuaries at Bethel and Dan. Jehu's engagement for the exclusive worship of Yahweh, however, was rewarded with a certain permanence of the dynasty (vv. 30-31). We see here a so-called *vaticinium ex eventu*

---

[1] Würthwein, *Könige*, 2:343.

(prophecy after the event), spoken from knowledge of the later course of the history of Israel. Jehu was succeeded in line by the kings Jehoahaz, Jehoash, Jeroboam, and Zechariah. Only Zechariah was killed by the usurper Shallum (15:10), who brought the dynasty to an end after nearly a century.

[10:32-33] This notice reports the military successes of the Aramean King Hazael. It seems that Hazael had managed to bring the entire area east of the Jordan under his control, a feat that indirectly shows up the military weakness of Israel under Jehu. It is of particular interest that one of the redactors adds the tribes of Gad, Reuben, and (half) Manasseh, which lie east of the Jordan River, to the territory called Gilead, which includes, also situated on the east bank of the Jordan River, the area north and south of the Jabbok. The subsequent geographical description of the territory notes expressly its extension from the river Arnon in the south to Bashan in the north, mentioning once more "Gilead" as the name for the northern part of the area east of the Jordan. The redactional addition thus corrects the geographical description according to the viewpoint and the terminology of the postexilic period.

Concluding Formula for Jehu

Text

10:34 Now the rest of the acts of Jehu, all that he did, and all his power, are they not written in the Book of the Annals of the Kings of Israel? 35 So Jehu slept with his ancestors, and they buried him in Samaria. His son Jehoahaz succeeded him. 36 The time that Jehu reigned over Israel in Samaria was twenty-eight years.

Commentary

[10:34-36] The concluding formula of Jehu follows the usual pattern and thus indicates the permanence of the dynasty. Nothing more is said about the twenty-eight years of his rule. He was a contemporary of Joash, king of Judah, after the latter became enthroned as such in Jerusalem, in the seventh year of his kingship, following the interim rule of Athaliah (see on 11:1-20). Apparently there was no attempt on Jehu's part to interfere in the running of the southern kingdom. The period of Jehu's rule can therefore be classed as weak with regard to foreign relations, but stable in the realm of internal politics.

The Fall of Queen Athaliah

Text

11:1 Now when Athaliah, Ahaziah's mother, saw that her son was dead, she set about to destroy all the royal family. 2 But Jehosheba, King Joram's daughter, Ahaziah's sister, took Joash son of Ahaziah, and stole him away from among the king's children who were about to be killed; she put him and his nurse in a bedroom. Thus she hid him from Athaliah, so that he was not killed; 3 he remained with her six years, hidden in the house of the LORD, while Athaliah reigned over the land.

4 But in the seventh year Jehoiada summoned the captains of the Carites and of the guards and had them come to him in the house of the LORD. He made a covenant with them and put them under oath in the house of the LORD; then he showed them the king's son. 5 He commanded them, "This is what you are to do: one-third of you, those who go off duty on the sabbath and guard the king's house 6 (another third being at the gate Sur and a third at the gate behind the guards), shall guard the palace; 7 and your two divisions that come on duty in force on the sabbath and guard the house of the LORD 8 shall surround the king, each with weapons in hand; and whoever approaches the ranks is to be killed. Be with the king in his comings and goings."

9 The captains did according to all that the priest Jehoiada commanded; each brought his men who were to go off duty on the sabbath, with those who were to come on duty on the sabbath, and came to the priest Jehoiada. 10 The priest delivered to the captains the spears and shields that had been King David's, which were in the house of the LORD; 11 the guards stood, every man with his weapons in his hand, from the south side of the house to the north side of the house, around the altar and the house, to guard the king on every side. 12 Then he brought out the king's son, put the crown on him, and gave him the covenant; they proclaimed him king, and anointed him; they clapped their hands and shouted, "Long live the king!"

13 When Athaliah heard the noise of the guard and of the people, she went into the house of the LORD to the people; 14 when she looked, there was the king standing by the pillar, according to custom, with the captains and the trumpeters beside the king, and all the people of the land rejoicing and blowing trumpets. Athaliah tore her clothes and cried, "Treason! Treason!" 15 Then the priest Jehoiada commanded the captains who were set over the army, "Bring her out between the ranks, and kill with the sword anyone who follows her." For the priest said, "Let her not be killed in the house of the LORD." 16 So they laid hands on her; she went through the horses' entrance to the king's house, and there she was put to death.

17 Jehoiada made a covenant between the LORD and the king and people, that they should be the LORD's people; also between the king and the people. 18 Then all the people of the land went to the house of Baal, and tore it down; his altars and his images they broke in pieces, and they killed Mattan, the priest of Baal, before the altars. The priest posted guards over the house of the LORD. 19 He took the captains, the Carites, the guards, and all the people of the land; then they brought the king down from the house of the LORD, marching through the gate of the guards to the king's house. He took his seat on the throne of the kings. 20 So all the people of the land rejoiced; and the city was quiet after Athaliah had been killed with the sword at the king's house.

Analysis

This chapter has some unusual features in content as well as style. Athaliah is not described along the pattern commonly employed for the kings of Judah. Her reign is acknowledged in the introductory formula of Joash of Judah and his chronology (12:1-4); in ignoring the usual pattern, however, the Deuteronomistic Historian does not include her years of reign in the official succession of the Davidic dynasty. Although the passage forms an independent narrative unit, it has been frequently reworked.[1] The redactional corrections were meant to elucidate but have caused rather more obscurity for the text as a whole. "The sequence of events is clearly broken up when the temple of Baal is destroyed between the royal covenant and the enthronement. Numerous details cause problems of interpretation: the location, the arraying of the guards, the anointing, and the judgment of Athaliah. Several doublets confuse the text in addition."[2]

Excluding the additions, vv. 1-5, 6a, 8a, 9aα, 11-13, 14*, 16, 17*, 18b, 19, 20a form the original narrative unit. Athaliah remains largely at the edge of events, with the exception of the introduction, vv. 1-3; the main actor in the installation of Joash

---

[1] On the textual criticism see Christoph Levin, *Der Sturz der Königin Atalja: Ein Kapitel zur Geschichte Judas im 9. Jahrhundert v. Chr.*, Stuttgarter Bibelstudien 105 (Stuttgart: Katholisches Bibelwerk, 1982).

[2] Ibid., 15.

as king of Judah is Jehoiada, who is introduced as a priest, with no further comment about his position. His authoritative stance toward Athaliah becomes clear if we assume that he held the office of "high priest" (25:18), the highest position in the administration of the cult, where he would be allowed to offer the sacrifice in lieu of the king and to make decisions regarding cultic matters.

The story is very different in style from the preceding two chapters. The events of the revolution of Jehu are narrated in a gripping fashion, and effective use is made of direct speech as a rhetorical tool to maintain its quick pace. The account of Athaliah's fall and Joash's enthronement, in contrast, is rather more sober, with only Athaliah's exclamation in v. 14 adding a dramatic note. The precise recording of location is also part of the terser style, while it is assumed that the reader is familiar with the geographical surroundings.

Despite its dry style the narrative has its own dramatic structure. The account of events preceding the actual story (vv. 1-3) is followed by Jehoiada's detailed instructions for the plan to overthrow the queen, with a short notice reporting its realization (vv. 4, 5, 6a, 8a, 9aα). Protected by the guard, Joash is installed as the new king of Judah (vv. 11-12). The move to a new setting then drives the narrative toward its high point (vv. 13, 14*, 16), which closes with the covenant and the celebration of king's entry into the palace, which signifies that his actions are validated by the people (vv. 17*, 18b, 19, 20a). The story thus falls into the following five parts with a clear structure:

vv. 1-3	Exposition
vv. 4, 5, 6a, 8a, 9aα	Preparation for revolution
vv. 11-12	Proclamation of the new king
vv. 13, 14*, 16	Assassination of Athaliah
vv. 17*, 18b, 19, 20a	Closing remarks

Apart from the exposition and the end, the scene is set in the temple forecourt throughout.

Although the enthronement of Joash should be central, the story reaches its high point with the assassination of Athaliah. As a granddaughter of Omri (8:26), Athaliah was a royal princess whose mother was Jezebel, a daughter of Ethbaal, king of Sidon, and a royal princess too (1 Kgs 16:31). The name "Athaliah" is glossed as "Yahweh has shown himself as a ruler," with reference to the Akkadian noun *etellu*, "ruler." Her marriage to Joram, king of Judah, was certainly politically motivated to strengthen the ties between the kingdoms of Judah and Israel. After the death of Joram and the succession of her son Ahaziah (2 Kgs 8:25), she occupied the influential court position of the queen mother (8:26).[3] Ahaziah was killed by Jehu in the first

---

[3] See Herbert Donner, "Art und Herkunft des Amtes der Königinmutter im Alten Testament," in *Festschrift Johannes Friedrich zum 65. Geburtstag am 27. August 1958,* ed. Richard von Kienle (Heidelberg: Winter, 1959), 105–45.

year of his rule (9:27). Jehu, moreover, had killed all of Ahaziah's brothers who could have claimed the throne of Judah (10:12-14). Neither did Ahaziah, aged only 22, himself have sons old enough to succeed him on the throne of David.

Athaliah, a royal princess of sufficient determination and with a strong motivation, had taken advantage of the situation and moved from her position of queen mother to that of queen herself, despite the succession of women to the throne being precluded by custom. The only detail imparted is that she did away with the last surviving members of the royal family (v. 1). Chr. Levin has already shown that this piece of information is altogether historically unfounded.[4] The murder of the royal house of David is clearly the deed of Jehu, and the suggestion that Athaliah murdered her own family has very little credibility. However, Athaliah does take advantage of the situation when she assumes power over Judah. We do not know whether she might have acted simply as a regent for her underage grandson Joash. In any case, the succession of a woman to the throne must have seemed so paradoxical to the Deuteronomistic Historian that he could explain it only by her murdering her own family. In this view it is only logical that the reign of a woman, founded upon murder, can only be brought to an end through murder.

Commentary

[11:1–3] The introduction describes the circumstances of Athaliah's rise to power and the saving of Joash. The extinction of the royal house, however, had been the work of Jehu (see 10:12-14). Joash, the son of Ahaziah and still an infant at the time, had been spared because he did not take part in that fateful trip to the northern kingdom. He was probably hidden for fear of further attacks and he owed his life to Jehosheba, a princess of the royal house of Judah, who brought him up in her home.

[11:4, 5, 6a, 8a, 9aα] A first scene has Jehoiada give detailed instruction to the guards. The revolutionary plan is laid out in detail: the guards are to split into three units and stand at attention at different positions within the palace and at the gates of the temple court. The temple and palace were within the same area (see on 1 Kings 6–7). The proximity of the buildings is the prerequisite for the "buildup" of the troops, although we cannot locate the two gates that lead from the palace area into the forecourt of the temple. The so-called captains of the [units of] hundred are the officers of the personal guard, later called "guards," who had access to the palace and temple areas. The driving force is Jehoiada, who has planned the coup in detail. The aim is to have forces in place to defend the underage king if necessary, that is, in the case of resistance from the supporters of Athaliah. In the planning stages it is only the officers of the guard who are informed, as they can safeguard the realization of the plan through the powers of their office.

---

4 Ibid., 85–87.

Even if Jehoiada, as the high priest, had no authority over the palace guard, he had been able to convince the captains of the necessity of revolution. The execution of the plan is mentioned succinctly in v. 9aα, because the assumption of tacit power is the prerequisite for the successful enthronement of Joash.

[11:11-12] The latter procedure is narrated in a factual and concise manner in a separate scene. The enthronement, overseen by the armed guard in the temple forecourt, is marked by two actions: anointing and jubilation. The handing over to him of the crown and the covenant is a secondary addition that need not be considered part of the ceremony. The crown seems to be mentioned with reference to the priestly habit; cf. Exod 29:6; 39:30; Lev 8:9. It is not specified who actually carries out the anointing, although in 2 Sam 2:4; 5:3; 19:11; 2 Kgs 23:30, too, the procedure is instigated by the people. (It is only as part of Deuteronomistic theology that the earlier anointing by a prophet signals the choice of Yahweh; cf. 1 Sam 10:1; 16:1-13; 2 Kgs 9:16.) The proclamation "Long live the king!" is the confirmation of the enthronement by the people (cf. 2 Sam 16:16; 1 Kgs 1:25, 39), and it can be accompanied by expressions of joy such as the clapping of hands or the sounding of trumpets. Elsewhere confirmed is the sounding of the ram's horn (shofar); see 2 Sam 15:10; 1 Kgs 1:39; 2 Kgs 9:13. The entire ceremony is acted out publicly under the eyes of the people thronging the temple court.

[11:13, 14*, 16] The next scene assumes that the queen, in her palace close by, has heard the events. Only after she has come to see the situation for herself does she proclaim her judgment of "treason." Her exclamation gives the name of conspiracy to the events, not a mistaken judgment (see on 9:14a). There can only be one ruler in Jerusalem; thus Joash's enthronement has brought Athaliah's reign to an end. In realizing this fact Athaliah rends her clothes. Her former guards, now sworn to the new king, lead her away from the cult area as a prisoner and she is subsequently killed in an unspecified alley of the palace. With Athaliah the last obstacle to the throne is removed from Joash's path.

[11:17*, 18b, 19, 20a] The closing passage mentions a covenant between the king and the people that took place before the enthronement. Nothing is said about its content, so we can conclude that its wording was fixed rather than open to negotiation. Since the proclamation as king precedes the covenant, we can assume that the latter was a regular part of the ceremony, even if such a covenant between king and people is not mentioned anywhere else.

About the specific content we can only speculate.[5] In contrast to the "law of the king" (1 Sam 8:11, 17), whose Deuteronomistic wording describes the negative effects

---

[5] See Georg Fohrer, "Der Vertrag zwischen König und Volk in Israel," in idem, *Studien zur alttestamentlichen Theologie und Geschichte (1949–1966),* BZAW 115 (Berlin: de Gruyter, 1969), 330–51.

of kingship on the possessions and the freedom of the individual, the covenant mentioned here is more likely a catalogue of the basic rights and obligations in accordance with the ancient Israelite code of conduct. The king of Judah was part of the preexisting legal system, in order to make his rule accord with the moral law and to prevent arbitrary acts.

The entry into the palace marks the beginning of his rule for good. The "gate of the guards" appears to have connected the temple forecourt and the palace area, taking its name from the frequent use the guards would make of it. (We have no information on the entryways to the temple for the common people of Jerusalem and Judah.) The throne, on which Joash is now seated, is likely to have stood in the Hall of the Throne (1 Kgs 7:7), where the king would publicly hold court. The remark in v. 20a suggests that the reactions of the city and of the country population differed.[6] It is possible that the revolution was mainly supported by the towns of Judah, whereas in Jerusalem there was stronger loyalty felt for Athaliah.

Disregarding the details and the distortion of the image of Athaliah, the narrative recounts an important moment in the history of Israel: the enthronement of Joash reestablishes the male succession to the throne of Judah and thus secures the continuation of the Davidic dynasty. A ceremony of enthronement is described nowhere else in such detail, with the exception of that of Solomon in 1 Kings 1. Its individual parts, as described here, point to an active role that the populace took. The additions and the comments seek to explain certain details, and they move only twice beyond the factual framework of the narrative: in the case of the crown and the covenant (v. 12) and with the destruction of a temple of Baal at Jerusalem, which is not mentioned anywhere else (v. 18a). Both instances are literary elaborations without any historical value. The original version of the narrative, however, relies on a tradition that was quite close to the events in time and that may have been contained in the "Book of the Annals of the Kings of Judah," which is frequently mentioned in the concluding formulas.

The story has also to be read in the context of 8:28—10:17. While Jehu's revolution establishes a new dynasty in the northern kingdom of Israel, the southern kingdom of Judah sees the restitution of the Davidic dynasty after the interim rule of Athaliah. The difference between Israel and Judah could not be made more obvious. As opposed to the north, where a usurper overthrows the ruling dynasty to set himself up on the throne, in the south the rule of the Davidides is reestablished while dynastic continuity is maintained.[7]

---

[6] On the "people of the land" see J. Alberto Soggin, "Der judäische ʿAm-haʾareṣ und das Königtum in Juda," *VT* 13 (1963) 187–95.

[7] See Albrecht Alt, "The Monarchy in the Kingdoms of Israel and Judah," in idem, *Essays on Old Testament History and Religion,* trans. R. A. Wilson (Oxford: Blackwell, 1966), 239–59.

Introductory Formula for
Jehoash of Judah

Text

12:1 Jehoash was seven years old when he began to reign. 2 In the seventh year of Jehu, Jehoash began to reign; he reigned forty years in Jerusalem. His mother's name was Zibiah of Beer-sheba. 3 Jehoash did what was right in the sight of the LORD all his days, because the priest Jehoiada instructed him. 4 Nevertheless the high places were not taken away; the people continued to sacrifice and make offerings on the high places.

Commentary

[12:1-4] The introductory formula for Joash gives the name of his mother as that of Zibiah of Beer-sheba. "Zibiah" translates as "gazelle" and shows the loving attention of the parents who name their child after this intelligent and nimble animal of the steppe. That she comes from Beer-sheba (Bir es-Seba') in the steppe of the Negev shows the close link of the royal house with the upper class families of the country. The positive judgment spoken by the Deuteronomistic Historian is repeated in 14:3.

The Temple Repaired

Text

12:5 Jehoash said to the priests, "All the money offered as sacred donations that is brought into the house of the LORD, the money for which each person is assessed—the money from the assessment of persons—and the money from the voluntary offerings brought into the house of the LORD, 6 let the priests receive from each of the donors; and let them repair the house wherever any need of repairs is discovered." 7 But by the twenty-third year of King Jehoash the priests had made no repairs on the house. 8 Therefore King Jehoash summoned the priest Jehoiada with the other priests and said to them, "Why are you not repairing the house? Now therefore do not accept any more money from your donors but hand it over for the repair of the house." 9 So the priests agreed that they would neither accept more money from the people nor repair the house.

10 Then the priest Jehoiada took a chest, made a hole in its lid, and set it beside the altar on the right side as one entered the house of the LORD; the priests who guarded the threshold put in it all the money that was brought into the house of the LORD. 11 Whenever they saw that there was a great deal of money in the chest, the king's secretary and the high priest went up, counted the money that was found in the house of the LORD, and tied it up in bags. 12 They would give the money that was weighed out into the hands of the workers who had the oversight of the house of the LORD; then they paid it out to the carpenters and the builders who worked on the house of the LORD, 13 to the masons and the stonecutters, as well as to buy timber and quarried stone for making repairs on the house of the LORD, as well as for any outlay for repairs of the house. 14 But for the house of the LORD no basins of silver, snuffers, bowls, trumpets, or any vessels of gold, or of silver, were made from the money that was brought into the house of the LORD, 15 for that was given to the workers who were repairing the house of the LORD with it. 16 They did not ask an accounting from those into whose hand they delivered the money to pay out to the workers, for they dealt honestly. 17 The money from the guilt offerings and the money from the sin

offerings was not brought into the house of the LORD; it belonged to the priests.

Analysis

The account of the repair work done to the temple focuses on the financing of the project, and the only decision that the king makes regards the way to guarantee funding. The dating of events to the twenty-third year of his reign does not point to an old source text but is taken straight from 13:1. The whole undertaking is rather perplexing, because it was the duty of the king to maintain the sanctuary as a royal foundation.[1]

Commentary

[12:5-9] The order given by Joash (vv. 5-6) changes the received legal practice. The offerings are donations made in association with prescribed sacrifices at the temple, which were taken by the priests for themselves. Originally consisting of natural produce, those dues, or voluntary gifts, could be replaced in postexilic times by money donations (cf. Leviticus 27). This practice is obviously implied here. From this the rule follows that the priests would have to pay for the upkeep of the temple out of their own pockets. Their income was distributed to them by the officials who apparently administered the donations for the priests. It becomes obvious why this method of financing did not work. The priests were not prepared to forgo their income in order to maintain the temple. Therefore the king revokes the first order expressly (vv. 7-9).

[12:10] The new regulation demands that all income be centrally collected in a box by the altar. This is the responsibility of the priests guarding the threshold, who would collect the amount of silver, according to the stipulations of the temple, by the entrance to the temple court. (With coins being yet unknown, pieces of silver served as currency, weighed by the standard of the shekel.)

[12:11-13] The system of payment for the repair work is next described in great detail. The exact amount of money received is registered by the scribe and the high priest. The scribe was one of the royal officials (see on 1 Kgs 4:3) and was responsible for the administration. The presence of the "high priest" is somewhat surprising, because this title was only instituted in the Second Temple period; during the First Temple the highest priest was called "chief priest," according to 2 Kgs 25:18. The view of the Deuteronomistic Historian is that both the secular power of the kingship and the cultic institution of the priesthood should be seen as acting together in this matter. Materials and workers are paid for according to the money received. The materials mentioned are quarried stone and timber, and the different workers and

---

[1] See Kurt Galling, "Königliche und nichtkönigliche Stifter beim Tempel von Jerusalem," *ZDPV* 68 (1951) 134–42.

artisans—carpenters, builders, masons, and stonecutters—were probably hired in the market and recruited for the duration of the work.

[12:14-16, 17] These verses record further details of the regulations; these details, which name extra specifications and limitations, are therefore likely to be later additions. First, the crafting of any silver or gold wares is prohibited. The provision of necessary equipment was the responsibility of the king (see 1 Kgs 7:50). All the money is to be spent on the necessary maintenance of the temple building; a transfer of the "budget" is explicitly rejected. Contrary to common practice, these payments need not be accounted for in detail. Second, the revenue from the guilt and sin offerings is allotted back to the priests, in accordance with Lev 7:7. Both kinds of offering serve to expiate individual offenses (cf. Lev 4:5), and the donations relating to them are deducted from the maintenance fund and redistributed to the priests who perform the sacrifices in question. The addition of vv. 14-16, 17 is probably the work of a postexilic redactor.

The detailed exploration of building works at the temple during the reign of Joash is somewhat puzzling, because the main theme appears to be the redistribution of funds from offerings, rather than the action or behavior of the king. The description also bears out conditions in the temple that are credible only for the period after the end of the kingship. It is thus best to interpret these expositions as an argument that legitimizes the situation prevailing during the Second Temple by connecting it back to the royal decrees during the First Temple. Throughout the monarchy it was part of the responsibilities of the king to provide for the maintenance of the temple. Joash's behavior is thus not likely to be historically accurate. Only during the Second Temple and with the end of kingship as an institution did the priests have to find solutions for the upkeep of the temple. Received contemporary practice of the postexilic period is thus explained by relating it back to the orders of the king and events of the past. Such justification of the legal status of those involved was appropriate, seeing that provision of means for the upkeep of the temple out of the cultic donations meant certain financial losses for the priesthood.

Hazael Threatens Jerusalem

Text

12:18 At that time King Hazael of Aram went up, fought against Gath, and took it. But when Hazael set his face to go up against Jerusalem, 19 King Jehoash of Judah took all the votive gifts that Jehoshaphat, Jehoram, and Ahaziah, his ancestors, the kings of Judah, had dedicated, as well as his own votive gifts, all the gold that was found in the treasuries of the house of the LORD and of the king's house, and sent these to King Hazael of Aram. Then Hazael withdrew from Jerusalem.

Commentary

[12:18-19] This short notice tells of Hazael's threat to Judah. Hazael had been mentioned earlier on, in 9:15 and 10:32-33, as the king of Aram and an enemy of Israel. The taking of Gath is the only detail of his campaign that is mentioned. The place cannot be identified as Gittaim (Ras Abu Ḥumeid) near er-Ramle; rather, it is the Philistine Gath, situated on the western edge of the Shephelah at Tell eṣ-Ṣafi.[1] The capture of Gath indicates a clear strategy: Hazael pushes south across the coastal plain in order to turn from there toward Judah and Jerusalem. The strategy resembles that of Sennacherib's invasion of Judah (see on 18:13-15).

Joash preempts a further advance by Hazael toward Jerusalem through the payment of tributes. No further details are given, although the tribute is paid out of the temple and palace treasury, over both of which the king had authority. Hezekiah's actions in 18:15 clearly parallel this incident.

The entire section thus seems to be modeled on the report given in 18:13-15, and it is doubtful whether the present notice relies on an old source. It is not unlikely that the section was formulated only by the Deuteronomistic Historian. At any rate, the advance of the king of Aram on Judah and the deep south is highly improbable, given that military conflicts with the Arameans would usually take place in the northern part of East Jordan.

---

[1] Anson F. Rainey, "The Identification of Philistine Gath—A Problem in Source Analysis for Historical Geography," *ErIsr* 12 (1975) 63*–67*. For Gittaim see Benjamin Mazar, "Gath and Gittaim," *IEJ* 4 (1954) 227–35.

Concluding Formula for Joash of Judah

Text

12:20 Now the rest of the acts of Joash, and all that he did, are they not written in the Book of the Annals of the Kings of Judah? 21 His servants arose, devised a conspiracy, and killed Joash in the house of Millo, on the way that goes down to Silla. 22 It was Jozacar son of Shimeath and Jehozabad son of Shomer, his servants, who struck him down, so that he died. He was buried with his ancestors in the city of David; then his son Amaziah succeeded him.

Commentary

[12:20-22] The concluding formula deviates from the usual pattern in that it places the murder of Joash in the fortieth year of his reign; cf. 12:2. The violent removal of a ruler at such a late stage is surprising, yet no further information is offered other than the names of the assassins. Whether they derive from a tradition or are sheer invention can no longer be determined. They are characterized as servants and thus belong to the small circle of courtiers, but nothing is said about their specific function. It therefore remains unclear whether the murder is an act of personal revenge or a planned insurrection; the smooth succession to the throne makes personal motives appear to be the more likely cause.

Millo is given as the location where events took place. According to 2 Sam 5:9; 1 Kgs 9:15, 24; 11:27, Millo is a quarter of the city that was built only during the reign of Solomon. Its precise location is lost, but is likely to have been in the area between the city on the southeastern hill and the palace and temple area north of it (see on 1 Kgs 9:15). To mention the place specifically is probably to forestall speculations about a conspiracy in the palace. The murder has no further consequence, and the dynastic succession remains guaranteed; on Ahaziah see 2 Kgs 14:1-7.

Jehoahaz of Israel

Text

13:1 In the twenty-third year of King Joash son of Ahaziah of Judah, Jehoahaz son of Jehu began to reign over Israel in Samaria; he reigned seventeen years. 2 He did what was evil in the sight of the LORD, and followed the sins of Jeroboam son of Nebat, which he caused Israel to sin; he did not depart from them. 3 The anger of the LORD was kindled against Israel, so that he gave them repeatedly into the hand of King Hazael of Aram, then into the hand of Ben-hadad son of Hazael. 4 But Jehoahaz entreated the LORD, and the LORD heeded him; for he saw the oppression of Israel, how the king of Aram oppressed them. 5 Therefore the LORD gave Israel a savior, so that they escaped from the hand of the Arameans; and the people of Israel lived in their homes as formerly. 6 Nevertheless they did not depart from the sins of the house of Jeroboam, which he caused Israel to sin, but walked in them; the sacred pole also remained in Samaria. 7 So Jehoahaz was left with an army of not more than fifty horsemen, ten chariots and ten thousand footmen; for the king of Aram had destroyed them and made them like the dust at threshing. 8 Now the rest of the acts of Jehoahaz and all that he did, including his might, are they not written in the Book of the Annals of the Kings of Israel? 9 So Jehoahaz slept with his ancestors, and they buried him in Samaria; then his son Joash succeeded him.

Analysis

Between the introductory formula (vv. 1-2) and the concluding formula (vv. 8-9) of Jehoahaz of Israel, vv. 3-5 add some comments on the wars against Aram. Verse 6 is a redactional addition repeating the negative judgment of the son of Jehu. The asherah or sacred pole that is mentioned belongs within the framework of the cult alien to Yahweh, although here it refers to the planting of a sacred pole by Ahab in particular (1 Kgs 16:33). With Jehoahaz a new dynasty is established in the northern kingdom too, which is then continued with Joash, the grandson of Jehu. Verse 7 is another addition in which the redactor points out the weakening of Israel during the reign of Jehoahaz.

Commentary

[13:1-2] As with all other Israelite kings, there is no mention of Jehoahaz's age. Since Jehu reigned for twenty-eight years, according to 10:36, we can assume that he succeeded to the throne as an adult. Following the synchronisms in v. 1 and 13:10, Jehoahaz reigned over Israel for fourteen years, not seventeen. One can account for the discrepancy in two ways: either his regency during the last years of Jehu's reign had been added in, or the system of counting the years of rule had changed.

[13:3-5] The episode of Israel being subjected to Aram is formulated in the style of the book of Judges (cf. Judg 2:18; 3:9, 15), most likely by the Deueronomistic Historian. The one who saves Israel from Aram is not mentioned by name, but it must be King Jehoahaz. The enemies in question are Hazael, mentioned several times already (cf. 8:7-15; 10:32; 12:18), and his son, also called Ben-hadad and counted as Ben-hadad III (see on 6:24). This Ben-hadad is mentioned in the inscription of King Zakkur of Hamath and he is probably identical with the Mari' of the inscriptions of Adadnirari III (811–783), since the Assyrian sources mistake the address Mari' (*Ma-ri-iɔ*), "my master," as a royal name.[1] The identity of the two is further strengthened by the fact that the father and predecessor Hazael is mentioned several times in the inscriptions of Shalmaneser III (859–824).[2] The figure of Hadadezer, also mentioned in the inscriptions of Shalmaneser III, is likely to be the same as King Ben-hadad II, who was destroyed by Hazael.[3] Even with the names of the two kings of Aram being consistent, there is no further information provided about the military campaigns. The text merely offers a general statement that Israel's subjection to Aram reached its peak during the reign of Jehoahaz.

[13:7] The addition of v. 7 confirms with numbers how weak the northern kingdom had become. Nothing can be said about either the origin or the accuracy of those figures. Compared to the two thousand chariots and ten thousand men commanded by Ahab in the battle of Qarqar against Shalmaneser III in 853,[4] the reduced size of the chariot regiment is noticeable, while the number of footmen remains equal. Even if there is no way to check those figures, it seems that the fighting power of the Israelite army was seriously diminished by the decrease in chariots. The remaining ten chari-

---

[1] See, respectively, *TUAT,* I/6, 626; I/4, 367–69.

[2] *TUAT,* I/4, 363–66.

[3] See Moshe Elat, "The Campaigns of Shalmaneser III against Aram and Israel," *IEJ* 25 (1975) 25–35.

[4] *TUAT,* I/4, 361.

ots are, next to the fifty horsemen, only of symbolic value: no field battle could have been won with such a small contingent. Although no more particulars about the conflict with Aram are given, the period of Jehoahaz's reign is characterized as one of the weakest of Israel that is improved only with the victories of Jehoahaz's successor (13:25).

[13:8-9] The concluding formula does not change from the usual pattern. The royal tomb around the capital of Samaria is as unknown as that of the Davidides at Jerusalem.

Introductory Formula for
Jehoash of Israel

Text

13:10 In the thirty-seventh year of King Joash of Judah, Jehoash son of Jehoahaz began to reign over Israel in Samaria; he reigned sixteen years.
11 He also did what was evil in the sight of the LORD; he did not depart
from all the sins of Jeroboam son of Nebat, which he caused Israel to sin,
but he walked in them.

Commentary

[13:10-11] With the succession of Jehoash of Israel, two kings of the same name rule
over Israel and Judah for about three years. The judgment on Jehoash of Israel is negative. The meaning of the name is "Yahweh gave as a gift." His name appears on a
stele of Adadnirari III from Tell er-Rime, where he is mentioned in the context of tributes from Damascus, Tyre, and Sidon, which presupposes the subjection of the entire
land west of the Euphrates down to the coast.[1] This area, today part of Syria and
Lebanon, is called "Amurru" and "the land of the Hittites" by the Assyrian text, and
it includes the small cities of Aram together with the Phoenician coastal settlements.
The stele thus gives proof of the Assyrian pressure on the Arameans of Damascus at
the end of the ninth century. The military victories of Joash of Israel in East Jordan
against Damascus (13:25) will also have to be seen from the perspective of the threat
to the Aramean state of Damascus by the Assyrians.

---

[1] *TUAT,* I/4, 368.

Concluding Formula for Joash of Israel

Text

13:12 Now the rest of the acts of Joash, and all that he did, as well as the might with which he fought against King Amaziah of Judah, are they not written in the Book of the Annals of the Kings of Israel? 13 So Joash slept with his ancestors, and Jeroboam sat upon his throne; Joash was buried in Samaria with the kings of Israel.

Commentary

[13:12-13] The concluding formula for Joash of Israel is actually put too early, since 13:22-25 goes on to mention his victories against the Arameans. The conflict with Amaziah of Judah is recounted only after the latter's introductory formula, in 14:8-14. Accordingly, the concluding formula of Joash of Israel is repeated in 14:15-17. It is unclear why it is already mentioned here, but it is likely to be the work of a redactor. The expression "Jeroboam sat upon his throne," however, differs from the usual wording and occurs only here.

Elisha's Prophecies of Victory
and His Death

Text

13:14 Now when Elisha had fallen sick with the illness of which he was to die, King Joash of Israel went down to him, and wept before him, crying, "My father, my father! The chariots of Israel and its horsemen!" 15 Elisha said to him, "Take a bow and arrows"; so he took a bow and arrows. 16 Then he said to the king of Israel, "Draw the bow"; and he drew it. Elisha laid his hands on the king's hands. 17 Then he said, "Open the window eastward"; and he opened it. Elisha said, "Shoot"; and he shot. Then he said, "The LORD's arrow of victory, the arrow of victory over Aram! For you shall fight the Arameans in Aphek until you have made an end of them." 18 He continued, "Take the arrows"; and he took them. He said to the king of Israel, "Strike the ground with them"; he struck three times, and stopped. 19 Then the man of God was angry with him, and said, "You should have struck five or six times; then you would have struck down Aram until you had made an end of it, but now you will strike down Aram only three times."

20 So Elisha died, and they buried him. Now bands of Moabites used to invade the land in the spring of the year. 21 As a man was being buried, a marauding band was seen and the man was thrown into the grave of Elisha; as soon as the man touched the bones of Elisha, he came to life and stood on his feet.

Analysis

This story of the prophet is to pave the way for the victories of Joash over Aram recounted in 13:22-25. The symbolic action in vv. 18-19 and the remark about the miracle at the tomb of the prophet are additions. Verse 20 appears to be the original ending of the narrative in vv. 14-17.

Commentary

[13:14-17] The symbolic action that is carried out by the king and Elisha at their meeting is Elisha's last prophetic act before his death. The short act is dramatized through the use of direct speech. The place of action is not specified, although the king has obviously left Samaria to visit Elisha, who has fallen ill. The address to the prophet repeats the wording of 2:12. The tears over Elisha and the honorific title "my father" express the king's high esteem.

The symbolic action is to represent the victory over the Arameans, indicating the enemy by pointing the arrow toward the east. The shot, which symbolically destroys the enemy, is accompanied by Elisha's interpretation prophesying the final victory at Aphek. Aphek is already mentioned as a site of battle with the Arameans in 1 Kgs 20:26-27, 29-34, 43; thus it is possible that the name has been taken from that tradition; on its location see on 1 Kgs 20:26.

[13:18-19] A second symbolic action is added with vv. 18-19, where the striking of the earth signifies the victory over the Arameans in battle. Its prophecy is repeated in the redactional statement 13:25b.

[13:20] The notice on the death and burial of Elisha formed the original ending of the story. It is possible that Elisha died at his birthplace, Abel-meholah (Tell Abu Sus); cf. 1 Kgs 19:16, although the Jewish and early Christian traditions localize his tomb at Samaria.[1] With the Arab conquest the knowledge and reverence of the site seems to have come to an end; although there is a tradition of the tomb of John the Baptist around Samaria, there is no trace of a tomb of Elisha. The disappearance of the tradition in Islamic times might not be altogether surprising, however, since the characteristics of Elisha recur in the Arabic figure of Chader, where they merge with those of the Christian knight St. George.

[13:21] The addition signals the power of the prophet that stretches beyond his death and is exemplary of the hyperbole through which Elisha's miraculous force is described in the later tradition: even the corpse that touches the man of God is brought back to life.

---

[1] See Joachim Jeremias, *Heiligengräber in Jesu Umwelt (Mt. 23,29; Lk. 11,47): Eine Untersuchung zur Volksreligion der Zeit Jesu* (Göttingen: Vandenhoeck & Ruprecht, 1958), 30.

The Victories over Aram

Text

13:22 Now King Hazael of Aram oppressed Israel all the days of Jehoahaz. 23 But the LORD was gracious to them and had compassion on them; he turned toward them, because of his covenant with Abraham, Isaac, and Jacob, and would not destroy them; nor has he banished them from his presence until now.
24 When King Hazael of Aram died, his son Ben-hadad succeeded him. 25 Then Jehoash son of Jehoahaz took again from Ben-hadad son of Hazael the towns that he had taken from his father Jehoahaz in war. Three times Joash defeated him and recovered the towns of Israel.

Commentary

[13:22-25] This passage relating Joash's final victories over Aram is kept in a quite general tone and is likely to be the work of the Deuteronomistic Historian. No details are put forward, but there is historical evidence for the change of rulership from Hazael to Ben-hadad III, confirmed by the Assyrian sources (see on 13:3-5). Even if there exists a tradition for the passage in question here, it cannot have been very detailed. Maybe the narrative version in 1 Kings 20 of a victory of Joash at Aphek was available. It seems, however, to be historically accurate that Joash did indeed recapture the territories in northern East Jordan that had been lost to Hazael. There is no mention of the significant part played by Assyria. Damascus was taken and Aram seriously weakened by Adadnirari III, as we can gather from the tribute lists.[1] On the stele from Tell er-Rime Joash, too, appears as a tributary next to Tyre and Sidon.[2] This means that, following Joash's succession to the throne, Ashur not only dealt a considerable blow to the strength of the Arameans at Damascus, but also gained temporary control

---

[1] *TUAT,* I/4, 368 and 369.
[2] *TUAT,* I/4, 368.

over Israel.[3] Notwithstanding the territorial gains against the Arameans and his recent coming into power, Joash would have had to acknowledge the supremacy of the Assyrian king soon.

We lack further sources about the duration of those tribute payments, although it appears to be a short one, followed by a period of political independence and economic stability for Israel until the succession of Tiglath-pileser III. This first conflict with the Assyrian power is not reflected further in the Book of Kings, yet it foreshadows the conquest of Israel by Assyria under Tiglath-pileser III (see on 15:19-20), which is, in turn, the prelude to the final destruction of the northern kingdom.

---

[3] On the dating see A. R. Millard and Hayim Tadmor, "Adadnirari III in Syria: Another Stele Fragment and the Dates of His Campaigns," *Iraq* 35 (1973) 57–64; Herbert Donner, "Adadnirari III. und die Vasallen des Westens," in *Archäologie und Altes Testament: Festschrift für Kurt Galling,* ed. Arnulf Kuschke and Ernst Kutsch (Tübingen: Mohr/Siebeck, 1970), 49–59.

Introductory Formula for
Amaziah of Judah

Text

14:1 In the second year of King Joash son of Joahaz of Israel, King Amaziah son of Joash of Judah, began to reign. 2 He was twenty-five years old when he began to reign, and he reigned twenty-nine years in Jerusalem. His mother's name was Jehoaddin of Jerusalem. 3 He did what was right in the sight of the LORD, yet not like his ancestor David; in all things he did as his father Joash had done. 4 But the high places were not removed; the people still sacrificed and made offerings on the high places. 5 As soon as the royal power was firmly in his hand he killed his servants who had murdered his father the king. 6 But he did not put to death the children of the murderers; according to what is written in the book of the law of Moses, where the LORD commanded, "The parents shall not be put to death for the children, or the children be put to death for the parents; but all shall be put to death for their own sins."

7 He killed ten thousand Edomites in the Valley of Salt and took Sela by storm; he called it Jokthe-el, which is its name to this day.

Commentary

[14:1-4] Apart from the usual information, this introductory formula offers a positive judgment of Amaziah, just like that of his father Joash. Its qualification added in v. 4 does not change the expected format either. His mother Jehoaddin ("Yahweh is delight") is likely to come from the upper classes of Jerusalem.

[14:5-6] The introductory formula is followed by two short notices. According to v. 5, Amaziah has had the murderers of his father killed. This seems to indicate that Amaziah had not risen to power by way of a palace revolution. The remark in v. 6, added at a later stage, about the sparing of the children is taken almost verbatim from Deut 24:16.

[14:7] The second notice testifies to a successful campaign against Edom, which was famously difficult to attack because of its geographical position. Although the place is not further specified, the "Valley of Salt" is likely to be found east of the Arabah. Sela is best identified as es-Sala^c (not as Petra), 8 km. southwest of et-Tafile, where there is ceramic evidence for an Iron Age settlement.[1] Its renaming as Jokthe-el is puzzling, but probably concerned a clan settling there. There is no reason to doubt the historicity of Amaziah's attack against Edom, although we do not know to what extent this advance could achieve a permanent rule there. The elaboration of the conflict between Amaziah and Joash of Israel in the narrative at 14:10 refers explicitly to this campaign.

---

[1] See M. Lindner, "Es-Sela^c: Eine antike Fliehburg 50 km nördlich von Petra," in *Petra und das Königreich der Nabatäer*, ed. Manfred Lindner (Munich: Delp, 1974), 271–85.

The Victory of Jehoash of Israel against Amaziah of Judah

Text

14:8 Then Amaziah sent messengers to King Jehoash son of Jehoahaz, son of Jehu, of Israel, saying, "Come, let us look one another in the face." 9 King Jehoash of Israel sent word to King Amaziah of Judah, "A thornbush on Lebanon sent to a cedar on Lebanon, saying, 'Give your daughter to my son for a wife'; but a wild animal of Lebanon passed by and trampled down the thornbush. 10 You have indeed defeated Edom, and your heart has lifted you up. Be content with your glory, and stay at home; for why should you provoke trouble so that you fall, you and Judah with you?"

11 But Amaziah would not listen. So King Jehoash of Israel went up; he and King Amaziah of Judah faced one another in battle at Beth-shemesh, which belongs to Judah. 12 Judah was defeated by Israel; everyone fled home. 13 King Jehoash of Israel captured King Amaziah of Judah son of Jehoash, son of Ahaziah, at Beth-shemesh; he came to Jerusalem, and broke down the wall of Jerusalem from the Ephraim Gate to the Corner Gate, a distance of four hundred cubits. 14 He seized all the gold and silver, and all the vessels that were found in the house of the LORD and in the treasuries of the king's house, as well as hostages; then he returned to Samaria.

Analysis

A tradition that recounts the basic events—the capture of the king of Judah and the partial destruction of the city walls of Jerusalem—is at the root of the narrative about the war between Amaziah of Judah and Jehoash of Israel. The story presupposes that the peaceful relations between the two states, which had been sealed with the marriage of Athaliah and Jehoram of Judah (see 8:25-26), had come to an end by the beginning of the eighth century.

Commentary

[14:8-10] The military action proper is prefaced by a verbal exchange in which Jehoash gives express warning against the campaign and its consequences. The exchange of words helps to elaborate the narrative, but the text gives no hint what the real causes were for the beginning of war. The most likely reason seems to be an attack by the stronger (Israel) against the weaker (Judah).

In an attempt to avoid armed conflict, Jehoash makes use of a fable whose imagery reflects the supremacy of Israel and the futility of Amaziah's plan. The point of comparison is the incompatibility between two plants, the cedar and the thornbush, which mirrors the hopeless undertaking of waging a war against a superior enemy. The genre of the plant parable was not uncommon in ancient Israel, as proven by the parable of Jotham in Judg 9:8-15a. Although the parable is not part of ancient Near Eastern literature, the characteristics of plants and animals find use in dialogues and short narratives that are predecessors of the parable.[1] The genre becomes increasingly common in Greek and Latin literature, where individual pieces are collected together.[2]

[14:11-12] Of the decisive battle at Beth-shemesh we are told only the result, that is, the defeat of Judah. Beth-shemesh was situated on the northern edge of the Shephelah at Khirbet er-Rumele and was, despite its frequent destruction, continuously settled during Iron Age I and II.[3] The city was of strategic value in that it marked the entrance to the ascent to Jerusalem, approaching from the coast. In addition, the plain and the low foothills were eminently suitable for the assembling of troops and therefore also as a battle site. It would appear that Amaziah deliberately sought out this important and opportune place.

[14:13] Still, the battle ended in defeat for him and turned into a disaster. The battle was won by the one who managed to turn the enemy army to flight. The king would usually take part in battle—standing on his chariot and visible to all. Yet while the army contingent takes to its heels, the king of Judah is taken captive by his enemy and thus stripped of his power. The defeat of Judah cleared the way for Jehoash of Israel to advance on Jerusalem, and he was apparently able to take the capital of Judah without any resistance. To strip the city of its protection, the walls were broken down over a length of about 200 m. Despite the detailed description we cannot locate the stretch of wall more precisely, because we lack the exact coordinates for the two gates that are mentioned. With early eighth-century Jerusalem essentially restricted to the southeastern hill and the area north of it, the stretch of wall is likely to have run above the Kidron Valley and the Tyropoeon Valley.

---

[1] See *TUAT,* III/1, 180–88.

[2] See Harry C. Schnur, *Fabeln in der Antike,* Tusculum-Bücherei (Munich: Heimeran, 1978).

[3] See Shlomo Bunimovitz and Zvi Lederman, "Beth-Shemesh," in *NEAEHL,* 1:249–53.

[14:14] In addition, a tribute was raised and hostages were taken. Nothing is said about the amount of the tribute, but, as under Rehoboam (1 Kgs 14:26), it was paid out of the treasures of the temple and the palace, which meant the loss of the entire treasury. Both practices conform to conventions of warfare. The conflict between Israel and Judah thus ended with the complete defeat of the southern kingdom, adding economic injury to insult. With the remark on Jehoash's return to his capital Samaria the story closes.

Concluding Formula for
Jehoash of Israel

Text

14:15 Now the rest of the acts that Jehoash did, his might, and how he fought with King Amaziah of Judah, are they not written in the Book of the Annals of the Kings of Israel? 16 Jehoash slept with his ancestors, and was buried in Samaria with the kings of Israel; then his son Jeroboam succeeded him.

17 King Amaziah son of Joash of Judah lived fifteen years after the death of King Jehoash son of Jehoahaz of Israel.

Commentary

[**14:15-17**] The concluding formula for Jehoash of Israel mentions again the war with Amaziah. Beyond that, it states only the seamless succession to the throne. The duration of Amaziah's remaining rule given in v. 17 is calculated from the synchronisms of 14:2 and 14:23; the calculation, in turn, is the work of a later redactor. The chronology of the kings of Judah in the eighth century is problematic; we finish with a surplus of 36 to 37 years if we add up the years of reign from Ahaziah to Hezekiah. The problem can be solved only if we assume coregency for at least some kings, with the years of coregency being counted as proper years of rule. Due to the lack of precise data the solutions differ considerably.[1] A decisive answer is simply beyond reach.

---

[1] See Alfred Jepsen and Robert Hahnhart, *Untersuchungen zur israelitisch-jüdische Chronologie,* BZAW 88 (Berlin: Töpelmann, 1964), 38; K. T. Andersen, "Die Chronologie der Könige von Israel und Juda," *ST* 23 (1969) 69–114.

Concluding Formula for
Amaziah of Judah

Text

14:18 Now the rest of the deeds of Amaziah, are they not written in the Book of the Annals of the Kings of Judah? 19 They made a conspiracy against him in Jerusalem, and he fled to Lachish. But they sent after him to Lachish, and killed him there. 20 They brought him on horses; he was buried in Jerusalem with his ancestors in the city of David. 21 All the people of Judah took Azariah, who was sixteen years old, and made him king to succeed his father Amaziah. 22 He rebuilt Elath and restored it to Judah, after King Amaziah slept with his ancestors.

Commentary

[14:18-21] Amaziah, like his father and predecessor Joash before him (cf. 12:21), falls victim to a conspiracy. Again, we are given no details, but the flight of the king to Lachish points to an insurrection at the court, most likely involving the captains of the guard and the army on an active planning level. Lachish had a royal palace and was probably the most important city of Judah besides Hebron; it certainly played a crucial role both in the defense of the kingdom during the invasion by Sennacherib in 701 and in the conquest of Judah by Nebuchadnezzar in 587. The conspirators manage to kill Amaziah at Lachish, despite the refuge he has taken there. Yet the country population, that is, the upper classes of the towns, prove once more to be the decisive factor in safeguarding the dynasty, in that they put Azariah, the son of Amaziah, on the throne to succeed his murdered father. Amaziah, too, is taken back to Jerusalem and buried in the family tomb of the Davidides.

[14:22] Although Azariah is formally introduced only in 15:1-7, the short notice in v. 22 refers to the events during his reign. The rebuilding of Elath presupposes control over the steppe of the Negev and its adjacent areas to the south. The place is dif-

322

ferent from the harbor of Ezion-geber established by Solomon (see commentary on 1 Kgs 9:26). Elath has not been located yet, but the settlement succeeding it in the Roman-Byzantine era, named Aila, lay at the western edge of modern 'Aqaba, where there is ceramic evidence for building activity during the period in question.[1] The rebuilding of Elath seems to be connected to the trade across the Red Sea being resumed, although no particulars are given. Once Amaziah had laid the foundations of the political sovereignty over Edom, his son Azariah was able to extend his sphere of power down to the Gulf of Aqaba. Already under his grandson Ahaz, however, Elath would fall back to the Edomites (2 Kgs 16:6).

---

[1] See the list in Othmar Keel and Max Küchler, *Orte und Landschaften der Bibel*, 2 vols. (Göttingen: Vandenhoeck & Ruprecht, 1982), 2:279–86.

Jeroboam of Israel

Text

14:23 In the fifteenth year of King Amaziah son of Joash of Judah, King Jeroboam son of Joash of Israel began to reign in Samaria; he reigned forty-one years. 24 He did what was evil in the sight of the LORD; he did not depart from all the sins of Jeroboam son of Nebat, which he caused Israel to sin. 25 He restored the border of Israel from Lebo-hamath as far as the Sea of the Arabah, according to the word of the LORD, the God of Israel, which he spoke by his servant Jonah son of Amittai, the prophet, who was from Gath-hepher. 26 For the LORD saw that the distress of Israel was very bitter; there was no one left, bond or free, and no one to help Israel. 27 But the LORD had not said that he would blot out the name of Israel from under heaven, so he saved them by the hand of Jeroboam son of Joash.

28 Now the rest of the acts of Jeroboam, and all that he did, and his might, how he fought, and how he recovered for Israel Damascus and Hamath, which had belonged to Judah, are they not written in the Book of the Annals of the Kings of Israel? 29 Jeroboam slept with his ancestors, the kings of Israel; his son Zechariah succeeded him.

Commentary

[14:23-24] To the usual framework three more verses are added: v. 25 and vv. 26-27. The judgment of Jeroboam, the second king of that name after Jeroboam, son of Nebat (see 1 Kgs 12:1-25), is negative. The name is also mentioned on a (lost) seal from Megiddo: "(Belonging to) Shema, servant of Jeroboam."[1] The duration of his reign is, at forty-one years, the longest of the northern kingdom. His reign during the early eighth century coincides with a period of Ashur's relative weakness, which meant a strengthened position of power for Israel. The era of Jeroboam is often considered the "last flourishing of Israel" before its decline after the Assyrian invasions

---

[1] *ANEP*, no. 276.

from Tiglath-pileser III onward. Within Israel, however, there is a noticeable increase in social conflict, as clearly mirrored, for example, in the book of Amos.[2]

[14:25] The same tradition o the victories over the Aramean states is drawn upon in v. 25 as in vv. 28-29. The same facts are related, this time in the form of geographical data mentioned in the context of the word of an otherwise unknown prophet. As in 1 Kgs 8:65, the description of the territory takes Lebo-hamath as the fictional border of Solomon's realm. The site of Lebo-hamath (Lebwe) had marked the boundary of Egyptian hegemony in Canaan as early as the second half of the second millennium.[3] The border between the realms of Damascus and Hamath, too, would have run through the area of this city in the first half of the first millennium. The same border was acknowledged in the eighth century when it was adopted as part of the Assyrian construction of provinces. It was only in postexilic times that Lebo-hamath became the northern boundary of the realm of David and Solomon (cf. Num 13:21; 34:8; Ezek 47:15; Josh 13:5). To mention Lebo-hamath means to indicate the extension of Israelite territory as far as the border of Hamath. Thus according to the Deuteronomistic Historian, Jeroboam has returned state territory to its former size of the Davidic-Solomonic realm. Its southern boundary is marked by the "Sea of the Steppe," that is, the Dead Sea (see Deut 3:17; 4:49; Josh 3:16; 12:3), where the East Jordanian areas of Israel border on Moab.

[14:26-27] The addition of vv. 26-27 is probably the work of a later redactor. It stresses that Jeroboam's victories were affected by Yahweh and that the king is therefore a tool of God. This not only strikes a positive chord as far as the judgment of Jeroboam is concerned, but it also justifies the unusually long period of his reign and its positive effects as an act of God. The basically negative judgment of v. 24 is thereby revised and modified. Verse 27 is certainly not an allusion to the prophet Amos, who is otherwise ignored in the Deuteronomistic History.[4]

[14:28-29] The concluding formula is enlarged to include a comment on the military successes of Jeroboam: "how he recovered for Israel Damascus and Hamath [. . .]." Following Eissfeldt, many read the lacuna as "of Ya'udi," although this link to the north Syrian state of the Arameans is not tenable.[5] "Damascus" and "Hamath" refer

---

[2] See Willy Schrottoff, "The Prophet Amos: A Socio-historical Assessment," in *God of the Lowly: Socio-historical Interpretations of the Bible,* ed. Willy Schottroff and Wolfgang Stegemann, trans. M. J. O'Connell (Maryknoll, N.Y.: Orbis, 1984), 27–46.

[3] See Nadav Na'aman, "The Canaanites and Their Land: A Rejoinder," *UF* 26 (1994) 397–418.

[4] *Pace* Frank Crüsemann, "Kritik an Amos im deuteronomistischen Geschichtswerk: Erwägungen zu 2. Könige 14,27," in *Probleme biblischer Theologie: Gerhard von Rad zum 70. Geburtstag,* ed. Hans Walter Wolff (Munich: Kaiser, 1971), 57–63.

[5] Otto Eissfeldt, "'Juda' in 2. Könige 14,28 und 'Judäa' in Apostelgeschichte 2,9," in idem, *Kleine Schriften,* 6 vols. (Tübingen: Mohr/Siebeck, 1968), 4:99–130; cf. Hayim Tadmor, "Azriyan of Yaudi," *Scripta Hierosolymitana* 8 (1961) 232–71.

to the two Aramean states that border Israel to the north.[6] With the threat from the Arameans of Damascus dispelled under Joash (see on 13:25), Joash's son and successor Jeroboam did apparently return the attack and eventually conquered the two states. No further details are mentioned, but the message behind the short notice is likely to be that "Jeroboam II achieved the supremacy of Israel across the northern Syrian territory."[7] More crucial military successes against the Arameans can also be inferred from the allusions to victories at Lo-debar and Karnaim (Seh Sa'd north of the Yarmuk River) in East Jordan as they occur in Amos 6:13-14. The mention of the successful campaigns against Damascus and Hamath seems to be independent of v. 25, which makes it possibly part of a reliable tradition available to the Deuteronomistic Historian. It is in any case a piece of information that is of historical value.

Jeroboam's obvious success is linked back to the word of the prophet Jonah from Gath-hepher and thus to the will of God. There is no mention of this prophet elsewhere, but his name was taken up again in postexilic times in the novella named after him. The book of Jonah was adopted into the Hebrew canon as one of the twelve Minor Prophets.[8] Gath-hepher in the area of the tribe of Zebulun (Josh 19:13) is given as Jonah's home; the site is to be located at Khirbet ez-Zerra' in Lower Galilee. The reference to the prophetic word remains vague, and it is likely that the Deuteronomistic Historian was relying on a historical figure about whom there existed no other tradition.

---

[6] See Martin Noth, "Das Reich von Hamath als Grenznachbar des Reiches Israel," in *ABLAK,* 2:148–60.

[7] Würthwein, *Könige,* 2:375.

[8] On its intention and composition see Wilhelm Rudolph, "Jona," in *Archäologie und Altes Testament: Festschrift für Kurt Galling,* ed. Arnulf Kuschke and Ernst Kutsch (Tübingen: Mohr/Siebeck, 1970), 233–39.

Azariah of Judah

Text

15:1 In the twenty-seventh year of King Jeroboam of Israel King Azariah son of Amaziah of Judah began to reign. 2 He was sixteen years old when he began to reign, and he reigned fifty-two years in Jerusalem. His mother's name was Jecoliah of Jerusalem. 3 He did what was right in the sight of the LORD, just as his father Amaziah had done. 4 Nevertheless the high places were not taken away; the people still sacrificed and made offerings on the high places. 5 The LORD struck the king, so that he was leprous to the day of his death, and lived in a separate house. Jotham the king's son was in charge of the palace, governing the people of the land. 6 Now the rest of the acts of Azariah, and all that he did, are they not written in the Book of the Annals of the Kings of Judah? 7 Azariah slept with his ancestors; they buried him with his ancestors in the city of David; his son Jotham succeeded him.

Commentary

[15:1-4] The regularity of the formulas for Azariah is interrupted only by the notice of his disease and the subsequent regency of his son Jotham in v. 5. However, his recapture and rebuilding of Elath had already been mentioned in 14:22. Given his long reign of fifty-two years, the information is extremely sparse. It is only in Chronicles that he is given credit for building activity and military campaigns (2 Chr 26:1-15), although those details do not rely on traditions of historical value and are therefore of no use in establishing the historical events during his reign.[1] Azariah, like his father Amaziah and his son Jotham, is judged positively by the Deuteronomistic Historian, although with the same exception of the high places, which have still not been abolished; that is, he continued to allow cultic sites outside Jerusalem.

---

[1] See Peter Welten, *Geschichte und Geschichtsdarstellung in den Chronikbüchern,* WMANT 42 (Neukirchen-Vluyn: Neukirchener, 1973).

His mother Jecoliah is from Jerusalem, yet without the name of her father there is little we can say about her pedigree from one of the Jerusalem families. It is possible that Jecoliah was not the first wife of the king, nor Ahaziah his firstborn son, but the lack of sources allows little more than speculation.

The fifty-two years of his reign include the fifteen years of his regency in lieu of his father Amaziah (14:17), after Joash of Israel took him captive (14:13). Toward the end of his reign he is succeeded by his son Jotham, who had become regent after his father was afflicted by a skin disease.

Apart from the name Azariah, "Yahweh has helped" (e.g., 14:21; 15:1, 6, 7, 8, 17, 23, 27), we also find the name Uzziah, "Yahweh is my strength" (e.g., 15:13, 30, 32, 34; Isa 1:1; 6:1; 7:1; Hos 1:1; Amos 1:1; Zech 14:5). The form Uzziah is, in all likelihood, the name that the king took on only when he succeeded to the throne.[2] There is no sure way to decide whether the figure of Azriyau mentioned in the Annals of Tiglath-pileser III is the same as Azariah of Judah.[3]

[15:5] The notice on Azariah's leprosy is certainly historical, but not properly dated; therefore we cannot specify when Jotham became regent. "Leprosy" is the generic term for a variety of skin diseases, without including the incurable leprosy proper. To be afflicted by a skin disease meant to become impure, and thus incapable of participating in cultic activity and subsequently to be isolated.[4] As done already in 5:1, the leprosy is attributed to Yahweh as punishment for an offense. The afflicted king could not continue his royal duties and was isolated in a "separate house" likely his royal retreat. The king was in any case dissolved from his cultic and royal duties, which passed on to his son Jotham during his lifetime, and who later also succeeded him to the throne (15:32-33). It is unclear to what extent Jotham would have maintained contact with the king during his regency. The rationale behind this solution is the continuation of the dynasty.

As indicated by the apposition, Jotham was also in charge of the palace; this office made him responsible for all the affairs of the royal palace and especially the administration of the royal estate (see on 1 Kgs 4:6). The notice thus informs us that members of the royal family could take on high offices. The king might have trusted members of his own family most and could at the same time delegate responsibilities to his son and designated successor, thus giving him insights into the execution of

---

[2] See A. M. Honeyman, "The Evidence of Royal Names among the Hebrews," *JBL* 67 (1948) 13–25.

[3] See Hayim Tadmor, *The Inscriptions of Tiglath-pileser III, King of Assyria: Critical Edition, with Introductions, Translations, and Commentary* (Jerusalem: Israel Academy of Sciences and Humanities, 1994), 273–74.

[4] The different types of skin disease are dealt with from a cultic perspective in Leviticus 13; see Erhard S. Gerstenberger, *Leviticus,* trans. Douglas W. Stott, OTL (Louisville: Westminster John Knox, 1996), 153–73. [Ed.] See also John J. Pilch, *Healing in the New Testament: Insights from Medical and Mediterranean Anthropology* (Minneapolis: Fortress Press, 2000), 39–54.

government. The regency of Jotham can preserve power and the Davidic dynasty in the exceptional case where the king is himself unable to rule. In this way both cultic and political demands can be fulfilled.

[15:7] According to v. 7 Azariah was buried in the tomb of the Davidic dynasty. Subsequent traditions, however, mention that he was buried outside the royal tomb because of his cultic impurity caused by leprosy (2 Chr 26:23; Josephus, *Ant.* 11.227). His name also appears in a four-line inscription of unknown origin from the area around Jerusalem: "To this place were brought (2) the bones of Uzziahu, (3) king of Judah, (4) and (it) must not be opened."[5] The inscription is found on an almost square slab (34 x 35 cm.) that served as the cover for a secondary burial; it is written in Aramaic and can be dated to the Roman-Hellenistic period. Since the second half of the nineteenth century the stone has been on display in the museum in the Eleona Church on the Mount of Olives, while the site where it was originally found remains unknown. The inscription is best interpreted in the context of secondary burials, as they became common in the Hasmonean period and onward.[6] The inscription offers evidence only on a secondary burial of Azariah/Uzziah in the Roman-Hellenistic period.

---

[5] *TGI*, 55.

[6] See L. Y. Rahmani, "Ancient Jerusalem's Funerary Customs and Tombs," *BA* 44 (1981) 171–77, 229–35; 45 (1982) 43–53, 109–19.

Zechariah of Israel

Text

15:8 In the thirty-eighth year of King Azariah of Judah, Zechariah son of Jeroboam reigned over Israel in Samaria six months. 9 He did what was evil in the sight of the LORD, as his ancestors had done. He did not depart from the sins of Jeroboam son of Nebat, which he caused Israel to sin. 10 Shallum son of Jabesh conspired against him, and struck him down in public and killed him, and reigned in place of him. 11 Now the rest of the deeds of Zechariah are written in the Book of the Annals of the Kings of Israel. 12 This was the promise of the LORD that he gave to Jehu, "Your sons shall sit on the throne of Israel to the fourth generation." And so it happened.

Commentary

[15:8-12] The formulas for King Azariah of Judah in 15:1-7 are followed by short notices on five kings of Israel who came to power during the reign of Azariah and ruled (almost all of them) for a short time only: Zechariah, Shallum, Menahem, Pekahiah, and Pekah. The changing political situation was to blame for this rapid turnover of kings in the northern kingdom. After the death of Jeroboam II, Assyrian hegemony started to spread quickly across the entire Near East. The ruling class of Israel was split over their attitude to the Assyrian Empire, and the resulting factions represented political choices: submission or resistance. Four kings (Zechariah, Shallum, Pekahiah, and Pekah) were killed quickly by their successors in order to enforce political claims. As a result no dynasty, and hence no stability, could be maintained, with only one exception.

With Zechariah, son of Jeroboam II, a king comes to the throne who is subjected to the same negative evaluation as the other rulers of the northern kingdom. After a reign that lasted for only six months, he was assassinated by Shallum at Jibleam (Khirbet Bel'ame). There is no hint as to why the king should be outside the capital at Jibleam on the northern edge of the Samaritan mountains. With his murder the dynasty of Jehu comes to an end. A redactor has, in v. 12, justified this fact by reference to the prophecy of 10:30.

Shallum of Israel

Text

15:13 Shallum son of Jabesh began to reign in the thirty-ninth year of King Uzziah of Judah; he reigned one month in Samaria. 14 Then Menahem son of Gadi came up from Tirzah and came to Samaria; he struck down Shallum son of Jabesh in Samaria and killed him; he reigned in place of him. 15 Now the rest of the deeds of Shallum, including the conspiracy that he made, are written in the Book of the Annals of the Kings of Israel. 16 At that time Menahem sacked Tiphsah, all who were in it and its territory from Tirzah on; because they did not open it to him, he sacked it. He ripped open all the pregnant women in it.

Commentary

[15:13-16] The reign of the usurper Shallum lasted only for a month, despite his attempt to secure the crown and power by taking over the palace at Samaria. It is doubtful whether we can link his father's name Jabesh with the East Jordanian site of the same name (Jabesh-gilead = Tell el-Maqlub). An internal division must have taken place within the army, because the capture of Samaria cannot have taken place without resistance and the support of troops. The office that Menahem held is not specified; he launched his campaign against Shallum from the old capital of Tirzah. His second campaign against Tappuach (Seh Abu Zarad), which is mentioned in v. 16, probably served to strengthen his position after the assassination of Shallum. Tappuach had apparently refused loyalty to the new king and was punished with the eradication of its entire population.

The extreme cruelty of the usurper's approach is expressed in the words "he ripped open their pregnant women."[1] One of the toponyms in the geographical description has unfortunately gone missing. According to the text, Tirzah belonged to the territory of Tappuach and therefore lay in the area south of Shechem (Tell Balatah).

---

[1] On this term, see Mordechai Cogan, "'Ripping open Pregnant Women' in Light of an Assyrian Analogue," *JAOS* 103 (1983) 755–57.

Menahem of Israel

Text

15:17 In the thirty-ninth year of King Azariah of Judah, Menahem son of Gadi began to reign over Israel; he reigned ten years in Samaria. 18 He did what was evil in the sight of the LORD; he did not depart all his days from any of the sins of Jeroboam son of Nebat, which he caused Israel to sin. 19 King Pul of Assyria came against the land; Menahem gave Pul a thousand talents of silver, so that he might help him confirm his hold on the royal power. 20 Menahem exacted the money from Israel, that is, from all the wealthy, fifty shekels of silver from each one, to give to the king of Assyria. So the king of Assyria turned back, and did not stay there in the land. 21 Now the rest of the deeds of Menahem, and all that he did, are they not written in the Book of the Annals of the Kings of Israel? 22 Menahem slept with his ancestors, and his son Pekahiah succeeded him.

Commentary

[15:17-18] Menahem, who had risen to power through a coup, was able to rule for ten years until his death. This stability is most likely due to the loyalty of the military and his support from Ashur. Menahem can thus be regarded as a loyal vassal to Ashur; his son Pekahiah would be overthrown by the anti-Assyrian party led by Pekah (15:25). If there is a shift in affiliation during the kingship, then Shallum, as Menahem's predecessor, can also be considered anti-Assyrian, while the dynasty of Jehu was pro-Assyrian.

[15:19-20] The formula for Menahem includes a notice on the tributes paid to the Assyrian King Tiglath-pileser III. The explicit remark on the political dependency to Ashur is surprising in that earlier payments by Jehu and Joash, which are mentioned in Assyrian sources, are silently glossed over in the Deuteronomistic History. By paying tribute Menahem has submitted to Tiglath-pileser III and become a vassal of Ashur. The payments are confirmed in the Assyrian sources.[1] In line with the general

---

[1] See Hayim Tadmor, *The Inscriptions of Tiglath-pileser III, King of Assyria* (Jerusalem: Israel Academy of Sciences and Humanities, 1994), 69, 107.

chronology assumed for the reign of Tiglath-pileser III (745–727), Menahem's tribute can be dated to 740. This makes the tribute predate the big campaigns by Tiglath-pileser III against Philistine and Damascus in 734–732 (see on 15:29). The appeasement policy of Menahem was brought to an end only by the revolution of Pekah (15:25).

The amount of the tribute, which is given as one thousand talents, is redistributed to the individual households, which have to contribute 50 shekels each. With one talent made up of 3,600 shekels (cf. Exod 21:32), we can calculate that there were 72,000 families in Israel. If we assume a standard family of four, the population amounts to 288,000 people overall. This tribute was apparently raised independently of land ownership and hence income of the families; undoubtedly this meant for the majority a serious financial strain beyond the usual taxation. The opposition to Ashur, which emerges more clearly during the last decades of the monarchy in Israel, has some of its roots certainly in the tax burden that Ashur had caused.

The name of the Assyrian ruler Tiglath-pileser III is given here as "Pul."[2] The use of the shorter alternative here is anachronistic, since it was adopted as the name of the Assyrian king only after the assumption of the Babylonian monarchy in 729, when it appears in the royal list "A" of Babylon; the tribute, however, can be dated to 740.[3] Tiglath-pileser III was the founder of the new Assyrian Empire, which existed until the conquest of Nineveh by the Babylonians and Medes in 612 and extended its power as far as Egypt under the rule of Ashurbanipal. Assyria's rise to world power began with Tiglath-pileser III's conquest of the neighboring states of Urartu and Arpad. The subsequent conquest of other small states in northern Syria led to their reorganization as Assyrian provinces, which meant that the Assyrian Empire extended as far as the Mediterranean.

The conquest was not only characterized by a particularly brutal type of warfare, but it was also accompanied by a no less brutal policy of deportations. "The novelty of Tiglath-pileser's action was not only its size, but its character. Deportation became a two-way exchange: from newly organized provinces in the West, he transferred populations to Assyria proper, and resettled those areas with people brought from the East and South. This radical procedure of population exchange sought to make the uprooted totally dependent on the central government, forcefully amalgamating them so that 'they became Assyrian.' This procedure, more than any other, created the new Assyrian empire."[4] The reign of Tiglath-pileser III is pivotal for the history of the ancient Near East in general and of Israel in particular. With this Assyrian king began a period of foreign rule that was to end with the destruction of Israel.

---

[2] See Otto Loretz and Walter Mayer, "Pulu-Tiglatpileser III. und Menahem von Israel nach assyrischen Quellen und 2. Kön.15, 19-20," *UF* 22 (1990) 221–31.

[3] See William H. Shea, "Menahem and Tiglath-pileser III," *JNES* 37 (1978) 43–49.

[4] Cogan and Tadmor, *II Kings,* 177.

Pekahiah of Israel

Text

15:23 In the fiftieth year of King Azariah of Judah, Pekahiah son of Menahem began to reign over Israel in Samaria; he reigned two years. 24 He did what was evil in the sight of the LORD; he did not turn away from the sins of Jeroboam son of Nebat, which he caused Israel to sin. 25 Pekah son of Remaliah, his captain, conspired against him with fifty of the Gileadites, and attacked him in Samaria, in the citadel of the palace along with Argob and Arieh; he killed him, and reigned in place of him. 26 Now the rest of the deeds of Pekahiah, and all that he did, are written in the Book of the Annals of the Kings of Israel.

Commentary

[15:23-26] The only thing we are told about Pekahiah, besides the formula with his negative evaluation, is his assassination by conspirators. As a son of Menahem, his is the last and unsuccessful attempt to establish a dynasty in Israel. His murder at the hand of Pekah takes place in the royal palace at Samaria. Within the party politics outlined so far (see on 15:19-20), the usurper Pekah belongs to those opposed to the pro-Assyrian policy. The fifty men who assist Pekah in his undertaking are specified as "Gileadites," that is, as a particular group from East Jordan. This might indicate that the formation of anti-Assyrian opposition was less dependent on social strata than on geographical distribution. Pekahiah lasted for two years before he was assassinated. Pekah, his assassin, was his captain (see on 7:2) and thus part of the court elite.

Pekah of Israel

Text

15:27 In the fifty-second year of King Azariah of Judah, Pekah son of Remaliah began to reign over Israel in Samaria; he reigned twenty years. 28 He did what was evil in the sight of the LORD; he did not depart from the sins of Jeroboam son of Nebat, which he caused Israel to sin. 29 In the days of King Pekah of Israel, King Tiglath-pileser of Assyria came and captured Ijon, Abel-beth-maacah, Janoah, Kedesh, Hazor, Gilead, and Galilee, all the land of Naphtali; and he carried the people captive to Assyria. 30 Then Hoshea son of Elah made a conspiracy against Pekah son of Remaliah, attacked him, and killed him; he reigned in place of him, in the twentieth year of Jotham son of Uzziah. 31 Now the rest of the acts of Pekah, and all that he did, are written in the Book of the Annals of the Kings of Israel.

Commentary

[15:27-28, 31] The duration of Pekah's reign at twenty years is certainly overestimated, as it cannot be made to agree with the chronology derived from the Assyrian sources. Due to a lack of further data, however, we cannot correct the estimate either. His reign is not likely to have exceeded the four years that Jepsen proposed, because the events of the reign of Tiglath-pileser III (745–727) and the last nine years of the last king Hoshea (17:1) could otherwise not be made to fit the chronology. Pekah is also mentioned, indirectly, as "son of Remaliah" in Isa 7:7-9 dating to the period of the so called Syro-Ephraimite War (see on 16:5, 7-9).

[15:29] The formula is interrupted in v. 29 with a notice on a campaign of Tiglath-pileser III. The captured cities, punished with deportation, of Ijon (Tell Dibbīn), Abel-beth-maacah (Tell Ābel el-Qamh), Janoah (Tell en-Nāᵓame), Kedesh (Tell Qedes), and Hazor (Tell el-Qedah) are spread across the upper Jordan Valley and seem to represent the marching route of the Assyrian army. The two area terms "Gilead and

Galilee" are added to the description of the Assyrian conquests. The same could be the case for the expression "all the land of Naphtali," since we have no other linguistic occurrence describing this particular area by reference to a tribe. The original list of captured cities in the north of Israel is therefore enlarged by some areas in order to show the full extent of the Assyrian conquests.

According to the eponym list, Tiglath-pileser III undertook three campaigns in the southern Levant between 734 and 732. In the canon, they are registered as "against Philistine" in 734, "against Damascus" in 733 and "against Damascus" in 732.[1] In the Annals we find only the report on the 733 campaign. It remains an open question whether the list of cities in v. 29 refers to this latter campaign or to either of the other two, and it cannot be answered without the help of further epigraphic material. According to Annals 18 and 24 Tiglath-pileser III conquered Galilee and therefore an area of Israel. The text of both versions is particularly badly preserved.[2] Of the cities mentioned only those of Hinatuna, Aruma, and Marum are completely legible; Yatbite as the fourth name can be restored with some certainty, while all other attempts at completion remain conjecture. Hinatuna is biblical Hannathon (Tell el-Bedēwīye) in Lower Galilee. Aruma is probably identical with Rumah (23:36) situated on Tell Rummān in the upper Jordan Valley. Marum is likely to be biblical Merom; the "waters of Merom" in Josh 11:5, 7 take their name from this place, which is probably the area of Lake Huleh, also in the upper Jordan Valley. Thus Merom must lie nearby. Yatbite equals Jotbah in 2 Kgs 21:19 and is located at Khirbet Ğefāt north of Hannathon in Lower Galilee.

Even if the toponyms of the Annals differ from those in v. 29, it is still very probable that they refer to the same campaign in 733. As a result of this campaign the largest part of Israel was reorganized into the Assyrian provinces Megiddo, Dor, and Gilead.[3] These events are also the background against which the new (and last) king Hoshea succeeds King Pekah.

[15:30] The sources differ on the succession by Hoshea. While v. 30 presumes the usual conspiracy-cum-assassination, Summary Inscription 4 makes the king of Assyria responsible for the act: "Peqah, their king [I/they] killed and I installed Hoshea [as king] over them."[4] It is likely that Tiglath-pileser III made Hoshea the new king of the remainder of Israel as part of the 733 campaign, in order to ensure a pro-Assyrian stance of the new vassal state. Pekah had been killed shortly before, either by Tiglath-pileser III or by his own people. The new king Hoshea was installed by the Assyrians and had to prove his loyalty through immense payments in gold and silver.

---

[1] Arthur Ungnad, *RLA,* 2:429.

[2] See Hayim Tadmor, *The Inscriptions of Tiglath-pileser III, King of Assyria* (Jerusalem: Israel Academy of Sciences and Humanities, 1994), 80–83.

[3] See Albrecht Alt, "Das System der assyrischen Provinzen auf dem Boden des Reiches Israel," in idem, *Kleine Schriften* (Munich: Beck, 1953), 2:188–205.

[4] Tadmor, *Inscriptions of Tiglath-pileser III,* 141.

According to the sources Tiglath-pileser III also began the deportations of the people of Israel.[5] Even if v. 29 does not give specific numbers, the Annals certainly do. Annal 18 gives the figure of 625 captives for an unknown city, 650 for Hannathon, and 656 for Jotbah, while Annal 24 mentions an overall figure of 13,520 deportees. The count represents the number of adult males who were accompanied into captivity by their wives and children. The figures for the individual cities should represent the surviving male population. The objective of deportation was "the destruction of national identity" and the attempt "to discourage the formation of resistance against the Assyrians."[6] It seems improbable, judging by the almost complete depopulation of the cities after 733, that the resettlement of other people instead of the Israelites had already begun at this point.

---

[5] See Bustenay Oded, *Mass Deportations and Deportees in the Neoassyrian Empire* (Wiesbaden: Reichert, 1979).

[6] Hermann Spieckermann, *Juda unter Assur in der Sargonidenzeit,* FRLANT 129 (Göttingen: Vandenhoeck & Ruprecht, 1982), 316.

Jotham of Judah

Text

15:32 In the second year of King Pekah son of Remaliah of Israel, King Jotham son of Uzziah of Judah began to reign. 33 He was twenty-five years old when he began to reign and reigned sixteen years in Jerusalem. His mother's name was Jerusha daughter of Zadok. 34 He did what was right in the sight of the LORD, just as his father Uzziah had done. 35 Nevertheless the high places were not removed; the people still sacrificed and made offerings on the high places. He built the upper gate of the house of the LORD. 36 Now the rest of the acts of Jotham, and all that he did, are they not written in the Book of the Annals of the Kings of Judah? 37 In those days the LORD began to send King Rezin of Aram and Pekah son of Remaliah against Judah. 38 Jotham slept with his ancestors, and was buried with his ancestors in the city of David, his ancestor; his son Ahaz succeeded him.

Commentary

[15:32-36, 38] Unlike his son and successor Ahaz, Jotham is evaluated positively by the Deuteronomistic Historian, save the complaint that the cult sites in the high places have not been abandoned—as was eventually done under Hezekiah (18:4). The reason for this positive judgment is mentioned in the sentence added to the formula: "He built the upper gate of the house of Yahweh." This is almost certain to be another direct access to the temple area from the north, that is, from outside the city (cf. Ezek 9:2). The sixteen years of his reign "fall into the period just before Judah became entangled in the political changes caused by Assur. Under Jotham, therefore, it enjoyed a relatively calm period compared to its neighboring states."[1]

---

[1] Würthwein, *Könige,* 2:385.

[15:37] Verse 37 is an addition that developed from 16:5, 7-9; it interrupts the flow of the concluding formula and does nothing to further our knowledge. Nothing else is remarked upon for the reign of Jotham, since the threat from the Assyrians became relevant for Judah only under Ahaz.

Introductory Formula for
Ahaz of Judah

Text

16:1 In the seventeenth year of Pekah son of Remaliah, King Ahaz son of Jotham of Judah began to reign. 2 Ahaz was twenty years old when he began to reign; he reigned sixteen years in Jerusalem. He did not do what was right in the sight of the Lord his God, as his ancestor David had done, 3 but he walked in the way of the kings of Israel. He even made his son pass through fire, according to the abominable practices of the nations whom the Lord drove out before the people of Israel. 4 He sacrificed and made offerings on the high places, on the hills, and under every green tree.

Commentary

[16:1-2] Ahaz is the short form of Jehoahaz, "Yahweh has taken"; its full form is mentioned in the inscriptions of Tiglath-pileser III as *Ia-a-ha-zi*. The judgment on the king is negative, and the name of his mother is not mentioned in the formula. The synchronism, too, is mistaken, since Pekah cannot have ruled for twenty years (see on 15:27).

[16:3-4] His introductory formula is enlarged by some further remarks on unlawful cult practices in vv. 3-4, an addition that justifies the negative evaluation retrospectively. Ahaz is found guilty of two different cult practices: child sacrifice and sacrifice outside the temple of Jerusalem. Both accusations are phrased in very general terms and give no hint about actual details of the practices. Child sacrifice was disapproved of in Israel and was not practiced in the Phoenician culture either.[1] The claim that

---

[1] See Otto Kaiser, "Den Erstgeborenen deiner Söhne sollst du mir geben: Erwägungen zum Kinderopfer im Alten Testament," in *Von der Gegenwartsbedeutung des Alten Testaments: Gesammelte Studien zur Hermeneutik und zur Redaktionsgeschichte,* ed. Volkmar Fritz et al. (Göttingen: Vandenhoeck & Ruprecht, 1984), 142–66; M. Gras, Pierre Rouillard, and Javier Teixidor, "The Phoenicians and Death," *Berytus* 39 (1991) 127–76.

Ahaz has killed his own children therefore amounts to slander. The repeated accusation of sacrifices "on the high places, on the hills, and under every green tree" is, likewise, a general condemnation without further evidence, whose aim is to discredit the king. In vv. 3-4 the redactor has tried to elaborate on the negative judgment of v. 1, without, however, moving beyond the sweeping accusations derived from Deuteronomistic theology.

The Conquest of Damascus
by Tiglath-pileser

Text

16:5 Then King Rezin of Aram and King Pekah son of Remaliah of Israel came up to wage war on Jerusalem; they besieged Ahaz but could not conquer him. 6 At that time the king of Edom recovered Elath for Edom, and drove the Judeans from Elath; and the Edomites came to Elath, where they live to this day. 7 Ahaz sent messengers to King Tiglath-pileser of Assyria, saying, "I am your servant and your son. Come up, and rescue me from the hand of the king of Aram and from the hand of the king of Israel, who are attacking me." 8 Ahaz also took the silver and gold found in the house of the LORD and in the treasures of the king's house, and sent a present to the king of Assyria. 9 The king of Assyria listened to him; the king of Assyria marched up against Damascus, and took it, carrying its people captive to Kir; then he killed Rezin.

Analysis

The introductory and concluding formulas of Ahaz frame two sections on his political and cultural activities: (1) the so-called Syro-Ephraimite War, vv. 5, 7-9, with an addition in v. 6; and (2) the building of a new altar in the temple at Jerusalem in vv. 10-16, with an addition in vv. 17-18.

Commentary

[16:5, 7-9] The events related in vv. 5, 7-9 are what the literature has called the Syro-Ephraimite War.[1] The opening situation is clearly laid out in v. 5: King Rezin of Aram

---

[1] See Joachim Begrich, "Der syrisch-efraimitische Krieg und seine weltpolitischen Zusammenhänge," *ZDMG* 83 (1929) 213–37; reprinted in idem, *Gesammelte Studien zum Alten Testament,* ThBü 21 (Munich: Kaiser, 1964), 99–120; Herbert Donner, *Geschichte des Volkes Israel und seiner Nachbarn in Grundzügen,* 2 vols., 2d ed., Grundrisse zum Alten Testament 4 (Göttingen: Vandenhoeck & Ruprecht, 1995), 2:334–47.

and Pekah, son of Remaliah and king of Israel, have marched on Judah and besieged Jerusalem in order to force King Ahaz of Judah to join the anti-Assyrian alliance. This presupposes that Ahaz had refused earlier on to side with the opposition against Ashur that had formed especially in the Aramean states of Syria and the Philistine cities of the coast.

Ahaz answers the threat by turning to the Assyrian king for protection, not without proving his loyalty by an appropriate tribute to Tiglath-pileser III and thus entering into a vassal relation. Tiglath-pileser III therefore numbers Ahaz among those who have accepted Assyrian hegemony through a tribute.[2] The threat for Ahaz is diverted by the campaign that Tiglath-pileser III launches on Damascus: Rezin has to abort the siege of Jerusalem to return to and protect his own capital.

The same situation immediately preceding the Syro-Ephraimite War is also presupposed in Isa 7:1-9.[3] The campaign of Rezin and Pekah against Ahaz can thus be dated with confidence to the period before the campaign of Tiglath-pileser III against Damascus in 733. It is possible that Ahaz's plea for support actually triggered the expedition of the Assyrian king against the Arameans as punishment. The conquest of Israel is likely to have taken place in the wake of this campaign against Damascus.

---

[2] *TUAT,* I/4, 375; also Hayim Tadmor, *The Inscriptions of Tiglath-pileser III, King of Assyria* (Jerusalem: Israel Academy of Sciences and Humanities, 1994), 171.

[3] See Otto Kaiser, *Isaiah 1–12,* trans. John Bowden, 2d ed., OTL (Philadelphia: Westminster, 1983), 136–50.

The New Altar in
the Temple at Jerusalem

Text

16:10 When King Ahaz went to Damascus to meet King Tiglath-pileser of Assyria, he saw the altar that was at Damascus. King Ahaz sent to the priest Uriah a model of the altar, and its pattern, exact in all its details. 11 The priest Uriah built the altar; in accordance with all that King Ahaz had sent from Damascus, just so did the priest Uriah build it, before King Ahaz arrived from Damascus. 12 When the king came from Damascus, the king viewed the altar. Then the king drew near to the altar, went up on it, 13 and offered his burnt offering and his grain offering, poured his drink offering, and dashed the blood of his offerings of well-being against the altar. 14 The bronze altar that was before the LORD he removed from the front of the house, from the place between his altar and the house of the LORD, and put it on the north side of his altar. 15 King Ahaz commanded the priest Uriah, saying, "Upon the great altar offer the morning burnt offering, and the evening grain offering, and the king's burnt offering, and his grain offering, with the burnt offering of all the people of the land, their grain offering, and their drink offering; then dash against it all the blood of the burnt offering, and all the blood of the sacrifice; but the bronze altar shall be for me to inquire by." 16 The priest Uriah did everything that King Ahaz commanded.

17 Then King Ahaz cut off the frames of the stands, and removed the laver from them; he removed the sea from the bronze oxen that were under it, and put it on a pediment of stone. 18 The covered portal for use on the sabbath that had been built inside the palace, and the outer entrance for the king he removed from the house of the LORD. He did this because of the king of Assyria.

Commentary

[16:10-16] The building of a new large stone altar was said to follow the model of a stone altar at Damascus, and it necessitated moving the bronze altar that had stood at the site before. As this altar is not listed among the bronze works of the temple in 1 Kgs 7:13-51, however, we have no other absolute evidence for its existence. Nor can we reconstruct the reasons for a new altar with certainty. Either it marked a change in cultic practice and more precisely the introduction of burnt offerings, or the creation of two adjacent altars is linked to the necessity of sacrifices for the Assyrian pantheon.[1] The background for these measures is not sufficiently clear as long as we do not know the degree of repression that the Assyrians imposed on Judah in cultic matters, for which we lack source evidence.

The new altar served for both grain offerings and burnt offerings, which established it as the center of the cult. For grain offerings vegetable goods were placed in bowls next to the altar and then burnt symbolically with the help of incense. Burnt offerings involved the burning of the entire animal on the altar, in order to consecrate it to God; thus "the act of burning is the essential component of the ritual."[2] One thing, however, is clear: "the cult of sacrifice to Yahweh is closely connected with the new altar."[3]

[16:17-18] The addendum tells first of the removal of all figurative decorations on temple equipment. According to the descriptions of temple equipment in 1 Kgs 7:27-39, items were decorated with lions, bulls, and cherubim. Ahaz removed these just like the bronze bulls on which the sea rested (1 Kgs 7:44). Pictorial representations of animals are thereby expelled from the temple.

The second notice refers to changes in the temple area. One thing is the removal of a special seat for the king from the temple court, another the walling up of the "king's entry." This "king's entry" is likely to be a passageway from the palace to the temple court, rather than a separate entrance into the temple (see on 1 Kgs 7:12). Both measures imply a loss of privileges for the king, which he enjoys as ruler and highest priest at the state sanctuary. The reasons for this reduction in royal privileges are beyond recovery. It seems to be motivated less by the Assyrian hegemony than by the increased position of the Zadokite priesthood at the temple in Jerusalem.

---

[1] For the former, see Volkmar Fritz, "'Bis an die Hörner des Altars': Erwägungen zur Praxis des Brandopfers in Israel," in *Gottes Recht als Lebensraum: Festschrift für Hans Jochen Boecker,* ed. Peter Mommer et al. (Neukirchen-Vluyn: Neukirchener, 1993), 61–70; for the latter, see Hermann Spieckermann, *Juda unter Assur in der Sargonidenzeit,* FRLANT 129 (Göttingen: Vandenhoeck & Ruprecht, 1982), 362–69.

[2] Rolf Rendtorff, *Studien zur Geschichte des Opfers im Alten Israel,* WMANT 24 (Neukirchen-Vluyn: Neukirchener, 1967), 235.

[3] Würthwein, *Könige,* 2:390.

Concluding Formula for Ahaz

Text

16:19 Now the rest of the acts of Ahaz that he did, are they not written in the Book of the Annals of the Kings of Judah? 20 Ahaz slept with his ancestors, and was buried with his ancestors in the city of David; his son Hezekiah succeeded him.

Commentary

[16:19-20] This is a standard formula including the reference to the "Annals of the Kings of Judah" and the information on death and burial. Prior to the positive report on King Hezekiah that follows (18:1—20:21), the Deuteronomistic Historian mentions Hoshea, the last king of Israel, the destruction of the northern kingdom (17:1-23), and its consequences for the history of the country with regard to the changes in cult practice (17:24-41).

Introductory Formula for
Hoshea of Israel

Text

17:1 In the twelfth year of King Ahaz of Judah, Hoshea son of Elah began to reign in Samaria over Israel; he reigned nine years. 2 He did what was evil in the sight of the LORD, yet not like the kings of Israel who were before him.

Commentary

[17:1-2] Hoshea rises to power in Samaria during the political conflict accompanying the campaigns of Tiglath-pileser III against Philistine and Damascus in 734–732; as a representative of pro-Assyrian policy he succeeds his assassinated predecessor, Pekah (see on 15:30). In any case, Hoshea was king by the grace of the Assyrians. The chronology of his nine-year reign is difficult to establish, because it is unclear whether those nine years reach up to his being taken captive by Shalmaneser V (17:4) or the conquest of Samaria by the Assyrian king (17:6). Suggestions reach from 731–723 (Jepsen and Donner) to 730–722 (Andersen), 732–724 (Cogan and Tadmor) and 732–723 (Thiele). As with other chronological problems, there is no straightforward solution. The judgment of Hoshea by the Deuteronomistic Historian is negative, even if we miss the usual reference to the "sin of Jeroboam." Compared to the other kings of Israel the judgment is even moderate, perhaps a gesture to honor his later opposition to Assyrian hegemony. We can, however, not draw any historical conclusions from this modified formula. The introductory formula marks also the beginning of the report of the end of the northern kingdom (17:36), which is given overall evaluation in 17:21-23. Further theological interpretations of the destruction of Israel are added later in 17:7-12, 18, and 17:13-17, 20.[1]

---

[1] See Würthwein, *Könige,* 2:396–97.

The Downfall of Israel

Text

17:3 King Shalmaneser of Assyria came up against him; Hoshea became his vassal, and paid him tribute. 4 But the king of Assyria found treachery in Hoshea; for he had sent messengers to King So of Egypt, and offered no tribute to the king of Assyria, as he had done year by year; therefore the king of Assyria confined him and imprisoned him.

5 Then the king of Assyria invaded all the land and came to Samaria; for three years he besieged it. 6 In the ninth year of Hoshea the king of Assyria captured Samaria; he carried the Israelites away to Assyria. He placed them in Halah, on the Habor, the river of Gozan, and in the cities of the Medes.

7 This occurred because the people of Israel had sinned against the LORD their God, who had brought them up out of the land of Egypt from under the hand of Pharaoh king of Egypt. They had worshiped other gods 8 and walked in the customs of the nations whom the LORD drove out before the people of Israel, and in the customs that the kings of Israel had introduced. 9 The people of Israel secretly did things that were not right against the LORD their God. They built for themselves high places at all their towns, from watchtower to fortified city; 10 they set up for themselves pillars and sacred poles on every high hill and under every green tree; 11 there they made offerings on all the high places, as the nations did whom the LORD carried away before them. They did wicked things, provoking the LORD to anger; 12 they served idols, of which the LORD had said to them, "You shall not do this." 13 Yet the LORD warned Israel and Judah by every prophet and every seer, saying, "Turn from your evil ways and keep my commandments and my statutes, in accordance with all the law that I commanded your ancestors and that I sent to you by my servants the prophets." 14 They would not listen but were stubborn, as their ancestors had been, who did not believe in the LORD their God. 15 They despised his statutes, and his covenant that he made with their ancestors, and the warnings that he gave them. They went after false idols and became false; they followed the

nations that were around them, concerning whom the LORD had commanded them that they should not do as they did. 16 They rejected all the commandments of the LORD their God and made for themselves cast images of two calves; they made a sacred pole, worshiped all the host of heaven, and served Baal. 17 They made their sons and their daughters pass through fire; they used divination and augury; and they sold themselves to do evil in the sight of the LORD, provoking him to anger. 18 Therefore the LORD was very angry with Israel and removed them out of his sight; none was left but the tribe of Judah alone.

19 Judah also did not keep the commandments of the LORD their God but walked in the customs that Israel had introduced. 20 The LORD rejected all the descendants of Israel; he punished them and gave them into the hand of plunderers, until he had banished them from his presence. 21 When he had torn Israel from the house of David, they made Jeroboam son of Nebat king. Jeroboam drove Israel from following the LORD and made them commit great sin. 22 The people of Israel continued in all the sins that Jeroboam committed; they did not depart from them 23 until the LORD removed Israel out of his sight, as he had foretold through all his servants the prophets. So Israel was exiled from their own land to Assyria until this day.

Commentary

[17:3-6] The historical account in vv. 3-6 covers the reign of the Assyrian King Shalmaneser V, who ruled from 727 to 722 as son and successor of Tiglath-pileser III. The following events regarding the history of Israel are mentioned in the correct order:

1. tribute by Hoshea (v. 3);
2. conspiracy with Egypt and ceasing of payment to Ashur (v. 4);
3. Hoshea taken captive by Shalmaneser V (v. 4), who besieges Samaria (v. 5);
4. conquest of Samaria and deportation of its population (v. 6).

The chronology of events is not entirely certain; in addition, we lack annals for this particular Assyrian king. The reign of Shalmaneser V and the destruction of Samaria are mentioned briefly in the Babylonian Chronicle.[1] The frame is established by the reign of Shalmaneser V (727–722).

1. Hoshea had paid tribute to Tiglath-pileser III already, which amounted to the sum of ten talents of gold and x talents of silver per year.[2] The payment of tribute was the outward sign that Assyria's hegemony was acknowledged. This acknowledgment was the condition for Hoshea to be made king over Israel by Tiglath-pileser

---

[1] *TGI*, 60; *TUAT*, I/4, 401–2.

[2] Hayim Tadmor, *The Inscriptions of Tiglath-pileser III, King of Assyria* (Jerusalem: Israel Academy of Sciences and Humanities, 1994), 141.

III. After his succession by Shalmaneser V Hoshea initially continued to pay the annual tribute.

2. It is not specified when Hoshea chose to discontinue the tribute. In any case, his decision signifies the end of the acceptance of hegemony. Hoshea switches to the camp of the anti-Assyrian coalition, a move that is unlikely to have happened without prior reassurance from the Egyptians. Hoshea had apparently entered negotiations with the former empire in order to shake off the yoke of tribute obligations. The Deuteronomistic Historian does not appear to have had more specific information at hand. The Egyptian pharaoh is not named; the name "So" that is given is more likely to be a distortion of the Egyptian word for the title of king (*nj-św.t*). The complex conditions of the late Egyptian period remain obscure, as does the identity of the unnamed pharaoh; it is possible that it is a minor king of the Delta. The political claims made by the pharaonic empire from the Twenty-second Dynasty must have come into conflict with those of Assyria by the end of the eighth century at the latest. Assyria subsequently conquered Egypt in the seventh century and ruled it under Esarhaddon.[3]

3. Shalmaneser V seems to have reacted promptly when Hoshea broke from him, and launched a military campaign. The capture of Hoshea precedes the siege of Samaria and might be connected to another battle that is not mentioned. During the siege Israel is already no longer under the rule of Hoshea. The duration of three years points to a strong anti-Assyrian coalition within the capital of Israel that had to survive and sustain resistance against the Assyrian power.

4. With Samaria the last bastion against Assyria is brought down. Even if the three years do not amount to a full thirty-six months, the duration of the siege reveals the intensity of the fight against Assyria in Israel. The capture of Samaria is also the only event that the Babylonian Chronicle mentions for the reign of Shalmaneser.[4] After the takeover the population is deported. Its resettlement to other areas of the Assyrian Empire is expressly mentioned: Halah is a province northeast of Nineveh,[5] and the name of the river Habor covers the upper area along the Habûr, specified further by the mention of Gozan (Tell Halâf). Finally, the "cities of the Medes" are to be found on the Iranian plateau north of the Tigris River, with no further specification. These statements indicate that deportation took place to three different areas of the new Assyrian Empire. It is not clear whether the reorganization of the former vassal state into the province of Samaria (Samerīna) occurred in the wake of the conquest by Shalmaneser V or after another punishment raid under Sargon II in 720. Sargon deported another 27,280 people and depopulated the country even further.[6] Repopu-

---

[3] See Kenneth A. Kitchen, *The Third Intermediate Period in Egypt (1100–650 BC)*, 2d ed. (Warminster: Aris & Phillips 1973), 362–93.

[4] See Stefan Timm, "Die Eroberung Samarias aus assyrisch-babylonischer Sicht," *WO* 20/21 (1989–90) 62–82.

[5] J. N. Postgate, *RLA*, 4:58.

[6] *TGI*, 60–70; *TUAT*, I/4, 382.

lation on former state territory may have begun under Shalmaneser V, and Sargon II may have continued the policy (see on 17:24). Once Shalmaneser V had ended the autonomy of the state of Israel, all further deportations by Sargon II finalized the destruction of the northern kingdom.

[17:21-23] In vv. 21-23 the Deuteronomistic Historian passes judgment on the events. The reason for the downfall of the northern kingdom is the "sin of Jeroboam," who made Bethel and Dan into state sanctuaries (see 1 Kgs 12:26-32). This accusation, which had run through the account like a red thread, is now reaching its final point: the end of Israel is to be sought in its beginning; the destruction of the kingdom founded by Jeroboam is seen as the punishment for turning away from the temple at Jerusalem as the central sanctuary, which amounts to a turning away from the cult of Yahweh. The involvement of the people in this act of turning away is explicitly underlined, since not only the king but the entire population are affected by the destruction. The concluding remark about the deportation, which thematizes once more the loss of the homeland, may be a later addition.

[17:7-12, 18] A first addition stresses again the turning from Yahweh as the reason for the destruction. To "fall away" implies both the worship of other gods and the inappropriate worship of Yahweh. The Israelites are responsible for their fate, because they did not follow the Deuteronomic stipulation to worship Yahweh alone (Deut 4:35, 39). This wrong cult is associated with the objects "pillars and sacred poles (asherahs)." In this case "pillars" signify stone images of foreign deities; asherahs are cultic wooden representations of the goddess Asherah. The symbolic representation in the form of a wooden plank or pole was seemingly appropriate for Asherah as a fertility goddess, and it might have its roots in the worship of her in the form of a tree. In the second millennium her worship was already widespread in the ancient Near East, and in the Ugaritic sources she is called the wife of El, father of the gods, and mother of all gods.[7] The worship of Asherah as giver of fertility and goddess beside Yahweh is attested for the time of the kingship by the inscriptions from Kuntillet 'Ajrūd, Khirbet el-Qom, and Khirbet el-Muqenna'.[8] With the worship of other deities Israel acts against the exclusivity of Yahweh in the temple at Jerusalem as it was stipulated by the Deuteronomic-Deuteronomistic theology. What other offenses were committed with the "wicked things" mentioned in v. 11 is not specified.

[17:13-17, 20, 19] The second addition (vv. 13-17, 20) focuses on how Israel has disregarded the words of the prophets who were sent to proclaim the will of Yahweh.

---

[7] See Hartmut Gese, Maria Höfner, and Kurt Rudolph, *Die Religionen Altsyriens, Altarabiens und der Mandäer,* Die Religionen der Menschheit 10/4 (Stuttgart: Kohlhammer, 1970), 149–55.

[8] See Saul M. Olyan, *Asherah and the Cult of Yahweh in Israel,* SBLMS 34 (Atlanta: Scholars, 1988).

The prophets are understood to be less workers of miracles than "proclaimers of the law, urging to repent."[9] "Disregard" means the disregard of the law of the covenant granted by Yahweh to his people; the historical development leading to the destruction is thus a punishment for the broken covenant. The covenant had obliged Israel to acknowledge and worship Yahweh as the only God and to fulfill his will by keeping his commandments (cf. Deut 26:16-18), and it is mutually binding.[10] Yahweh punishes the broken covenant by abolishing Israel's sovereignty as a people at the hand of the Assyrians. The Deuteronomistic redactor once more makes clear that Israel alone is to blame for its bitter fate; he also adds a negative judgment on Judah in v. 19, comparing its behavior to that of Israel.

---

[9] Würthwein, *Könige,* 2:397.

[10] On the "covenant" as the defining aspect of the relation between God and his people see Lothar Perlitt, *Bundestheologie im Alten Testament,* WMANT 36 (Neukirchen-Vluyn: Neukirchener, 1969), 54–128.

The Foreign Nations in
the Cities of Samaria

Text

17:24 The king of Assyria brought people from Babylon, Cuthah, Avva, Hamath, and Sepharvaim, and placed them in the cities of Samaria in place of the people of Israel; they took possession of Samaria, and settled in its cities. 25 When they first settled there, they did not worship the LORD; therefore the LORD sent lions among them, which killed some of them. 26 So the king of Assyria was told, "The nations that you have carried away and placed in the cities of Samaria do not know the law of the god of the land; therefore he has sent lions among them; they are killing them, because they do not know the law of the god of the land." 27 Then the king of Assyria commanded, "Send there one of the priests whom you carried away from there; let him go and live there, and teach them the law of the god of the land." 28 So one of the priests whom they had carried away from Samaria came and lived in Bethel; he taught them how they should worship the LORD.

29 But every nation still made gods of its own and put them in the shrines of the high places that the people of Samaria had made, every nation in the cities in which they lived; 30 the people of Babylon made Succoth-benoth, the people of Cuth made Nergal, the people of Hamath made Ashima; 31 the Avvites made Nibhaz and Tartak; the Sepharvites burned their children in the fire to Adrammelech and Anammelech, the gods of Sepharvaim. 32 They also worshiped the LORD and appointed from among themselves all sorts of people as priests of the high places, who sacrificed for them in the shrines of the high places. 33 So they worshiped the LORD but also served their own gods, after the manner of the nations from among whom they had been carried away. 34 To this day they continue to practice their former customs.

They do not worship the Lord and they do not follow the statutes or the ordinances or the law or the commandment that the Lord commanded the children of Jacob, whom he named Israel. 35 The Lord had made a covenant with them and commanded them, "You shall not worship other gods or bow yourselves to them or serve them or sacrifice to them, 36 but you shall worship the Lord, who brought you out of the land of Egypt with great power and with an outstretched arm; you shall bow yourselves to him, and to him you shall sacrifice. 37 The statutes and the ordinances and the law and the commandment that he wrote for you, you shall always be careful to observe. You shall not worship other gods; 38 you shall not forget the covenant that I have made with you. You shall not worship other gods, 39 but you shall worship the Lord your God; he will deliver you out of the hand of all your enemies." 40 They would not listen, however, but they continued to practice their former custom.

41 So these nations worshiped the Lord, but also served their carved images; to this day their children and their children's children continue to do as their ancestors did.

Analysis

This section on the resettlement of foreign nations and their cults in the northern kingdom features two additions. The first, vv. 25-28, tells of the instruction of the new settlers in the cult of Yahweh; the second, vv. 5-30, focuses once more on the theology of the covenant and the duty to fulfill its commandments. With v. 34b also a later addition, the original core narrative on the foreign nations and their cult it is reduced to vv. 24, 29-34a, 41. Its aim is not an all-encompassing account; rather, the details exemplify the new, detestable state of affairs.

Commentary

[17:24] This verse states the origin of the new settlers: Babylon, mentioned first because of its importance, is the capital of Babylonia, situated on the lower banks of the Euphrates River. It is unlikely that part of an urban population would have been resettled, and we are probably dealing with a delegation of officials. Cuthah is a site in northern Babylonia, between the cities of Babylon and Sippar, probably at Tell Ibrahīm. Nothing can be said about the location of Avva.[1] Hamath can hardly indicate the Aramean capital on the Orontes River; its distance to the new kingdom of Samaria would be too short.[2] Hamath is thus more likely identical with Akkadian *Amati* in southern Mesopotamia.[3] Sepharvaim is scarcely a misspelled version of Babylonian

---

[1] For various suggestions see Gray, *I & II Kings,* 651.

[2] See the list of place names mentioned for the deportations in Bustenay Oded, *Mass Deportations and Deportees in the Neo-Assyrian Empire* (Wiesbaden: Reichert, 1979), 116–35.

[3] See Ran Zadok, "Geographical and Onomastic Notes," *JANESCU* 8 (1976) 117 [113–26].

Sippar;[4] instead, it is reminiscent of Akkadian *Sipíra'ni* near Nippur. Like Babylonia and Cuthah, the remaining places can therefore be located in southern Mesopotamia; this far-flung region is the origin of the new settlers of the newly established province of Samaria. The method of the Assyrian deportations to settle people as far away from their former homes as possible curtails their hope for return from the beginning. Deportation in this case did not involve the resettling of an entire population; rather, part of the country's population would stay put and mix with the new settlers over time.

[17:29-34a, 41] That those settlers brought their own pantheon with them is considered most relevant by the Deuteronomistic Historian. The worship of Yahweh and of foreign gods are juxtaposed in practice (vv. 29-34a, 41), and the individual deities, some of whose names have been distorted in the biblical account, are associated with individual communities. "Succoth-benoth" is the wife of Marduk (Sarpanitu), who is surprisingly not mentioned in the text, and the main goddess of Babylon. Nergal is the god of the underworld, whose main site was established at Cuth. In mythology and hymns he is given both terrifying and life-giving attributes: "He was considered the god of burning destroying heat, . . . of epidemics, fevers and the plague; . . . he is the master of Hades, the lord of battle and hunt. . . . He is also a benevolent god of the fields who grants fertility and life, and a wise judge."[5] Ashima, worshiped by the people of Hamath, reappears in Amos 8:14 as the goddess Ashima, although to this day there is no evidence from the Akkadian sources that would help clarify her origin and function.[6] The Avvite god Nibhaz remains entirely obscure. In the name "Tartak" the two goddesses 'Anat and 'Astarte have merged, both well-known members of the Ugaritic parthenon.[7] In Hellenistic times Atagartis became the main goddess of greater Syria, and in the Roman period she was finally the Goddess of the East, the Dea Syria.[8] The Sepharvites are accused of child sacrifice, which was forbidden in Israel (see on 16:3). There is no evidence from the Israelite environment for the next two deities that are mentioned; their names might have been formed in analogy to the divine name of Adadmilki, "King Adad," as it is contained in the late Assyrian name *Adad-milki-ila-a*, "Adadmilki is my god."[9] Adrammelech would then have to be read as "King Adad," Anammelech as "Anat of Melech" (i.e., of Adrammelech). Both names are therefore artificial creations with no real equivalent in the religious history

---

[4] *Pace* G. R. Driver, "Geographical Problems," *ErIsr* 5 (1958) 16*–20*.

[5] Franz Marius Theodor Böhl, *Opera Minora* (1953), 211.

[6] See E. Koenig, "Die Gottheit Aschima," *ZAW* 34 (1914) 16–30.

[7] See Hartmut Gese, Maria Höfner, and Kurt Rudolph, *Die Religionen Altsyriens, Altarabiens und der Mandäer,* Die Religionen der Menschheit 10/4 (Stuttgart: Kohlhammer, 1970), 156–64.

[8] See Monika Hörig, *Dea Syria: Studien zur religiösen Tradition der Fruchtbarkeitsgöttin in Vorderasien,* AOAT 208 (Neukirchen-Vluyn: Neukirchener, 1978).

[9] See Otto Eissfeldt, "Adrammelek und Demarus," in idem, *Kleine Schriften,* 6 vols. (Tübingen: Mohr/Siebeck, 1966), 3:335–39.

of the ancient Near East. The intention of the Deuteronomistic Historian is to name one or two of the deities of each ethnic group and in this way to add credibility to his descriptions of foreign cults. In consequence we are better advised to treat his account as a polemical strategy rather than as an accurate description of the political and religious circumstances.

[17:32] This verse, accordingly, discredits even the worship of Yahweh, because it is practiced in the high places. Whatever the cult practice behind those "high places" may actually have been, the Deuteronomistic Historian uses it as a synonym for unlawful worship, as its site is outside Jerusalem; the Deuteronomic-Deuteronomistic attitude considers each form of worship of Yahweh outside the temple of Jerusalem incorrect and detestable.[10]

[17:33-34a, 41] Verse 33 continues to state the juxtaposition of the worship of Yahweh and foreign cults, a juxtaposition that contradicts the first rule of Deuteronomic-Deuteronomistic theology, the exclusivity of Yahweh.[11] Thus according to v. 41, the population of Samaria, worshiping both Yahweh and other gods, did not comply with this commandment. "The account endeavors to show that the present inhabitants of Samaria are of foreign origin and that they practice a mixed religion that contradicts the first and second commandments."[12] It follows that the later history of Samaria is seen in the context of the northern kingdom, not Judah, judging by its cultic affinity. The foundation for the later rejection of the Samaritans is laid here. Although they are considered worshipers of Yahweh, the Samaritans are not keepers of the covenant with God, a judgment that has colored the relationship of Judaism and the Samaritans until today.[13]

[17:25-28] The two interpolations are to bolster the negative judgment: vv. 25-28 claim that the Assyrian king ordered the reintroduction of the cult of Yahweh, an order that implies that the cult had completely disappeared in the past. The reintroduction is linked to the priesthood at Bethel and is therefore discredited a priori: Bethel was the site where Jeroboam had established the state sanctuary (see on 1 Kgs 12:26-30). Bethel and its sanctuary symbolize the "abomination of Jeroboam," that is, the falling away of the northern kingdom from the lawful worship of Yahweh in the south. The Deuteronomistic Historian rejects the new cult of Yahweh in the area of the former northern kingdom from the beginning, without giving any further details on actual practice.

---

[10] See Patrick H. Vaughan, *The Meaning of "bamâ" in the Old Testament: A Study of Etymological, Textual and Archaeological Evidence,* SOTSMS 4 (London: Cambridge Univ. Press, 1974).

[11] See Norbert Lohfink, *Das Hauptgebot: Eine Untersuchung literarischer Einleitungsfragen zu Dtn 5–11,* AnBib 20 (Rome: Pontifical Biblical Institute Press, 1963).

[12] Würthwein, *Könige,* 2:400.

[13] See Shemaryahu Talmon, *Die Samaritaner in Vergangenheit und Gegenwart* (1972).

[17:35-40] In the second interpolation a redactor has again spelled out the basic parameters of Deuteronomic-Deuteronomistic theology: the link among history, covenant, and obligation. Würthwein has rightly pointed out that this is a direct address to the new settlers. The explicit reference to the exodus from Egypt as the foundational deed of Yahweh makes clear that the new peoples "cannot ever be true worshipers of Yahweh: the worship of Yahweh is inseparable from its [Israel's] history."[14] Once more it is stressed that the inhabitants of the province of Samaria have no part in the covenant of Yahweh and Israel; the Samaritans, as they are later called, are therefore not part of the community of Judaism.[15]

---

[14] Würthwein, *Könige,* 2:401.

[15] On the Samaritans in antiquity see Jürgen Zangenberg, *Samareia: Antike Quellen zur Geschichte und Kultur der Samaritaner in deutscher Übersetzung,* Texte und Arbeiten zur neutestamentlichen Zeitalter 15 (Tübingen: Francke, 1994).

The Kingdom of Judah
after the Destruction of Israel

2 Kings 18:1-8

Introductory Formula for Hezekiah

Text

18:1 In the third year of King Hoshea son of Elah of Israel, Hezekiah son of King Ahaz of Judah began to reign. 2 He was twenty-five years old when he began to reign; he reigned twenty-nine years in Jerusalem. His mother's name was Abi daughter of Zechariah. 3 He did what was right in the sight of the LORD just as his ancestor David had done. 4 He removed the high places, broke down the pillars, and cut down the sacred pole. He broke in pieces the bronze serpent that Moses had made, for until those days the people of Israel had made offerings to it; it was called Nehushtan. 5 He trusted in the LORD the God of Israel; so that there was no one like him among all the kings of Judah after him, or among those who were before him. 6 For he held fast to the LORD; he did not depart from following him but kept the commandments that the LORD commanded Moses. 7 The LORD was with him; wherever he went, he prospered. He rebelled against the king of Assyria and would not serve him. 8 He attacked the Philistines as far as Gaza and its territory, from watchtower to fortified city.

Analysis

The formula differs in some respects from its usual pattern. Its bulk, composed by the Deuteronomistic Historian, is contained in vv. 1-7a, while vv. 7b-8 add historical information lifted straight from the Annals or another source. The deviations regard mainly the so-called cult reform in v. 4 and the description of the piety of the king in vv. 5-7a.

Commentary

[18:1-3] The synchronism of v. 1 does not agree with 18:3, although it offers, in my opinion, the more accurate chronology (see on 20:6). The name "Hezekiah," with the meaning, "Yahweh is my strength" is confessional in character and is attested on a Hebrew seal as well as in Assyrian inscriptions.[1] His mother, Abi, probably hails from Jerusalem, even if this is not explicitly said of her father, Zechariah. Hezekiah's reign of twenty-nine years is long compared to the sixteen years of his father, Ahaz. Both figures point to increased political stability in Judah during the second half of the eighth century. Initially, Hezekiah continued the pro-Assyrian policy of his father and paid the annual tribute.

[18:4] The positive judgment of Hezekiah is founded on his measures taken in cultic matters, summarized in v. 4. Hezekiah abolished the cult sites outside Jerusalem and in this way advanced cult centralization, that is, the limitation of worship to the temple in Jerusalem as the only seat of Yahweh. It is unclear which precise measures are behind the reform; what is clear is that the measures were not imposed in an attempt to abolish the Assyrian state cult, which was probably introduced out of duty toward the sovereign. The breaking of the bronze serpent in the temple cannot be accurately established either. As a cult symbol it was linked back to Moses and authorized through the short episode in Num 21:4b-9; still, it seems to have been a ritual object whose veneration in the temple was at least questionable. The general statements of this passage are therefore "a proof that cult centralization was attributed to Hezekiah at a later stage, rather than proof that he actually carried out such a reform."[2]

[18:5-7a] These verses elevate Hezekiah as a paradigm of trust in Yahweh and of keeping the commandments. The language is characteristic of that of the Deuteronomistic redactor who also formulated Joshua 23.[3]

[18:7b-8] With vv. 7b and 8 two undated historical notices are added to the formula. The victory over the Philistines as far as Gaza implies a campaign against the cities of Philistia, although Hezekiah is not likely to have gained rule over the entire coastal plain as a result. The events are best dated before the campaign of Sennacherib against Judah, with further details unfortunately lacking. The move on Gaza means also an offensive against the Assyrian Empire, since Gaza had already been subjected to Ashur under Sargon II.[4] A military strength has to be presupposed that might also

---

[1] For the former, see Ruth Hestrin and Mikhal Dayagi, "A Seal Impression of a Servant of King Hezekiah," *IEJ* 24 (1974) 27–29; for the latter, *TUAT,* I/4, 389–90.

[2] Würthwein, *Könige,* 2:411.

[3] See Volkmar Fritz, *Das Buch Josua,* HAT 7 (Tübingen: Mohr/Siebeck, 1994), 227–32.

[4] See *TUAT,* I/4, 379.

have played a part in falling away from Ashur. The objective of the campaign may have been to win additional support for the fight against Ashur; in its wake Hezekiah may also have conquered the city of Ekron by taking captive and dethroning King Padi, as is suggested by the account on the prism.[5] Hezekiah's anti-Assyrian turn came probably shortly after Sennacherib's accession to the throne in 705 or 704.[6]

---

[5] *TUAT,* I/4, 389; see Siegfried Mittmann, "Hiskia und die Philister," *JNSL* 16 (1990) 91–106.

[6] On the fate of the Philistine cities under Assyrian hegemony in the second half of the eighth century see Hayim Tadmor, "Philistia under Assyrian Rule," *BA* 29 (1966) 86–102.

Shalmaneser's Advance on Samaria

Text

18:9 In the fourth year of King Hezekiah, which was the seventh year of King Hoshea son of Elah of Israel, King Shalmaneser of Assyria came up against Samaria, besieged it, 10 and at the end of three years, took it. In the sixth year of Hezekiah, which was the ninth year of King Hoshea of Israel, Samaria was taken. 11 The king of Assyria carried the Israelites away to Assyria, settled them in Halah, on the Habor, the river of Gozan, and in the cities of the Medes, 12 because they did not obey the voice of the LORD their God but transgressed his covenant—all that Moses the servant of the LORD had commanded; they neither listened nor obeyed.

Commentary

[**18:9-12**] This section repeats briefly the information on the conquest of Samaria by Shalmaneser V, which brought the northern kingdom to an end. It is the work of a redactor who recounts the events known from 17:5-6, with a special focus on their chronology (see on 17:5-6).

Hezekiah Pays Tribute to Sennacherib

Text

18:13 In the fourteenth year of King Hezekiah, King Sennacherib of Assyria came up against all the fortified cities of Judah and captured them. 14 King Hezekiah of Judah sent to the king of Assyria at Lachish, saying, "I have done wrong; withdraw from me; whatever you impose on me I will bear." The king of Assyria demanded of King Hezekiah of Judah three hundred talents of silver and thirty talents of gold. 15 Hezekiah gave him all the silver that was found in the house of the LORD and in the treasuries of the king's house. 16 At that time Hezekiah stripped the gold from the doors of the temple of the LORD, and from the doorposts that King Hezekiah of Judah had overlaid and gave it to the king of Assyria.

Commentary

[18:13-16] Hezekiah appears to have been the driving force of the anti-Assyrian coalition of the southern Levant. In 701 Sennacherib launched a massive campaign in order to suppress the insurrection, well documented in his inscriptions.[1] The inscriptions do not say which of those cities and states paying tribute submitted again, so we cannot determine the extent of the coalition. However, that the kings of Egypt and Ethiopia (probably the minor kings of the Delta and Shabaka, the pharaoh of the so-called Ethiopian Dynasty) intervened in the struggle is evidence enough of the scope of opposition against Ashur. The battle between the opposition and the Assyrian army in the coastal plain near Elteke (Tell eš-Šallāf) resulted in utter defeat for the coalition

---

[1] *TUAT,* I/4, 388–91. For a detailed historical account according to Assyrian and biblical sources, see Herbert Donner, *Geschichte des Volkes Israel und seiner Nachbarn in Grundzügen,* 2 vols., 2d ed., Grundrisse zum Alten Testament 4/1-2 (Göttingen: Vandenhoeck & Ruprecht, 1995), 2:347–60.

forces and ended once and for all their aspirations of political independence from Ashur. The consequences for Hezekiah and the kingdom of Judah were devastating. What followed were the conquest of forty-six unnamed cities and the deportation of their inhabitants (the number given by Sennacherib is, at 200,150, too high), the siege of Jerusalem by Assyrian troops, and the annexation of large parts of territory. Judah did not become a province of Assyria, however, but was added to the territories of the pro-Assyrian kings of Philistia: Mitinti of Ashdod, Padi of Ekron, and Silbel of Gaza. Once Hezekiah had resubmitted to Ashur by paying tribute, he remained king by name only and his rule was limited to Jerusalem and its immediate surroundings. Judah was reduced to a city-state after areas like the Shephelah and the mountain ranges had been cut off, yet it did not cease to exist.[2] Judah apparently did not recover from this defeat; there was no further insurrection until the end of the Neo-Assyrian Empire in the last two decades of the seventh century. Judah was probably restored within its former boundaries under Manasseh, the successor of Hezekiah, who remained a loyal vassal of Ashur all his life (see on 21:1-18).

Contemporary with his campaign against Judah is Sennacherib's siege and conquest of Lachish, which are represented on reliefs in his palace at Nineveh, even if they are not expressly mentioned in the biblical account.[3] Represented is a sequence of events that gives a vivid impression of the siege and conquest of a Judean city by Assyrian troops. Excavation has shown that the city conquered by Sennacherib is identical with the settlement in stratum III at Lachish.[4] At the same time Hezekiah renewed his vows of submission to Ashur and in this way saved Jerusalem from destruction.

Submission was accompanied by payment of a new tribute, which is given in v. 14 as 30 talents of gold and 300 talents of silver, while the prism inscription claims an amount of 30 talents of gold and 800 talents of silver. There is no obvious explanation for the discrepancy; what is obvious, however, is that Sennacherib stresses the amount of tribute paid when he refers to Hezekiah's further contributions. The amount of 800 talents of silver may include the annual tribute, and the prism inscription states explicitly that the tribute was delivered to the Assyrian capital, Nineveh. The exceptional amount that Sennacherib demanded was paid out of the temple treasure and the royal treasury, over both of which Hezekiah had authority.

---

[2] See Albrecht Alt, "Die territorialgeschichtliche Bedeutung von Sanheribs Eingriff in Palästina," in idem, *Kleine Schriften zur Geschichte des Volkes Israels* (Munich: Beck, 1953), 2:242–49; M. Elat, "The Political Status of the Kingdom of Judah within the Assyrian Empire in the 7th Century B.C.E.," in *Investigations at Lachish: The Sanctuary and the Residency (Lachish V)*, ed. Yohanan Aharoni, Publications of the Institute of Archaeology 4 (Tel Aviv: Gateway, 1975), 61–70.

[3] See their reproduction in David Ussishkin, *The Conquest of Lachish by Sennacherib*, Publications of the Institute of Archaeology 6 (Tel Aviv: Tel Aviv Univ., Institute of Archaeology, 1982).

[4] See David Ussishkin, "The Destruction of Lachish by Sennacherib and the Dating of the Royal Judean Storage Jars," *TA* 4 (1977) 28–60.

[18:16] The redactional notice is to stress the sacrifices involved in raising the tribute; the temple decorations donated by Hezekiah himself are removed to hand over the metal to the Assyrian king.[5]

---

[5] On the historical events see in more detail Leo L. Honor, *Sennacherib's Invasion of Palestine* (New York: AMS, 1966); Tomislav Vuk, *Wiedererkaufte Freiheit: Der Feldzug Sanheribs gegen Juda nach dem Invasionsbericht 2. Kön. 18,13-16* (Jersualem: Studium Biblicum Franciscanum, 1984); Ernst Vogt, *Der Aufstand Hiskijas und die Belagerung Jerusalems 701 v. Chr.,* AnBib 106 (Rome: Pontifical Biblical Institute Press, 1986).

Sennacherib at Jerusalem

Text

18:17 The king of Assyria sent the Tartan, the Rabsaris, and the Rabshakeh with a great army from Lachish to King Hezekiah at Jerusalem. They went up and came to Jerusalem. When they arrived, they came and stood by the conduit of the upper pool, which is on the highway to the Fuller's Field. 18 When they called for the king, there came out to them Eliakim son of Hilkiah, who was in charge of the palace, and Shebnah the secretary, and Joah son of Asaph, the recorder.

19 The Rabshakeh said to them, "Say to Hezekiah: Thus says the great king, the king of Assyria: On what do you base this confidence of yours? 20 Do you think that mere words are strategy and power for war? On whom do you now rely, that you have rebelled against me? 21 See, you are relying now on Egypt, that broken reed of a staff, which will pierce the hand of anyone who leans on it. Such is Pharaoh king of Egypt to all who rely on him. 22 But if you say to me, 'We rely on the LORD our God,' is it not he whose high places and altars Hezekiah has removed, saying to Judah and to Jerusalem, 'You shall worship before this altar in Jerusalem'? 23 Come now, make a wager with my master the king of Assyria: I will give you two thousand horses, if you are able on your part to set riders on them. 24 How then can you repulse a single captain among the least of my master's servants, when you rely on Egypt for chariots and for horsemen? 25 Moreover, is it without the LORD that I have come up against this place to destroy it? The LORD said to me, Go up against this land, and destroy it."

26 Then Eliakim son of Hilkiah, and Shebnah, and Joah said to the Rabshakeh, "Please speak to your servants in the Aramaic language, for we understand it; do not speak to us in the language of Judah within the hearing of the people who are on the wall." 27 But the Rabshakeh said to them, "Has my master sent me to speak these words to your master and to you, and not to the people sitting on the wall, who are doomed with you to eat their own dung and to drink their own urine?"

28   Then the Rabshakeh stood and called out in a loud voice in the language of Judah, "Hear the word of the great king, the king of Assyria! 29 Thus says the king: 'Do not let Hezekiah deceive you, for he will not be able to deliver you out of my hand. 30 Do not let Hezekiah make you rely on the LORD by saying, The LORD will surely deliver us, and this city will not be given into the hand of the king of Assyria.' 31 Do not listen to Hezekiah; for thus says the king of Assyria: 'Make your peace with me and come out to me; then every one of you will eat from your own vine and your own fig tree, and drink water from your own cistern, 32 until I come and take you away to a land like your own land, a land of grain and wine, a land of bread and vineyards, a land of olive oil and honey, that you may live and not die. Do not listen to Hezekiah when he misleads you by saying, The LORD will deliver us. 33 Has any of the gods of the nations ever delivered its land out of the hand of the king of Assyria? 34 Where are the gods of Hamath and Arpad? Where are the gods of Sepharvaim, Hena, and Ivvah? Have they delivered Samaria out of my hand? 35 Who among all the gods of the countries have delivered their countries out of my hand, that the LORD should deliver Jerusalem out of my hand?'"

36   But the people were silent and answered him not a word, for the king's command was, "Do not answer him." 37 Then Eliakim son of Hilkiah, who was in charge of the palace, and Shebna the secretary, and Joah son of Asaph, the recorder, came to Hezekiah with their clothes torn and told him the words of the Rabshakeh.

19:1   When King Hezekiah heard it, he tore his clothes, covered himself with sackcloth, and went into the house of the LORD. 2 And he sent Eliakim, who was in charge of the palace, and Shebna the secretary, and the senior priests, covered with sackcloth, to the prophet Isaiah son of Amoz. 3 They said to him, "Thus says Hezekiah, This day is a day of distress, of rebuke, and of disgrace; children have come to the birth, and there is no strength to bring them forth. 4 It may be that the LORD your God heard all the words of the Rabshakeh, whom his master the king of Assyria has sent to mock the living God, and will rebuke the words that the LORD your God has heard; therefore lift up your prayer for the remnant that is left." 5 When the servants of King Hezekiah came to Isaiah, 6 Isaiah said to them, "Say to your master, 'Thus says the LORD: Do not be afraid because of the words that you have heard, with which the servants of the king of Assyria have reviled me. 7 I myself will put a spirit in him, so that he shall hear a rumor and return to his own land; I will cause him to fall by the sword in his own land.'"

8   The Rabshakeh returned, and found the king of Assyria fighting against Libnah; for he had heard that the king had left Lachish. 9 When the king heard concerning King Tirhakah of Ethiopia, "See, he has set out to fight against you," he sent messengers again to Hezekiah, saying, 10 "Thus

shall you speak to King Hezekiah of Judah: Do not let your God on whom you rely deceive you by promising that Jerusalem will not be given into the hand of the king of Assyria. 11 See, you have heard what the kings of Assyria have done to all lands, destroying them utterly. Shall you be delivered? 12 Have the gods of the nations delivered them, the nations that my predecessors destroyed, Gozan, Haran, Rezeph, and the people of Eden who were in Telassar? 13 Where is the king of Hamath, the king of Arpad, the king of the city of Sepharvaim, the king of Hena, or the king of Ivvah?"

14 Hezekiah received the letter from the hand of the messengers and read it; then Hezekiah went up to the house of the LORD and spread it before the LORD. 15 And Hezekiah prayed before the LORD, and said: "O LORD the God of Israel, who are enthroned above the cherubim, you are God, you alone, of all the kingdoms of the earth; you have made heaven and earth. 16 Incline your ear, O LORD, and hear; open your eyes, O LORD, and see; hear the words of Sennacherib, which he has sent to mock the living God. 17 Truly, O LORD, the kings of Assyria have laid waste the nations and their lands, 18 and have hurled their gods into the fire, though they were no gods but the work of human hands—wood and stone—and so they were destroyed. 19 So now, O LORD our God, save us, I pray you, from his hand, so that all the kingdoms of the earth may know that you, O LORD, are God alone."

20 Then Isaiah son of Amoz sent to Hezekiah, saying, "Thus says the LORD, the God of Israel: I have heard your prayer to me about King Sennacherib of Assyria. 21 This is the word that the LORD has spoken concerning him:
She despises you, she scorns you—
> virgin daughter Zion;
she tosses her head—behind your back,
> daughter Jerusalem.

22 Whom have you mocked and reviled?
> Against whom have you raised your voice
and haughtily lifted your eyes?
> Against the Holy One of Israel!

23 By your messengers you have mocked the Lord,
> and you have said, 'With my many chariots
I have gone up the heights of the mountains,
> to the far recesses of Lebanon;
I felled its tallest cedars,
> its choicest cypresses;
I entered its farthest retreat,
> its densest forest.

24 I dug wells
> and drank foreign waters,

I dried up with the sole of my foot
all the streams of Egypt.'
25   Have you not heard
that I determined it long ago?
I planned from days of old
what now I bring to pass,
that you should make fortified cities
crash into heaps of ruins,
26   while their inhabitants, shorn of strength,
are dismayed and confounded;
they have become like plants of the field
and like tender grass,
like grass on the housetops,
blighted before it is grown.
27   "But I know your rising and your sitting,
your going out and coming in,
and your raging against me.
28   Because you have raged against me
and your arrogance has come to my ears,
I will put my hook in your nose
and my bit in your mouth;
I will turn you back on the way
by which you came.

29   "And this shall be the sign for you: This year you shall eat what grows of itself, and in the second year what springs from that; then in the third year sow, reap, plant vineyards, and eat their fruit. 30 The surviving remnant of the house of Judah shall again take root downward, and bear fruit upward; 31 for from Jerusalem a remnant shall go out, and from Mount Zion a band of survivors. The zeal of the LORD of hosts will do this.

32   "Therefore thus says the LORD concerning the king of Assyria: He shall not come into this city, shoot an arrow there, come before it with a shield, or cast up a siege ramp against it. 33 By the way that he came, by the same he shall return; he shall not come into this city, says the LORD. 34 For I will defend this city to save it, for my own sake and for the sake of my servant David."

35   That very night the angel of the LORD set out and struck down one hundred eighty-five thousand in the camp of the Assyrians; when morning dawned, they were all dead bodies. 36 Then King Sennacherib of Assyria left, went home, and lived at Nineveh. 37 As he was worshiping in the house of his god Nisroch, his sons Adrammelech and Sharezer killed him with the sword, and they escaped into the land of Ararat. His son Esar-haddon succeeded him.

Analysis

The section 18:17—19:37 offers a version of events that moves, contrary to 18:13-16, toward the miraculous saving of Jerusalem. There is an almost word-for-word parallel passage of this long section in Isaiah 36–37, although the version of the Deuteronomistic Historian is undoubtedly its precedent.[1] The narrative is not uniform, and the section 19:9b-35 containing the second message to Hezekiah and its consequences is indeed a doublet. The repetition forms a separate version and was included at a later stage as 18:17-37; 19:19a, 36-37. It was complemented with the story of the appeal to Isaiah in 19:1-7 and several other redactional comments (18:21-22, 25, 30, 32b-35); the original text is thus restricted to 18:17-20, 23-24, 26-29, 31a, 32a, 36-37; 19:8-9a, 36-37.

The taunt in 19:21-28, in turn, is a further addition within the later version, 19:9b-35. We can therefore distinguish two versions that develop differently from the same starting point, namely Sennacherib's demand that Hezekiah capitulate. The end to the threat is reported differently too. In the older version Sennacherib rushes back to Nineveh, where he is assassinated by his sons (19:36-37). According to the later version, however, the Assyrian army suffers a catastrophic defeat before the walls of Jerusalem (19:35). It is only in this version that Isaiah appears as the proclaimer of God's will, who foretells the salvation from the Assyrian assault.

Scholarship has tried to bridge the gap between the contradictory accounts of 18:17—19:37 and 18:13-15 by assuming two separate campaigns of Sennacherib.[2] No second campaign is mentioned anywhere in the Assyrian sources; what is more, such an assumption would misjudge the character of both the older and newer versions of the text. The text is not only silent about the shameful submission of Hezekiah, but it also integrates events from later Assyrian history in the form of literary motifs. A case in point is the assassination of Sennacherib in 681, which is mentioned in the Babylonian Chronicle.[3] The hasty retreat of the Assyrian army could reflect the defeat of Esarhaddon in Egypt in 674/673.[4] The later version of the sudden death of the entire Assyrian contingent before Jerusalem would then be a hyperbole to describe the salvation, a type of hyperbole that has a parallel in Herodotus's account (2.141) of the apparent destruction of the Assyrian weapons by mice.

The two versions on how Jerusalem was spared make recourse to miraculous events in order to gloss over the real happenings—Hezekiah's submission and the payment of a high tribute. It is a historical fact that Sennacherib did not conquer Jerusalem. Yet neither of the versions makes the political negotiating of the king of Judah responsible for this turn of events: the older version refers to external circum-

---

[1] See Otto Kaiser, *Isaiah 13–39,* trans. R. A. Wilson, OTL (Philadelphia: Westminster, 1974), 369–97.

[2] See Cogan and Tadmor, *II Kings,* 246–51.

[3] *TUAT,* I/4, 402.

[4] Cogan and Tadmor, *II Kings,* 250.

stances, the later one to the powerful intervention of Yahweh. In this sense both versions in 18:17—19:37 are later elaborations of the events surrounding Sennacherib's campaign against Jerusalem, in an effort to come to terms with the defeat. Even if the accounts take their cue from historical events, they do nothing to increase our historical understanding.

The Older Version (18:17-20, 23-24, 26-29, 31a, 32a*, 36-37; 19:8-9a, 36-37)

It is likely that the older version included two speeches of the Rabshakeh, one directed toward the three negotiators sent by the king to meet with the Rabshakeh before the city (18:19-20, 23-24), and a second one addressed to the people (18:28-29, 31a, 32a*). Both are linked by 18:26-27. Disregarding the sense of conclusion, the narrative continues with the return of the Rabshakeh to the king of Assyria and comes to a proper finish only with the retreat and death of Sennacherib in 19:36-37. The structure of the older version is therefore as follows:

18:17-18	The Rabshakeh before Jerusalem
18:19-20, 23-24	First speech of the Rabshakeh
18:26-27	Linking passage
18:28-29, 31a, 32a*	Second speech of the Rabshakeh
18:36-37	Response by the people and the emissaries of Hezekiah
19:8-9a	Return of the Rabshakeh to Sennacherib
19:36-37	Retreat and death of Sennacherib

Commentary

[18:17-18] The Rabshakeh before Jerusalem. 18:17 presumes Sennacherib's siege of Lachish, while 19:8 later confirms its conquest indirectly. The fall of this city, which came next to Jerusalem in importance, testifies to the hopelessness of the situation faced by Hezekiah. The Rabshakeh is sent to Jerusalem as the representative of the Assyrian king, in expectation of the final submission of Hezekiah, in order to start negotiations for a peaceful handover without siege or assault. Sennacherib remained at his camp at Lachish, as is shown on the reliefs from his palace at Nineveh. The Rabshakeh was a high official from the circle of the Assyrian king, whose exact function we cannot establish; the other two officials mentioned must be an addition, as they do not appear again later on. The exact site where negotiations take place, "the conduit of the upper pool," is not known, but it is likely to be found north of the city and certainly outside the city walls.[5] The same location is mentioned in Isa 7:3, which allows the conclusion that we are dealing with a reservoir and a canal predating Hezekiah. The "highway to the Fuller's Field" then led away from the city toward the north or northwest. The name gives a hint that the area of the so-called upper pool was used as a tannery requiring large water supplies.

---

[5] See David Ussishkin, "The 'Camp of the Assyrians' in Jerusalem," *IEJ* 29 (1979) 137–42.

The Judean delegation is made up of three officials, who are authorized by the king to enter into negotiations with the Rabshakeh. Steward, scribe, and recorder are, from the time of Solomon, among the highest offices (see on 1 Kgs 4:16). The steward oversaw the administration of the royal possessions, especially the royal estate, whereas the scribe, as a secretary of state, had responsibility for the royal chancellery. The portfolio of the recorder or spokesman, as a minister of state, included the execution of royal decrees and judgments. Of the three named officials it is Eliakim and Shebnah who appear again in Isa 22:15-23, although their names there are later additions.[6] A tomb at Silwān, which bears an epitaph to an unnamed steward, may belong to Shebnah, although this is unlikely.[7] Overall, the present section offers a convincing and detailed introduction to the historical circumstances.

[18:19-20, 23-24] First speech of the Rabshakeh. The first speech of the Rabshakeh is formulated as a message from Sennacherib to Hezekiah, pointing out forcefully the supremacy of Ashur. "The theme of the speech is the military strength of Hezekiah; because it is found lacking, he has no reason for confidence."[8] Verse 23 formulates it rather pointedly: even if he was given two thousand horses, Hezekiah would be unable to muster the appropriate number of horsemen. The cavalry had played an important part in the Assyrian military since Tiglath-pileser I and was successively adopted by the small states of Syria and the southern Levant. Its maintenance demanded not only the costly acquisition and upkeep of horses, but also a special training of the horsemen. Verse 23, therefore, underlines the strength of the Assyrian army particularly forcefully.

[18:24] The reference to Egypt stems probably from the coalition with the pharaoh and the small kingdoms of the Delta into which Hezekiah had entered (see on 18:13-15). Trust in the once mighty Egypt for support would explain why Hezekiah challenged Assyria; also, it was an Egyptian army that was present at the decisive battle at Eltekeh.[9] In his message, Sennacherib heaps nothing but scorn on the two coalition parties, following his victory and the restitution of Assyrian hegemony.

[18:21] The addition expresses the lack of strength of Egypt in the image of the broken reed.

[18:26-27] Linking passage. The scene prepares for the second speech addressed to the public and implies that the negotiations between Hezekiah's delegation and the

---

[6] See Kaiser, *Isaiah 13–39,* 379–80

[7] See Nahman Avigad, "The Epitaph of a Royal Steward from Siloam Village," *IEJ* 3 (1953) 137–52.

[8] Würthwein, *Könige,* 2:421.

[9] See *TUAT,* I/4, 389.

Rabshakeh are held in public or, at any rate, publicly audible. The three Judean emissaries ask the Rabshakeh to speak to them in Aramaic, which had become the language of diplomacy across the Levant. Aramaic, like Hebrew, belongs to the family of Northwest Semitic languages and is well attested in texts from the Aramean small states between the tenth and eighth centuries.[10] In the Assyrian Empire Aramaic was in wide use west of the Euphrates River, and it became the language of common use in all of the Near East and Egypt in the Babylonian and Persian periods.[11] The request by the delegation implies that Aramaic was spoken only by the officials of Jerusalem and not yet by its population.

The suggestion put to the Rabshakeh does not have the desired result, quite the contrary. The representative of the Assyrian king now turns to address the people in their native language, which is termed "the language of Judah" (as opposed to "the language of Israel"), which means the local form of Hebrew spoken in Judah. The difference between the two dialects is also visible in its writing.[12] The Rabshakeh's change to Judahite is accompanied by strong words describing the consequences of the siege.

[18:28-29, 31a, 32a*] Second speech of the Rabshakeh. The aim of the speech before the people is to turn them away from Hezekiah. Hezekiah is portrayed as a powerless loser; in addition, the Assyrian king pleads for a peace treaty and invites the population to show him loyalty. The people are to be separated from their king so that Sennacherib can take his place. The redactor has filled this part of the speech, in vv. 31a, 32a*, with imagery well known in Deuteronomistic usage. In the further addition, vv. 32b-35, the might of Yahweh is put into doubt by reference to the powerlessness of the deities of other peoples; with the exception of Arpad, the redactor has recourse to the place names of 17:30-31.

[18:36-37] Response of the people and the emissaries of Hezekiah. Both the people and the delegates respond with silence. The order of the king would have applied only to the three officials sent to negotiate with the Rabshakeh. Their duty was to hear the demands of Sennacherib and to pass them on to the king. The tearing of clothes is a mourning ritual that can be understood almost as a commentary on the Rabshakeh's speech. The seriousness of the situation is made clear: there is nothing to hope for, and it is mourning that remains to be done.

---

[10] See Rainer Degen, *Altaramäische Grammatik der Inschriften des 10–8. Jh. v. Chr.,* Abhandlungen für die Kunde des Morgenlandes 38/3 (Mainz: Deutsche Morgenländische Gesellschaft, 1969).

[11] See Hayim Tadmor, "The Aramaization of Assyria," in *Mesopotamien und seine Nachbarn: Politische und kulturelle Wechselbeziehungen im alten Vorderasien vom 4. bis 1. Jahrtausend v. Chr.,* ed. Hans-Jörg Nissen and Johannes Renger, Berliner Beiträge zum Vorderen Orient 1 (Berlin: Reimer, 1983), 449–70.

[12] See Frank Moore Cross and David Noel Freedman, *Early Hebrew Orthography: A Study of the Epigraphic Evidence,* AOS 36 (New Haven: American Oriental Society, 1952).

[19:8-9a] Return of the Rabshakeh to Sennacherib. Both of the Rabshakeh's speeches have a programmatic character and therefore demand no response. "Like the Judean ministers return to their king, so the Rabshakeh returns to his master who is pitching battle against Libnah."[13] Libnah is another town of the Shephelah, situated at Tell Bornāt. In all likelihood this implies the preceding fall of Lachish, although we cannot be certain. The capture of the city is at any rate portrayed on the reliefs in Sennacherib's palace at Nineveh. The mention of Tirhakah in v. 9a is an anachronism, since the pharaoh of this name, of the Twenty-fifth Dynasty, reigned only from 690. He is mentioned in order to explain Sennacherib's hasty retreat from Judah. Although Egypt was conquered by Esarhaddon during the reign of Tirhakah (690–664), the same pharaoh made the Assyrians suffer a serious defeat in 673, and he would conquer Memphis, the old capital, once more in 669. Only after his death was Egypt finally made a vassal state by Ashurbanipal.[14] Tirhakah, who made a name for himself as an enemy of Ashur later on, had therefore not yet appeared as a player on the historical stage in the time of Sennacherib. His name is mentioned here because of its associations with a policy of resisting Assyrian expansion after Sennacherib. Any interpretation that Sennacherib left Judah for fear of an Egyptian assault under Tirhakah is therefore ruled out on historical grounds.

[19:36-37] Retreat and death of Sennacherib. With the retreat of Sennacherib and his assassination by his sons in Nineveh, the narrative comes to its intended end. The Assyrian king, who had expressed his power in his contempt before the walls of Jerusalem, now not only has to retreat without success, but he also finds a dishonorable end, being assassinated by his own sons.[15] The name of his son given as Adrammelech probably derives from Arda-Mulissu, mentioned again as Adramelos, son of Sennacherib, in Berossus.[16] The other name, Sharezer, is not as yet verified.[17] The name of Nisroch, whose temple is mentioned as the locale of the assassination, is corrupt; a god of this name is unknown in Mesopotamia, but it might indicate a deity such as Marduk or Nusku.[18]

The closing episode is the murder of Sennacherib: his inglorious end offsets his self-assured display of power in Judah. It is in this way that the historical events as they are known from 18:13-15 and the inscriptions of Sennacherib are sidelined in favor of a different historical account. Jerusalem was not saved by the submission of

---

[13] Würthwein, *Könige*, 2:422.

[14] See Erik Hornung, *History of Ancient Egypt: An Introduction,* trans. David Lorton (Ithaca: Cornell Univ. Press, 1999), 134–37.

[15] *TUAT,* I/4, 402.

[16] See Simo Parpola, "The Murderer of Sennacherib," in *Death in Mesopotamia,* ed. Bendt Alster, Mesopotamia 8 (Copenhagen: Akademisk, 1980), 171–82.

[17] See Riekele Borger, *TUAT,* I/4, 391–92.

[18] Cogan and Tadmor, *II Kings,* 239.

Hezekiah but by the powerful intervention of Yahweh as the master of history. The sparing of Jerusalem brought about by tribute payment and the survival of the kingdom of Judah are interpreted as a miracle. It was not King Hezekiah who turned away the danger from the state and the people, the kingdom and the temple, at the last moment, but Yahweh alone. This tendency is even more pronounced in the later version.

The Later Version (19:9b-20, 32-33, 35)

The later version sets out with a new message by Sennacherib, which takes the form of a letter and is decisive for the further course of the events. Verse 35 is likely to be the end of this version with the fulfillment of the word of God in vv. 32-33. The prophecy of the sign does not fit the context, so v. 29 is probably a redactional addition. Leaving aside for the moment the redactional contributions of vv. 30-31 and 34, the structure is as follows:

19:9b-13	Message from Sennacherib to Hezekiah
19:14-19	Hezekiah's prayer
19:20, 32-33	Isaiah's word to Hezekiah
19:35	Destruction of the Assyrian army

The later version is distinguished from the older by its lack of specific demands. In accordance with Deuteronomistic ideals, Hezekiah appears as a pious ruler who by a visit to the temple seeks the answer in God to the problem he faces. The letter from Sennacherib, before that, is also crafted along the lines of Deuteronomistic theology; history is understood in terms of acts of God, and the question of power is phrased as the question of the power of Yahweh.

[19:9b-13] Message from Sennacherib to Hezekiah. The literary link to the new version is built on the older one. Sennacherib's message puts the power of Yahweh into question. The historical events are therefore interpreted as a challenge to the God of Israel. The crucial question is: will Yahweh save Jerusalem after it has become apparent that the deities of other peoples could not save them from the Assyrians? To compare Yahweh with other deities amounts to relativizing his claim to exclusivity.

Of the names put forward in v. 12, Gozan had already been mentioned in the context of the deportations of the Israelites in 17:6. Gozan is to be read as Akkadian *Guzāna* (Tell Halāf), the capital of the Assyrian province of Bīt Bahian on the Upper Habûr from the second half of the ninth century. Haran, Akkadian *Harrāun* (Altınbaşak), was an important cult site of the moon-god Sîn located on the Upper Balih; it was incorporated into Assyria already in the ninth century.[19] The city of Rezeph (Akkadian *Rasappa*) was also the capital of an Assyrian province in northern

---

[19] See J. N. Postgate, *RLA*, 4:122–25.

Mesopotamia, also from the ninth century. The expression "the people of Eden who were in Telassar" refers to the resettlement of people from the Assyrian province of Bīt-Adini to Til Aššuri, here called Telassar, under Shalmaneser III in the ninth century. Til Aššuri, "the hill of the Assyrians," is best located in the Zagros region on the Lower Diyala.

The list of names in v. 13 is almost identical with that of the redactor in 18:34, which misses only the name of Lair [not mentioned in NRSV]. Irvah, Hamath, and Sepharvaim were mentioned before in 17:24.[20] Hamath is identical with Akkadian *Amati* in southern Mesopotamia. Arpad (Tell Refāt) was an Aramean city-state that had come under Assyrian control already at the end of the ninth century. Lair is echoed in Akkadian *Lahiru* and refers to an Assyrian province in northeastern Babylonia. Sepharvaim may be identical with Akkadian *Sipiraʾni* in eastern Babylonia. No equivalent for Hena has as yet been suggested. Ivvah is most probably the same as Akkadian *Amaa* in eastern Babylonia, although its exact site has not been determined. All names refer to places or areas that had been under Assyrian control from the ninth century. The author, therefore, utilizes more obviously an identifiably Assyrian geography rather than real historical events.

[19:14-19] Hezekiah's prayer. This prayer praises Yahweh not only as enthroned above the cherubim and as the creator of heaven and earth, but also as the only God. The prayer is clearly informed by Deuteronomic-Deuteronomistic theology, which first articulated the profession of Yahweh as the only God (cf. Deut 4:35, 39). It is only the deliberate exclusion of other gods beside Yahweh that marks the monotheism later expressed in the postexilic period in such striking words as Isa 44:6 and 45:5-6, 18.[21] Hezekiah's prayer is a firm testimony to monotheism, for example, when the gods of other peoples are called "the work of human hands," while Yahweh is the only God. Drawing from this theology with a monotheistic claim, the author has clearly formulated the profession of Yahweh as the only God.

[19:20, 32-33] Isaiah's words to Hezekiah. In 19:20 the narrator introduces Isaiah, the prophet of the word of God, who is to answer the lament with the forecast that is expected (19:32-33). The inclusion of Isaiah's appearance before Hezekiah presupposes an existing tradition of this prophet. Its extent is unknown, but the book of Isaiah contains, together with the judgments, a number of prose narratives collected in the so-called Isaiah memorial (Isa 6:1—9:6). We find an equivalent insofar as we can infer from several words of the Assyrian cycle (Isaiah 28–30) that Isaiah was

---

[20] On place names see Ran Zadok, "Geographical and Onomastic Notes," *JANESCU* 8 (1976) 113–26.

[21] Hans Wildberger, "Der Monotheismus Deuterojesajas," in *Beiträge zur alttestamentlichen Theologie: Festschrift für Walther Zimmerli zum 70. Geburtstag,* ed. Herbert Donner (Göttingen: Vandenhoeck & Ruprecht, 1977), 506–30.

probably active before 701, at the time of the Assyrian danger coming from Sennacherib. Isaiah is the only writing prophet who is mentioned in the Deuteronomistic History, even if as part of a later stratum and even if the precise paths of transmission are unknown.

The word of Yahweh (19:32-33) predicts the salvation of Jerusalem: no battle or siege will take place, and Sennacherib will return to Ashur without entering the city. The pronouncement is justified by the events of the year 701, in that Sennacherib did indeed not take Jerusalem; Hezekiah bought the city out of the threat from the Assyrian superpower by agreeing to pay tribute. The payment of the tribute is expressly mentioned in 18:14-15, and it is confirmed by the inscriptions of Sennacherib.[22] Isaiah's promise of salvation reduces the course things have taken to the will of Yahweh alone and offers a new interpretation of the events.

[19:35] Destruction of the Assyrian army. Verse 35 describes the fulfilled prophecy in terms of Yahweh interfering in the course of history: the entire army is dead within one night. Ashur is ruled out as an enemy of Hezekiah and Jerusalem is miraculously saved. In contrast to the older version, which has Sennacherib return without further explanation to Ashur and Nineveh (19:36), where he is assassinated by his sons, the later version chooses a place closer to Jerusalem as the site of miraculous liberation: the angel of death comes to kill the entire Assyrian army outside the city gates. The prophecy of Isaiah is thus fulfilled: God himself has averted disaster.

In the last instance, this interpretation points back to the singularity of Yahweh. Yahweh has intervened in the course of history, while the gods of all the other nations were powerless in the face of Ashur; Sennacherib has been unable to take Jerusalem and is forced to abandon the campaign against Hezekiah. History proves the power of Yahweh over both the king of Ashur and the foreign gods. The fact that Sennacherib left Jerusalem unconquered, together with the belief in the uniqueness of Yahweh, gave rise to the tradition of a "paradigmatic religious narrative that aims to show that Yahweh surpasses other gods in might, that he is the God of all and can be trusted."[23]

The Consultation of Isaiah (19:1-7)

Analysis

Within the later version, the Deuteronomistic redactor had introduced Isaiah as the prophet of God in 19:20, 32, 33, in order to make the miraculous rescue by divine intervention appear as an event announced through the prophet. Isaiah had lived in the decades before 701, during the threat from Assyria, which explains his selection. The older version is enlarged by the present episode in 19:1-7, where Hezekiah deliber-

---

[22] *TUAT,* I/4, 390.
[23] Würthwein, *Könige,* 2:430.

ately turns to a prophet for consultation. The king thus appears as a faithful servant of Yahweh who aligns his life along the will of God. The scene is a direct continuation of 18:37.

Commentary

[19:1-4] First, the king expresses his grief with ritual gestures (v. 1). Next, he sends to Isaiah two of the delegates who have spoken with the Rabshakeh (v. 2). The message they carry is formulated in the spirit of Deuteronomistic theology and focuses on the uniqueness of Yahweh, which is put into doubt by the Rabshakeh (vv. 3-4). The political situation is portrayed in the imagery of women entering into the labor of childbirth—an image, of course, which glides over the fact that Hezekiah's own anti-Assyrian policy is the cause of the present crisis. Hezekiah is seeking an escape route from the impending danger; he lacks a concrete vision. His turn to the prophet and thus to Yahweh is to an extent also guided by the present plight.

[19:5-7] The prophet replies with a promise of salvation. As the mediator of the word of God he can predict the turn of affairs. The promise begins with the words: "Do not be afraid," an assurance against the false threat of the Assyrian king. Then follows the announcement of the divine work. Yahweh acts on Sennacherib through a spirit. The deception makes him depart from Jerusalem early. The behavior of the Assyrian king, who thus spares the city, is caused by Yahweh; Sennacherib cannot resist the spirit sent by Yahweh. Yahweh is the one who has power over the Assyrian king and is able to control his will through a spirit. The prophecy interprets the events again as commanded by God.

The Taunt (19:21-28)

Analysis

The taunt is addressed to Ashur and consists of three parts:

vv. 21-22	Introduction and judgment
vv. 23-24	Boasting of the enemy
vv. 25-28	Yahweh's judgment of the enemy

The taunt resembles the oracles against the foreign nations, where misfortune is predicted to other peoples (Isaiah 13–21, 23; Jeremiah 25, 46–51; Ezekiel 25–32, 35; Amos 1:3—2:3; Obadiah). Another parallel is the word against the king of Babel in Isa 14:4-21. The prophecy follows a pattern of deeds and consequences: Ashur's hybris causes its fall: in its own striving for power it has despised the power of Yahweh. Yahweh, as the Lord of history, holds true power, whatever the might of the Assyrian king. This power of Yahweh is expressed as a universal claim through the words against the foreign nations.

Commentary

[19:21] The song opens with the scorn that Jerusalem pours over its enemy, who has suffered a defeat before the city. The shaking of the head is an expression of this scorn (cf. Pss 22:8; 44:15; Lam 2:15; Job 16:4; Jer 18:16). Jerusalem is given the poetic address "Daughter of Zion" (cf. Isa 3:16-17; 4:4).

[19:22] This verse turns toward God, formulaically addressed as the "Holy One of Israel." This mode of speech is grounded especially in the story of calling (Isaiah 6), foregrounding two aspects: the utter alterity of God on the one hand, and his relation to his chosen people on the other.

[19:23-24] The second stanza talks of the irresistible rise of the Assyrian military power, using their self-praise as a formal vehicle: no other power in the world can match the Assyrian army in force and organization; even the mountains of Lebanon and the Nile River in Egypt cannot stop them. (The reference to the Egyptian campaigns are anachronistic, since it was only under Esarhaddon, the successor of Sennacherib, that Ashur marched against Egypt.) The references to the brilliant logistics of the Assyrian army, which contributed significantly to their military prowess, are borne out by the inscriptions of the Assyrian kings. The specific historical allusions of the song cannot be verified. The general thought expressed in the song is the complete power of Ashur, which prevails even in unusual circumstances.

[19:25-28] The negative prophecy in vv. 25-28 states that Sennacherib will be led back to his own country like an animal that is dragged to the slaughter by its nose ring. This prophecy shapes the end: as Yahweh leads away Sennacherib, Jerusalem is delivered from the Assyrian danger. The song refers to the events of 701 and interprets them as Yahweh's necessary intervention against an enemy whose hybris has made him an enemy of Yahweh too. "It celebrates the liberation of 701 in full acknowledgment of the downfall of Ashur."[24] The king symbolizes the proud superpower, humiliated and broken in being led away. The king of Ashur does not take the inhabitants of Jerusalem as prisoners, but instead is taken hostage himself. Yahweh has prepared the same fate for the king of Ashur that Ashur had prepared for other peoples after the conquest. Thus Yahweh has reduced the powerful to a powerless prisoner, who is in turn scorned by the inhabitants of Jerusalem.

The Sign (19:29)

The sign does not fit the historical context, because it does not predict the immediate change of the situation that the context would lead to expect. Rather, it suggests an

---

[24] Würthwein, *Könige*, 2:431.

improvement after three years, and in this it is less the announcement of a sign than a parable. After years without harvest and lack of agriculture, normality will return to the fields. The image is taken from the experience of the farming life. If agriculture comes to a halt in times of war, then there will be some natural growth in the first year, while in the second season fields will lie fallow and overgrow. For the third year a return to the familiar farming cycle of sowing and harvesting is foretold. The prophecy refers to the agricultural life in Judah, but we cannot be sure when it was included in the text.

Hezekiah's Illness and Recovery

Text

20:1   In those days Hezekiah became sick and was at the point of death. The prophet Isaiah son of Amoz came to him, and said to him, "Thus says the LORD: Set your house in order, for you shall die; you shall not recover." 2 Then Hezekiah turned his face to the wall and prayed to the LORD: 3 "Remember now, O LORD, I implore you, how I have walked before you in faithfulness with a whole heart, and have done what is good in your sight." Hezekiah wept bitterly. 4 Before Isaiah had gone out of the middle court, the word of the LORD came to him: 5 "Turn back, and say to Hezekiah prince of my people, Thus says the LORD, the God of your ancestor David: I have heard your prayer, I have seen your tears; indeed, I will heal you; on the third day you shall go up to the house of the LORD. 6 I will add fifteen years to your life. I will deliver you and this city out of the hand of the king of Assyria; I will defend this city for my own sake and for my servant David's sake." 7 Then Isaiah said, "Bring a lump of figs. Let them take it and apply it to the boil, so that he may recover."

8   Hezekiah said to Isaiah, "What shall be the sign that the LORD will heal me, and that I shall go up to the house of the LORD on the third day?" 9 Isaiah said, "This is the sign to you from the LORD, that the LORD will do the thing that he has promised: the shadow has now advanced ten intervals; shall it retreat ten intervals?" 10 Hezekiah answered, "It is normal for the shadow to lengthen ten intervals; rather let the shadow retreat ten intervals." 11 The prophet Isaiah cried to the LORD; and he brought the shadow back the ten intervals, by which the sun had declined on the dial of Ahaz.

Analysis

To the story of Hezekiah's illness and recovery (vv. 1-7) is added another story (vv. 8-11) in which a sign is sent to confirm Yahweh's promise of v. 6. Both narratives originated separately, and the inclusion of v. 6 might have prepared the addition of vv.

8-11. Verse 6 disrupts the first narrative in that the promise of another fifteen years' of life exceeds the tale of illness and recovery. The first narrative is, however, not of one piece in the first place, because Hezekiah's prayer and the prediction of his recovery in vv. 2b, 3a, 4, 5 are later additions. The original narrative, comprising vv. 1, 2a, 3b, 7, was very short.

Commentary

[20:1, 2a, 3b, 7] In the original version Isaiah appears as a miracle worker and a man of God closer to the figure of Elisha than to the prophet of judgment uttering oracles of doom in the book of Isaiah. The story reaches its peak with Hezekiah's recovery. Verse 1 does not mention the cause of the illness, but presupposes that it was inflicted by God as punishment for an offense. Isaiah's announcement of the king's imminent death is proof of its seriousness. His recovery later on contradicts this announcement, and Isaiah, like Elisha before him, is both miracle worker and mediator of God's will. No reason is given for the change in divine will, but it would appear that Hezekiah's behavior in vv. 2a, 3b is responsible. His action may well be a sign of scrutiny and return to Yahweh following the insight into his own wrongdoing. The actual healing (v. 7) is expressed in a visible sign. Dried figs were generally known in antiquity for their healing powers; the sign thus makes use of a remedy with a proven therapeutic effect. The proclamation of recovery brings the story to an end.

[20:2b-3a, 4-5] The redaction adds a prayer by Hezekiah in vv. 2b-3a and a prophecy in vv. 4-5. The prayer is clearly marked by its Deuteronomistic language and the notion that Hezekiah has acted faithfully and true to the will of God (cf. 18:5-7a). With the pronouncement of the will of God to Hezekiah through Isaiah (vv. 4-5) the recovery is explicitly attributed to Yahweh. It is Yahweh himself who effects the healing, not the miracle worker Isaiah, so that Hezekiah can get up from his sickbed and resume his royal duties. The priests in the temple are supposed to confirm his complete recovery, that is, his unlimited participation in the cult, on the third day. It is only after the restoration of cultic purity that Hezekiah can return to his royal and priestly offices.

[20:6] An addition smooths the way for the second story and puts the events into their historical context. The reference to Sennacherib's retreat and the liberation of Jerusalem dates illness and recovery to before the events of 701 as they are recorded in 18:17—19:37. The promise of extending Hezekiah's life for another fifteen years points in the same direction and presumes the dating of Sennacherib's 701 campaign into the fourteenth year of Hezekiah in 18:13. The twenty-nine years of his rule would therefore be estimated to last from 715/714 to 686, in order to account for the fifteen extra years. The dating of the synchronisms in 18:1, 9-10, according to which

Hezekiah ruled from about 727 to 698, is conflicting.[1] This last chronology can be upheld only if the narrative predates the events of 701 by a long time. It seems likely that the redactor worked with the dating from 18:13 when he formulated and included v. 6, without harmonizing it with the synchronisms of 18:1, 9-10.

[20:8-11] The narrative of vv. 1-7 is followed by the report of an actual sign in vv. 8-11, which is to prove the promise of recovery and the granting of a longer life. The retreating of the shadow by ten intervals has in all likelihood to do with a form of measuring time where the hours were counted by the shadow thrown onto a flight of steps.[2] Yahweh, as the master of history, is also the master of time, as the shortening of the shadow implies a stepping back in time.

Both stories appear again in the appendix to the book of Isaiah, Isaiah 38, although in this case the story of the sign precedes, not unreasonably, the announcement of recovery. Also, there is added a long prayer of thanks spoken by Hezekiah. This reorganization proves the version of 2 Kgs 20:1-11 to be the older one.

---

[1] See Nadav Na'aman, "Hezekiah and the Kings of Assyria," *TA* 21 (1994) 235–54.

[2] For details see Yigael Yadin, "The Dial of Ahaz," *ErIsr* 5 (1958) 94–96 (Hebrew).

The Threat against Hezekiah

Text

20:12 At that time King Merodach-baladan son of Baladan of Babylon sent envoys with letters and a present to Hezekiah, for he had heard that Hezekiah had been sick. 13 Hezekiah welcomed them; he showed them all his treasure house, the silver, the gold, the spices, the precious oil, his armory, all that was found in his storehouses; there was nothing in his house or in all his realm that Hezekiah did not show them. 14 Then the prophet Isaiah came to King Hezekiah, and said to him, "What did these men say? From where did they come to you?" Hezekiah answered, "They have come from a far country, from Babylon." 15 He said, "What have they seen in your house?" Hezekiah answered, "They have seen all that is in my house; there is nothing in my storehouses that I did not show them."

16 Then Isaiah said to Hezekiah, "Hear the word of the LORD: 17 Days are coming when all that is in your house, and that which your ancestors have stored up until this day, shall be carried to Babylon; nothing shall be left, says the LORD. 18 Some of your own sons who are born to you shall be taken away; they shall be eunuchs in the palace of the king of Babylon." 19 Then Hezekiah said to Isaiah, "The word of the LORD that you have spoken is good." For he thought, "Why not, if there will be peace and security in my days?"

Analysis

The story of the delegation sent by Merodach-baladan to Hezekiah culminates in a threat spoken by Isaiah. His utterance is a premonition of the Babylonian exile of Judah after the conquest of Jerusalem by Nebuchadnezzar in 587, an event as yet far away. This type of prediction is called a *vaticinium ex eventu* (prophecy after the event), that is, a "prediction" of an event that has already taken place. The narrative as such is therefore of no historical value, even if the figure of Merodach-baladan is historically attested.[1] Merodach-baladan was a prince of the Bit-Yakin tribe from southern Babylonia who managed to become king twice, in 730 and 721–710, and thus stood in opposition to the Assyrian kings who had assumed the kingship in Babylon since the time of Tiglath-pileser III. A meeting between Hezekiah, who had been in conflict with the empire since his breaking away from Ashur, and an envoy from the usurper Merodach-baladan is still relatively unlikely, despite the historical information available. Rather, Merodach-baladan is mentioned here as a forerunner of the Neo-Babylonian Empire, since Isaiah's utterance of doom points ahead to events taking place under Nebuchadnezzar, its founder.

The critical slant of the narrative with regard to Hezekiah is difficult not to notice. Yahweh may have saved Judah from the assault of the Assyrians under Sennacherib (18:13—19:37), but Hezekiah is to blame for the later deportation by the Babylonians. The reason lies in Hezekiah's behavior: "The prophetic narrative interprets the pride with which Hezekiah shows off his riches as hubris; it reveals an undue trust in his own wealth and strength."[2] Because the narrative justifies the later fate of Judah with misguided behavior on the part of Hezekiah, who is so positively judged by the Deuteronomistic Historian, the latter is hardly likely to be the author of this section. Instead, it must be the work of a redactor who composed the section in the knowledge of the entire work, taking a historical figure as his model.

Commentary

[20:12-13] The sequence of events is consistent. We lack the sources on the diplomatic relations between the states rebelling against Ashur, but we can assume that there was contact in order to negotiate a common course of action. A personal interest in each other's well-being seems to have been part of the established practice of communication, and this habit forms the background of v. 12. Hezekiah receives the envoys sent by Merodach-baladan with great honors (v. 13). As a sign of special honor they are given a tour of the entire palace, to be impressed by the display of royal wealth. The access of visitors to all parts of the palace seems not to have been the rule; the palace was usually reserved for the royal family and the royal household that had to fulfill its private and public duties.

The "treasure house" is expressly mentioned as the destination of the tour. The term is not attested anywhere else in the Bible and is a loanword from Akkadian (*bīt nakkamti*). We know nothing more about either the design or location of the treasure house within the palace, but it is likely to have been a separate building. Its function as a storehouse for the royal possessions is obvious. Here the revenue from the

---

[1] See J. A. Brinkman, "Merodach-Baladan II," in *Studies Presented to A. Leo Oppenheim, June 7, 1964* (Chicago: Univ. of Chicago, Oriental Institute, 1964), 6–53.
[2] Würthwein, *Könige,* 2:437.

royal estates was put, together with tax money and trade profits. The "treasure" consisted largely of precious metals and expensive objects or products.

[20:14-15] Hezekiah's behavior while welcoming the envoy brings Isaiah, the prophet of the divine will, onto the scene. It is inferred that he has received the word of God regarding Hezekiah before. Isaiah is portrayed as a prophet of judgment in this narrative, just as he is in the collection of sayings in the book of Isaiah.

[20:16-18] The word of doom is prepared well through the deceptively innocent questions asked by Isaiah and the fatal replies given by Hezekiah. The prediction of doom aims at the later Babylonian exile and the end of Judah. Two facets are especially pronounced against the framework of the narrative: the loss of the accumulated treasures and the enslavement of the royal princes to become court officials at the palace in Babylon. The personal humiliation that princes will have to serve in the palace of another ruler is thus added to the loss of riches. The prophecy of doom is developed from the perspective of the end of the Deuteronomistic History. Hezekiah, too, has contributed with his own guilt to the downfall of Judah. A later time did not see Hezekiah with the same positive eyes as the Deuteronomistic Historian does, but has him added to the list of those who were responsible for the national disaster that struck in the year 587.

[20:19] The reply by the king deconstructs the Deuteronomistic image of Hezekiah even further. The piety that he shows in response to the utterance is only pretended; in truth he is, as a human being, considering only his well-being in his own time.

Concluding Formula for Hezekiah

Text

20:20 The rest of the deeds of Hezekiah, all his power, how he made the pool and the conduit and brought water into the city, are they not written in the Book of the Annals of the Kings of Judah? 21 Hezekiah slept with his ancestors; and his son Manasseh succeeded him.

Commentary

[20:20-21] A comment is included with this concluding formula, which mentions a building project improving the water supply of Jerusalem. This is the tunnel that leads from the Gihon spring to the pool of Siloam inside the city, which was rediscovered in the nineteenth century.[1] This tunnel, which transported water from the spring outside the city walls to the southern parts of the city, was a significant improvement. Up to that time the only water supply available in case of a siege came through the so-called Warren's Shaft.[2]

The technical achievement of this measure is praised in a six-line inscription chiseled into the rock not long before the end of the tunnel:

> [This] was the tunnel, and [these] were the circumstances of the tunnel: while the stone workers were still [swinging] their pick axes, one toward the other, and there were still three yards to hack through, the voice of each calling out to his colleague [was] heard, for there was a gap in the rock from the south and [from the no]rth. And on the day of breaking through the stone workers were hacking toward each other, axe against [a]xe, and the waters flowed from the source into the pool for a length of

---

[1] See Robert Wenning and Erich Zenger, "Die verschiedenen Systeme der Wassernutzung im südlichen Jerusalem und die Bezugnahme darauf in biblischen Texten," *UF* 14 (1982) 279–94.

[2] See Yigal Shiloh, "The Rediscovery of the Ancient Water System Known as 'Warren's Shaft,'" in *Ancient Jerusalem Revealed*, ed. Hillel Geva (Jerusalem: Israel Exploration Society, 1994), 46–54.

1,200 yards. And the rock above the head of the stone workers was 100 yards high.[3]

This tunnel, named after its constructor, Hezekiah, is one of the few examples where the biblical text can be verified by the archaeological record. Other than that, the concluding formula comprises the usual notices and leads to the successor.

---

[3] Johannes Renz, *Die althebräischen Inschriften* (Darmstadt: Wissenschaftliche Buchgesellschaft, 1995), 1:178–89. [Ed.] See also Robert B. Coote, "Siloam Inscription," in *ABD,* 6:23–24.

Manasseh

Text

21:1 Manasseh was twelve years old when he began to reign; he reigned fifty-five years in Jerusalem. His mother's name was Hephzibah. 2 He did what was evil in the sight of the LORD, following the abominable practices of the nations that the LORD drove out before the people of Israel. 3 For he rebuilt the high places that his father Hezekiah had destroyed; he erected altars for Baal, made a sacred pole, as King Ahab of Israel had done, worshiped all the host of heaven, and served them. 4 He built altars in the house of the LORD, of which the LORD had said, "In Jerusalem I will put my name." 5 He built altars for all the host of heaven in the two courts of the house of the LORD. 6 He made his son pass through fire; he practiced soothsaying and augury, and dealt with mediums and with wizards. He did much evil in the sight of the LORD, provoking him to anger. 7 The carved image of Asherah that he had made he set in the house of which the LORD said to David and to his son Solomon, "In this house, and in Jerusalem, which I have chosen out of all the tribes of Israel, I will put my name forever; 8 I will not cause the feet of Israel to wander any more out of the land that I gave to their ancestors, if only they will be careful to do according to all that I have commanded them, and according to all the law that my servant Moses commanded them." 9 But they did not listen; Manasseh misled them to do more evil than the nations had done that the LORD destroyed before the people of Israel.

10 The LORD said by his servants the prophets, 11 "Because King Manasseh of Judah has committed these abominations, has done things more wicked than all that the Amorites did, who were before him, and has caused Judah also to sin with his idols; 12 therefore thus says the LORD, the God of Israel, I am bringing upon Jerusalem and Judah such evil that the ears of everyone who hears of it will tingle. 13 I will stretch over Jerusalem the measuring line for Samaria, and the plummet for the house of Ahab; I will

wipe Jerusalem as one wipes a dish, wiping it and turning it upside down. 14 I will cast off the remnant of my heritage, and give them into the hand of their enemies; they shall become a prey and a spoil to all their enemies, 15 because they have done what is evil in my sight and have provoked me to anger, since the day their ancestors came out of Egypt, even to this day."

16 Moreover Manasseh shed very much innocent blood, until he had filled Jerusalem from one end to another, besides the sin that he caused Judah to sin so that they did what was evil in the sight of the LORD.

17 Now the rest of the acts of Manasseh, all that he did, and the sin that he committed, are they not written in the Book of the Annals of the Kings of Judah? 18 Manasseh slept with his ancestors, and was buried in the garden of his house, in the garden of Uzza. His son Amon succeeded him.

Analysis

The Deuteronomistic Historian has significantly enlarged the introductory formula for Manasseh by including vv. 3-9. Verses 10-15 are a further addition to which v. 16 has been added yet later on. Verses 3-9 are not a compilation of notes, but rather an independent creation of the Deuteronomistic Historian that aims to show the degree of the king's depravity. The list of offenses in this case does not match up with real historical events but instead is oriented to the stipulations of the book of Deuteronomy. The introductory formula does therefore not contain information about other events during his rule; it throws the negative judgment of Manasseh into sharper relief when it blames him for an extra series of cultic offenses, practices that are ruled out by the book of Deuteronomy.

Commentary

[21:1-2] Introductory formula. Of all the Judean kings, Manasseh reigns longest. The length of his reign is due to his young age at succession. We can infer from 18:2 that Hezekiah died at fifty-four, which makes him already forty-two years old when his son Manasseh was born. Manasseh is therefore unlikely to be the firstborn, and it is not clear why he succeeded his father. Other brothers or half-brothers might have died or been passed over.

Manasseh is mentioned twice in Assyrian sources. He is one of the "twelve kings of the coast" under Esarhaddon who were obliged to supply building materials to Nineveh. Also, he appears in a similar list of Ashurbanipal among the vassals who had to support the Assyrian king during a campaign against Egypt.[1] Manasseh was a loyal vassal under Esarhaddon and Ashurbanipal. Still, with regard to vv. 3-9, "there is no evidence that Assyria demanded adherence to Assyrian religious practices or interfered in any way in the native cults of their vassals."[2]

---

[1] *TUAT,* I/4, 397.
[2] Cogan and Tadmor, *II Kings,* 272.

The long years of Manasseh's reign indicate that his loyalty to Ashur was beyond doubt. Ashur was at the height of its power after the conquest of Egypt in 671, and an attempt to break away, such as Hezekiah had undertaken with disastrous consequences, was out of the question for Manasseh. This loyalty must have given extra impetus to the negative judgment proclaimed on him by the Deuteronomistic Historian, made explicit in the list of cultic offenses in vv. 3-9. The reference to the "abominable practices of the nations" in v. 2 takes up an expression from Deut 18:9 on the cult practices not in accordance with Yahweh.

[21:3-9] The cult practices. Every cult practice that is prohibited in the legal code of the book of Deuteronomy is here attributed to Manasseh. The necessity for such negative stipulations is proof that such offenses were actually practiced. The list of the various manifestations of cults of foreign deities under Manasseh is, however, a work of literature by the Deuteronomistic Historian and not a description of the reality of religious practices in seventh-century Judah. The establishing of sanctuaries in the high places or, alternatively, the refusal to abolish them, is a stock charge made against the kings of Israel and Judah (see 1 Kgs 12:13; 14:23; 22:44; 2 Kgs 12:4; 14:4; 15:4, 35; 17:11, 29, 32).

The special twist of the episode here lies in the reference that Hezekiah had destroyed the sanctuaries in the high places (cf. 18:4). Manasseh returns to the cult of foreign gods by setting up more altars to Baal and constructing new sacred poles (asherahs). The reference to Ahab puts Manasseh in a line with this particularly depraved king of the northern kingdom (cf. 1 Kgs 16:29—22:40). The charge to have worshiped all the host of heaven in vv. 3 and 5 explicitly contradicts Deut 4:19 and 17:3 and implies the worship of sun, moon, and stars as cosmic features with individual powers, whereas the creation order of Israel gives no independent religious significance to those heavenly bodies.

[21:5] The two courts around or in front of the temple, mentioned in v. 5, are referred to again in 23:19. The description of the upper court in Jer 36:10 also makes two courts seem likely, although the description of the outer wall surrounding the temple area given in 1 Kgs 6:36 and 7:12 presupposes only one court. It is only the draft constitution of Ezekiel that first distinguishes two separate temple courts with different degrees of sacredness (see Ezek 44:19, 21). The solution could lie in a small walled enclosure between the walled temple area and the palace, which during the time of kings was adjacent to the temple; this space would then form an outer court as opposed to the inner forecourt of the temple proper.

[21:6] The practices named in v. 6 stand in direct opposition to Deut 18:10-11. The phrase "he made his son pass through fire" is a euphemism for the practice of child sacrifice, which was banned in Israel (see on 16:3). "Soothsaying and augury" refer to the mantic practices that were widespread in the environment of Israel. Their main aim was to foretell the future through oracles. Their best-known forms are dream oracles, casting lots, observing the flight and call of birds, and augury from a liver. Only two forms of oracle by lots are attested for prestate Israel and the early kingship: the ephod (see 1 Sam 23:9-12; 30:7-9) and the Urim and Thummim (see 1 Sam 14:41; 28:6; and compare 1 Sam 23:2; 2 Sam 5:19). Both were used to reveal the will of God, but were suppressed early on as inappropriate means to access hidden knowledge of the future. The terms "soothsaying and augury" recall Deut 18:10-11, and they include the practice of necromancy; in this practice the dead are asked to reveal desired information that is inaccessible to the living. An example is Saul's visit to the female medium at Endor (1 Sam 28:4-25).[3] Apart from extracting knowledge about the future, necromancy was also used to placate wandering spirits who were potentially harmful.

[21:7] The goddess Asherah has to be distinguished from the wooden cult object of the same name, probably a wooden symbol of that deity. In the mythical texts from Ugarit she often appears together with El, the father of the gods, although she was apparently worshiped by the Israelite kings too as a female counterpart of Yahweh, according to biblical and nonbiblical sources (cf. 1 Kgs 15:13; 16:33; 2 Kgs 13:6). Epigraphic evidence for the goddess Asherah is found at Kuntillet 'Ajrūd in the Sinai desert, at Khirbet el-Qom in the Judean mountains, and at Ekron (Khirbet el-Muqanna'). The configuration of words "Yahweh . . . and his Asherah" is of particular interest in those cases, and it is still a contentious question in the literature whether Asherah is to be interpreted as Yahweh's companion.[4]

[21:10-13] Verses 10-13, part of the extension vv. 10-15, are a scolding by a Deuteronomistic redactor: Judah is threatened with the fate of the northern kingdom, namely the conquest of the capital and the subsequent loss of independence. The mention of Ahab is an explicit reference to the conflict between the royal house and the prophets (see 1 Kgs 16:29—22:40). The analogy centers essentially on the figure of Jeroboam, "who sinned and led his people astray, with disastrous consequences, as does Manasseh."[5] The Deuteronomistic Historian thus condemns Manasseh's policy, which bought peace with submission to Ashur, as contradicting the will of Yahweh. Manasseh has brought about the destruction of his people precisely through his

---

[3] On the ancient Near Eastern parallels see J. L. Finkel, "Necromancy in Ancient Mesopotamia," *AfO* 29/30 (1983–84) 1–17.

[4] See Judith M. Hadley, "Yahweh and 'His Asherah': Archaeological and Textual Evidence for the Cult of the Goddess," in *Ein Gott allein? JHWH-Verehrung und biblischer Monotheismus im Kontext der israelitischen und altorientalischen Religionsgeschichte,* ed. Walter Dietrich, Martin A. Klopfenstein, OBO 139 (Göttingen: Vandenhoeck & Ruprecht, 1994), 235–68.

[5] Würthwein, *Könige,* 2:442.

pro-Assyrian attitude. His policy is uncompromisingly opposed to the judgment based on Deuteronomistic theology.

[21:16] The negative judgment reaches its climax. The phrase "to shed innocent blood" usually refers to the oppression of the poor and socially weak (cf. Jer 7:6; 22:3, 17; Ezek 22:6-16, 25-31). The later redactor thus viewed the reign of Manasseh not only as a period of cultic malpractice but also as an epoch of social injustice and violent oppression.

[21:17-18] Concluding formula. Apart from the usual statements there is one reference to a new burial site "in the garden of Uzza." All the kings of Judah down to Hezekiah were buried in the royal tomb in the city of David, a site that has not been located yet, if it has survived at all. The old burial site of the Davidides is thus as unspecific as the new one, even if "the garden of Uzza" seems to indicate a site outside the city walls. The reasons for this change we do not know; lack of space is highly unlikely, given that the bones were collected in a single grave according to ancient Israelite burial custom. A better reason is the extension of the city at the beginning of the ninth or end of the eighth century.[6] The inclusion into the settlement of new areas west of the city may have forced the royal family too to shift its burial ground. It is unlikely that this new site "in the garden of Uzza" can be identified with the caves of the kings mentioned in Josephus (*War* 5.147) or the graves on the grounds of the École Biblique et Archéologique.[7]

---

[6] See Dan Bahat, *The Illustrated Atlas of Jerusalem,* trans. Shelomo Ketko (New York: Simon & Schuster, 1990), 24–33.

[7] *Pace* Amos Kloner, "The 'Third Wall' in Jerusalem and the 'Cave of the Kings' (Josephus, *War* V,147)," *Levant* 18 (1986) 121–29.

Amon

Text

21:19 Amon was twenty-two years old when he began to reign; he reigned two years in Jerusalem. His mother's name was Meshullemeth daughter of Haruz of Jotbah. 20 He did what was evil in the sight of the LORD, as his father Manasseh had done. 21 He walked in all the way in which his father walked, served the idols that his father served, and worshiped them; 22 he abandoned the LORD, the God of his ancestors, and did not walk in the way of the LORD. 23 The servants of Amon conspired against him, and killed the king in his house. 24 But the people of the land killed all those who had conspired against King Amon, and the people of the land made his son Josiah king in place of him. 25 Now the rest of the acts of Amon that he did, are they not written in the Book of the Annals of the Kings of Judah? 26 He was buried in his tomb in the garden of Uzza; then his son Josiah succeeded him.

Commentary

[21:19-26] The short reign of Amon is subjected to the same negative judgment by the Deuteronomistic Historian as that of his father Manasseh. If Manasseh, following 21:1, died at sixty-one, Amon was born when his father was already forty-five years old, which makes him probably not one of the oldest sons. No explanation is given why he succeeded to the throne; given Manasseh's long reign, however, he might have survived one or more of his older sons. Amon's mother is not from Jerusalem but from Jotbah. This is the same place in Lower Galilee that is mentioned by Tiglath-pileser III and Josephus, probably identical with Khirbet Shifat, about 14 km. north of Nazareth.[1] Manasseh's marriage to a woman from northern Israel shows that no tensions had yet arisen between the populations, but there is no indication whether this was an expression of a deliberate policy.

---

[1] See Hayim Tadmor, *The Inscriptions of Tiglath-pileser III, King of Assyria* (Jerusalem: Israel Academy of Sciences and Humanities, 1994), 80.

[21:23] Amon is assassinated by his own men after only two years. No reasons are given, but several motives could be brought forward in order to elucidate the background: (1) The deed is the attempt of an older brother in order to usurp the power by assassinating the king. (2) The assassination is carried out by an anti-Assyrian party that thinks its hour of action has come.[2] (3) The responsible party is an oppositional faction within the priesthood, demanding the exclusive worship of Yahweh.[3]

[21:24] Whatever the reason for the assassination (and we cannot establish any of them with complete certainty), it did not have the desired effect, since the people chose Josiah (probably Amon's firstborn son) to succeed him as king. The "people of the land" are the full citizens of Judah, who maintain the dynasty by their choice. Whether the mother of the new king, who came from the Shephelah, was a link to the full citizens of Judah is not known.

---

[2] See Abraham Malamat, "The Historical Background of the Assassination of Amon, King of Judah," *IEJ* 3 (1953) 26–29.

[3] See Eduard Nielsen, "Political Conditions and Cultural Developments in Israel and Judah during the Reign of Manasseh," in *Proceedings of the Fourth World Congress of Jewish Studies* (Jerusalem: World Union of Jewish Studies, 1967), 1:103–6.

Introductory Formula for Josiah

Text

22:1 Josiah was eight years old when he began to reign; he reigned thirty-one years in Jerusalem. His mother's name was Jedidah daughter of Adaiah of Bozkath. 2 He did what was right in the sight of the LORD, and walked in all the way of his father David; he did not turn aside to the right or to the left.

Commentary

[22:1-2] Josiah, the last of the significant kings of Judah, is evaluated positively by the Deuteronomistic Historian. The reason is undoubtedly Josiah's cult reform, which was entirely in line with the Deuteronomistic call for the monotheistic worship of Yahweh. With Josiah still being underage at the time of succession, the regency was likely overseen by high officials. His mother is from the Shephelah, and although we do not know the precise location of Bozkath, Josh 15:39 tells us that it was part of the same administrative district as Lachish (Tell ed-Duwēr), Eglon (Tell Etûn), and Makkedah (Khirbet el-Qom near Bēt Maqdûm). Josiah was thus linked through his mother to the "people of the land," who chose him as a successor.

Several stories (2 Kgs 22:3-11, 12-20; 23:1-3) are told between the opening and concluding formula (23:28-30), which all serve to prepare for the great cult reform (23:4-27), the high point of Josiah's reign and of its account. Nothing is said about other political activities of the king.

Since the date of Josiah's death is a known reference point, we can infer that his reign lasted from 639 to 609, thus coinciding with the decline of Ashur, which had begun with the death of Ashurbanipal between 631 and 627.[1] After Babylonia gained independence under Nabopolassar in 626, Assyria was not able to regain control over this area. The end of the Neo-Assyrian Empire is marked by the capture of Nineveh

---

[1] See Herbert Donner, *Geschichte des Volkes Israel und seiner Nachbarn in Grundzügen,* 2 vols., 2d ed., Grundrisse zum Alten Testament 4 (Göttingen: Vandenhoeck & Ruprecht, 1995), 2:370–89.

in 612; the final attempt to cling to control with the help of Egypt was defeated in the battle of Carchemish in 605. Although we lack sources for a political history of Judah itself at the time, the reign of Josiah has to be seen against the background of the political upheavals of the Near East.[2] The liberation from the Assyrian yoke led to an extensive cult reform in Judah as well as (unspecified) territorial changes. The Deuteronomistic History passes over other political events and focuses on the cult reform of Josiah alone.

---

[2] See Nadav Na'aman, "The Kingdom of Judah under Josiah," *TA* 18 (1991) 3–71.

The Discovery of the Book of the Law

Text

22:3 In the eighteenth year of King Josiah, the king sent Shaphan son of Azaliah, son of Meshullam, the secretary, to the house of the LORD, saying, 4 "Go up to the high priest Hilkiah, and have him count the entire sum of the money that has been brought into the house of the LORD, which the keepers of the threshold have collected from the people; 5 let it be given into the hand of the workers who have the oversight of the house of the LORD; let them give it to the workers who are at the house of the LORD, repairing the house, 6 that is, to the carpenters, to the builders, to the masons; and let them use it to buy timber and quarried stone to repair the house. 7 But no accounting shall be asked from them for the money that is delivered into their hand, for they deal honestly."

8 The high priest Hilkiah said to Shaphan the secretary, "I have found the book of the law in the house of the LORD." When Hilkiah gave the book to Shaphan, he read it. 9 Then Shaphan the secretary came to the king, and reported to the king, "Your servants have emptied out the money that was found in the house, and have delivered it into the hand of the workers who have oversight of the house of the LORD." 10 Shaphan the secretary informed the king, "The priest Hilkiah has given me a book." Shaphan then read it aloud to the king.

11 When the king heard the words of the book of the law, he tore his clothes.

Commentary

[22:3-11] The extensive report of the reform begins with the discovery of a book in the temple and its handing over to the king. The starting point is the regular control of the money collected for the upkeep of the temple, as it was established in 12:10ff. Verses 4-7, 9 are a continuation of 12:10ff. in terms of style and content, and the framing narrative establishes the whole episode as a secondary composition.[1] Shaphan the scribe, who came to oversee the funds at the temple, is on this occasion presented with a book found there by the high priest Hilkiah. Nothing is said about the circumstances of its discovery. The name "book of the law" in 22:8, 11; 23:24 and "book of the covenant" in 23:2, 3, 21 indicates that it is the collection of laws and stipulations from Deuteronomy 12–26, referred to as *Urdeuteronomium*.[2] This *Urdeuteronomium* is presented in the shape of a speech of Moses and a revelation of the divine will at the same time.

The narrative leads on to the handing over of the book to the king, who is the first to recognize its true significance. Its meaning is manifested by the king's reaction; accordingly, from now on no further action is taken without the explicit order of the king. The king is thus made the driving force behind the cult reform from early on, and he acts not from his own will but rather fulfills the task given by God in the "book of law." The discovery of the book in the temple guarantees its authenticity. The reaction of the king, who rends his clothes in a gesture of mourning, mirrors not only his shock at the discovery but also his despair at the present situation. The necessity for reform is thus firmly established.

---

[1] See Walter Dietrich, "Josia und das Gesetzbuch (2 Reg. 22)," *VT* 27 (1977) 13–35.

[2] See Otto Kaiser, *Grundriss der Einleitung in die kanonischen und deuterokanonischen Schriften des Alten Testaments,* 3 vols. (Gütersloh: Gütersloher, 1992), 1:90–99.

The Prediction of the Prophetess Huldah

Text

22:12 Then the king commanded the priest Hilkiah, Ahikam son of Shaphan, Achbor son of Micaiah, Shaphan the secretary, and the king's servant Asaiah, saying, 13 "Go, inquire of the LORD for me, for the people, and for all Judah, concerning the words of this book that has been found; for great is the wrath of the LORD that is kindled against us, because our ancestors did not obey the words of this book, to do according to all that is written concerning us."

14 So the priest Hilkiah, Ahikam, Achbor, Shaphan, and Asaiah went to the prophetess Huldah the wife of Shallum son of Tikvah, son of Harhas, keeper of the wardrobe; she resided in Jerusalem in the Second Quarter, where they consulted her. 15 She declared to them, "Thus says the LORD, the God of Israel: Tell the man who sent you to me, 16 Thus says the LORD, I will indeed bring disaster on this place and on its inhabitants—all the words of the book that the king of Judah has read. 17 Because they have abandoned me and have made offerings to other gods, so that they have provoked me to anger with all the work of their hands, therefore my wrath will be kindled against this place, and it will not be quenched. 18 But as to the king of Judah, who sent you to inquire of the LORD, thus shall you say to him, Thus says the LORD, the God of Israel: Regarding the words that you have heard, 19 because your heart was penitent, and you humbled yourself before the LORD, when you heard how I spoke against this place, and against its inhabitants, that they should become a desolation and a curse, and because you have torn your clothes and wept before me, I also have heard you, says the LORD. 20 Therefore, I will gather you to your ancestors, and you shall be gathered to your grave in peace; your eyes shall not see all the disaster that I will bring on this place." They took the message back to the king.

Commentary

[22:12-20] In order to learn the will of God, the king dispatches a delegation to the court prophetess. Huldah is the only woman who is mentioned as the holder of this office during the kingship; the incumbent was usually male. Of the five named men of the delegation, the priest Hilkiah and the scribe Shaphan have been mentioned earlier in vv. 3-11. The remaining three are not identified by their function, but are likely to be members of the upper class holding high state offices. Ahikam, son of Shaphan, is mentioned again in Jer 26:24, where he saves Jeremiah from the angry people. According to Jer 26:22 and 36:12, Achbar is the father of Elnathan, who held a high office under King Jehoiachin. Shaphan, too, appears again in Jer 36:12 as the father of Gemariah, a high official under Jehoiachin. Asaiah is the only figure who is not named elsewhere.

[22:12-14] The official delegation from the king seeks out the prophetess in her home in the new town. Judging by archaeological evidence, the new town was built on the western hill as part of the city's expansion.[1] The quarter was built sometime in the eighth century; it was fortified by a wall and included within the city only under Hezekiah. Verse 13b is offered as an additional explanation for the delegation within the exposition of vv. 12-14.

As stressed in 23:26-27 and 24:3, 20a, the reason for Yahweh's anger is the disobedience of the ancestors. Spoken by the king, these words claim that the fate of Judah is ineluctable. The will of God is therefore already set on the destruction of the southern kingdom at the time when the book of the law is discovered, and even Josiah's reform can do nothing to avert disaster. The events of the year 587 are thus justified by the guilt of the people before the reign of Josiah (see 22:18-20).

[22:15-20] The answer that the prophetess gives to the king's question is in two parts. The general prophecy of doom (vv. 15-17) is followed by a personal address to Josiah (vv. 18-20a). The latter part has an explanatory function and is therefore a later addition. The original prophecy of doom justifies the impending catastrophe with the wrongdoing of the people. The argument is in line with the intention of the newly discovered book of the law: Israel has not fulfilled the demand to worship Yahweh as the one and only God and therefore has to suffer punishment. Yahweh will give the chosen dwelling place of his name over to destruction. History thus becomes the execution of the judgment of Yahweh according to Deuteronomistic theology. The fate suffered is appropriate to the deeds done, even if the fate arrives late and not immediately after the wrongdoing. The world order established through this principle remains in place. The prophetess repeats and interprets the doom toward which history inevitably moves.

---

[1] See Nahman Avigad, *Discovering Jerusalem* (Nashville: Nelson, 1983), 23–60.

[22:18-20a] The addition belongs within the same horizon and it gives a positive interpretation to the fate of Josiah. His penitence and uprightness save him from having to witness the destruction of the temple and the kingdom. His violent death at Megiddo (23:29) lets Josiah escape the fate ordained by Yahweh. The later catastrophe shows up his premature end as a way of being saved from becoming an eyewitness to the wrath of God. Coming from the lips of the prophetess, his being spared the final fate is also part of the divine plan manifested in history.

[22:20b] Nothing is said on the king's reaction after the prophecy has been delivered to him.

The Covenant

Text

23:1 Then the king directed that all the elders of Judah and Jerusalem should be gathered to him. 2 The king went up to the house of the LORD, and with him went all the people of Judah, all the inhabitants of Jerusalem, the priests, the prophets, and all the people, both small and great; he read in their hearing all the words of the book of the covenant that had been found in the house of the LORD. 3 The king stood by the pillar and made a covenant before the LORD, to follow the LORD, keeping his commandments, his decrees, and his statutes, with all his heart and all his soul, to perform the words of this covenant that were written in this book. All the people joined in the covenant.

Commentary

[23:1-3] The covenant validates the law as it was set out in the discovered book, "covenant" indicating the special relationship granted by God to his people. The covenant means a special commitment on the part of God, while his people were obliged to keep the law of the covenant.[1] The "book of the law" spells out a new obligation under the covenant that regulates the appropriate behavior of the people through its commandments, decrees, and statutes.

The king serves as mediator of the covenant between God and his people. To this end he stands in a "high place," probably meaning a pedestal rather than a pillar. Following 11:4 this pedestal was the stand of the king on formal occasions. The elders represent the people and their individual places in the ceremony; the entire population becomes included only in v. 2. The covenant under Josiah stands in the tradition of the covenants under Moses on Sinai (Exodus 24) and under Joshua at

---

[1] See Moshe Weinfeld, "ברית, covenant," in *TDOT* 2:253–79.

Shechem (Joshua 24). With the renewed covenant the people were committed to a new law.

Thus it is for the first time in the history of the kingship that the state is founded on the basis of a religious legal corpus; the confusion resulting from the "amalgamation of the religious order and the state" is not considered further.[2] For the Deuteronomistic Historian the history of Israel has reached its high point: the nation has not only entered into a covenant with God, but the covenant has also become the legal foundation of the political order. The reform of Josiah is portrayed consequently as the prevailing of the law of God with regard to the worship of Yahweh as the one and only God.

---

[2] Martin Noth, *The History of Israel,* 2d ed., trans. P. R. Ackroyd (New York: Harper & Row, 1960), 275.

The Cult Reform of Josiah

Text

23:4 The king commanded the high priest Hilkiah, the priests of the second order, and the guardians of the threshold, to bring out of the temple of the Lord all the vessels made for Baal, for Asherah, and for all the host of heaven; he burned them outside Jerusalem in the fields of the Kidron, and carried their ashes to Bethel. 5 He deposed the idolatrous priests whom the kings of Judah had ordained to make offerings in the high places at the cities of Judah and around Jerusalem; those also who made offerings to Baal, to the sun, the moon, the constellations, and all the host of the heavens. 6 He brought out the image of Asherah from the house of the Lord, outside Jerusalem, to the Wadi Kidron, burned it at the Wadi Kidron, beat it to dust and threw the dust of it upon the graves of the common people. 7 He broke down the houses of the male temple prostitutes that were in the house of the Lord, where the women did weaving for Asherah. 8 He brought all the priests out of the towns of Judah, and defiled the high places where the priests had made offerings, from Geba to Beer-sheba; he broke down the high places of the gates that were at the entrance of the gate of Joshua the governor of the city, which were on the left at the gate of the city. 9 The priests of the high places, however, did not come up to the altar of the Lord in Jerusalem, but ate unleavened bread among their kindred. 10 He defiled Topheth, which is in the valley of Ben-hinnom, so that no one would make a son or a daughter pass through fire as an offering to Molech. 11 He removed the horses that the kings of Judah had dedicated to the sun, at the entrance to the house of the Lord, by the chamber of the eunuch Nathan-melech, which was in the precincts; then he burned the chariots of the sun with fire. 12 The altars on the roof of the upper chamber of Ahaz, which the kings of Judah had made, and the altars that Manasseh had made in the two courts of the house of the Lord, he pulled down from there and broke in pieces, and threw the rubble into the Wadi Kidron. 13 The king defiled the high places that were east of Jerusalem, to the south of the Mount of Destruction, which King Solomon of Israel had built for Astarte the abomination of the Sidonians, for Chemosh the abomination of Moab, and for Milcom the abomination of the Ammonites. 14 He broke the pillars in pieces, cut down the sacred poles, and covered the sites with human bones.

15 Moreover, the altar at Bethel, the high place erected by Jeroboam son of Nebat, who caused Israel to sin—he pulled down that altar along with the high place. He burned the high place, crushing it to dust; he also burned the sacred pole. 16 As Josiah turned, he saw the tombs there on the mount; and he sent and took the bones out of the tombs, and burned them on the altar, and defiled it, according to the word of the LORD that the man of God proclaimed, when Jeroboam stood by the altar at the festival; he turned and looked up at the tomb of the man of God who had predicted these things. 17 Then he said, "What is that monument that I see?" The people of the city told him, "It is the tomb of the man of God who came from Judah and predicted these things that you have done against the altar at Bethel." 18 He said, "Let him rest; let no one move his bones." So they let his bones alone, with the bones of the prophet who came out of Samaria. 19 Moreover, Josiah removed all the shrines of the high places that were in the towns of Samaria, which kings of Israel had made, provoking the LORD to anger; he did to them just as he had done at Bethel. 20 He slaughtered on the altars all the priests of the high places who were there, and burned human bones on them. Then he returned to Jerusalem.

21 The king commanded all the people, "Keep the passover to the LORD your God as prescribed in this book of the covenant." 22 No such passover had been kept since the days of the judges who judged Israel, or during all the days of the kings of Israel or of the kings of Judah; 23 but in the eighteenth year of King Josiah this passover was kept to the LORD in Jerusalem.

24 Moreover Josiah put away the mediums, wizards, teraphim, idols, and all the abominations that were seen in the land of Judah and in Jerusalem, so that he established the words of the law that were written in the book that the priest Hilkiah had found in the house of the LORD. 25 Before him there was no king like him, who turned to the LORD with all his heart, with all his soul, and with all his might, according to all the law of Moses; nor did any like him arise after him.

26 Still the LORD did not turn from the fierceness of his great wrath, by which his anger was kindled against Judah, because of all the provocations with which Manasseh had provoked him. 27 The LORD said, "I will remove Judah also out of my sight, as I have removed Israel; and I will reject this city that I have chosen, Jerusalem, and the house of which I said, My name shall be there."

Analysis

The reform includes numerous measures that may have been introduced over a long period of time; no chronology is suggested by the text. The carrying through of the reform is limited by and large to Jerusalem; the sanctuaries of the land are, with the exception of Bethel, mentioned only summarily. The report goes back to a number of phrases coined earlier on, and its original version is enlarged by three further sections:

vv. 16-18   Preservation of a prophet's tomb
vv. 19-20   Extension to Samaria
vv. 24-27   Positive judgment of Josiah

The report mentions the following specific measures:

1. Abolition of the worship of foreign deities
2. Destruction of the sanctuaries in the high places
3. Individual measures in the temple
4. Destruction of the altar at Bethel
5. Centralization of the Passover

Commentary

[23:4-9] The abolition of the worship of foreign deities is mentioned prominently in vv. 4 and 5. Baal and Asherah are Canaanite deities that were worshiped beside Yahweh during the kingship, as shown by extrabiblical evidence.[1] The "host of heaven" must indicate the worship of the heavenly bodies, naming the sun and moon separately (cf. Deut 4:17; 17:3). Just as the worship of foreign gods is condemned in toto (cf. 2 Kgs 17:16; 21:3), here its abolition is reported without any further details on the character of the gods or the form of worship. "Baal, Asherah, and heavenly host form an unholy alliance that stands in for any and all foreign worship."[2] Baal is linked to a fertility cult, while Asherah represents the female element missing from Yahweh. The heavenly bodies were thought to have great influence on daily life. The worship of foreign gods questions the exclusive power of Yahweh, while the exclusive worship of Yahweh returns to him the claim to power. All measures introduced by Josiah help to enforce the first commandment that Yahweh is the only God of Israel who has no other gods beside him.

"Sanctuaries in the high places" is the name given by the Deuteronomistic Historian to all cult sites outside the temple at Jerusalem. For the period of kings there is

---

[1] See Johannes C. de Moor and M. J. Mulder, "בעל, baʿal," in *TDOT* 2:181–200; Johannes C. de Moor, "אשרה, ʾasherah," in *TDOT* 1:438–44.

[2] Hermann Spieckermann, *Juda unter Assur in der Sargonidenzeit,* FRLANT 129 (Göttingen: Vandenhoeck & Ruprecht, 1982), 81.

only one temple of Yahweh attested, at the fortress at Arad.[3] The temple at Arad was, however, abandoned some time during the eighth century and no longer existed by the seventh century. For the time being, the abolition of sanctuaries in the country cannot be verified by archaeological findings. The only case of open-air sites that could be brought forward is that of the round platforms near Jerusalem that were indeed abandoned; however, we would have to be sure that these are sanctuaries and not threshing floors.[4] With clear evidence of sites outside Jerusalem still missing, there is no proof for the effects of Josiah's reform across Judah. It appears that his measures were by and large restricted to Jerusalem.

Numerous credible details are related for Jerusalem and its immediate environs. The "houses of the male temple prostitutes" probably does not refer to cultic prostitution, for which there is no evidence in ancient Israel. They might be rooms connected to the cult of Asherah. A wooden cult statue of Asherah was also removed from the temple and burned (v. 6). As was customary in the ancient Near East, cult statues were clothed and fed. The mention of "weaving for Asherah" envisages a group of women tending to her. When the cult statue is removed, the building housing them is destroyed as well. The reform not only brings changes to cult practice, but also does away with the buildings connected to it. We do not know anything about the cult site at the gate mentioned in v. 8b, but its attribution to demons marks it clearly as a site not dedicated to Yahweh. It is possible that in Israel cultic activity did indeed take place at the gates, but evidence does not bear out this hypothesis as yet.

[23:10] It is unclear what is behind the "fire" in the Hinnom Valley, for the meaning of Hebrew "Topheth" is uncertain. It is in any case definitely not a place of child sacrifice, an assumption that is based on a misinterpretation of Punic burial sites (see the notes on 16:1-4). The Hinnom Valley is identical with the Wādi er-Rababi southwest of Jerusalem, which meets the Kidron Valley (Wādi en-Nār) near the ʿĒn Rogel. The phrase "to make a son or a daughter pass through fire as an offering to Molech" does not help to illuminate the cult practice. It concerns most likely "a rite of purification through which children are presented to the deity."[5] The name Molech is probably a corruption of the Hebrew word for king (*melek*), and might here be a cover for the Aramean-Assyrian weather-god Adad.[6] The origin of the cult practiced at Topheth lies certainly outside Judah and was abolished as being incompatible with the worship of Yahweh.

---

[3] See Z. Herzog, M. Aharoni, Anson F. Rainey, and Sh. Moshkovitz, "The Israelite Fortress at Arad," *BASOR* 254 (1984) 1–34.

[4] See Ruth Amiran, "The Tumuli West of Jerusalem: Survey and Excavations, 1953," *IEJ* 8 (1958) 205–27.

[5] Rainer Albertz, *A History of Israelite Religion in the Old Testament Period,* 2 vols., trans. John Bowden, OTL (Louisville; Westminster John Knox, 1994), 1:190–94.

[6] See Moshe Weinfeld, "The Worship of Molech and of the Queen of Heaven and Its Background," *UF* 4 (1972) 133–54.

[23:11] The horses and chariot of the sun are likely to be a carriage for the Babylonian-Assyrian god Shamash. Whether this was a chariot drawn by real horses or a representation is not clear. What the processional vehicle does indicate, however, is the entry of the sun-god into, and thus the Assyrian influence upon, the temple at Jerusalem. Following the liberation from Assyrian hegemony Josiah is also removing the signs of the Assyrian state cult from the temple of Yahweh. The objective of the cult reform was also to shake off the yoke of Assyrian authority in religious matters.[7]

[23:12-14] The purity of the cult of Yahweh, demanded by the book of the law, leads to a cleansing of the temple from all syncretistic elements. Accordingly, all the altars are removed (v. 12), without indication to which gods they belonged. In general, we have no means to verify the historical accuracy of those details. It is obvious, however, that the account is shaped in such a way as to present the fulfillment of the demands made by the book of the law or *Urdeuteronomium* (Deuteronomy 12–26). The details give a glimpse of the actual concerns of the measures. The list of the gods of foreign nations in v. 13, lastly, makes explicit reference to the introduction of their cult by Solomon (see on 1 Kgs 11:7).

[23:15] The only measure of Josiah that does not concern Jerusalem is the destruction of Bethel. The notice is best seen as the work of a later redactor who felt he had to mention the destruction of the rival sanctuary set up by Jeroboam (cf. 1 Kgs 12:26-30), once the Deuteronomistic Historian had already condemned it as contradicting Yahweh. Thus the "sin of Jeroboam" is removed by Josiah. If v. 15 is mainly a literary formulation, then it is not necessary to decide whether Bethel had been reintegrated into Judah under Josiah, after the territory of the tribe of Benjamin had been lost to the Assyrian province of Samaria some time under Hezekiah. The report of the destruction of the sanctuary there cannot therefore be verified; it mainly serves to extol the glory of Josiah.

[23:21-23] The move of the Passover to Jerusalem, briefly summarized here, is modeled on the demand of Deut 16:5-6, which is fulfilled now. The notice refers deliberately to the Passover celebrated by all of Israel after the crossing of the Jordan.[8] We do not know to what extent a centralized Passover kept its character as a family celebration. Passover was originally a celebration of sacrifice of unknown provenance; during the monarchy it was conflated with the Feast of Unleavened Bread and tied to the Exodus tradition.[9] In the present context, the move of the Passover to Jerusalem is the high point of Josiah's reform; the king, now that he has established the worship of

---

[7] See Spieckermann, *Juda unter Assur*.

[8] On Josh 5:10-12, see Volkmar Fritz, *Das Buch Josua*, HAT 7 (Tübingen: Mohr/Siebeck, 1994), 59–63.

[9] See Martin Rösel, *TRE*, 26:231–36.

Yahweh as the one and only God in the temple at Jerusalem, consistently carries out the stipulations of the book of the law regarding the cult.

[23:16-20] The additional verses continue to praise Josiah. According to vv. 16-18 he preserved a tomb near Bethel, because it contained the bones of the prophet mentioned in 1 Kgs 13:2, who had foretold Josiah's destruction of the altar built at Bethel by Jeroboam. The passage is the literary link back to the earlier episode. Verses 19-20 extend the reform of Josiah retrospectively to all of Samaria, which was under Assyrian authority. The destruction of all cult sites in the former northern kingdom excludes all illegitimate worship from the area.

[23:24-27] The last addition underlines once more the exceptionality of Josiah, who has fulfilled the demands imposed by the book of the law. Despite the king's penitence, however, and his return to Yahweh, the will of God remains set on the destruction of Judah. The reason is seen in the sin of Manasseh. To the rejection of his will "Yahweh answered with the destruction of Judah, the rejection of Jerusalem, the chosen city, and of the place which was to be the house of his name."[10] Not even Josiah and his reform could turn away the decreed fate of Judah and the destruction of the Davidic kingship.

---

[10] Würthwein, *Könige,* 2:462.

Concluding Formula for Josiah

Text

23:28 Now the rest of the acts of Josiah, and all that he did, are they not written in the Book of the Annals of the Kings of Judah? 29 In his days Pharaoh Neco king of Egypt went up to the king of Assyria to the river Euphrates. King Josiah went to meet him; but when Pharaoh Neco met him at Megiddo, he killed him. 30 His servants carried him dead in a chariot from Megiddo, brought him to Jerusalem, and buried him in his own tomb. The people of the land took Jehoahaz son of Josiah, anointed him, and made him king in place of his father.

Commentary

[23:28-30] Following the long account of the reform, the section on Josiah is rounded off quickly with the concluding formula. Nothing is said about other internal measures or external politics during the decline of the Assyrian power. Only a single notice on Josiah's death is added to the usual pattern in v. 29, whose brevity stands in stark contrast with the elaborate account preceding it. The vagueness of the note gives the impression that events were deliberately left obscure. The exact circumstances of his death are not mentioned and are not illuminated either by the parallel section 2 Chr 35:20ff., which does not add further sources but simply elaborates on what is already there.

Even if there is no reference to a military conflict, we can assume, given the political situation, that Josiah's death is connected to a military campaign. The place of his death makes sense only when we assume a battle or at least its preparations. Egypt had shaken off the Assyrian hegemony already under Psammetik I (664–610).[1] When the Assyrian Empire had to fight for its supremacy in the Near East after 626, the former vassal turned into an ally. Maybe the pharaohs of the Twenty-sixth Dynasty wanted to put their own position in Syria and Palestine on a more secure

---

[1] See Hermann Spieckermann, *Juda und Assur in der Sargonidenzeit*, FRLANT 129 (Göttingen: Vandenhoeck & Ruprecht, 1982), 138–53.

footing by stabilizing Assyria. When Ashuruballit II, the last Assyrian king, formed a rump state around Harran in 612, after the fall of Nineveh, Egypt supported him with troops. The march of Neco's army toward the Euphrates in 609 is directly linked to the Egyptian support of Ashur.

Josiah, whose liberation from Ashur had come before its final decline, had to defend the independence of Judah against the Egyptians by military action. Megiddo, capital of an Assyrian province in the seventh century (stratum III) and seat of a governor, occupied a key strategic position, independent of whether Josiah captured the city or the Egyptians had set up a military camp there. Josiah's presence at Megiddo could be a hint that he intended to take over the parts of the former northern kingdom, which had been turned into Assyrian provinces under Tiglath-pileser III, after the collapse of the empire and integrate them into his own territory. Such thoughts of expansion must have met with strong resistance by the pharaoh, especially in the light of Egypt's attempts in the late period to regain its sovereignty over Canaan that it had held during the New Kingdom of the Eighteenth and Nineteenth Dynasties.

Neco must have followed two goals when marching toward the Euphrates: the assumption of power in the former Assyrian provinces and the support of the last Assyrian king against the Babylonians. Both hopes were defeated in the final battle at Carchemish in 605 from which the Babylonians emerged victorious as the heirs of the Assyrian Empire. Josiah was obviously unable to withstand the Egyptian offensive in 609; all further attempts to take advantage of the Assyrian decline in order to further Judah's own independence come to a halt after the death of the king. Neco II (610–595) establishes himself as the true ruler of Syria and Palestine, at least for the time being. Josiah's corpse is brought back to Jerusalem, disregarding the new political circumstances, to be buried in the new tomb of the kings of Judah. No reason is given why Jehoahaz is chosen as a successor.

Jehoahaz of Israel

Text

23:31 Jehoahaz was twenty-three years old when he began to reign; he reigned three months in Jerusalem. His mother's name was Hamutal daughter of Jeremiah of Libnah. 32 He did what was evil in the sight of the LORD, just as his ancestors had done. 33 Pharaoh Neco confined him at Riblah in the land of Hamath, so that he might not reign in Jerusalem, and imposed tribute on the land of one hundred talents of silver and a talent of gold. 34 Pharaoh Neco made Eliakim son of Josiah king in place of his father Josiah, and changed his name to Jehoiakim. But he took Jehoahaz away; he came to Egypt, and died there. 35 Jehoiakim gave the silver and the gold to Pharaoh, but he taxed the land in order to meet Pharaoh's demand for money. He exacted the silver and the gold from the people of the land, from all according to their assessment, to give it to Pharaoh Neco.

Commentary

[23:31-35] Jehoahaz was the royal name that Shallum adopted when he acceded to the throne (cf. Jer 22:10-12). Shallum was the fourth son of Josiah, according to the chronology of the Davidides given in 1 Chr 3:15. The judgment on him is negative. His mother came from the countryside of the Shephelah, with Libnah lying probably at today's Tell Bornāt. The hope that he would continue the reform policy of his father, Josiah, might explain why his brothers were passed over. His reign lasted for only three months, though, until Neco intervened in the succession.

Neco took him captive during an official visit to Riblah. Jehoahaz was taken to Egypt as a prisoner at the court of the pharaoh, where he died sometime later. Riblah was the military and administrative center of the Assyrians in Syria, located on Tell Zerra'a near Rableh, south of Hamath on the Orontes River. Neco installed Eliakim, another son of Josiah, as the new king of Judah; he took the crown name Jehoiakim, and he is referred to in 1 Chr 3:15 as the second of the four sons of Josiah. By imposing a tribute, Neco made the king a vassal of Egypt.

The sum of one talent of gold and one hundred talents of silver is redistributed and claimed from the population as a special tax, just as it happened under Menahem of Israel. Yet here no information is given about the tax amount claimed from each household, so we cannot calculate the population figures (see on 15:20). It is noticeable, however, that the tribute in silver amounts to only a tenth of that demanded from Menahem by Tiglath-pileser III. There is no concluding formula for Jehoahaz either. Since he died in Egypt, he was not buried in Jerusalem, and his tomb remains unknown.

Jehoiakim

Text

23:36 Jehoiakim was twenty-five years old when he began to reign; he reigned eleven years in Jerusalem. His mother's name was Zebidah daughter of Pedaiah of Rumah. 37 He did what was evil in the sight of the LORD, just as all his ancestors had done.

24:1 In his days King Nebuchadnezzar of Babylon came up; Jehoiakim became his servant for three years; then he turned and rebelled against him. 2 The LORD sent against him bands of the Chaldeans, bands of the Arameans, bands of the Moabites, and bands of the Ammonites; he sent them against Judah to destroy it, according to the word of the LORD that he spoke by his servants the prophets. 3 Surely this came upon Judah at the command of the LORD, to remove them out of his sight, for the sins of Manasseh, for all that he had committed, 4 and also for the innocent blood that he had shed; for he filled Jerusalem with innocent blood, and the LORD was not willing to pardon. 5 Now the rest of the deeds of Jehoiakim, and all that he did, are they not written in the Book of the Annals of the Kings of Judah? 6 So Jehoiakim slept with his ancestors; then his son Jehoiachin succeeded him. 7 The king of Egypt did not come again out of his land, for the king of Babylon had taken over all that belonged to the king of Egypt from the Wadi of Egypt to the River Euphrates.

Commentary

[23:36-37] The new king Jehoiakim is, with his twenty-five years, only marginally older than his predecessor Jehoahaz when he is installed by Neco. His mother comes from the former territory of Israel. Rumah is to be found at Tell er-Rummān in the Upper Jordan Valley and is mentioned along with Merom in the Annals of Tiglath-pileser III.[1] The judgment on him is negative. He reigned for eleven years and appar-

---

[1] See Hayim Tadmor, *The Inscriptions of Tiglath-pileser III, King of Assyria* (Jerusalem: Israel Academy of Sciences and Humanities, 1994), 83.

ently died a natural death, after which he was buried in Jerusalem, although this is not explicitly recorded.

[24:1-7] With 24:1-4 a section is included, between introductory and concluding formulas, that gives an account of the political situation and its interpretation by the Deuteronomistic Historian. Verse 7 adds a further comment on the changed balance of power. The Babylonian king Nabopolassar succeeded in stabilizing Babylonia's position after the fall of Nineveh in 612. When the Egyptians were finally defeated in the battle of Carchemish in 605, Babylonia firmly established its supremacy.[2] Nebuchadnezzar, crown prince of Babylon and leader of its army, advanced as far as Hamath on the Orontes River in the same year and thus removed the Egyptians entirely from Syro-Palestine. It is unclear why Jehoiakim became a vassal of Babylon and when he withdrew again.

After Nebuchadnezzar succeeded to the throne in 605, he advanced on Ashkelon in 604 to establish his rule over Syria and Palestine more firmly. The Neo-Babylonian Empire had become heir to the Neo-Assyrian Empire. The attempted defeat of Egypt in 601 appears to have failed.[3] Nebuchadnezzar did not lead a campaign in 600, which left it to the Aramean and East Jordanian vassals to fight against disloyal Judah. Jehoiakim's fall from Babylon is thus best dated to the year 601. The Babylonian king finally marched on Jerusalem in 598, when he besieged and sacked the city and installed a new king, reported in detail in 24:10-17.

---

[2] See *TUAT,* I/4, 403.

[3] *TGI,* 74.

Jehoiachin

Text

24:8 Jehoiachin was eighteen years old when he began to reign; he reigned three months in Jerusalem. His mother's name was Nehushta daughter of Elnathan of Jerusalem. 9 He did what was evil in the sight of the Lord, just as his father had done.

10 At that time the servants of King Nebuchadnezzar of Babylon came up to Jerusalem, and the city was besieged. 11 King Nebuchadnezzar of Babylon came to the city, while his servants were besieging it; 12 King Jehoiachin of Judah gave himself up to the king of Babylon, himself, his mother, his servants, his officers, and his palace officials. The king of Babylon took him prisoner in the eighth year of his reign.

13 He carried off all the treasures of the house of the Lord, and the treasures of the king's house; he cut in pieces all the vessels of gold in the temple of the Lord, which King Solomon of Israel had made, all this as the Lord had foretold. 14 He carried away all Jerusalem, all the officials, all the warriors, ten thousand captives, all the artisans and the smiths; no one remained, except the poorest people of the land. 15 He carried away Jehoiachin to Babylon; the king's mother, the king's wives, his officials, and the elite of the land, he took into captivity from Jerusalem to Babylon. 16 The king of Babylon brought captive to Babylon all the men of valor, seven thousand, the artisans and the smiths, one thousand, all of them strong and fit for war. 17 The king of Babylon made Mattaniah, Jehoiachin's uncle, king in his place, and changed his name to Zedekiah.

Commentary

[24:8-17] When Jehoiakim dies in the eleventh year of his reign, aged thirty-six, his son Jehoiachin succeeds him. His mother is from the upper classes of Jerusalem; her father Elnathan is mentioned as a high court official in Jer 26:22; 36:12, 25. The judgment on him is negative, even though he rules for only three months until he is deported to Babylon (v. 15). A concluding formula is missing, but the lack is com-

416

pensated for by the pardon of this king reported in 25:27-30, which closes off the entire Deuteronomistic History.

[24:10-17] Verses 10-17 are a detailed account of the punitive expedition of Nebuchadnezzar, an account that is verified in the Babylonian Chronicle: "In the seventh year [= 598], in the month of Kislev, the king of Akkad gathered his troops and advanced on Hattu. He attacked the city of Judah (*Ia-a-hu-du*). On the second of Adar he took the city. He set up a king after his own heart. He took a heavy tribute and brought (it) to Babel."[1] To this brief summary the biblical text adds the deportation of the king, his family, and the entire royal household (vv. 12, 15). The army and part of the population were also led into captivity, numbers ranging from 10,000 men (v. 14) to 7,000 (v. 16), with women and children to be added. Together with the ruling class, also the serving military and the artisans and metalworkers are taken into exile, the rationale being, of course, that without soldiers or the help of smiths to forge new weapons, no further insurrection was possible. The kingdom under the new king remained a dependent vassal state by the grace of Nebuchadnezzar. The new king Mattaniah was a younger son of Josiah, who took the royal name of Zedekiah. Verse 17 makes the name change appear to be the suggestion of Nebuchadnezzar, yet it is more likely that it was part of the customs surrounding the accession to the throne.

We do not learn the value of the objects taken away, but it is clear that all objects made from precious metal are included and that the treasure house of the palace is plundered. Everything valuable is taken as booty. With this measure the royal house is emptied of all movable goods; poverty is another way to pressure the new king into loyal submission.

Despite being ransacked, Jerusalem is not destroyed. Jehoiachin may have capitulated even before the storming of the city by the Babylonian troops, given the hopeless situation, an act that left the city inhabitable and the temple preserved. Still, Jehoiachin, taken prisoner and being deported, paid a high price for the policy of his father Jehoiakim and his striving for independence from Babylonia.

---

[1] *TGI*, 74.

Zedekiah

Text

24:18 Zedekiah was twenty-one years old when he began to reign; he reigned eleven years in Jerusalem. His mother's name was Hamutal daughter of Jeremiah of Libnah. 19 He did what was evil in the sight of the LORD, just as Jehoiakim had done. 20 Indeed, Jerusalem and Judah so angered the LORD that he expelled them from his presence.

Zedekiah rebelled against the king of Babylon. 25:1 And in the ninth year of his reign, in the tenth month, on the tenth day of the month, King Nebuchadnezzar of Babylon came with all his army against Jerusalem, and laid siege to it; they built siegeworks against it all around. 2 So the city was besieged until the eleventh year of King Zedekiah. 3 On the ninth day of the fourth month the famine became so severe in the city that there was no food for the people of the land. 4 Then a breach was made in the city wall; the king with all the soldiers fled by night by the way of the gate between the two walls, by the king's garden, though the Chaldeans were all around the city. They went in the direction of the Arabah. 5 But the army of the Chaldeans pursued the king, and overtook him in the plains of Jericho; all his army was scattered, deserting him. 6 Then they captured the king and brought him up to the king of Babylon at Riblah, who passed sentence on him. 7 They slaughtered the sons of Zedekiah before his eyes, then put out the eyes of Zedekiah; they bound him in fetters and took him to Babylon.

Commentary

[24:18-20a] Zedekiah, who was installed by Nebuchadnezzar as a vassal king, was a younger son of Josiah not mentioned in 1 Chr 3:15. He and his predecessor Jehoahaz had the same mother, and he became the last king on the throne of David. The kingship in Judah comes to an end with him: after a new act of disobedience by the Judean ruler, Nebuchadnezzar abolishes the vassal kingship, turns Judah into a province, and

418

installs a governor instead. The negative judgment of Zedekiah is complemented in v. 20a by another mention of the wrath of Yahweh as the reason for the destruction of Judah and the temple at Jerusalem. From 24:20b there follows a detailed account of the siege of Jerusalem and the fate of the king.

[24:20b—25:3] No explanation is offered for why Zedekiah breaks his loyalty oath as a vassal. The new insurrection is proof that the king was either unwilling or unable to draw the right conclusions from the events of 598. He also appears to have misjudged the balance of power, possibly because Egypt was still maintaining its independence from Babylonia during the Twenty-sixth Dynasty. The act of disobedience may have consisted in refusing to pay the annual tribute or the annual paying of homage in front of the Babylonian master. Nebuchadnezzar answers the provocation with a campaign in order to force the vassal into submission. It is uncertain how much of Judah was conquered en route to Jerusalem. Despite the precise dating available up to the fall of the city, the year of the actual conquest is not attested with certainty. Following the arguments of Ernst Kutsch, 587 is the most likely date for Zedekiah's eleventh year of rule and the year of the conquest.[1] The famine caused by the siege is expressly mentioned (see on 6:24—7:20).

[25:4-7] When the Babylonian army manages to cut a breach in the city wall, the king and his soldiers drop their resistance and flee the city. The term "soldiers" indicates the troops stationed in Jerusalem, which was probably not a large contingent. The flight leads (rather unspecifically) through the eastern gate into the Judean desert. It is an act born of despair and condemned to failure from the beginning. Zedekiah is pursued, overtaken, and captured. Nebuchadnezzar's punishment for the renegade king is a cruel one. Like Neco before him (23:33), Nebuchadnezzar takes up residence in Riblah, the former Assyrian administrative center on the Orontes River. The sons of Zedekiah are executed, the king himself is blinded. In this way all successors are removed and the king is led to Babylon as a prisoner. The kingship founded by David has come to an end.

---

[1] Ernst Kutsch, "Das Jahr der Katastrophe: 587 v Chr: Kritische Erwägungen zu neueren chronologischen Versuchen," *Bib* 55 (1974) 520–45.

The Destruction of Jerusalem

Text

25:8 In the fifth month, on the seventh day of the month—which was the nineteenth year of King Nebuchadnezzar, king of Babylon—Nebuzaradan, the captain of the bodyguard, a servant of the king of Babylon, came to Jerusalem. 9 He burned the house of the LORD, the king's house, and all the houses of Jerusalem; every great house he burned down. 10 All the army of the Chaldeans who were with the captain of the guard broke down the walls around Jerusalem. 11 Nebuzaradan the captain of the guard carried into exile the rest of the people who were left in the city and the deserters who had defected to the king of Babylon—all the rest of the population. 12 But the captain of the guard left some of the poorest people of the land to be vinedressers and tillers of the soil.

13 The bronze pillars that were in the house of the LORD, as well as the stands and the bronze sea that were in the house of the LORD, the Chaldeans broke in pieces, and carried the bronze to Babylon. 14 They took away the pots, the shovels, the snuffers, the dishes for incense, and all the bronze vessels used in the temple service, 15 as well as the firepans and the basins. What was made of gold the captain of the guard took away for the gold, and what was made of silver, for the silver. 16 As for the two pillars, the one sea, and the stands, which Solomon had made for the house of the LORD, the bronze of all these vessels was beyond weighing. 17 The height of the one pillar was eighteen cubits, and on it was a bronze capital; the height of the capital was three cubits; latticework and pomegranates, all of bronze, were on the capital all around. The second pillar had the same, with the latticework.

18 The captain of the guard took the chief priest Seraiah, the second priest Zephaniah, and the three guardians of the threshold; 19 from the city he took an officer who had been in command of the soldiers, and five men of the king's council who were found in the city; the secretary who was the commander of the army who mustered the people of the land; and sixty

men of the people of the land who were found in the city. 20 Nebuzaradan the captain of the guard took them, and brought them to the king of Babylon at Riblah. 21 The king of Babylon struck them down and put them to death at Riblah in the land of Hamath. So Judah went into exile out of its land.

Analysis

The passage describing the events after the conquest of Jerusalem focuses on three themes:

vv. 8-12	Fate of the city
vv. 13-15, [16-17]	Plunder of the temple
vv. 18-20	Deportation of the people

Commentary

[25:8-21] The new dating in v. 8 suggests that the destruction of the temple and the palace is the result of a separate punitive expedition by the Babylonians, led by Nebuzaradan. The city walls are razed, at least in several places, so that even the remains of the wall would not be able to support a defense. The craftsmen who had remained in the city or were repatriated after the exile of 598 are led into captivity together with the deserters. The only group remaining in Jerusalem is therefore the lower class of simple farmers.

The temple is plundered, as was the case under Jehoiachin (24:13). This time it is all bronze objects that are taken away to be melted down, together with the bronze covers of the two pillars of the temple (see on 1 Kgs 7:13-51). The mention of further equipment and gold and silver in v. 15 seems to be a later addition. The explanation of the pillars in vv. 16-17 is certainly later, modeled on the description in 1 Kgs 7:15-22. The number of the people led into captivity is not specified. The parallel passage in Jer 52:28-30 speaks of 4,600 men in three separate actions.[1] In contrast to the Assyrians, who would deport entire nations, the Babylonians led away only a fraction of the population, without resettling others in their place. Because of this crucial difference between the Assyrian and Babylonian practices of exile, Judah is spared the fate of the northern kingdom of Israel. Even if the capture of Jerusalem by Nebuchadnezzar means the end of the kingdom and the destruction of the temple, the people are spared from extinction and could largely remain in their country.

[25:18-21] The list of the people of Jerusalem led away by Nebuzaradan amounts to just over sixty persons, separated into small subgroups. They include priests and

---

[1] On this section missing from the Deuteronomistic History see Wilhelm Rudolph, *Jeremia,* 3d ed., HAT 12 (Tübingen: Mohr/Siebeck, 1968), 323–25.

temple staff as much as court officials, although no names are given. The section shows clearly that the number of those deported was relatively small. After the deportations of 587 the country was not entirely depopulated, even if the consequences for the social setup must have been drastic. It is the poor, that is, the lower social class, that remains, a group that had always formed the largest part of the population.

Gedaliah

Text

25:22 He appointed Gedaliah son of Ahikam son of Shaphan as governor over the people who remained in the land of Judah, whom King Nebuchadnezzar of Babylon had left. 23 Now when all the captains of the forces and their men heard that the king of Babylon had appointed Gedaliah as governor, they came with their men to Gedaliah at Mizpah, namely, Ishmael son of Nethaniah, Johanan son of Kareah, Seraiah son of Tanhumeth the Netophathite, and Jaazaniah son of the Maacathite. 24 Gedaliah swore to them and their men, saying, "Do not be afraid because of the Chaldean officials; live in the land, serve the king of Babylon, and it shall be well with you." 25 But in the seventh month, Ishmael son of Nethaniah son of Elishama, of the royal family, came with ten men; they struck down Gedaliah so that he died, along with the Judeans and Chaldeans who were with him at Mizpah. 26 Then all the people, high and low and the captains of the forces set out and went to Egypt; for they were afraid of the Chaldeans.

Commentary

[25:22-26] Jeremiah 40:7—41:18 offers a much more detailed parallel tradition of this episode. Both accounts are likely to rely on a common source.[1] Within the framework of the Deuteronomistic History the present short narrative is an addition from exilic times that attempts to continue the history of Judah beyond the end of the kingship and the fulfillment of the wrath of God. After the conquest the Babylonians began to set up a central form of administration in Judah—modeled on Assyria's treatment of Israel.

Gedaliah, who is appointed as governor, comes from a Jerusalem family with a tradition of holding high official functions. His father, Ahikam, served under Josiah (2 Kgs 22:12; Jer 26:24), while his grandfather was a scribe under the same king

---

[1] See Gunther Wanke, *Untersuchungen zur sogenannten Baruchschrift*, BZAW 122 (Berlin: de Gruyter, 1971), 115–16.

(2 Kgs 22:39). It is unclear whether Gedaliah himself might already have held a high office under the kings of Judah; a seal from Lachish carries the inscription *lgdlyhw ʾšr ʿl hbyt* "(belonging) to Gedaliah, the steward,"[2] but it is not possible to identify the bearer of the name with certainty. The steward oversaw the royal estates and the domestic affairs of the court (see on 1 Kgs 4:6). According to Jer 40:1-6, the prophet Jeremiah remained loyal to Gedaliah. Gedaliah chose as his residence Mizpah (Tell en-Nasbeh), north of Jerusalem, probably because the city was not destroyed during the campaign of Nebuchadnezzar in the early sixth century.[3]

The office that Gedaliah held was beset by difficulty from the beginning. On the one hand, as an overseer of Judah he was accountable to the king of Babylon; on the other hand, as a Judean he was bound to his own people. It is for this reason that he promises impunity to the former captains, who are concerned about prosecution for their actions. It would appear, though, that splinter groups formed in the wake of the dissolution of the king's central authority who disregarded the political situation and were intent on continuing resistance against Babylon. Thus Ishmael, who is of unspecified royal lineage and does not appear elsewhere in the account, gathers a small group of ten men and assassinates Gedaliah at Mizpah, despite the latter's well-balanced promise. Gedaliah's death is a political murder that, although it is directed against the empire, has little effect on it. Instead, the deed is eventually responsible for the flight of the remaining population, who fear yet more reprisals. About the actual reaction of the Babylonian king the text keeps silence.

The appointment of a Judean as governor remains a brief report, and we lack sources on the way Judah was administrated subsequently. The attempt by the Babylonians to rule through a governor from the upper strata of Judean society failed, stalled by a supporter of the Davidic monarchy who wanted to resist Babylonian sovereignty.

---

[2] Olga Tufnell and Harry Torczyner, *Lachish,* 4 vols., Wellcome-Marston Archaeological Research Expedition to the Near East (London: Oxford Univ. Press, 1938–58), 3:348.

[3] See E. Stern, "Israel at the Close of the Period of the Monarchy: An Archaeological Survey," *BA* 38 (1975) 32–37.

The Pardon of Jehoiachin

Text

25:27 In the thirty-seventh year of the exile of King Jehoiachin of Judah, in the twelfth month, on the twenty-seventh day of the month, King Evil-merodach of Babylon, in the year that he began to reign, released King Jehoiachin of Judah from prison; 28 he spoke kindly to him, and gave him a seat above the other seats of the kings who were with him in Babylon. 29 So Jehoiachin put aside his prison clothes. Every day of his life he dined regularly in the king's presence. 30 For his allowance, a regular allowance was given him by the king, a portion every day, as long as he lived.

Analysis

The episode of the pardon of Jehoiachin in Babylonian exile is a further epilogue to the Deuteronomistic History. It probably relies on a folk tradition well known among the exiles. Its origin is lost, but its aim is to introduce a note of hopefulness that the Davidic monarchy might not be finally destroyed.

Commentary

[25:27-30] In 598 Nebuchadnezzar brought Jehoiachin to Babylon, where he was held hostage in the interest of Babylonia's hold on power. He was accompanied by his mother, his wives, and his relatives as well as his court (24:15). According to 1 Chr 3:17-18, seven sons were born to him in exile, and he remained a prisoner at the court of the Babylonian king, together with his family. His presence in Babylon is attested in cuneiform documents on the supply of oil for the year 592.[1] With circumstances being so vague, it is not clear what his privileges granted by Evil-merodach meant in reality. They probably did not mean a decisive change of his actual conditions at court, but rather a modification of the protocol, which raised his standing as the erstwhile king of Judah among the other prisoners of royal origin.

---

[1] *TGI*, 78–79.

This short and quite vague epilogue helps to soften the end of the Deuterono-mistic History a little, in that it now finishes with an act of mercy that allows hope for the continuation of the Davidic dynasty without voicing specific expectations. The end is still the destruction of Judah, interpreted by the Deuteronomistic Historian as the fulfillment of the divine judgment. The epilogue does nothing to change this, but by referring to King Jehoiachin as still being alive, it not only saves from despair but introduces a glimmer of hope for the future. As opposed to the unknown fate of the blinded rebel Zedekiah, the treatment of Jehoiachin by Evil-merodach gives rise to a more positive image of the future. The influence of those high expectations linked to the Davidides is reflected in the hopes arising from the fact that Zerubbabel, Jehoiachin's grandson, is made governor of Judah at the beginning of the Persian hegemony (cf. Haggai 1).

Select Bibliography

1. Commentaries on the Books of Kings

Auld, A. Graeme. *I & II Kings*. DSBOT. Philadelphia: Westminster, 1986.

Brueggemann, Walter. 1 & 2 Kings. SHBC. Macon: Smyth & Helwys, 2000.

Cogan, Mordechai. *I Kings*. AB 10. New York: Doubleday, 2001.

———, and Hayim Tadmor. *II Kings*. AB 11. New York: Doubleday, 1988.

Cohn, Robert L. *2 Kings*. BerO. Collegeville, Minn.: Liturgical, 2000.

De Vries, Simon J. *1 Kings*. WBC 12. Waco, Tex.: Word, 1985.

Dietrich, Walter. "1 and 2 Kings." In *Oxford Bible Commentary,* edited by John Barton and John Muddiman, 232–66. Oxford: Oxford Univ. Press, 2001.

Gray, John. *I and II Kings*. 3d ed. OTL. Philadelphia: Westminster, 1979.

Hobbs, T. R. *2 Kings*. WBC 13. Waco: Word, 1985.

Jones, G. H. *1 and 2 Kings*. 2 vols. NCB. Grand Rapids: Eerdmans, 1994.

Long, Burke O. *1 Kings*. FOTL 9. Grand Rapids: Eerdmans, 1984.

———. *2 Kings*. FOTL 10. Grand Rapids: Eerdmans, 1991.

Montgomery, James A., and Henry Snyder Gehman. *The Book of Kings*. ICC. Edinburgh: T. & T. Clark, 1951.

Mulder, Martin J. *1 Kings 1–11*. Translated by John Vriend. HCOT. Leuven: Peeters, 1998.

Nelson, Richard D. *First and Second Kings*. IBC. Louisville: Westminster John Knox, 1987.

Noth, Martin. *Könige: 1 Könige 1–16*. BKAT 9.1. Neukirchen-Vluyn: Neukirchener, 1968.

O'Brien, Mark A., and Antony F. Campbell. "1–2 Kings." In *The International Bible Commentary,* edited by William R. Farmer et al., 608–43. Collegeville, Minn.: Liturgical, 1998.

Polzin, Robert. *David and the Deuteronomist: A Literary Study of the Deuteronomic History*. Part 3. Bloomington: Indiana Univ. Press, 1993.

Provan, Iain W. *1 and 2 Kings*. NIBC. Peabody, Mass.: Hendrickson, 1995.

Seow, Choon-Leong. "1 & 2 Kings." In *New Interpreter's Bible,* vol. 3. Nashville: Abingdon, 1999.

Thiel, Winfried. *Könige (1 Kgs 17:1-24)*. BKAT 9.2,1. Neukirchen-Vluyn: Neukirchener, 2000.

Select Bibliography

Walsh, Jerome T. *1 Kings*. BerO. Collegeville, Minn.: Liturgical, 1996.

Wiseman, D. J. *1 and 2 Kings*. TOTC. Leicester: InterVarsity, 1993.

Würthwein, Ernst. *Die Bücher der Könige: 1. Kön. 17—2. Kön. 25*. ATD 11/2. Göttingen: Vandenhoeck & Ruprecht, 1984.

———. *Das Erste Buch der Könige, Kapitel 1–16*. ATD 11/1. Göttingen: Vandenhoeck & Ruprecht, 1977.

2. Studies on the Books of Kings

Ackerman, Susan. "The Queen Mother and the Cult in Ancient Israel." *JBL* 112 (1993) 385–401.

Aharoni, Yohanan. "The Solomonic Districts." *TA* 3 (1976) 5–15.

Ahlström, Gösta. *Royal Administration and National Religion in Ancient Palestine*. SHANE 1. Leiden: Brill, 1982.

Alt, Albrecht. "The Monarchy in the Kingdoms of Israel and Judah." In *Essays on Old Testament History and Religion*, 239–59. Translated by R. A. Wilson. Oxford: Blackwell, 1966.

Auld, A. Graeme. *Kings Without Privilege: David and Moses in the Story of the Bible's Kings*. Edinburgh: T. & T. Clark, 1994.

Avishur, Yitzhak, and Michael Heltzer. *Studies on the Royal Administration in Ancient Israel in the Light of Epigraphic Sources*. Jerusalem: Akademon. [Hebrew]

Bach, Alice, editor. *Women in the Hebrew Bible: A Reader*. London: Routledge, 1999.

Barrick, W. Boyd. *The King and the Cemeteries: Toward a New Understanding of Josiah's Reform*. VTSup 88. Leiden: Brill, 2002.

———. "Loving Too Well: The Negative Portrayal of Solomon and the Composition of the Kings History." *Estudios Biblicos* 59 (2001) 419–49.

———. "The Meaning of בית־ה/במות and בתי־במות and the Composition of the Kings History." *JBL* 115 (1996) 621–41.

Becking, Bob. *The Fall of Samaria: An Historical and Archaeological Study*. SHANE 2. Leiden: Brill, 1992.

Ben-Zvi, Ehud. "The Account of the Reign of Manasseh in II Reg 21,1-18 and the Redactional History of the Book of Kings." *ZAW* 103 (1991) 355–74.

———. "Prophets and Prophecy in the Compositional and Redactional Notes in I–II Kings." *ZAW* 105 (1993) 331–51.

Bin-Nun, Shoshana R. "Formulas from Royal Records of Israel and of Judah." *VT* 18 (1968) 14–32.

Brettler, Marc Zvi. "The Structure of 1 Kings 1–11." *JSOT* 49 (1991) 87–97.

Broshi, Magen, and Israel Finkelstein. "The Population of Palestine in Iron Age II." *BASOR* 287 (1992) 47–60.

Campbell, Antony F. *Of Prophets and Kings: A Late Ninth Century Document (1 Samuel 1—2 Kings 10)*. CBQMS 17. Washington, D.C.: Catholic Biblical Association of America, 1986.

Carroll, Robert P. "The Elijah–Elisha Sagas: Some Remarks on Prophetic Succession in Ancient Israel." *VT* 19 (1969) 400–415.

Cazelles, Henri. "David's Monarchy and the Gibeonite Claim." *PEQ* 87 (1955) 165–75.

Coote, Robert B., editor. *Elijah and Elisha in Socioliterary Perspective.* SemSt. Atlanta: Scholars, 1992.

de Pury, Albert, and Thomas Römer, editors. *Die sogenannte Thronfolgegeschichte Davids: Neue Einsichten und Anfragen.* OBO 176. Göttingen: Vandenhoeck & Ruprecht, 2000.

Eynikel, Erik. *The Reform of King Josiah and the Composition of the Deuteronomistic History.* OtSt 33. Leiden: Brill, 1996.

Frisch, Amos. "Structure and Its Significance: The Narrative of Solomon's Reign (1 Kings 1–11)." *JSOT* 51 (1991) 3–14.

Gottwald, Norman K. *The Hebrew Bible: A Socio-Literary Introduction with CD-ROM.* Minneapolis: Fortress Press, 2002.

Halpern, Baruch, and David S. Vanderhooft. "The Editions of Kings in the 7th –6th Centuries B.C.E." *HUCA* 62 (1991) 179–244.

Handy, Lowell, editor. *The Age of Solomon: Scholarship at the Turn of the Millennium.* SHCANE 11. Leiden: Brill, 1997.

Haran, Menahem. "The Books of the Chronicles 'of the Kings of Judah' and 'of the Kings of Israel': What Sort of Books Were They?" *VT* 49 (1999) 156–64.

———. "The Rise and Decline of the Empire of Jeroboam ben Joash." *VT* 17 (1967) 266–97.

Heaton, E. W. *Solomon's New Men: The Emergence of Ancient Israel as a National State.* London: Thames & Hudson, 1974.

Herrmann, Siegfried. "The Royal Novella in Egypt and Israel: A Contribution to the History of Genre in the Historical Books of the Old Testament." In *Reconsidering Israel and Judah: Recent Studies on the Deuteronomistic History,* edited by Gary N. Knoppers and J. Gordon McConville, 493–515. SBTS 8. Winona Lake, Ind.: Eisenbrauns, 2000.

Ishida, Tomoo. *The Royal Dynasties in Ancient Israel: A Study on the Formation and Development of Royal-Dynastic Ideology.* BZAW 142. Berlin: de Gruyter, 1977.

Knoppers, Gary N. "Prayer and Propaganda: Solomon's Dedication of the Temple and the Deuteronomist's Program." *CBQ* 57 (1995) 229–54.

Koopmans, William T. "The Testament of David in 1 Kings II 1–10." *VT* 41 (1991) 429–49.

Machholz, Christian. "Die Stellung des Königs in der israelitischen Gerichtsverfassung." *ZAW* 84 (1972) 157–81.

Malamat, Abraham. "Aspects of the Foreign Policies of David and Solomon." *JNES* 22 (1963) 1–17.

————. "The Last Kings of Judah and the Fall of Jerusalem." *IEJ* 18 (1968) 137–56.

Matthews, Victor H., and Don C. Benjamin. *Social World of Ancient Israel, 1250–587 BCE.* Peabody, Mass.: Hendrickson, 1993.

McKenzie, Steven L. *The Trouble with Kings: The Composition of the Book of Kings in the Deuteronomistic History.* VTSup 42. Leiden: Brill, 1991.

Mettinger, Tryggve N. D. *King and Messiah: The Civil and Sacral Legitimation of the Israelite Kings.* CBOT 8. Lund: Gleerup, 1976.

————. *Solomonic State Officials: A Study of the Civil Government Officials of the Israelite Monarchy.* CBOT 5. Lund: Gleerup, 1971.

Miller, J. Maxwell. "Another Look at the Chronology of the Early Divided Monarchy." *JBL* 86 (1967) 276–88.

————. "The Elisha Cycle and the Accounts of the Omride Wars." *JBL* 85 (1966) 441–55.

Na'aman, Nadav. "Prophetic Stories as Sources for the Histories of Jehoshaphat and the Omrides." *Bib* 78 (1997) 153–73.

Porten, Bezalel. "The Structure and Theme of the Solomon Narrative (I Kings 3–11)." *HUCA* 38 (1967) 93–128.

Rad, Gerhard von. "The Deuteronomic Theology of History in I and II Kings." In *The Problem of the Hexateuch and Other Essays,* 205–21. Translated by E. W. T. Dicken. New York: McGraw-Hill, 1966.

Savran, George W. "1 and 2 Kings." In *The Literary Guide to the Bible,* edited by Robert Alter and Frank Kermode, 146–64. Cambridge: Harvard Univ. Press, 1987.

Sweeney, Marvin A. "The Critique of Solomon in the Josianic Edition of the Deuteronomic History." *JBL* 114 (1995) 607–22.

————. *King Josiah of Judah: The Lost Messiah of Israel.* Oxford: Oxford Univ. Press, 2001.

Trebolle Barrera, Julio C. "Redaction, Recension, and Midrash in the Book of Kings." *BIOSCS* 15 (1982) 12–35.

Walsh, Jerome T. "The Characterization of Solomon in First Kings 1–5." *CBQ* 57 (1995) 471–93.

Weippert, Helga. "Die 'deuteronomistischen' Beurteilungen der Könige von Israel und Juda und das Problem der Redaktion der Königsbücher." *Bib* 53 (1972) 301–39.

White, Marsha C. *The Elijah Legends and Jehu's Coup.* BJS 311. Atlanta: Scholars, 1997.

3. The Deuteronomistic History

Campbell, Antony F. "Martin Noth and the Deuteronomistic History." In *The History of Israel's Traditions: The Heritage of Martin Noth,* edited by Steven L.

McKenzie and M. Patrick Graham, 31–62. JSOTSup 182. Sheffield: Sheffield Academic, 1994.

Campbell, Antony F., and Mark A. O'Brien. *Unfolding the Deuteronomistic History: Origins, Upgrades, Present Text.* Minneapolis: Fortress Press, 2000.

Cross, Frank Moore. "The Themes of the Book of Kings and the Structure of the Deuteronomistic History." In *Canaanite Myth and Hebrew Epic: Essays in the History of the Religion of Israel,* 274–89. Cambridge: Harvard Univ. Press, 1973.

de Pury, Albert, Thomas Römer, and Jean-Daniel Macchi, editors. *Israel Constructs Its History: Deuteronomistic Historiography in Recent Research.* JSOTSup 306. Sheffield: Sheffield Academic, 2000.

Dietrich, Walter. *Prophetie und Geschichte: Eine redaktionsgeschichtliche Untersuchung zum deuteronomistischen Geschichtswerk.* FRLANT 108. Göttingen: Vandenhoeck & Ruprecht, 1972.

Knoppers, Gary N. "The Deuteronomist and the Deuteronomic Law of the King: A Reexamination of a Relationship." *ZAW* 108 (1996) 329–46.

———. *Two Nations Under God: The Deuteronomistic History of Solomon and the Dual Monarchies.* 2 vols. HSM 52, 53. Atlanta: Scholars, 1993–94.

———, and J. Gordon McConville, editors. *Reconsidering Israel and Judah: Recent Studies on the Deuteronomistic History.* SBTS 8. Winona Lake, Ind.: Eisenbrauns, 2000.

Mayes, A. D. H. *The Story of Israel between Settlement and Exile: A Redactional Study of the Deuteronomistic History.* London: SCM, 1983.

McKenzie, Steven L. "The Book of Kings in the Deuteronomistic History." In *The History of Israel's Traditions: The Heritage of Martin Noth,* edited by Steven L. McKenzie and M. Patrick Graham, 281–307. JSOTSup 182. Sheffield: Sheffield Academic, 1994.

———. "The Deuteronomistic History." In *ABD* 2:160–68.

———, and M. Patrick Graham, editors. *The History of Israel's Traditions: The Heritage of Martin Noth.* JSOTSup 182. Sheffield: Sheffield Academic, 1994.

Nelson, Richard D. *The Double Redaction of the Deuteronomistic History.* JSOTSup 18. Sheffield: JSOT Press, 1981.

Noth, Martin. *The Deuteronomistic History.* Translation supervised and edited by David J. A. Clines. JSOTSup 15. 2d ed. Sheffield: JSOT Press, 1991.

O'Brien, Mark A. *The Deuteronomistic History Hypothesis: A Reassessment.* OBO 92. Freiburg: Freiburg Universitätsverlag, 1989.

Provan, Iain W. *Hezekiah and the Books of Kings: A Contribution to the Debate about the Composition of the Deuteronomistic History.* BZAW 172. Berlin: de Gruyter, 1988.

Rost, Leonhard. *The Succession to the Throne of David.* Translated by M. D. Rutter and D. M. Gunn. HTIBS 1. Sheffield: Almond, 1982.

Select Bibliography

Veijola, Timo. *Das Königtum in der Beurteilung der deuteronomistischen Histori-ographie: Eine redaktionsgeschichtliche Untersuchung.* STTB 198. Helsinki: Suomalainen Tiedeakatemia, 1977.

Wolff, Hans Walter. "The Kerygma of the Deuteronomic Historical Work." In *The Vitality of Old Testament Traditions,* by Walter Brueggemann and Hans Walter Wolff, 83–100. Atlanta: John Knox, 1982.

4. The Geography and Archaeology of Ancient Israel

Aharoni, Yohanan. *The Archaeology of the Land of Israel: From the Prehistoric Beginnings to the End of the First Temple Period.* Edited by Miriam Aharoni. Translated by Anson F. Rainey. Philadelphia: Westminster, 1982.

———. *The Land of the Bible: A Historical Geography.* Rev. ed. Translated by Anson F. Rainey. Philadelphia: Westminster, 1979.

———, and Michael Avi-Yonah. *The Macmillan Bible Atlas.* 3d ed. Revised by Anson F. Rainey and Ze'ev Safrai. New York: Macmillan, 1993.

Albright, William F. *Archaeology and the Religion of Israel.* 5th ed. Garden City, N.Y.: Doubleday, 1969.

Baly, Denis. *Basic Biblical Geography.* Philadelphia: Fortress Press, 1987.

Barkay, Gabriel. "The Iron Age II–III." In *The Archaeology of Ancient Israel,* edited by Amnon Ben-Tor. Translated by R. Greenberg. New Haven: Yale University Press, 1992.

Ben-Tor, Amnon, and D. Ben-Ami. "Hazor and the Archaeology of the Tenth Century B.C.E." *IEJ* 48 (1998) 1–37.

Cogan, Michael D., J. Cheryl Exum, and Lawrence E. Stager, editors. *Scripture and Other Artifacts: Essays on the Bible and Archaeology in Honor of Philip J. King.* Louisville: Westminster John Knox, 1994.

Dever, William G. "Monumental Architecture in Ancient Israel in the Period of the United Monarchy." In *Studies in the Period of David and Solomon and Other Essays,* edited by Tomoo Ishida, 269–306. Winona Lake, Ind.: Eisenbrauns, 1982.

———. *What Did the Biblical Writers Know and When Did They Know It? What Archaeology Can Tell Us about the Reality of Ancient Israel.* Grand Rapids: Eerdmans, 2001.

Edelman, Diana Vikander, editor. *The Fabric of History: Text, Artifact and Israel's Past.* JSOTSup 127. Sheffield: JSOT Press, 1991.

Finkelstein, Israel. "On Archaeological Methods and Historical Considerations: Iron Age II Gezer and Samaria." *BASOR* 277/278 (1990) 109–30.

———, and Neil Asher Silberman. *The Bible Unearthed: Archaeology's New Vision of Ancient Israel and the Origin of Its Sacred Texts.* New York: Free Press, 2001.

Fritz, Volkmar. *Das Buch Josua.* HAT 7. Tübingen: Mohr/Siebeck, 1994.

————. *The City in Ancient Israel.* BibSem 29. Sheffield: Sheffield Academic, 1995. German ed. 1990.

————. *An Introduction to Biblical Archaeology.* JSOTSup 172. Sheffield: JSOT Press, 1994. German ed. 1985.

————. "Die Kapitelle der Säulen des Salomonischen Tempels." *ErIsr* 23 (1992) 36*–42*.

————. *Kleines Lexikon der biblischen Archäologie.* Bibel, Kirche, Gemeinde 26. Konstanz: Christliche Verlagsanstalt, 1987.

————. "Monarchy and Re-urbanization: A New Look at Solomon's Kingdom." In *Origins of the Ancient Israelite States,* edited by Volkmar Fritz and Philip R. Davies, 187–95. JSOTSup 228. Sheffield: Sheffield Academic, 1996.

————. *Tempel und Zelt: Studien zum Tempelbau in Israel und zu dem Zeltheiligtum der Priesterschrift.* WMANT 47. Neukirchen-Vluyn: Neukirchener, 1977.

————. "What Can Archaeology Tell Us about Solomon's Temple?" *BAR* 13.4 (1987) 38–49.

Gitin, Seymour, and William Dever, editors. *Recent Excavations in Israel: Studies in Iron Age Archaeology.* AASOR 49. Winona Lake, Ind.: Eisenbrauns, 1989.

Hertog, Cornelius G., et al., editors. *Saxa loquentur: Studien zur Archäologie Palästinas/Israel: Festschrift für Volkmar Fritz zum 65. Geburtstag.* AOAT 302. Münster: Ugarit Verlag, 2003.

Isserlin, B. S. J. *The Israelites.* Minneapolis: Fortress Press, 2001.

Kallai, Zecharia. *Historical Geography of the Bible: The Tribal Territories of Israel.* Leiden: Brill, 1986.

Kempinski, Aharon, and Ronny Reich, editors. *The Architecture of Ancient Israel: From the Prehistoric to the Persian Periods—In Memory of Immanuel (Munya) Dunayevsky.* Jerusalem: Israel Exploration Society, 1992.

Kenyon, Kathleen. *Archaeology in the Holy Land.* 4th ed. New York: Norton, 1979.

King, Philip J., and Lawrence E. Stager. *Life in Biblical Israel.* LAI. Louisville: Westminster John Knox, 2001.

Mazar, Amihai. *Archaeology of the Land of the Bible, 10,000–586 B.C.E.* ABRL. New York: Doubleday, 1990.

————, editor. *Studies in the Archaeology of the Iron Age in Israel and Jordan.* JSOTSup 331. Sheffield: Sheffield Academic, 2001.

Mazar, Benjamin. "Iron Age I." In *The Archaeology of Ancient Israel,* edited by Amnon Ben-Tor. Translated by R. Greenberg. New Haven: Yale Univ. Press, 1992.

Mazar, Eilat, and Benjamin Mazar. *Excavations in the South of the Temple Mount: The Ophel of Biblical Jerusalem.* Jerusalem: Institute of Archaeology, the Hebrew University of Jerusalem, 1989.

Silberman, Neil Asher, and David Small, editors. *The Archaeology of Israel: Constructing the Past, Interpreting the Present.* JSOTSup 237. Sheffield: Sheffield Academic, 1997.

Stern, Ephraim. *Archaeology of the Land of the Bible. Volume II: The Assyrian, Baby-lonian, and Persian Periods, 732–332 B.C.E.* ABRL. New York: Doubleday, 2001.

Thompson, Thomas L. *The Mythic Past: Biblical Archaeology and the Myth of Israel.* New York: Basic, 1999.

Ussishkin, David. "Jezreel, Samaria and Megiddo: Royal Cities of Omri and Ahab." In *Congress Volume: Cambridge,* edited by J. A. Emerton, 351–64. VTSup 66. Leiden: Brill, 1997.

———. "King Solomon's Palaces." *BA* 36 (1973) 78–105.

Vaughn, Andrew G., and Ann E. Killebrew, editors. *Jerusalem in Bible and Archae-ology: The First Temple Period.* SBL Symposium Series. Atlanta: Society of Biblical Literature, 2003.

5. The History of Ancient Israel

Ahlström, Gösta W. *The History of Ancient Palestine.* Edited by Diana Edelman. Minneapolis: Fortress Press, 1993.

Alt, Albrecht. *Essays on Old Testament History and Religion.* Translated by R. A. Wilson. Oxford: Blackwell, 1966.

———. *Kleine Schriften zur Geschichte des Volkes Israels.* 3 vols. Munich: Beck, 1953–59.

Barnes, William Hamilton. *Studies in the Chronology of the Divided Monarchy of Israel.* HSM 48. Atlanta: Scholars, 1991.

Brettler, Marc Zvi. *The Creation of History in Ancient Israel.* London: Routledge, 1995.

Bright, John. *A History of Israel.* 4th ed. Introduction and Appendix by William P. Brown. Louisville: Westminster John Knox, 2000.

Cross, Frank Moore. *Canaanite Myth and Hebrew Epic: Essays in the History of the Religion of Israel.* Cambridge: Harvard Univ. Press, 1973.

Dearman, J. Andrew, and M. Patrick Graham, editors. *The Land That I Will Show You: Essays on the History and Archaeology of the Ancient Near East in Honor of J. Maxwell Miller.* JSOTSup 343. Sheffield: Sheffield Academic, 2001.

Donner, Herbert. *Geschichte des Volkes Israel und seiner Nachbarn in Grundzügen.* 2 vols. 2d ed. Grundrisse zum Alten Testament 4. Göttingen: Vandenhoeck & Ruprecht, 1995.

Freedman, David Noel. "Kingly Chronologies: Then and Later." *ErIs* 24 (1993) 41*–65*.

Fritz, Volkmar. *Die Entstehung Israels in der 12. und 11. Jahrhundert v. Chr.* Bibli-sche Enzyklopädie 2. Stuttgart: Kohlhammer, 1996.

———. *Israel in der Wüste: Traditionsgeschichtliche Untersuchung der Wüstenüber-lieferung des Jahwisten.* Marburger theologische Studien 7. Marburg: Elwert, 1970.

————. *Studien zur Literatur und Geschichte des alten Israel.* Stuttgarter biblische Aufsatzbände 22. Stuttgart: Katholisches Bibelwerk, 1997.

————, and Philip J. Davies, editors. *The Origins of the Ancient Israelite States.* JSOTSup 228. Sheffield: Sheffield Academic, 1996.

Galil, Gershon. *The Chronology of the Kings of Israel and Judah.* SHCANE 9. Leiden: Brill, 1996.

Grabbe, Lester L., editor. *Can a History of Israel Be Written?* JSOTSup 245. Sheffield, England: Sheffield Academic, 1997.

Halpern, Baruch. *The Constitution of the Monarchy in Israel.* HSM 25. Chico, Calif.: Scholars, 1981.

————. *The First Historians: The Hebrew Bible and History.* San Francisco: Harper & Row, 1988.

Hayes, John H., and J. Maxwell Miller, editors. *Israelite and Judaean History.* OTL. Louisville: Westminster John Knox, 1977.

Herrmann, Siegfried. *A History of Israel in Old Testament Times.* Rev. ed. Translated by John Bowden. Philadelphia: Fortress Press, 1981.

Holloway, Steven W., and Lowell K. Handy, editors. *The Pitcher is Broken: Memorial Essays for Gösta W. Ahlström.* JSOTSup 190. Sheffield: Sheffield Academic, 1995.

Ishida, Tomoo. *History and Historical Writing in Ancient Israel: Studies in Biblical Historiography.* SHCANE 16. Leiden: Brill, 1999.

Knoppers, Gary N. "The Vanishing Solomon? The Disappearance of the United Monarchy in Recent Histories of Ancient Israel." *JBL* 116 (1997) 19–44.

Miller, J. Maxwell, and John H. Hayes. *A History of Ancient Israel and Judah.* Philadelphia: Westminster, 1986.

Noth, Martin. *The History of Israel.* 2d ed. Translated by Peter R. Ackroyd. New York: Harper & Row, 1960.

Shanks, Hershel, editor. *Ancient Israel: From Abraham to the Roman Destruction of the Temple.* Rev. ed. Washington, D.C.: Biblical Archaeology Society, 1999.

Soggin, J. Alberto. *An Introduction to the History of Israel and Judah.* 3d ed. Translated by John Bowden. London: SCM, 1999.

Index of Ancient Sources

Editor's note: The indexing of passages in 1 and 2 Kings is only to those places outside of the primary commentary sections.

Ancient Near Eastern Sources

Adadnirari III Inscriptions
308, 310, 314

Amarna Tablets
EA 33:9   60

Ashurbanipal Inscriptions
389

Babylonian Chronicle
349–50, 369

Dan Inscription
167

Famine Stele
273

Gedaliah Seal
424

Hezekiah Seal
359

Khirbet el-Muqenna'
Inscription
351, 391

Khirbet el-Qom
Inscription
351, 391

Kuntillet 'Ajrūd
Inscription
98, 351, 391

Lachish Letters
2:4   275
5:4   275
6:3   275

Mesha Inscription
131, 244–45

Papyrus Anastasi
VI, 51-61   273

Sam'āl Inscriptions
287

Sargon II Inscriptions
350, 359

Sennacherib Inscriptions
360, 362–63,
373, 376

Shalmaneser III
Inscriptions
126–27, 223,
274, 308

Shema Seal
324

Siloam Inscription
386–87

Tiglath-pileser III
Inscriptions
332, 336, 340,
343, 349, 393,
414

Treaties of Esarhaddon
448-50   269

Zakkur Inscription
308

Uzziah Burial Inscription
329

Yzbl Seal
179

Hebrew Bible

Genesis
5:24   235
8:20   102
12–37   192
12:2   38
12:7   99
13:16   38
15:5   38
15:18   54
19   277
22:17   38, 55
26:3   37
26:4   38
28:14   38
28:16   37
31:10-11   37
31:24   37
32:3   50
32:13   55
32:32   145
34   142
36:31-39   132, 225
36:35   134

437

Genesis (*cont.*)

37:34	207	11:18	269	4:39	193, 208, 260, 375
38:14	183	13	328		
40:5	37	14:4	58	4:49	325
41:25-32	273	14:6	58	5:2	197
46:2ff.	37	14:49	58	6:4	193
		14:51-52	8	6:5	34
		16:18	23	7:1	112
Exodus		21:1	161	7:2	112
3:2	193, 235	24:16	213	7:6-8	38
3:6	192	25:23	211	7:9	208
3:8	112	27	303	7:24	246
3:13	192			7:26	112
3:15-16	192	Numbers		8:6	24
3:17	112	11:28	201	9:8	197
4:5	192	12	259	10:1-5	89, 97
9:3	99	13:21	102, 325	10:1	224
9:15	99	14:12	99	10:14–15	38
12:12	58	19:6	58	11:1	24, 34
13:5	112	19:18	58	12–26	100, 398
13:21	235	21:4b-9	59	12	2, 35, 97
15:23-25a	237	21:13	112	12:2	161
19:16-18	198	23:1-2	102	12:5	97
19:18	193, 235	23:14	102	12:11	61, 97
20:12	201	23:29-30	102	12:21	97
20:24	40	27:18-23	234	13:14	34
21:32	333	29:7	212	14:2	38
23:23	112	33	197	14:3-8	269
24:13	201	34:5	54	14:23-24	97
25–32	86	34:8	325	14:23	61
25:10-22	88	35:30	213	16:2	61, 97
25:13-15	88	43:8	102	16:5-6	408
25:23-30	86			16:6	61, 97
25:31-39	86	Deuteronomy		16:7	102
28:17-20	119	1:2	197	16:11	61, 97
29:6	299	1:6	197	16:22	161
30:1-10	86	1:19	197	17:3	390, 406
30:10	23	1:38	100	17:6	213
30:35	238	2:24	246	18:9	390
32:6	40	2:30	246	18:10-11	390–91
32:13	99	2:34-35	112	18:16	197
33:1	201	3:2-3	246	19:15	213
34:28	197	3:6-7	112	20:10-18	208
39:30	299	3:17	50, 325	20:13	246
40:34-35	89	3:28	100	20:16-18	112
43:11	112	4:10	197	20:17	112
		4:15	197	20:19	245
Leviticus		4:17	406	21:10	246
1–7	101	4:19	390	24:16	316
2:13	238	4:20	100	26:2	61, 97
4:5	304	4:29	24	26:16-18	352
7:7	304	4:35	99, 193, 208, 260, 375	27:6	40
8:9	299			28:52-58	269

28:69	197	18:11-20	51	Ruth	
29:8	24	18:16	113	1	273
31:7	100	18:28	113		
31:67	24	19:10-16	48	1 Samuel	
34:3	277	19:18	14, 250	1–4	154
		19:24-31	51	1:1-20	251
Joshua		19:27	107	2:27-36	29
1:1	201	19:32-39	50	3:4ff.	37
1:2-9	24	22:3	24	3:20	55
1:6	24	22:4	102	4:4	74
1:7	24	22:6-8	102	6:18	230
1:9	24	23	359	7:6	212
2:10	112	23:14	24	8:10-17	141
2:11	208	24	96, 104,	8:11	299
2:24	208		142, 191, 403	8:17	299
3:10	112	24:8	112	9:4	255
3:16	325	24:11	112	9:6	184
4:19	234			9:13-19	35
5:9	234	Judges		9:16	21–22
5:10-12	408	1	112	9:27—10:1	135
5:10	234	1:21	113	10:1	21–22,
6:2	208	2:18	308		283, 299
6:26	179, 238	3:3	102, 113	10:5-12	192
8:1	208	3:5	112	12	96, 104
8:10-22	270	3:9	308	12:20	132
8:18	208	3:15	308	13:9	40
8:30	40	5:4-5	198	13:14	22
9:1	112	5:10	21	14:41	391
9:10	112	5:28	286	15:1	126
10:8	208	6:26	102	15:17	21
10:13	90	8:8	145	15:27-28	136
10:18	208	8:9	145	16:1-13	299
10:25	24	8:17	145	16:12-13	21
10:41	54	9	142	16:13	283
11:3	112–13	9:5	287	17:11	55
11:5	336	9:8-15a	319	18:8	40
11:7	336	9:34-41	270	18:30	230
12:3	50, 325	9:42-45	270	19:18-24	192
12:7	49	9:45	238	21:1-16	31
12:8	112	10:4	21	22:20-22	29
13:5	102, 325	10:8	112	23:2	391
13:27	50	11:20	112	23:6	29
15:4	54	13	251	23:9-12	391
15:8	113	14:1-19	119	23:9	29
15:21	17	14:18	85	24:2	55
15:35	49	19:11	113	24:7	21
15:39	395	20:1	55	24:11	21
15:47	54	20:26	40	24:14	275
15:48	49	20:29-48	270	24:15	55
15:63	113	21:4	40	25:22	284
16:4-9	48			25:30	22

Ancient Sources

1 Samuel (*cont.*)		8:5-6	134	3:3	138
25:34	284	8:13-14	133	3:6-9	78
26:9	21	8:15-18	44	4:2-6	113
26:11	21	8:16	46	4:3	303
26:16	21	9:1-13	54	4:6	141, 328,
26:23	21	9:8	275		424
27:1—28:2	31	10:12	24	4:8-19	136
28:4-25	391	12:7	21	4:13	283
28:4	250	13:29	21	4:16	371
28:6	391	15:10	21, 299	4:20	57
29:3	230	15:36	23	5:1—6:8	53
29:4	230	16:1-12	26	5:4	102
29:9	230	16:5-14	26	5:15-26	77, 107
30:7-9	391	16:16	299	5:17	97
30:7	29	17:17ff.	23	6:1-38	61
31:1	48	17:17-24	252	6:24—7:20	259
31:8	48	17:24-29	25	6:36	390
		17:24	50	7:7	125, 300
2 Samuel		17:27	50	7:8	114
1:5	48	18:9-15	25	7:12	345, 390
1:14	21	19:11	299	7:13-51	345, 421
1:16	21	19:16	234	7:15-22	421
1:18	90	19:22	21	7:27-39	345
1:23	85	19:24	26	7:44	345
2:4	21, 283, 299	19:32-41	26	7:50	304
2:8-10	50	19:33	50	8:9	197
2:8	46	19:41	234	8:12-13	147
2:25	30	20:9-10	25	8:14-53	92
2:31	30	20:23-26	44	8:64	40
3:3	131	20:23	46	8:65	54, 325
3:26-30	25	20:24	141	9:14	119
3:31	207	20:25	44	9:15	306
5:1-10	27	21:1-9	37	9:20-22	141
5:2	22, 220	22:11	74	9:22	291
5:3	21, 141,	24:25	102	9:24	306
	283, 299			9:25	40
5:4-5	26	1 Kings		9:26-28	118
5:9	109, 306	1–11	1	9:26	323
5:19	391	1:1—2:46	xiv	10:1	116
6	154	1:1-4	250	10:26	53, 112
6:2	74	1:1	1	10:29	113
6:14	191	1:5	126	11:7	408
6:16	286	1:11-40	141	11:14-22	225
6:17-18	40	1:11	284	11:27	306
6:17	22	1:13	284	11:28	109
6:21	22	1:18	284	11:29-30	144
7:8	22	1:25	299	11:41	2
7:12-15	24	1:28-29	40	12:1-25	157, 324
7:12-13	61	1:34	283	12:13	390
7:13	97	1:39	283, 299	12:25-32	85
7:16	98	2:35	45	12:25	156
8:1-14	54	3:1	114	12:26-32	351
8:3-8	134	3:3-15	103	12:26-30	356, 408

13	157	21	284
13:1	184	21:17	182
13:2	409	21:19	285
14	157	21:20bβ-24	172
14:1-18	135	21:21	284
14:7-11	172	21:23-24	172
14:7	22	21:23	284
14:10-11	172	21:24	287–88
14:10	284	21:27	207
14:15	179	22	259
14:17	145	22:1-38	180, 283
14:23	179, 390	22:4	244
14:26	320	22:29-37	236
14:27-28	291	22:39-40	178, 180
15:13	160, 391	22:44	390
15:18-20	268	22:52-54	229, 232
15:18	134	22:52	229
15:27	285	22:54	230
16:2	22, 169		
16:9	285	2 Kings	
16:11	284	1:1	227
16:15-20	286	1:2-17	227
16:16	285	1:3	182
16:20	285	1:8	182
16:29—22:40	390–91	1:9-16	184
16:31	297	1:17b-18	229
16:32-33	241	1:18	227
16:32	284	2:1-15	200
16:33	307, 391	2:1-8	201
17:1—22:38	178	2:5—8:17a	230
17–21	230	2:8	50
17–19	180, 284	2:26-27	45
17–18	180	3:1-3	283
17:1	180	3:1	229
17:2-7	180	3:2	161
17:8-16	180	3:4-27	229
17:17-24	180, 201	3:5	229
18:1	180, 183	3:7	218
18:2a	180, 183	3:14	182
18:2b-16	180, 220	3:15	192
18:15	182	4:7	184
18:17-40	180	5:16	182
18:39	191, 209	6:1-7	201
18:41-46	180, 183	6:30	207
19:16	313	7:2	291
19:19-21	198, 234	7:6	113
19:19	235	7:7	291
20	259	7:19	291
20:1-43	180, 218	8:7-15	283
20:26	313	8:18	225
20:26-27	313	8:25	286, 297
20:29-34	313	8:26	297
20:43	313	8:28—10:17	232
9:1-15	198		
9:1-14a	198		
9:5-6	135		
9:7-10a	172		
9:10	172		
9:11-29	241		
9:13	299		
9:16	299		
9:30-37	196		
9:36	21		
10:13	160		
10:18-27	194		
10:27	161, 241		
11:4	291		
11:6	291		
11:12	21, 283		
12:4	390		
12:21	109		
13:1	303		
13:6	391		
13:17	206		
13:24-25	268		
14:1-7	306		
14:4	390		
14:25	102		
15:4	390		
15:10	169, 285		
15:14	169		
15:15	285		
15:25	169, 285, 291		
15:30	169, 285		
15:35	390		
16:3	390		
16:6	323		
16:10-17	101		
16:13	40		
16:17	85		
17:7-10	291		
17:10	179		
17:11	390		
17:16	179, 406		
17:29	390		
17:32	390		
18–25	1		
18:4	161, 390		
18:6	132		
18:8	54		
18:13-15	371		
19:15	74		
20:1-11	382		
20:5	22		
20:12-15	60		

Ancient Sources

2 Kings (*cont.*)

21:1	166
21:2	179
21:3	406
21:19	336
22:3-11	395
22:12-20	395
22:12	423
22:39	424
23:1-3	395
23:4-27	395
23:13	131
23:14	161
23:16	150
23:28-30	395
23:30	21, 283, 299
23:30a	286
24:7	54
24:13	421
25:13ff.	86
25:18	303

1 Chronicles

1:23	116
2:6	57
2:15	61
2:16	16
3:15	412, 418
3:17-18	425
5:29-34	45
10:1	48
10:8	48
11:4	113
13:6	74
15–18	99

2 Chronicles

4:6	84–85
9:21	125
9:25	53
11:5-12	161
12:5-8	144
12:16	164
13:1	164
13:2	164
13:4	164
13:22	164
13:23	164
22:9	286
26:1-15	327
26:23	329
35:20ff.	410

Ezra

8:36	54

Nehemiah

2:7	54
2:9	54
3:7	54
9:1	99

Job

2:1-6	221
16:4	378
22:24	116

Psalms

18:8-16	198
18:10-11	91
18:11	74
22:8	378
41:14	23
44:15	378
46	92
48	92
76	92
78:50	99
78:72	220
80:2	74
89:53	23
91:3	99
91:6	99
99:1	74
105:8	99
105:11	99
106:48	23
119:12	23
132:13-14	91
135:21	23
149:3	191
150:4	191

Proverbs

4:1	57
4:5	57
4:7	57
16:16	57
23:23	57
30:30	85

Ecclesiastes

9:10	26

Canticles

2:9	286

4:10	119
4:14	119
4:16	119
5:1	119
5:13	119
6:2	119
8:14	119

Isaiah

1:1	328
1:6	100
2:16	125
3:16-17	378
4:4	378
6:1—9:6	375
6	378
6:1	328
6:13	221
6:19	88
7:1-9	343
7:1	328
7:3	370
7:7-9	335
11:23	100
13–21	377
13:6-7	100
14:4-21	377
15:5	277
19:44	111
21:9	206
22:15-23	371
23	377
27:12	54
28–30	375
36–37	369
37:16	74
38	382
38:17	206
44:6	99, 193, 260, 375
45:5-6	193, 260, 375
45:18	193, 260, 375
46:9	193
60:6	119

Jeremiah

2:20	161
7	72, 92
7:6	392
11:4	100
13:18	160

18:16	378	1:2	285	**New Testament**
22:3	392	2:4	285	
22:10-12	412	4:11	285	Matthew
22:17	392	4:14	161	8:28-29	201
22:19	284	6:10	285	9:18-26	185
25	377	9:3	260	10:25	230
26:22	400, 416	10:2	161	14:13-21	184, 256
26:24	400, 423	14:1	275	15:32-39	256
29:2	160			
31:13	191	Joel		Mark
35	288	1:14	212	3:22	230
36:10	390	2:15	212	5:21-43	185
36:12	400, 416			6:30-44	184, 256
36:25	416	Amos		8:1-9	184, 256
40:1-6	424	1:1	328	9:10b-17	256
40:7—41:18	423	1:3—2:3	377	9:49	238
46–51	377	1:3	275	
48:4	277	1:13	275	Luke
52:21b	83	6:13-14	326	4:26	183
52:28-30	421	6:14	102	8:40-56	185
		7:13	147	9:10-17	184
		7:17	260	9:61-62	201
Lamentations		8:14	355	11:15	230
2:15	378			
2:20	269	Obadiah		John
4:10	269		377	11:1-45	185
		Micah		
Ezekiel		1:1	220	
5:10	269	4:4	55	**Josephus**
9:2	338	5:12	161	*Antiquities*
14:19	99			8.3	60
22:6-16	392	Habakkuk		8.141-43	119
22:25-31	392	3:5	99	9.62	269
25–32	377			11.227	329
27:22	119	Haggai		13.146	48
28:13	119	1	426	
35	377			*Apion*
40–48	86	Zechariah		17-18	60
43:24	238	3:10	55	106-27	60
44:19	390	14:5	328	
44:21	390			*War*
47:14	99			5.147	392
47:15	325	**Apocrypha**		
Hosea		1 Maccabees		
1:1	328	11:59	48	

Index of Divine Names

Editor's note: Since the name of Yahweh appears throughout, it is not included here.

Adad, 355, 407
Adadmilki, 355
Adrammelech, 355
Anammelech, 355
'Anat, 355
Asherah, 156, 160, 166, 351, 391, 406–7
Ashima, 355
'Astarte, 131, 136, 355
Atagartis, 355

Baal, 91, 156, 178–80, 182, 190–94, 227, 230, 241, 284–86, 288, 290–92, 296, 300, 390, 406

Chemosh, 131, 136

El, 179, 351, 391,

Hadad, 179, 260

Marduk, 355, 373
Milcom, 131, 136
Molech, 407

Nergal, 355
Nibhaz, 355
Nisroch, 373
Nusku, 373

Rimmon, 260

Shamash, 408
Sîn, 374

Tartak, 355

Yamm, 164

Zedek, 45

Index of Geographical Names

Editor's note: Since Judah and Israel appear throughout, they have not been included in this index. The pages refer only to the commentary and not the biblical text.

Abana River (Bavadā), 259
Abdon (Khirbet 'Abde), 51
Abel-beth-maacah (Tell Abel el-Qamḥ), 167, 335
Abel-meholah (Tell Abu Sus), 201, 313
Achzib (ez-Zib), 51, 107
Acre, 51–52, 107, 194
Aegean Sea, 17
Africa, 125
Aloth, 47–48
Altin-baṣak—see Haran
Amarna (Tell el-Amarna), 79
Ammon, 51, 126, 131
Amuru, 113, 310
Anata, 29
Anathoth (Khirbet Der es-Sidd), 29
Anatolia, 113
Aphek, 204–6, 313–14
Aqabah, Gulf of, 111, 116, 133, 323
Arabah, 82, 111, 115, 133, 317
Arabia, 116, 118–20, 126
Arad, 73, 102, 111, 407
Arnon River (Sēl el Mōğib), 244, 293
Arpad (Tell Refāt), 333, 372, 375
Arubboth, 49
Aruma—see Rumah
Ashdod, 363
Asher, 47–48, 51–52, 107
Ashur, 223, 314, 324, 332–33, 343, 349, 359–60, 362–63, 371, 373, 376–78, 384, 390–91, 395, 411
Asia Minor, 113, 127
Assyria, 75, 83, 100, 271, 314–15, 333, 350, 359, 363, 369, 371–72, 395

Baalath, 110–11
Baal-shalishah, 255
Babylonia, 354–55, 375, 384, 395, 415, 417, 419, 425

Bahurim, 26, 30
Barruka, 30
Bashan, 293
Bāṭen el-Hawa, 131
Bavadā River—see Abana River
Beer-sheba (Bī'r es-Seba'), 55, 196, 301
Beitin—see Bethel
Beit Qad, 288
Benjamin, 30, 37, 48–49, 51–52, 136, 145, 164, 167–68, 225, 255, 408
Bethel, (Beitin), 2, 48, 51–52, 146–47, 150–51, 156, 234, 236, 292, 351, 356, 406, 408–9
Beth-haggan, 286
Beth-horon (Bēt 'Ūr), 110–11
Bethlehem, 30
Beth-shean, Bay of, 48, 50, 201
Beth-shemesh, (Khirbet er-Rumele), 49, 319
Bēt Maqdûm, 395
Bēt 'Ūr—see Beth-horon
Biqa', 102
Bir Ayyub—see Rogel Spring
Bī'r es-Seba'—see Beer-sheba
Bēt Adini, 375
Bēt Bahian, 374
Byblos, 65, 124

Cabul, 107
Canaan, 2, 52, 101, 111, 113, 411
Carchemish, 396, 411, 415
Carmel, Mount, 48, 52, 188–94, 240, 251
Chinneroth, 167
Cilicia, 127
Cuth, 354–55
Cuthah, 354–55

Damascus, 326, 343

445

Geographical Names

Dan (Tell el-Qaḍi), 2, 55, 86, 146–47, 156, 167, 292, 351
Dead Sea, 50, 52, 111, 244, 277, 325
Dibban, 244
Dor (et-Tantura), 49, 336

Edom, 132–34, 225–26, 244–45, 276–77, 317, 323
Eglon (Tell Etûn), 395
Egypt, 33–34, 45, 69, 97, 100, 111, 127, 133–35, 142, 161, 235, 271, 277, 325, 333, 349–50, 357, 362, 369, 371–72, 378, 389–90, 396, 410–13, 415, 419
Ekron (Khirbet el-Muqanna'), 170, 230, 351, 391
Elath, 322–23, 327
el-Anwağ—see Pharpar River
el-Ğuwēr Plain, 167
el-Ḥisiā, 133
el-Jib—see Gibeon
el-Lebwe—see Lebo-hamath
el-Muğar, 111
el-Muḥraqa, 190
Elon/Aialon (Yalo), 49
Elteke (Tell eš-Šallaf), 362, 371
Endor, 391
'En Gel'ad, 51
'Ēn Ḥusb—see Tamar
'En-rogel—see Rogel Spring
'En Samiya, 255
Ephraim, 48, 51–52
er-Ramle, 305
er-Remta, 50
et-Tantura—see Dor
Ethiopia, 121, 362
Euphrates River, 54, 223, 310, 354, 372, 411
Ezion-geber, 111, 115–16, 225–26, 323
ez-Zib—see Achzib

Fiq, 206

Galilee, 50–51, 106–7, 167, 326, 336, 393
Galilee, Sea of, 50, 167
Gath (Tell eṣ-Ṣafi), 31, 305
Gath-hepher (Khirbet ez-Zerra'), 326
Gaza (Gazze), 54, 359, 363
Gazze—see Gaza
Gebal (Jebeil), 65
Genezareth, Sea of, 206
Gezer, 110
Gibbethon (Tell el-Melat), 170

Gibeon, (el-Jib), 35, 37–39, 41
Gihon Spring, 20–21, 386
Gilboa, 48
Gilead, 50–52, 182, 283, 293, 335–36
Gilgal, 234–36, 253, 255
Gittaim (Ras abu-Ḥameid), 305,
Golan Heights, 206–7
Gozan (Tell Halāf), 350, 374
Greece, 101, 191
Gur, 286

Habor River, 350, 374
Hamath, 126, 308, 325–26, 354–55, 375, 412, 415
Hannathon (Tell el-Bedēwīye), 336–37
Haran (Altin-başak), 374
Hazor (Tell el-Qedah), 110, 222, 335
Hebron, 15, 21, 27, 32, 322
Hena, 375
Hepher, 49
Hinnom Valley (Wadi er-Rababi), 407
Hippo (Khirbet Susita), 206
Huleh, Lake, 50, 336

Ijon (Tell Dibbin), 167, 335
Irvah, 375
Issachar, 14, 51
Ivvah, 375

Jabbok River, 25, 50–51, 145, 293
Jabesh-gilead (Tell el-Maqlub), 331
Jaffa, 61
Janoah (Tell en-Na'ame), 335
Jarcon (Nahr el-'Auga), 49
Jebeil—see Gebal
Jebel Gel'ad, 51
Jebus, 113
Jenin, 286, 288
Jericho, 234, 236
Jerusalem, 1–2, 16–17, 20–21, 25–27, 30, 35, 37, 39–40, 45–46, 51, 61, 64, 71, 73–74, 79, 88, 91–92, 99–100, 109–11, 113, 125, 131, 135–36, 141, 147, 152, 154, 156, 160, 166–67, 207, 224, 235, 276, 278, 282, 286, 292, 294, 299–300, 305, 309, 316, 318–19, 322, 327–29, 340, 342–43, 345, 351, 356, 359, 363, 369–70, 372–74, 376–78, 381, 383, 386, 393, 406-9, 411, 413, 415-17, 419, 421, 423–24
Jezreel (Zer'in), 14, 48–51, 189–90, 194, 211, 250, 283, 285–86, 288

Jibleam (Khirbet Bel'ame), 286, 330
Jordan River, 183, 234–36, 259, 262, 293
Jordan Valley, 50
Jotbah (Khirbet Ğefāt), 336–37, 393

Kabūl, 107
Kabzeel, 17
Kedesh (Tell Qedesh), 50, 335
Khirbet 'Abde—see Abdon
Khirbet Bel'ame—see Jibleam
Khirbet Der es-Sidd—see Anathoth
Khirbet el-Marjameh, 255
Khirbet el-Muqqena'—Ekron
Khirbet el-Qom, 351, 391
Khirbet er-Rumele—see Beth-shemesh
Khirbet ez-Zerra'—see Gath-hepher
Khirbet Ğefat—see Jotbah
Khirbet Gel'ad, 51
Khirbet Ras ez-Zetun, 107
Khirbet Shifat, 393
Khirbet Susita—see Hippo
Khirbet Zertun er-Rame—see Ramah
Kidron Valley, (Wadi en-Nār), 17, 21, 319
Kinnereth, 50
Kiriath-jearim (Tell el-Azhar), 40
Kue, 127
Kuntillet 'Ajrūd, 98, 351, 391

Lachish (Tell ed-Duwēr), 111, 322, 363,
   370, 373, 395, 424
Lebanon, 61, 63,–64, 77–78, 102, 123,
   125, 310, 378
Lebo-hamath (el-Lebwe), 102, 325

Machir, 52
Mahanaim, 25–26, 30, 50
Makaz, 49
Makkedah (Khirbet el-Qom), 395
Marum—see Merom
Mediterranean Sea, 54, 60–61, 115, 125,
   188, 194, 333
Megiddo (Tell el-Mutesellim), 50, 78, 85,
   110–11, 124, 222, 278, 286, 324,
   336, 401, 411
Merom (Marum), 336, 414
Mesopotamia, 75, 354–55, 373, 375
Midian, 133, 197
Mizpah (Tell en-Nasbeh), 424
Moab, 131, 133, 227, 229, 235, 243–45,
   277, 325
Musri, 127

Nahr el-'Auga—see Jarcon

Naphath-dor, 49
Naphtali, 50–52, 167, 336
Nazareth, 393
Negev, 17, 51, 161, 196, 301, 322
Nile River, 378
Nineveh, 333, 350, 363, 369–70, 373, 376,
   389, 395, 411, 415
Nippur, 355
Nob (Ras el-Mesharif), 16, 29

Orontes River, 84, 354, 412, 415, 419

Pharpar River (el-Anwağ), 259
Philistia, 359, 363
Phoenicia, 60–61, 64–65, 78, 101, 106–7,
   179, 183, 196, 222–23, 310, 340

Qal'at el-Ḥuṣu, 206
Qatre, 111

Ramah (Khirbet Zertun er-Rame), 50–51
Ramoth-gilead, 50, 218, 220, 283
Ras abu-Ḥameid—see Gittaim
Ras el-Mesharif—see Nob
Rās Ṣarafandi—see Sidon
Reuben, 52
Rezeph, 374
Ribla, Bay of, 102
Rogel Spring (Bir Ayyub), 17, 407
Rumah (Tell er-Rummān), 336, 414

Sahl 'Arraba, 49
Sahl Battof, 48, 51
Samaria, 48, 71, 79, 111, 142, 145, 156,
   177–79, 188–89, 204–5, 207, 213,
   218–19, 222, 240–41, 259, 264, 268,
   270–71, 284, 286–88, 290–91, 309,
   313, 320, 331, 334, 347, 349–50,
   354–57, 361, 406, 408–9
Selbit—see Shaalbim
Sēl el Mōğib—see Arnon River
Shaalbim (Selbit), 49
Sharon, 49
Sheba, 118
Shechem (Tell Balatah), 48–49, 141–42,
   145, 331, 403
Shephelah, 31, 125, 305, 319, 363, 373,
   394–95, 412
Shiloh, 29, 39, 88, 135–36, 154
Sidon (Rās Ṣarafandi), 60, 178–79, 183,
   284, 297, 310, 314
Silwān, 371

Geographical Names

Sinai, 89, 133, 147, 197, 237, 391, 402
Sippar, 354–55
Socoh (Suweke), 49
Spring of Mary ('En Sitti Miryam), 21
Ṣūr—see Tyre
Suweke—see Socoh
Syria, 54, 70–71, 75, 83–84, 113, 127,
    222–23, 310, 325–26, 333, 343, 355,
    371, 410–12

Taanach (Ta'anek), 50,
Ta'anek—see Taanach
Tabor, Mount, 50–51
Tamar ('Ēn Ḥusb), 110–11
Tappuach (Tell Seh Abu Zarad), 48–49,
    331
Taurus Mountains, 127
Tawahin es-Sukkar, 277
Telassar (Til Aššuri), 375
Tell Abel el-Qamḥ—see Abel-beth-maacah
Tell Abu Sus—see Abel-meholah
Tell Balatah—see Shechem
Tell Dibbin—see Ijon
Tell el-Amarna—see Amarna
Tell el-Azhar—see Kiriath-jearim
Tell el-Bedēwīye—see Hannathon
Tell el-Duwēr—see Lachish
Tell el-Hulēfi, 115
Tell el-Ḥusn, 50, 218, 283
Tell el-Maqlub—see Jabesh-gilead
Tell el-Melat—see Gibbethon
Tell el-Muhaffar, 49
Tell el-Mutesellim, 50
Tell el-'Oreme, 167
Tell el-Qaḍi—see Dan
Tell el-Qedah—see Hazor
Tell en-Na'ame—see Janoah
Tell en-Nasbeh—see Mizpah
Tell er-Rummān—see Rumah
Tell eṣ-Ṣafi—see Gath
Tell eš-Šallaf—see Elteke
Tell es-Sultan (Tell Ǧalǧûl), 234
Tell Etûn—see Eglon
Tell Halāf—see Gozan

Tell Qedesh—see Kedesh
Tell Refāt—see Arpad
Tell Seh Abu Zarad—see Tappuach
Tell Soreg, 206
Thapsakos—see Tiphsah
Tigris River, 350
Til Aššuri—see Telassar
Tiphsah (Thapsakos), 54
Tirzah, 145, 156, 158, 167, 171, 176–77,
    286, 331
Topheth, 407
Transjordan, 2, 48, 132
Tulkarm, 49
Tyre (Ṣūr), 48, 51–52, 60, 82, 107, 115,
    125, 196, 310, 314
Tyropoeon Valley, 319

Urartu, 333

Wadi Cherith, 180, 183, 197
Wadi el-'Arish, 54
Wadi el-Fâra', 48
Wadi el-Gazze, 102
Wadi el-Ḥesā, 133, 244, 277
Wadi el-Lahhem, 30
Wadi en-Nar, 17
Wadi er-Rababi—see Hinnom Valley
Wadi es-Sallale, 50
Wadi es-Sarar, 49
Wadi Fēran, 133
Wadi Kishon, 193–94
Wadi of Egypt, 102
Wadi Nablus, 48–49
Wadi Semme, 286
Wadi Zemir, 49

Yalo—see Elon
Yemen, 121
Yarmuk River, 326

Zagros Mountains, 375
Zebulun, 48, 52, 326
Zered River (Wadi el-Hesā), 244, 277
Zer'in—see Jezreel